Lecture Notes in Artificial Intelligence   **13462**

Subseries of Lecture Notes in Computer Science

More information about this subseries at https://link.springer.com/bookseries/1244

Valeria Giardino · Sven Linker · Richard Burns ·
Francesco Bellucci · Jean-Michel Boucheix ·
Petrucio Viana (Eds.)

Diagrammatic Representation and Inference

13th International Conference, Diagrams 2022
Rome, Italy, September 14–16, 2022
Proceedings

Springer

Editors
Valeria Giardino 🆔
CNRS, Ecole Normale Supérieure
Paris, France

Richard Burns 🆔
West Chester University
West Chester, PA, USA

Jean-Michel Boucheix
Université Bourgogne Franche-Comté
Dijon, France

Sven Linker 🆔
Lancaster University in Leipzig
Leipzig, Germany

Francesco Bellucci 🆔
Universitá di Bologna
Bologna, Italy

Petrucio Viana 🆔
Universidade Federal Fluminense
Niterói, Brazil

ISSN 0302-9743   ISSN 1611-3349 (electronic)
Lecture Notes in Artificial Intelligence
ISBN 978-3-031-15145-3   ISBN 978-3-031-15146-0 (eBook)
https://doi.org/10.1007/978-3-031-15146-0

LNCS Sublibrary: SL7 – Artificial Intelligence

This Springer imprint is published by the registered company Springer Nature Switzerland AG
The registered company address is: Gewerbestrasse 11, 6330 Cham, Switzerland

Preface

The 13th International Conference on Theory and Application of Diagrams (Diagrams 2022) was held at the Sapienza University of Rome during September 13–17, 2022. The conference was co-located with the IEEE Symposium on Visual Languages and Human-Centric Computing (VL/HCC 2022).

After two years of online conferences, Diagrams 2022 was planned from the beginning as a fully physical event. While this added additional uncertainty to the organization, we envisioned that a physical event would foster natural collaboration and communication among researchers in the Diagrams community more strongly.

Submissions to Diagrams 2022 were solicited in the form of long papers, short papers, posters, and abstract submissions. Each submission received at least three peer reviews. Afterwards, the authors were given the opportunity to respond to the reviews in the form of a rebuttal. During the lively discussion among the Program Committee, both the reviews and the rebuttal were taken into account. This robust process ensured that only the highest-quality papers were accepted for presentation at the conference. We thank all members of the Program Committee for their hard work and the time they spent on the discussion.

Diagrams 2022 received 58 submissions across the Main, Philosophy, and Psychology and Education tracks. Out of all these submissions, 11 were accepted as long papers, 19 as short papers, and five as posters. Furthermore, one submission was accepted as a full abstract, one as a short abstract, and, one as a non-archived poster. This program was complemented by four tutorials, and a workshop on "Diagrams of Life and Evolution". The conference included two keynote presentations by prestiguous researchers in the Diagrams community:

– Gem Stapleton on "The Power of Diagrams: Observation, Inference and Overspecificity". This keynote was shared with VL/HCC.
– Sun-Joo Shin on "Visual Representation and Abductive Reasoning".

In addition, Diagrams 2022 hosted an Inspirational Early Career Researcher speaker, who was invited to open the Graduate Symposium. We were delighted to host Lorenz Demey from KU Leuven to give this talk with the title "From Aristotelian Diagrams to Logical Geometry".

Of course, the organization would not have been possible without the help of many others. First of all, we would like to thank Paolo Bottoni and Francesco Sapio for their outstanding work as local organizers. Furthermore, we thank Amy Fox for her help as the Publicity Chair, Petrucio Viana for his work as the Proceedings Chair, and Reetu Bhatthacharjee for her support to the next generation of researchers by serving as the Graduate Symposium Chair. Our institutions, CNRS, Lancaster University Leipzig, West Chester University, University of Bologna, and Université de Bourgogne, provided us with additional support, for which we are thankful.

Finally, we would like to thank the Steering Committee for their continuous support throughout the organization of the conference, and in particular the Chair of the Steering Committe, Amirouche Moktefi, who was always willing to help with additional advice.

July 2022   Valeria Giardino
                                                                              Sven Linker
                                                                            Richard Burns
                                                                       Francesco Bellucci
                                                                     Jean-Michel Boucheix

Organization

Program Committee

Mohanad Alqadah	Umm Al-Qura University, Saudi Arabia
Amrita Basu	Jadavpur University, India
Francesco Bellucci (Co-chair)	University of Bologna, Italy
Reetu Bhattacharjee	Scuola Normale Superiore di Pisa, Italy
Andrew Blake	University of Brighton, UK
Ben Blumson	National University of Singapore, Singapore
Leonie M. Bosveld-De Smet	University of Groningen, The Netherlands
Jean-Michel Boucheix (Co-chair)	Université de Bourgogne, France
Richard Burns (Co-chair)	West Chester University, USA
Peter Chapman	Edinburgh Napier University, UK
Peter Cheng	University of Sussex, UK
Daniele Chiffi	Tallinn University of Technology, Estonia
Lopamudra Choudhury	Jadavpur University, India
James Corter	Columbia University, USA
Gennaro Costagliola	Università di Salerno, Italy
Silvia De Toffoli	Princeton University, USA
Erica de Vries	Université Grenoble Alpes, France
Aidan Delaney	Bloomberg, UK
Lorenz Demey	KU Leuven, Belgium
Maria Giulia Dondero	Université de Liège, Belgium
George Englebretsen	Bishop's University, Canada
Jacques Fleuriot	University of Edinburgh, UK
Amy Fox	University of California, San Diego, USA
Valeria Giardino (General Chair)	CNRS, Ecole Normale Supérieure, France
Nathan Haydon	Tallinn University of Technology, Estonia
Mateja Jamnik	University of Cambridge, UK
Mikkel Willum Johansen	University of Copenhagen, Denmark
Yasuhiro Katagari	Future University Hakodate, Japan
John Kulvicki	Dartmouth College, USA
Brendan Larvor	University of Hertfordshire, UK
John Lee	University of Edinburgh, UK
Javier Legris	Universidad de Buenos Aires, Argentina
Jens Lemanski	FernUniversität in Hagen, Germany
Sven Linker (Co-chair)	Lancaster University in Leipzig, Germany
Emmanuel Manalo	Kyoto University, Japan
Kim Marriott	Monash University, Australia

Mark Minas	Universität der Bundeswehr München, Germany
Amirouche Moktefi	Tallinn University of Technology, Estonia
Martin Nöllenburg	Vienna University of Technology, Austria
Mario Piazza	Scuola Normale Superiore di Pisa, Italy
Ahti Pietarinen	Tallinn University of Technology, Estonia
Margit Pohl	Vienna University of Technology, Austria
Uta Priss	Ostfalia University, Germany
Joao Queiroz	Federal University of Juiz de Fora, Brazil
Peter Rodgers	University of Kent, UK
Dirk Schlimm	McGill University, Canada
Stephanie Schwartz	Millersville University, USA
Sumanta S. Sharma	Shri Mata Vaishno Devi University, India
Atsushi Shimojima	Doshisha University, Japan
Hans Smessaert	KU Leuven, Belgium
Gem Stapleton	University of Cambridge, UK
Yuri Uesaka	University of Tokyo, Japan
Jean Van Bendegem	Vrije Universiteit Brussel, Belgium
Peggy Van Meter	Pennsylvania State University, USA
Petrucio Viana	Federal Fluminense University, Brazil
Reinhard von Hanxleden	Christian-Albrechts-Universität zu Kiel, Germany
Michael Wybrow	Monash University, Australia

Additional Reviewers

Kasperowski, Maximilian
Petzold, Jette
Raggi, Daniel
Rentz, Niklas
Smola, Filip

Contents

Logical Diagrams

Posters

Theoretical Perspectives

Introducing the Diagrammatic Semiotic Mode

Tuomo Hiippala[1]([email]) and John A. Bateman[2]

[1] University of Helsinki, Helsinki, Finland
`tuomo.hiippala@helsinki.fi`
[2] Bremen University, Bremen, Germany
`bateman@uni-bremen.de`

Abstract. As the use and diversity of diagrams across many disciplines grows, there is an increasing interest in the diagrams research community concerning how such diversity might be documented and explained. In this article, we argue that one way of achieving increased reliability, coverage, and utility for a general classification of diagrams is to draw on recently developed semiotic principles developed within the field of multimodality. To this end, we sketch out the internal details of what may tentatively be termed the *diagrammatic semiotic mode*. This provides a natural account of how diagrammatic representations organising lines of research integrate natural language, various forms of graphics, diagrammatic elements such as arrows, lines and other expressive resources into coherent organisations, while still respecting the crucial diagrammatic contributions of visual organisation. We illustrate the proposed approach using two recent diagram corpora and show how a multimodal approach supports the empirical analysis of diagrammatic representations, especially in identifying diagrammatic constituents and describing their interrelations in a manner that may be generalised across diagram types and be used to characterise distinct kinds of functionality.

Keywords: Diagrams · Semiotics · Multimodality · Corpora · Annotation

1 Introduction

Diagrams appear to be playing an ever greater range of roles in a similarly increasing range of application contexts. Several authors have consequently called for more efforts to characterise this diversity so as to establish more finely articulated accounts of just what kinds of diagrams there are and how they might serve different communicative and cognitive functions. Norman, for example, considers a two-dimensional characterisation in terms of 'discretion' and 'assimilability' to distinguish more clearly the role of diagrams among the traditionally drawn categories of descriptions, diagrams, and depiction [18]. Smessaert and Demey offer a typology of types of diagrams used in linguistics, focusing on more

© The Author(s) 2022
V. Giardino et al. (Eds.): Diagrams 2022, LNAI 13462, pp. 3–19, 2022.
https://doi.org/10.1007/978-3-031-15146-0_1

content-oriented 'linguistic parameters' and specific semiotically-motivated diagrammatic parameters distinguishing iconic and symbolic representations [21]. Johansen *et al.* offer a typology of mathematical diagrams based on their use by mathematicians, identifying 'resemblance', 'abstract' and 'Cartesian' diagrams [15]. And Purchase and colleagues propose a multidimensional classification of infographics by analysing how users grouped a selection of 60 infographics [19].

Work of this kind raises important research questions, including questions of the particular cognitive capabilities demanded or supported by distinct diagram types [15, p. 107], the ways in which diagram usage has developed and expanded over time [15, p. 106], and how studies might be extended to address entire collections of diagrams, thereby focusing and organising lines of research on a broader scale than hitherto [19, p. 210]. Strengthening the empirical basis for diagrams research by drawing on broader sets of examples and providing more finely articulated characterisations of the properties of diagrams that go beyond existing categories, such as the fundamental distinctions offered by Peirce in terms of iconicity, indexicality and symbolicity and so on, are consequently now well established as aims. As Johansen *et al.* argue, Peirce's functional definition, particular of iconicity, "is too broad and does not allow for making cognitively and practically meaningful distinctions in the category of diagrams" [15, p. 107]. Nevertheless, developing convincing classifications of diagrams – even in specific areas – has proved challenging.

Both the conceptually-based development of frameworks [8,15,18,21,24] and more bottom-up clustering based on human judgements [19] continue to face issues of exhaustivity, discriminability, and reliability. Several significant problems are noted by Johansen *et al.*:

> "Although such a classification gave a more fine-grained resolution in the diagram classification ... it turned out to be difficult to carry out in practice ... Consequently, counting the number of diagrams of a specific type requires making judgements based on the visual appearance of diagrams to classify them correctly." [15, p. 116]

Indeed, "we also encountered cases where we had to involve the textual or intellectual context of diagrams to classify them, and in other cases, we could only give educated guesses." [15, p. 116]. Moreover, even in Purchase *et al.*'s 'user-based' classification, the Likert scores used to evaluate the infographics were found to be poor predictors of class with "their values bear[ing] little relation to the groupings created by the participants" [19, p. 216]; again, visual grouping of diagrams appeared to give stronger results.

Consequently, despite the generally positive reports and indications of considerable utility of working with diagram collections, it is less clear whether the classifications proposed to date can be scaled-up in a reliable fashion. Certain gaps appear to occur due to the context-dependent nature of any functional categories employed. In this article, therefore, we address these issues from a complementary perspective and argue that the resulting multiply-dimensioned classification promises a more robust approach to diagram classification, capable not only of respecting visual appearance in a systematic and philo-sophically sound fashion, but also of providing a principled approach to context-dependent interpretations as well.

This approach draws on classification work in the field of multimodality research, an emerging discipline that studies how communication builds on appropriate combinations of multiple modes of expression, such as natural lan-guage, illustrations, drawings, photography, gestures, layout and many more [6]. One product of this work is a battery of theoretical concepts that strongly sup-port *empirical* analysis of complex communicative situations and artefacts. We describe how this can now be applied directly to the analysis of diagrams within the context of the challenges set out above. For this, we define what we ten-tatively term the *diagrammatic semiotic mode*. This bridges discussions in the diagrams research and multimodality communities by introducing an explicitly multimodal, discourse-oriented perspective to diagrams research. We illustrate this in relation to two recently published multimodal diagram corpora.

2   A Multimodal Perspective on Diagrams

The framework of multimodality adopted here offers a common set of concepts and an explicit methodology for supporting empirical research regardless of the 'modes' and materials involved [6]. The result is capable of addressing all forms of multimodal representation, including diagrammatic representations of all kinds. The core theoretical concept within the framework is that of the *semiotic mode*, a graphical definition of which we show on the left-hand side of Fig. 1. Here we see three distinct 'semiotic strata' that the model claims are always needed for a fully developed semiotic mode to operate [3].

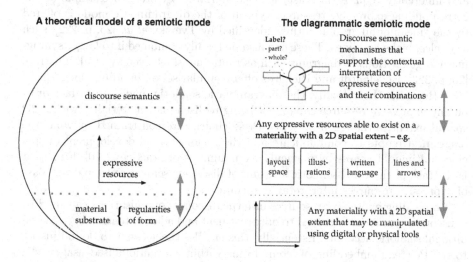

Fig. 1. A theoretical model of a semiotic mode and a sketch of the fundamentals for a diagrammatic semiotic mode [12, p. 408]

Starting from the lower portion of the inner circle, the model requires that all semiotic modes work with respect to a specified *materiality* which a community of users regularly 'manipulates' in order to leave traces for communicative purposes; second, these traces are organised (paradigmatically and syntagmatically) to form *expressive resources* that characterise the material distinctions that are specifically pertinent for the semiotic mode at issue; and finally, those expressive resources are mobilised in the service of communication by a corresponding *discourse semantics*, whose operation we show in a moment.

In general, no ordering is imposed on the flow of information across these three strata, although methodologically it can often be beneficial to begin with the more observable material traces. Different semiotic modes also provide differing degrees of constraint at the various levels: for example, whereas the semiotic mode of verbal language offers substantial form-driven constraints guiding discourse interpretation, pictorial semiotic modes often require more discourse constraints when selecting between perceptually plausible readings – Bateman, Wildfeuer and Hiippala [6, p. 33] discuss an example offered by Gombrich [9, p. 7] further from this perspective, showing how variability in interpretation is naturally supported. Finally, the model places no restrictions on the kinds of materiality that may be employed; for current purposes, however, we illustrate the approach by focusing on static two-dimensional diagrams. As Bateman [4] shows, however, the approach generalises equally to both dynamic and 3D cases.

Building on this scheme, we set out on the right-hand side of the figure an initial characterisation of the specific properties of the diagrammatic semiotic mode. The 2D materiality of this mode not only allows the creation of spatial organisations in the form of layout, but is also a prerequisite for realising many of the further expressive resources commonly mobilised in diagrams, such as written language and arrows, lines, glyphs and other diagrammatic elements, which also inherently require (at least) a 2D material substrate. An example of the corresponding expressive resources typical of the diagrammatic mode is offered by the "meaningful graphic forms" identified by Tversky *et al.* [25, p. 222], such as circles, blobs and lines. These can also be readily combined into larger syntagmatic organisations in diagrams such as route maps, as Tversky et al. illustrate [25, p. 223]; Engelhardt and Richards offer a similar set of 'building blocks' [8, p. 201]. However, theoretically, the diagrammatic semiotic mode can in fact draw on any expressive resource capable of being realised on a materiality with a 2D spatial extent, although in practice these choices are constrained by what the diagram attempts to communicate and the sociohistorical development of specific multimodal *genres* by particular communities of practice [2,10]. Finally, it is the task of the third semiotic stratum of discourse semantics to make the use of expressive resources interpretable in context.

Embedding expressive resources into the discourse organisations captured by a discourse semantics is crucial to our treatment and a key extension beyond traditional semiotic accounts. Essentially, this enables the account to do full justice to the Peircean embedding of iconic forms within conventionalised usages [22]. It is this addition that explains formally how (and why) fundamental graphic forms, such as those identified by Engelhardt and Richards, Tversky *et al.* and others, may receive different interpretations in different contexts of use – a problem noted for several of the classifications introduced above – while also allowing certain intrinsic properties of those forms (such as connectivity and directionality) to play central roles in finding interpretations as well. The combination of materiality, expressive forms and discourse interpretations then provides a robust foundation for considerations of diagrammatic reasoning quite generally.

3   Multimodal Diagram Corpora

We now illustrate the potential of a characterisation of diagrams drawing on our multimodal framework for dealing with collections of diagrams by considering two concrete, interrelated diagram corpora: AI2D [16] and AI2D-RST [11]. These corpora build on one another, as AI2D-RST covers a subset of AI2D. We describe the corpora and how they have been characterised and show how an increasing orientation to multimodality successively raises the accuracy and utility of the classification applied. We will argue that the characterisation provided supports a general methodology for building classifications for collections of diagrams.

3.1   The Allen Institute for Artificial Intelligence Diagrams Dataset

The Allen Institute for Artificial Intelligence Diagrams dataset (AI2D) was developed to support research on computational processing of diagrams [16]. AI2D contains a total of 4903 diagrams that represent topics in elementary school natural sciences, ranging from life and carbon cycles to human physiology and food webs, to name just a few of the 17 categories in the dataset. Because the diagram images were scraped from the web using school textbook chapter headings as search terms, the corpus covers a wide range of diagrams created by producers with various degrees of expertise with the diagrammatic semiotic mode, such as students, teachers and professional graphic designers. As the diagrams have been removed from their original context during scraping, little may be said about the medium they originated in. For this reason, it may be suggested that AI2D *approximates* how diagrams are used in learning materials realised using various media.

AI2D models four types of diagram elements: text, blobs (graphic elements), arrows and arrowheads. Although these elements cover the main expressive resources mobilised in these diagrams, no further distinctions are made between drawings, illustrations, photographs and other visual expressive resources [12]. Each diagram in the dataset is nevertheless provided with several layers of description. Instances of the four diagram element types were first segmented from the original diagram images by crowdsourced workers [16, p. 243]. The elements identified during this *layout segmentation* provide a foundation for a *Diagram Parse Graph* (DPG), which represents the diagram elements as nodes and semantic relations between elements as edges. Ten relations are used, drawing from the framework proposed by Engelhardt [7]. Crowdsourcing annotations is a promising way of creating larger-scale collections of classified diagrams – it also, however, demands that the classifications constructed are sufficiently clear and well-defined to avoid the drawbacks observed by other approaches reported in the introduction above [11, pp. 683–684].

Figure 2 shows as an example the treatment given to a diagram originally scraped from the web, diagram #4210 in AI2D. Below the original shown at the top of the figure, we see the diagram's crowdsourced layout segmentation and, at the bottom, its corresponding DPG. The original diagram represents a rock cycle, that is, transitions between different types of rock, using a combination of an illustration (a cross-section) whose parts are described using written language. These parts set up the stages of the rock cycle, which are then related to one another using arrows.

For the formation of the AI2D corpus, annotators were instructed to identify units and relationships. As the resulting layout segmentation image in the middle of the figure shows, text blocks and arrowheads were segmented using rectangular bounding boxes, whereas more complex shapes for arrows and various types of graphics were segmented using polygons. The layout segmentation illustrates a common problem with crowdsourced annotations: annotators tend to segment diagrams to quite uneven degrees of detail. Here the entire cross-section is assigned to a single blob (B0), although a more accurate description would be to segment separate parts of the cross-section, such as magma and various layers of rock. We will see shortly how such omissions readily compromise the accurate description of semantic relations in the DPG.

Referring again to the layout segmentation and DPG in the figure, we can see for example that the semantic relations carried by the edges in the DPG cover ARROWHEADTAIL between arrow A2 and arrowhead H2 in the upper part of the diagram, which together act as a connector in an INTEROBJECTLINKAGE relation between text blocks T1 ('Magma flows to surface ...') and T2 ('Weathering and erosion'). As these relations illustrate, Engelhardt's [7] relations cover local relations holding between diagram elements that are positioned close to one another or connected using arrows or lines. They neglect, however, the relations needed to describe the global organisation of the diagram, that is, relations between units that are made up of multiple elements [16, p. 239]. Crowdsourcing coherent graph-based descriptions of diagrams thus turns out to be a challenging task. AI2D DPGs often include isolated nodes and multiple connected components, as exemplified by the DPG in Fig. 2. Furthermore, the DPG does not feature a cyclic structure, although the diagram clearly describes a rock *cycle*. The AI2D annotation scheme provides the relation definitions necessary for describing this process in principle, such as INTEROBJECTLINKAGE and INTRAOBJECTREGIONLABEL [16, p. 239], but annotators following a more shallow visual grouping would not be led to this option from the diagram at hand. As we shall see, this is one of many problems that an explicit discourse semantic orientation can address.

The crowdsourced annotators were not explicitly instructed to decompose cross-sections or other visual expressive resources capable of demarcating meaningful regions, which results in an insufficiently detailed layout segmentation.

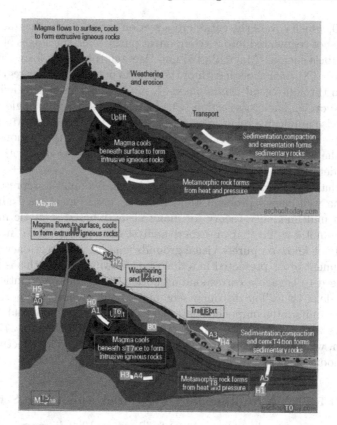

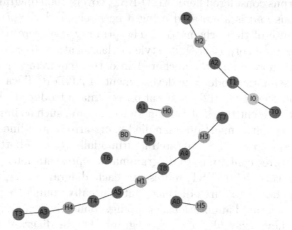

Fig. 2. Original diagram image (top), layout segmentation (middle) and Diagram Parse Graph (bottom) for diagram #4210 in the AI2D corpus. In the layout segmentation, the original image has been converted into grayscale to highlight the crowd-sourced layout segmentation. Each layout segment is coloured according to diagram element type (blue: text; red: blob; arrow: green; arrowhead: orange) and assigned a unique identifier. These colours and identifiers are carried over to the Diagram Parse Graph. (Color figure online)

The blob B0, which covers the entire cross-section shown in the diagram, is as a consequence not segmented into its component parts – i.e., the stages of the rock cycle with labels such as 'Magma' (T5) and 'Metamorphic rock forms from heat and pressure' (T8) even though each of these picks out a particular region of the cross-section through visual *containment* [7, p. 47] as necessary for defining the stages of the cycle. The cross-section (B0) instead constitutes a single unit and so an otherwise applicable relation such as INTRAOBJECTREGIONLABEL cannot be used to pick out corresponding regions simply because those regions are not present in the inventory of identified elements. As such, the description is not sufficiently detailed to represent a cyclic structure.

These challenges relating to decomposing diagrammatic representations relate to the well-known problem of identifying 'units' mentioned above and discussed in multimodality theory for many visually-based semiotic modes. In general an annotator, be that an expert analyst or a crowdsourced non-expert worker, will not know on purely visual grounds whether it is necessary, or bene-ficial, to segment areas presented in a diagram. As we shall see, this is precisely where we need to engage a corresponding notion of discourse semantics for the semiotic mode at issue. The discourse semantics simultaneously supports *decomposing* larger units into component parts and *resolving* their potential interrela-tions, always with the goal of maximising *discourse coherence* [5, p. 377]. In the next section, we show how this approach can be used for a more effective design of a multimodal corpus of diagrams.

3.2   AI2D-RST – A Multimodally-Motivated Annotation Schema

The second corpus considered here, AI2D-RST, covers 1000 diagrams taken from the AI2D corpus and is annotated using a new schema by experts specifically trained in the use of that schema [11]. The primary goal here was precisely to compare the original corpus, with its style of classification, to a corpus adopting a classification more explicitly anchored into the requirements raised by the diagrammatic semiotic mode. The development of AI2D-RST was motivated by the observation that the AI2D annotation schema introduced above conflates descriptions of different types of multimodal structure, such as implicit semantic relations and explicit connections signalled using arrows and lines, into a single DPG [13]. These can now be separated multimodally so as to better understand how such structures contribute to diagrammatic representations.

To achieve this, AI2D-RST represents each diagram using three distinct graphs corresponding to three distinct, but mutually complementary, layers of multimodally motivated annotations: grouping, connectivity and discourse struc-ture. Figure 3 shows examples of all three graphs for the diagram from Fig. 2. To begin, the grouping layer (top right) organises diagram elements that are likely to be perceived as belonging together into visual perceptual groups loosely based on Gestalt properties [26]. The resulting organisation is represented using a hier-archical tree graph, with grouping nodes with the prefix 'G' added to the graph as parents to nodes grouped together during annotation. Such grouping nodes can be picked up in subsequent annotation layers to refer to a group of diagram elements and thereby serve as a foundation for the description of both the connectivity and discourse structure layers.

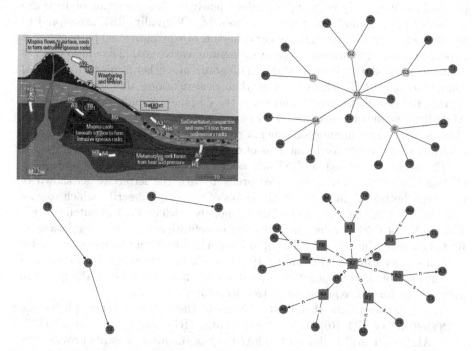

Fig. 3. The original crowd-sourced layout segmentation from AI2D (top left) and AI2D-RST grouping (top right), connectivity (bottom left; with two subgraphs) and discourse structure (bottom right) graphs for diagram #4210. Note that unlike AI2D, AI2D-RST does not model arrowheads as individual units, which is why they are absent from the graphs. This information can be retrieved from the original AI2D annotation if needed.

The connectivity layer (bottom left) is represented using a cyclic graph, in which edges represent visually explicit connections signalled using arrows and lines in the diagram. As the connectivity graph in Fig. 3 shows, it is important that these cover explicit connections only since this reveals the diagram to leave several gaps in its characterisation of the rock cycle, namely between the stages represented using text blocks T7 ('Magma cools beneath surface ...') and T1 ('Magma flows to surface ...'), and between T2 ('Weathering and erosion) and T3 ('Transport'). It is consequently left to the viewer to fill in such connections during discourse interpretation. Not including such connections in the description of connectivity allows us to capture discrepancies between explicit visual signals, such as arrows and lines, and implicit meanings that are only derivable from the discourse structure.

In AI2D-RST, such implicit discourse relations are handled by the third layer, that of discourse structure, which uses Rhetorical Structure Theory (RST) [17,23] to describe semantic relations between diagram elements. RST was originally developed as a theory of text organisation and coherence in the 1980s [17] and has frequently been applied subsequently to the description of discourse semantics in multimodality research as well [2]. Originally, RST attempted to describe why well-formed texts appear coherent, or why individual parts of a text appear to contribute towards a common communicative goal [23], and so this is a relatively natural perspective to take on diagrams and other forms of multimodal communication. RST defines a set of 'rhetorical relations' that are intended to capture the communicative intentions of the designer, as judged by an analyst. AI2D-RST applies these relations to diagrams from the AI2D dataset to provide an alternative annotation schema offering a more multimodally informed description of the intended functions of diagrammatic representations [11].

The relations defined by RST are added to the discourse structure graph of diagrams in the corpus as nodes prefixed with the letter 'R' as shown in the graph bottom right in Fig. 3; the edges of the graph describe which role an element takes in the discourse relation, namely nucleus ('n') or satellite ('s'). This notion of *nuclearity* is a key criterion in definitions of semantic relations in RST. Following the original RST definitions, AI2D-RST represents the discourse structure layer using a strict tree graph: if a diagram element is picked up as a part of multiple rhetorical relations, a duplicate node is added to the graph to preserve the formal requirement of tree structure.

In Fig. 3, the specific rhetorical relations in the bottom right graph include IDENTIFICATION (R1–R6), CYCLIC SEQUENCE (R7) and BACKGROUND (R8). Since AI2D-RST still builds on the inventory of diagram elements provided by the original layout segmentation in AI2D, this requires some compromises in the RST analysis. Here the original annotator of the diagram had concluded that most text instances serve to identify what the arrows stand for, namely stages of the rock cycle. The image showing the cross-section (B0), in turn, is placed in a BACKGROUND relation to the CYCLIC SEQUENCE relation. The definition of a BACKGROUND relation [17] states that the satellite (B0) increases the ability to understand the nucleus (R7), which is the top-level relation assigned to the diagram's representation of the entire cycle.

Although this offers a first incremental step for including discourse information in a diagram corpus, building directly on the original AI2D corpus and its segmentation is also a severe limitation. In fact, this offers only a rather crude description of the discourse structure of the diagram in Fig. 3 because the cross-section B0 is actually providing far more information. This information is crucial for understanding what the diagram is attempting to communicate *but we cannot know that such a decomposition is necessary without considering the rhetorical discourse organisation of the diagram as a whole.* The particular decomposition of diagrams must often be pursued in a top-down direction therefore, emphasising the discourse structure from the outset [5]. Without methodologically prioritising the analysis of discourse structure, it is difficult to know which aspects of the diagrammatic mode are being drawn on and which elements should actually be included in the description of discourse structure.

This is one of the basic problems underlying several of the limitations discussed for previous diagram classifications above. A visually-accessible cross-section such as the one shown in Fig. 2 is, in fact, very likely to use *illustration* or other expressive resources capable of representing and demarcating meaningful regions in 2D layout space [20]. This possibility makes the question of whether the capability is actually being drawn on pertinent and, if the capability is used, raises further the issue of the extent to which the illustration must be decomposed so as to achieve the inventory of elements needed for making appropriate inferences about the discourse structure. Analytical problems arising from the original layout segmentation are consequently still being propagated from AI2D to AI2D-RST.

3.3   Next Step: Adding Discourse-Driven Decomposition to AI2D-RST

To solve the analytical problems described above, we propose an alternative, discourse-driven layout segmentation that overcomes the limitations discussed above by incorporating the distinctions provided by our definition of a semiotic mode (see Fig. 1). Figure 4 shows a decomposition motivated by discourse structure for diagram #4210, which picks out relevant parts of the cross-section. In contrast to the crowdsourced segmentation in Fig. 2, the cross-section has been decomposed with the goal of maximising the coherence of discourse structure, which involves making available all the elements needed for such a representation of the diagram and its communicative intentions using the AI2D-RST annotation schema.

This is shown in Fig. 4, which applies the AI2D-RST annotation schema to the diagram elements identified through discourse-driven decomposition. When provided with a sufficient inventory of diagram elements, the grouping graph more accurately reflects key structural properties of the diagram. The grouping graph (top right) contains two subgraphs, whose root nodes G10 and I0 correspond to the cross-section and cycle, respectively. Keeping in mind that the grouping graph seeks to capture visual groupings, this already provides a strong cue for two visually distinct configurations, which the AI2D-RST annotation schema refers to as *macro-groups*. These constitute established configurations of the diagrammatic mode that may be flexibly combined in diagrams [11, p. 681]. To summarise, the grouping graph then already pulls these macro-groups apart and provides a foundation for their further analysis. We will shortly show how these macro-groups are integrated in the discourse structure graph.

The connectivity graph (bottom left) reveals that the diagram makes perhaps surprisingly limited use of arrows and lines as an expressive resource despite the intention that the diagram represents a cycle. This is one of the typical complicating factors contributing to the problems for annotation mentioned in the introduction above. The diagram does use arrows to set up connections between some individual elements and their groups, but the connectivity graph

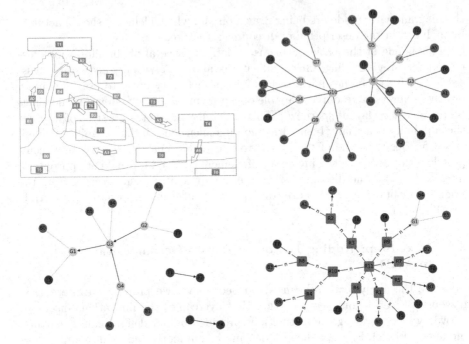

Fig. 4. A discourse-driven decomposition of diagram layout (top left) with grouping (top right), connectivity (bottom left) and discourse structure (bottom right) graphs for diagram #4210.

does not exhibit a cyclic structure. Some arrows, such as A2, have clear sources (T1; 'Magma flows to surface ...') and targets (T2; 'Weathering and erosion'), whereas other arrows, such as A4, do not. This encourages two alternative frames of interpretation for arrows [1]: some clearly signal transitions between stages (A2, A3), whereas others indicate the overall direction of the cycle (A4, A0).

The disconnections in the connectivity graph raise a crucial question: how does an interpretation involving a cyclic structure emerge if it is not clearly signalled using arrows? The answer to this question lies in the discourse structure of the graph as a whole, which here relies largely on *written* language as an expressive resource. This allows the diagram to describe stages of the rock cycle explicitly using clausal structures, e.g. "Metamorphic rock forms from heat and pressure", but does not express the relationships diagrammatically using arrows. The verbal descriptions are instead placed in relation with specific regions of the cross-section, as shown in the discourse structure graph (bottom right).

The discourse structure graph illustrates how the cross-section and the cycle, which form separate subgraphs in the grouping graph, are tightly integrated in the discourse structure graph, capturing their *joint* contribution towards a shared communicative goal and moving beyond the information in visual grouping alone. The specific rhetorical relations in Fig. 4 and criteria for their application, based loosely on Bateman [2, pp. 149–162], are given in abbreviated form in

Table 1. Beginning from the top of the table, several IDENTIFICATION relations are used to name regions (R1) and arrows (R6, R3). In relation R3, identification is extended to both arrows A0 and A1, which are joined together using the JOINT relation R2. ELABORATION relations R4–R5 and R7–R9, which assign descriptions to specific regions of the cross-section. This explains most of the phenomena depicted in the diagram.

Table 1. Rhetorical relations in the discourse structure graph in Fig. 4

Identifier(s)	Relation	Nucleus	Satellite
R1, R3, R6	IDENTIFICATION	Identified	Identifier
R2	JOINT	No constraints	No constraints
R4–5, R7–9	ELABORATION	Basic information	Additional information
R10	DISJUNCTION	Two or more alternatives	–
R11	CYCLIC SEQUENCE	Repeated steps	–

All of these descriptions contribute towards an interpretation involving a cycle, which requires not only world knowledge, but is also supported using cohesive ties between lexical elements, such as the nouns 'magma' and 'rock' and the verb 'to form'. The cycle itself is represented by the CYCLIC SEQUENCE relation R11, which joins together the individual descriptions that form its steps. The cycle also includes two possible alternatives, that is, whether magma cools below or above ground to form rocks, which is also explicitly captured by the DISJUNCTION relation R10 visible in the figure.

This analysis illustrates several of the methodological benefits of adopting a discourse-driven approach to unpacking the structure of diagrammatic representations. We can now move in a principled fashion beyond visual grouping and the individual sources of information in any diagram analysed to produce classifications more sensitive to the likely functions of the diagram as a whole.

4   Discussion

We now briefly discuss some of the principal implications of our analysis for diagrams research more generally. The analysis has shown how a multimodal perspective can yield valuable insights into diagrammatic representations by drawing on the broader basis provided by an appropriately differentiating view of the diagrammatic semiotic mode. Instead of building pre-defined inventories of diagrammatic elements, for example, which are rapidly exhausted when faced with data that do not fall neatly into the categories defined, one can focus more on mapping the expressive resources available to the diagrammatic semiotic mode and describing the kinds of discourse structures they participate in.

This can be approached both empirically and with respect to existing proposals for the graphical elements and properties of diagrams. A recent example of such a proposal is that of Engelhardt and Richards, who seek to define "universal building blocks of all types of diagrams and information graphics" [8, p. 201]. However, this still excludes "context-related aspects" of diagram use [8, p. 203], which, as we have seen above, can be problematic when characterising larger collections of diagrams. A multimodal perspective is inherently geared towards addressing all of the aforementioned aspects of diagrammatic representations and naturally spans from form to contextually-motivated use. Furthermore, such frameworks can be applied reliably to diagrams, as exemplified by substantial inter-annotator agreement achieved for the AI2D-RST corpus [11, pp. 674–679].

Multimodality research can also contribute towards a deeper understanding of *signification* in diagrams, as this is precisely the work that expressive resources perform as part of the diagrammatic mode. As our analysis shows, diagrams that represent cycles do not necessarily need to draw on arrows for this purpose: the diagrammatic mode provides alternatives, such as written language, whose structural features (here: cohesive ties) may be used to cue a discourse seman-tic interpretation involving cyclicity. This allows a fine-grained decomposition of the proposed building blocks of diagrammatic representations [8,14]. Conversely, multimodality research is likely to benefit from the concepts developed in dia-grams research for producing systematic descriptions of expressive resources. This will, however, require a significant effort in triangulating what has been done previously in multimodality and diagrams research, and aligning their the-oretical concepts as necessary. Previous approaches to diagram classification as described above are the logical place to start such investigations.

Finally, our findings also carry implications for the computational modelling of diagrams. In particular, problems with the AI2D annotation [16] echo the need remarked on for mathematical diagrams above by Johansen and colleagues for domain expertise in describing the diagrammatic mode in order to achieve a description that respects its specific features. When applied to diagrams, com-puter vision tasks such as instance-level semantic segmentation and visual ques-tion answering must acknowledge particular characteristics of the diagrammatic mode. They should not be based simply on assumptions concerning how such tasks are defined for processing pictorial representations, since pictures con-stitute a quite different family of semiotic modes and exhibit rather different properties. Particularly important here is the issue of the appropriate level of semantic segmentation, that is, to what extent the mode in question needs to be decomposed into its components. Developing appropriate descriptions of the diagrammatic mode for computational modelling is therefore a task that needs to involve research communities working on both diagrams and multimodality.

5   Conclusion

We have introduced a multimodal perspective on diagrammatic representations, and presented a description of the diagrammatic semiotic mode, exemplifying the proposed approach using two recent multimodal diagram corpora. Multi-modal analysis involves decomposing diagrammatic representations into their component parts, and we have argued for supporting decompositions driven by discourse structure – that is, what the diagrammatic representations attempt to communicate and how their organisations explicitly guide readers to candidate interpretations. Capturing segmentations of this kind explicitly in appropriately designed corpora ensures that the necessary diagrammatic elements are available for further analysis. We suggest that given the widespread use of diagrams and their variation in different domains, an extensive programme of corpus-driven research of the kind we have proposed is now essential for developing an empirically-motivated account of the diagrammatic semiotic mode.

References

1. Alikhani, M., Stone, M.: Arrows are the verbs of diagrams. In: Proceedings of the 27th International Conference on Computational Linguistics, Santa Fe, New Mexico, USA, pp. 3552–3563 (2018)
2. Bateman, J.A.: Multimodality and Genre: A Foundation for the Systematic Analysis of Multimodal Documents. Palgrave Macmillan, London (2008)
3. Bateman, J.A.: The decomposability of semiotic modes. In: O'Halloran, K.L., Smith, B.A. (eds.) Multimodal Studies: Multiple Approaches and Domains. Routledge Studies in Multimodality, pp. 17–38. Routledge, London (2011)
4. Bateman, J.A.: Dimensions of materiality: towards an external language of description for empirical multimodality research. In: Pflaeging, J., Wildfeuer, J., Bateman, J.A. (eds.) Empirical Multimodality Research: Methods, Evaluations, Implications, pp. 35–64. De Gruyter, Berlin and Boston (2021)
5. Bateman, J.A., Wildfeuer, J.: Defining units of analysis for the systematic analysis of comics: a discourse-based approach. Stud. Comics 5(2), 373–403 (2014)
6. Bateman, J.A., Wildfeuer, J., Hiippala, T.: Multimodality: Foundations. Research and Analysis - A Problem-Oriented Introduction. De Gruyter Mouton, Berlin (2017)
7. Engelhardt, Y.: The language of graphics: a framework for the analysis of syntax and meaning in maps, charts and diagrams. Ph.D. thesis, Institute for Logic, Language and Computation, University of Amsterdam (2002)
8. Engelhardt, Y., Richards, C.: A framework for analyzing and designing diagrams and graphics. In: Chapman, P., Stapleton, G., Moktefi, A., Perez-Kriz, S., Bellucci, F. (eds.) Diagrams 2018. LNCS (LNAI), vol. 10871, pp. 201–209. Springer, Cham (2018). https://doi.org/10.1007/978-3-319-91376-6_20
9. Gombrich, E.: Art and Illusion: A Study in the Psychology of Pictorial Representation. Pantheon Books, New York (1960)
10. Hiippala, T.: The Structure of Multimodal Documents: An Empirical Approach. Routledge, New York and London (2015)
11. Hiippala, T., et al.: AI2D-RST: a multimodal corpus of 1000 primary school science diagrams. Lang. Resour. Eval. 55(3), 661–688 (2020). https://doi.org/10.1007/s10579-020-09517-1
12. Hiippala, T., Bateman, J.A.: Semiotically-grounded distant view of diagrams: insights from two multimodal corpora. Digit. Scholarsh. Human. 37(2), 405–425 (2021). https://doi.org/10.1093/llc/fqab063
13. Hiippala, T., Orekhova, S.: Enhancing the AI2 diagrams dataset using rhetorical structure theory. In: Proceedings of the Eleventh International Conference on Language Resources and Evaluation (LREC 2018), pp. 1925–1931. European Language Resources Association (ELRA), Paris (2018)

14. Hullman, J., Bach, B.: Picturing science: design patterns in graphical abstracts. In: Chapman, P., Stapleton, G., Moktefi, A., Perez-Kriz, S., Bellucci, F. (eds.) Diagrams 2018. LNCS (LNAI), vol. 10871, pp. 183–200. Springer, Cham (2018). https://doi.org/10.1007/978-3-319-91376-6_19

15. Johansen, M.W., Misfeldt, M., Pallavicini, J.L.: A typology of mathematical diagrams. In: Chapman, P., Stapleton, G., Moktefi, A., Perez-Kriz, S., Bellucci, F. (eds.) Diagrams 2018. LNCS (LNAI), vol. 10871, pp. 105–119. Springer, Cham (2018). https://doi.org/10.1007/978-3-319-91376-6_13

16. Kembhavi, A., Salvato, M., Kolve, E., Seo, M., Hajishirzi, H., Farhadi, A.: A diagram is worth a dozen images. In: Leibe, B., Matas, J., Sebe, N., Welling, M. (eds.) ECCV 2016. LNCS, vol. 9908, pp. 235–251. Springer, Cham (2016). https://doi.org/10.1007/978-3-319-46493-0_15

17. Mann, W.C., Thompson, S.A.: Rhetorical structure theory: toward a functional theory of text organization. Text 8(3), 243–281 (1988)

18. Norman, J.: Differentiating diagrams: a new approach. In: Anderson, M., Cheng, P., Haarslev, V. (eds.) Diagrams 2000. LNCS (LNAI), vol. 1889, pp. 105–116. Springer, Heidelberg (2000). https://doi.org/10.1007/3-540-44590-0_13

19. Purchase, H.C., et al.: A classification of infographics. In: Chapman, P., Stapleton, G., Moktefi, A., Perez-Kriz, S., Bellucci, F. (eds.) Diagrams 2018. LNCS (LNAI), vol. 10871, pp. 210–218. Springer, Cham (2018). https://doi.org/10.1007/978-3-319-91376-6_21

20. Richards, C.: Technical and scientific illustration: picturing the invisible. In: Black, A., Luna, P., Lund, O., Walker, S. (eds.) Information Design: Research and Practice, pp. 85–106. Routledge, London (2017)

21. Smessaert, H., Demey, L.: Towards a typology of diagrams in linguistics. In: Chapman, P., Stapleton, G., Moktefi, A., Perez-Kriz, S., Bellucci, F. (eds.) Diagrams 2018. LNCS (LNAI), vol. 10871, pp. 236–244. Springer, Cham (2018). https://doi.org/10.1007/978-3-319-91376-6_24

22. Stjernfelt, F.: Diagrammatology. An investigation on the borderlines phenomenology, ontology, and semiotics. Int. J. Semiot. Law 21, 297–301 (2007). Springer, Dordrecht

23. Taboada, M., Mann, W.C.: Rhetorical structure theory: looking back and moving ahead. Discourse Stud. 8(3), 423–459 (2006)

24. Tversky, B.: Diagrams: cognitive foundations for design. In: Black, A., Luna, P., Lund, O., Walker, S. (eds.) Information Design: Research and Practice, pp. 349–360. Routledge, London (2017)

25. Tversky, B., Zacks, J., Lee, P., Heiser, J.: Lines, blobs, crosses and arrows: diagrammatic communication with schematic figures. In: Anderson, M., Cheng, P., Haarslev, V. (eds.) Diagrams 2000. LNCS (LNAI), vol. 1889, pp. 221–230. Springer, Heidelberg (2000). https://doi.org/10.1007/3-540-44590-0_21

26. Ware, C.: Information Visualization: Perception for Design, 3rd edn. Elsevier, Amsterdam (2012)

On Computing Optimal Linear Diagrams

Alexander Dobler[✉][iD] and Martin Nöllenburg[iD]

Algorithms and Complexity Group, TU Wien, Vienna, Austria
{adobler,noellenburg}@ac.tuwien.ac.at

Abstract. Linear diagrams are an effective way to visualize set-based data by representing elements as columns and sets as rows with one or more horizontal line segments, whose vertical overlaps with other rows indicate set intersections and their contained elements. The efficacy of linear diagrams heavily depends on having few line segments. The underlying minimization problem has already been explored heuristically, but its computational complexity has yet to be classified. In this paper, we show that minimizing line segments in linear diagrams is equivalent to a well-studied NP-hard problem, and extend the NP-hardness to a restricted setting. We develop new algorithms for computing linear diagrams with minimum number of line segments that build on a traveling salesperson (TSP) formulation and allow constraints on the element orders, namely, forcing two sets to be drawn as single line segments, giving weights to sets, and allowing hierarchical constraints via PQ-trees. We conduct an experimental evaluation and compare previous algorithms for minimizing line segments with our TSP formulation, showing that a state-of-the art TSP-solver can solve all considered instances optimally, most of them within few milliseconds.

Keywords: Linear diagrams · Consecutive ones · TSP · NP-hardness · Algorithm benchmarking

1 Introduction

Many real-world datasets represent set systems, and there is a vast landscape of different visualization techniques for set-based data. Two well-known techniques are Euler and Venn Diagrams that draw sets as closed curves and set intersections are represented by intersections of the boundaries of these curves. For a detailed survey of these and other set visualizations we refer to Alsallakh et al. [1].

The set visualization that we study in this paper are linear diagrams. It has been demonstrated that they are simple and effective, and have advantages when compared with other set visualizations [7,21,29]. Linear diagrams represent elements as columns and sets as rows of a matrix or table, where in each row there are one or more horizontal line segments indicating which elements are contained

This work is supported by the Vienna Science and Technology Fund (WWTF) under grant ICT19-035.

V. Giardino et al. (Eds.): Diagrams 2022, LNAI 13462, pp. 20–36, 2022.
https://doi.org/10.1007/978-3-031-15146-0_2

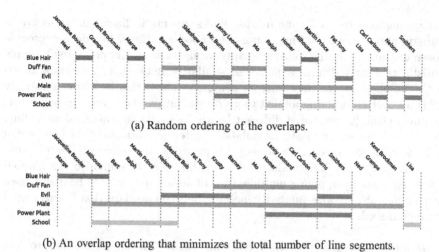

(a) Random ordering of the overlaps.

(b) An overlap ordering that minimizes the total number of line segments.

Fig. 1. Linear diagrams representing the Simpsons.

in a specific set. Vertical overlaps of these line segments in different rows show set intersections, and the corresponding elements. Figure 1a shows a linear diagram representing a Simpsons data set introduced by Jacobsen et al. [18]. For example, the set Blue Hair contains the elements Jacquelin Bouvier, Marge, and Milhouse, and is drawn with three line segments. Mr. Burns is contained in the sets Evil, Male, and Power Plant, as represented by the corresponding vertical overlap of the line segments in these three rows with the column of Mr. Burns.

Linear diagrams can be drawn in many ways, e.g., by choosing different permutations of the rows/sets and columns/overlaps. It has been shown that there are several quality criteria for linear diagrams, while the most important one is finding an ordering of the elements that minimizes the number of line segments [26]. For example, the linear diagram depicted in Fig. 1b shows the same set system as before, but with an ordering of the overlaps that minimizes the number of line segments, here using 8 segments instead of 23.

The underlying computational problem of finding an ordering of the overlaps that minimizes line segments seems hard, as for n overlaps, there are $n!$ different orderings of these overlaps. Finding orderings that minimize line segments is mainly done via heuristics in the literature [6,17,26]. The main topic of this paper is computing *optimal linear diagrams* – those which realize the minimum possible number of line segments that have to be drawn.

Related Work. Several user studies were performed to compare the efficacy of linear diagrams and other diagram types; they showed that linear diagrams perform equally well or better than other diagram types including Euler and Venn diagrams [7,21,27]. Linear diagrams have then been used, e.g., to visualize sets over time [24], and Lamy et al. [20] extended linear diagrams to allow multiple sets per row.

Existing algorithms for minimizing line segments in linear diagrams are of heuristic nature, i.e., they may often find good solutions, but do not provide proven guarantees on the solution quality. Rodgers et al. [26] presented a simple heuristic that first defines a pair-wise similarity between two overlaps based on the number of sets they have in common. Then, this heuristic iteratively builds an overlap ordering aiming to group similar overlaps next to each other. Chapman et al. [6] compared different heuristics based on simulated annealing, a travelling salesperson (TSP) formulation, and other variants of the heuristic of Rodgers et al. [26]. A GitHub project [17] provides an implementation of linear diagrams in Python. The underlying algorithm tries to minimize the number of line segments by applying multiple runs of an iterative greedy heuristic, each with a different pair-wise similarity measure between overlaps that is augmented by random seeds.

Contribution and Structure. We further investigate the computational problem of computing optimal linear diagrams. Section 2 defines general preliminaries and notation for permutations, matrices, and graphs. In Sect. 3, we describe how the problem of computing optimal linear diagrams can be modelled as a known problem on binary matrices, thus bridging the gap missing in the literature. This problem is known to be NP-complete; we further strengthen this NP-completeness result by showing that computing optimal linear diagrams is even NP-complete for set systems where each set contains exactly two elements and each element is contained in exactly three sets. Moreover, we present further literature on matrix problems that are relevant with regard to linear diagrams.

In Sect. 4, we present a way to compute optimal linear diagrams by reducing the problem to TSP, thus, completing the work of Chapman et al. [6]. They also presented an algorithm based on a TSP formulation, but this algorithm sometimes produces non-optimal overlap orderings. We further expand on this formulation, showing that we can model specific constraints on the overlap orders. Namely, we can force up to two sets to be drawn as single line segments while still minimizing the number of line segments. This is particularly interesting for allowing interactivity in linear diagrams [5]. We also show how to model constraints based on weighted sets and hierarchical ordering constraints represented by PQ-trees, which is of interest for certain set visualization tasks.

In Sect. 5, we conduct an experimental evaluation of our algorithms from Sect. 4, and compare them with the state-of-the art heuristics. We show that a state-of-the-art TSP-solver can solve all considered instances optimally, most of them within few milliseconds. We also verify that the considered heuristics from the literature perform well with regard to the number of line segments, where the average optimality gaps of the heuristics are less than ten percent.

2   Preliminaries

Let A be a matrix with m rows and n columns; we set $n_A = n$ and $m_A = m$. We write $A_{i,j}$ with $1 \leq i \leq m$ and $1 \leq j \leq n$ for the *entry* of A at row i and column j. Furthermore, by r_i^A and c_j^A we denote the i-th row and j-th column of A, respectively. A matrix is a *binary matrix* if all its entries are either 0 or 1. If it is clear from the context, we might omit explicitly mentioning the matrix A in the above notations.

We denote by $[k]$ the set of elements $\{1, \ldots, k\}$. A *permutation* $\pi : [k] \to X$ is a bijective function from $[k]$ to a set X. Sometimes we write permutations π as sequences of elements, that is, $\pi = (x_1, \ldots, x_n)$ is the permutation such that $\pi(i) = x_i$ for $1 \leq i \leq n$. We denote by Π_k the set of all permutations from $[k]$ to $[k]$. For two permutations $\pi_1 = (x_1, \ldots, x_n)$ and $\pi_2 = (y_1, \ldots, y_m)$, we denote by $\pi_1 \star \pi_2$ their *concatenation* $(x_1, \ldots x_n, y_1, \ldots, y_m)$. For two sets Π_1 and Π_2 of permutations, we define $\Pi_1 \star \Pi_2 = \{\pi_1 \star \pi_2 \mid \pi_1 \in \Pi_1, \pi_2 \in \Pi_2\}$.

For a matrix A and a permutation $\pi : [n_A] \to [n_A]$ we denote by $\pi(A)$ the matrix such that $\pi(A)_{i,j} = A_{i,\pi(j)}$. Equivalently $\pi(r_i^A) = r_{\pi(i)}^A$ for a row r_i^A. By "a permutation of the columns of the matrix A" we mean a permutation $\pi : [n_A] \to [n_A]$.

A block of *consecutive ones* in a row r_i^A of a matrix A with n columns is a maximal non-empty sequence $A_{i,p}, A_{i,p+1}, \ldots, A_{i,q}$ satisfying

- $A_{i,j} = 1$ for all $p \leq j \leq q$,
- $p = 1$ or $A_{i,p-1} = 0$, and
- $q = n$ or $A_{i,q+1} = 0$.

For a row r_i^A, $\mathrm{cons1}(r_i^A)$ is the number of blocks of consecutive ones in r_i^A. Additionally, $\mathrm{splits}(r_i^A)$ (the number of gaps between the blocks) is defined as $\mathrm{cons1}(r_i^A) - 1$ if r_i^A contains a 1-entry, and 0 otherwise. We define $\mathrm{cons1}(A) = \sum_{i=1}^{m_A} \mathrm{cons1}(r_i^A)$ for a matrix A. Equivalently, $\mathrm{splits}(A) = \sum_{i=1}^{m_A} \mathrm{splits}(r_i^A)$. Let c_i^A and c_j^A be two columns of a binary matrix. By $d_h(c_i^A, c_j^A)$ we denote the Hamming distance between c_i^A and c_j^A, that is, the number of rows with different values.

In this paper we assume graphs G as simple and undirected. By $V(G)$ and $E(G)$ we denote the vertex set and edge set of G, respectively. For a binary matrix A, let $G(A)$ be the complete graph that consists of the vertices $V = \{v_i \mid c_i^A \text{ is a column in } A\}$. If we talk about a vertex v_i with index i in $G(A)$, we mean the vertex v_i that corresponds to column c_i^A.

Sometimes we consider graphs $G(A)$ obtained from a matrix A with a quadratic and symmetric *distance matrix* D of size $|V(G)| \times |V(G)|$, such that $D_{i,j}$ is the *length* of the edge between v_i and v_j. A *tour* T in $G(A)$ is a sequence of vertices $(v_{i_1}, \ldots, v_{i_n})$ that contains each vertex of $G(A)$ exactly once. (We do not require adjacency, as $G(A)$ is complete.) The *length* of T in $G(A)$ under a distance matrix D is $D_{i_n,i_1} + \sum_{k=1}^{n-1} D_{i_k,i_{k+1}}$. Finding a tour of minimum length in $G(A)$ under a distance matrix D is known as the *Travelling Salesperson Problem* (TSP) and is NP-complete [25].

3 Complexity of Linear Diagrams

The most important quality aspect supporting the cognitive effectiveness of linear diagrams is the number of line segments [26]. To minimize the number of line segments that have to be drawn, we have to find an appropriate horizontal ordering of the overlaps. There is a one-to-one correspondence between linear diagrams and binary matrices: Let $(\mathcal{S}, \mathcal{U})$ be a set system with universe $\mathcal{U} = \{u_1, \ldots, u_n\}$ and sets $\mathcal{S} = \{S_1, \ldots, S_m\}$, hence, for all $i \in [m]$, $S_i \subseteq \mathcal{U}$. The system $\mathcal{S}$ can be represented by a binary matrix A s.t. $A_{i,j} = 1$ if and only if element u_j belongs to set S_i. The rows and columns of A are exactly the rows and columns of the linear diagram, respectively. Line segments in the linear diagram correspond to blocks of consecutive ones in the matrix A. The problem of finding a horizontal ordering of the overlaps that minimizes the number of line segments is equivalent to the problem of finding a permutation $\pi \in \Pi_n$ that minimizes $\mathrm{cons1}(\pi(A))$.

A matrix A is said to have the *consecutive ones property* (C1P) if there is a permutation $\pi \in \Pi_{n_A}$ with $\mathrm{splits}(\pi(A)) = 0$. There are several linear-time algorithms for testing if a matrix has the C1P and for computing the corresponding permutation, the first due to Booth and Lueker [3]. Thus, we can decide in linear time if a linear diagram can be drawn such that each set is represented by exactly one line segment.

Most of the time though, linear diagrams cannot be drawn in this way. In this case we want to minimize the number of required line segments. The corresponding binary matrix problem is known as *consecutive block minimization* in the literature, its decision problem is given below.

CONSECUTIVE BLOCK MINIMIZATION
Instance: A binary matrix A and a non-negative integer k.
Question: Does there exist a permutation $\pi \in \Pi_{n_A}$ such that
   $\mathrm{cons1}(\pi(A)) \leq k$?

The problem has been shown to be NP-complete [19], even if each row contains exactly two ones [13]. We give here an alternative proof of NP-completeness for binary matrices with two ones per row and three ones per column, thus further strengthening the NP-completeness result.

Theorem 1. CONSECUTIVE BLOCK MINIMIZATION *is* NP-*complete for matrices with two ones per row and three ones per column.*

Proof. Membership in NP is evident. For hardness, we give a reduction from HAMILTONIAN PATH on graphs of degree 3, which is NP-complete [11]. HAMILTONIAN PATH asks for a given graph G, if there is a path in G that visits every vertex exactly once. Let G be an instance of HAMILTONIAN PATH such that $E(G) = \{e_1, \ldots, e_m\}$ and $V(G) = \{v_1, \ldots, v_n\}$ and G has degree 3. We construct an instance (A, k) of CONSECUTIVE BLOCK MINIMIZATION as follows. Let A be the incidence matrix of G, which has $n_A = |V(G)|$ columns and $m_A = |E(G)|$ rows with $A_{i,j} = 1$ if and only if $v_i \in e_j$. Clearly, this matrix has two ones per row, as each edge contains two vertices and 3 ones per column, as G has degree 3. We show that G contains a Hamiltonian path if and only if there exists a permutation π of the columns of A such that $\mathrm{cons1}(\pi(A)) \leq 2 \cdot m - (n-1)$.

"$\Rightarrow$": Let $P = (v_{\ell_1}, v_{\ell_2}, \ldots, v_{\ell_n})$ be a Hamiltonian path in G. We claim that $\pi = (\ell_1, \ell_2, \ldots, \ell_n)$ satisfies $\mathrm{cons1}(\pi(A)) \leq 2 \cdot m - (n-1)$. Consider the edges $\{v_{\ell_i}, v_{\ell_{i+1}}\}$ for $1 \leq i \leq n-1$, which exist because P is a path. As v_{ℓ_i} and $v_{\ell_{i+1}}$

are consecutive in P, the columns $c_{\ell_i}^A$ and $c_{\ell_{i+1}}^A$ are consecutive in $\pi(A)$. Thus, the row in A corresponding to the edge $\{v_{\ell_i}, v_{\ell_{i+1}}\}$ contributes to exactly one block of consecutive ones. The remaining $m - (n - 1)$ rows can contribute to at most two blocks of consecutive ones as they only contain two 1-entries each. Together, there are at most $n - 1 + 2 \cdot (m - (n - 1)) = 2 \cdot m - (n - 1)$ blocks of consecutive ones in $\pi(A)$.

"$\Leftarrow$": Let $\pi = (\ell_1, \ell_2, \ldots, \ell_n)$ be a permutation of the columns of A that satisfies $\mathrm{cons1}(\pi(A)) \leq 2 \cdot m - (n - 1)$. We claim that $P = (v_{\ell_1}, v_{\ell_2}, \ldots, v_{\ell_n})$ is a Hamiltonian path in G. There are at least $n - 1$ blocks of consecutive ones of size two in $\pi(A)$ as otherwise $\mathrm{cons1}(\pi(A)) > 2 \cdot m - (n - 1)$. As G is a simple graph, no two rows of A contain ones in the same columns and thus each of these blocks of consecutive ones has to start at a different column. By the pigeonhole principle, for each $1 \leq i \leq n - 1$, there exists such a block of consecutive ones that starts at the i-th column of $\pi(A)$. Hence, $\{v_{\ell_i}, v_{\ell_{i+1}}\}$ is an edge in G for all $1 \leq i \leq n - 1$, and P is a Hamiltonian path. $\square$

CONSECUTIVE BLOCK MINIMIZATION has been further studied from an algorithmic view. Several heuristic methods for finding permutations π with small $\mathrm{cons1}(\pi(A))$ have been given [14,15,28]. Haddadi and Layouni [16] transformed CONSECUTIVE BLOCK MINIMIZATION to a travelling salesperson problem, we will go into more details on their results in Sect. 4.

Further variations of consecutive-ones problems that could be interesting for linear diagrams have been studied, mostly giving hardness results or polynomial algorithms assuming that some underlying parameters of the problems are constant: It has been shown that the problem of finding a permutation π of the columns of a binary matrix A such that for all $i \in [m_A]$, $\mathrm{cons1}(r_i^A) \leq k \in \mathbb{N}$ is NP-complete [12], which translates to the problem of having at most k line segments per set in a linear diagram. Another more involved problem has been studied, called GAPPED CONSECUTIVE ONES, in which we are given a binary matrix A and want to find a permutation π of the columns of A such that for all $i \in [m_A]$, $\mathrm{cons1}(r_i^A) \leq k \in \mathbb{N}$, and the gaps between two consecutive blocks of ones in a row of $\pi(A)$ is at most some maximum gap parameter δ [8,22,23]. Here gaps refer to maximal blocks of zeros between two blocks of ones.

Furthermore, there is literature devoted to turning a binary matrix into a binary matrix that has the C1P by deleting rows, deleting columns, or flipping entries (turning 1-entries into 0-entries and/or turning 0-entries into 1-entries). Dom et al. [10] give a summary of results.

4 TSP Model

In this section, we describe the procedure of minimizing the number of line segments in a linear diagram by using a TSP model, and give a runtime optimization. We also show how to incorporate further constraints into this model.

4.1 Solving Linear Diagrams with TSP

We now present how to solve the task of minimizing the number of line segments drawn in a linear diagram. Let us start with the key lemma for our model.

Lemma 1 ([16]). *Let A be a binary matrix with n columns and let A' be the binary matrix obtained from A by appending a column of zeros to the right of A. Let $(v_{i_1}, v_{i_2}, \ldots, v_{i_{n+1}})$ be a tour of length L in $G(A')$ under distance matrix $D_{i,j} = d_h(c_i^{A'}, c_j^{A'})$. Assume that $v_{i_k} = v_{n+1}$, corresponding to the appended column of zeros, and let $\pi = (i_{k+1}, \ldots i_{n+1}, i_1, \ldots, i_{k-1})$. Then $L = 2 \cdot \mathrm{cons1}(\pi(A))$.*

As discussed in Sect. 3, the task of minimizing line segments in linear diagrams is the same as finding a permutation π of the columns of a binary matrix A that minimizes $\mathrm{cons1}(\pi(A))$. One way to find such a permutation is with a TSP-model as outlined by Lemma 1: Let A be a binary matrix with n columns. We construct the binary matrix A' by appending a column of zeros to the right of A. From the matrix A', we construct the complete graph $G(A')$, such that vertices correspond to columns in A'. A distance matrix D for $G(A')$ is constructed such that $D_{i,j}$ is the Hamming distance $d_h(c_i^{A'}, c_j^{A'})$. We then compute a TSP tour $(v_{i_1}, v_{i_2}, \ldots, v_{i_{n+1}})$ of minimal length in $G(A')$. Assume that v_{i_k} is the vertex corresponding to the column $c_{n_{A'}}^{A'}$. Then, by Lemma 1, $\pi = (i_{k+1}, \ldots, i_{n+1}, i_1, \ldots, i_{k-1})$ is the permutation with minimal $\mathrm{cons1}(\pi(A))$. The intuition for this is that choosing an edge $\{v_i, v_j\}$ of small length in $G(A')$ is the same as starting or ending few consecutive blocks of ones (corresponding to line segments in a linear diagram) when going from the column c_i to c_j. With this argumentation each block of consecutive ones is started and ended exactly once, and the length of the tour is $2 \cdot \mathrm{cons1}(\pi(A))$. Note that adding the extra column at the end is necessary, as otherwise it could be that some consecutive blocks of ones, those that start at the first column or end at the last column, are "not counted in the tour".

There is a small runtime optimization that can be applied to decrease the size of the graph $G(A')$. Columns of A that have ones in the same rows, their Hamming distance being zero, can be collapsed into a single column. The above procedure may be applied to compute the desired permutation of columns, and then the collapsed columns can be expanded again to appear consecutively. Clearly, this does not influence the number consecutive blocks of ones in the resulting matrix. In terms of set systems, this corresponds to collapsing multiple overlaps that contain the same sets into a single representative. In an optimal linear diagram, such overlaps would never be separated.

We tested this method of computing optimal column orderings by applying a state-of-the art TSP-solver. We will report on experimental results for real-world and previously considered set visualization instances in Sect. 5. Note that the same procedure has already been applied to instances from consecutive block minimization [28].

4.2   Priorities for Sets

In some contexts certain sets in a linear diagram might be considered more important than others. We would want to compute a linear diagram, in which these sets are drawn with a single line segment, but the other sets should be drawn with as few line segments as possible. It is clear that forcing more than two sets to be drawn as one line segment is not always possible, as there are binary matrices with three rows that do not have the C1P. We can solve the problem on binary matrices as a TSP model due to the following result.

Lemma 2. *Let A be a binary matrix with n columns and exactly p 1-entries and let $C_1, \ldots, C_q \subseteq \{c_1, \ldots, c_{n_A}\}$ be a family of non-empty sets of columns of A satisfying*

$$\exists \pi \in \Pi_n \forall k \in [q] : \text{the columns in } C_k \text{ appear consecutively in } \pi(A).$$

Let A' be the matrix obtained from A by appending a column of zeros. We consider the graph $G(A')$ with distance matrix D s.t.

$$D_{i,j} = d_h(c_i, c_j) + (2p+1) \cdot \sum_{k=1}^{q} |\mathbb{1}_{C_k}(c_i) - \mathbb{1}_{C_k}(c_j)|,$$

where $\mathbb{1}_{C_k}$ is the indicator function for set C_k. Let $T = (v_{i_1}, v_{i_2}, \ldots, v_{i_{n+1}})$ be a tour of minimal length in $G(A')$ under distance matrix D. Let $v_{i_k} = v_{n+1}$, corresponding to the appended column of zeros. Then the permutation $\pi = (i_{k+1}, \ldots, i_{n+1}, i_1, \ldots, i_{k-1})$ has the following properties

(1) For all $k \in [q]$ the columns in C_k appear consecutively in $\pi(A)$.
(2) Of all $\pi' \in \Pi_n$ that satisfy (1), π is the one with minimum $\text{cons1}(\pi(A))$.

Proof. Let π be the permutation as defined above. We first show by contradiction that π satisfies (1). Assume to the contrary that π does not satisfy (1) and consider any permutation π' of the columns of A that satisfies (1). This permutation exists by assumption. Consider the tour $T' = (v_{n+1}) \star \pi$. The length of T' is at most $2q(2p+1) + 2p$, as there can be at most p consecutive blocks of ones in $\pi'(A)$, each contributing two to the length of T'. The value $2q(2p+1)$ is due to the fact that we "leave" or "enter" vertices corresponding to the set of columns C_k, $1 \le k \le q$, exactly twice. To the contrary, the length of T is at least $2(q+1)(2p+1)$. Hence, T cannot be a tour of minimal length, yielding a contradiction. It is clear that π also satisfies (2), as increases in the length of the tour T, also increases the number of consecutive ones of the matrix $\pi(A)$ due to the same reasoning as in Lemma 1. □

We can directly apply the above lemma to find a permutation of the columns of a matrix A with minimum blocks of consecutive ones among the permutations π that have $\text{cons1}(r_{i_1}^{\pi(A)})) = \text{cons1}(r_{i_1}^{\pi(A)}) = 1$ for $i_1, i_2 \in m_A$: We simply define $C_1 = \{j \in [n_A] \mid A_{i_1,j} = 1\}$ and $C_2 = \{j \in [n_A] \mid A_{i_2,j} = 1\}$, and apply the reduction to TSP as outlined in Lemma 2. Clearly, C_1 and C_2 satisfy the requirements of Lemma 2, as a matrix with two rows always has the C1P. In our experiments we show how adding these constraints affects the runtime and the number of blocks of consecutive ones. Note, however, that the result of Lemma 2 allows us to constrain column orders of a matrix in far more general ways.

4.3 A Weighted Version

The shortcoming of the approach described in Sect. 4.2 is that we can only restrict two sets to be drawn in one line segment. If we want to involve more sets in this, we can use a model with weighted sets (corresponding to rows in a binary matrix A). Then, if a weight of row r_i^A is bigger than a weight of r_j^A, it is "worse" to have more blocks of consecutive ones for r_i^A than it is for r_j^A. Formally, we are given a binary matrix A and a weight function $f : [m_A] \to \mathbb{N}$, and we want to find a permutation π of the columns of A that minimizes $\sum_{i=1}^{m_A} f(i) \mathrm{cons1}(r_i^{\pi(A)})$. Solving this problem is straight-forward with a TSP-model: We construct the matrix A' by appending a column of zeros to the right of A. We then create a distance matrix D for $G(A')$ such that $D_{i,j} = \sum_{k=1}^{m_A} f(k)|A'_{k,i} - A'_{k,j}|$. This distance matrix corresponds to weighted Hamming distances. Then, we simply find the tour T of minimal total distance in $G(A')$ under D, and obtain the desired permutation π from T as in Lemma 1. We conduct experiments for this weighted version of consecutive block minimization in Sect. 5.

4.4 Hierarchical Constraints

We now to present an algorithm that allows for more general constraints on the allowed column orders of a binary matrix, restricting column orders by *PQ-trees*. We adopt the definition of PQ-trees of Burkard et al. [4], as our algorithm directly applies their results. A PQ-tree T over the set $[n]$ is a rooted, ordered tree whose *leaves* are pairwise distinct elements of $[n]$ and whose *internal* nodes are distinguished as either *P*-nodes or *Q*-nodes. The set LEAF(T) denotes the leaves of T.

Every PQ-tree T represents a set $\Pi(T)$ of permutations of LEAF(T) as follows. If T consists of a single leaf $i \in [n]$, then $\Pi(T) = \{(i)\}$. Otherwise, the root $r(T)$ of T is a *P*-node or a *Q*-node. Let $v_1, \ldots, v_m$ denote the children of $r(T)$, ordered from left to right, and let T_i denote the maximal subtrees rooted at v_i, $1 \le i \le m$. If $r(T)$ is a *P*-node, then

$$\Pi(T) = \bigcup_{\psi \in \Pi_m} \Pi(T_{\psi(1)}) \star \Pi(T_{\psi(2)}) \star \cdots \star \Pi(T_{\psi(m)}),$$

and if $r(T)$ is a *Q*-node, then

$$\Pi(T) = \Pi(T_1) \star \Pi(T_2) \star \cdots \star \Pi(T_m) \cup \Pi(T_m) \star \Pi(T_{m-1}) \star \cdots \star \Pi(T_1).$$

Informally, children of *P*-nodes can be permuted arbitrarily, while children of *Q*-nodes can only be reversed.

For applications of PQ-trees we refer to Booth and Lueker [3]. They can be used to model allowed column orders of a binary matrix or, equivalently, the orders of overlaps in a linear diagram; for example, if overlaps illustrated by a linear diagram have some hierarchical relations between them and should not be permuted arbitrarily, then we might represent this by a PQ-tree accordingly. If the maximum degree of the PQ-tree T that represents column orders of a

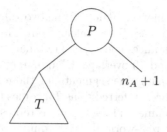

Fig. 2. Construction of PQ-tree in Theorem 2.

binary matrix A has small maximum degree, then the permutation $\pi \in \Pi(T)$ that minimizes $\mathrm{cons1}(\pi(A))$ can be computed efficiently.

Theorem 2. *Let A be a binary matrix and let T be a PQ-tree of maximum degree d such that $\Pi(T) \subseteq \Pi_{n_A}$. The permutation $\pi \in \Pi(T)$ that minimizes $\mathrm{cons1}(\pi(A))$ can be found in time $\mathcal{O}(\max(m_A \cdot n_A^2, 2^d \cdot n_A^3))$.*

Proof. We apply a result of Burkard et al. [4] that states that for a PQ-tree T with maximum degree d, and an $n \times n$ distance matrix D, the shortest TSP tour for the matrix D contained in $\Pi(T)$ can be computed in $\mathcal{O}(2^d \cdot n^3)$ overall time.

Let A be a binary matrix and let T be a PQ-tree of maximum degree d such that $\Pi(T) \subseteq \Pi_{n_A}$. Let A' be the binary matrix obtained from A by appending a column of zeros to the right of A. We construct a PQ-tree T' such that $\Pi(T') \subseteq \Pi_{n_A+1}$. The PQ-tree T' consists of a P-node that has two children: The leaf $n_A + 1$ and the tree T rooted at $r(T)$, see Fig. 2. Notice that the maximum degree of T' is at most $d + 1$. Let D be the distance matrix corresponding to edge weights $D_{i,j} = d_h(c_i^{A'}, c_j^{A'})$ in $G(A')$. Due to the result of Burkard et al. we can find in time $\mathcal{O}(2^d \cdot n_A^3)$ a tour of minimum length in $G(A')$ that is contained in $\Pi(T')$. By Lemma 1 and the construction of T', we can obtain from this tour a permutation $\pi \in \Pi(T)$ that minimizes $\mathrm{cons1}(\pi(A))$. We need $m_A \cdot n_A^2$ time to construct the distance matrix D, thus we need to account for the possibility that $m_A \cdot n_A^2 > 2^d \cdot n_A^3$, taking the maximum of both. $\qquad\square$

5 Experiments

In this section, we present an experimental evaluation of the algorithms proposed in Sect. 4, comparing them with state-of-the art heuristics.

5.1 Setup and Test Data

Setup. All experiments were performed on a desktop machine with an Intel i7-8700K processor. The implementations of algorithms were done in Python 3.7. To solve our TSP models, we used the Concorde TSP solver[1] with the QSopt linear programming solver[2]. The code is available online [9].

---

[1] https://www.math.uwaterloo.ca/tsp/concorde.html.
[2] http://www.math.uwaterloo.ca/~bico/qsopt/.

Test Data. We consider binary matrices from two different sources. The first set of instances, referred to as T_1, is taken from Chapman et al. [6] and is available online[3]. These instances consist of 440 binary matrices with 5 sets and 10 overlaps up to 50 sets and 70 overlaps. Chapman et al. [6] provide results of their algorithms for minimizing line segments for these instances.

The second set of instances, referred to as T_2, comes from a work by Jacobsen et al. [18] and is available online[4]. The set systems represented by these instances are taken out from a large real-world dataset coming from the Kaggle "What's Cooking" competition [2]. The sizes of these instances range from 20 overlaps and 6 sets to 160 overlaps and 20 sets. Overall, there are a total of 4060 instances.

5.2   Computing Optimal Linear Diagrams

The first set of experiments considers the task of computing optimal linear diagrams, or equivalently, finding column orderings of the instances that minimize the number of blocks of consecutive ones.

Algorithms. We include comparisons of the following algorithms.

- TSPConcorde: This algorithm from Sect. 4.1 uses our TSP model and the Concorde TSP solver to solve the problem optimally. The reported runtimes include generating input files for the Concorde solver and reading its output.
- HeuristicRodgers: This algorithm is a python implementation of a greedy algorithm by Rodgers et al. [26]. A pairwise similarity measure between overlaps is defined, and then an overlap order is computed iteratively, trying to place similar overlaps next to each other. Rodgers et al. provide an online demo that implements this algorithm[5].
- Supervenn: This algorithm is from a recent GitHub project [17]. For a set of 10000 seeds it defines a pairwise similarity measure between overlaps and then applies a heuristic to compute an overlap order.
- BestChapman: Chapman et al. [6] compare several heuristic methods to compute overlap orderings of linear diagrams that minimize the drawn line segments. They report the number of line segments of overlap orders computed by their algorithms for test set T_1. As they do not provide the code for all algorithms, and the explanation of the remaining algorithms is incomplete, we had to restrict the evaluation of their approaches to test set T_1. For an instance of T_1, we assume that the algorithm BestChapman is any algorithm of Chapman et al. that computes an overlap ordering with the least amount of blocks of consecutive ones. They do not provide the runtimes of their algorithms in their abstract [6], so we cannot either.

---

[3] https://doi.org/10.17869/enu.2021.2748170.
[4] https://osf.io/nvd8e/.
[5] http://www.eulerdiagrams.com/linear/generator/.

Table 1. Results for test set T_1. White columns depict the mean relative/absolute optimality gaps (except TSPConcorde); gray columns depict the mean runtimes. For the algorithms of Chapman we do not know the runtimes.

| #columns | TSPConcorde | | HeuristicRodgers | | Supervenn | | Best Chapman |
	blocks / row	t [ms]	gap [rel./abs.]	t [ms]	gap [rel./abs.]	t [ms]	gap [rel./abs.]
10	1.7	7	3.3/0.9	0	1.6/0.8	853	0.0/0.0
20	2.8	13	6.0/3.0	1	3.3/1.8	1360	0.0/0.0
30	4.0	22	6.0/5.2	1	3.4/3.1	1861	0.2/0.3
50	6.0	69	6.9/9.3	4	3.7/5.6	2969	0.4/0.5
70	7.9	340	8.1/13.3	7	4.7/8.0	4192	0.5/0.8

Comparison. TSPConcorde by design computes optimal column orderings. Hence, we report the relative and absolute optimality gaps for the other algorithms. That is, let blocks$(\mathcal{A}, I)$ be the number of blocks of consecutive ones of a column ordering computed by algorithm $\mathcal{A}$ for instance I. Then the relative optimality gap in percent is $100 \cdot \left(\frac{\text{blocks}(\mathcal{A}, I)}{\text{blocks}(\text{TSPConcorde}, I)} - 1 \right)$ and the absolute optimality gap is blocks$(\mathcal{A}, I)$ − blocks(TSPConcorde, I). For a set of instances, we report these value averaged. For TSPConcorde we provide the average number of consecutive blocks of ones per row, as the optimality gap is always zero. We also provide the mean runtime for the same set of instances. Results are broken down by the number of columns, as the factorial of the number of columns determines the size of the possible search space for an algorithm.

Test Set T_1. Table 1 shows the results for test set T_1. The simple heuristic of Rodgers et al. [26] has the smallest runtimes, while also performing worst with regard to optimality gaps. The runtimes of Supervenn are rather high, while the optimality gaps are lower when compared to HeuristicRodgers, resulting from the 10000 runs of a heuristic, each skewed with a different seed value. While the problem of consecutive block minimization is NP-complete, TSPConcorde solved all instances optimally. The average runtime for the largest class of instances from T_1 is still less than a second. It is worth mentioning that optimality gaps of mostly under 10% indicate that the heuristics are quite good.

The heuristics of Chapman et al. [6] solved 340 of the 440 instances optimally. For the remaining instances, the maximum difference between the optimal number of consecutive blocks and their best solution is 3. This yields the fairly small optimality gaps for BestChapman, while we expect that these values would increase for larger instances, a pattern that just starts to appear in Table 1.

Test Set T_2. Table 2 shows results for test set T_2. TSPConcorde is able to solve all instances optimally, the mean runtime still being well below 100 ms, even for instances with up to 160 columns. For Supervenn and HeuristicRodgers we see similar results as in the previous test set. While Supervenn has slightly better optimality gaps, HeuristicRodgers takes only a thousandth of the time of

Table 2. Results for test set T_2. White columns depict the mean relative/absolute optimality gaps (except TSPConcorde); gray columns depict the mean runtimes.

	TSPConcorde		HeuristicRodgers		Supervenn	
#columns	blocks / row	t [ms]	gap [rel./abs.]	t [ms]	gap [rel./abs.]	t [ms]
20-50	1.7	17	8.4/2.0	1	7.7/1.8	1949
55-80	1.8	23	10.0/2.5	2	8.4/2.2	3642
85-110	1.9	36	10.9/2.8	4	9.2/2.5	5408
115-140	2.0	82	11.1/3.1	6	9.8/2.8	7782
145-160	2.0	71	10.7/3.0	9	9.8/2.9	10133

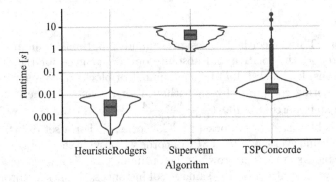

Fig. 3. Violin and box plot showing runtimes for all instances from T_1 and T_2.

Supervenn. Again, optimality gaps increase with increasing number of columns to about 10% compared to the optimal solutions.

Runtimes. Figure 3 shows a boxplot and violin plot of the runtimes of the three algorithms HeuristicRodgers, Supervenn, and TSPConcorde for the combined test set $T_1 \cup T_2$. The y-axis is scaled logarithmically. It again reflects that Supervenn takes much longer than HeuristicRodgers, while the runtimes for both algorithms do not contain outliers as their runtime is rather "deterministic", in the sense that their runtime is accurately represented as a polynomial function of the number of columns of an instance. On the contrary, the runtimes of TSPConcorde contain a multitude of outliers, while most runtimes are still below 100 ms. Only two instances take more than 10 s to solve.

5.3   Constraints

Next, we present experiments on how constraints on the column order affect the runtime and the number of blocks of TSPConcorde. Namely, we implemented the constraints from Sects. 4.2 and 4.3 that either specify that two sets/rows

Table 3. Results for test set T_1 and constrained versions. White columns depict mean relative/absolute optimality gaps (except TSPConcorde); gray columns depict mean runtimes.

#columns	TSPConcorde blocks / row	t [ms]	TSPConcordeFS gap [rel./abs.]	t [ms]	TSPConcordeW gap [rel./abs.]	t [ms]
10	1.7	7	4.1/1.7	8	2.6/0.9	7
20	2.8	13	4.8/3.7	17	4.5/3.0	11
30	4.0	22	6.2/6.7	37	6.5/5.9	25
50	6.0	69	6.4/10.2	104	8.7/12.1	61
70	7.9	340	7.0/14.8	210	9.4/16.7	84

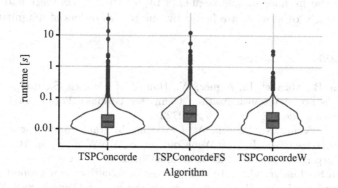

Fig. 4. Runtimes of constrained algorithms for all instances from T_1 and T_2.

have to be represented as a single line segment/consecutive blocks of ones, or give specific weights to sets. The evaluation for both constraints works as follows.

- Two sets as single line segment: We pick uniformly at random for each instance in our test set $T_1 \cup T_2$ two sets that have to be drawn as a single line segments, and then apply the reduction to TSP described in Sect. 4.2, and solve the resulting TSP-instance with the Concorde TSP-solver. We identify this approach by TSPConcordeFS for "fixed sets".
- Weighted sets: For each matrix A in the test set $T_1 \cup T_2$ we specify a weight function $f : [m_A] \to \mathbb{N}$ that assigns to each set a unique integer weight in $[m_A]$ uniformly at random. Then, we apply the reduction to TSP as described in Sect. 4.3 and solve the resulting TSP-instance with the Concorde TSP-solver. We identify this approach by TSPConcordeW for "weighted".

Table 3 shows runtimes and optimality gaps for test set T_1. We observe that adding constraints does not influence runtimes of the TSP solver significantly. Furthermore, by adding constraints we may not be able to reach the optimal number of line segments anymore and see a maximum optimality gap of 10%. The results for test set T_2 are similar. Figure 4 shows a box and violin plot of runtimes for TSPConcorde and the constrained versions thereof, further suggesting that adding constraints does not significantly influence runtimes.

6   Conclusion

We have studied the algorithmic complexity of computing optimal linear diagrams and observed that it is equivalent to a related problem on binary matrices. Despite its NP-completeness, even in a restricted setting, we have formulated a TSP model for solving the problem optimally. In an experimental study, we have seen that a state-of-the-art TSP solver can in fact solve a large set of instances obtained from our model optimally, most of them within few milliseconds. Hence it is feasible to strive for optimal linear diagrams in most practical settings and thus reduce the number of line segments by up to 10% compared to the best heuristics, which, otherwise, are faster by one to two orders of magnitude.

References

1. Alsallakh, B., Micallef, L., Aigner, W., Hauser, H., Miksch, S., Rodgers, P.: The state-of-the-art of set visualization. Computer Graphics Forum **35**(1), 234–260 (2016). https://doi.org/10.1111/cgf.12722
2. Amburg, I., Veldt, N., Benson, A.: Clustering in graphs and hypergraphs with categorical edge labels. In: The Web Conference (WWW 2020), pp. 706–717. ACM (2020). https://doi.org/10.1145/3366423.3380152
3. Booth, K.S., Lueker, G.S.: Testing for the consecutive ones property, interval graphs, and graph planarity using PQ-tree algorithms. J. Comput. Syst. Sci. **13**(3), 335–379 (1976). https://doi.org/10.1016/S0022-0000(76)80045-1
4. Burkard, R.E., Deineko, V.G., Woeginger, G.J.: The travelling salesman and the PQ-Tree. Math. Oper. Res. **23**(3), 613–623 (1998). https://doi.org/10.1287/moor.23.3.613
5. Chapman, P.: Interactivity in linear diagrams. In: Basu, A., Stapleton, G., Linker, S., Legg, C., Manalo, E., Viana, P. (eds.) Diagrams 2021. LNCS (LNAI), vol. 12909, pp. 449–465. Springer, Cham (2021). https://doi.org/10.1007/978-3-030-86062-2_47
6. Chapman, P., Sim, K., Chen, H.: Drawing algorithms for linear diagrams. In: Talk Abstracts of Diagrams 2021, pp. 1–3 (2021), http://www.diagrams-conference.org/2021/wp-content/uploads/2021/08/Peter-Chapman-6-chapman.pdf
7. Chapman, P., Stapleton, G., Rodgers, P., Micallef, L., Blake, A.: Visualizing sets: an empirical comparison of diagram types. In: Dwyer, T., Purchase, H., Delaney, A. (eds.) Diagrams 2014. LNCS (LNAI), vol. 8578, pp. 146–160. Springer, Heidelberg (2014). https://doi.org/10.1007/978-3-662-44043-8_18
8. Chauve, C., Maňuch, J., Patterson, M.: On the gapped consecutive-ones property. Electron. Notes Discret. Math. **34**, 121–125 (2009). https://doi.org/10.1016/j.endm.2009.07.020
9. Dobler, A.: On computing optimal linear diagrams: Code (2022). https://doi.org/10.5281/zenodo.6637911
10. Dom, M., Guo, J., Niedermeier, R.: Approximation and fixed-parameter algorithms for consecutive ones submatrix problems. J. Comput. Syst. Sci. **76**(3), 204–221 (2010). https://doi.org/10.1016/j.jcss.2009.07.001

11. Garey, M.R., Johnson, D.S., Tarjan, R.E.: The planar Hamiltonian circuit problem is NP-complete. SIAM J. Comput. **5**(4), 704–714 (1976). https://doi.org/10.1137/0205049

12. Goldberg, P.W., Golumbic, M.C., Kaplan, H., Shamir, R.: Four strikes against physical mapping of DNA. J. Comput. Biol. **2**(1), 139–152 (1995). https://doi.org/10.1089/cmb.1995.2.139

13. Haddadi, S.: A note on the NP-hardness of the consecutive block minimization problem. Int. Trans. Op. Res. **9**(6), 775–777 (2002). https://doi.org/10.1111/1475-3995.00387

14. Haddadi, S.: Exponential neighborhood search for consecutive block minimization. Int. Trans. Op. Res. (2021). https://doi.org/10.1111/itor.13065

15. Haddadi, S.: Iterated local search for consecutive block minimization. Comput. Oper. Res. **131**, 105273 (2021). https://doi.org/10.1016/j.cor.2021.105273

16. Haddadi, S., Layouni, Z.: Consecutive block minimization is 1.5-approximable. Inf. Process. Lett. **108**(3), 132–135 (2008). https://doi.org/10.1016/j.ipl.2008.04.009

17. Indukaev, F.: Supervenn python package (v0.3.2) (2021). https://doi.org/10.5281/zenodo.4424381

18. Jacobsen, B., Wallinger, M., Kobourov, S., Nöllenburg, M.: MetroSets: visualizing sets as metro maps. IEEE Trans. Vis. Comput. Graph. **27**(2), 1257–1267 (2021). https://doi.org/10.1109/TVCG.2020.3030475

19. Kou, L.T.: Polynomial complete consecutive information retrieval problems. SIAM J. Comput. **6**(1), 67–75 (1977). https://doi.org/10.1137/0206004

20. Lamy, J.B., Berthelot, H., Capron, C., Favre, M.: Rainbow boxes: a new technique for overlapping set visualization and two applications in the biomedical domain. J. Vis. Lang. Comput. **43**, 71–82 (2017). https://doi.org/10.1016/j.jvlc.2017.09.003

21. Luz, S., Masoodian, M.: A comparison of linear and mosaic diagrams for set visualization. Inf. Vis. **18**(3), 297–310 (2019). https://doi.org/10.1177/1473871618754343

22. Maňuch, J., Patterson, M.: The complexity of the gapped consecutive-ones property problem for matrices of bounded maximum degree. J. Comput. Biol. **18**(9), 1243–1253 (2011). https://doi.org/10.1089/cmb.2011.0128

23. Maňuch, J., Patterson, M., Chauve, C.: Hardness results on the gapped consecutive-ones property problem. Discret. Appl. Math. **160**(18), 2760–2768 (2012). https://doi.org/10.1016/j.dam.2012.03.019

24. Masoodian, M., Koivunen, L.: Temporal visualization of sets and their relationships using time-sets. In: Information Visualisation (IV 2018), pp. 85–90. IEEE (2018). https://doi.org/10.1109/iV.2018.00025

25. Papadimitriou, C.H.: The Euclidean travelling salesman problem is NP-complete. Theor. Comput. Sci. **4**(3), 237–244 (1977). https://doi.org/10.1016/0304-3975(77)90012-3

26. Rodgers, P., Stapleton, G., Chapman, P.: Visualizing sets with linear diagrams. ACM Trans. Comput. Hum. Interact. **22**(6), 1–39 (2015). https://doi.org/10.1145/2810012

27. Sato, Y., Mineshima, K.: The efficacy of diagrams in syllogistic reasoning: a case of linear diagrams. In: Cox, P., Plimmer, B., Rodgers, P. (eds.) Diagrams 2012. LNCS (LNAI), vol. 7352, pp. 352–355. Springer, Heidelberg (2012). https://doi.org/10.1007/978-3-642-31223-6_49

28. Soares, L.C.R., Reinsma, J.A., Nascimento, L.H.L., Carvalho, M.A.M.: Heuristic methods to consecutive block minimization. Comput. Oper. Res. **120**, 104948 (2020). https://doi.org/10.1016/j.cor.2020.104948

29. Stapleton, G., Chapman, P., Rodgers, P., Touloumis, A., Blake, A., Delaney, A.: The efficacy of Euler diagrams and linear diagrams for visualizing set cardinality using proportions and numbers. PLoS ONE **14**(3), e0211234 (2019). https://doi.org/10.1371/journal.pone.0211234

Visual Proofs as Counterexamples to the *Standard View* of Informal Mathematical Proofs?

Simon Weisgerber$^{(\boxtimes)}$ [ID]

University of Vienna, Universitätsstraße 7, 1010 Vienna, Austria
`simon.weisgerber@univie.ac.at`

Abstract. A passage from Jody Azzouni's article "The Algorithmic-Device View of Informal Rigorous Mathematical Proof" in which he argues against Hamami and Avigad's *standard view* of informal mathematical proof with the help of a specific visual proof of $1/2 + 1/4 + 1/8 + 1/16 + \cdots = 1$ is critically examined. By reference to mathematicians' judgments about visual proofs in general, it is argued that Azzouni's critique of Hamami and Avigad's account is not valid. Nevertheless, by identifying a necessary condition for the visual proof to be considered a proper proof in the first place, and suggesting an appropriate way to establish its correctness, it is shown how Azzouni's assessment of the epistemic process associated with the visual proof can turn out to be essentially correct. From this, it is concluded that although visual proofs do not constitute counterexamples to the *standard view* in the sense suggested by Azzouni, at least the visual proof mentioned above shows that this view does not cover all the ways in which mathematical truth can be justified.

Keywords: Visual proofs · Mathematical rigor · Standard view · Mathematical practice

1 Introduction

The relation between informal mathematical proofs and formal derivations in (suitable) formal systems is a much debated topic in the philosophy of mathematics in general and the philosophy of mathematical practice in particular. Here I concentrate on the epistemological side of the topic and am concerned with the question whether and, if so, to what extent this relation has something to do with how mathematicians' informal proofs secure mathematical knowledge. The focus is on a specific "derivational account of informal mathematical proof" together with a particular critique of it. According to the derivationists, as named by Tanswell [25], the rigor and correctness of informal proofs depend (in some sense) on associated formal derivations.

© The Author(s) 2022
V. Giardino et al. (Eds.): Diagrams 2022, LNAI 13462, pp. 37–53, 2022.
https://doi.org/10.1007/978-3-031-15146-0_3

While Jody Azzouni has defended a derivational account of informal mathematical proof himself [4], he has developed an alternative approach to informal rigorous proof in his recent article [7] which he calls "the algorithmic-device view." In this article, he explains why derivational accounts of mathematical proofs do not work and argues for the "superiority" of his algorithmic-device view. He argues explicitly against a specific derivational account, namely Hamami and Avigad's *standard view* of informal mathematical rigor and proof, among other things with the help of the visual/diagrammatic proof of the fact that $1/2 + 1/4 + 1/8 + 1/16 + \cdots = 1$ shown in Fig. 1.[1] Note that when the talk is of "Hamami and Avigad's *standard view*" I am referring to two separate papers, namely [20] and [3]. Insofar as Avigad's work can be understood as an augmentation of Hamami's model of the "standard view of mathematical rigor" which we will see later, and for the purposes of this text, it is convenient to talk about "Hamami *and* Avigad's derivational account/*standard view*," as sometimes Azzouni himself does.

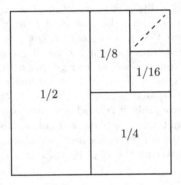

Fig. 1. A visual proof of $1/2 + 1/4 + 1/8 + 1/16 + \cdots = 1$.

In the following, I will critically examine Azzouni's account of the visual proof and the conclusions he draws regarding Hamami and Avigad's *standard view*. In particular, using mathematicians' evaluations of visual proofs in general, which play a fundamental role in Hamami and Avigad's *standard view*, I will argue that Azzouni's criticism of their account is not valid. Nevertheless, by identifying a necessary condition for the visual proof to be considered a proper proof in the first place, and suggesting an appropriate way to establish its correctness, I will argue that his assessment of the epistemic process associated with the visual proof proves to be essentially correct. From this, I will conclude that although visual proofs do not constitute "counterexamples" to the *standard view* in the sense suggested by Azzouni, at least the one presented in Fig. 1 shows that this view does not cover all the ways in which mathematical truth can be justified.

---

[1] A possible description of what is going on in the figure can be found in the initial paragraphs of Sect. 5.

After having introduced, in Sect. 2, Azzouni's account of the visual proof and his critique towards Hamami and Avigad's *standard view*, their work is briefly discussed in Sect. 3. Section 4 is about how mathematicians themselves regard visual proofs. This is followed by a critical examination of Azzouni's critique in Sect. 5, which discusses, inter alia, the conditions under which the visual proof can turn out to be a proper proof (5.1) and what this means for the *standard view* (5.2).

2   Azzouni's Counterexample to the *Standard View*

In [7], Azzouni uses the visual proof of $1/2 + 1/4 + 1/8 + 1/16 + \cdots = 1$ shown in Fig. 1 to argue against Hamami and Avigad's *standard view*. In particular, he argues that this proof constitutes a counterexample to the "normativity thesis" which is "in a way" part of Avigad's *standard view*. We will see to what extent this is true in Sect. 3, where I will discuss their *standard view* in more detail. In Azzouni's own words:

> I've suggested in earlier work [5] – in a way related to Avigad's [3] approach to a normative role for formal derivations – that transcribability to a formal derivation has, in the contemporary setting, become a norm for informal rigorous proof. I want to end this section by revisiting considerations that cut against that idea. The problem is that there are informal rigorous mathematical proofs that are *counterexamples* to the normativity thesis. [7, p. 77]

Besides in this passage, he does not mention the expression "normativity thesis" again. Since he writes shortly after that whether "derivations correspond to informal proofs" is actually a norm is "ultimately, a sociological matter" [7, pp. 77f.], I take him to mean by the normativity thesis something like "the transcribability to a formal derivation *should* be considered a norm for informal rigorous proof." In the earlier work he is referring to in the indented quote above, he explains that

> The first point to observe is that formalized proofs have become the norms of mathematical practice. And that is to say: should it become clear that the implications (of assumptions to conclusion) of an informal proof cannot be replicated by a formal analogue, the status of that informal proof as a successful proof will be rejected. [...] The norm is this: *There is* a formal analogue of a purported informal mathematical proof or else the latter fails to be a proof. [5, p. 14]

Based on this passage, I present the following characterization as a first attempt to specify what this thesis might amount to:

(NT*) Should it become clear that the implications (of assumptions to conclusion) of an informal rigorous proof cannot be replicated by a formal analogue, the status of that informal rigorous proof as a successful proof *should* be rejected.

His reasoning for the visual proof being a counterexample to the normativity thesis is as follows (cf. [7, p. 77]): **(i)** "Phenomenologically – notice – this proof is *utterly convincing* as it stands" and **(ii)** "there is no sense in which it looks like it needs to be completed or filled in" from which he concludes that **(iii)** "neither epistemically nor normatively does this proof and many other informal rigorous proofs [...] need supplementation of any sort." Finally, he states that **(iv)** this and many other informal rigorous mathematical proofs do not themselves "indicate the existence of formalizations that, in turn, justify why they're true: their content, that is, does nothing of this sort."[2]

Because of this—especially because of his statement **(iv)** —and the fact that the implications of the visual proof can in fact be captured and to a certain degree replicated by a formal analogue, which is also admitted by Azzouni himself,[3] the following appears to be a more appropriate characterization of the normativity thesis:

(NT) The transcribability to a formal derivation should be considered a *norm* for informal rigorous proof, i.e., an informal rigorous proof should indicate the existence of a formal counterpart that, in turn, justifies why it is true.

Besides the reference to an "indication relation" between informal rigorous proofs and their formal counterparts in the sense that an informal proof should indicate the existence of a formal analogue, there is a second essential component of Azzouni's "normativity thesis," namely that it deals exclusively with informal *rigorous* proofs. In accordance with this, he describes the visual proof shown in Fig. 1 as a rigorous one. With respect to the (alleged) rigorousness of visual proofs, Azzouni explains in [6] that

it's been quite common, historically, to describe diagrammatic proofs as lacking 'in rigor'. This is so to the extent that, in the nineteenth century, if not before, it seemed reasonable to expunge diagrams altogether from mathematical proof along with reliance on 'intuition'. [6, p. 324]

---

[2] Notice that statement **(iv)** is closely related to one of Tanswell's five "minimal desiderata" of any derivational account of informal proofs, namely **(Content)** (cf. [25, pp. 297f.]), which are all approved by Azzouni. That is to say that any derivational account needs to provide an explanation for each of these aspects of mathematical practice in general or informal mathematical proofs in particular. In Azzouni's words, **(Content)** says that "[a]ny derivational explanation must explain how the perceived content of an informal rigorous mathematical proof – what the sentences of that proof are experienced to *say* – determines which formal proof(s) it indicates" [7, p. 10].

[3] In [6], Azzouni explains with respect to this visual proof that he does not want to deny "that there is a sense in which the (visual) concepts involved in the pictorial-proof have been embedded or reconstrued in the ϵ-δ proof" [6, p. 330], where for the "ϵ-δ proof" he has in mind the standard proof with ϵ-δ techniques such as the one presented in [12]. So, it seems that according to Azzouni, the now-standard proof is an appropriate semi-formal *analogue* of the visual proof, which, in turn, can be replicated rather straightforwardly by a formal analogue itself.

In this article, however, Azzouni argues that it is false to claim that diagrammatic proofs lack in rigor. He identifies several factors which people mistakenly regard as reasons to deny rigor to them. In particular, he argues against the suggestion that these proofs are not rigorous or defective because they involve unarticulated mathematical content. Although he does not give a very detailed account of mathematical rigor, I take him to implicitly assume something like the following sufficient condition for (informal) rigorousness that is related to his statement **(ii)** from above (cf. [6, p. 333], where also the following expressions in quotation marks come from): If there are no missing steps in the mathematical content of a proof—where the content does not need to be "explicit" (e.g. "explicated by axioms"), but which is nevertheless "playing a role enabling the proof procedure"—then this proof should count as rigorous. Except for one qualification, I think that statements **(ii)** and **(iii)** show that Azzouni in [7] still holds on to this view. Since he states in footnote 142 on page 77 of [7], that if "language-based transcriptions of something we see visually" are treated to be more explicit or as making something explicit in the first place, then only *by fiat*, let me reformulate the condition as follows:

(R) If there are no missing steps in the content of a proof—where the content does not necessarily have to be presented in a language-based form, but which is nevertheless playing a role enabling the proof-procedure—then this proof counts as *rigorous*.

Furthermore, with respect to the visual proof, Azzouni argues that **(v)**

The epistemic process, rather, is the exact *reverse* of what normative and descriptive derivational accounts hypothesize. The intuitively effective procedures such proofs exhibit right on their surfaces, when preserved formally, simultaneously preserve the epistemic qualities (the phenomenology) of those informal proofs. The formalization inherits, that is, what it is about the informal proof that convinces us – what *justifies* our being convinced of the result of the proof. It's not, that is, that the formalization reveals what's convincing about that proof or that the formalization justifies that proof. [7, p. 77]

He concludes that **(vi)**a6 this "is enough to show that – at least with respect to *many* informal rigorous mathematical proofs – derivation accounts are intrinsically misleading" (ibid.).

The "intuitively effective (recognition) procedures" which are mentioned in statement **(v)**, lie at the heart of Azzouni's algorithmic-device view of informal rigorous mathematical proofs. These are procedures that "mathematicians grasp directly and not via formal transcriptions of those procedures into the medium of formal languages" [7, p. 20]. The notion of "intuitive" involved in the characterization is meant to refer to something which is computable or executable by a human being while an "effective procedure" or "effective method" which is expressible as a finite set of precise instructions is closely related to the notion of an algorithm [7, pp. 11–17].

Let us now take a closer look at Hamami and Avigad's account(s).

3 The *Standard View* of Mathematical Rigor and Proof

In a recent article, Yacin Hamami [20] offers an elaborated formulation of, what he calls, "the standard view of mathematical rigor" [20, p. 411]. He traces this view back to the work by Saunders Mac Lane and Bourbaki. Hamami differentiates between a descriptive and a normative part of the *standard view*. The descriptive part—which might be called an account of *informal mathematical rigor*—is meant to "provide a characterization of the process by which mathematical proofs are judged to be rigorous in mathematical practice, i.e., by which the quality of being rigorous is attributed to mathematical proofs in mathematical practice" [20, p. 420]. His general characterization of a descriptive account of mathematical rigor is given as follows [20, pp. 420f.]:

A mathematical proof P is rigorous$_M$

$\Leftrightarrow$

P can be verified by a typical agent in mathematical practice M, using the resources commonly available to the agents engaged in M.

$\Leftrightarrow$

Every mathematical inference I in P can be verified by a typical agent in mathematical practice M, using the resources commonly available to the agents engaged in M.

Hamami's particular description of the descriptive part of the *standard view* expresses the last specification of the characterization above in terms of decomposition and verification processes. That is to say that when confronted with a proof P, agents in a practice M verify specific proof steps by decomposing these steps into smaller steps (if needed) until they can verify them with the help of mathematical inference rules that were acquired during their former studies [20, pp. 422ff.].

Hamami explains that in general, "a *normative account* of mathematical rigor stipulates one or more conditions that a mathematical proof ought to satisfy in order to qualify as rigorous" [20, p. 411]. The specific normative part of the *standard view* is now given by the following characterization [20, p. 428]: A mathematical proof P is rigorous in the normative sense if and only if it "can be *routinely translated* into a formal proof." It is with respect to this part of the view that Hamami claims that it is "almost an orthodoxy among contemporary mathematicians" [20, p. 409]. He develops in his article a precise conception of the notion of "routine translation" by first differentiating between four "levels of granularity" and then elaborating three successive translations, i.e., algorithmic procedures, each from one level of granularity to the next finer level. At the coarsest level, which he calls the "vernacular level," the mathematical proof "is a sequence of inferences as commonly presented in the ordinary mathematical texts of mathematical practice M" [20, p. 429].

With the help of the machinery presented in his article, Hamami can show that if a proof is informally rigorous, it is also rigorous in the normative sense, i.e., it can be routinely translated into a formal proof [20, pp. 433f.].

In [3], in which the philosopher and mathematician Jeremy Avigad defends the *standard view*, he explains that according to this view, "an informal mathematical statement is a theorem if and only if its formal counterpart has a formal derivation" and that a judgment as to the correctness of a mathematical proof "is tantamount to a judgment as to the existence of a formal derivation, and whatever psychological processes the mathematician brings to bear, they are *reliable insofar as they track the correspondence*" [3, p. 7379, emphasis added]. Avigad further explains that informal proof texts are "high-level sketches that are intended to *indicate* the existence of formal derivations" [3, p. 7381, emphasis original] and that informal proofs "work" in this way [3, p. 7394]. To be sure, when Avigad talks about "informal proofs" he is referring to informal mathematical proofs that are in line with mathematicians' *contemporary* proof practice. Since he explicitly mentions Hamami's work, among others, as an example in which his general viewpoint has been articulated [3, p. 7379] (another example is Burgess's account expressed in [13] where he characterizes *rigor* as, among other things, "[t]he quality whose presence in a purported proof makes it a genuine proof by present-day journal standards" [13, p. 2]), we may take him to be talking about informal *rigorous* proofs. Together with Avigad's statements above, one can see that the normativity thesis **(NT)** is indeed—at least "in a way"—part of his *standard view*, which is in accordance with Azzouni's assessment. (Notice the subtle difference that while Avigad speaks of the existence of formal derivations, Hamami (only) speaks of the existence of a routine translation which is able to turn a proof P into a formal one (cf. [20, p. 432, footnote 25]).)

Now, with respect to Hamami's model of informal rigor, i.e., the descriptive part of the *standard view*, Avigad, while broadly accepting it, nevertheless has some reservations. He believes that

> Hamami's model is essentially correct: when we read an informal mathematical proof, we really do try to expand inferences in order to gain confidence that a much more detailed version could be given, down to the kinds of basic inferences that twentieth century logic has shown can be reduced to axiomatic primitives. At the same time, we can be convinced by an informal proof without carrying out a fully detailed expansion, and it is too much to ask that we reach the point where each inference is an instance of a known theorem or an explicit rule we have stored in memory. [3, pp. 7393f.]

In order to bridge this gap with respect to Hamami's criterion of informal rigor, Avigad discusses in his article several strategies, such as *modularize, generalize* and *visualize*, which are employed by mathematicians to ensure reliable and robust assessments concerning the correctness of informal mathematical proofs. In fact, he presents these "common features of mathematical practice" as "normative dictates, strategies that one might urge upon an aspiring young mathematician" [3, p. 7388].

Since the judgments and evaluations of (contemporary) mathematicians play a fundamental role in Hamami's (and Avigad's) descriptive part of the *standard view*, we will now have a look at how mathematicians themselves regard visual proofs such as the one shown in Fig. 1.

4   Mathematicians on *Visual Proofs*

How do (contemporary) mathematicians regard visual proofs? Roger Nelsen, for instance, who has edited three volumes on "proofs without words" (PWWs) (as visual proofs are often referred to in the mathematical literature), states in the introduction of the first volume in which Fig. 1 can be found on page 118, that "[o]f course, 'proofs without words' are not really proofs" [21, p. vi]. This statement is somewhat weakened in the introduction of the second volume, where he explains that "[o]f course, some argue that PWWs are not really 'proofs'" but goes on by quoting a passage by James Brown from his "Philosophy of Mathematics – An Introduction to the World of Proofs and Pictures" [12] in which Brown states that "pictures can prove theorems" [22, p. x]. However, this is again relativized in [2], where Nelsen and his co-author Claudi Alsina describe PWWs as "pictures or diagrams that help the reader see *why* a particular mathematical statement may be true, and also to see *how* one might begin to go about proving it true" [2, p. 118].

As another example, consider the two mathematicians Peter Borwein and Loki Jörgenson who write in their article "Visible Structures in Number Theory" (for which they won a "Paul R. Halmos – Lester R. Ford Award" from the "Mathematical Association of America" which recognizes "authors of articles of expository excellence published in *The American Mathematical Monthly*" [24]) that

> The value of visualization hardly seems to be in question. The real issue seems to be what it can be used for. Can it contribute directly to the body of mathematical knowledge? Can an image act as a form of "visual proof"? Strong cases can be made to the affirmative [they mention two references, one of which is an article again by James Brown; S.W.] (including in number theory), with examples typically in the form of simplified, heuristic diagrams such as Fig. [2 a) (see below); S.W.]. These carefully crafted examples call into question the epistemological criteria of an acceptable proof. [10, pp. 898f.]

Note that although Borwein and Jörgenson seem inclined to grant specific diagrams the status of "visual proofs" ("strong cases can be made"), they nevertheless refer to them as "heuristic diagrams."

Besides what these individual mathematicians have to say about visual proofs, there is also a survey study conducted by Weber and Czocher [26] in which the executors asked ninety-four mathematicians from universities in the United Kingdom to judge the visual proof shown in Fig. 2 b)—in addition to an empirical, a computer-based and two "prototypical" proofs—regarding its validity. When the participants were asked "If you were forced to choose, would you say that this argument is a valid proof?," 38% chose "This is not a valid proof" [26, pp. 259f.]. Note that this visual proof is quite different from the proofs shown in Fig. 1 and 2 a) which raises the question whether the evaluations of mathematicians concerning this specific visual proof should be considered representative of a whole class of proofs. However, the general handling of visual proofs, especially the fact that they are almost all listed in the mathematical literature under the heading of PWWs, suggests this.[4]

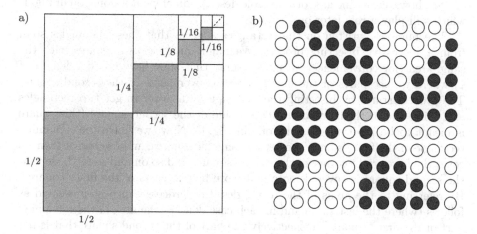

Fig. 2. a) A visual proof of $(1/2)^2 + (1/4)^2 + (1/8)^2 + (1/16)^2 + \cdots = 1/3$. b) A visual proof that n odd implies $n^2 \equiv 1 \pmod 8$ [23, p. 8].

These findings suggest that the general status of visual proofs, i.e., whether they should count as "proper" or "valid" proofs, is (at least to some degree) controversial among (contemporary) mathematicians. Obviously, whether these "proofs" should count as "rigorous proofs"—insofar as one can legitimately (or wants to in the first place) distinguish between *valid* and *rigorous* proofs—is

---

[4] In the introduction of [1], the authors write that

> Mathematical drawings related to proofs have been produced since antiquity in China, Arabia, Greece and India but only in the last thirty years has there been a growing interest in so-called "proofs without words." Hundreds of these have been published in *Mathematics Magazine* and *The College Mathematics Journal,* as well as in other journals, books and on the World Wide Web. Popularizing this genre was the motivation for the second author of this book in publishing the collections [21, 22]. [1, p. ix]

The visual proof shown in Fig. 2 b) appears in this work on page 145 as a proof of $8T_n + 1 = (2n+1)^2$, where $T_n = 1 + 2 + \cdots + n$ denotes the nth triangular number.

46 S. Weisgerber

then not less controversial.[5] This assessment is consistent with Azzouni's own statement which we have already seen in Sect. 2 that "it's been quite common, historically, to describe diagrammatic proofs as lacking 'in rigor'" [6, p. 324].[6]

5 Azzouni's Critique Towards the *Standard View* Revisited

In this section, I have a closer look at Azzouni's critique of the normativity thesis and Hamami and Avigad's *standard view* in general. Before I go into more detail on this, however, let me give one possible description of what is going on in Fig. 1, which will play a role later on.

The numbers written on the rectangles suggest that these rectangles stem from a successive bisecting process. We might imagine two squares with the same area (for convenience, we may assume that they have an edge length of 1) where we use parts of the first square to cover parts of the second square. The process starts by bisecting the first square in order to get two rectangles and using one of them to cover the left side of the second square (this square is meant to be positioned as the one in Fig. 1). Now, we halve the remaining rectangle of the first "square" to get two smaller squares, and use one of them to cover the lower right corner of the second square, and so on and so forth, so that the second square is covered more and more by the parts of the first "square." By referring to the areas of the rectangles, this process can be represented as follows (where the last summand in each case denotes the area of the remaining part of the first "square," respectively the part of the second square that is not yet covered):

---

[5] One can speculate that Weber and Czocher's study shows even more than what has been said so far. Mathematicians were also asked to evaluate the visual proof shown in Fig. 2 b) with respect to a "more fine-grained view of validity" as Weber and Czocher call it. In that regard, even 78% of the participants characterize this proof as invalid in at least some contexts. I think it is not too much of a stretch to suggest that probably many were thinking of mathematical contexts in which rigorous proof is required. But this is pure speculation, as participants were not asked to specify the contexts more precisely.

[6] The case of visual proofs or proofs without words discussed here is a rather extreme one. Many recent studies in the philosophy of mathematical practice do not focus on these particular diagrams, but on those that play an important role in (contemporary) mathematical reasoning and that can even be part of a published modern proof (see, for instance, [15], [19] and [16]). See also footnote 8 in this context.

$$1 = \frac{1}{2} + \frac{1}{2}$$
$$= \frac{1}{2} + \frac{1}{4} + \frac{1}{4}$$
$$= \frac{1}{2} + \frac{1}{4} + \frac{1}{8} + \frac{1}{8} \tag{1}$$
$$= \frac{1}{2} + \frac{1}{4} + \frac{1}{8} + \frac{1}{16} + \frac{1}{16}$$
$$= \frac{1}{2} + \frac{1}{4} + \frac{1}{8} + \frac{1}{16} + \frac{1}{32} + \frac{1}{32}$$

and so forth, so that in the nth step we have $1 = (\sum_{k=1}^{n}(1/2)^k) + (1/2)^n$ or, equivalently, $1 - (1/2)^n = \sum_{k=1}^{n}(1/2)^k$. That is, in each step, the last summand of the previous step is expressed as the summation of its bisection with its bisection. This process could in principle be performed infinitely often, so that the last summand (or the remaining area of the first "square," respectively the part of the second square that is not yet covered) becomes infinitesimally small and the series $1/2+1/4+1/8+1/16+\ldots$ should be assigned the value 1 (if any at all). Note that I propose here "to make the jump to an infinite summation" as a "modern reader is inclined to" do, as expressed by David Bressoud in his "radical approach" to real analysis [11, p. 11], while this would have been avoided, for instance, by the Greeks of the classical era, such as Archimedes [11, pp. 9ff.].

5.1   Figure 1 and the Corresponding Epistemic Process

I think that Azzouni's characterization of the epistemic process with respect to the visual proof shown in Fig. 1 which he gives in (**v**), in particular that it is not the case that a formalization would reveal what is convincing about the visual proof in the first place or that it justifies this proof, is essentially correct. However, I think there is an implicit assumption by Azzouni that needs to be made explicit and argued for in a proper way to give a full explanation of why his characterization in (**v**) is appropriate.

   With that in mind, let us distinguish between an intuitive, pre-formal notion of something that could in principle be repeated infinitely often or that refers to infinity in one way or another and an exact, i.e., "rigorous" (with respect to modern standards) mathematical definition thereof, such as the modern definition of an infinite series or the sum of a convergent infinite series. Let us write the "mathematical theorem" suggested by the visual proof which corresponds to the first, pre-formal understanding as "$1/2 + 1/4 + 1/8 + \cdots = 1$," where the dots "$\ldots$" are referring to the involved (potential) infinite process, and let "$\sum_{k=1}^{\infty}(1/2)^k = 1$" denote the theorem which appears in modern mathematical textbooks or exercise sheets. The description of what is going on in Fig. 1 which I gave above shows that it is quite reasonable to judge the figure as a proof of "$1/2 + 1/4 + 1/8 + \cdots = 1$" or why one is inclined to judge it as "utterly convincing" as Azzouni does in (**i**). But of course Azzouni wants the visual proof to be understood as a proof of "$\sum_{k=1}^{\infty}(1/2)^k = 1$" and his comments (**v**) and

(vi) are to be interpreted in this sense (see also [6, pp. 329f.]). This means that he has to assume some sort of link between these two interpretations, probably something like the following:

(Lim) The (an) intuitive notion of the sum of the series involved in the intuitively effective procedure that Fig. 1 exhibits right on its surface is compatible with the now-standard, "rigorous" definition of the sum as the limit of the sequence of partial sums using the ϵ-δ terminology.

By "compatible with" I mean that the now-standard definition should not rule out the (an) intuitive notion of the sum of the series which one is inclined to read into the diagram.

So I claim that the correctness of **(Lim)** is a necessary condition for Fig. 1 to constitute a (visual) proof of the mathematical theorem "$\sum_{k=1}^{\infty}(1/2)^k = 1$." If there were no such connection between the visual proof and the mathematical theorem that appears in current textbooks, I cannot see how the former could ever constitute a proof of the latter.

Now, how can we know that **(Lim)** is correct? One way would be to simply verify that the now-standard ϵ-δ technique proves this series to be convergent. Azzouni claims in **(v)**, however, that it is not the formalization of the visual proof that justifies it, but the diagram itself. This would not follow if we justified **(Lim)**—which, as I have just pointed out, is a necessary condition for the visual proof to constitute a proof of the mathematical theorem "$\sum_{k=1}^{\infty}(1/2)^k = 1$"— with reference to the semi-formal version of it. Note that if this were the only way to establish **(Lim)**, the visual proof could not be considered a real proof either, since one would have to prove the theorem by another method before one could prove it using the diagram. I submit, however, that there is another way of justifying **(Lim)** which does not lead to this result so that Azzouni's evaluation of the epistemic process in **(v)** can still turn out to be valid: One can also establish **(Lim)** by showing that mathematicians in the development of the calculus tried to capture the (main) intuitions underlying the visual proof shown in Fig. 1—possibly in the form of the equations (1)—with their definitions of the sum of a series.

Even though the following two excerpts from the history of mathematics might not necessarily prove the correctness of **(Lim)** themselves, they strongly suggest that one can justify **(Lim)** in the way just described: For instance, in his "De seriebus divergentibus" from 1760 (which was roughly a century before "[w]ith Weierstrass, the now-accepted ϵ-δ terminology became part of the language of rigorous analysis" [14, p. 620]), Leonhard Euler refers to the series $1 + 1/2 + 1/4 + 1/8 + \cdots = 2$ in his characterization of a convergent series as a clear example of this "phenomenon":

> And now, series are said to be convergent when their terms steadily become smaller and at length completely vanish, such as this one: $1 + 1/2 + 1/4 + 1/8 + 1/16 + 1/32 + etc.$, whose sum is in fact $= 2$, without any doubt. For as you add in more terms, you draw closer to 2; thus the sum of 100 terms

falls short of 2 by a very small amount, indeed a fraction with numerator 1 and a denominator made up of 30 digits. Therefore, with such a series, there is no doubt that it indeed has a sum and that the sum which is assigned in analysis is correct. [8, p. 143]

As another example, consider Cauchy's still "unrigorous" definition (with respect to modern standards) of the convergence of series presented in his "Cours d'Analyse" from 1821. Especially when the calculations or relations indicated by the visual proof are written as in (1), one can see how they fit nicely with this definition: Cauchy calls a series convergent if and only if its sequence of partial sums s_n "tends to a certain limit s for increasing values of n" [9, p. 3] where by "limit" he means that "[w]hen the values successively attributed to the same variable approach indefinitely a fixed value, eventually differing from it by as little as one could wish, that fixed value is called the *limit* of all the others" [9, p. 2]. Immediately after the presentation of his definition of the convergence of series, Cauchy briefly discusses "one of the simplest sequences" which is the geometric progression $1, x, x^2, x^3, \ldots$ for which one finds that

$$1 + x + x^2 + \cdots + x^{n-1} = \frac{1}{1-x} - \frac{x^n}{1-x}$$

and whose sum is $1/(1 - x)$ if the magnitude of x is less than unity [9, p. 3]. If we start with the term $u_1 = x$ (or subtract the value 1) and set $x = 1/2$, we of course get the series that is currently being discussed.

Let me conclude this section with a comment on Azzouni's statement **(vi)**. Insofar as mathematicians throughout history tried to capture with their definitions of the convergence of series the intuitive notion of the sum of the series involved in the intuitively effective procedure that Fig. 1 exhibits right on its surface as the historical findings from above suggest (at least to a certain degree), I think that an account of informal mathematical proof would in fact be "intrinsically misleading"—as Azzouni states in **(vi)**—if it suggested that the truth of the visual proof can be justified only by its formalization. However, that Hamami and Avigad's account is not susceptible to the accusation of being "intrinsically misleading" in this respect will be shown, inter alia, in the next section.

5.2 Visual Proofs as Counterexamples to the *Standard View*?

As we have already seen in Sect. 2, Azzouni argues in [7] against the normativity thesis **(NT)** with the help of the visual proof shown in Fig. 1 which is meant to constitute a counterexample towards it. Insofar as **(NT)** is part of the *standard view* (which it actually appears to be as indicated in Sect. 3), does this imply that the visual proof constitutes a counterexample to this view itself? I claim that the answer is no, even if one were to agree with Azzouni's estimation expressed in **(iv)**, that the visual proof does not indicate a formalization—which seems not to be uncontroversial, since it is a general statement about all possible "indication relations" (where his own from his earlier work [4] and Hamami's "routine translation" are only two of them).

The reason for this is that crucial to Hamami and Avigad's models of informal rigor is the assessment of proofs by mathematicians themselves (keyword "descriptive part"). The findings of Sect. 4—especially the quotations of the individual mathematicians—suggest that even the general status of visual proofs among mathematicians is controversial, i.e., whether Fig. 1, for example, qualifies as a proof of "$\sum_{k=1}^{\infty}(1/2)^k = 1$" (referring to the interpretation introduced in Sect. 5.1) in the first place, not to mention whether they should be considered rigorous.[7]

As we have seen in Sect. 3, Hamami's descriptive part of the *standard view* is meant to characterize the process by which "a typical agent in mathematical practice $\mathcal{M}$" attributes the quality of being rigorous to mathematical proof. But even if one granted that the creation of PWWs constituted one of these practices, Nelsen's statements above suggest that "a typical agent" of this practice would not characterize these proofs as rigorous. Due to Avigad's generally affirmative attitude towards Hamami's account and his own focus on contemporary mathematical practice and its practitioners, I take this to mean that the visual proof shown in Fig. 1 does not constitute a counterexample to **(NT)** from the perspective of the *standard view*, since this view is simply not concerned with this genre of proofs. This also means that if Fig. 1 would indeed constitute a counterexample to **(NT)** as claimed by Azzouni, this interpretation of the normativity thesis would not be part of the *standard view*, since it would deal with a different notion of informal *rigorous* proof, (partially) expressed, for instance, in **(R)**.

As I have argued in Sect. 5.1, the visual proof shown in Fig. 1 can indeed be seen as a proper proof of the mathematical theorem "$\sum_{k=1}^{\infty}(1/2)^k = 1$," although one has to establish the correctness of the necessary condition **(Lim)** first without having to confirm that the now-standard ϵ-δ technique proves this series to be convergent. In light of this, the corresponding epistemic process as described by Azzouni in **(v)** turns out to be essentially correct. However, this does not imply that Hamami and Avigad's account of the *standard view* is intrinsically misleading. This is due to the same reason that the visual proof is not a counterexample to the normativity thesis from the point of view of their account: It is not intrinsically misleading with respect to visual proofs, because it does not deal with that type of proof. What it shows, however, is that the *standard view* does not cover all the ways in which mathematical truth can be justified. Hamami starts his investigation with the words

> Mathematical proof is the primary form of justification of mathematical knowledge. But in order to count as a *proper* mathematical proof, and thereby to function *properly* as a justification for a piece of mathematical knowledge, a mathematical proof must be *rigorous*. [20, p. 409]

---

[7] My speculation in footnote 5 even suggests that a criterion such as **(R)** and/or that visual proofs satisfy the necessary condition for **(R)** that there must be no missing steps in the content of the proofs—which Azzouni addresses with his statement **(ii)** regarding the visual proof shown in Fig. 1—are not commonly accepted by mathematicians.

However, as the discussion of the "epistemic process" of the visual proof of Fig. 1 has shown, an informal mathematical proof can be *proper*—in the sense that it functions properly as a justification for a piece of mathematical knowledge—without being *rigorous* (in Hamami's descriptive sense).[8]

6   Conclusion

We have seen that, according to Azzouni, the visual proof shown in Fig. 1 constitutes a counterexample to the "normativity thesis" that is part of Avigad's *standard view* and which says that the transcribability to a formal derivation should be considered a norm or standard of correctness for informal rigorous proof. It has been argued, however, that from the point of view of Hamami and Avigad's *standard view*, the visual proof does not constitute a counterexample to this thesis and thereby no counterexample to their *standard view* in general. This is the case, because the *standard view* is not concerned with this genre of proofs: Crucial to the view are the judgments about the rigorousness of a mathematical argument by the mathematicians themselves. And many comments made by mathematicians and a survey study suggested that even the general status of visual proofs is controversial, not to mention whether they should be considered rigorous.

Furthermore, we have seen that from an evaluation of the epistemic process associated with the visual proof, Azzouni concludes that with respect to this specific one and many other informal proofs the *standard view* is "intrinsically misleading." This conclusion was rejected for the same reason that the visual proof is not a counterexample to the normativity thesis from the perspective of the *standard view*: It is not intrinsically misleading with respect to visual proofs, because it does not deal with that type of proof. I further identified the need for a connection between the intuitive notion of the sum of the series one

---

[8] Note that although we have seen that visual/diagrammatic proofs are not too much of a problem for Hamami and Avigad's *standard view*, there is a legitimate concern, especially with respect to Hamami's model: His characterization of the *standard view* appears to preclude any mathematical diagram from being an essential part of a rigorous mathematical proof. That this would indeed be a real deficit confirms a quick look at, for instance, contemporary homological-algebraic, category-theoretical or knot-theoretical proof practice. While adapting Hamami's account to diagrams from homological-algebraic and category-theoretical proof practice, such as commutative diagrams and the accompanying method of "diagram-chasing," appears to be relatively unproblematic, since these can be expressed rather straightforwardly with the help of sequences of equations—which is also mentioned by Avigad (cf. [3, p. 7380])—more work seems to be necessary concerning what Silvia De Toffoli calls "geometric-topological diagrams," such as knot diagrams [18]. A promising first step of how one might try to adapt the *standard view* is by distinguishing between the criterion of informal rigor itself and criteria of acceptability for rigorous proofs as suggested by her in [17] which appears to fit nicely with Avigad's augmentation of Hamami's model of informal rigor which I have briefly mentioned at the end of Sect. 3. However, this is not the right place to go into this in more detail.

is inclined to read into the diagram and the now-standard, rigorous definition of it, as a necessary condition for the visual proof to constitute a proper proof, and suggested a way in which one can establish its correctness, namely with the help of the history of mathematics, that also proves Azzouni's assessment of the epistemic process to be essentially correct. From this, I concluded that although visual proofs do not show that the *standard view* is intrinsically misleading, at least the one mentioned above shows that this view does not cover all the ways in which mathematical truth can be justified.

Acknowledgment and Copyright. This research was funded in whole by the Austrian Science Fund (FWF) [DOC 5 doc.funds]. For the purpose of open access, the author has applied a CC BY public copyright licence to any Author Accepted Manuscript version arising from this submission.

References

1. Alsina, C., Nelsen, R.: Math Made Visual - Creating Images for Understanding Mathematics. The Mathematical Association of America, Washington (2006)
2. Alsina, C., Nelsen, R.: An invitation to proofs without words. Eur. J. Pure Appl. Math. **3**(1), 118–127 (2010)
3. Avigad, J.: Reliability of mathematical inference. Synthese **198**(8), 7377–7399 (2020). https://doi.org/10.1007/s11229-019-02524-y
4. Azzouni, J.: The derivation-indicator view of mathematical practice. Philos. Math. **III**(12), 81–105 (2004)
5. Azzouni, J.: Why do informal proofs conform to formal norms? Found. Sci. **14**, 9–26 (2009)
6. Azzouni, J.: That we see that some diagrammatic proofs are perfectly rigorous. Philosophia Mathematica (III) **21**(3), 323–338 (2013)
7. Azzouni, J.: The Algorithmic-Device View of Informal Rigorous Mathematical Proof. In: Sriraman, B. (ed.) Handbook of the History and Philosophy of Mathematical Practice, pp. 1–82. Springer, Cham. (2020). https://doi.org/10.1007/978-3-030-19071-2_4-1
8. Barbeau, E., Leah, P.: Euler's 1760 paper on divergent series. Hist. Math. **3**(2), 141–160 (1976)
9. Birkhoff, G.: A Source Book in Classical Analysis. Harvard University Press, Cambridge (1973)
10. Borwein, P., Jörgenson, L.: Visible structures in number theory. Am. Math. Mon. **108**(10), 897–910 (2001)
11. Bressoud, D.: A Radical Approach to Real Analysis, 2nd edn. The Mathematical Association of America, Washington (2007)
12. Brown, J.: Philosophy of Mathematics - An Introduction to the World of Proofs and Pictures. Routledge, London (1999)
13. Burgess, J.: Rigor and Structure. Oxford University Press, Oxford (2015)
14. Burton, D.: The History of Mathematics - An Introduction, 7th edn. McGraw-Hill, New York (2011)
15. Carter, J.: Diagrams and proofs in analysis. Int. Stud. Philos. Sci. **24**(1), 1–14 (2010)
16. De Toffoli, S.: 'Chasing' the diagram the use of visualizations in algebraic reasoning. Rev. Symbol. Logic **10**(1), 158–186 (2017)

17. De Toffoli, S.: Reconciling rigor and intuition. Erkenntnis **86**, 1783–1802 (2021)

18. De Toffoli, S.: What are mathematical diagrams? Synthese **200**(86), 1–29 (2022)

19. De Toffoli, S., Giardino, V.: An inquiry into the practice of proving in low-dimensional topology. In: Lolli, G., Panza, M., Venturi, G. (eds.) From Logic to Practice, pp. 315–336. Springer (2015). https://doi.org/10.1007/978-3-319-10434-8_15

20. Hamami, Y.: Mathematical rigor and proof. Rev. Symbol. Logic **15**(2), 409–449 (2022)

21. Nelsen, R.: Proofs without Words - Exercises in Visual Thinking. The Mathematical Association of America, Washington (1993)

22. Nelsen, R.: Proofs without Words II - More Exercises in Visual Thinking. The Mathematical Association of America, Washington (2000)

23. Nelsen, R.: Visual gems of number theory. Math Horizons **15**(3), 7–31 (2008)

24. Paul R. Halmos - Lester R. Ford Awards, https://www.maa.org/programs-and-communities/member-communities/maa-awards/writing-awards/paul-halmos-lester-ford-awards. Accessed June 2022

25. Tanswell, F.: A problem with the dependence of informal proofs on formal proofs. Philosophia Mathematica (III) **23**(3), 295–310 (2015)

26. Weber, K., Czocher, J.: On mathematicians' disagreements on what constitutes a proof. Res. Math. Educ. **21**(3), 251–270 (2019)

Representational Interpretive Structure: Theory and Notation

Peter C.-H. Cheng[1][(✉)] , Aaron Stockdill[1] , Grecia Garcia Garcia[1] ,
Daniel Raggi[2] , and Mateja Jamnik[2]

[1] University of Sussex, Brighton, UK
{p.c.h.cheng,a.a.stockdill,g.garcia-garcia}@sussex.ac.uk
[2] University of Cambridge, Cambridge, UK
{daniel.raggi,mateja.jamnik}@cl.cam.ac.uk

Abstract. A cognitive theory of the interpretive structure of visual representations (*RIST*) was proposed by Cheng (2020), which identified four classes of schemas that specify how domain concepts are encoded by graphical objects. A notation (*RISN*) for building RIST models as networks of these schemas was also introduced. This paper introduces common RIST/RISN network structures – *idioms* – that occur across varied representations. A small-scale experiment is presented in which three participants successfully modelled their own interpretation of three diverse representations using RIST/RISN and idioms.

Keywords: Cognition · Representations · Interpretation · Schemas · Idioms

1 Introduction

To advance the study of Diagrams, and visual representations in general, the field requires a comprehensive cognitive account of how readers of representations *interpret representations*. Such a theory is needed for multiple reasons.

(A) Although it is tempting to assume, say, for the sake of theoretical analysis, that a representation has one 'correct' reading, this mask the full diversity of the readers' interpretations. It is unlikely that two readers of a given representation will naturally construct identical interpretations. So, some approach to systemically describe those varied interpretations could be valuable; for example, the mastery of visual representations is critical in STEM subjects, so there is pedagogic utility in being able to characterise what differs between novice and competent readers of a target representation.

(B) The particular content of any given topic can be encoded in quite distinct representations, with dramatic differential impacts on problem solving and learning across those representations (e.g., [3, 10, 22]). Thus, an approach to estimating the relative cognitive benefits of alternative interpretations of representations could be useful. For instance, such measures could be deployed in the development of automated systems to select effective representations tailored to individuals and classes of problems (e.g., [8, 20]).

V. Giardino et al. (Eds.): Diagrams 2022, LNAI 13462, pp. 54–69, 2022.
https://doi.org/10.1007/978-3-031-15146-0_4

(C) Related to the previous point, but more fundamental, is the issue of how even to compare representations with substantially different formats that encode the same informational content. Conventionally, comparison of alternative representations involves laborious task analyses (e.g., [2, 3]) or cognitive modelling (e.g., [10, 11]), or empirical studies (e.g., [2, 3, 22]). Instead, an approach at an intermediate level of abstraction could obviate the toil of ultra-fine-grained analyses and costly experiments. The approach will require the formulation of generic, format-independent, theoretical constructs that are applicable to all representations. Such constructs could serve as "natural" explanatory entities for interpretations. For these reasons, a cognitive theory of the structure of interpretations of representations is a worthy goal.

A contrast with linguistics is instructive. Linguistics has produced accounts of the interpretation of natural language which specify cognitive structures and processes of meaning extraction from verbal representations (e.g., [9, 16]). Many accounts of the nature of diagrams address structure (e.g., [10, 17, 18, 21, 22]) but comparatively less attention has been paid to how individuals interpret or comprehend diagrams ([11, 12]).

Our purpose here is to take the next step towards a general cognitive theory of the interpretation of representations, by testing the "sketch" of the theory developed by Cheng [4], which we will call *Representational Interpretative Structure Theory* (RIST). The RIST sketch proposed that the human interpretation of representations deploys four elementary types of mental schemas. Critically, the schemas coordinate information about concepts from a target topic with information about how those concepts are encoded in the graphical components of the representations. To operationalise RIST, Cheng [4] also outlined a *graphical notation* for constructing models of interpretations under RIST, which we will call *RISN* (RIS Notation). RIST and RISN[1] are described in Sect. 2 of this paper.

In Sect. 2 we introduce RIST and RISN, and take the opportunity to increase the precision of the definition of RIST's components and to more tightly specify how RISN captures particular interpretive constructs. In Sect. 3, we introduce and describe patterns of elementary schemas – *idioms* – that commonly occur in interpretations, which we discovered in RIST/RISN networks across diverse representations. Idioms have the potential to meet the requirement that RIST identifies "design patterns" as standard interpretive structures for constructing RISN models [4]. As noted above (reason A), different readers of a given representation will naturally construct alternative interpretations of that representation, so the requirement that RIST accounts for, and for RISN to model, alternative interpretations is investigated in a small-scale experiment in Sect. 4. Drawing these advances together, in Sect. 5, we will briefly consider how RIST and RISN may yield estimates of the cognitive cost of making alternative interpretations of a representation (reason B), and how RIST and RISN may provide a neutral approach to the cognitive analysis of representations that is independent of the particular format of representations (reason C).

---

[1] Pronounced like "wrist" (/ˈɹɪst/) and "risen" (/ˈɹɪzən/), respectively.

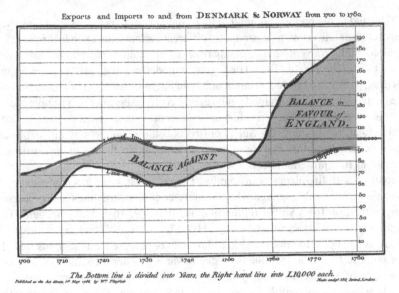

Fig. 1. William Playfair's line graph, in *Commercial and Political Atlas*, 1786.

2 Representation Interpretation Theory/Notation – RIST/RISN

To introduce RIST and RISN [4], we adopt a running example of the analysis of the interpretation of a famous diagram – Playfair's line graph, Fig. 1. Following Cheng's [4] analysis guidelines, Fig. 2 annotates the important graphical components of Playfair's line graph, and Fig. 3 is a RISN model of the graph[2].

2.1 Four Schemas

RIST hypothesises that four *schemas* underpin our ability to interpret representations[3]. The fundamental purpose of these schemas is to tightly coordinate concepts from the target topic with the graphic objects in the representation that stand for those concepts. Networks of these schemas encode the rich hierarchical structure of the encoding relations that constitutes an interpretation of a representation. RISN is a system for modelling such networks; Fig. 3 is an example. At the highest level is the *Representation* schema, capturing an entire representation. *R-Scheme* schemas capture intermediate level substructures. *R-Dimension* schemas deal with varying quantities; they describe R-symbol domains. The *R-symbol* schema identifies the 'unitary' concepts of the target topic. Their depiction in RISN models is shown in Fig. 4 and examples are scattered throughout Fig. 3. Let us consider them in turn, in reverse order.

---

[2] Figure 3 was drawn in a web browser tool, RIS Editor (RISE), that was specifically developed for creating RISN models. The tool will be presented in a paper to follow.

[3] A schema is a mental knowledge representation for a category defined by a set of attributes (slots) for which a particular instance of a concept is assigned values (fillers); e.g., [16].

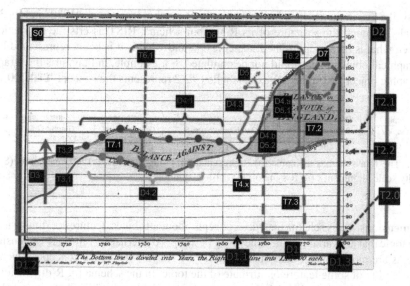

Fig. 2. Playfair's line graph as annotated for modelling (by R1).

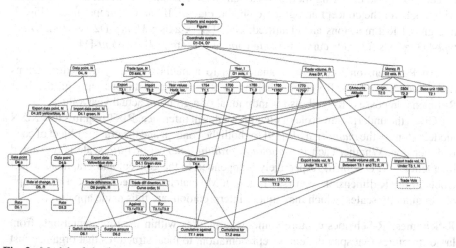

Fig. 3. Model of the interpretation of Playfair's line graph (by R1). Colour shadings are for reference and not part of the model (Color figure online).

R-symbols [4]. R-symbols are the 'fixed' elements of a representation. Their role is to code the association of concept with the graphic object representing it. In RISN, R-symbols are rounded rectangles, with labels identifying the concept and graphical object (Fig. 4d). In Fig. 2, the overlaid annotations with labels beginning with a "T" are instances of R-symbols, and these labels are written in the slots of the corresponding R-symbol icons in Fig. 3. The graphic object may also be described (e.g., *altitude*). For textual graphic

---

[4] *R-symbol* supersedes *Token* used in [4] for reasons of notational and theoretical consistency.

objects, the text in quotes may be written in the R-symbol icons (e.g., "1770" in Fig. 3). Critically, through the structure of its R-symbol schema, RIST asserts the distinction between what is being represented, the concept, and what is it is being represented by, the graphical object: they should not be conflated. For example, in Playfair's line graph the graphic object "80" on the y-axis, labelled *T2.2* represents the concept '£80,000'.

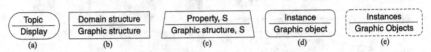

Fig. 4. The four schemas as icons: (a) Representation; (b) R-Scheme; (c) R-Dimensions (S = quantity scale alignment); (d) R-symbol; (e) class R-symbol.

R-Dimensions. This schema encodes concepts about attributes, features or dimensions of the topic that are variable in that they may be assigned alternative values. R-dimension concepts are more general than those encoded by R-symbols. These concepts concern the variability of some feature or attribute of the topic. In the schema for R-dimensions, RIST simultaneously distinguishes the concept of variable quantities from its graphic object whilst also declaring their association. R-dimensions are drawn as a trapezium, with labels for the concept and graphic object, Fig. 4c. In the line graph model, Fig. 3, five global R-dimensions are identified: *Year*-D1 (x-axis); *Money*-D2 (y-axis); *Trade type*-D3 (z-axis for trade curves); *Trade volume*-D7 (area); *Data point*-D4.

An R-dimension's concept is analogous to a mathematical type: R-dimensions range over R-symbols. R-symbols belong to at least one R-dimension; e.g., the *Year* R-dimension possess R-symbols for individual or a group of actual year values.

Given the underpinning role of quantity scales in inference, RIST requires that RISN models identify the *quantity scale* [19] for both the concept and the graphic object of each R-dimension. Whether each is a *nominal, ordinal, interval* or *ratio* scale is registered by a letter – *N, O, I* or *R,* respectively – appended to the concept and graphical object labels in the R-dimension icon (see Fig. 4c). Mismatches between concept and graph object quantity scales, which may hinder interpretation, are thus made apparent.

R-Schemes. R-Schemes capture complex structures within the representations, from large structures that span the entire representation, to local structures that organize just a few R-symbols. While R-Dimensions collect many R-symbols of a similar kind, R-Schemes are typically heterogeneous: they link together different R-Dimensions, R-symbols, or other R-Schemes, into some larger structure. R-Schemes are drawn as a rectangle in RISN (Fig. 4b). The RISN model (Fig. 3) for the interpretation of Playfair's graph (Fig. 1) has an overarching R-scheme composed of five R-dimensions.

Representations. At the highest level is the Representation schema. Representation schemas are drawn as lozenges (Fig. 4a). This schema defines a complete representation and a RISN model always has a Representation schema at its root. However, sub-Representations can occur in other parts of a RISN model, when there is a distinct nested representation within a larger representation (see anchoring below).

2.2 Linking Schemas

RIST conceptualizes interpretations of representations as rich hierarchical networks of relations among the four schemas. With the schemas defined, we can begin linking them together. RISN models must be connected. Here, we introduce a more precise definition of the three kinds of links proposed: *hierarchy*, *anchoring*, and *equivalence*.

Hierarchy. This most fundamental link asserts when one schema is conceptually enclosed by another. For example, R-symbols enclosed under R-Dimensions will represent a specific value from that R-dimension. The hierarchy link can be formed between any two schemas, with the following exceptions:

- The 'child' of a hierarchy link is never a Representation schema, because a Representation schema stands for a complete representation (but see anchoring below).
- An R-symbol schema can only be the parent of another R-symbol schema, because they are the base-level components of RIST/RISN (but see anchoring below).
- An R-dimension schema cannot be the parent of an R-Scheme schema, because R-dimensions only range over R-symbols.

We notate hierarchy using a thin solid line (no arrow heads). The hierarchy link is directed: the direction is indicated by connecting to the parent schema from below, and the child schema from above. Some subsequent properties of RISN models are:

- All schemas, except for the root Representation schema, must have at least one parent schema.
- All schemas must have at least one child, except for R-symbol schemas and non-root Representation schemas: they are the 'leaves' of a RISN model.
- A schema may not be the parent of any schemas that are its ancestors – that is, RISN models are acyclic. However, a schema may have multiple parents, and so parallel paths may exist.

Anchoring. *Anchoring* links denote a new substructure that exists as a direct result of the parent R-symbols. Anchoring is a rich relation where a new concept emerges. We denote anchoring using solid thin line, with a bullet terminal at the parent. The link is thus directed, with the direction being shown by the position of the bullet. The parents *must* be R-symbol schemas, but there is no restriction on the children except that they are not an ancestor of the parent – that is, anchors must not introduce cycles into the RISN model. For example, in Fig. 3 (left), the sequence of hierarchy and anchor relations from the D3 R-dimension through to the D5.1 R-symbol, via D4.2/3, D4.a and D5, expresses the notion that export data points are identified by the export curve and that it is only meaningful to speak of a specific rate of change of the curve with reference to a particular data point. Anchoring is more than just a sub-R-symbol relationship, such as a segment of a line, or the digits in a number.

A (sub-)Representation schema may be anchored to an R-symbol; for example, a Representation Schema for Hindu-Arabic numbers can be added to some of the leaf nodes in Fig. 3, if we wish to elaborate the inner workings of that numeration system.

Equivalence. It is useful to register cases of repeated symbols for concepts (e.g., the two 'x' in $x \times 2 = x + 3$), because of their potential impact to the cognitive efficacy of a representation. Further, a single sophisticated concept in a representation may be encoded by quite different subnetworks of schemas in a RISN model; for instance, imagine that the areas for trade *against* and *in favour* in Fig. 1 are equal. The *equivalence* link captures the 'mental bookkeeping' that occurs during such interpretations, in which the reader must hold in mind the relationships between different parts of the representation. It is not intended to capture "mathematical" equivalence – although it may do, if this is part of the mental bookkeeping. Equivalence links are undirected and represented by a thick, dashed line with no terminals. There are no restrictions on what can be connected via the equivalence relation, allowing cycles in RISN models.

That completes the summary of RIST and RISN. We have outlined RIST's "words" and "grammar" for composing "sentences" that express interpretations of representations. RIST makes strong claims about the fundamental mental knowledge structures we use to interpret representations (the four schemas) and how interpretation occurs (construction of networks of those schemas). In this paper, the adequacy of the theory has been enhanced by more rigorously specifying RIST's components; in particular, the circumstances under which each type of link is applicable. Some of the ambiguity in Cheng's original theory sketch [4] has been eliminated, which provides greater constraint on the permissible schema networks.

3 Idioms: Higher-Order Structures

Consider an analogy. Chemical theory is successful because it identifies elements and has rules by which atoms may be composed into molecules, but moreover it provides general categories of structures and processes; benzene rings, alcohol groups, or multi-bonded carbon atoms are substructures of organic molecules, each providing local information about the molecule as a whole. Similarly, we observe substructures of schemes within RIST models. Through many applications of RIST to diverse representations, both sentential and diagrammatic, we observed repeated substructures capturing common ideas emerge naturally: we call these *idioms*. Idioms serve dual purposes: first, they are an aid to interpreting RISN models; second, they can serve as guides when building RISN models. Three particularly common classes of idioms are introduced and described here: *collections*, *R-dimension* idioms, and *coordinate systems*.

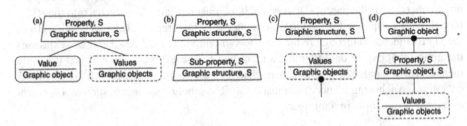

Fig. 5. Templates for (a) *pick*, (b) *filter*, (c) *for-each*, and (d) *reduce*.

3.1 Collections

We have found, frequently, that R-symbols are not just 'one-off' symbols within a representation: there are many points on a chart, many regions in an Euler diagram, and so forth. To capture this regularity, we allow for *class* R-symbols, Fig. 4e. However, we might want to discuss R-symbols as a group, or talk in general about the R-symbols without specifying an R-symbol in the class. We define four idioms on collections of representations: *pick*, *filter*, *for-each*, and *reduce*. Some readers might note that these names were inspired by functional programming, and draw helpful analogies [1].

The simplest collection idiom is *pick*: a single R-symbol is extracted from the class of R-symbols. This idiom can identify a single R-symbol as being of particular interest in an interpretation. We connect a new R-symbol(s) below the dimension and exclude it from the sibling class R-symbol, shown in Fig. 5a. An example in the Playfair's line graph model is shown by the purple shading in Fig. 3 (and Fig. 9).

When the model requires some subset of the R-symbol collection, we use the *filter* idiom. While all the R-symbols in a collection might belong to the same R-Dimension, that R-Dimension might be very general: sometimes, a specific subset is more useful in some context. In effect, this is a sub-R-Dimension, so is notated by introducing new sub-R-Dimensions below the original R-Dimension, Fig. 5b. The name of the *filter* idiom is inspired by the *filter* function common in programming languages: given a collection of values, extract just the values that match some predicate. For example, in the orange shading in Fig. 3, if a modeller wanted to just talk about the 'import data point' then only this schema would have been drawn, and thus considered as a *filter* idiom.

Often, some interpretation is true for all R-symbols in a class, regardless of which specific R-symbol is being considered. In RISN, we call this idiom *for-each*, Fig. 5c: any schemas under a class R-symbol in the model are true for all members of the class. We can draw analogy to the standard mathematical phrase 'without loss of generality': something true for every member of a set. For example, in the model of Playfair's line graph, Fig. 3 (left), the anchoring of the 'Export data' class R-symbol under the 'Year values' class R-symbol expresses the idea that each year has an export data value. In functional programming, this would be a *map*.

For the sake of clarity, class R-symbols merit further comment in the context of the *for-each* idiom. Class R-symbols are limited in how they connect to descendent schemas: like single R-symbols, they connect either to sub-R-symbols, or via anchoring. We discussed both types of connection in Sect. 2. In both cases, they apply to *each individual concept* included in the class R-symbol, not to the 'class' of R-symbols. For example, in Fig. 3, we have a class R-symbol 'Year values' under the 'Year' R-dimension plus individual R-symbols for year '1754' and four others. It would have been *incorrect* to make the '1754' R-symbol a child of the 'Year values' class R-symbol as it is not a sub-R-symbol of *every* R-symbol in the class 'Year values'.

Finally, when the individual R-symbols within the class are not specifically interesting, but the grouping of them is, we *reduce* them to a single R-symbol capturing the concept of the collection of R-symbols, Fig. 5d. The R-symbol for the concept of the collection is at the top, the class R-symbol for all the members of the collection is at the bottom of the structure, and in between we include an R-Dimension to identify the aspect common to the members that define the category.

This idiom is inverse to *for-each*: while *for-each* allows us to consider every member of a collection identically but individually, *reduce* allows us to consider the entire collection as a single unit. A common use for the *reduce* idiom is in plots of data, where there are emergent structures that exist only as collections of 'simpler' R-symbols. For example, in Fig. 9 below (grey shading), the 'Value of exports in a year' class R-symbol is reduced to the 'Line of exports' R-symbol via the 'Value of Exports' R-dimension.

Together, these collection idioms provide succinct, expressive modelling options for collections of R-symbols.

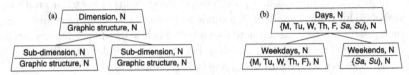

Fig. 6. (a) General model of sum R-dimensions. (b) Example using weekdays.

3.2 R-Dimension Idioms

As mentioned earlier, we may think of an R-Dimension as a 'type' of R-symbols – all the R-symbols that are under the same R-Dimension in the hierarchy fill the same semantic role in the representation. Taking inspiration from this 'type' analogy, we present two idioms named after algebraic data types [6]: *sum* R-Dimensions, and *product* R-Dimensions.

A sum R-Dimension is an R-Dimension that has two or more sub-R-Dimensions. Just as a sum type is the union of its constituents, a sum R-Dimension is the union of the sub-R-Dimensions. We encode a sum R-Dimension in RISN in the obvious way: the sum R-Dimension is directly above its sub-R-Dimensions in the hierarchy. Figure 6a presents the general idiom, while Fig. 6b is a diary example from a "week to a view" diary that differentiates weekday and weekend blocks. An example of sum R-dimensions in the Playfair line graph model, orange shading in Fig. 3, states that all datapoints are comprised of export plus import datapoints (see Fig. 10 for another example).

A product R-Dimension is an R-Dimension that combines two or more R-Dimensions. Just as a product type is the cartesian product of constituent types, the R-symbols of a product R-Dimension can be considered as some combination of the R-symbols of the constituent R-Dimensions. The direct analog in algebraic data types would be a tuple type. Product R-Dimensions are encoded in RISN as being directly under their constituent R-Dimensions in the hierarchy. The general idiom is shown in Fig. 7a, and an alternative shortcut of the idiom is in Fig. 7b for convenience. Figure 7c is an example about citations that code the idea that combining author's surname, an ordinal quantity, with a year of publication, an interval quantity, produces a citation, which is an ordinal quantity. An example in the Playfair line graph model, green shading in Fig. 3, captures the idea that a datapoint for equal amounts of trade occurs when the data points for export and import data are identical.

For both sum and product R-Dimensions, the quantity scales of their resulting R-dimensions require careful consideration; the interaction in particular for a product R-dimension is complex, with no simple domain-independent rules governing the quantity scale of the resulting R-dimension.

Although R-Dimension idioms were presented in isolation, they can compose in powerful ways. With these R-Dimension structures for sums and products, we have a concise, powerful way to model rich interpretations by composing R-symbols or decomposing R-schemes.

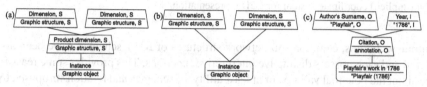

Fig. 7. (a) General model of product R-dimension. (b) Alternative shortcut for (a). (c) Example model of citations as product of author and year.

3.3   Coordinate Systems

Representations are often structured around *coordinate systems*: literally, systems that coordinate information. In addition to the obvious cases – such as tables, and the Cartesian axes of graphs – coordinate systems occur when one or more R-Dimensions provide an indexing system for one, or more, R-Dimensions for sets of data. Coordinate systems setup linked conceptual and graphical spaces within which individuals are located. In practice, we find two idioms for modelling coordinate systems; *explicit* and *implicit*. In the case of explicit coordinate systems, the modeller specifically identifies a fixed set of R-dimensions that constitute the coordinate system that are distinct from the R-dimension(s) that categorises the dataset(s). A template for this case is shown in Fig. 8a. Information visualisations with graphical objects that define quantities, such as axes with scales or legends setting up categories, are typically interpreted as explicit coordinate systems. Alphanumerical index systems, such as book classification schemes, are explicit coordinate systems. Books in an unorder collection are indexed by R-dimensions for subject areas, sub-topics, author, year and the like.

In contrast, in an *implicit* coordinate system the distinction between what is an indexing R-dimension and a data R-dimension is not taken by the interpreter to be fixed but interchangeable. What counts as data depends on the user's current context. Figure 8b shows the template for this idiom; the nested R-Scheme has gone, so the R-Dimensions all occur at the same level. The particular interpretation for Playfair's line graph in Fig. 3 includes an *implicit* coordinate system (yellow rectangle), because the modeller did not wish to single out points in the graph as the only dataset. Rather, the 'Data point' R-dimension is used as an index along with the 'Money' R-dimension to make a coordinate system dealing with 'Trade directions' and 'Trade differences' (centre left).

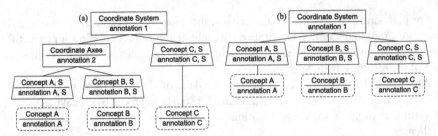

Fig. 8. (a) Template for a nested (explicit) coordinate system for a 2D representation. (b) Template of flat (implicit) coordinate system for a 2D representation.

Summary. Idioms, common sub-network structures of RIST schemas, have been discovered and each possess distinctive interpretive functions. This provides some reassurance about the potential validity, or at least utility, of schemas and relations proposed by RIST. Idioms introduce a new layer of interpretations between the elementary schemas and whole networks, which imposes theoretically desirable constrains on the space of possible network structures for modelling. In turn, this suggests that attempts to model the interpretations of representations could profitably focus on interpretive functions of idioms, an idea that is to be outlined in the last section.

4   Diversity of Interpretations

So far, we have presented refinements to RIST's schema relations and introduced idioms to encode particular interpretive functions, both of which improve the adequacy of the theory. This section considers our first, albeit small-scale, empirical test of RIST and the capabilities of RISN. In particular, we wish to show that the theory and modelling notation are able to capture the alternative interpretations of a representation made by different readers, as mentioned in the Introduction. In the test, three of the authors ("reviewers"), who are experienced users of representational systems, independently created RISN models for 3 different representations. The representations were Playfair's line graph (Fig. 1), the Home tab from Microsoft PowerPoint's toolbar, and a chart about monetary flows in an economy depicted as a hydraulic model[5]. They were selected due to their diversity in both their form and function. Here, just the model for Playfair's line graph will be examined in detail, see Fig. 3, Fig. 9 and Fig. 10, but we summarize the outcomes of the other two representations.

---

[5] 'The Round Flow of Money Income and Expenditure, 1922': https://commons.wikimedia.org/wiki/File:The_Round_Flow_of_Money_Income_and_Expenditure,_1922.jpg.

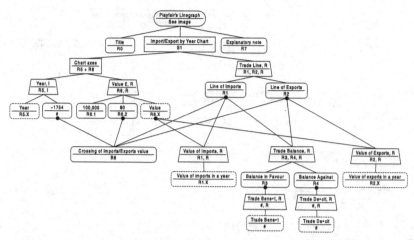

Fig. 9. Interpretation of Playfair's line graph by R2. Colour shadings are for reference and not part of the model (Color figure online).

All reviewers had experience creating RISN models. They reviewed the guidelines for RIST/RISN before starting the task. They were instructed to model their own interpretation of the content of the representations. R1, R2 & R3, started by annotating the original line graph, Fig. 1: R1's annotations are shown in Fig. 2, where *T*, *D*, and *S* labels stand for R-symbols, R-Dimensions, and R-schemes, respectively. The reviewers' RISN models for the line graph are shown in Figs. 3, 9 and 10. For reference, we highlighted parts of the models with coloured shadings. After finishing their individual models, the reviewers discussed the models and made edits that just corrected the invalid schema relations, which were few in number. We wished to determine if the models revealed meaningful differences in the reviewers' interpretations, and what the principal differences were.

R1's overall interpretation treats that representation as a complex coordinate system with five R-dimensions (Fig. 3, yellow shading). The concept of trade balance, 'Equal trade' R-symbol, depends on four of the R-dimensions, directly or indirectly, so is central to the network of schemas conceptually and happens to be positioned centrally in the diagram. Derived quantities, such as 'Trade volume (over a period of time)' and 'Rate (of change of trade)', are defined within the overarching coordinate system as a sub-R-dimension anchored on an R-symbol of some other R-dimension.

R2's interpretation has global coordinate system which incorporates the two graph axes as sub-system alongside an R-dimension for the lines in the graph (Fig. 9). Other R-dimensions, which were primary for R1, are derived concepts in R2's interpretation, defined relative to the context of particular values of the overarching coordinate system.

R3's model (Fig. 10) contrasts to R1 and R2 in terms of its overall interpretation. It gives the concepts of trade 'Balance' and 'Region' primacy and uses them to examine the relation of imports and exports relative to England. The coordinate system for the graph axes is seen as subservient to those ideas and is providing specific values as required.

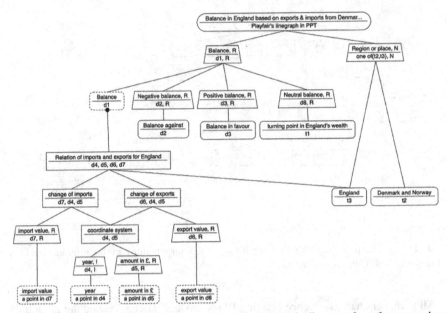

Fig. 10. Interpretation of Playfair's line graph by R3. Colour shadings are for reference and not part of the model (Color figure online).

Comparing the topology of the models, all three models have approximately similar depth, but R1's model has greater breadth, which reflects concepts not in R2 and R3's interpretation. Examining the range and priority of concepts, R3's interpretation focuses on the topic's conceptual content – *what* is represented – whereas R1 and R2 are oriented more towards the means by which the line graph conveys the information – *how* the content is represented – using a global, high-level, coordinate system.

The idioms introduced in Sect. 3 provide a useful level of abstraction for our analysis of the models; like molecules being understood through their functional groups, we can understand our RISN models through their idioms. The coloured areas in Figs. 3, 9 and 10 exemplify some of them. The coordinate system idiom (in yellow) appears across all models, as described in the summaries above, but at different levels. The sum R-dimension is present in two of models: examples are shown Fig. 3 and Fig. 10 (orange shading). R1 splits the 'Data points' global R-dimension into exclusive sub-R-dimensions for 'Export' and 'Import' data. R3 divides trade 'Balance' into the three categories of 'Negative', 'Positive' and 'Neutral'. R1 and R2 also make equivalent distinctions related to trade balance, but a lower level.

There are also differences among how reviewers use idioms. All three use coordinate systems (Figs. 3, 9 and 10, yellow shading) and the 'for-each' idiom (blue shading), but their primacy in the interpretations varies. For R1 and R2, the coordinate takes precedence, with the 'for-each' idiom serving a narrower role. In contrast, R3 gives the 'for-each' idiom priority and hangs a coordinate system under that idiom. Another case is that of important "trade balance" concept, which is encoded in different ways by all three reviewers: R1 uses a product R-dimension idiom (Fig. 3, light green); R2 has a single R-symbol for a concept anchored on other R-symbols (Fig. 9, 'Crossing of Imports/Export values'); and for R3 it is an R-symbol of a sub-R-dimension of the primary 'Balance' R-dimension.

Similar observations apply to the PowerPoint toolbar and the economic flowchart modelling. For example, for the PowerPoint toolbar, R2's model includes the use of R-schemes for concepts extensively, whereas R1 and R3 tend to categorize and group concepts with R-dimensions. In spite of this, there is little variation in terms of the depth of the models across reviewers. The models for the economic flow are also diverse across reviewers. R3's model focusses on the topic, R2's model focusses more on the structure of the diagram, and R1's model is a mixture.

The modelling activities were followed by a session of reflection by the reviewers. From instances of ambiguity among the reviewer interpretations, it was apparent that there are some specific limitations to RISN expressiveness that need to be addressed. In particular, the semantics of the relation links between R-dimension and class R-symbol schemas needs clarifying, and when R-dimensions and class R-symbols have "common elements" or are disjoint.

5 Discussion

We presented Representational Interpretive Structure Theory, RIST. It proposes that interpretation of representations is cognitively grounded in four schemas whose primary function is to associate (a) concepts from the to-be represented target domain with (b) graphical objects in the representation that stand for those concepts. RIST specifies a small number of relations that link these schemas. RIST contends that an interpretation of a representation consists of a network of schemas that are linked by the relations. Different interpretations have alternative network structures. By examining numerous networks that model diverse representations, idioms were discovered that are common to representations with distinct formats. Idioms appear to perform specific interpretive functions and operate at an intermediate level between the elementary schemas and complete networks for whole representations.

RISN is a modelling notation for RIST, which possess distinct modelling symbols for each class of schemas. The symbols are connected together with lines that stand for relations between the schemas. RIST schema networks are modelled as networks of RISN symbols.

A small-scale experiment was conducted in which three reviewers produced models of their own interpretations of three heterogenous representations. The RISN networks produced across the different representations were varied and the networks produced by different reviewers, of the same representation, were also distinctive. The models varied both in the content and in their topology. Further, close examination of the models reveals that the overall interpretations are readily explicable in terms of the idioms. In other words, a reviewer could use the idioms to guide their understanding of the meaning of a RISN model produced by another reviewer. Some idioms were shared across all the reviewer's models for a given representation and in other cases different idioms were deployed in the interpretations of alternative reviews on the same representation. Thus, this small study provides some tentative preliminary evidence of the acceptability of

RIST and the utility of RISN. However, further studies are needed in order to make more definite claims. Such studies are planned.

The Introduction proposed three desiderata for a cognitive theory of the interpretation of representations. The first concerns the facility to model alterative interpretations made by different individuals. The present study begins to demonstrate that RIST/RISN has this capability. Further, although anecdotal, the authors recognise that R1 has particular expertise with Cartesian plots, so it is no surprise that R1's model of the line graph had a greater breadth than the models of R2 and R3, as it included a greater range of concepts. Also, R3 was the least familiar with PowerPoint, so it is also not unexpected that the network models of R1 and R2 were broader. All this suggests that RIST/RISN could be used in an approach to model differences in the interpretative structure of learners with different level of experience of target representations.

The outcome of the small study also suggests that it may be feasible to model the different interpretive structures of alternative representations of the same subject matter. RIST/RISN might provide a useful method for the evaluation of alternative representations for particular topics. This would satisfy the second and third requirements described in the Introduction.

Finally, we note that this research was conducted as part of a wider project that is developing automated systems for the selection of representations for individual problem solvers with varying levels of competence on different classes of problems [13–15]. One aspect of the project is to devise a measure of the cognitive cost of representations [5], which can be used to assess the relative difficulty a user will likely experience with alternative representations. We note that RIST/RISN may provide an addition route to such assessments though the analysis of the contents of the schemas and the nature of their networks.

Acknowledgements. This work was supported by the EPSRC grants EP/R030642/1, EP/T019603/1, EP/T019034/1 and EP/R030650/1.

References

1. Bird, R., Wadler, P.: Introduction to Functional Programming. Hemel Hempstead: Prentice Hall International (UK) (1988)
2. Cheng, P.C.-H.: Electrifying diagrams for learning: principles for effective representational systems. Cogn. Sci. **26**(6), 685–736 (2002). https://doi.org/10.1016/S0364-0213(02)00086-1
3. Cheng, P.C.-H.: Probably good diagrams for learning: representational epistemic re-codification of probability theory. Top. Cogn. Sci. **3**(3), 475–498 (2011)
4. Cheng, P.C.-H.: A sketch of a theory and modelling notation for elucidating the structure of representations. In: Pietarinen, A.-V., Chapman, P., Bosveld-de Smet, L. Giardino, V., Corter, J., Linker, S. (eds.) Diagrams 2020, LNCS (LNAI), vol. 12169, pp. 93–109. Springer Cham (2020). https://doi.org/10.1007/978-3-030-54249-8_8
5. Cheng, P.-H., Garcia Garcia, G., Raggi, D., Stockdill, A., Jamnik, M.: Cognitive properties of representations: a framework. In: Basu, A., Stapleton, G., Linker, S., Legg, C., Manalo, E., Viana, P. (eds.) Diagrams 2021. LNCS (LNAI), vol. 12909, pp. 415–430. Springer, Cham (2021). https://doi.org/10.1007/978-3-030-86062-2_43

6. Gordon, M., Milner, R., Wadsworth, C.P.: Edinburgh LCF: A Mechanised Logic of Computation. LNCS. Springer, Berlin (1979). https://doi.org/10.1007/3-540-09724-4

7. Gurr, C.A.: On the isomorphism, or lack of it, of representations. In: Marriott, K., Meyer, B. (eds.) Visual Language Theory, pp. 293–306. Springer, New York (1998). https://doi.org/10.1007/978-1-4612-1676-6_10

8. Jamnik, M., Cheng, P.C.-H.: Endowing machines with the expert human ability to select representations: why and how. In: Muggleton, S., Chater, N. (eds.) Human-Like Machine Intelligence, pp. 355–378. Oxford University Press, Oxford (2021)

9. Kintsch, W.: Comprehension: A Paradigm for Cognition. Cambridge University Press, New York (1998)

10. Larkin, J.H., Simon, H.A.: Why a diagram is (sometimes) worth ten thousand words. Cogn. Sci. **11**, 65–99 (1987)

11. Peebles, D.J., Cheng, P.C.-H.: Modelling the effect of task and graphical representations on response latencies in a graph-reading task. Hum. Factors **45**(1), 28–45 (2003). https://doi.org/10.1518/hfes.45.1.28.27225

12. Pinker, S.: A theory of graph comprehension. In: Freedle, R. (ed.) Artificial Intelligence and the Future of Testing, pp. 73–126. Lawrence Erlbaum, Hillsdale (1990)

13. Raggi, D., Stockdill, A., Jamnik, M., Garcia Garcia, G., Sutherland, H.E.A., Cheng, P.C.-H.: Dissecting representations. In: Pietarinen, A.-V., Chapman, P., Bosveld de Smet, L., Giardino, V., Corter, J., Linker, S. (eds.) Diagrams 2020. LNCS (LNAI), vol. 12169, pp. 144–152. Springer, Cham (2020). https://doi.org/10.1007/978-3-030-54249-8_11

14. Raggi, D., Stapleton, G., Stockdill, A., Jamik, M., Garcia Garcia, G., & Cheng, P. C.-H. (2020). How to (re)represent it? In S. Pan (Ed.), *32nd International Conference on Tools with Artificial Intelligence*: IEEE

15. Raggi, D., Stockdill, A., Jamnik, M., Garcia Garcia, G., Sutherland, H.E.A., Cheng, P.-H.: Inspection and selection of representations. In: Kaliszyk, C., Brady, E., Kohlhase, A., Sacerdoti Coen, C. (eds.) CICM 2019. LNCS (LNAI), vol. 11617, pp. 227–242. Springer, Cham (2019). https://doi.org/10.1007/978-3-030-23250-4_16

16. Schank, R.C., Abelson, R.P.: Scripts, Plans, Goals, and Understanding: An Enquiry into Human Knowledge Structures. Erlbaum, Mahwah (1977)

17. Shimojima, A.: Semantic Properties of Diagrams and Their Cognitive Potentials. CSLI Press, Stanford (2015)

18. Stenning, K., Oberlander, J.: A cognitive theory of graphical and linguistic reasoning: logic and implementation. Cogn. Sci. **19**(1), 97–140 (1995)

19. Stevens, S.S.: On the theory of scales of measurement. Science **103**(2684), 677–680 (1946)

20. Stockdill, A., Raggi, D., Jamnik, M., Garcia Garcia, G., Cheng, P.-H.: Considerations in representation selection for problem solving: a review. In: Basu, A., Stapleton, G., Linker, S., Legg, C., Manalo, E., Viana, P. (eds.) Diagrams 2021. LNCS (LNAI), vol. 12909, pp. 35–51. Springer, Cham (2021). https://doi.org/10.1007/978-3-030-86062-2_4

21. Zhang, J.: A representational analysis of relational information displays. Int. J. Hum. Comput. Stud. **45**, 59–74 (1996)

22. Zhang, J.: The nature of external representations in problem solving. Cogn. Sci. **21**(2), 179–217 (1997)

Mixing Colors, Mixing Logics

José-Martín Castro-Manzano[(✉)] [iD]

School of Philosophy, UPAEP University, 72410 Puebla, Mexico
josemartin.castro@upaep.mx

Abstract. In this contribution we combine some term logics as to produce a synthetic term logic. We accomplish this goal by following a color mixing metaphor: the way color addition and substraction work are pretty much like joints and meets between logics, and so we can think of combining logics as a process of color mixing.

Keywords: Term logic · Tableaux · Combining logics

1 Introduction

Combining logics is a quite interesting task: it is a regular practice and yet a required exercise. It is a pervasive habit in the sense that we use combined logics virtually all the time, but it is also an imperative since it is instrumental for solving problems [1]. Typically, however, the combination of logics is done with respect to Fregean-Tarskian-Kripkean systems [5], but since logic needs not be constrained by this received view [4,8], in this contribution we combine some term logics as to produce a synthetic term logic. We accomplish this goal by following a color mixing metaphor: the way color addition and substraction work are pretty much like joints and meets between logics, and so we can think of combining (term) logics as a process of color mixing. To reach this goal we briefly sketch four logics designed to capture four aspects of natural language reasoning—assertion, numeracy, modality, and relevance—and we assign said logics a color; then, using the aforementioned metaphor, we produce a synthetic logic.

2 Term Logics

Assertoric syllogistic is a term logic that captures a basic notion of assertion using categorical statements. A categorical statement is a statement of the form $\langle Quantity\ \mathsf{S}\ Quality\ \mathsf{P}\rangle$ where $Quantity = \{All,\ Some\}$, $Quality = \{is,\ is\ not\}$, and S and P are term-schemes. From the standpoint of Sommers & Englebretsen's (assertoric) Term Functor Logic (TFL^α, from now on) [4,8], we say a categorical statement is a statement of the form $\pm\mathsf{S}\pm\mathsf{P}$ where $\pm$ are functors, and S and P are term-schemes.

© Springer Nature Switzerland AG 2022
V. Giardino et al. (Eds.): Diagrams 2022, LNAI 13462, pp. 70–77, 2022.
https://doi.org/10.1007/978-3-031-15146-0_5

Given this language (say, $\mathcal{L}_{\mathsf{TFL}^\alpha} = \langle \mathcal{T}, \pm \rangle$, where $\mathcal{T} = \{\mathsf{A}, \mathsf{B}, \mathsf{C}, \ldots\}$ is a set of terms, and $\pm$ is shorthand for $+$ and $-$ functors), TFL^α offers a sense of validity as follows [4, p. 167]: a syllogism is valid (in TFL^α) iff *1)* the algebraic sum of the premises is equal to the conclusion, and *2)* the number of particular conclusions (*viz.*, zero or one) is equal to the number of particular premises. These components define a pair $\mathsf{TFL}^\alpha = \langle \mathcal{L}_{\mathsf{TFL}^\alpha}, (1,2) \rangle$ where "$(1,2)$" stands for rules 1 and 2 of TFL^α. We will assign TFL^α the (achromatic) color black.

Murphree's Numerical Term Logic (TFL^ν) is a term logic that tries to capture numeracy by representing and performing inference with numerical quantifiers [7]. In this logic, a numerical statement is a statement of the form $\langle Quantity\ \mathsf{n}\ \mathsf{S}\ Quality\ \mathsf{P} \rangle$ where $Quantity = \{All,\ All\ but,\ At\ most,\ At\ least,\ Some\}$, $\mathsf{n} \in \mathbb{R}^+$, $Quality = \{is,\ is\ not\}$, and S and P are term-schemes. Formally, since TFL^ν is a conservative extension of TFL^α, we say a numerical statement in TFL^ν is a statement of the form $\pm_\mathsf{n}\mathsf{S} \pm_\varepsilon \mathsf{P}$ where $\pm$ are functors, $\mathsf{n}, \varepsilon \in \mathbb{R}^+$, and S and P are term-schemes.

Consequently, given this language ($\mathcal{L}_{\mathsf{TFL}^\nu} = \langle \mathcal{T}, \pm, \mathbb{R}^+ \rangle$), TFL^ν offers the next notion of validity: a syllogism is valid (in TFL^ν) iff *1)* the algebraic sum of the premises is equal to the conclusion, *2)* the number of particular conclusions (*viz.*, zero or one) is equal to the number of particular premises, and *3)* either *(a)* the value of a universal conclusion is equal to the sum of the values of the universal premises, or *(b)* the value of a particular conclusion is equal to the difference of the universal premise minus the particular. We will assign this logic (i.e. $\mathsf{TFL}^\nu = \langle \mathcal{L}_{\mathsf{TFL}^\nu}, (1,2,3) \rangle$) the color blue.

Englebretsen's Modal Term Functor Logic (TFL^μ) tries to capture modality by extending TFL^α with $\Box$ and $\Diamond$ [3]. So, given a term T, TFL^μ allows the next combinations: $+\Box + \mathsf{T}$ (i.e. $\Box + \mathsf{T}$), $+\Box - \mathsf{T}$ (i.e. $\Box - \mathsf{T}$), $-\Box + \mathsf{T}$ (i.e. $-\Box\mathsf{T}$), $-\Box - \mathsf{T}$, and, as usual, the operator $\Diamond$ is defined as $-\Box-$. Thus, we can say a *de dicto* modal statement is a statement of the form $\langle Modality\ (Quantity\ \mathsf{S}\ Quality\ \mathsf{P}) \rangle$; and a *de re* modal statement is a statement of the form $\langle Quantity\ \mathsf{S}\ Quality\ Modality\ \mathsf{P} \rangle$ where $Modality = \{\Diamond, \Box\}$, $Quantity = \{All,\ Some\}$, $Quality = \{is,\ is\ not\}$, and S and P are term-schemes. Thus, formally, a modal statement in TFL^μ is a statement of one of the following forms: $\mu(\pm\mathsf{S} \pm \mathsf{P})|\pm\mathsf{S} \pm \mathsf{P}|\pm\mathsf{S} \pm \mu\mathsf{P}$ where $\pm$ are functors, μ is a modality, and S and P are term-schemes.

Given this language ($\mathcal{L}_{\mathsf{TFL}^\mu} = \langle \mathcal{T}, \pm, \mathcal{M} \rangle$, where $\mathcal{M} = \{\Diamond, \Box\}$), we have the next notion of validity: a syllogism is valid (in TFL^μ) iff *1)* the algebraic sum of the premises is equal to the conclusion, *2)* the number of particular conclusions (*viz.*, zero or one) is equal to the number of particular premises, *4)* the conclusion is not stronger than any premise (*peiorem*), and *5)* the number of *de dicto*-$\Diamond$ premises is not greater than the number of *de dicto*-$\Diamond$ conclusions. We will assign this logic (i.e. $\mathsf{TFL}^\mu = \langle \mathcal{L}_{\mathsf{TFL}^\mu}, (1,2,4,5) \rangle$) the color red.

Relevance Term Logic (TFL^ρ) is an extension of TFL^α that captures a notion of relevance by following some insights of the Aristotelian sense of causal relevance (cf. [9]). It represents pieces of complex discourse (insofar as they include at least two premises and one conclusion) with mood and figure (because the order of statements and terms matters) in which a conclusion that is different from the premises (thus avoiding *petitio principii*) necessarily (and hence deductively) follows from and depends on said premises (thus avoiding irrelevance, *non causa ut causa*). In this logic we say a relevant statement is a statement of the form ⟨*Quantity* S *Quality* P *Flag*⟩ where *Quantity* = {*All, Some*}, *Quality* = {*is, is not*}, S and P are term-schemes, and *Flag* = {p_i, c} for $i \in \{1, 2, 3, \ldots\}$ is a set of (premise or conclusion) flags. So, formally, we say a relevant statement is a statement of the form $\pm$S $\pm$ P$_f$ where $\pm$ are functors, S and P are term-schemes, and f is a flag.

With this language ($\mathcal{L}_{\text{TFL}^\rho} = \langle \mathcal{T}, \pm, \mathcal{F} \rangle$, where $\mathcal{F}$ is a set of flags), TFL$^\rho$ offers a notion of validity as follows: a syllogism is valid (in TFL$^\rho$) iff *1)* the algebraic sum of the premises is equal to the conclusion, *2)* the number of particular conclusions (*viz.*, zero or one) is equal to the number of particular premises, and *6)* all the flags of the premises are reclaimed for reaching the conclusion while the flags of the conclusion are different to the flags of the premises. We will assign this logic (i.e. TFL$^\rho$ = ⟨$\mathcal{L}_{\text{TFL}^\rho}$, (1, 2, 6)⟩ the color green.

3 Mixing Colors, Mixing Logics

In general, color mixing can be done in either of two ways: by addition or by substraction. The addition process is understood by the tenets of the RGB model (■■■), while substraction is given by the postulates of the CMY model (■■■). All details aside, additive colors produce white (□) when combined, while subtractive colors produce black (■) (Table 1). In an integrated mixture model (Table 2), the coherent combinations of colors can only be displayed in six arrangements which correspond to each path of the Küppers' rhombohedral model so that, bottom-up, we have the RGB model of addition, and top-down, the CMY model of substraction (Fig. 1).

Table 1. Additive/Substractive mixture models [6].

Additive color	Mixture	Substractive color
■	■	■■■
■	■	■■
■	■	■■
■	■	■■
■■	■	■
■■	■	■
■■	■	■
■■■	□	□

Table 2. Integrated mixture model [6].

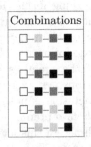

Combinations
□–■–■–■
□–■–■–■
□–■–■–■
□–■–■–■
□–■–■–■
□–■–■–■

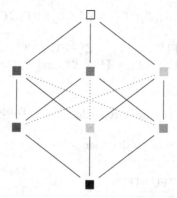

Fig. 1. Küppers' rhombohedral color space [6]. Solid lines represent the paths of the integrated mixture model. Dotted lines represent complementary colors, that is, colors that produce white if combined. (Color figure online)

After a while, it does not take much time to realize that the structure of this model induces a lattice, an order of colors. Thus, a metaphor comes to mind: addition and substraction between colors is analogous to joints and meets between logics, and so we can think of combining logics as a process of color mixing. To work with this metaphor, start by recalling that the different term logics we have displayed try to capture different, basic aspects of natural language reasoning, namely, assertion (TFL^α), numeracy (TFL^ν), modality (TFL^μ) and causal relevance (TFL^ρ). Each logic is like a color hue. Now, given the structure of each logic, we can combine them by addition (joint-combination) and substraction (meet-combination) of syntactical elements and rules in such a way that $\mathsf{TFL}^{\alpha\nu} = \mathsf{TFL}^\nu$, $\mathsf{TFL}^{\alpha\mu} = \mathsf{TFL}^\mu$, $\mathsf{TFL}^{\alpha\rho} = \mathsf{TFL}^\rho$, $\mathsf{TFL}^{\alpha\nu\mu} = \mathsf{TFL}^{\nu\mu}$, $\mathsf{TFL}^{\alpha\nu\rho} = \mathsf{TFL}^{\nu\rho}$, $\mathsf{TFL}^{\alpha\mu\rho} = \mathsf{TFL}^{\mu\rho}$ and, finally, $\mathsf{TFL}^{\alpha\nu\mu\rho}$.

In order to *see* these combinations, use the colors we have previously assigned to each logic and notice that additive logics produce a particular, top logic when combined; while substractive logics produce a particular, bottom logic (Table 3) and, in the same way we have an integrated mixture model, we have six arrangements which correspond to each path of Küppers' rhombohedral model (Table 4). Consequently, this model induces a lattice of term logics such that TFL^α is the bottom logic, and $\mathsf{TFL}^{\alpha\nu\mu\rho}$ is the top logic. Thus, we can *see* that these combined logics set up an order in such a way that $(\mathsf{TFL}, \subseteq)$ is a hierarchy of term logics (Fig. 2).

If this metaphor makes sense then we can also say, although trivially, that for term logics $\mathcal{L}_i, \mathcal{L}_j, \mathcal{L}_k$, the following combinations hold:

- Association of logics: $\mathcal{L}_i \cup (\mathcal{L}_j \cup \mathcal{L}_k) = (\mathcal{L}_i \cup \mathcal{L}_j) \cup \mathcal{L}_k$, and $\mathcal{L}_i \cap (\mathcal{L}_j \cap \mathcal{L}_k) = (\mathcal{L}_i \cap \mathcal{L}_j) \cap \mathcal{L}_k$.
- Commutation of logics: $\mathcal{L}_i \cup \mathcal{L}_j = \mathcal{L}_j \cup \mathcal{L}_i$, and $\mathcal{L}_i \cap \mathcal{L}_j = \mathcal{L}_j \cap \mathcal{L}_i$.
- Idempotence of logics: $\mathcal{L}_i \cup \mathcal{L}_i = \mathcal{L}_i$, and $\mathcal{L}_i \cap \mathcal{L}_i = \mathcal{L}_i$.
- Absorption of logics: $\mathcal{L}_i \cup (\mathcal{L}_i \cap \mathcal{L}_j) = \mathcal{L}_i$, and $\mathcal{L}_i \cap (\mathcal{L}_i \cup \mathcal{L}_j) = \mathcal{L}_i$.

- Distribution of logics: $\mathcal{L}_i \cup (\mathcal{L}_j \cap \mathcal{L}_k) = (\mathcal{L}_i \cup \mathcal{L}_j) \cap (\mathcal{L}_i \cup \mathcal{L}_k)$, and $\mathcal{L}_i \cap (\mathcal{L}_j \cup \mathcal{L}_k) = (\mathcal{L}_i \cap \mathcal{L}_j) \cup (\mathcal{L}_i \cap \mathcal{L}_k)$.
- Extrema: $\bigcap_{i=1}^{8} \mathcal{L}^i = \mathsf{TFL}^{\alpha}$, and $\bigcup_{i=1}^{8} \mathcal{L}^i = \mathsf{TFL}^{\alpha\nu\mu\rho}$.
- Complementary logics: $\mathcal{L}_i \cup \overline{\mathcal{L}}_i = \mathsf{TFL}^{\alpha\nu\mu\rho}$, and $\mathcal{L}_i \cap \overline{\mathcal{L}}_i = \mathsf{TFL}^{\alpha}$.

Table 3. Additive/Substractive mixture models.

Additive logic	Mixture	Substractive logic
TFL^{α}	TFL^{α}	$\mathsf{TFL}^{\mu\rho}\mathsf{TFL}^{\nu\mu}\mathsf{TFL}^{\nu\rho}$
TFL^{ν}	TFL^{ν}	$\mathsf{TFL}^{\nu\mu}\mathsf{TFL}^{\nu\rho}$
TFL^{ρ}	TFL^{ρ}	$\mathsf{TFL}^{\mu\rho}\mathsf{TFL}^{\nu\rho}$
TFL^{μ}	TFL^{μ}	$\mathsf{TFL}^{\mu\rho}\mathsf{TFL}^{\nu\mu}$
$\mathsf{TFL}^{\nu}\mathsf{TFL}^{\rho}$	$\mathsf{TFL}^{\nu\rho}$	$\mathsf{TFL}^{\nu\rho}$
$\mathsf{TFL}^{\nu}\mathsf{TFL}^{\mu}$	$\mathsf{TFL}^{\nu\mu}$	$\mathsf{TFL}^{\nu\mu}$
$\mathsf{TFL}^{\rho}\mathsf{TFL}^{\mu}$	$\mathsf{TFL}^{\mu\rho}$	$\mathsf{TFL}^{\mu\rho}$
$\mathsf{TFL}^{\nu}\mathsf{TFL}^{\rho}\mathsf{TFL}^{\mu}$	$\mathsf{TFL}^{\nu\mu\rho}$	$\mathsf{TFL}^{\nu\mu\rho}$

Table 4. Integrated mixture model.

Combinations
$\mathsf{TFL}^{\nu\mu\rho}$–$\mathsf{TFL}^{\mu\rho}$–$\mathsf{TFL}^{\mu}$–$\mathsf{TFL}^{\alpha}$
$\mathsf{TFL}^{\nu\mu\rho}$–$\mathsf{TFL}^{\mu}$–$\mathsf{TFL}^{\nu\mu}$–$\mathsf{TFL}^{\alpha}$
$\mathsf{TFL}^{\nu\mu\rho}$–$\mathsf{TFL}^{\nu\mu}$–$\mathsf{TFL}^{\nu}$–$\mathsf{TFL}^{\alpha}$
$\mathsf{TFL}^{\nu\mu\rho}$–$\mathsf{TFL}^{\nu}$–$\mathsf{TFL}^{\nu\rho}$–$\mathsf{TFL}^{\alpha}$
$\mathsf{TFL}^{\nu\mu\rho}$–$\mathsf{TFL}^{\nu\rho}$–$\mathsf{TFL}^{\rho}$–$\mathsf{TFL}^{\alpha}$
$\mathsf{TFL}^{\nu\mu\rho}$–$\mathsf{TFL}^{\rho}$–$\mathsf{TFL}^{\mu\rho}$–$\mathsf{TFL}^{\alpha}$

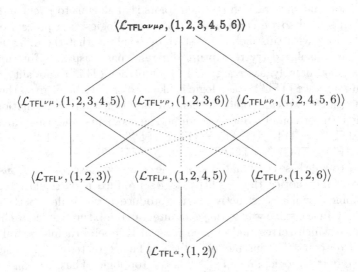

Fig. 2. A lattice of languages and rules.

Now, let us focus on the top logic, which is a synthethic logic, and say a synthetic statement in $\mathsf{TFL}^{\alpha\nu\mu\rho}$ is a statement of the form $\mu(\pm_n \mathsf{S} \pm_\varepsilon \mathsf{P})_f | \pm_n \mathsf{S} \pm_\varepsilon \mathsf{P}_f | \pm_n \mathsf{S} \pm \mu_\varepsilon \mathsf{P}_f$ where μ are modalities, $\pm$ are functors, $n, \varepsilon \in \mathbb{R}^+$, f is a flag, and S and P are term-schemes. Hence, following our exposition pattern, we can say a syllogism is valid (in $\mathsf{TFL}^{\alpha\nu\mu\rho}$) iff rules 1 through 6 hold.

Given this brief exposition, one could think the notion of validity for this logic is constrained to monadic or syllogism-like inferences, but that would be a hasty conclusion. We can extend said notion of validity either by enlarging the rules of inference [4] or by implementing tableaux proof methods [2]: since we are interested in diagrammatic procedures, we will follow the second path. So, we can follow our procedural metaphor and mix tableaux rules as in Diagram 1.1.

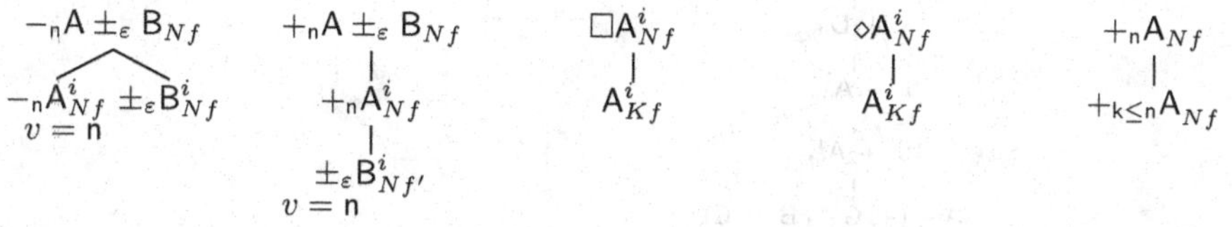

$$
\begin{array}{ccccc}
-_nA \pm_\varepsilon B_{Nf} & +_nA \pm_\varepsilon B_{Nf} & \square A^i_{Nf} & \diamond A^i_{Nf} & +_nA_{Nf} \\
\overbrace{\quad\quad} & | & | & | & | \\
-_nA^i_{Nf} \pm_\varepsilon B^i_{Nf} & +_nA^i_{Nf} & A^i_{Kf} & A^i_{Kf} & +_{k\le n}A_{Nf} \\
v = \mathsf{n} & | & & & \\
& \pm_\varepsilon B^i_{Nf'} & & & \\
& v = \mathsf{n} & & &
\end{array}
$$

Diagram 1.1. TFL$^{\alpha\nu\mu\rho}$ expansion rules

For this synthetic system we say a branch is *open* if and only if there are no terms of the form $\pm A^i_{Nf}$ and $\mp A^i_{Nf}$ on it; a branch is *semi-open* (resp. *semi-closed*) if and only if there are terms of the form $\pm A^i_{Nf}$ and $\mp A^i_{Nf}$; otherwise it is *closed*. An open branch is indicated by writing ∞ at the end of it; a semi-open (semi-closed) branch is indicated by writing $\propto_{f,f}$ (resp. $\infty_{f,f}$); and a closed branch, as usual, is denoted by $\perp_{f,f'}$.

As an example, consider a multipremissed inference that encompasses assertion (plus relations), numeracy (both exceptive and non-exceptive), modality (both *de dicto* and *de re*) and causal relevance: call it a synthetic syllogism (Table 5, Diagram 1.2).

Table 5. A synthetic syllogism.

Statement	TFL$^{\alpha\nu\mu\rho}$
1. Necessarily all but 2 A give 4 B to some C	$\square(-_2A + (+G +_4 B + C))_{0p_1}$
2. At least 5 D are necessarily A	$+_5D + \square A_{0p_2}$
3. Every B is E	$-_0B + E_{0p_3}$
$\vdash$ Possibly 3 D give 4 E to some possible C	$\diamond(+_3D + (+G +_4 E + \diamond C))_{0c}$

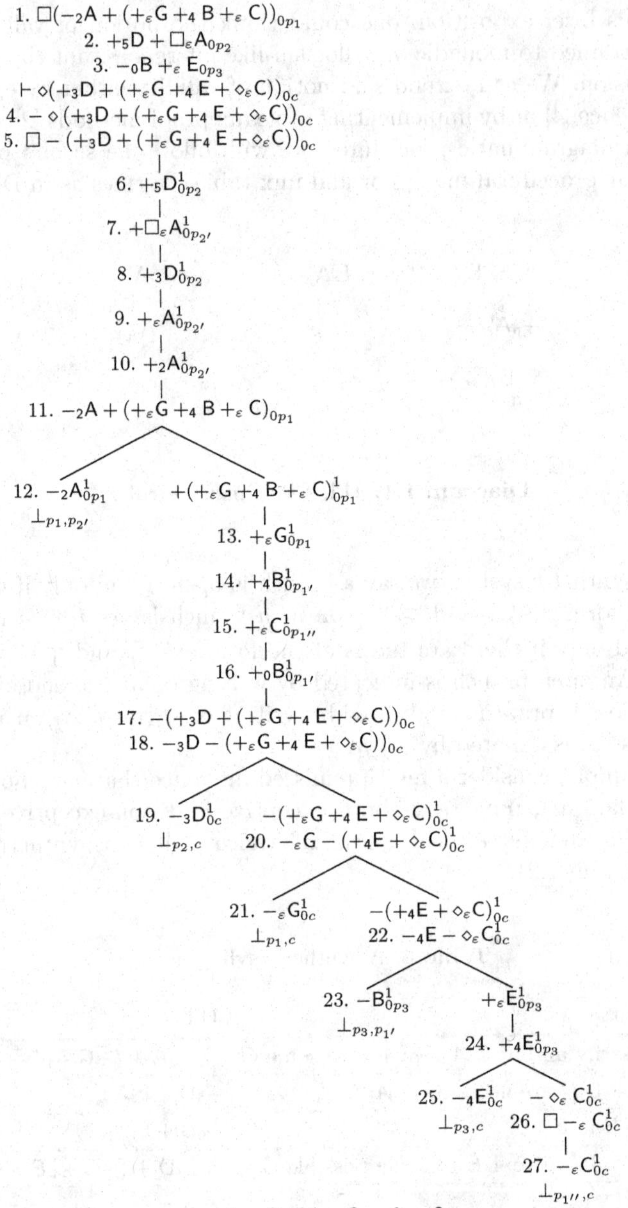

1. $\Box(-_2A + (+_\varepsilon G +_4 B +_\varepsilon C))_{0p_1}$
2. $+_5D + \Box_\varepsilon A_{0p_2}$
3. $-_0B +_\varepsilon E_{0p_3}$
$\vdash \Diamond(+_3D + (+_\varepsilon G +_4 E + \Diamond_\varepsilon C))_{0c}$
4. $- \Diamond (+_3D + (+_\varepsilon G +_4 E + \Diamond_\varepsilon C))_{0c}$
5. $\Box - (+_3D + (+_\varepsilon G +_4 E + \Diamond_\varepsilon C))_{0c}$
    |
6. $+_5D^1_{0p_2}$
    |
7. $+\Box_\varepsilon A^1_{0p_{2'}}$
    |
8. $+_3D^1_{0p_2}$
    |
9. $+_\varepsilon A^1_{0p_{2'}}$
    |
10. $+_2A^1_{0p_{2'}}$
    |
11. $-_2A + (+_\varepsilon G +_4 B +_\varepsilon C)_{0p_1}$

12. $-_2A^1_{0p_1}$ $+(+_\varepsilon G +_4 B +_\varepsilon C)^1_{0p_1}$
$\perp_{p_1,p_{2'}}$ |
                    13. $+_\varepsilon G^1_{0p_1}$
                         |
                    14. $+_4B^1_{0p_{1'}}$
                         |
                    15. $+_\varepsilon C^1_{0p_{1''}}$
                         |
                    16. $+_0B^1_{0p_{1'}}$
                         |
                    17. $-(+_3D + (+_\varepsilon G +_4 E + \Diamond_\varepsilon C))_{0c}$
                    18. $-_3D - (+_\varepsilon G +_4 E + \Diamond_\varepsilon C))_{0c}$

                19. $-_3D^1_{0c}$ $-(+_\varepsilon G +_4 E + \Diamond_\varepsilon C)^1_{0c}$
                $\perp_{p_2,c}$ 20. $-_\varepsilon G - (+_4E + \Diamond_\varepsilon C)^1_{0c}$

                    21. $-_\varepsilon G^1_{0c}$ $-(+_4E + \Diamond_\varepsilon C)^1_{0c}$
                    $\perp_{p_1,c}$ 22. $-_4E - \Diamond_\varepsilon C^1_{0c}$

                        23. $-B^1_{0p_3}$ $+_\varepsilon E^1_{0p_3}$
                        $\perp_{p_3,p_{1'}}$ |
                                        24. $+_4E^1_{0p_3}$

                            25. $-_4E^1_{0c}$ $- \Diamond_\varepsilon C^1_{0c}$
                            $\perp_{p_3,c}$ 26. $\Box -_\varepsilon C^1_{0c}$
                                                    |
                                            27. $-_\varepsilon C^1_{0c}$
                                                $\perp_{p_{1''},c}$

$$v = 5 - 2 + 4 - 3 - 4 = 0$$

Diagram 1.2. A valid synthetic syllogism.

4   Conclusions

In this contribution we have combined some term logics as to produce a synthetic term logic. We accomplished this goal by following a color mixing metaphor. We sketched four logics designed to capture four aspects of natural language reasoning and then, using the aforementioned metaphor, we produced a synthetic logic.

Finally, due to reasons of space, we would like to close this contribution with a statement of the following results:

Theorem 1 (Relevance-completeness for TFL$^{\alpha\nu\mu\rho}$). *An inference is relevant in* TFL$^{\alpha\nu\mu\rho}$ *iff there is a closed complete tableau with $v = 0$ for said inference.*

Theorem 2 (Validity-completeness for TFL$^{\alpha\nu\mu\rho}$). *An inference is valid in* TFL$^{\alpha\nu\mu\rho}$ *iff there is a semi-closed/semi-open complete tableau with $v = 0$ for said inference.*

References

1. Blackburn, P., de Rijke, M.: Why combine logics? Studia Logica: Int. J. Symbol. Logic **59**(1), 5–27 (1997). http://www.jstor.org/stable/20015923
2. Castro-Manzano, J.M.: Distribution tableaux, distribution models. Axioms **9**(2) (2020). https://doi.org/10.3390/axioms9020041, https://www.mdpi.com/2075-1680/9/2/41
3. Englebretsen, G.: Preliminary notes on a new modal syllogistic. Notre Dame J. Formal Logic **29**(3), 381–395 (1988). https://doi.org/10.1305/ndjfl/1093637935
4. Englebretsen, G.: Something to Reckon with: The Logic of Terms. Canadian Electronic Library: Books Collection, University of Ottawa Press (1996)
5. Gabbay, D.: Fibring Logics. Oxford Logic Guides, Clarendon Press (1998)
6. Küppers, H.: The Basic Law of Color Theory. Pocket Art Series, Barron's (1982)
7. Murphree, W.A.: Numerical term logic. Notre Dame J. Formal Logic **39**(3), 346–362 (1998). https://doi.org/10.1305/ndjfl/1039182251
8. Sommers, F.: The Logic of Natural Language. Clarendon Library of Logic and Philosophy, Clarendon Press; Oxford University Press, Oxford; New York (1982)
9. Woods, J.: Aristotle's Earlier Logic. Studies in Logic. College Publications (2014)

Normatively Determined Propositions

Matteo Pascucci[1]([⊠]) [iD] and Claudio E. A. Pizzi[2] [iD]

[1] Department of Analytic Philosophy, Institute of Philosophy,
Slovak Academy of Sciences, v.v.i., Bratislava, Slovakia
matteopascucci.academia@gmail.com
[2] Emeritus, University of Siena, Siena, Italy

Abstract. In the present work we provide a logical analysis of normatively determined and non-determined propositions. The normative status of these propositions depends on their relation with another proposition, here named reference proposition. Using a formal language that includes a monadic operator of obligation, we define eight dyadic operators that represent various notions of "being normatively (non-)determined"; then, we group them into two families, each forming an Aristotelian square of opposition. Finally, we show how the two resulting squares can be combined to form an Aristotelian cube of opposition.

Keywords: Normatively determined propositions · Aristotelian squares · Aristotelian cubes · Modal logic · Deontic logic

1 Introduction

Formal logic has been used for decades in the analysis of normative concepts, shedding light on their properties and relations. In the area of normative reasoning, logic has been employed to deal with several families of concepts. Just to mention a few of these, much has been written about the notions of obligation, permission, prohibition (see, e.g., the surveys by Åqvist [1] or Hilpinen and McNamara [6]), right and duty (see, e.g., Lindahl [7] or Makinson [8]). Other concepts, such as the ones of power, liability and responsibility, are receiving increasing attention (see, e.g., Glavaničová and Pascucci [5], Markovich [9] or Pascucci and Sileno [10]). In the present work we propose an inquiry on a topic that has not received attention in the logical literature, namely the formal characterization of *normatively determined propositions*.

Saying that a proposition B is determined by a proposition A, in general, means that either (i) B holds in all circumstances in which A holds or (ii) B holds in no circumstances in which A holds. In this informal definition A can be

Matteo Pascucci was supported by the *Štefan Schwarz Fund* for the project "A fine-grained analysis of Hohfeldian concepts" (2020–2023) and by the VEGA project no. 2/0125/22 "Responsibility and modal logic". The article results from a joint work of the two authors.

V. Giardino et al. (Eds.): Diagrams 2022, LNAI 13462, pp. 78–85, 2022.
https://doi.org/10.1007/978-3-031-15146-0_6

said to be the *reference proposition* (i.e., the proposition with reference to which the status of B is assessed). It can be easily checked that "being determined" is a *bilateral* notion, since, according to the above definition, B is determined by A iff $\neg B$ is determined by A (where $\neg$ is the classical operator of negation).[1]

Here we propose to focus on a deontic variant of the notion at issue. Let N be a set of normatively relevant scenarios: a proposition B is *normatively determined* by a proposition A in N iff either (i) the truth of A implies the truth of B in every scenario of N or (ii) the truth of A implies the falsity of B in every scenario of N. Consequently, a proposition B is *normatively non-determined* by a proposition A in N iff the truth of A is conjoined with the truth of B in some scenarios of N and with the falsity of B in other scenarios of N. The framework introduced here will not be committed to any particular choice of normatively relevant scenarios; in the simplest interpretation, one can take them to be the normatively ideal scenarios (along the lines of Åqvist [1]).

Determination is a crucial issue in the normative domain, since sets of norms are associated with layers: norms belonging to one layer may depend on norms belonging to an upper-level layer. Logical accounts of normative conditionals and contrary-to-duty reasoning (see Hilpinen and McNamara [6] for an extended discussion) capture some aspects of this; yet, the notion of normative determination offers a broader perspective, since it covers other forms of dependency among norms. In fact, one can distinguish various kinds of determination for a proposition B on the basis of the normative status of a proposition A (the reference proposition). Here we will focus on the following two issues:

- whether the normative status assigned to A is that of an obligation or of a permission;
- whether the normative status of A is claimed to be of a certain kind or simply supposed to be of a certain kind.

Combining these options with the two possible ways in which the normative status of B depends on the normative status of A, namely "being determined by A" or "being non-determined by A", one gets as a result a set of eight normative relations between A and B.

The following are a few examples of claims taken from everyday normative discourse illustrating the meaning of some of the notions at issue:

1. it is obligatory to pay for the goods at the time of delivery and it is permitted (although not obligatory) to use a credit card.
2. it is obligatory to pay for the goods in advance but it is forbidden to pay via a bank transfer.
3. if an online payment for the goods is permitted, then one can pay via a bank transfer or with a different method.

---

[1] More precisely, "being determined" is a *dyadic* notion of *non-contingency*. An axiomatic characterization of dyadic non-contingency has been recently proposed by Pizzi [13]. For more on the logic of (non-)contingency, see Cresswell [2].

In example (1) the proposition that one pays with a credit card is *not* normatively determined by the proposition that one pays at the time of delivery. Indeed, we know that a customer has to pay at the time of delivery but also that she can choose whether to pay with a credit card or not (neither of the two options is forced). In example (2) the proposition that one pays via a bank transfer is normatively determined by the proposition that one pays in advance. Indeed, we know that customers have to pay in advance and this forces them to avoid using a bank transfer; hence, this option is ruled out.[2] In example (3) the proposition that one uses a bank transfer is *not* normatively determined by the proposition that one pays online. Indeed, if we suppose that a customer is allowed to pay online, then she can choose between using a bank transfer or a different method.

These relations will be analysed via a language of propositional modal logic in terms of dyadic deontic operators. Two Aristotelian squares of opposition will be drawn which, in turn, will clarify logical connections between pairs of the normative relations at issue. Finally, we will show how the two squares can be combined in order to form an Aristotelian cube of opposition. Aristotelian diagrams are known for their didactic efficacy. A long-term objective of the present work is contributing to the development of graphical interfaces based on these diagrams for human-machine interaction. For instance, imagine that a user specifies a set of normative statements in a simplified language (as initial hypotheses) and gives it as input to a program that builds an Aristotelian diagram out of this set; then, the user can explore the displayed diagram and make inferences from the nodes associated with the initial hypotheses to other nodes, by following the available paths of edges. For the user, this may be an effective help in reasoning on normative problems (e.g., on the content of a contract).

2   Formal Setting

The formal language which will be used here consists of (i) a set of propositional variables, denoted by a, b, c, etc., (ii) the monadic operators $\neg$ (negation) and $\Box$ (obligation), (iii) the dyadic operator $\rightarrow$ (material implication). We take $\Diamond$ (permission) to be a shorthand for $\neg\Box\neg$ and other propositional connectives, such as $\wedge$ (conjunction), $\vee$ (disjunction) and $\leftrightarrow$ (material equivalence) to be defined in terms of the primitive ones, as usual. Arbitrary formulas will be denoted by A, B, C, etc. If N is the chosen set of normatively relevant scenarios, we read $\Box A$ as "A is true in all scenarios of N", which essentially means that A is obligatory. Furthermore, we read $\Diamond A$ as "A is true in some scenarios of N", which essentially means that A is permitted.

---

[2] Since "being normatively determined" is a bilateral notion, in examples (1)-(3), if a proposition B is normatively (non-)determined by a proposition A, then so is $\neg B$. For instance, in example (2) both the proposition that one pays via a bank transfer and the proposition that one does not pay via a bank transfer are normatively determined by the reference proposition that one pays in advance, since the latter excludes one of the two alternatives and forces the other. Furthermore, we highlight that our analysis covers also cases of (non-)determination with respect to forbidden propositions, as long as one defines "A is forbidden" as "$\neg A$ is obligatory" ($\Box\neg A$).

The following is a list of definitions for the auxiliary modal operators representing the *eight dyadic modalities* that will be the object of our inquiry:

- $\triangle(A, B) := \Diamond A \wedge (\Box(A \to B) \vee \Box(A \to \neg B))$, meaning that A is permitted and B is normatively determined by A.
- $\triangle^*(A, B) := \Box A \wedge (\Box(A \to B) \vee \Box(A \to \neg B))$, meaning that A is obligatory and B is normatively determined by A.
- $\blacktriangle(A, B) := \Diamond A \to (\Box(A \to B) \vee \Box(A \to \neg B))$, meaning that if A is permitted, then B is normatively determined by A.
- $\blacktriangle^*(A, B) := \Box A \to (\Box(A \to B) \vee \Box(A \to \neg B))$, meaning that if A is obligatory, then B is normatively determined by A.
- $\triangledown(A, B) := \Diamond A \wedge (\Diamond(A \wedge B) \wedge \Diamond(A \wedge \neg B))$, meaning that A is permitted and B is not normatively determined by A.[3]
- $\triangledown^*(A, B) := \Box A \wedge (\Diamond(A \wedge B) \wedge \Diamond(A \wedge \neg B))$, meaning that A is obligatory and B is not normatively determined by A.
- $\blacktriangledown(A, B) := \Diamond A \to (\Diamond(A \wedge B) \wedge \Diamond(A \wedge \neg B))$, meaning that if A is permitted, then B is not normatively determined by A.
- $\blacktriangledown^*(A, B) := \Box A \to (\Diamond(A \wedge B) \wedge \Diamond(A \wedge \neg B))$, meaning that if A is obligatory, then B is not normatively determined by A.

Notational conventions for dyadic operators are as follows: (i) operators expressing the *claim* that the reference proposition A has a certain status are white triangles ($\wedge$ is the main operator in the *definiens*), whereas those expressing the *supposition* that A has a certain status are black triangles ($\to$ is the main operator in the *definiens*); (ii) operators saying that B is *determined* by A are up-pointing triangles, whereas those saying that B is *non-determined* by A are down-pointing triangles (cf. the use of the symbols 'delta' and 'nabla' by authors working on contingency logic, such as Cresswell [2]); (iii) operators treating the reference proposition A as an *obligation* (rather than a *permission*) are distinguished by $*$.

The three examples discussed in Sect. 1 can be rendered as follows ($d =$ one pays for the goods at the time of delivery, $c =$ one pays with a credit card, $b =$ one pays via a bank transfer, $a =$ one pays in advance, $o =$ one pays online):

1. $\Box d \wedge (\Diamond(d \wedge c) \wedge \Diamond(d \wedge \neg c))$;
2. $\Box a \wedge \Box \neg b$;
3. $\Diamond o \to (\Diamond(o \wedge b) \wedge \Diamond(o \wedge \neg b))$.

Notice that the formula encoding (1) corresponds to $\triangledown^*(d, c)$ and the formula encoding (3) corresponds to $\blacktriangledown(o, b)$; moreover, in any normal modal system, the formula encoding (2) entails $\triangle^*(a, b)$.

There are several ways of grouping the eight dyadic modalities. Here we take $\triangle(A, B)$ and $\triangledown(A, B)$ to be the basic notions: they express the conjunction of a statement describing a normative relation between A and B with the statement that A represents a permission. We will use each of these two operators to build an Aristotelian square of opposition.

---

[3] In normal modal systems $\triangledown(A, B)$ boils down to $\Diamond(A \wedge B) \wedge \Diamond(A \wedge \neg B)$.

3   Geometrical Representations

In Pizzi [12] an *Aristotelian square of opposition over a logical system* **S**, or simply an *Aristotelian* **S**-*square*, is a 4-tuple of formulas $Q = (W, X, Y, Z)$, where each formula in the 4-tuple is said to be a *vertex* of Q and the pairs of formulas (W, X), (Y, Z), (W, Y) and (X, Z) are the *edges* of Q. The first formula W in Q is said to be its *origin*. The logical relations in an Aristotelian **S**-square Q are as follows: W and X represent *contrary* propositions in **S**; Y and Z *subcontrary* propositions in **S**; W and Y, as well as X and Z *connected* propositions (more precisely, Y is a *subalternant* of W and Z is a *subalternant* of X) in **S**; W and Z, as well as X and Y, *contradictory* propositions in **S**.[4] We will be here working within modal system **KD**, i.e., the smallest normal system closed under the schema $\Box A \to \Diamond A$ and whose models are serial[5].

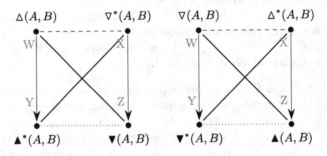

Fig. 1. $\triangle$-rooted (left) and ∇-rooted (right) Aristotelian **KD**-squares

Figure 1 graphically represents two Aristotelian **KD**-squares of opposition, one having $\triangle(A, B)$ at its origin, the other having $\nabla(A, B)$ at its origin. The former will be said to be a $\triangle$-*rooted* square, the latter a ∇-*rooted* square. In each square an arrow from one vertex to another stands for subalternation, a full line between two vertices for contradiction, a dashed line between two vertices for contrariety and a dotted line between two vertices for subcontrariety.

The construction of the $\triangle$-rooted square can be justified as follows. In **KD**, from the assumption $\triangle(A, B)$, namely $\Diamond A \wedge (\Box(A \to B) \vee \Box(A \to \neg B))$, one can infer $\Box A \to (\Diamond A \wedge (\Box(A \to B) \vee \Box(A \to \neg B)))$ via the Propositional Calculus (**PC**), whence $\Box A \to (\Box(A \to B) \vee \Box(A \to \neg B))$, namely $\blacktriangle^*(A, B)$, again via **PC**. By contrast, the inference from $\blacktriangle^*(A, B)$ to $\triangle(A, B)$ is not supported by **KD**, since any **KD**-model including a world w that has access to no worlds is such that $\blacktriangle^*(A, B)$ is true at w and $\triangle(A, B)$ is false at w. This means that $\blacktriangle^*(A, B)$ is a subalternant of $\triangle(A, B)$ in **KD**. Moreover, $\Diamond A \to (\Diamond(A \wedge B) \wedge \Diamond(A \wedge \neg B))$ is equivalent to $\neg(\Diamond A \wedge (\Box(A \to B) \vee \Box(A \to \neg B)))$ thanks to the definition

---

[4] We assume familiarity with the meaning of the Aristotelian relations at issue. For details, see Pizzi [11, 12].

[5] For details, see Åqvist [1]. For Aristotelian squares built on non-normal modal systems, see Demey [3].

of $\Diamond$ and **PC**. This means that $\triangle(A, B)$ and $\blacktriangledown(A, B)$ are contradictories in **KD**. Finally, $\Diamond A \wedge (\Box(A \to B) \vee \Box(A \to \neg B))$ entails $\neg(\Box A \wedge (\Diamond(A \wedge B) \wedge \Diamond(A \wedge \neg B)))$, since $\Box(A \to B) \vee \Box(A \to \neg B)$ is equivalent to $\neg(\Diamond(A \wedge B) \wedge \Diamond(A \wedge \neg B))$; however, $\neg(\Diamond A \wedge (\Box(A \to B) \vee \Box(A \to \neg B)))$ is equivalent to $\Diamond A \to (\Diamond(A \wedge B) \wedge \Diamond(A \wedge \neg B))$ and the latter does not entail $\Box A \wedge (\Diamond(A \wedge B) \wedge \Diamond(A \wedge \neg B))$; for instance, any **KD**-model including a world w having access to a unique world v where A is false is such that $\Diamond A \to (\Diamond(A \wedge B) \wedge \Diamond(A \wedge \neg B))$ is true at w and $\Box A \wedge (\Diamond(A \wedge B) \wedge \Diamond(A \wedge \neg B))$ is false at w. This means that $\triangle(A, B)$ and $\nabla^*(A, B)$ are contraries in **KD**. The fact that $\blacktriangle^*(A, B)$ and $\blacktriangledown(A, B)$ are sub-contraries in **KD** follows from the rest.[6]

In the case of the ∇-rooted square, the construction can be justified as follows. In **KD**, starting with the assumption $\nabla(A, B)$, namely $\Diamond A \wedge (\Diamond(A \wedge B) \wedge \Diamond(A \wedge \neg B))$, one can infer $\Box A \to (\Diamond A \wedge (\Diamond(A \wedge B) \wedge \Diamond(A \wedge \neg B)))$ via **PC**, whence (again, via **PC**) $\Box A \to (\Diamond(A \wedge B) \wedge \Diamond(A \wedge \neg B))$, namely $\blacktriangledown^*(A, B)$. By contrast, the inference from $\blacktriangledown^*(A, B)$ to $\nabla(A, B)$ is not supported by **KD**, since any **KD**-model including a world w that has access to a single world v where A is false is such that $\blacktriangledown^*(A, B)$ is true at w and $\nabla(A, B)$ is false at w. This means that $\blacktriangledown^*(A, B)$ is a subalternant of $\nabla(A, B)$ in **KD**. Moreover, $\Diamond A \wedge (\Diamond(A \wedge B) \wedge \Diamond(A \wedge \neg B))$ is equivalent to $\neg(\Diamond A \to (\Box(A \to B) \vee \Box(A \to \neg B)))$ thanks to the definition of $\Diamond$ and **PC**. This means that $\nabla(A, B)$ and $\blacktriangle(A, B)$ are contradictories in **KD**. Finally, $\Diamond A \wedge (\Diamond(A \wedge B) \wedge \Diamond(A \wedge \neg B))$ entails $\neg(\Box A \wedge (\Box(A \to B) \vee \Box(A \to \neg B)))$, since $\Box(A \to B) \vee \Box(A \to \neg B)$ is equivalent to $\neg(\Diamond(A \wedge B) \wedge \Diamond(A \wedge \neg B))$; however, $\neg(\Diamond A \wedge (\Diamond(A \wedge B) \wedge \Diamond(A \wedge \neg B)))$ is equivalent to $\Diamond A \to (\Box(A \to B) \vee \Box(A \to \neg B))$ and the latter does not entail $\Box A \wedge (\Box(A \to B) \vee \Box(A \to \neg B))$; for instance, any **KD**-model including a world w that has access to a unique world v where A is false is such that $\Diamond A \to (\Box(A \to B) \vee \Box(A \to \neg B))$ is true at w and $\Box A \wedge (\Box(A \to B) \vee \Box(A \to \neg B))$ is false at w. This means that $\nabla(A, B)$ and $\triangle^*(A, B)$ are contraries in **KD**. The fact that $\blacktriangledown^*(A, B)$ and $\blacktriangle(A, B)$ are sub-contraries in **KD** follows from the rest.

The two squares can be combined in system **KD** to form an Aristotelian cube. The notion of an Aristotelian cube has been defined in various ways (see, for instance, Dubois, Prade and Rico [4]). Here we follow Pizzi [11] and first introduce the notion of a semiaristotelian square. A *semiaristotelian* **S**-*square* is a 4-tuple $Q = (W, X, Y, Z)$, where each edge represents one of the Aristotelian relations of connectedness, contrariety, subcontrariety and contradiction.[7] An *Aristotelian* **S**-*cube* is a set $K = \{Q1, ..., Q6\}$ where:

- every Qi, for $1 \leq i \leq 6$, is a semiaristotelian square;
- for some j, k s.t. $1 \leq j \neq k \leq 6$, Qj, Qk are Aristotelian **S**-squares;
- each edge of each square in K is also an edge of some other square in K.

---

[6] As observed by Pizzi [13], the notion of absolute (non-)determination may be defined in terms of dyadic (non-)determination by replacing the reference proposition with a tautology $\top$. For instance: $\triangle(\top, B)$.

[7] Thus, a semiaristotelian **S**-square is a square whose edges are associated with *some* of the relations holding between the edges of an Aristotelian **S**-square.

Looking at the graphical representation of the cube in Fig. 2, the two formulas occupying corners W and W', as well as the two formulas occupying corners X and X' are contraries in **KD**. For instance, in such system $\triangle(A, B)$ logically entails $\neg\triangledown(A, B)$, whereas $\neg\triangle(A, B)$ does not entail $\triangledown(A, B)$. Furthermore, the two formulas occupying corners Y and Y', as well as the two formulas occupying corners Z and Z' are sub-contraries in **KD**. For instance, in such system $\neg\blacktriangle^*(A, B)$ entails $\blacktriangledown^*(A, B)$, whereas $\blacktriangle^*(A, B)$ does not entail $\neg\blacktriangledown^*(A, B)$. Thus, the squares (W, W', X, X'), (W, W', Y, Y'), (X, X', Z, Z') and (Y, Y', Z, Z') are all semiaristotelian and one can conclude that the cube at issue is an Aristotelian **KD**-cube, according to the definition in Pizzi [11].

Yet, the 16 relations graphically represented in Fig. 2 are not the only relations between pairs of vertices of the two squares. Indeed, the total number of relations on 8 formulas is $(8 \times (8 - 1))/2 = 28$ and the following 12 hold too: $\triangledown(A, B)$ is a subalternant of $\triangledown^*(A, B)$; $\triangle(A, B)$ is a subalternant of $\triangle^*(A, B)$; $\blacktriangledown^*(A, B)$ is a subalternant of $\blacktriangledown(A, B)$; $\blacktriangle^*(A, B)$ is a subalternant of $\blacktriangle(A, B)$; $\triangle(A, B)$ and $\blacktriangledown^*(A, B)$ are subcontraries; $\triangledown(A, B)$ and $\blacktriangle^*(A, B)$ are subcontraries; $\blacktriangle(A, B)$ and $\triangledown^*(A, B)$ are contraries; $\blacktriangledown(A, B)$ and $\triangle^*(A, B)$ are contraries; $\blacktriangle(A, B)$ is a subalternant of $\triangle(A, B)$; $\blacktriangledown(A, B)$ is a subalternant of $\triangledown(A, B)$; $\blacktriangle^*(A, B)$ is a subalternant of $\triangle^*(A, B)$; $\blacktriangledown^*(A, B)$ is a subalternant of $\triangledown^*(A, B)$.

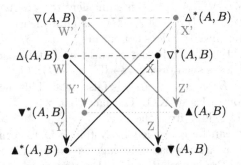

Fig. 2. Aristotelian **KD**-cube for the eight dyadic operators

4   Final Remarks

Our logical analysis of normatively determined and non-determined propositions can be extended in many respects. From the point of view of Aristotelian diagrams, alternative combinations of the operators introduced here can be taken into account. For instance, consider the formulas $\triangle(A, B)$ and $\triangledown(A, B)$ at the origins of the two Aristotelian squares in Fig. 1: it might be possible to build other Aristotelian squares having the same origins, by finding new formulas C and D that are respectively contrary to $\triangle(A, B)$ and to $\triangledown(A, B)$ in system **KD** or in stronger systems. Dyadic operators can be also used to define the monadic operators $\Box$ and $\Diamond$, as shown by Pizzi [13]. For instance, in normal modal systems $\Diamond A$ is definable as $\triangle(A, A)$. Moreover, $\triangle(A, B)$ entails $\triangle(A, A)$ (i.e., $\Diamond A$) whereas there is no entailment in the opposite direction: thus, $\Diamond A$ is a subalternant of $\triangle(A, B)$. In the light of the latter observation, one can check whether it is possible to build Aristotelian squares and cubes involving both monadic and dyadic operators.

References

1. Åqvist, L.: Deontic logic. In: Gabbay, D., Guenthner, F. (eds.) Handbook of Philosophical Logic, vol. 8, pp. 147–264. Kluwer, Dordrecht (2002)
2. Cresswell, M.J.: Necessity and contingency. Stud. Logica. **47**, 145–149 (1988)
3. Demey, L.: Logic-sensitivity of Aristotelian diagrams in non-normal modal logics. Axioms **10**, 128–152 (2021)
4. Dubois, D., Prade, H., Rico, A.: The cube of opposition - a structure underlying many knowledge representation formalisms. In: Proceedings of IJCAI 2015, pp. 2933–2939 (2015)
5. Glavaničová, D., Pascucci, M.: Formal analysis of responsibility attribution in a multimodal framework. In: Baldoni, M., Dastani, M., Liao, B., Sakurai, Y., Zalila Wenkstern, R. (eds.) PRIMA 2019. LNCS (LNAI), vol. 11873, pp. 36–51. Springer, Cham (2019). https://doi.org/10.1007/978-3-030-33792-6_3
6. Hilpinen, R., McNamara, P.: Deontic logic: a historical survey and introduction. In: Gabbay, D., et al. (eds.) Handbook of Deontic Logic and Normative Systems, vol. 1, pp. 1–134. College Publications, London (2013)
7. Lindahl, L.: Position and Change: A Study in Law and Logic. Reidel, Dordrecht (1977)
8. Makinson, D.: On the formal representation of rights relations. J. Philos. Log. **15**, 403–425 (1986)
9. Markovich, R.: Understanding Hohfeld and formalizing legal rights: the Hohfeldian conceptions and their conditional consequences. Stud. Logica. **108**, 129–158 (2020)
10. Pascucci, M., Sileno, G.: The search for symmetry in Hohfeldian modalities. In: Basu, A., Stapleton, G., Linker, S., Legg, C., Manalo, E., Viana, P. (eds.) Diagrams 2021. LNCS (LNAI), vol. 12909, pp. 87–102. Springer, Cham (2021). https://doi.org/10.1007/978-3-030-86062-2_9
11. Pizzi, C.: Aristotle's cubes and consequential implication. Log. Univers. **2**, 143–153 (2008)
12. Pizzi, C.: Generalization and composition of modal squares of opposition. Log. Univers. **10**, 313–325 (2016)
13. Pizzi, C.: Possibility and dyadic contingency. J. Logic Lang. Inf. (Forthcoming)

A Diagram Must Never Be Ten Thousand Words: Text-Based (Sentential) Approaches to Diagrams Accessibility Limit Users' Potential for Normative Agency

David Barter[1,2]([☒]) [iD] and Peter Coppin[1,2,3] [iD]

[1] Perceptual Artifacts Lab, OCAD University, Toronto, ON M5T 1W1, Canada
{david.barter,pcoppin}@ocadu.ca
[2] Inclusive Design Program, OCAD University, Toronto, ON M5T 1W1, Canada
[3] Faculty of Design, OCAD University, Toronto, ON M5T 1W1, Canada

Abstract. Web Content Accessibility Guidelines (WCAG) require digital diagrams to be tagged with screen readable text descriptions for access by blind and partially sighted individuals (BPSI). The aim of these guidelines is to comply with human rights-based accessibility legislation, which aims to preserve the normative agency of BPSI (the ability to reflect on, evaluate and act upon a conception of what constitutes a worthwhile life for themselves). However, theories from the Diagrams community suggest that text and diagrams offer distinctly different constraints. For example, Shimojima's Constraint Hypothesis (the relationship of structural constraints to target problem constraints in a mode of representation establish the variance of inferential potential) and the interrelated free ride phenomenon (additional inferences can be made in a representation if the relationship of constraints is a good match). Therefore, a guideline that requires the text description of a diagram (such as via the WCAG) might limit the normative agency diagram users who are BPSI. Despite the apparent necessity of providing non-visual alternatives of diagrammatic properties for accessibility, they are rarely explored or developed sufficiently to be consistently provided to BPSI. Thus, we argue that the affordances of diagrammatic representations provide possibilities for normative agency that are lost if not represented non-visually in diagrams designed for accessibility.

Keywords: Free Rides · Minimum Provision of Information · Accessibility · Normative Agency

1 Introduction

Diagrams display spatial and topological relations of ideas, phenomena, and the material world and are thus in many cases an indispensable, part of everyday reasoning, decision making, communication and expression for many people [1, 2]. The Diagrams community, in their attempt to better understand why a diagram is "worth ten thousand words" [1], aims to demonstrate how diagrams offer beneficial features not provided

© Springer Nature Switzerland AG 2022
V. Giardino et al. (Eds.): Diagrams 2022, LNAI 13462, pp. 86–93, 2022.
https://doi.org/10.1007/978-3-031-15146-0_7

by sentences alone [3, 4]. Unfortunately, blind and partially sighted individuals (BPSI) experience text descriptions of diagrams in most cases [5–7]. Human rights-based accessibility requirements, such as the Web Content Accessibility Guidelines (WCAG) [7], aim to extend human rights principles of autonomy and agency to digital media by requiring visual content to be accessible via alternative (non-visual) formats. However, because WCAG [7] offers no technical way to distinguish diagrams relative to sentences, most diagrams are made accessible through screen-readable text descriptions (or interpretations) of diagrams [3, 4]. Previously, we demonstrated how sentences are more effective for conveying abstract conceptual categories whereas diagrams are more effective for conveying concrete structures (specific spatial-topological arrangements) [3, 4]. However, many potential impacts on audiences who cannot sufficiently access them [3, 4] have yet to be explored in depth.

In this paper, we propose that there is a need for a technical understanding of the affordances, or constraints, of diagrams as opposed to text descriptions for accessibility experts. Several traditional theories from the diagrams community demonstrate that diagrams have distinct properties that provide information that text descriptions cannot. These include the distinction between "diagrammatic and sentential representations" [1], Shimojima's [2] concept of a Constraint Hypothesis (the relationship of structural constraints to target problem constraints in a mode of representation establish the variance of inferential potential) and phenomenon of "free rides" (additional inferences can be made in a representation if its structural constraints match the constraints of the targets of representation effectively). Reliance on text descriptions to present diagrams to BPSI for accessibility often results in perceptual ambiguity [3, 4, see Fig. 1] and with it, a reduction of possibilities for action [8]. This ambiguity results from an inappropriate relationship of constraints within the problem context that calls for diagrammatic representations [1] in the first place. We argue that it is feasible to set the stage for future work on accessibility standards through this technical understanding of diagram affordances for accessibility. This effort should be incentivized when considering how the potential "normative agency" [9] a BPSI might possess is limited relative to sighted individuals by limiting their possibilities for action [8]. After all, accessibility specialists are guided by standards to use text descriptions for diagram accessibility so predominantly.

2   Diagrammatic Representation and "Free Rides"

The disadvantages of limiting the provision of pictures, diagrams, charts and icons for accessibility to text descriptions is noted by Coppin [4]. The existence of pictorial and diagrammatic representations implies that a complete translation into text or speech cannot be sufficient, as otherwise, it would be unnecessary in the first place [4]. This echoes the work of Shimojima [2], who describes a "Constraint Hypothesis," which predicts that coding information into a two-dimensional plane with geometric and topological relations provides additional information without requiring additional inferences. This is a "free ride", a phenomenon that exemplifies how diagrams offer "consequential information with little inferential effort [that is] *observable* from [a diagram], not just *inferable*" [10]. For this information to be observable from a representation, there must be an appropriate match of representational choices to goals or problems that necessitate the use of a diagram [2]. A relationship of structural constraints of diagrams to target problem constraints [2] in the context of accessibility for BPSI must further consider the constraints of the sensory modalities available to this audience.

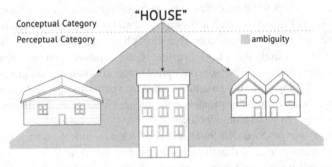

Fig. 1. Per Coppin [3, p. 108], this demonstrates "perceptual ambiguity", as the abstract conceptual category "house" (top) produces many possible concrete perceptual categories (bottom).

Coppin [3] adds that this relationship of constraints upon a structure of representation with its target problem also functions in the context of symbolic representations, such as text. However, both diagrammatic and symbolic representations have a drawback of conceptual (see Fig. 2) and perceptual ambiguity (see Fig. 1), respectively [3]. Consequently, these forms of representation are not equivalent in their information providing capacities. The free ride [2] may therefore have a constraint of conceptual ambiguity [3]. However, understanding the free ride's constraints and how they may be effectively complemented by other representation methods to increase may account for this issue. For example, one may label a picture or diagram, and in doing so, use symbolic representations in combination with pictorial and diagrammatic [1, 3].

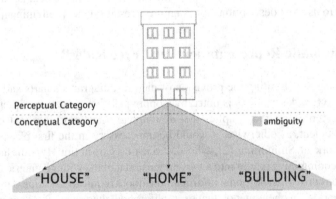

Fig. 2. Per Coppin [3, p.104], this demonstrates "conceptual ambiguity", as the concrete perceptual category of the image (top) produces many possible abstract conceptual categories (bottom).

Minimizing perceptual ambiguity means utilizing the spatial and topological relations among marks (a diagram [1]) to represent the spatial and topological properties of an item. To minimize conceptual ambiguity, one should rely on conventions that refer to familiar abstract meanings to a target audience [3]. The perceptual certainty of a diagrammatically represented item recruits capabilities to perceive and act in the physical world [8]. For example, the choice of whether to eat an apple is structured by the certainty with which one perceives that eating the apple is a beneficial or harmful action (is the apple rotten or is it fresh?). These options can be conveyed visually or through the physical properties that characterize an apple as "rotten". This demonstrates that our understanding of diagrammatic properties can be expanded to other sensory modalities, such as through 3D models and spatial audio [11]. The possibilities for action are therefore also a result of a relationship of constraints between the structural constraints (of the diagram) and the target problem's constraints (environment) [3, 8, 12].

With an understanding of this idea, we may view diagrams as possessing affordances and producing possibilities for action [8]. However, are the geometric and topological properties of diagrams (and their "free rides") afforded consistently to BPSI? Do BPSI have sufficient access to the quantity and certainty of information in diagrams to possess equal potential for choices and actions by interpreting them?

3 Accessibility Issues of Diagrams

BPSI have faced challenges with digital information access needs limiting them mainly to symbolic representations, such as alternative text and Braille, rather than diagrammatic representations (e.g. raised line diagrams, which are costly and quickly made obsolete when used for digital documents: discussed in [13]). High costs and a lack of guidelines for multi-sensory representations [13–15] limited the use of these alternatives in the past, however, barriers to making the necessary representational choices have been reduced. The possibilities for providing cross-sensory correlates for diagrammatic properties has only increased in options and decreased in cost over time [14, 16, 17].

In conjunction with this issue, note that a majority of practitioners and researchers in the accessible diagrams and data visualizations fields prioritize symbolic representations for information access needs of BPSI [5, 18, 19]. Examples of this approach include: a presentation delivered at the data visualizations conference "Outlier 2021", which demonstrated a standard approach used for graphics accessibility at Microsoft [5]. It overviews graphics delivered in speech through a screen reader, including descriptions of the meaning that a user should acquire from the visual properties (produced by mapping large quantities of data to a chart). Second, perceptual and linguistic processing in BPSI were shown to be linked in Fryer [18]. Linguistic audio descriptions were claimed to be capable of producing an equivalent to multi-sensory experiences for them [18]. Finally, Lundgard and Satyanarayan [19] only argue for better informed accessibility standards for using natural language to describe complex images. The authors did not address whether this complexity makes representation solely through language appropriate in the first place [19]. Text descriptions for accessibility support a multitude of information perception and interpretation tasks [6] and uphold accessibility standards that minimize costs and barriers to availability [7]. However, considering how limited and perceptually ambiguous (see Fig. 1) strictly symbolic forms of representation of diagrams are [3], representational choices and related standards should be reconsidered to provide greater equity in information provision for BPSI.

These limitations persist in practice despite some examples that represent diagrammatic properties non-visually and show promise for more effective and beneficial outcomes for accessibility. In Bassett-Bouchard et al. [16], a web application provides a sonification of financial charts that translate diagrammatic properties into non-linguistic sounds. Pitch and tempo convey positive or negative relationships between chart values and a mean over time, or the change rate of data values at any set of points on the chart [16]. Biggs et al. [20] explored binaural audio labeling via an augmented reality application for a 3D scale model map of a playground. The project leveraged the constraints of spatial audio and cross-sensory tangible interactions that assist BPSI with way finding and orientation relative to the features of the playground without needing visual representation [20]. Finally, an audio-tactile globe [21] provided cross-sensory interactions through spatial-topological properties of the Earth's land masses and bodies of water combined with auditory labels. It augments the perceptual specificity (see Fig. 2) of the shapes of continents with the conceptual specificity of the continents' and oceans' names (see Fig. 1) to communicate geography insights to BPSI in an alternative format to the diagrammatic representations of visual maps [21].

In each case, effective representations are constructed for BPSI by recognizing what is afforded by the relationship of constraints between representation options and their abilities. This builds upon the Constraint Hypothesis [2], since using and combining different sensory modalities have inherent constraints that may guide design decisions. For example, whereas visual perception effectively processes a visual diagram composed of items indexed to different elevations of a rectangle [1], audio perception is more effective for detecting items at different directions on a virtual ground plane. An audio diagram should translate visual relations to auditory relations of this kind. Doing so would provide additional possibilities for action [8] compared to text descriptions alone and foster equivalent access to information for BPSI as users with sight. With only text descriptions for accessibility, however, their available action-possibilities [8] would be comparatively limited, considering that their sole resource for action would be a conceptually specific interpretation [3, see Fig. 1] provided for them.

The examples above demonstrate scenarios in which BPSI possess an equal potential for "normative agency" by virtue of having the same available resources for making choices and taking action in pursuit of what they consider worthwhile [9] as their peers with sight. Without these resources, they have limited potential normative agency [9] in comparison, making said restriction a possible issue of human rights that should be explored in addition to the challenges of accessibility.

4   Relationships of Constraints, Possibilities for Action, and Connections with Human Rights

Philosophies of human rights [22] relate strongly to the perception-action cycle and the behaviour of organisms in an environment [8, 12]. An organism's available choices for action are built upon the relationship between themselves and the environment that they occupy [8], establishing them as an agent that "competently inhabit[s their surroundings]" [12]. A relationship of constraints emerges, including those of perceptual affordances [8], perception of information, and the representation-structure-to-target-problem constraints theorized to provide "free rides" [2].

In this context of human rights, consider the relationship of constraints that yields a "social contract" [22]. This theory explains that without a society, humans and their status as agents give them "natural rights" that would cause conflict (over resources, territory, etc. [22]). However, humans are not known to have existed in such a "state of nature", rather than form societies [22]. A "social contract", implies that all members of a society agree to cede an equal aggregate of their "natural rights" to achieve peace and security, and minimize the threat of individuals' agency causing conflict [22].

"Natural rights" meaning to be ceded equally in a society [22] emphasizes why agency is an important criterion for developing diagrammatic representation practices for accessibility. To support this agency for BPSI more equally relative to those with sight, understanding what actions are available, which are taken, and why they are taken is critical. For a human being in an environment, in a society, and in engagement with a problem concerning information that possesses topological and geometric relations, the provision of more or less information to users solely on the basis of differing abilities clearly indicates unequal, limited agency potential.

5   Providing Normative Agency with Accessible Diagram Design

To address this inequality in potential agency, we propose a consideration of the term "normative agency" and its components, as outlined in Griffin [9]. "Normative agency" is defined here as having the capacity to "choose one's own path through life... [in pursuit of] what one sees as ... worthwhile" [9]. How this pursuit can be supported by the design of diagrams for accessibility can be determined by examining the three structural components of "normative agency" that are defined by Griffin [9]. First, it must support "autonomy", the phenomenon of averting domination or control by someone or something external to the agent [9]. Second, it must comply with "minimum provision of resources and capabilities", which includes minimum standards for access to education and information allowing agents to choose between and take actions that are informed by accurate information [9]. Finally, diagrams must not conflict with the agent's "liberty", the quality of being free from being "forcibly stop[ped] ... from pursuing one['s chosen path for] ... a worthwhile life" [9].

From this perspective, the norms and standards of accessible diagram design in research and practice [5–7, 18, 19] are clearly compromising the normative agency [9] of BPSI when one considers the inequity of information accessible to them when restricted solely to text descriptions [4]. The normative agency component of "autonomy" [9] emphasizes the need for users to interpret the meaning of diagrammatic properties for themselves. If they cannot, they are restricted to a biased interpretation likely provided by the creator of the representation. Similarly, the "minimum provision of resources and capabilities" component includes "minimum education and information" for the purpose of ensuring that "one's choice[s are] real ... and having chosen, one must be able to act" [9]. This again shows the relation to the perception-action cycle, as these actions that emerge from having the necessary minimum information become possibilities for action, as though they were affordances [8, 12].

Note that the capacity for agency differs between individuals: for example, a factor such as age (children develop to possess greater capacity for agency as they gain life experience) [9]. There are also differences in abilities that specifically affect the capacity for agency, such as developmental disabilities that impair judgment and decision making, requiring in many cases supervision and having decisions made by caretakers to avert inappropriate risks [9]. However, BPSI would have equal potential for normative agency [9] as any sighted individual if neither is impacted by disabilities with these effects. That potential is unfulfilled if living in an environment in which as a standard, diagrams lack the necessary properties to materialize their potential agency [4, 9].

Consequently, this effect should set the stage for the standards of diagram design to change. This practice can be improved by using approaches that provide first-hand interpretation of diagrammatic properties for BPSI whenever necessary [1, 16, 20, 21], which can be achieved with ever-decreasing cost [13, 16, 17]. The implications for future work on accessibility standards for diagram design are that the potential for normative agency [9] for BPSI equal to that of their peers with sight must be a consideration when the target problem places it at risk of limitations from the choice to represent diagrammatic properties solely with text descriptions.

6 Conclusion

The concepts reviewed in this paper aim to set the stage for the development of non-visual diagrammatic representation approaches when designing accessible diagrams for blind and partially sighted individuals (BPSI). Diagrams have distinct properties [1, 2] that text descriptions cannot sufficiently replace if provided as the sole accessibility approach, as the resulting perceptual ambiguity causes a loss of information [3, 4]. This technical understanding of the affordances [8] of diagrammatic properties has not significantly affected the standards in research or practice of diagram design for accessibility [5–7, 18, 19], despite the consequences of BPSI having limited potential normative agency [9] relative to their peers with sight as a result. While they do not represent standards of non-visual diagram design, there are numerous examples that demonstrate the potential for representing diagrammatic properties [1, 3] in forms that may be perceived firsthand, without reliance on text descriptions [16, 20, 21].

References

1. Larkin, J.H., Simon, H.A.: Why a diagram is (sometimes) worth ten thousand words. Cogn. Sci. **11**(1), 65–100 (1987)
2. Shimojima, A.: On the efficacy of representation. Indiana University (1996)
3. Coppin, P.: Perceptual-cognitive properties of pictures, diagrams, and sentences: Toward a science of visual information design. University of Toronto (2014)
4. Coppin, P., Abrose L., Carnevale, M.: Iconic properties are lost when translating visual graphics to text for accessibility. Cognitive Semiotics (2016)
5. Elavsky, F., Le Gassick, L., Fossheim, S.: Are your data visualizations excluding people? Outlier 2021 (2021). https://www.youtube.com/watch?v=SWB-KLXN-Ok

6. Jung, C., Mehta, S., Kulkarni, A., Zhao, Y., Kim, Y.S.: Communicating visualizations without visuals: Investigation of visualization alternative text for people with visual impairments. IEEE Trans. Visual Comput. Graphics **28**(1), 1095–1105 (2021)
7. Web Content Accessibility Guidelines (WCAG): Understanding conformance (2022). https://www.w3.org/WAI/WCAG21/Understanding/conformance#levels, last accessed 2022/03/16
8. Gibson, J.J.: The Ecological Approach to Visual Perception. Taylor & Francis LLC, New York (1986)
9. Griffin, J.: On human rights. OUP Oxford (2009)
10. Stapleton, G., Jamnik, M., Shimojima, A.: What makes an effective representation of information: a formal account of observational advantages. J. Logic Lang. Inform. **26**(2), 143–177 (2017)
11. Coppin, P., Windeyer, R.: Sonifying Napoleon's march by identifying auditory correlates of the graphic-linguistic distinction. In: Chapman, P., Stapleton, G., Moktefi, A., PerezKriz, S., Bellucci, F. (eds.) Diagrams 2018. LNCS (LNAI), vol. 10871, pp. 228–235. Springer, Cham (2018). https://doi.org/10.1007/978-3-319-91376-6_23
12. Warren, W.H.: Direct perception: the view from here. Philos. Top. **33**(1), 335–361 (2005)
13. Han, R.: Translating scientific content into accessible formats with visually impaired learners: Recommendations and a decision aid based on haptic rules of perception. Master's thesis, OCAD University (2020)
14. Dragicevic, P., Jansen, Y., Vande Moere, A.: Data physicalization. In: Vanderdonckt, J., Palanque, P., Winckler, M. (eds.) Handbook of Human Computer Interaction, pp.1–51. Springer, Cham (2020). https://doi.org/10.1007/978-3-319-27648-9_94-1
15. Hogan, T., Hornecker, E.: Towards a design space for multisensory data representation. Interact. Comput. **29**(2), 147–167 (2017)
16. Bassett-Bouchard, C., Saltz, E., Tane, N., Marie Carroll, C., Prathipati, J.: Stockgrok: A sonic chart analysis tool for Google Chrome (2017). https://stockgrok.github.io/index.html. Accessed 20 Mar 2022
17. Goncu, C., Marriott, K.: GraVVITAS: generic multi-touch presentation of accessible graphics. In: Campos, P., Graham, N., Jorge, J., Nunes, N., Palanque, Philippe, Winckler, Marco (eds.) INTERACT 2011. LNCS, vol. 6946, pp. 30–48. Springer, Heidelberg (2011). https://doi.org/10.1007/978-3-642-23774-4_5
18. Fryer, L.: Putting it into Words: The Impact of Visual Impairment on Perception, Experience and Presence. University of London, Goldsmiths (2013)
19. Lundgard, A., Satyanarayan, A.: Accessible visualization via natural language descriptions: a four-level model of semantic content. IEEE Trans. Visual Comput. Graphics **28**(1), 1073–1083 (2021)
20. Biggs, B., Coughlan, J., Coppin, P.: Design and evaluation of an interactive 3D map. Rehabilitation Engineering and Assistive Technology Society of North America 2021 (2021)
21. Ghodke, U., Yusim, L., Somanath, S., Coppin, P.: The cross-sensory globe: participatory design of a 3D audio-tactile globe prototype for blind and low-vision users to learn geography. In: Proceedings of the Designing Interactive Systems Conference 2019 (DIS 2019), pp. 399–412 (2019)
22. Seabright, P., Stieglitz, J., Van der Straeten, K.: Evaluating social contract theory in the light of evolutionary social science. Evol. Hum. Sci. 3 (2021)

History

Combing Graphs and Eulerian Diagrams in Eristic

Reetu Bhattacharjee[1(✉)] and Jens Lemanski[2,3]🆔

[1] Classe di Lettere e Filosofia (Faculty of Humanities), Scuola Normale Superiore, Pisa, Italy
reetu.bhattacharjee@sns.it
[2] Philosophical Seminar, University of Münster, Münster, Germany
[3] Institute of Philosophy, FernUniversität in Hagen, Hagen, Germany
jens.lemanski@fernuni-hagen.de

Abstract. In this paper, we analyze and discuss Schopenhauer's n-term diagrams for eristic dialectics from a graph-theoretical perspective. Unlike logic, eristic dialectics does not examine the validity of an isolated argument, but the progression and persuasiveness of an argument in the context of a dialogue or even controversy. To represent these dialogue situations, Schopenhauer created large maps with concepts and Euler-type diagrams, which from today's perspective are a specific form of graphs. We first present the original method with Euler-type diagrams, then give the most important graph-theoretical definitions, then discuss Schopenhauer's diagrams graph-theoretically and finally give an example of how the graphs or diagrams can be used to analyze dialogues.

Keywords: Arthur schopenhauer · Logic diagrams · Graph-theory · Eristic · Dialectics · Euler diagrams

1 Introduction

In several phases of his work, the post-Kantian philosopher Arthur Schopenhauer (1788–1860) was not only intensively concerned with logic, but also with eristic. Whereas formal logic is for him primarily the study of the correct use of concepts, judgements, and inferences, eristic examines the techniques and artifices of deliberately using them incorrectly in order to emerge victorious in a debate. Logic is thus a monological discipline, whereas eristic is a dialogical one.

Although the two disciplines pursue different goals, Schopenhauer uses similar diagrams for visualisation in both fields. In recent years, Schopenhauer's logic diagrams in particular have been intensively researched: V. Pluder and also A.-S. Heinemann have pointed out that Schopenhauer's logic was pioneering, among others because of the Euler-type diagrams used [8,18]. L. Demey has shown that Schopenhauer's logic is built compositionally from a certain number of basic diagrams. These basic diagrams use circles to depict all possible positional relations in space and also depict oppositional relations [6]. M. Dobrzański

V. Giardino et al. (Eds.): Diagrams 2022, LNAI 13462, pp. 97–113, 2022.
https://doi.org/10.1007/978-3-031-15146-0_8

and K. Matsuda have illustrated how Schopenhauer's diagrams can be used to map and analyse semantic and ontological relations [7,14].

Schopenhauer's eristic diagrams are less known so far and only two research approaches can be found from the last decades: A. Moktefi and J. Lemanski have shown that Schopenhauer used some of the basic diagrams in eristic, and he was perhaps the first to introduce diagrams for n-terms [12]. M. Tarrazo has argued that these diagrams can be seen as a visualization of fuzzy logic [24].

Schopenhauer wrote several treatises on eristic, but not all of them contain diagrams (for details cf. [22, Sect. 10.2]). In the texts without diagrams, Schopenhauer describes mainly eristic fallacies, artifices or stratagemata so that one can protect oneself from those argumentation partners who deliberately use such techniques to deceive others and achieve their goal [3,9]. Although Schopenhauer's eristic diagrams are hardly known, the interest in Schopenhauer's texts on eristic, which do not contain diagrams, is all the greater in recent years: There are research approaches to these texts in the field of argumentation theory [17], proof theory [4], communication ethics [10], and pedagogy [13]. These texts on eristic are also used in the area of social sciences, especially in the field of law, economics and politics (cf. e.g. [2,23]).

This paper is a contribution to a large-scale research on diagrams in eristic, which began with the works mentioned above. Here, we discuss a graph-theoretical interpretation of eristic diagrams since it is striking that these diagrams for n-terms have a structure similar to a graph. Individual areas of these diagrams have also already been called 'routes' or 'paths' by scholars [15]. Beyond that, there is a long tradition in research of representing argumentation processes as graphs, e.g. the classic methods of argument maps by Whately, Wigmore, Toulmin or Dung [19] or current ones such as ConvGraph [16].

So it is not unlikely that Schopenhauer also had an idea in mind when he drew the diagrams, which today we would perhaps implement primarily in terms of graph theory. However, even if Schopenhauer was well versed in the mathematics of his time, his early 19th-century drawings predate the beginnings of graph theory by many years. Thus, a graph-theoretic interpretation cannot rely on Schopenhauer's descriptions of the diagram. It is our task to present and discuss the different graph-theoretic interpretation possibilities and then to select, combine and apply the best of them.

The present paper is motivated by the hope of soon having a diagrammatic tool or argument map that combines the best of both worlds – Euler-type circle diagrams and graph theory. Apart from that, however, it may simply offer a suitable means of describing eristic diagrams. Our roadmap is as follows: In Sect. 2, we introduce eristic diagrams and summarize some of the previous research on diagrams. Section 3 defines the elements of graph theory that we use in subsequent sections. Then, in Sect. 4, we present two graph-theoretic interpretations of the eristic diagrams and discuss advantages and problems. In Sect. 5, we bring together the diagrams and a particular graph-theoretical interpretation to map an exemplary controversy between two dialogue partners. However, as we also emphasize in conclusion of Sect. 6 this is only one way of combining graphs and Euler-type diagrams to apply the new technique of argument mapping in human-human or human-machine interaction.

2   Current Research Results and Problems

In this section, we introduce Schopenhauer's eristic diagrams and combine this with a presentation of results and problems that have been discussed in research in recent years.

Schopenhauer sees eristic as a discipline separate from logic. However, since eristic takes many components from logic (such as diagrams), one can say that eristic is an extension of logic by a new subject area. In the chapters on logic, Schopenhauer starts with five basic diagrams in 1819 [21, §9] and with six basic diagrams in later manuscripts of the 1820s. These six basic diagrams show the position of two circles in space to each other or to a third one (then including arc, sector, and segment). Each of these diagrams denotes the relationship of two concepts to each other or in relation to a third. Schopenhauer speaks of 'representations of possible relations' [20, p. 272] which can also be called 'relational diagrams', or RD in short. The six RD are shown in Fig. 1.

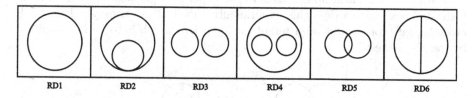

Fig. 1. Schopenhauer's Relational Diagrams (RD) taken from [20, 269–284] (*Euler diagrams* = {RD2, RD3, RD5}; *Gergonne relations* = Euler diagrams ∪ {RD1}; *Partition diagrams* = {RD4, RD6}).

A concept is symbolized by a circle (often called 'sphere' by Schopenhauer) or, as in RD6, by a semicircle. This can be concretized by some examples, but for our purposes it is sufficient to explain RD2, RD3 and RD5. A more detailed description of the RDs can be found in [11].

RD2 shows that the concept indicated by the inner circle is completely contained in the other. For example, the term 'cat' is completely contained in the concept 'animal'.

RD3 shows that two concepts are completely separate and have no commonality. For example, the concepts 'good' and 'evil' (as understood by Schopenhauer).

RD5 shows that two concepts are partially connected or have some commonality. As an example, we can take the terms 'red' and 'flower', because there are things that are only red, but are not a flower, that are both or that are only a flower, but not red.

Schopenhauer uses these three diagrams, RD2, RD3, RD5, and transfers them to eristic. Therewith he constructs diagrams to show two different perspectives: On the one hand an "in-depth view", on the other hand, a "superficial view". The in-depth view shows the actual, neutral or factual relations between two or more terms employing one RD, whereas the superficial view shows a distorted, subjective, biased or prejudiced relation by resorting to another RD. The superficial relation is the one that may seem plausible at first, i.e. when viewed superficially, but is often only used and accepted by one dialog partner, maybe only to intentionally deceive another.

> The sphere of a concept A, which lies partly in another B, but partly also in C quite different from this one, can now be represented according to its subjective intention as lying entirely in the sphere B, or in C, just as the speaker prefers [20].

Schopenhauer describes here that the thorough relation of two terms corresponds to RD5, but a dialog partner may treat the terms as if RD2 is present. One can imagine this change of the relations or views at the two diagrams of Fig. 2. In this case, the dialog partner represents $A \subset B$ (right diagram of Fig. 2) instead of $A \cap B$ (left diagram of Fig. 2). Similarly, the dialog partner represents $B \subset C$ instead of $B \cap C$, which finally leads to the superficial perspective $A \subset C$. And if the dialogue partner does this intentionally, then it is not simply a dialectical or dialogical process, but an attempt at deception, which is to be investigated by the discipline of eristic.

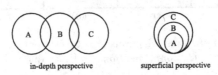

in-depth perspective   superficial perspective

Fig. 2. Interchange of RDs

In his later works, Schopenhauer believes that this interchange of RDs is the basic principle of the entire eristic [20, p. 365]. In several treatises, Schopenhauer listed eristic artifices, which are intentionally committed fallacies, sophisms, paralogisms, etc., which are repeatedly used by dishonest discussion partners for the purpose of being right [3,17]. According to Schopenhauer's opinion, these eristic artifices can all be traced back to the interchange of RDs, which is why the diagrammatic representation of eristic was of great importance to him. This can be seen in the diagrams for n-terms, which have a strong resemblance to modern argument maps.

In Fig. 3, one finds such a diagram, which shows the in-depth view of several terms. These diagrams show numerous spheres of terms, the relationships of these terms in the form of RDs. An interchange of the RDs is not to be seen, but initially only the in-depths perspective on possible propositions of arguments, which in sum depict possible dialogues. Thus they are not only applicable to eristic, but can also be used as an argument map for any kind of dialogue. Schopenhauer, however, initially reads these diagrams in a very specific way, namely for their use in eristic. Figure 3 is supposed to show, according to Schopenhauer,

> how the conceptual spheres interlock in manifold ways and thus give room for arbitrariness to pass from each concept to this or that other. [...] I have chosen the concept of travel as an illustrative example. Its sphere reaches into the area of four others, from each of which the persuader can pass over at will: these reach again into other spheres, some of them at the same time into two and more, through which the persuader takes his way at will, always as if it were the only one, and then finally, depending on his intention, arrives at good or evil. [20]

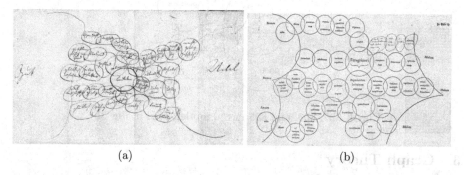

(a)   (b)

Fig. 3. Schopenhauer's Argument Maps: (a) taken from *Berlin Lectures*, StB PK, Na 50, NL Schopenhauer, 1428, Bl. 170 (urn:nbn:de:hebis:30:2-417557); (b) taken from Schopenhauer's hand copy of *The World as Will and Representation*, §9, Fondation Martin Bodmer, S. 73 (urn:nbn:de:hebis:30:2-259336).

Schopenhauer explains that the eristic diagram describes how a possible dialogue partner **P** starts from the term in the centre and then uses several term connections, usually represented by RD5, to finally arrive in the periphery, i.e., on the far left or right of the diagram. Once the other dialogue partner **Q** has accepted this path, **P** can conclude that the term in the centre is a component of the periphery term. Let us take Fig. 3 again as an example: **P** wants to argue that travel is something evil. So he uses multiple RD5 as a path from 'travelling' to 'evil'. If **Q** has accepted this, **P** can conclude that traveling is something evil. **P** thus presents the relation of travel and evil in the conclusion as RD2, whereas, according to Fig. 3, it is actually both terms that are connected only by RD5. (We will take up this example again in Sect. 5 and then see that graph theory offers us many possibilities to describe and analyse this example more precisely.)

The few interpreters of this diagram mentioned above seem to share this interpretation. However, it is problematic that numerous RD3 appear in Fig. 3, which only in a few cases make sense from the logical perspective or often even seem irritating. In logic, RD3 (and RD4) indicate contrary relations between two terms or classes (and RD6 shows contradictory relations [6]). However, this does not make sense for all RD3 in Fig. 3, so RD3 have little crucial meaning in eristic: True, terms such as good and bad are shown to be logically correct in RD3 because they are contrary terms. However, most of the terms that stand between the middle term and the peripheral terms within a sequence of RD5 are usually not contrary [15, sect. 5]: In Fig. 4, for example, we see several RDs in a section of the diagram, but terms such as 'profitable' and 'good' are not usually taken as being contradictory.

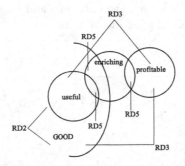

Fig. 4. RD2, RD3, and RD5 in the top left area of Fig. 3b

3   Graph Theory

We have seen in previous section that Schopenhauer established six fundamental relation diagrams, RD (Fig. 1) in logic. In eristic, we find at least three RDs again. However, it turned out that RD2 and RD3 were problematic and one would have to either clarify their meaning or ignore them altogether in the eristic diagram. If they are ignored, only a series of RD5s is relevant, which seem to make up the core idea of the diagram. Now, however, one can argue that if usually only RD5 in Fig. 3 is important, then perhaps one can get a clearer idea of Fig. 3 by ignoring the circles altogether and interpreting all RD5 as edges and vertices. That is, one turns what appear to be Euler-type eristic diagrams for n-terms into a graph. This will indeed be discussed in more detail in Sect. 4 (and we can anticipate that we will later argue for linking diagrams and graphs together). However, in order to make such a graph-theoretic interpretation of Fig. 3, we revisit certain important graph theoretic notions that we need for our interpretation in Sect. 4. In the following we define most of these notions in a much simpler way than their actual mathematical definition. Graph can be defined as

an ordered triple $G = (V(G), E(G), I_G)$, where $V(G)$ is a nonempty set, $E(G)$ is a set disjoint from $V(G)$, and I_G is an "incidence" relation that associates with each element of $E(G)$ an unordered pair of elements (same or distinct) of $V(G)$ [1].

The sets, V(G) and E(G) are called 'Vertex set' and 'Edge set' respectively. We write $I_G(e) = \{u, v\}$, when the edge 'e' is connected by the two vertices 'u' and 'v'. Here, u and v are called the 'end vertices' of the edge e. A 'degree' of a vertex is basically the number of edges incident on it. Two vertices are called 'adjacent' if and only if they are end vertices on an edge. Two edges are called 'adjacent' if and only if they have a common end vertex.

A 'path' is defined as an alternating sequences of vertices and edges where neither edges nor vertices appears more than once. A graph G is said to be 'connected' if for every pair of vertices in G there is at least one path between them. Otherwise, G is said to be a 'disconnected' graph. Subgraph is defined as follows:

A graph H is called a subgraph of G if $V(H) \subseteq V(G)$, $E(H) \subseteq E(G)$; and I_H is the restriction of I_G to E(H). If H is a subgraph of G; then G is said to be a supergraph of H: A subgraph H of a graph G is a proper subgraph of G if either $V(H) \neq V(G)$ or $E(H) \neq E(G)$ [1].

For example, in Fig. 5, $V(G) = \{v_1, v_2, v_3, v_4\}$ and $E(G) = \{e_1, e_2, e_3, e_4\}$ are the vertex set and edge set of the graph G respectively. Here, $I_G(e_1) = \{v_1, v_2\}$, $I_G(e_2) = \{v_1, v_3\}$ and so on. The degree of the vertices v_1 and v_3 is two, whereas, the degrees of the vertices v_2 and v_4 are three and one respectively. Except for v_1 and v_4, every other vertices is adjacent to one another. The two edges e_2 and e_4 are not adjacent. Rest of the edges are adjacent to one another. One example of a path in G is $v_1e_1v_2e_4v_4$. Graph G is a connected graph as for every pair of vertices $\{v_i, v_j\}$ ($1 \leq i \leq 4$, $1 \leq j \leq 4$ and $i \neq j$), there exist a path between them. Graph H is a subgraph of G [see Fig. 5].

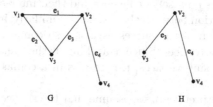

Fig. 5. Example of Graph and Subgraph

The Graph G in Fig. 5 is an undirected graph, where the incidence relation $I_G(e_k)$ associates the edge e_k to an unorderderd pair of vertices (v_i, v_j). For a 'directed graph', the incidence relation associates every edge onto some 'ordered pair' of vertices. In directed graph, every edge is represented by an line segment with an arrow to from one vertex to another vertex. In a directed graph, a 'source vertex' is the vertex where the number of incoming edges is zero and a 'sink vertex' is the vertex where the number of outgoing edges is zero. For example, Fig. 6, represents a directed graph, where v_1 is the source vertex and v_2 and v_3 are both sink vertices.

Fig. 6. Example of directed graph

4   Interpretations and Discussion

As shown in Sect. 2, Schopenhauer gave little information on how to interpret
Fig. 3. Since there was no graph theory in the early 19th century either, Schopenhauer could not provide any precise statements about it. There are probably
many ways of interpreting Fig. 3 in terms of graph theory. For example, three criteria such as (1) directed/ undirected graph, (2) connected/ unconnected graph,
(3) display of all RDs/ display only RD5, result in 6 possible graph-theoretical
interpretations. In the following, we will introduce only two interpretations (I),
which we will then discuss. We cannot present these two interpretations in every
detail either, but we only want to clarify certain aspects for the reader in order
to awaken an understanding of how we combine the Euler-type diagrams and
graph in the next chapter. We have chosen the following two interpretations as
we think they are the most suitable to be applied. As envisaged in Sect. 3, only
RD5s will be considered as showing dialogue transition.[1]

(I1) The first interpretation assumes that the concepts are the vertices and the
edges connect the concepts with each other. Figure 3 shows almost only RD5
and in RD5s, curves represents concepts and their intersection represents the
relation or connection between the concepts. Similarly, in a graph, edges acts
like the intersection of the curves as it is also connects the concepts that
are represented by vertices. Since 'travelling' is the source vertex and 'good'
and 'evil' are the sink vertices, this results in a connected directed graph,
as shown in Fig. 7.

(I2) In the second interpretation, we assume that the vertices are represented by
the intersections of RD5 and edges connects these vertices with one another.
Here we have four source vertices which we obtained by the intersection
of the circle 'travelling' with four adjacent conceptual spheres, namely
'healthy', 'expansive', 'ample opportunity for storing experience' and 'dis-
pelling boredom'. This interpretation results in a disconnected directed
graph, as shown in Fig. 8. Here, each edge and vertex are traversed only
once for a single path.

Both interpretations assume a directed graph, since there is a source vertex and
several possible sink vertices, but (I1) and (I2) differ in whether the graph is

---

[1] In the following we use the graph-theoretical labels v and e only if we directly refer
to the graphs and not to the RDs.

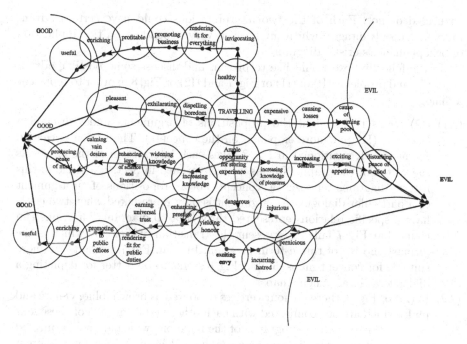

Fig. 7. (I1)

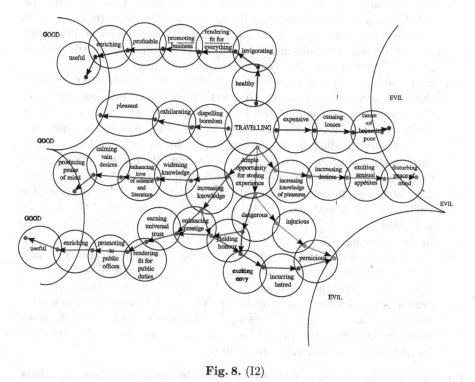

Fig. 8. (I2)

connected or not. Each of the two interpretations could have certain advantages and disadvantages, which might even vary depending on the application of Schopenhauer's eristic diagram.

In the following, we would like to present and discuss some possible advantages (A) and problems (P) of (I1) or Fig. 7 and (I2) or Fig. 8 in order to represent a dialogue.

(A1) (I2) seems to highlight the propositions of arguments under discussion (whereas (I1) put more emphasis on the concepts). The reason is that in the approach mentioned in Fig. 8 takes each intersection of the circles as the vertex of the graph. Now as we have argued in Sect. 2, a circle in this n-term diagrams represent a 'concept' not a propositions of an argument or a particular dialogue. An argument is only represented when two circle have a specific relation represented through a RD diagram. Thus, one can claim that Fig. 7 fails to represent the transition of dialogue which is the primary motive of this n-term diagram. In sum, Fig. 7 seems to be more suitable for concept maps [5], but Fig. 8 seems to be better for depicting a dialogue as in argument maps.

(A2) In (I2) or Fig. 8, there are four vertices (coloured as brown, blue, violate and pink) which are not connected with each other and from each of these four vertices generates four subgraphs of the main one which are not connected to one another. In a dialogue, for example, **P** have at least four different ways to convince **Q** whether 'travelling' is either good or bad. If suppose **P** beliefs that travelling is bad then **P** can consider the subgraph Fig. 9 which is the shortest path from 'travelling' to 'evil'. The disconnected graph (I2) thus shows the possibilities of having different opinions in the form of subgraphs better than the connected graph (I1) does.

(A3) Each path in (I2) could immediately indicate the direction, i.e. whether the path leads from 'traveling' to 'good' or to 'evil'. Thus, already at the first transition, the path of the dialogue would be clearly foreseeable. If Fig. 8 were used as an argument map, this would have the advantage that the course of the dialogue would be recognizable by its direction: In Fig. 8, the brown and green path are neutral at first, since they only go up or down and only approach good or evil later. But even with this advantage, as soon as a path turns to the right or to the left (e.g. as the pink one), the neutrality is removed and an 'ethical value' (good or evil) of the depicted argument arises. This is one of the problem of (I2), that will be discussed in the following.

(A4) Both (I1) and (I2) have a great advantage over the diagrams (Fig. 3) because the directed graphs can accurately represent the flow of the dialogue. They show the beginning and the end of a series of propositions or arguments. However, as mentioned in (A1), the (I1) graph does not show the transition accurately. Therefore, (I2) has advantages over (I1). Moreover, the definitions in graph theory allow a more precise description of individual elements than do the diagrams.

But there are also certain problems that accrue to one or both interpretations, which we would now like to address.

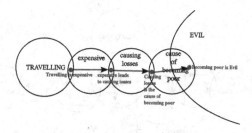

Fig. 9. Example of dialogue transition to show 'Travelling is bad'

(P1) We have to keep the following in mind. If dialogue transition strictly depends on RD5 diagrams, we cannot connect two vertices by an edge unless the circles where these vertices lies are connected by RD5. For example, in Fig. 10, the vertex v_1 can be connected with vertex v_2 as the circle C_1 is in RD5 relation with the circle C_2. But we cannot connect v_1 with v_3 as C_1 is not in a RD5 relation with the circle C_3 but in a RD3 relation. Of course, this reduces the entire diagram to only one RD, which means that the expressivity is not very high. One can even argue that the original diagram (Fig. 3) shows more possible arguments than (I1) or (I2).

(P2) However, if one wanted to try to solve (P1) graph theoretically, one would run into a new problem. If we imagine a connected graph in which all RDs are entered, the expressivity is similar to Fig. 3, but the graph would be very confusing. We would have a network of numerous RD3s and RD5s that would be almost impossible to trace. Although one could introduce RD3s into graphs by a rule, e.g. that all vertices that are not directly connected by an edge map an RD3, this would only be implicit information. The expressivity of the original diagram thus seems to be higher than one of the graph-theoretical interpretations.

(P3) As noted above, (I2) bears most resemblance to an argument map as used today in many different variations in fields such as critical thinking, argumentation theory, argument mapping etc. [25], [19]. Overall, however, there are unfortunately numerous points that (I2) do not fulfil and which are also important for Schopenhauer's eristic as well as for most argument maps today: the graphs show arguments, but it do not show which dialogue partner made the argument and how another reacted to it. The graph also does not show the interchange of RDs that was discussed in Sect. 2. The graph also does not show a counter-argument, e.g. an attack by another dialogue partner. In some cases, it is already sufficient to use the diagrams from Sect. 2 with the graph, but in other cases more diagrammatic elements must be used to meet all requirements.

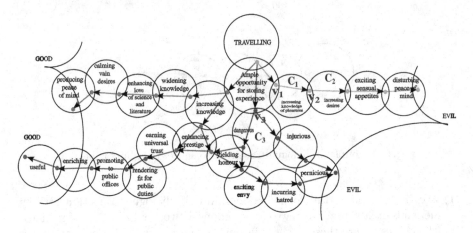

Fig. 10. Importance of RD5 in eristic

5 An Example of a Controversy

Schopenhauer's n-term diagrams can be interpreted in terms of graph theory, as we have seen in Sect. 4. This gives clearer possibilities of description by the definitions mentioned in Sect. 3 as well as some advantages mentioned in Sect. 4.

Nevertheless, the graphs discussed in Sect. 4 also have disadvantages, which concern expressivity, for example. If Schopenhauer's diagrams were to be completely replaced by graphs, as argued in Sect. 3, there would be some advantages, but also some disadvantages and problems, which would ultimately lead potential users to use graph systems that are already established in the field of argumentation, e.g. Toulmin, Scriven, Dung maps, etc. [19]. Our goal should therefore be to combine the best of both worlds and to adapt the graphs and diagrams in such a way that they are well-suited for the respective purpose.

The n-term diagrams were actually intended to be applied to Schopenhauer's own treatises on eristic. Nevertheless, the diagrams and graphs of eristic can also be applied in many other areas of human-to-human or human-to-machine interaction [19]. In this section, we will stay in the field of human agents and try to *represent* a fictitious controversy with Schopenhauer's diagrams and graphs. (However, it should be taken into account that one can also *analyse* or even *plan* possible arguments with Schopenhauer's diagrams and, on the other hand, other areas such as political debates, sales talks, negotiations, legal pleadings can be represented with the help of Schopenhauer's eristic.)

In our fictitious controversy, however, we stay in eristic with the topic of 'travelling' using Schopenhauer's example. Thus, we take up the fictional dialogue between **P** and **Q** already announced in Sect. 2, in which **P** wants to argue that travelling is something evil. The dialogue could go as follows:

Q	$\mathcal{K}1$	Dear P, what do you actually think about travelling?
P	$\mathcal{K}2$	I'd like to tell you. Travelling gives you plenty of opportunities to store experience.
Q	$\mathcal{K}3$	You could say that.
P	$\mathcal{K}4$	But experiences can also be dangerous.
Q	$\mathcal{K}5$	Well...
P	$\mathcal{K}6$	And everything that is dangerous is also injurious.
Q	$\mathcal{K}7$	No, I have to disagree. For one thing, it has nothing to do with travelling, and for another, not everything that is dangerous is also injurious. Dangerous experiences can also bring honour, and that is not injurious.
P	$\mathcal{K}8$	Yes, I agree with you. But this honour can also cause envy, so that you incur hatred.
Q	$\mathcal{K}9$	That is possible, of course.
P	$\mathcal{K}10$	If you incur hatred, that is something pernicious, and so travelling is an evil.

The entire dialogue consists of 10 actions ($\mathcal{K}$), whereby not every action represents an argument: $\mathcal{K}1$ is a question, $\mathcal{K}3$ and $\mathcal{K}5$ are agreements. On the other hand, in some cases there are several arguments in one action: whereas $\mathcal{K}2$, $\mathcal{K}4$, $\mathcal{K}6$ represent only one argument, $\mathcal{K}7$, $\mathcal{K}8$, $\mathcal{K}10$ each contain several arguments ($a, b, c, \ldots$).

$\mathcal{K}7$ even plays a special role overall: here an attack or counter-argument is found. **Q** does not initially accept **P**'s argument in $\mathcal{K}6$. **Q** notices that **P** could have the intention to connect 'travelling' with something evil. Therefore, **Q** anticipates such an argument $\mathcal{K}7a$ (For one thing,...), excludes it, and negates $\mathcal{K}6$ in $\mathcal{K}7b$ explicitly (and for another...). As a counter-argument, **Q** falls back on $\mathcal{K}4$, which **Q** still accepted in $\mathcal{K}5$, and turns it to the positive, i.e. $\mathcal{K}7c$ (Dangerous experience can also bring honour). At the same time, **Q** uses $\mathcal{K}7c$ to refer to RD3 between 'bringing honour' and 'is injurious', i.e. $\mathcal{K}7d$.

In $\mathcal{K}8$, **P** recognises the chance that the positive argument put forward by **Q** in $\mathcal{K}7c$ can still lead to the goal, even though **Q** has rejected $\mathcal{K}6$. In order not to give **Q** too much leeway for the new argument $\mathcal{K}7c$, **P** turns it to the negative, $\mathcal{K}8a$ (But this honour can), and immediately connects it with the next argument, $\mathcal{K}8b$ (so that you...), which is presented as a consequence. **Q** seems to have been caught off guard by this in $\mathcal{K}9$. **Q** at least admits that $\mathcal{K}8$ is possible.

This then allows **P** to present a series of arguments in $\mathcal{K}10$, i.e. $\mathcal{K}10a$, $\mathcal{K}10b$, which finally appears as a consequence of the whole controversy and also as an answer to $\mathcal{K}1$: travelling is an evil. Should **P** have the last word with $\mathcal{K}10$ in the dialogue and if **Q** not contradict, the conclusion ($\mathcal{K}10b$) should be accepted by both.

Let us look again at the transition from $\mathcal{K}6$ to $\mathcal{K}7$. What is expressed here is what we called the interchange of RDs in Sect. 2. This concerns the transition between 'dangerous' and 'injurious', which is evaluated differently by **P** and **Q**, which is why the controversy comes to a head here: **P** argues in $\mathcal{K}6$ that the transition between 'dangerous' and 'injurious' is justified. **P**'s argument is even so strong that it can be seen as an exaggeration: **P** makes an RD2 out of the

RD5 between the two terms; for if everything that is dangerous is injurious, then 'dangerous' is also completely contained in 'injurious'. But **Q** does not accept this transition: **Q** points out that there are dangerous experiences that are not harmful and gives a counterexample that even constructs an RD3 argument.

This illustrates the interchange of RDs that expresses between the two speakers regarding a particular argument. Since we have chosen our example in such a way that **P** intentionally wanted to deceive **Q** with $\mathcal{K}6$, i.e. an intentional interchange from RD5 to RD2 was intended by **Q** in order to quickly support the main argument (travelling is something evil), the fictional dialogue can be taken as an example of eristic.

Our aim in this section, however, is now to apply the diagrams and their graph-theoretical interpretations to represent the dialogue just presented. To represent this dialogue, $\mathcal{K}1 - \mathcal{K}10$, we now use Schopenhauer's original diagram, Fig. 3, which represents the RDs, and an overlying subgraph of (I2), which is to represent the concrete course in the diagram. The result is Fig. 11 Here the broken line represent the path taken by **P** and the straight line represent the path taken by **Q**. We thus see in Fig. 11 two argument transitions: first the path that **P** takes, but which ends at 'dangerous' and 'injurious' without having reached the goal. The second path then continues via **Q**'s argument until **P** reaches the sink node at 'evil'[2]. The argument $\mathcal{K}7c$ remains implicit in Fig. 11, but could be supplemented by further diagrammatic elements.

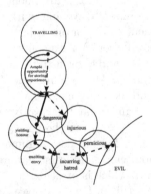

Fig. 11. Dialogue Graph

This connection of diagram and subgraph should enable a reader to read out a fictitious dialogue from Fig. 11 which, although it does not correspond to the flow of words of $\mathcal{K}1 - \mathcal{K}10$, can at least reproduce the arguments, i.e. the dialectical essence of the controversy.

---

[2] The first step in Fig. 11 have both dotted and straight lines as P and Q both agrees on the argument 'travelling' is 'ample opportunity for storing experience', viz. $\mathcal{K}2$ and $\mathcal{K}3$.

6   Summary and Outlook

In this paper, our aim has been to develop a graph-theoretical interpretation of the Eulerian diagrams that Schopenhauer uses in eristic and to combine the advantages of both. In doing so, we have found that there are numerous ways in which Schopenhauer's diagrams can be read and also how they can be used. While Schopenhauer primarily had application in eristic in mind, however, the diagrams can initially only show possibilities of dialogue progressions. We have understood these possible dialogues as subgraphs of a main graph, which can describe the structure of the diagrams more precisely than the diagrams do. Nevertheless, we have also seen that the Euler-type diagrams have the advantage of displaying numerous relations between terms and arguments that would no longer be intuitively understandable in complex graphs or networks.

Having explained Schopenhauer's diagrams in Sect. 2, defined the basic graph-theoretical terms in Sect. 3 and presented some possible graph-theoretical interpretations of the diagrams in Sect. 4, we have presented in Sect. 5, using an exemplary controversy, how graph and diagram can be combined to represent the course of conversation. However, numerous other applications in the field of human-human or human-machine interaction are conceivable with the help of this technique: Pointing out alternative or counterfactual arguments, strategically planning the course of arguments, analysing possible false conclusions, etc. This versatility is likely to be particularly applicable in areas where arguments play a central role in communication, such as law, politics, commerce, the sciences. In this context, Schopenhauer's eristic diagrams occupy a special position to all argument maps known so far: they combine the intuitive advantages of graphs with those of Euler-type diagrams. Moreover, their interpretation possibilities and extensions are numerous, so that one can adapt the diagram graphs depending on the field of application.

Acknowledgements. This research benefited from the research grant "Quod erat videndum: heuristic, logical and cognitive aspects of diagrams in mathematical reasoning" as part of the research project MIUR - "Departments of Excellence", call 2017 - Faculty of Humanities at Scuola Normale Superiore, Pisa, Italy received by Reetu Bhattacharjee in 2022. The research of the second author was supported by the project 'History of Logic Diagrams in Kantiansm' (AZ.10.22.1.037PH) from the Fritz Thyssen-Stiftung.

References

1. Balakrishnan, R., Ranganathan, K.: A Textbook of Graph Theory. Springer, New York (2012)
2. C. Rocha, E. Solano, J.M.: The Bolsonaro paradox. Latin American societies (current challenges in social sciences). In: D. Béchet, A.D. (ed.) The New Brazilian Right: Radical and Shameless, pp. 11–57. Springer (2021)
3. Chichi, G.M.: Die Schopenhauersche Eristik: Ein Blick auf ihr Aristotelisches Erbe. Schopenhauer-Jahrbuch **83**, 163–183 (2002)

4. Fouqueré, C., Quatrini, M.: Ludics and natural language: first approaches. In: Béchet, D., Dikovsky, A. (eds.) LACL 2012. LNCS, vol. 7351, pp. 21–44. Springer, Heidelberg (2012). https://doi.org/10.1007/978-3-642-31262-5_2

5. Davies, M.: Concept mapping, mind mapping and argument mapping: what are the differences and do they matter? High. Educ. **62**, 279–301 (2011)

6. Demey, L.: From Euler diagrams in Schopenhauer to Aristotelian diagrams in logical geometry. In: Lemanski, J. (ed.) Language, Logic, and Mathematics in Schopenhauer. SUL, pp. 181–205. Springer, Cham (2020). https://doi.org/10.1007/978-3-030-33090-3_12

7. Dobrzański, M.: Problems in reconstructing Schopenhauer's theory of meaning: with reference to his influence on Wittgenstein. In: Lemanski, J. (ed.) Language, Logic, and Mathematics in Schopenhauer. SUL, pp. 25–45. Springer, Cham (2020). https://doi.org/10.1007/978-3-030-33090-3_3

8. Heinemann, A.-S.: Schopenhauer and the equational form of predication. In: Lemanski, J. (ed.) Language, Logic, and Mathematics in Schopenhauer. SUL, pp. 165–179. Springer, Cham (2020). https://doi.org/10.1007/978-3-030-33090-3_11

9. Hordecki, B.: Dialektyka erystyczna jako sztuka unikania rozmowcow nieadekwatnych. Res Rhetorica **8**(2), 118–129 (2021)

10. Lemanski, J.: Discourse ethics and eristic. Polish J. Aesthetics **62**, 151–162 (2022)

11. Lemanski, J., Demey, L.: Schopenhauer's partition diagrams and logical geometry. In: Basu, A., Stapleton, G., Linker, S., Legg, C., Manalo, E., Viana, P. (eds.) Diagrammatic Representation and Inference. In: 12th International Conference, Diagrams 2021, Virtual, 28–30 September, 2021, Proceedings, pp. 149–165 (2021)

12. Lemanski, J., Moktefi, A.: Making sense of Schopenhauer's diagram of good and evil. In: Chapman, P., Stapleton, G., Moktefi, A., Perez-Kriz, S., Bellucci, F. (eds.) Diagrams 2018. LNCS (LNAI), vol. 10871, pp. 721–724. Springer, Cham (2018). https://doi.org/10.1007/978-3-319-91376-6_67

13. Marciniak, A.: Wprowadzenie do erystyki dla pedagogow. Studia z Teorii Wychowania **11**, 59–84 (2020)

14. Matsuda, K.: Spinoza's redundancy and Schopenhauer's concision. An attempt to compare their metaphysical systems using diagrams. Schopenhauer-Jahrbuch **97**, 117–131 (2016)

15. Moktefi, A.: Schopenhauer's Eulerian diagrams. In: Lemanski, J. (ed.) Language, Logic, and Mathematics in Schopenhauer. SUL, pp. 111–127. Springer, Cham (2020). https://doi.org/10.1007/978-3-030-33090-3_8

16. Muñoz, M., Vicente, E., González, I., Mateos, A., Jiménez-Martín, A.: Convgraph: Community detection of homogeneous relationships in weighted graphs. Mathematics **9**(4) (2021)

17. Nickerson, R.S.: Argumentation: The Art of Persuasion. Cambridge University Press (2021)

18. Pluder, V.: Schopenhauer's logic in its historical context. In: Lemanski, J. (ed.) Language, Logic, and Mathematics in Schopenhauer. SUL, pp. 129–143. Springer, Cham (2020). https://doi.org/10.1007/978-3-030-33090-3_9

19. Reed, C., Walton, D., Macagno, F.: Argument diagramming in logic, law and artificial intelligence. Knowl. Eng. Rev. **22**, 87–109 (2007)

20. Schopenhauer, A.: Philosophische Vorlesungen (Sämtliche Werke IX. Ed. by P. Deussen and F. Mockrauer). Piper & Co. (1913)

21. Schopenhauer, A.: The World as Will and Representation. 2 vols, ed. and transl. by J. Norman, A. Welchman, and C. Janaway. Cambridge University Press (2010)

22. Schubbe, D., Koßler, M. (eds.): Schopenhauer-Handbuch. Leben - Werk - Wirkung. 2nd ed. Metzler (2018)

23. Stelmach, B.: Methods of Legal Reasoning. Springer (2006)
24. Tarrazo, M.: Schopenhauer's prolegomenon to fuzziness. Fuzzy Optim. Decis. Making **3**, 227–254 (2004)
25. Thomas, S.N.: Practical Reasoning in Natural Language. Prentice-Hall (1986)

Taming the Irrational Through Musical Diagrams – from Boethius to Oresme and Nemorarius

Daniel Muzzulini[✉] [iD]

Zurich University of the Arts, Zurich, Switzerland
`daniel.muzzulini@zhdk.ch`

Abstract. Boethius and his followers used diagrammatic methods to esti-mate musical intervals with epimoric ratios, they determined geometric num-ber sequences with triangular tables, and they treated the converse problem of dividing musical intervals equally. The collection of mathematical manuscripts Codex Basel F II 33 (ca. 1360) contains treatises by Nicolaus Oresme, Jordanus Nemorarius and others. Images in Nemorarius' treatise combine number triangles into complex spider webs and they display recursive algorithms. Oresme diagrams make use of irrational ratios. These little known images and their relationship to music theory are the focus of this paper.

Keywords: Ratios of ratios · Geometric proportions · Recursion · Pythagorean music theory

1 Ratios, Measuring Intervals and Proportions

Musical ratio theory in the Pythagorean tradition is a theory of positive rational numbers that focuses on multiplication rather than addition. The mathematics required to address the topics of adding musical intervals and of multiplying musical intervals by numbers or dividing them equally by numbers involves magnitude comparisons of rational numbers, geometric sequences as well as fractional powers of integers and rational numbers.

Traditionally, the natural numbers are *discrete quantities* which do not exhibit metrical structures per se. They are means for counting, and ratios are relationships between pairs of *countable quantities*. Since Boethius (ca. 480–525), arc diagrams are used to visualize whole numbers and their relationships. This widespread mode of representation, typically assigns numbers to positions on a line – in ascending or descending order – and ratios to semi-circular arcs within undirected graphs (see Fig. 1, 5 and 6). The ratio interpretation of musical intervals was rejected by Aristox-enus (c. 375–335 BC), who maintained a geometrical sensualistic approach to inter-vals not anchored in Pythagorean ratios. Instead he admitted microtonal division of intervals as if they were spatial distances [1, 2, 12]. The collocation "proportio pro-portionum" (ratio of ratios) [7, 18] coined in the 14th century raises the ratio the-ory to a higher level, by proclaiming a comprehensive theory for musical intervals

V. Giardino et al. (Eds.): Diagrams 2022, LNAI 13462, pp. 114–122, 2022.
https://doi.org/10.1007/978-3-031-15146-0_9

generalizing the Pythagorean ratio concept and accounting for the perceptual space metaphor of musical pitches and intervals [8, 13].

Measuring the length of a line means comparing it to a *unit* length defined by convention – by expressing it as a multiple of the unit. If there were a smallest and hence indivisible musical interval of which all the others were integer multiples, this interval could serve as a musical unit interval. The so-called Pythagorean comma was sometimes considered indivisibly small – at least perceptually. Rather than being a proper musical interval to be sung or played, it served as a *tertium comparationis* for larger musical intervals and pitch configurations. For this purpose, Jacobus Leodiensis in the 14th century proposed a division of the octave into 53 micro-intervals or commas so that measuring intervals comes close to counting commas. [11].

2 Epimoric Ratios as a Measure for Musical Intervals

The musical octave, defined with the proportion 1 : 2, plays a crucial role in Western musical pitch systems. Pitches one or more octaves apart are usually considered closely related to each other and – presented simultaneously – they often seem to merge to a single sound. Traditional harmonic theory is developed to a wide extent within the frame of an octave. *Epimoric ratios* are fractions defined by successive numbers. Throughout the course of history epimoric ratios of small numbers were used to explain the perceptual phenomenon of consonance. All internal ratios within the proportion 12 : 9 : 8 : 6 are epimoric because of 12/8 = 9/6 = 3/2, 12/9 = 8/6 = 4/3. In medieval source this division of the octave, which relates the whole tone to the consonances within the octave, is frequently visualized with a symmetric arc diagrams (see Fig. 1).

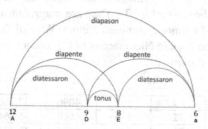

Fig. 1. Symmetric division of the octave Aa into two fourths, AD and Ea, and a whole tone DE. Connecting arcs corresponds to adding musical intervals.

The epimoric ratios can be used to partition the "octave space". Because they form a sequence of decreasing rational numbers approaching one (the unison)

$$2/1 > 3/2 > 4/3 > 5/4 > \ldots$$

they provided a convenient way to measure and compare small musical intervals at a time where decimal fractions and logarithms were not yet invented. A method to find for a given interval the closest epimoric ratios was described by Boethius and sometimes visualized in medieval treatises (see Fig. 2). Walter Odington (ca. 1253–1328) in *De speculatione musice* illustrates the estimation of the Pythagorean comma.

$$75/74 < 531,441/524,288 < 74/73$$

in this way [17].

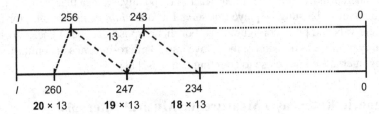

Fig. 2. Epimoric estimation for the Pythagorean semitone. The terms 243 and 256 are compared with multiples of their difference. Therefore, 20/19 < 256/243 < 19/18.

The horizontal lines represent monochord strings of equal length l and tension, the ticks are fret positions for the respective sounds. The reasoning uses the difference of the terms under consideration (13 for the semitone, 7153 for the Pythagorean comma) and compares the terms with the closest multiples of the difference [4].

3   Boethius Triangles and Nemorarius Webs

The medieval copies of Boethius' writings on arithmetic and music contain matrix like triangular tables of numbers (see Fig. 3). They are diagrammatical tools to calculate geometrical sequences of epimoric common factors. We call them *Boethius triangles* although they probably go back to Nicomachus of Gerasa, a main source for Boethius' writings on arithmetic and music [9].

1	8	64	512	4096	32,768	262,144
	9	72	576	4608	36,864	294,912
		81	648	5184	41,472	331,776
			729	5832	46,656	373,248
				6,561	52,488	419,904
	a	$8\,a$			59,049	472,392
		$9\,a$	$+\,a$			531,441

Fig. 3. Boethius triangle for the common ratio 9/8. The small interpretive diagram at the bottom shows that the table can be created from the numbers in the first row with additions only (a stands for the value in any cell).

The numbers in the last column contain the proportion for a pile of six Pythagorean tones (9/8). The quotient of the last term of this column (531,441) and twice the first (2 × 262,144 = 524,288) defines the Pythagorean comma, the tiny difference between six tones and an octave: 531,441/524,288. It was explained in the previous section that it is of similar size as the epimoric intervals for 75/74 and 74/73.

Beside the powers of 8 in the first row there are no further multiplications required in order to create the table at arbitrary depth. Medieval copies of Boethius' writings and related texts usually have diagrams for the common factors 3/2, 4/3 and 5/4, sometimes also for 9/8 as for example an early 10th century copy of Boethius' "De institutione musica" [5].

The positions of the matrix elements viewed as locations in a (discrete) system of coordinates permit a geometric interpretation of the related interval arithmetic. Hereby, vector addition corresponds to the addition of musical intervals, and the multiplication of a vector by an integer is equivalent with the multiplied musical interval vector of the same direction. In other words, the tables can serve as two dimensional look-up tables for various geometric sequences and combinations of intervals. This interpretation is implied in some medieval triangles for the common factor 3/2 used to describe binary and ternary rhythmic divisions [14, 20].

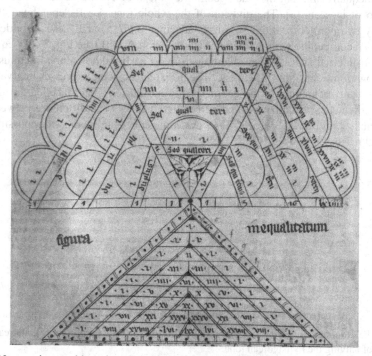

Fig. 4. Nemorarius combines three Boethius triangles for "dupli" (2/1), "sesquialteri" (3/2) and "sesquiteri" (4/3) to a web of geometric sequences. The lower part of the picture is an early "Pascal triangle". **Source**: Basel Universitätsbibliothek (UBH F II 33, fol. 83r).

A diagram by Jordanus Nemorarius [15] shows that the totality of the Boethius triangles can be calculated iteratively and completely without multiplication (see Fig. 4).

The left part serves to calculate the powers of 2, the octaves. The powers of 2 can be used to calculate the sequences for the fifths (3/2) in the middle and the powers of 3, which in turn can be used to calculate the sequences of fourths (4/3) and powers of 4, etc.

Nemorarius was aware that the binomial coefficients, the numbers in Pascal's triangle (see the lower part of Fig. 4), are useful for the iterative calculation of powers when the base is increased. Whereas powers of epimoric ratios can be determined without multiplications at all, the more general case of non-epimoric ratios is based on sums weighted by the binomial coefficients. Nemorarius solves this task for selected ratios with a full spider web combining six triangular parts.

4   Geometric Division of the Pythagorean *Tetraktys* in Theory and Practice

It is known since antiquity that the proportion 16 : 17 : 18 divides the whole tone (18/16 = 9/8) unequally and that the true "geometric" mean of 16 and 18 cannot be written as a ratio of integers [3]. The division of the whole tone A : B "epogdovs" (9/8 = 18/16) by two epimoric ratios "sesquisextadecima" (17/16) and "sesquisept'decima" (18/17) is incompatible with the geometrical division A:D:B (see Fig. 5). By equating radius and interval size, this arc diagram from an early 10th century Boethius copy reveals logarithmic insights into music: The horizontal spacing expresses interval sizes so that the arcs belonging to the geometrically halved tones and labelled "medietas" are equal diameters visualizing equal perceptual distance. The difference between the two unequal semitones, 18/17 and 17/16, is exaggerated in the drawing, possibly for didactical reasons.

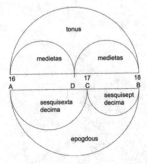

Fig. 5. The arc diagram, transcribed from a late 10th century Boethius copy [5], addresses the problem of halving the Pythagorean tone.

Nicolaus Oresme applies the novel concept of fractional powers to the very heart of the Pythagorean dogma, the numbers and intervals of the *tetraktys*, that is, the set of pair relationships between the first four natural numbers, and he ventures to illustrate his transformed tetraktys as an ordinary arc diagram. In other words, he applies the square root function to the set X = {1, 2, 3, 4} and to the ratios formed by number pairs from X (see Fig. 6).

Two other arc diagrams in the same treatise by Oresme concern the problem of tripling the cube, and the calculation of regular polygons inscribed and circumscribed to a circle of a fixed radius. They use musical terminology to denote irrational ratios. Oreseme's "Algorismus proportionum" was rediscovered and published only in the 19th century [6]. To our knowledge, his diagrams and their ability to describe finite systems with irrational proportions have hardly been noted in the literature.

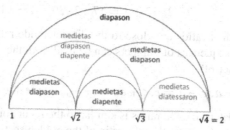

Fig. 6. Besides the octave, all intervals in the diagram transcribed from a 14th century manuscript of Nicole Oresme's "Algorismus proportionum" form irrational ratios [6, 19]. The numbers are obtained by applying the square root function to the numbers and ratios in the standard tetraktys $1 : 2 : 3 : 4$.

How Jordanus Nemorarius determined the square root of two, the bisected octave, algorithmically, is illustrated in the "flowchart" shown in Fig. 7.

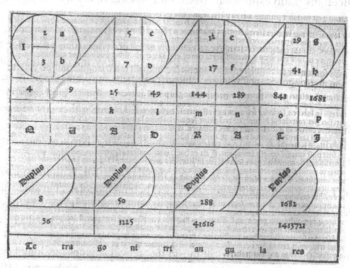

Fig. 7. Jordanus Nemorarius' algorithm to determine the twelve tempered tritonus $\sqrt{2}$ from the Pythagorean fifth 3/2 in an early printed edition by Jacobus Faber Stapulensis (1496). **Source:** Basel Universitätsbibliothek (UBH AM V 8:2, VIII).

Musically speaking, he begins with the perfect fifth (3/2) of the Pythagoreans and approaches the tritonus recursively: an irrational ratio, which simply did not exist in the Pythagorean universe.

The sequence of ratios b/a = 3/2 = 1.5, d/c = 7/5 = 1.4, f/e = 17/12 = 1.4171, h/g = 41/29 = 1.414 approaches the square root of two in an oscillating manner. This can be seen by comparing the squares and doubled squares of the terms of the ratios, shown in the lower part of the chart:

$$2 \cdot 5 - 1 = 7^2, 2 \cdot 12 + 1 = 17^2, 2 \cdot 29 - 1 = 41^2$$

Therefore, the original ratios are close to the diameter/side ratio of a square. The rules to derive the two sequences of numbers can be read from the chart (and are better explained in the manuscript):

$$a + c = d, c + d = e, c + e = f, e + f = g, e + g = h$$

The procedure to determine the ratios is similar to the recursion in the well-known Fibonacci sequence, which approaches the ratio of the golden section in the same way. Because they avoid multiplications the calculations could be done easily with Roman numerals – as it was done in the Basel manuscript [15].

5 Conclusion

Mathematicians in the 14th century used diagrammatic means to illustrate and explain their algorithms needed in arithmetic and music theory. Walter Odington, for instance, visualized Boethius' ratio estimations based on epimoric ratios with a generally valid diagram.

Boethius used number triangles as means to find the proportions of number sequences whose successive terms form epimoric ratios. These proportions can be used to describe uniform musical ladders and they are suited to measure other intervals. Boethius' triangles were picked up and generalized to arbitrary ratios by Jordanus Nemorarius. These novel mathematical concepts and methods were taken up and refined only in the 16th century by Michael Stifel [21] and Simon Stevin [22], paving the way to exponential and logarithmic functions in the modern sense.

The multiplication of a musical interval with a number n is equivalent to raising its ratio to the power of k, and dividing a musical interval by n is equivalent to extracting the n-th root of the ratio or raising it to the fractional power $1/n$. With fractional powers, however, the Pythagorean number concept is left behind. Nicolaus Oresme was able to formally describe fractional powers of rational numbers and their rules. In his diagrams summarizing the solution of geometrical problems he gives algebraic results in a musical language.

The value of diagrams in historical music-theoretical sources has long been underrated, and only recently have they been duly acknowledged in philosophy [10]. In this text, musical and mathematical diagrams were examined as objects in their own right. The images are interpreted by excluding the surrounding text and historical context as much as possible. The art of diagramming is also an art of reduction – to bring the essential to the point and into an aesthetic form with lines, numbers – and almost without words.

References

1. Barker, A. (ed.): Greek Musical Writings, vol. II. Harmonic and Acoustic Theory. Cambridge University Press, Cambridge (1989)
2. Barker, A.: Scientific method in Ptolemy's Harmonics. Cambridge University Press, Cambridge (2001). https://doi.org/10.1017/CBO9780511481765
3. Borzacchini, L.: Incommensurability, Music and continuum: a cognitive approach. Arch. Hist. Exact Sci. **61**, 273–302 (2007). https://doi.org/10.1007/s00407-007-0125-0
4. Boethius A.: Fundamentals of Music. In: Bower, C.M., Palisca, C.V. (eds.) Yale University Press, New Haven (1989)
5. Boethius, A.M.S.: De institutione arithmetica – De institutione musica, Staatsbibliothek Bamberg Msc. Class. 9 (late 10th century)
6. Curtze E.L.W.M. (ed.): Der Algorismus Proportionum des Nicolaus Oresme. Zum ersten Male nach der Lesart der Handschrift R. 4. 2. der Königlichen Gymnasial-Bibliothek zu Thorn (1868)
7. Grant, E.: Nicole Oresme and his De proportionibus proportionum. Isis **51**(3), 293–314 (1960). www.jstor.org/stable/226509
8. Hoyrup, J.: In measure, number, and weight: studies in mathematics and culture, SUNY Series in Science, Technology, and Society (1994)
9. Kárpati, A.: Translation or Compilation? Contributions to the Analysis of Sources of Boethius' De institutione musica. In: Studia Musicologica Academiae Scientiarum Hungaricae, T. 29, Fasc. 1/4, pp. 5–33 (1987)
10. Krämer, S.: Figuration, Anschauung, Erkenntnis – Grundlinien einer Diagrammatologie. Suhrkamp, Berlin (2016)
11. Leodiensis, J.: Compendium de Musica. In: Royale Albert Ier, Smits van Waesberghe et al. (eds.) Bibl, 10162-66, 48r–54v. Frits Knuf, Buren (1988)
12. Lindley, M.: Stimmung und Temperatur. Geschichte der Musiktheorie Bd. 6,. Hören, Messen und Rechnen in der frühen Neuzeit, Wissenschaftliche Buchgesellschaft, Darmstadt, pp. 109–331 (1987)
13. Merzbach, U.C., Boyer, C.B.: A History of Mathematics, 3rd edn. Wiley, Hoboken (2011)
14. Muzzulini, D.: The Geometry of Musical Logarithms. Acta Musicologica **LXXXVII/2**, 193–216 (2015)
15. Nemorarius, J.: Arithmetica Iordani, Cod. Basel F II 33, 65r–86v
16. Nemorarius, J.: Artithmetica decem libris demonstrata. In: Stapulensis, J.F., Paris (1496)
17. Odington, W.: De speculatione musicae. The Parker Library, Corpus Christi College, Cambridge MS 410, 1r–36v
18. Oresme, N.: De proprtionibus proportionum, E. Grant (ed. with Engl. trans.), Publications in Medieval Science 9, Madison (1966)
19. Oresme, N.: Algorismus proportionum, Cod. Basel F II 33, 95v–98v
20. Torkesey, Johannes. Declaratio trianguli et scuti. Biblioteca Apostolica Vaticana, Reginensis lat. 1146 (14th c.)
21. Stevin, S.: De Thiende, Nijhoff, La Haye (1585)
22. Stifel, M.: Arithmetica Integra, Johannes Petreius, Nürnberg (1544)

A Database of Aristotelian Diagrams: Empirical Foundations for Logical Geometry

Lorenz Demey[1]([✉])(iD) and Hans Smessaert[2](iD)

[1] Center for Logic and Philosophy of Science, KU Leuven
Kardinaal Mercierplein 2, 3000 Leuven, Belgium
lorenz.demey@kuleuven.be
[2] Department of Linguistics, KU Leuven
Blijde-Inkomststraat 21, 3000 Leuven, Belgium
hans.smessaert@kuleuven.be

Abstract. Aristotelian diagrams, such as the square of opposition, are among the oldest and most well-known types of logical diagrams. Within the burgeoning research program of logical geometry, we have been developing a comprehensive database of Aristotelian diagrams that occur in the extant literature: Leonardi.DB (the Leuven Ontology for Aristotelian Diagrams, and its corresponding Database). This paper presents an (intermediate) report on this development. We describe the philosophical background and main motivations for Leonardi.DB, focusing on how the database provides a solid empirical foundation for theoretical research within logical geometry. We also discuss some of the main methodological and technical aspects of the database development. As a proof-of-concept, we provide some examples of the new kinds of research that will be facilitated by Leonardi.DB, e.g. regarding broad trends in the usage and visual properties of Aristotelian diagrams.

Keywords: Aristotelian diagram · Square of opposition · Logical geometry · Leonardi.DB · Diagram database · Semantic Web

1 Introduction

Aristotelian diagrams are among the oldest and most well-known types of logical diagrams. The most famous example is the square of opposition (cf. Fig. 1), but there also exist many other, more complex examples. These diagrams have a rich history in philosophy and logic, and nowadays they are also used extensively in

The first author holds a Research Professorship (BOFZAP) from KU Leuven. This research was funded through the KU Leuven research projects 'Empirical Foundations for Logical Geometry: A Database of Aristotelian Diagrams' (3H180236, 2018–2020) and 'BITSHARE: Bitstring Semantics for Human and Artificial Reasoning' (3H190254, 2019–2023).

© Springer Nature Switzerland AG 2022
V. Giardino et al. (Eds.): Diagrams 2022, LNAI 13462, pp. 123–131, 2022.
https://doi.org/10.1007/978-3-031-15146-0_10

124   L. Demey and H. Smessaert

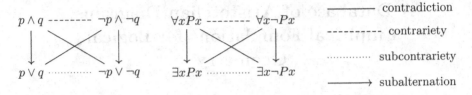

Fig. 1. Squares of opposition for propositional logic and first-order logic.

various other disciplines that deal with logical reasoning, such as linguistics, psychology and artificial intelligence [3,20]. Furthermore, in the past 15 years, it has become increasingly clear that Aristotelian diagrams are not only useful tools to explain or illustrate some logical notion, but can also be fruitfully studied as objects of independent mathematical and philosophical interest. This has given rise to the burgeoning research program of *logical geometry*.

One of the main aims of this research program has been to develop a comprehensive database of Aristotelian diagrams that occur in the extant literature. This has recently led to Leonardi.DB, i.e., the Leuven Ontology for Aristotelian Diagrams, and its corresponding Database, which is now fully available online.[1] The goal of this paper is to present a new (intermediate) report on this development.[2] Sect. 2 describes the philosophical background and main motivations for the development of this database. Section 3 describes some of its main methodological and technical (Semantic Web) aspects. Finally, Sect. 4 provides some examples of the new kinds of research that have become possible, and sketches some avenues for future research.

2 Background and Motivation

Aristotelian diagrams are widely used across reasoning-related disciplines. After a relative decline in popularity in the 20th century,[3] they have witnessed a renewed surge of interest in the first two decades of the 21st century. To a considerable extent, this interest has crystallized around the SQUARE [1,2], and recently also the DIAGRAMS conference series. For example, recent research has focused on the role of Aristotelian diagrams in authors such as John Buridan [5] and Arthur Schopenhauer [14] and topics such as privative negation [12] and Hohfeld's legal concepts [16]. In logical geometry, Aristotelian diagrams are studied as objects of independent interest. From a logical perspective, we study the Boolean properties of these diagrams [18], the interface between opposition and implication relations [10,20], and their broader category-theoretic setting [26]. From a visual-geometric perspective, we study Aristotelian diagrams in terms of notions such as symmetry groups [7], central symmetry [19], vertex-first projections [21] and Euclidean distance [8]; from a visual-cognitive perspective,

---

[1] Cf. https://leonardi.logicalgeometry.org/.
[2] A first and very preliminary report can be found in [25].
[3] See [13] for the broader religious-cultural context of this temporary setback.

we focus on notions such as free rides [22] and derivative meaning [23]. Finally, there is ongoing research on the interface of Aristotelian diagrams with other types of logical diagrams, such as Hasse, duality and Euler diagrams [4, 6, 9, 11].

Until now, systematic research on Aristotelian diagrams has largely remained an armchair enterprise. When a new theory about some logical, geometric, cognitive or other feature of Aristotelian diagrams is developed, it is checked against and/or illustrated by means of a small and well-delineated set of very well-known applications. Similarly, historical and philosophical reflection also starts from that same limited stock of well-known Aristotelian diagrams, coming from the historical canon of philosophy (e.g. Buridan, Schopenhauer).

To address this situation, we are currently developing a comprehensive database, which aims to collect all Aristotelian diagrams that have ever appeared in the extant literature, along with rich metadata annotations. This database will include the well-known Aristotelian diagrams mentioned above, but the vast majority of diagrams will come from lesser-known authors and applications. After all, it can reasonably be assumed that the distribution of Aristotelian diagrams throughout the literature obeys a version of *Zipf's law* [15]: the occurrence frequency of an Aristotelian diagram is inversely proportional to its frequency rank. We thus hypothesize that there is a small number of diagrams that are used very frequently (clearest example: the square of opposition), but that the overwhelming majority of diagrams is used less often. If the database is to be truly comprehensive in nature, it should not only include the small sample of frequently-used diagrams, but also the much larger number of rarely-used diagrams.

Once the database is sufficiently comprehensive, we envisage it will deliver three main benefits. First of all, it will provide a firm empirical basis for logical geometry, and thus help us to avoid idle armchair theorizing. Rather than developing, illustrating and testing our theories on the basis of a limited stock of well-known diagrams, we will be forced to take the lesser-known cases into account as well, which will lead to more empirically informed and nuanced theories. Secondly, we even expect to discover altogether new types of logical behavior in Aristotelian diagrams. After all, if a certain phenomenon only occurs in some lesser-known diagrams, then it will likely have gone unnoticed until now. However, by forcing us to take these lesser-known diagrams into account as well, the database will allow us to discover the new type of behavior after all. Finally, historical and philosophical research on Aristotelian diagrams often focuses on broader trends in the usage of Aristotelian diagrams across time periods or across scientific disciplines. For example, at the beginning of this section we already mentioned that in the 20th century, there was somewhat of a decline in the use of Aristotelian diagrams, and noted that [13] explains this in religious-cultural terms. To investigate this further, we first need to get a clearer quantitative picture of the situation: is there indeed a (statistically significant) decline in the use of Aristotelian diagrams in the 20th century? A comprehensive diagram database will enable us to carry out precisely such quantitative analyses.

3   Methodological and Technical Aspects

In this section we will describe some of the main methodological and technical aspects of the database that we are currently developing. The database is based on the Leuven Ontology for Aristotelian Diagrams (Leonardi), which was developed specifically for this purpose. The ontology consists of four main categories:

1. persons: e.g. authors, editors, translators, early Modern printers, etc.
2. sources: e.g. monographs, edited volumes, book chapters, journal articles, medieval manuscripts, incunabula, etc.
3. organization: e.g. publishing houses, libraries, national archives, etc.
4. diagrams: most importantly, the actual Aristotelian diagrams

Persons, sources and organizations are clearly auxiliary categories, and are thus annotated with only fairly basic metadata. For example, persons get annotated with their dates of birth and death, if these are known, and also with the most important renderings of their name. The latter is particularly relevant for medieval and early Modern people, e.g. *Jean Buridan* vs. *Johannes Buridanus*, or more extremely, *Juraj Dragišić* vs. *Georgius Benignus*. Whenever possible, we also provide links with other important datasets, e.g. the CERL Thesaurus concerning European book heritage.[4] The ontology is designed primarily to facilitate rich annotation of the actual diagrams. Every diagram in the database is annotated along the following dimensions:

1. administrative: e.g. dates of initial data entry and last modification, etc.
2. bibliographic: e.g. author, source, page/folio number, etc.
3. logical: e.g. Aristotelian family, Boolean complexity, formulas unique up to logical equivalence, presence of logical errors in the diagram, etc.
4. geometric: e.g. geometric shape, central symmetry, colinearity, etc.
5. vertices: e.g. words/symbols, logical system, linguistic/conceptual field, shape, presence of mnemonic support (e.g. the typical vowels A, E, I, O), etc.
6. edges: e.g. words/symbols, solid/dashed/dotted lines, arrowheads, etc.
7. style: e.g. presence of color, embellishments, etc.
8. additional info: e.g. research notes, connections with other diagrams, etc.

The Leonardi ontology has been implemented according to Semantic Web standards such as the Resource Description Framework (RDF), Linked Open Data (LOD) and (a computationally tractable subset of) the Web Ontology Language (OWL). More technical details and motivation are provided in our earlier paper [25]. Figure 2 displays a small but important part of the ontology, which can be used to describe a diagrams' vertices, edges, shape and general style features. The full ontology can be accessed online at https://logicalgeometry.org/assets/pdf/leonardi-schemata.pdf.

---

[4] See https://data.cerl.org/thesaurus/_search?lang=en. Note that these other datasets concern *people, books*, etc.; setting aside Leonardi.DB, we currently do not know of any comprehensive database which primarily consists of (logical) *diagrams*.

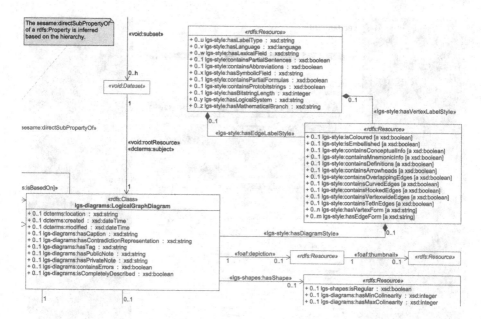

Fig. 2. A small part of the Leonardi ontology.

Data collection has thus far proceeded in a fairly straightforward fashion: we have focused on the numerous diagrams that are readily available, e.g. in research papers, textbooks, (digitized versions of) medieval manuscripts, incunabula, early Modern printed books, etc. In a later stage, data collection and processing will be done in a more comprehensive fashion, e.g. by systematically perusing bibliographic resources such as Risse's *Bibliographia Logica* [17] and online databases such as those of the Bibliothèque nationale de France (BnF) and the Bayerische Staatsbibliothek (BSB). We will return to this point in Sect. 4.

Leonardi.DB is freely available online (cf. Footnote 1), as a service to the wider research community, but also in order to further increase its empirical coverage. In particular, database users are encouraged to submit new diagrams (along with the relevant metadata) that they have created or discovered in the extant literature. All data can be explored and queried via a user-friendly graphical user interface (GUI), and can be exported in various formats (BibTeX, HTML, RDF); cf. Fig. 3 for a simple example. The data can be queried and filtered in full detail using the RDF query language SPARQL. However, in order to optimize user-friendliness, the database GUI also enables quite advanced searches by simply clicking some buttons and ticking some boxes. We mention just one example. Suppose that a given diagram D in the database cannot be dated precisely; the most accurate dates that are available are the range 1000–1200. Now suppose that the user wants to query the database to return all diagrams from the period 1100–1500. Should D be among the results for this query? According to a loose interpretation, D should be included, since it is

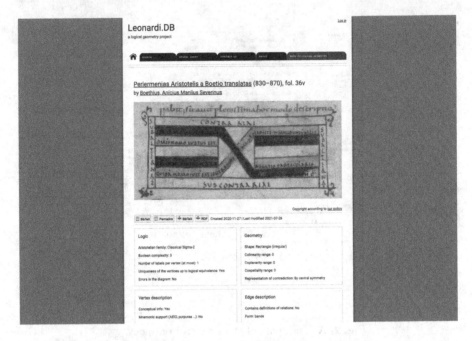

Fig. 3. A concrete diagram in Leonardi.DB, together with its annotation.

possible that D was created within the period specified in the query (mathematically: $[1000; 1200] \cap [1100; 1500] \neq \emptyset$); however, according to a strict interpretation, D should not be included, since it is not *certain* that D was created during the specified period (mathematically: $[1000; 1200] \not\subseteq [1100; 1500]$). Whenever the user wants to query the database based on chronological constraints like these, the GUI provides a simple checkbox that they can tick in order to indicate whether they want to adopt the 'loose' or rather the 'strict' interpretation.

4   New and Future Research Directions

At the time of writing (3 March 2022), Leonardi.DB contains annotations for 2461 Aristotelian diagrams (along with 1676 persons, 273 organizations, and 1616 sources). Although these numbers are not even close to the level of comprehensiveness that we are ultimately aiming for, the data volume and diversity are already sufficiently high to allow us to illustrate some of the new kinds of research that are facilitated by the diagram database. To make matters concrete, consider the following statement, taken from an earlier paper on logical geometry which was presented at DIAGRAMS 2016:

> we will only deal with Aristotelian diagrams in which negation is visually represented by means of central symmetry [. . .] both the logical condition (closed under negation) and the geometrical condition (central symmetry) are satisfied in nearly every Aristotelian diagram [7, p. 71]

Furthermore, when assessing this statement, it might make sense to set aside the last few decades, when more and more 'exotic' Aristotelian diagrams have begun to be studied (in the context of logical geometry and its immediate predecessors). Querying Leonardi.DB yields the following numerical results:

	Before 1950	After 1951	
Closed under negation, central symmetry	484	1584	2068
Closed under negation, no central symmetry	25	141	166
Not closed under negation	23	204	227
	532	1929	2461

We thus find that $(2068 + 166)/2461 = 90.8\%$ of all Aristotelian diagrams are closed under negation, and $2068/2461 = 84\%$ visualize negation by means of central symmetry. Furthermore, if we only consider the diagrams produced before 1950, these numbers further increase to 95.7% and 91%, respectively. Time period is clearly statistically significant; $\chi^2(2, N = 2461) = 25.78; p < 0.00001$. Furthermore, by further exploring the diagrams that are closed under negation but do not visualize this by means of central symmetry, we observed that many of them nevertheless do obey a kind of 'local' central symmetry. For example, in a cube diagram, we often found central symmetry *within* the front and back faces (so that the negation of the upper left front vertex occurs at the lower right *front* vertex, rather than at the lower right *back* vertex, as global central symmetry would require). This nicely illustrates how Leonardi.DB not only allows us to make more quantitatively precise statements about Aristotelian diagrams, but also triggers entirely new research questions and hypotheses.

In future research, we plan to scale up data collection and annotation through machine learning algorithms. The Aristotelian diagrams that have already been manually annotated are sufficiently representative to constitute a good training set. We hope to draw inspiration from the work of Sørensen and Johansen [24]: they have developed a regional convoluted neural network (r-CNN) within the Python-based deep learning platform Keras, which can quite accurately detect diagrams in a corpus of mathematical texts.

References

1. Béziau, J.Y., Jacquette, D. (eds.): Around and Beyond the Square of Opposition. Springer, Basel (2012). https://doi.org/10.1007/978-3-0348-0379-3
2. Béziau, J.Y., Vandoulakis, I. (eds.): The Exoteric Square of Opposition. Springer, Basel (2022)
3. Ciucci, D., Dubois, D., Prade, H.: Structures of opposition induced by relations. The Boolean and the gradual cases. Ann. Math. Artif. Intell. **76**, 351–373 (2016)
4. Demey, L.: Algebraic aspects of duality diagrams. In: Cox, P., Plimmer, B., Rodgers, P. (eds.) Diagrams 2012. LNCS (LNAI), vol. 7352, pp. 300–302. Springer, Heidelberg (2012). https://doi.org/10.1007/978-3-642-31223-6_32

5. Demey, L.: Boolean considerations on John Buridan's octagons of opposition. Hist. Philos. Logic **40**(2), 116–134 (2019)
6. Demey, L., Smessaert, H.: The relationship between Aristotelian and Hasse diagrams. In: Dwyer, T., Purchase, H., Delaney, A. (eds.) Diagrams 2014. LNCS (LNAI), vol. 8578, pp. 213–227. Springer, Heidelberg (2014). https://doi.org/10.1007/978-3-662-44043-8_23
7. Demey, L., Smessaert, H.: The interaction between logic and geometry in Aristotelian diagrams. In: Jamnik, M., Uesaka, Y., Elzer Schwartz, S. (eds.) Diagrams 2016. LNCS (LNAI), vol. 9781, pp. 67–82. Springer, Cham (2016). https://doi.org/10.1007/978-3-319-42333-3_6
8. Demey, L., Smessaert, H.: Logical and geometrical distance in polyhedral Aristotelian diagrams in knowledge representation. Symmetry **9**(10), 204 (2017)
9. Demey, L., Smessaert, H.: Aristotelian and duality relations beyond the square of opposition. In: Chapman, P., Stapleton, G., Moktefi, A., Perez-Kriz, S., Bellucci, F. (eds.) Diagrams 2018. LNCS (LNAI), vol. 10871, pp. 640–656. Springer, Cham (2018). https://doi.org/10.1007/978-3-319-91376-6_57
10. Demey, L., Smessaert, H.: Using multigraphs to study the interaction between opposition, implication and duality relations in logical squares. In: Pietarinen, A.-V., Chapman, P., Bosveld-de Smet, L., Giardino, V., Corter, J., Linker, S. (eds.) Diagrams 2020. LNCS (LNAI), vol. 12169, pp. 385–393. Springer, Cham (2020). https://doi.org/10.1007/978-3-030-54249-8_30
11. Demey, L., Smessaert, H.: From Euler diagrams to Aristotelian diagrams. In: V. Giardino et al. (eds.) Diagrams 2022. LNCS (LNAI), vol. 13462, pp. 279–295. Springer, Cham (2022). https://doi.org/10.1007/978-3-031-15146-0_24
12. García Cruz, J.D.: What kind of opposition-forming operator is privation? In: Basu, A., Stapleton, G., Linker, S., Legg, C., Manalo, E., Viana, P. (eds.) Diagrams 2021. LNCS (LNAI), vol. 12909, pp. 118–131. Springer, Cham (2021). https://doi.org/10.1007/978-3-030-86062-2_11
13. Jaspers, D., Seuren, P.: The square of opposition in Catholic hands: a chapter in the history of 20th-century logic. Logique et Anal. (N.S.) **59**(233), 1–35 (2016)
14. Lemanski, J., Demey, L.: Schopenhauer's partition diagrams and logical geometry. In: Basu, A., Stapleton, G., Linker, S., Legg, C., Manalo, E., Viana, P. (eds.) Diagrams 2021. LNCS (LNAI), vol. 12909, pp. 149–165. Springer, Cham (2021). https://doi.org/10.1007/978-3-030-86062-2_13
15. Li, W.: Zipf's law everywhere. Glottometrics **5**, 14–21 (2002)
16. Pascucci, M., Sileno, G.: The search for symmetry in Hohfeldian modalities. In: Basu, A., Stapleton, G., Linker, S., Legg, C., Manalo, E., Viana, P. (eds.) Diagrams 2021. LNCS (LNAI), vol. 12909, pp. 87–102. Springer, Cham (2021). https://doi.org/10.1007/978-3-030-86062-2_9
17. Risse, W.: Bibliographia Logica. 4 vols., esp. I: 1472–1800 and II: 1801–1969. Georg Olms, Hildesheim (1965–1979)
18. Smessaert, H.: Boolean differences between two hexagonal extensions of the logical square of oppositions. In: Cox, P., Plimmer, B., Rodgers, P. (eds.) Diagrams 2012. LNCS (LNAI), vol. 7352, pp. 193–199. Springer, Heidelberg (2012). https://doi.org/10.1007/978-3-642-31223-6_21
19. Smessaert, H., Demey, L.: Logical and geometrical complementarities between Aristotelian diagrams. In: Dwyer, T., Purchase, H., Delaney, A. (eds.) Diagrams 2014. LNCS (LNAI), vol. 8578, pp. 246–260. Springer, Heidelberg (2014). https://doi.org/10.1007/978-3-662-44043-8_26
20. Smessaert, H., Demey, L.: Logical geometries and information in the square of opposition. J. Logic Lang. Inform. **23**, 527–565 (2014)

21. Smessaert, H., Demey, L.: Visualising the Boolean Algebra $\mathbb{B}_4$ in 3D. In: Jamnik, M., Uesaka, Y., Elzer Schwartz, S. (eds.) Diagrams 2016. LNCS (LNAI), vol. 9781, pp. 289–292. Springer, Cham (2016). https://doi.org/10.1007/978-3-319-42333-3_26

22. Smessaert, H., Shimojima, A., Demey, L.: Free rides in logical space diagrams versus Aristotelian diagrams. In: Pietarinen, A.-V., Chapman, P., Bosveld-de Smet, L., Giardino, V., Corter, J., Linker, S. (eds.) Diagrams 2020. LNCS (LNAI), vol. 12169, pp. 419–435. Springer, Cham (2020). https://doi.org/10.1007/978-3-030-54249-8_33

23. Smessaert, H., Shimojima, A., Demey, L.: On the cognitive potential of derivative meaning in Aristotelian diagrams. In: Basu, A., Stapleton, G., Linker, S., Legg, C., Manalo, E., Viana, P. (eds.) Diagrams 2021. LNCS (LNAI), vol. 12909, pp. 495–511. Springer, Cham (2021). https://doi.org/10.1007/978-3-030-86062-2_51

24. Sørensen, H.K., Johansen, M.W.: Counting mathematical diagrams with machine learning. In: Pietarinen, A.-V., Chapman, P., Bosveld-de Smet, L., Giardino, V., Corter, J., Linker, S. (eds.) Diagrams 2020. LNCS (LNAI), vol. 12169, pp. 26–33. Springer, Cham (2020). https://doi.org/10.1007/978-3-030-54249-8_3

25. Termont, W., Demey, L., Smessaert, H.: First steps toward a Digital Access to Textual Cultural Heritage. In: Poster presentation at the third international conference on digital access to textual cultural heritage (DATeCH 2019) (2019)

26. Vignero, L.: Combining and relating Aristotelian diagrams. In: Basu, A., Stapleton, G., Linker, S., Legg, C., Manalo, E., Viana, P. (eds.) Diagrams 2021. LNCS (LNAI), vol. 12909, pp. 221–228. Springer, Cham (2021). https://doi.org/10.1007/978-3-030-86062-2_20

Origami and the Emergence of Hybrid Diagrams

Francesca Ferrara⑩ and Giulia Ferrari[(✉)] ⑩

Università degli Studi di Torino, Turin, Italy
{francesca.ferrara,giulia.ferrari}@unito.it

Abstract. The paper discusses the emergence of *hybrid diagrams* in the context of origami practice with respect to the study of the crease pattern, a particular diagram that can be associated with any origami model. We introduce the expression "hybrid diagram" to refer to a 2D diagram that embeds physical parts of the origami model and information about transformations occurred in space, or to an origami model on which attempts to grasp parts of the crease pattern appear. We focus on some university students working with the crease pattern for a given origami model. A first analysis of the work of these students allows for a preliminary characterization of hybrid diagrams: they encapsulate relations between the 3D model and the crease pattern and reveal the entanglement of diagrammatic activity with the gestural and the material. Drawing on the cognitive perspective of semiotic representations by R. Duval and diagrammatic thinking by C. Peirce, we interpret the emergence of hybrid diagrams as relevant to the conversion between different (mathematical) registers.

Keywords: Origami · Crease pattern · Hybrid diagram · Mathematical thinking

1 Origami and Diagrams

In this paper we use the idea of "hybrid diagram" drawing on observations made in the context of a teaching experiment that involved a group of university students in activities with origami models and the crease pattern, a diagram that consists of all or most of the creases that are folded in the final origami model.

The making of an origami consists in repeatedly folding one or more squared sheets of paper to obtain other (three-dimensional) shapes which can resemble animals or flowers, as well as recall geometric shapes or patterns. Far from being just a recreational activity, in recent years it has had important applications in many fields, like the aero-spatial and medical field. From an educational perspective, a major interest in paper folding lies in the possibility of exploring geometric properties through material activity. The geometry of origami has its mathematical formalization in a set of seven axioms, which identify the ways in which it is possible to create a fold. These axioms have become famous as Huzita-Justin or Huzita-Hatori Axioms [9]. The list is also complete [2]. Most of the movements that contribute to the creation of an origami model are based on axioms, making the underlying mathematical theory particularly rich and interesting from the didactic point of view for they allow the discovery and study of mathematical relations in a concrete context (e.g., [6] and [8]).

V. Giardino et al. (Eds.): Diagrams 2022, LNAI 13462, pp. 132–139, 2022.
https://doi.org/10.1007/978-3-031-15146-0_11

Most of the available books on origami illustrate the process of making a model through instruction diagrams. In such diagrams, the sheet of paper is shown generally as a square, and each step of the construction is accompanied by arrows that indicate the direction of the movements to be performed and by marks that capture the position and type of fold (valley or mountain creases). The instruction diagrams provide an iconic representation of the steps in the construction, while the final model incorporates all the transformations made by paper folding. The relationships between an origami model and the set of transformations undergone by the sheet of paper through the activity of folding is captured by another diagram: the *crease pattern*. Some beautiful examples of crease patterns are available on the site of the origamist Robert J. Lang [12]. In the initial page of the website, Lang points out how in a crease pattern, one can see everything that is hidden in the folded work.

Intuitively, we can revisit the definition of crease pattern given by Hull [7], introducing it as the plane diagram that consists of the lines representing the fundamental valley and mountain folds, i.e., all the folds that are folded in the origami in its final form. An example of an origami model and the relative crease pattern is given in Fig. 1.

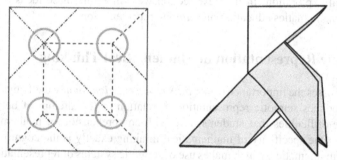

Fig. 1. The crease pattern and the model of the Pajarita, a classical origami. The vertexes of the crease pattern are circled in the first diagram.

The crease pattern is therefore a plane diagram that contains important information about the nature of the folds composing the final model, but only the expert eye can "reconstruct" (or imagine) a model starting from its crease pattern. Even the reverse process (i.e., building the crease pattern starting from a folded origami model) is not obvious, because it requires a considerable effort of three-dimensional visualization. It is not sufficient, indeed, to reopen the origami model and highlight the traces of the folds. Two distinctions must be made: (1) fundamental folds must be recognized and distinguished from those that are folded in the construction but no longer in the final model; (2) these fundamental folds can be *valley* or *mountain* creases. Following Hull [7], in a crease pattern generally valley folds are represented with dashed lines and mountain folds with dash-dot lines. Moreover, when drawing a crease pattern while looking at the relative origami model, it is necessary to "always look at the sheet of paper from the same side", since when the sheet is turned upside down, mountain folds become valley folds and vice versa.

In a crease pattern, which is a square-shaped diagram within which folds are represented through segments, we call a *vertex* each point inside the square where at least two distinct lines concur (see Fig. 1 again). In our work we have focused our attention on the characteristics of particular origami, called flat origami. Intuitively, a flat origami can be closed in a book without creating further folds and without removing any fundamental fold: it is therefore an object that, despite being three-dimensional, since it is made up of multiple layers folded over each other, can be treated as two-dimensional.

Studying the crease pattern is of interest for many reasons. We select here two of them, which are relevant to this paper. First, the crease pattern *shows* what is hidden in the model once folded, therefore it opens a different window on the creation process of an origami and the relations among folds in the origami. Secondly, properties of a flat origami can be illustrated and expressed through the crease pattern, so this is a space for rich mathematical explorations.

In this paper, we will focus on some students working on the task of drawing the crease pattern of an origami model, and we will describe the emergence of types of diagrams in their activity, which we call *hybrid diagrams*. We will present a qualitative analysis of the students' activity that shows how such diagrams emerge and sustain the mathematical exploration. In the next section we will frame these ideas drawing on research in mathematics education on semiotic representation.

2 Semiotic Representation in Mathematical Thinking

Duval [5] stresses the importance of *semiotic representation* for any mathematical activity. He introduces semiotic representation in relation to the attempt of better understanding the difficulties that students have with comprehension of mathematics, and their nature. One specificity of mathematical thinking exactly is the cognitive activity required by mathematics, which makes use of semiotic systems of representation. Signs, or semiotic systems of representation, play a role not only to designate mathematical objects or to communicate but also to work on, and with, mathematical objects. For Duval, no kind of mathematical process is performed without using a semiotic system of representation: mathematical processes always involve "*substituting some semiotic representation for another*" (p. 107, *emphasis in the original*). Therefore, in mathematical activity what matters is not representations but the transformation of representations. Semiotic activity is so relevant to mathematics (and mathematics education) because signs and semiotic representations allow access to mathematical objects. Ambiguity can emerge when learners must distinguish objects and their representations. According to Duval, the ability to change from one representation system to another is critical to progress and problem solving. Mathematical activity has different semiotic representation systems, called *registers*: the verbal, the numerical, the graphical, the symbolic, each providing specific possibilities for performing mathematical processes. There are two different types of transformations of semiotic representations: treatments and conversions. Treatments occur within the same register and can be carried out depending on the possibilities of semiotic transformation which are specific to the register used. Conversions instead are transformations of representation that consist of changing a register without changing the objects, like when we pass from the algebraic notation for a function to its graph. Briefly speaking, these transformations capture changes in or of register.

Today, semiotic activity in mathematics is regarded as more complex than just implying treatments of and conversions between the semiotic registers à la Duval and has been expanded to incorporating bodily-based signs, like gesture, gazes, tones of voice, sketches, tool usages, and so on, so that we speak of *multimodal* or *sensuous* mathematical cognition [11], meaning that mathematical cognition involves multiple modalities and senses, besides registers. Thus, we refer to *semiotic sets* instead of registers. Arzarello [1], for example, has introduced the notion of *semiotic bundle* to capture the relationships in and within different semiotic sets. In this paper, we consider *diagrams* as one possible semiotic resource that is activated in mathematical thinking. In so doing, we must refer to Peirce's theory of cognitive activity and his attempt to rescue the import of perception [10]. Peirce considers diagrammatic thinking as central to discovery of new conceptual relations, which remained hidden before or beyond the realm of our attention and are instead made apparent by perceptual inspection.

What matters to us in respect to Peirce's consideration of diagrams is therefore the role that they can play in reasoning about mathematical relations. We are not interested in the appearance of diagrams but more in their nature (how they emerge) and function (why they emerge), because this helps us to better investigate cognitive activity in mathematics. In addition, the history of mathematics shows that relevant mathematical ideas were discovered or advanced with a productive semiotic activity involving an interplay of gestures and diagrams [3]. Borrowing from these ideas, we see diagrams as a semiotic set consisting of graphs, sketches, figures, and any form of visual thinking expressed in the written. Focus is put on the emergence of kinds of diagrams in mathematical activity, which we call *hybrid diagrams*.

3 The Emergence of Hybrid Diagrams

3.1 The Mathematical Activity

For this paper, whose purpose is to present and discuss the emergence of hybrid diagrams in the context of mathematical paper folding, we centre our attention on a specific task. Some university students were asked to draw the crease pattern corresponding to each step of the construction process of an origami model. This task is relevant to the issue of conversion between different registers in mathematics, considering the origami model and the crease pattern as two different registers for the same object. The teaching experiment was aimed at creating the opportunity for university students to engage with origami and their representations and explore the features of flat origami regarding the mathematical properties of their crease pattern. The experiment was designed by the authors and carried out during the first semester of the academic year 2020/21, when university courses were held online because of the Covid pandemic. It engaged 29 master's degree students in mathematical explorations of origami models using 7 worksheets and the Google Meet platform. The conditions of distance teaching and learning are relevant to our research study. Initially, main interest was in the creation and study of mathematical activities involving origami to make the students explore non-elementary properties of flat origami. Additional interest arose concerning the understanding of the way in which the online environment could trigger new strategies for mathematical exploration and communication. Data for the analysis mostly consists of the video recordings of the Google Meet rooms in which the students worked in groups to face the tasks of the worksheets. Also, the written materials produced by the groups were uploaded to online shared folders. Our qualitative analysis employed techniques from micro-ethnography [13] to understand how the students make sense of the paper folding activities.

The first two worksheets focused on the creation and analysis of the crease patterns of two simple origami: the triangle base and the square base, which generally are the basis of folds for more complex origami constructions. In the third worksheet, the focus was on the analysis of the crease pattern created by another group and on the concept of vertex in the crease pattern. Worksheet 4 was divided into two parts (a and b) and centred on the request to create the sequence of crease patterns corresponding to the various steps of the construction of the "crane". The tasks of worksheets 5 to 7 finally guided the investigation of flat origami and the exploration and discovery of the theorems of Maekawa and Kawasaki, which advance peculiar properties of the flat origami's crease pattern. In this paper, we draw attention to the request given by the first part of Worksheet 4. The students were given the instruction diagrams for the origami model and a sequence of squares, which each group was asked to fill in with the crease pattern at each construction step. The first step was the crease pattern of the square base, which the students had already encountered. The last step was the complete crease pattern of the crane (Fig. 2). The students were also asked to assign a different role to different members of the group, as a folder or sketcher.

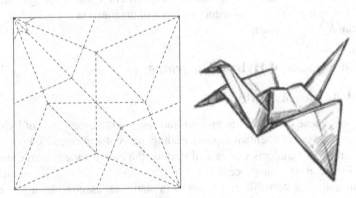

Fig. 2. The crease pattern (left) of the crane (right).

3.2 The Work of Two Groups

In this section we analyse the work of two groups (1 and 2). Group 1 is made up of three female students (S, G, H) and one male student (A). In solving the worksheet, S and A create the origami, while G and H create the crease pattern at each step (Fig. 3c).

Interestingly, S, in addition to building the model, draws the crease pattern directly on the model step by step, re-opening it and tracing the basic lines on paper, where it is possible to see the trace of the crease and therefore detect both the position and the nature of the fold (Fig. 3a).

To check the correspondence with what the groupmates do on paper, the model is often opened and closed again, but only halfway (Fig. 3b), as the model is substantially symmetric, for almost the whole process, with respect to the diagonals of the square.

We see that the group creates a type of hybrid diagram, given by the origami with folds added and marked with the same notation used in the crease pattern. We consider it *hybrid* because we recognize that the characteristics of origami are crucially merged with those of the crease pattern, and the model then is manipulated with different interest and in new ways (for example, just half-opened). The model thus modified can be conceived as a diagram, since the set of relations it contains becomes predominant perceptually other than semiotically, and such information is conveyed through appropriate conventions. The diagram is hybrid also in that it combines the material nature of the model with the usual way of representing the nature of the folds in a plane drawing.

We observe that the diagram is used by the students to operate a conversion between the register of the origami model and that of the crease pattern, which entails to check relations and modifications in space and in the plane and to discern the fundamental folds and their nature.

a   b   c

Fig. 3. (a) - (b) The hybrid diagram of group 1, then folded in half; (c) the crease pattern of the crane created by group 1.

Group 2 works in a different manner: a student (M) shares his tablet screen, in particular the window of a graphic editor software through which he modifies the assigned worksheet drawing the crease pattern; the rest of the group work on the origami model. The group is convinced that they are not allowed to reopen the model and observe the position of the folds with respect to the initial square. Therefore, they all proceed by imagining the changes occurred in the ongoing crease pattern, without comparing this directly with the folds traced on the paper sheet.

Each time the group works on a new crease pattern, M copies and pastes the crease pattern created in the previous step and then adds the changes directly on that diagram. The new added lines are of a different colour (Fig. 4a; as already done by group 1 in the hybrid diagram) and the online worksheet is rotated several times through the editor to show the crease pattern in the same position in which the other members of the group hold the origami. New folds are often first drawn as segments and, only later, the nature of the fold is captured by means of the appropriate marks.

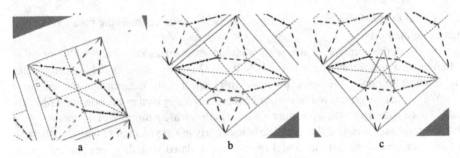

Fig. 4. (a) - (b) - (c) Lines and arrows added by group 2 on the crease pattern.

Other signs are also drawn on the crease pattern to support the students' conjectures: in particular, arrows refer to the folding movement (Fig. 4b) or materialize parts of the origami in that passage, as they look like in the 3D space (Fig. 4c).

We observe the emergence of a "hybrid" diagram also in the case of group 2: the crease pattern, phase by phase, incorporates folding movements or captures representations of elements of the three-dimensional model.

3.3 Conclusions

Although at the very end the crease pattern of the crane produced by the groups is not entirely correct, we observe that the emergence of hybrid diagrams fosters the students' mathematical reasoning on the conversion between the origami and the crease pattern. In this paper, we analyse these diagrams focusing on the work of two groups. The ways in which we talk about the hybrid nature of the diagrams for the two groups are dual of each other. In the case of the first group, the 3D model incorporates qualities of the plane representation. In the case of the second group, during the process of diagramming, the crease pattern is transiently inhabited by arrows that literally bring in folding movements or new elements that mirror actual parts of the 3D origami. This seems to be an important characteristic of a hybrid diagram, which is provisionally arranged to incorporate aspects that usually belong to different registers and do not appear together.

In this sense, we see hybrid diagrams as semiotic and cognitive tools to operate a conversion, borrowing from Duval's language, between the register of the origami model and that of the crease pattern. The crease pattern crystallizes the process of folding, which essentially is a movement that happens in space but leaves a material trace, a material modification on the piece of paper. This is probably the reason why hybrid diagrams either capture movements (group 2) or are manipulated to perform such movements while controlling the nature and position of the folds (group 1). This way of addressing students' diagramming and gesturing aligns with de Freitas and Sinclair's [4] vision of them "as inventive and creative acts by which "immovable mathematics" can come to be seen as a deeply material enterprise" (p. 134).

Moreover, a hybrid diagram is nonstandard (does not belong entirely to one system of representation or another) and open to new modification and configuration. These features fundamentally evoke the dynamic character that Châtelet [3] sees as constitutive of diagrams. Tracing the emergence of hybrid diagrams allows us to better illuminate the semiosis that is at play in the process of conversion in mathematics.

Despite the huge interest in the field of origami practice and its relationship with mathematics, research that focuses on the cognitive side of this relationship is missing. Other studies, even in other contexts, might enhance the characterization of hybrid diagrams and help elucidate their role in mathematical thinking. Further qualitative research is needed to enlarge understanding of hybrid diagrams and their cognitive and didactical relevance. Wider implications could build on these first observations to better characterize hybrid diagrams and their cognitive value in mathematical activity.

References

1. Arzarello, F.: Semiosis as a Multimodal Process. Revista Latinoamericana de Investigación en Matemática Educativa, RELIME **9**(Special Issue), 267–299 (2006)
2. Alperin, R.C., Lang, R.J.: One-, two-, and multi-fold origami axioms. In: Lang, R.J. (ed.) Proceedings of the Fourth International Meeting of Origami in Science, Mathematics, and Education, pp. 371–393 (2006)
3. Châtelet, G.: Figuring space: Philosophy, mathematics and physics (R. Shore, & M. Zagha, Trans.) Kluwer. (2000; Original work published 1993)
4. de Freitas, E., Sinclair, N.: Diagram, gesture, agency: theorizing embodiment in the mathematics classroom. Educ. Stud. Math. **80**, 133–152 (2012)
5. Duval, R.: A cognitive analysis of problems of comprehension in a learning of mathematics. Educ. Stud. Math. **61**, 103–131 (2006)
6. Haga, K.: Origamics. Mathematical Explorations through Paper Folding. World Scientific Publishing Co., Singapore (2008)
7. Hull, T.: On the Mathematics of Flat Origamis. Congr. Numer. **100**, 215–224 (1994)
8. Hull, T.: Project Origami: Activities for exploring mathematics. CRC Press, New York (2013)
9. Huzita, H.: Axiomatic Development of Origami Geometry. In: Huzita, H. (ed.) Proceedings of the First International Meeting of Origami Science and Technology, pp. 143–158 (1989)
10. Peirce, C.S.: Collected Papers, vol. 1–8. Harvard University Press, Cambridge (1931–1958)
11. Radford, L.: Sensuous cognition. In: Martinovic, D., Freiman, V., Karadag, Z. (eds.) Visual mathematics and cyberlearning, pp. 141–162. Springer, New York (2013)
12. Robert J. Lang Homepage, https://langorigami.com, last accessed 2022/04/08
13. Streeck, J., Mehus, S.: Microethnography: the study of practices. In: Fitch, K.L., Sanders, R.E. (eds.) Handbook of language and social interaction, pp. 381–404. Lawrence Erlbaum Associates, Mahwah (2005)

On Lambert Quadrilaterals and Why They Cannot Be Diagrams (According to Lambert)

Theodor Berwe[⊠] [iD]

Ruhr University Bochum, Bochum, Germany
theodor.berwe@rub.de

Abstract. Johann Heinrich Lambert characterizes geometrical diagrams by the fact that in them the "thing itself", its concept and the corresponding sign coincide. Remarkably, in one of his geometrical works, the *Theory of Parallel Lines*, he makes use of objects that challenge this very characterization. In his attempt to proof the parallel axiom, Lambert introduces a set a set of peculiar quadrilaterals, the so-called Lambert quadrilaterals, which depict non-Euclidean objects. This is baffling, since Lambert explicitly states at the beginning of the *Theory of Parallel Lines* to proceed "purely symbolically". However, he repeatedly refers to what appear to be diagrams in the form of Lambert quadrilaterals. In my talk I address this puzzle. I argue that if we take Lambert's remarks on geometrical diagrams seriously, non-Euclidean Lambert quadrilaterals cannot possibly be diagrams in the strict sense, since they neither represent a concept nor a "thing itself". Instead, they can be considered as symbolic representations.

Keywords: History of mathematics · Semiotics · J. H. Lambert · Non-euclidean geometry

1 Introduction

In the context of the history of diagrams, polymath J. H. Lambert (1728–1777), is well known for his linear diagrams [3, 9, 13]. This paper, however, focuses on Lambert's notion of geometrical diagrams. I investigate what role diagrams play in Lambert's foundation of geometry. For this purpose I take a look on an example which is an excellent basis for discussing what constitutes a geometrical diagram for Lambert. Namely, his *Theory of Parallel Lines*, which he wrote in 1766, but which was published only after his death in 1786.

Here, Lambert tries to prove the parallel axiom via a proof of contradiction similar to Saccherie half a century earlier. The parallel axiom states, as Lambert puts it, "that, when two lines CD, BD are intersected by a third, and the two inner angles DCB, DBC taken together, are less than two right angles, then the

© Springer Nature Switzerland AG 2022
V. Giardino et al. (Eds.): Diagrams 2022, LNAI 13462, pp. 140–147, 2022.
https://doi.org/10.1007/978-3-031-15146-0_12

two lines CD, BD meet on the side of D, or the side where theses angles are found". [7, §1, trans. Ewald].[1]

Although Lambert does at no point doubt the truth of this principle, it is, "by no means as clear and evident as the others". Thus, "one somehow feels that it is capable of proof, that there must exist a proof of it" [7, §1, trans. Ewald]. He is not alone in this. The parallel axiom has been considered a source of discontent since antiquity [1, p. 599], because it is a dark spot on the otherwise clear field of geometry. Therefore, already in Lambert's time, the parallel axiom has a long history of failed proof attempts. So the issue at stake is not a sub-problem within geometry, but a vital flaw in its foundations.

To overcome this difficulty, Lambert attempts a proof by contradiction. He develops three different 'hypotheses', one of which corresponds to Euclidean geometry, the other two to a hyperbolic and spherical geometry. He then tries to proof the first one by deriving contradictions from the latter. Such a proof, Lambert states, proceeds "purely symbolically":

> And since Euclid's postulates and other axioms have been expressed in words, it can and should be demanded that the proof never appeals to the thing itself [die Sache selbst], but that the proof should be carried out purely symbolically—when it is possible. In this respect, Euclid's postulates are as it were like so many algebraic equations which one already has in front of oneself and from which one is to compute x, y, z, etc. without looking back to the thing itself [7, §11, trans. Ewald].

Lambert's claim not to refer to the thing itself, but to operate with symbols, i.e. words or even characters, suggests at first glance that he will refrain from using diagrams. This is especially plausible if one considers that his claim originates from a time in which there was a strong urge to detach geometry from all visual reference and to dispense completely with diagrams.

However, if we take a look at the *Theory of Parallel Lines*, we are surprised to find that this does not appear to be the case here. Lambert opens his proof with the introduction of a figure, a quadrilateral, on which the three different hypotheses within his proof are subsequently based. The so-called Lambert quadrilateral *ABDC*, in which three of the angles are right angles. The fourth angle *BDC* is 90°C in Euclidean geometry, and smaller or larger than 90°C in a hyperbolic or spherical geometry (see Fig. 1). Given his previous claim to proceed purely symbolically, Lambert extensively utilizing diagrams seems puzzling.

The simplest explanation is to assume Lambert to be inconsistent. After all, Lambert did not publish his work for certain reasons. So how seriously should we take his remarks? Perhaps he himself was dissatisfied with the approach. I believe, however, that there is more behind this puzzle. A second possible explanation would be that our first, intuitive understanding of what Lambert means by his characterization of his procedure is mistaken. Perhaps our contemporary

---

[1] The parallel axiom, which Lambert addresses as the 11th principle, originally served as a postulate in Euclid's *Elements* for all we know. However, since Clavius's edition of the *Elements* in 1589, it was common to consider postulate 5 as an axiom [11].

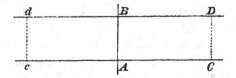

Fig. 1. So-called Lambert quadrilaterals [7, § 29].

understanding of a symbolic proof does not correspond to Lambert's. Perhaps, and this is the line of reasoning I want to follow here, our contemporary understanding of a what a diagram is does not match that of Lambert.

In fact, a closer look at Lambert's philosophical writings shows that he has a very strict and specific understanding of what diagrams are and do in geometry. Applying this understanding of geometrical diagrams, it follows that Lambert quadrilaterals are not diagrams at all, but rather types of symbolic knowledge. Hence, there is no inconsistency on the part of Lambert, but a mistaken expectation on our part, regarding what diagrams are in the first place.[2]

I proceed as follows: I will first examine the nature of geometrical diagrams according to Lambert as presented in his philosophical writings. Subsequently, I will have a closer look at the Lambert quadrilaterals. As I just described, I argue that they do not meet the previously developed criteria and therefore cannot be considered geometrical diagrams in the strict sense. Third, I outline and discuss a suggestion on how to understand them instead. I argue that Lambert quadrilaterals can be understood as a form of symbolic knowledge.

2 Lambert's Methodological Remarks on Geometrical Diagrams

Lambert considers geometry a paradigm of a proper axiomatized science in general. In this regard, he is a child of his time. In the 17th and 18th centuries, the geometric method (*mos gemetricus*) was regarded by innumerable thinkers as the ideal of science. In his methodological and philosophical writings, Lambert himself is concerned with designing a blueprint for science based on the example of geometry. Against this background, it is easy to understand why geometry plays such an important role in his philosophical work. In contrast to, say, Wolff, the renowned mathematician Lambert is quite aware of the flaws of geometry and the problems connected to the parallel axiom. His project of a universal science stands and falls with the possibility of a well-founded geometry.

Likewise, it is typical for the time that Lambert does not claim a *transfer* of the geometrical method to other sciences. Instead, geometry is considered as an example of a universal method which is applied first in geometry [8, § 22]. Why is that the case? Lambert pinpoints the main reason as follows:

---

[2] Lambert does not use the term 'diagram' in his writings, which was uncommon in the 18th century. Instead, he speaks of 'figures' both in reference to geometric figures and to logic diagrams. For consistency, I will nevertheless use 'diagrams' throughout.

It was easy for Euclid to give definitions and define the use of his words. He could put lines, angles and figures in front of the eyes and thus directly connect words, concepts and things. The word was only the name of the thing, and because one could see it before one's eyes, one could not doubt the possibility of the concept [6, § 12].

The decisive advantage of geometry is that here words, concepts and things are immediately connected. Understanding what he means by this and how diagrams contribute requires some background on Lambert's epistemological beliefs.

Lambert advocates a representationalist epistemology. He distinguishes between the thing itself, the idea representing it (the concept), and the sign, which in turn stands as a representative for the concept. We form general concepts by means of abstraction and refer to them by signs or symbols, for example, words, although signs are by no means limited to words. Most often, the relation between sign and concept is arbitrary in that it is based on convention.

Whenever we imagine something corresponding to an abstract concept, the imagination creates a concrete image, an individual instance of the abstract concept, so to speak, e.g. a concrete triangle with defined place, size and position. While the representation of a thing is usually not identical with the represented thing (an imagined dog is not a dog), this is not the case with geometrical objects. To imagine a triangle is to "trace it in thought along the outline of the figure ... just about as if we wanted to draw it" [5, *Alethiologie* § 17]. Thus, whenever we imagine a triangle, we represent the thing itself. In the case of geometric objects, there is no surplus of the thing over the representation. The geometrical diagram then is the result of a construction, accomplished in thought. In this sense, Lambert understands the diagram as a mental object. At the same time, of course, the diagram is also a sign. A drawn, i.e. sensually perceivable triangle, is an immediate sign for the concept of the triangle and the thing itself. No mediation is necessary here unlike in the case of words based on arbitrary conventions. Consequently, every diagram-based proof in geometry is *also* a symbolic proof. But conversely, of course, not every symbolic proof is also diagrammatic.

Due to diagrams, Euclid could "directly connect words, concepts and things" [6, § 12]. This gives geometry an immense advantage over other sciences, in which objects can neither be produced at will, nor do the concepts have immediate signs. This advantage, however, is not what elevates geometry to a science. Diagrammaticity in this sense is not a necessary condition for science. It merely made things easier for Euclid. Why this is the case becomes clear, if we consider a possible objection against Euclid's way of proceeding as well as the counter argument, which can be brought forward against it following Lambert.

"The figure thus represented the concept whole and pure", Lambert writes [6, § 12]. This is odd, as we have seen that a figure always represents an individualized instance of a geometrical object. Under these circumstances, how can one arrive at universal concepts on the basis of diagrams? In Lambert's terminology, this question concerns the "universal possibility" of geometric concepts. The imagined or drawn diagram may prove beyond doubt the possibility of a particular triangle, but it cannot prove the general possibility of all triangles which

correspond to the concept. This exposes, at least for Lambert, a more fundamental problem, which Katherine Dunlop reconstructs as a skeptical objection
against geometry [2]. Lambert brings into play a fictional radical skeptic who
notoriously questions the universal possibility of geometrical objects in a sort
of hyperbolic doubt [8, § 79]. Euclid meets the skeptic by stating the rules of
construction of geometrical figures in the form of problems. He begins with the
construction of an equilateral triangle in prop. 1, book 1 of the *Elements*, which
requires only the postulates. On this basis he proves that it is possible to draw
a straight line of a given length and in the consequence to construct further
triangles. The skeptic may then doubt a theorem as much as he likes. Euclid's
proof shows him how he can construct every possible figure himself (in thought
or on paper) and therefore he cannot possibly uphold his doubt.

The basis for the construction are the postulates, which Lambert also calls
"general, unconditional, and in themselves thinkable or simple possibilities or
doabilites [Tulichkeiten]" [6, § 12]. For this reason, Lambert repeatedly emphasizes the importance of postulates for the Euclidean method of proof, especially
in his criticism of Wolff, who almost completely banishes postulates and problems from geometry. The "categorical in his theorems", as Lambert puts it in
the *Theory of Parallel Lines*, Euclid takes "not from definitions, but actually
and primarily from the postulates" [7, § 7]. A rigorous geometric proof in Lambert's eyes is therefore not based on particular and therefore inevitably concrete
diagrams, but on the universal rules of construction, which show how *all* possible diagrams can be constructed. From this follows that geometrical diagrams
are in principle dispensable. Provided that the rules of construction established
by the postulates retain their validity, the diagrams can be replaced at will by
other signs, for example by words. Using diagrams as signs increases the clarity
of geometry due to their immediate relation to the concepts, but it is not a
necessary condition for their certainty.

Against this background we can now take another look at Lambert quadrilaterals. My thesis is that Lambert does not consider these quadrilaterals named
after him as geometrical diagrams in the sense just developed. Why this is the
case, I will show in the following.

3   Lambert Quadrilaterals Versus Geometrical Diagrams

If Lambert quadrialterals were geometrical diagrams, they would have to combine sign, concept and representation of the thing itself in the aforementioned
way. That Lambert could have hold such a view seems to me exceedingly implau-
sible for two reasons.

First, it would imply that the general possibility of Lambert diagrams would
have to be ensured by a construction based on the Euclidean postulates. Just like
a triangle, the Lambert quadrilaterals would have to be vindicated against the
objection of the skeptic questioning their general possibility. It seems blatantly
impossible to me that Lambert could have considered this to be possible. The
entire indirect proof attempt within the *Theory of Parallel Lines* is based on

the idea that contradictions can be derived from the non-Euclidean hypotheses, which are, after all, based on the Lambert quadrilaterals, in combination with Euclid's principles.

Second, it would have to be possible to form a concept of the Lambert quadrilaterals. To Lambert, this presupposes that the concept does not contain a logical contradiction, because "insofar as someone thinks something erroneous, he indeed thinks nothing, or as much as nothing" [6, § 196]. The contradiction is, as Lambert phrases it, the "criterion of the unthinkable and in itself impossible" [6, § 108]. The Lambert quadrilaterals, however, contradict the parallel axiom— again, this is the whole idea of the indirect proof—the truth of which Lambert does not doubt.

So we can conclude: Lambert diagrams cannot be constructed by the means of Euclidean postulates, nor can they be represented. Therefore, they do not satisfy the epistemological criteria Lambert places on geometric diagrams. Lambert nevertheless addresses the quadrilaterals in his proof as "figures". If the previous reasoning is correct, he does not use the term in the specific sense that sign, concept and the thing itself coincide. This seems anything but unlikely. In the 18$^\text{th}$ century, the German term 'Figur' was not limited to geometric figures, but was also used, prominently for example by Wolff in his *German Metaphysics*, to denote signs in a much broader sense [12]. This interpretation is also supported by the fact that Lambert uses dashed lines for the line DC that constitutes the non-Euclidean variants (see Fig. 1). Unlike the regular lines, which are the result of an imagined or real movement (of the pen on paper), this is not true for the dashed lines. Rather, they can be understood to indicate something unrepresentable, unimaginable, and impossible.

If Lambert quadrilaterals cannot be diagrams according to Lambert's own criteria, what might they be instead? A clue is given already by Lambert's claim, that his proof "never appeals to the thing itself" but proceeds "*purely* symbolically" [my emphasis]. Whereas diagrams to Lambert are *also* signs, the Lambert quadrilaterals are *mere* signs in that they lack any corresponding concept. In the third book of his *New Organon*, *Semiotics*, Lambert deals with a type of knowledge that fits this description perfectly. It operates on the basis of signs, but abstracts completely from the representation of the thing itself. Lambert calls this type of knowledge "symbolic knowledge".

4 Lambert Quadrilaterals as Symbolic Knowledge

In the tradition of Leibniz's *characteristica universalis*, Lambert develops a semiotic approach to science according to which the "theory of the thing" should be reduced to the "theory of the signs". In the process, the mediating level of representation is eliminated. Thus, "the dark knowledge of concepts can be exchanged with the intuitive knowledge, with the sensation and clear representation of signs" [6, § 24]. Symbolic knowledge does not only offer the possibility to exclude a main source of errors in the form of concepts, but moreover provides a positive potential. With the help of symbols we can operate with objects which exceed the limits of our imagination by far. Lambert mentions in a letter to Kant from October 13th, 1770 as an example both infinite series and, more interesting in our context, thought constructs like imaginary numbers.

> No one has yet formed himself a clear representation of all the members of an infinite series, and no one is going to do so in the future. But we are able to do arithmetic with such series, to give their sum, and so on, by virtue of the laws of symbolic knowledge. We thus extend ourselves far beyond the borders of our actual thinking. The sign $\sqrt{-1}$ represents an unthinkable nonthing. And yet it can used very well in finding theorems [10, 109 f.].

Symbolic knowledge allows us to denote the conceptual impossible. And this is because the expressive power of language goes far beyond the range of possible concepts. It is only subject to certain rules according to which we construct the signs. That means that the signs have to be well formed. Semantically such a sign has no meaning. It does not represent a thing, but a "thing impossible in itself, a nonthing, non-ens".

I suggest to understand Lambert's proof attempt as symbolical insofar as it includes elements of symbolic knowledge in this sense. Lambert carries out the proof of contradiction starting from hypotheses, which we can make use of merely in a mode of a symbolic knowledge. Lambert quadrilaterals with obtuse and acute angle are "unthinkable nonthings" in the same vein as the square root of a negative number. We can use these symbols in operations or in proofs to arrive at new theorems or, in the case of the indirect proof in the *Theory of Parallel Lines*, contradictions. But we cannot possibly obtain a representation of them, let alone put them in front of our eyes as concrete figures.[3]

5   Conclusion

An examination of Lambert's philosophical writings reveals that his approach in the *Theory of Parallel Lines* is methodologically quite coherent, although the proof itself is of course invalid. Today we know that a proof of the parallel axiom is not possible, at the latest since Beltrami proved the consistency of hyperbolic geometry in 1868. Lambert understands geometrical diagrams in a very specific sense that is closely related to his epistemology. Against this background, it is unlikely that he regarded Lambert quadrilaterals as diagrams in this sense.

To conclude, I will take a very brief look at the relation between symbolic and diagram-based proofs. From our contemporary perspective, it is quite natural to relate Lambert's remark about a "purely symbolical" proof to this relation which is nowadays often regarded as a strict opposition. Proofs that use diagrams are often contrasted with 'rigorous', i.e. formal or symbolic proofs.

---

[3] Note that it is irrelevant whether these signs are actual drawings (i.e. Fig. 1 above) or consist of words. To Lambert, a verbal description of a Lambert quadrilateral yields symbolic knowledge in exactly the same manner as a drawn figure.

For Lambert, however, the matter is more complex and the contrast between diagram-based and symbolic proof is not as clear-cut. As mentioned above, a diagram-based proof is also symbolical in that it involves symbols or signs in the form of diagrams. But as long as these diagrams are geometrical, they provide us at the same time with the representation of the thing itself and thus cannot be an element in a proof that is "purely symbolical". As a matter of fact, this is the great value of geometrical diagrams according to Lambert. A "purely symbolical" proof, on the other hand, must do completely without diagrams. However, it does not necessarily have to contain elements like the Lambert quadrilaterals that are categorically beyond our imagination. That Lambert reaches for such an instrument is rather due to the extraordinary difficulty associated with the parallel axiom, which he believes he can only overcome in this way.

References

1. De Risi, V.: The development of Euclidean axiomatics. Arch. Hist. Exact Sci. **70**, 591–676 (2016)
2. Dunlop, K.: Why Euclid's geometry brooked no doubt: J. H. Lambert on certainty and the existence of models. Synthese. **167**, 33–65 (2009)
3. Englebretsen, G.: Figuring it Out: Logic Diagrams. De Gruyter, Berlin and Boston (2019)
4. Ewald, W. (ed.): From Kant to Hilbert: A Source Book in the Foundations of Mathematics. Clarendon Press, Oxford (1996)
5. Lambert, J.H.: Neues Organon: Oder Gedanken über die Erforschung und Bezeichnung des Wahren und dessen Unterscheidung vom Irrthum und Schein. Johann Wendler, Leipzig (1764)
6. Lambert, J.H.: Anlage zur Architektonic. Johann Friedrich Hartknoch, Riga (1771)
7. Lambert, J.H.: Theorie der Parallellinien. In: Engel, F., Stäckel, P. (eds.) Die Theorie der Parallellinien: Von Euklid bis Gauss, pp. 137–207. Teubner, Leipzig (1895)
8. Lambert, J.H.: Abhandlung vom Criterium Veritatis, Kant-Studien Ergänzungshefte, vol. 36. Reuther und Reichard, Berlin (1915)
9. Moktefi, A., Bellucci, F., Pietarinen, A.: Diagrammatic autarchy: linear diagrams in the 17th and 18th centuries. In: Burton, J., Choudhury, L. (eds.) DLAC 2013: Diagrams, Logic and Cognition. Proceedings of the First International Workshop on Diagrams, Logic and Cognition, vol. 1132, pp. 23–30. CEUR Workshop Proceedings (2014)
10. Preussische Akademie der Wissenschaften zu Berlin (ed.): Kant's gesammelte Schriften, vol. 10. De Gruyter, Berlin and Leipzig (1922)
11. Shabel, L.: Mathematics in Kant's Critical Philosophy. Routledge, New York (2003)
12. Wolff, C.: Vernünfftige Gedancken von Gott, der Welt und der Seele des Menschen, auch allen Dingen überhaupt: den Liebhabern der Wahrheit mitgetheilet. Renger, Halle (1720)
13. Wolters, G.: Basis und Deduktion: Studien zur Entstehung und Bedeutung der Theorie der axiomatischen Methode bei J. H. Lambert (1728–1777). De Gruyter, Berlin and Boston (1980)

Cognition and Diagrams

Euler vs Hasse Diagrams for Reasoning About Sets: A Cognitive Approach

Dimitra Bourou[1,2]([✉]), Marco Schorlemmer[1,2], and Enric Plaza[1]

[1] Artificial Intelligence Research Institute (IIIA), CSIC,
Bellaterra (Barcelona), Catalonia, Spain
dbourou@iiia.csic.es

[2] Dept. Ciències de la Computació, Universitat Autònoma de Barcelona,
Bellaterra (Barcelona), Catalonia, Spain

Abstract. The literature on diagrammatic reasoning includes theoretical and experimental work on the effectiveness of diagrams for conveying information. One influential theoretical contribution to this field proposes that a notation that is more effective than another would have an observational advantage over it; that is, it would make certain pieces of information observable—by means of some visual, meaning-carrying relationships—that were not observable in the other. Although the notion of observational advantage captures a relevant aspect of the benefit of using one notation over another, we present here an example where this notion is not sufficient to distinguish between a more and a less effective diagram. We suggest to take the theory of observational advantage one step further by linking it to cognitive theories of human conceptualisation and reasoning. Following our previous work, we propose that the act of observing facts about set theory from the geometry of a diagram can be modeled as a conceptual blend of image schemas with parts of the geometric configuration of a diagram. Image schemas are elementary mental structures that crystallize early embodied experiences, allowing agents to make sense of what they perceive by conceptualising it in terms of these structures (e.g., CONTAINER, LINK, SCALE etc.). With our approach, we can extend the theory of observational advantage to take into account the cognitive complexity of the act of observation. Concretely, we present an example of an Euler and a Hasse diagram, and we posit that, while their observational advantage is equivalent, the Hasse diagram requires a much more complex network of conceptual blends to model certain observations made from it. Thus, to reason about certain set-theoretic claims, a Hasse diagram is less cognitively effective than an Euler diagram with equivalent observational advantage. We believe our approach contributes to the theoretical discussion on what factors affect the effectiveness of a diagram, and provides new avenues for the exploration of how the embodied experiences of the users contribute to the way they reason with diagrams.

Keywords: Conceptual blending · Image schemas · Sense-making · Diagram effectiveness · Observational advantage

© The Author(s) 2022
V. Giardino et al. (Eds.): Diagrams 2022, LNAI 13462, pp. 151–167, 2022.
https://doi.org/10.1007/978-3-031-15146-0_13

1   Introduction

What makes a certain choice of representation better suited than another for conveying the same information? Stapleton et al. made a contribution towards a general theory that may provide an answer to this question [27]. They put forward a formal theory of 'observation' and 'observational advantage' that distinguishes between the information that is observable in, and the one that needs to be inferred from, a given representation. This theory allows to formally prove the observational advantage of Euler diagrams over set-theoretic sentences when it comes to conveying information about set-theoretic claims concerning set equality and inclusion. In order to achieve that, Stapleton et al. resort to an abstract notation for Euler diagrams that is detached from cognitive aspects of the act of observing and making sense of a diagram. This leaves open the possibility of some diagrammatic formalisms where observation is much more cognitively costly, having an equivalent observational advantage, and thus be judged as equally effective. For instance, as we will show in this paper, Hasse and Euler diagrams can have equivalent observational advantage over set-theoretic sentences. Thus, to account for the cognitive aspects of observation, we will model the act of observing and making sense of a diagram as a network of conceptual blends of image schemas with the geometric configuration of the diagram, and show that observation on the Hasse diagram is modeled with a much more complex network of blends. We believe the latter fact indicates that the observation act has a higher cognitive cost for the user.

Our work is based on various theories of cognitive science. First, the notion of sense-making refers to how agents actively create meaning by perceiving and acting within their environment [20,28]. Image schemas are mental structures acquired through infancy, as humans interact with their environment, and reflect the basic structure of sensorimotor contingencies experienced repeatedly, such as CONTAINER, LINK, and PATH [13,15]. Conceptual blending is a theory that posits that novel meaning emerges as we integrate existing concepts with each other [11]. Integrating all these theories, and applying them to the domain of diagrammatic reasoning, our proposal is the following: The geometry of a diagram is not meaningful on its own. We make sense of it, and reason with it, by integrating with it certain image schemas that are suitable to actively draw conclusions about its semantics [1–3].

To realise the above proposal, we must decide which image schemas are blended with each diagram, which can be done by following the approach that the advocates of the theories of image schemas and conceptual blending have followed for language. In this literature (e.g., [11,16]), in order to argue that humans make sense of certain concepts by integrating certain image schemas with them, it is shown that:

- the components of the image schema correspond, in a one-to-one manner, to the components of the concept to be made sense of,
- there is a transfer of a more detailed inferential structure, that allows reasoning about the new concept.

For example, to explain the concept of being depressed, a conceptual metaphor is described using the CONTAINER schema to convey the experience of being trapped, when one says: "I am in a deep depression." By uttering this sentence, we put in correspondence the inside of a CONTAINER with the state of being depressed, and the outside of the CONTAINER with the non-depressed mental state. The inferences here originate in our embodied experience with containers: if I am inside a depressed state, I cannot be outside of it; if my depression is deep, then getting out of it will be hard. Transferring this approach from language to diagrams, in this paper we will show that:

- certain image schemas can be put in correspondence, in a way that is almost one-to-one, with the geometric configuration of certain diagrams
- certain blends of these image schemas with certain mathematical diagrams are apt to model the sense-making of the latter, because they can give rise to inferences that are valid in the reference domain of these diagrams.

Integrating image schemas with the geometry of our diagrams, using the guidelines described above, we will be able to compare the resulting networks of conceptual blends. Our hypothesis is that, between two diagrams for both of which such networks exist, the most cognitively effective one would be that with the simplest network of blends. We will argue that users reason about sets with Hasse diagrams by conceptualising them as vertically linked paths along a scale, and with Euler diagrams by conceptualising them as a configuration of containers that may contain other containers. We present an Euler and a Hasse diagram that have equivalent observational advantage with respect to set-theoretical notation, but we argue the Euler diagram is more cognitively effective than the Hasse one because the network of conceptual blends modeling observation with it is much simpler. We believe our approach reaps the benefits of a formal but abstract approach, such as that of Stapleton et al. [27], while accounting for the cognitive aspects of reasoning when comparing the effectiveness of two diagrams.

2   Background

The term *sense-making* is defined within the framework of enactive cognition, which takes cognition and sense-making to refer to the process of an autonomous agent bringing its own meaning upon its environment, as a result of trying to grow and sustain itself [20,28]. This process is dependent on the embodiment of the agent, because a specific body—including a brain, sensory organs, and actuators—constrains the ways an agent can perceive, and interact with, its environment. Cognition and sense-making are therefore understood as emerging through the interaction of an embodied agent with its environment.

One concrete way to approach *sense-making* is through image schemas and conceptual blending. Image schemas are mental structures formed early in life, constituting structural contours of repeated sensorimotor contingencies, such as CONTAINER, SUP-PORT, VERTICALITY and BALANCE [13,15]. They are not acquired by learning a set of propositions, rules, or criteria, but by experiencing, for instance, our bodies being balanced, trying to maintain our balance, supporting an object, etc. Repeated experiences of the same kind lead to the formation of a mental structure capturing what is invariant and shared among them. The most important function of image schemas is their capacity to structure our experience. For example, we can perceive bees as being in a swarm, through the CONTAINER and COUNT-MASS schemas, even though there is no single physical object in the environment, corresponding to 'swarm' [17, p. 31]. Image schemas are Gestalts; they consist of a set of necessary components with a specific relational structure, whereby each component becomes meaningful only through its relation to all the others [17, p. 31]. By way of this structure, agents can—unconsciously but systematically—integrate image schemas with their experience, thus making sense and drawing meaning out of it. In order to fulfill this function, the image-schematic structure has to be preserved during this integration [17, p. 42]. Consequently, when putting image schemas in correspondence with the geometry of a diagram, it would be desirable to put in correspondence as many elements of the image schemas as possible, and in a one-to-one manner, with the geometrical shapes. Finding the right schema for a given state of a affairs is unconscious and immediate, but is nonetheless a cognitive process that uses our mental resources.

The image schemas of relevance for our case study are: LINK, PATH, VERTICALITY, SCALE, and CONTAINER. We will now discuss their cognitive structure according to the literature, and explain what kind of geometrical configurations they should be put in correspondence with. However, these correspondences are not written in stone, but are flexible and could change depending on the context the diagrams are used in. We have previously described and formalised similar correspondences for Hasse, Euler, and some more diagrams [3].

LINK. This schema can capture associations of various types, ranging from a physical chain tying two objects together, to two events abstractly linked by occurring at the same time. The prototypical LINK schema associates two distinct, usually contiguous, entities linked with each other through a link. Therefore, the LINK schema structure comprises two objects of the same type (entities), and a third object of a different type (link). Being in this particular configuration makes it so that the two entities have the property of being 'linked'. This structure fits well with a geometrical configuration of two regions or points that both intersect with a line. The objects identified as linked entities are typically "spatially contiguous within our perceptual field." [13, p. 118], which holds for points linked by a line.

PATH. This schema gives rise to our understanding of things moving from one point to the other [13, pp. 113–114]. It underlies the conceptualisation of objects following trajectories through space, irrespective of the details of the trajectory [18]. The PATH schema has the cognitive structure of a sequence of pairwise adjacent locations, naming the first one as a source and the last one as a goal. There can optionally be a trajector on some location of the path [13,15]. The structure of the schema necessitates that, if someone is on a certain location of the path, then they have already traversed all prior locations, and that contiguous locations serially lead from the source to the goal without branching. Given its structure, we believe the PATH schema should be put in correspondence with a series of shapes that are neighboring with each other in some way, and the source and the goal with shapes that do not have the same neighboring relation with any shape. This description is quite general, and could apply to almost any diagram. We will later see how it can be applied it to the diagrams studied here.

VERTICALITY. This schema obtains its structure from our experience of standing upright with our bodies resisting gravity, or from perceiving upright objects like trees. It comprises the axis of an upright object, the axis reflecting the trajectory an object would follow if free-falling, or an axis that is merely mentally visualised by an observer upon a scene [25]. Regarding the latter case, for example, when observing the sun on the horizon, the horizon is the base, and a visualised vertical axis runs upward from it, reaching the sun. This axis is always unique, and has an up-down polarity, so it is associated with a base at the bottom, or the ground, as a reference point. The base corresponds to the point where the axis meets the ground, or, if discussing an upright object, to the bottom part of an object by which it can stand [25]. Given the above, the VERTICALITY schema could be put in correspondence with diagrams with configurations along a vertical axis. More precisely, there must be a single shape that is geometrically lower than all others, serving as a base, and a geometric configuration resembling a vertical axis, e.g., shapes being one above the other.

SCALE. This image schema pertains to a gradient of quantity, and has the following four properties: a fixed directionality, a cumulative property (if one has 15 euros, they also have 10), it can be open or closed, i.e., have a specific endpoint or not, and finally, numerical gradients or normative judgements can be projected on it [13, pp. 122–123]. The SCALE schema is proposed to underlie the MORE-IS-UP metaphor, whereby a higher position in the vertical axis implies a higher quantity of something; that is, a larger number of rocks, or amount of water, means the top/surface reaches a higher position. Thus, the fixed directionality of SCALE is always upward [13, p. 121]. However, we believe that horizontal or circular scales (e.g., rulers and measuring tapes, or mechanical weighting scales respectively) also satisfy the other properties of SCALE and so perhaps SCALE is not inherently vertical, and a separate VERTICALITY schema is additionally involved in the MORE-IS-UP metaphor. Therefore, for us SCALE simply comprises an order of several discrete levels. Given the above, a SCALE schema could be put in correspondence with a geometrical structure of shapes that have a graded property. Such a structure could comprise, for example, shapes with a color or size grading, or shapes that are positioned one above the other, one to the right of the other, etc.

CONTAINER. This schema captures the structure of entities that are hollow, and can enclose and protect other entities in various ways, ranging from a fence enclosing a plot of land, to a balloon enclosing the air inside it. CONTAINER consists of a boundary, separating an inside and an outside, and this structure gives it certain properties; that is, an entity can be either in the inside or on the outside of a boundary, but not both. Also, several axioms hold, such as: if object A is inside boundary B, and boundary B is inside boundary C, then object A is inside boundary C; if object A is inside boundary B, and boundary B is outside boundary C, then object A is outside boundary C [17, p. 44]. We can see that the boundary of a CONTAINER can be put in correspondence very naturally with a closed curve of any shape on the 2D plane. The inside and outside regions of the CONTAINER also correspond naturally with the areas inside and outside the curve in this 2D space, respecting all the aforementioned properties of CONTAINER [17, pp. 45, 122].

In our approach, sense-making as the integration of image schemas with our experience can be described though the theory of conceptual blending, following [11, pp. 104–105]. Conceptual blending operates on mental spaces, which we introduce below based on the descriptions of Fauconnier [10] and Gärdenfors [12]. Mental spaces are mental representations that structure our perception and action. They comprise coherent and integrated chunks of information, containing entities, and relations or properties that characterise them. Mental spaces can be constructed from knowledge we have acquired previously, or from current experience, including exposure to language. Therefore, they operate in working memory but long-term memory can play an important role in their construction. Last but not least, the elements of one mental space can be put in correspondence with those of others, allowing cognitive access to them.

The central claim of the theory of conceptual blending is that a systematic process of building correspondences between different, preexisting mental spaces—called *input spaces*—can result in the emergence of novel meaning. This process gives rise to a new mental space—called *blended space*—that contains some elements of the input spaces with new relations among them. To construct a blend, some pairs of entities, relations, or attributes from input spaces must be put in correspondence with each other, and related in a new way, or even merged with each other, in the blend. This process leads to the emergence of novel structure and thus novel meaning. The entire network comprising the input spaces, the blended space, the generic space—reflecting the common structure among input and blended spaces—as well as the correspondences among all spaces, is called the integration network. Meaning emerges in the integration network as a whole.

Now we can put the aforementioned theories in the context of sense-making of diagrams. An enactive cognition approach to diagrammatic reasoning would entail that no geometric configuration is meaningful in itself, but it prompts the user to unconsciously structure it into a meaningful diagram by activating suitable frames, and integrating them appropriately with the configuration. The logical approaches taken to diagrammatic reasoning are very different from this paradigm. Such approaches formally study the informational content, and the effectiveness of diagrams for reasoning. To that end, a mapping between the syntax (geometric configuration) and the semantics of the diagram is typically assumed [19]. The theory of observational advantage put forward by Stapleton et al. [27], which stems from Shimojima's early work on the effectiveness of representations [26], follows an equally abstract approach. We believe such abstract approaches overlook the active, embodied role of the user in diagrammatic reasoning. Indeed, in agreement with enactive cognition, it has been suggested that the interpretation of diagrams entails a constructive and imaginative process on the part of the user [7, 19]. We wish to extend the theory of Stapleton et al. [27] to take into account the embodied and enactive aspect of our capacity to understand diagrams, and explain observation as emerging from the structure of the image schemas.

3　Related Work

In this section we will briefly summarise the theory of observational advantage of Stapleton et al. [27], and a cognitively-inspired framework for the analysis of representations, developed by Cheng et al. [6]. The former work put forth a formal criterion to compare the effectiveness of two notations of any kind; including diagrammatic or sentential. First, any notation has some meaning-carrying relationships among its components, i.e., visuo-spatial relationships that express a certain meaning. A mathematical diagrammatic notation, in particular, is drawn with certain meaning-carrying relationships intended to express some sentences in another notation, e.g., logical or set-theoretical. In some cases drawing this notation can result in the appearance of additional meaning-carrying relationships that allow reading even more sentences, that would require additional inference steps in the second notation, directly off of the first one. In this case, the first notation has an observational advantage over the second. For example, someone intending to express the sentences $P \cap Q = \emptyset$ and $R \subseteq P$ with an Euler diagram, will have to draw a diagram that is topologically equivalent to that of Fig. 1(a),[1] and will, in doing so, inadvertently also express that $R \cap Q = \emptyset$. In contrast, to obtain that $R \cap Q = \emptyset$ from the sentential notation, an inference step is required. Observation is therefore seen as a kind of immediate inference rule by which we extract, by merely looking at the notation, some atomic fact (that evaluates to either true or false) that is already 'within' that notation. Finally, a notation can also be observationally complete with respect to a set of facts (in the same or other notation), meaning that any inferences that can be drawn from these statements can be observed from the first notation.

With these definitions of 'observation' and 'observational advantage', Stapleton et al. go about proving the observational advantage of Euler diagrams [27] over set-theoretical sentential notation. This is done in a very abstract way, disconnected from the embodied, enactive nature of observation and from the spatial properties of the geometry. The visuo-spatial relationship of a 'region' r_1 being contained in a 'region' r_2 is not a visuo-spatial relationship anymore in this abstract treatment of Euler diagrams. As we will see in the next section, this gives rise to the possibility of defining an alternative diagrammatic notation with an equivalent abstract observational advantage, but in which observation would arguably have a higher cognitive cost.

Regarding other work with similar goals to ours, Cheng et al. [6] develop a comprehensive formal framework for characterising the formal and cognitive properties of representations, ultimately aiming to build an AI system to automatically select effective representations for particular problem solving tasks. They systematically classify cognitive properties of representation systems, allowing them also to discuss cognitive cost, and thus effectiveness, of using a certain representation system for solving a problem. Important variables assessed have to do with both the components of the representation (e.g., symbols, sentences etc.) and their characteristics, as well as cognitive processes from symbol parsing to problem solving.

4 Approach

In this section we introduce an Euler and a Hasse diagram that have equivalent observational advantage, in that, any entailment about sets that can be observed in one diagram can be also be observed in the other. However, the act of observing a particular set-theoretic claim is more complicated in the Hasse diagram. We will show this by describing the act of observation in these diagrams as integration networks that make the conceptual blends of the image schemas with the geometrical elements of the diagram explicit, and show that the integration network corresponding to the Hasse diagram is more complex then the one corresponding to the Euler diagram.

---

[1] This is because the meaning-carrying relationships of Euler diagrams are topological ones.

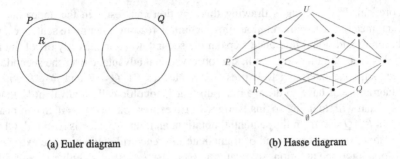

(a) Euler diagram   (b) Hasse diagram

Fig. 1. Observationally complete Euler and Hasse diagrams (and thus of equivalent observational advantage) that are semantically equivalent to the set of set-theoretical sentences $\mathscr{S} = \{P \cap Q = \emptyset, R \subseteq P\}$.

4.1 Working Example

Take, for example, the set of set-theoretic sentences $\mathscr{S} = \{P \cap Q = \emptyset, R \subseteq P\}$ over a set of labels $\mathscr{L} = \{P, Q, R\}$ (two additional symbols, $\emptyset$ and U, are also part of the syntax, to denote the empty set and the universal set, respectively). An observationally complete Euler diagram that is semantically equivalent[2] to $\mathscr{S}$ is shown in Fig. 1(a). All set-theoretic sentences that are entailed by $\mathscr{S}$ can be observed from this Euler diagram. We can also draw a semantically equivalent Hasse diagram for $\mathscr{S}$, such as the one shown in Fig. 1(b). This Hasse diagram represents the lattice of all regions of the Euler diagram, generated as the lattice of sets closed under finite union and intersections, such that $A \vee B = A \cup B$ and $A \wedge B = A \cap B$.[3] Put more simply, the nodes of the second level from the bottom of the Hasse diagram, correspond to the four minimal disjoint sets R, $P \setminus R$, $\overline{P \cup Q}$, and Q. The bottom level corresponds to their intersection, which is empty, the third level is generated by all possible unions of the minimal disjoint sets, and finally the top level is generated by the unions of the previous unions. As with the Euler diagram of in Fig. 1(a), all set-theoretic sentences that are entailed by $\mathscr{S}$ can be observed from the Hasse diagram of Fig. 1(b). In what follows, we will describe these observations using integration networks of image schemas with the geometry, and compare the complexity of the integration networks corresponding to the two diagrams.

4.2 Enactive Observation in Hasse Diagrams

To observe if a certain set-theoretic claim $S \subseteq T$ or $S = T$ holds in a given Hasse diagram (where S and T are labels or complex set-theoretic expressions formed using the

---

[2] Two (sets of) statements are semantically equivalent if they have the same models.

[3] Formally, all labels in $\mathscr{L}$ are attached to some of the lattice elements (i.e., there exists a labeling function $\lambda : \mathscr{L} \to \mathfrak{L}$, where $\mathfrak{L}$ denotes this lattice of regions), the maximum is labeled with the additional symbol U, and the minimum is labeled with the additional symbol $\emptyset$. In general, given an Euler diagram whose curves are labeled with labels $\mathscr{L}$, the corresponding Hasse diagram will represent a lattice with 2^n elements, where $0 \leq n \leq 2^{|\mathscr{L}|}$.

operators ∩, ∪, \, and ⁻), we must first identify the nodes of the Hasse diagram representing set-expressions S and T, and then check if there is an upward path between these nodes (for set inclusion) or if they are the same (for set equality). The existence of an upward path can be immediately ruled out if the nodes representing S and T are distinct nodes at the same level of the Hasse diagram. Let us denote this identification task with a function node that assigns to each set-theoretic expression S over a set of labels $\mathscr{L}$ a node node(S) in the Hasse diagram:

- if $S \in \mathscr{L}$, then node(S) = $\lambda(S)$, the node labeled with S
- if $S = S_1 \cup S_2$, then
  - if there is a downward path from node(S_1) to node(S_2), then node(S) = node(S_1)
  - if there is a upward path from node(S_1) to node(S_2), then node(S) = node(S_2)
  - if there is neither an upward nor a downward path between node(S_1) and node(S_2), then node(S) is the lowest of all those nodes that are on a meeting point between an upward path from node(S_1) to node(U), and a upward path from node(S_2) to node(U)
- if $S = S_1 \cap S_2$, then
  - if there is a downward path from node(S_1) to node(S_2), then node(S) = node(S_2)
  - if there is a upward path from node(S_1) to node(S_2), then node(S) = node(S_1)
  - if there is neither an upward nor a downward path between node(S_1) and node(S_2), then node(S) is the highest of all those nodes that are on a meeting point between a downward path from node(S_1) to node($\emptyset$), and a downward path from node(S_2) to node($\emptyset$)
- if $S = S_1 \setminus S_2$, then
  - if there is a downward path from node(S_1) to node(S_2), then
    * if node(S_2) = node($\emptyset$), then node(S) = node(S_1)
    * if node(S_2) ≠ node($\emptyset$), then node(S) is the highest among all those nodes (excluding node(S_1)) that are on all downward paths from node(S_1) to node($\emptyset$) that do not go through node(S_2)
  - if there is a upward path from node(S_1) to node(S_2), then node(S) = node($\emptyset$);
  - if there is neither an upward nor a downward path between node(S_1) and node(S_2), then
    * if node($S_1 \cap S_2$) ≠ node($\emptyset$), then node(S) is the highest among all those nodes (excluding node(S_1)) that are on all downward paths from node(S_1) to node($\emptyset$) that do not go through node($S_1 \cap S_2$)
    * if node($S_1 \cap S_2$) = node($\emptyset$), then node(S) = node(S_1)
- if $S = \overline{S_1}$, then
  - if node(S_1) = node($\emptyset$), then node(S) = node(U),
  - if node(S_1) ≠ node($\emptyset$), then node(S) is the highest among all those nodes (excluding node(U)) that are on all downward paths from node(U) to node($\emptyset$) that do not go through node(S_1)

As is evident from the above description, we can observe set-theoretic claims in a given Hasse diagram by realising these observations in an enactive, experiential way through the image schemas LINK, PATH, VERTICALITY, and SCALE. Notice that all operations between sets are expressed as spatial relations between the objects in the diagram, therefore satisfying the definition of observation. We thus describe the cognitive process of observation as constructing a network of blends involving some instances of the aforementioned image schemas, and parts of the geometric configuration of the Hasse diagram.

Apart from the PATH schema, a VERTICALITY schema is also involved. Specifically, the base of the VERTICALITY schema is put in correspondence with the point that is geometrically lowest. This schema provides the polarity required in order to disambiguate which correspondences of the source and the goal of a PATH schema are needed in order to go 'upwards' or 'downwards'; that is, to go upward, we put in correspondence the source with the point closer to the base, i.e., lower, and the goal with the point further from the base, i.e., higher. To move downward, we build the reverse correspondence. The LINK schema also plays a crucial role because what counts as a path, given the desired interpretation of a Hasse diagram, is formed only by those points connected by lines, not e.g., merely neighboring points, as the PATH schema structure dictates. Therefore, adjacency on the path is determined by lines drawn between node locations. In summary, we can model observations on the Hasse diagram through the involvement of a VERTICALITY schema to specify upward and downward orientation, several LINK schemas blended on pairs of nodes that are connected by some line, and also a PATH schema blended on the sequence of linked node locations from a source location (node) to a target location, capturing our experiential understanding of advancing, step by step, node by node, along the lines of the Hasse diagram.

Concretely, to observe, for instance, whether $Q \subseteq P \setminus R$, we need to check if we can reach a target location node$(P \setminus R)$ starting from a source location node(Q) by traversing a path of contiguous node locations going upwards. Since Q is already denoted in the diagram, there is no need to locate it by way of our enactive cognition. We would, however, need to identify the target location node$(P \setminus R)$ in the Hasse diagram. To do so, we would need to check first if we can reach node(R) on a downward path from node(P), blending the base of the VERTICALITY schema to the lowest node, i.e., node$(\emptyset)$, and a LINK schema and a PATH schema on the edge from node(P) to node(R) of the Hasse diagram, so that we can "walk down the path" from node(P) to node(R). Since this is possible, we next need to find all downward paths from node(P) to node$(\emptyset)$ that do not go through node(R). This blends a VERTICALITY schema, two LINK schemas and a PATH schema on the Hasse diagram, in order to traverse the two steps on the path from node(P) to node$(\emptyset)$ via the node location that is not labeled with R. The highest location on our path down (excluding node(P)) is the node we were looking for. Subsequently, we return to our original question, whether $Q \subseteq P \setminus R$. Now, we have to check whether there is an upward path from node(Q) to the node we have identified as node$(P \setminus R)$. Here, the SCALE schema comes into play. The way this particular Hasse diagram is drawn,[4] a user can easily put in correspondence the base of the

---

[4] This Hasse diagram represents a poset that is ranked, meaning that all its maximal chains have the same finite length. This is why it can be represented as a lattice, and is thus guaranteed to have what we call here 'levels,' corresponding to elements with the same rank, i.e., elements that are the same number of steps away from the minimum element.

VERTICALITY schema with the geometrically lowest shape of the Hasse diagram, i.e., the node representing $\emptyset$, and one level of a SCALE to each group of points that are on the same horizontal plane.[5] This way, the user can observe that node(Q) and the node we identified as node($P \setminus R$) are on the same level. Our embodied experience with paths, scales and the vertical dimension equips us with the knowledge that if two objects are on the same level of a vertical scale, it is impossible to traverse an upward path from one towards the other. Thus, it is immediately clear to us that there is no upward path from node(Q) to node($P \setminus R$) and therefore $Q \subseteq P \setminus R$ does not hold.

To summarise: although the fact that $Q \not\subseteq P \setminus R$ is observable from the Hasse diagram, it requires from the user to walk many paths with different source and target locations, stepping through several linked node locations, sometimes following an upwards, sometimes a downwards orientation, and finding the highest node locations traversed. From our description it is evident that a complex network of blends involving many instances of the PATH, LINK, VERTICALITY and SCALE schemas, and correspondences with many different shapes, is involved.

4.3   Enactive Observation in Euler Diagrams

To observe if a certain set-theoretic claim $S \subseteq T$ or $S = T$ holds in a given Euler diagram, as the one in Fig. 1(a), we must first identify the regions of the Euler diagram representing set-expressions S and T, and then check if the first region is inside the second (for set inclusion), or if they are the same region (for set identity). Let us denote this identification task with a function region that assigns to each set-theoretic expression S over a set of labels $\mathscr{L}$ a region region(S) in the Euler diagram:

- if $S \in \mathscr{L}$, then region(S) is the region inside the closed curve labeled with S
- if $S = S_1 \cup S_2$, then region(S) is the region made up of the combination of the insides of region(S_1) and region(S_2)
- if $S = S_1 \cap S_2$, then region(S) is the region that is both inside region(S_1) and inside region(S_2)
- if $S = S_1 \setminus S_2$, then region(S) is the part of region(S_1) outside of region(S_2)
- if $S = \overline{S_1}$, then region(S) is the region outside region(S_1)

As is evident from the above description, any set-theoretic claim in a given Euler diagram is enactively observed by way of the CONTAINER image schema. We model this cognitive process as a network of conceptual blends involving some instances of the CONTAINER schema and parts of the geometric configuration of the Euler diagram.

For instance, to observe $Q \subseteq P \setminus R$, we need to check if region(Q) is contained in region($P \setminus R$). This points to two instances of the CONTAINER schema blended upon the geometric configuration of the Euler diagram, capturing our sense-making of the inside, boundary, and outside of region($P \setminus R$), and of region(Q), together with the containment relationship between the two CONTAINER schemas. Concretely, the integration network involved is as follows: first, to identify $P \setminus R$, we put in correspondence the boundary of one CONTAINER schema with the curves labeled P and R, the inside with the area

---

[5] The VERTICALITY here is necessary in order to put in correspondence horizontal planes to levels; SCALE in itself does not necessarily correspond to vertical configurations.

between curves P and R, and the outside with the area outside curve P and the area inside curve R. With this blend, we model the way we observe region$(P \setminus R)$ in the diagram as a container. Subsequently, to check if $Q \subseteq P \setminus R$, we construct another blend between a second CONTAINER schema and the same geometrical configuration. This time the boundary, inside and outside of the CONTAINER will correspond to the curve labeled Q, its interior, and its exterior. Checking whether $Q \subseteq P \setminus R$ amounts to observing that the boundary of the CONTAINER schema we put in correspondence with the former is located on the outside of the CONTAINER schema we put in correspondence with the latter. This observation again comes from our experience with containers, leading to the realisation that if Q is on the outside of $P \setminus R$ then it cannot be on its inside, and thus $Q \subseteq P \setminus R$ does not hold.

Regarding the complexity of the integration network required to model the observations of $Q \subseteq P \setminus R$ from the Euler versus from the Hasse diagram, we can note that the integration network for the Euler diagram contains fewer different image schemas, fewer instances of image schemas, the diagram geometry itself contains much fewer elements, and the correspondences are also fewer. Concerning the blended space, blending the boundaries of CONTAINER schemas with the closed curves in a diagram imbues the latter with a sense of enclosure and separation. This sense emerges in the conceptual blends, where geometrical and image-schematic elements are integrated with each other, into elements that are simultaneously geometric and image-schematic. As we have seen, what constitutes the interior, boundary and exterior of a configuration of closed curves representing a set-theoretic expression, such as $P \setminus R$, arises in the way a CONTAINER schema is blended with said configuration; not from the geometry itself.

5   Discussion

The predominant logical approaches to diagrammatic reasoning and effectiveness usually view the diagram as a mapping between an abstract geometry and an abstract semantics. These approaches seem to overlook the enactive cognitive processes on the user's part, despite the fact that the term *effectiveness* can only be conceptualised and tested with respect to a user. We believe the user's embodied experiences—whose invariants are crystallized in the form of image schemas—can help bridge that gap. Using them, we can propose a conceptual model of the sense-making of a diagram as the integration of image schemas with the geometry of a diagram. This way, we can provide a more cognitively-plausible approach to diagrammatic reasoning whereby the users act cognitively upon the geometry of the diagram.

According to our framework, the effectiveness of Euler diagrams for representing set inclusion and disjointness (demonstrated in behavioral experiments [5, 24]) can be explained as follows: The geometry of an Euler diagram can be put in correspondence with instances of the CONTAINER schema. Through the process of constructing these correspondences, and thus integration networks, facts like $R \cap Q = \emptyset$ in Fig. 1(a) become immediately apparent. This integration network models how a user cognitively structures set P as a container, surrounding curve R, enveloping it, thus preventing its exiting and coming into contact with set Q—in agreement with [21]. Furthermore, it has been proposed that classes and Boolean logic are conceptualised via the CONTAINER schema [17]. Elements are understood as being in or out of a class, and Boolean logic has intersections and unions, which also emerge from a blend with the CONTAINER schema. Moreover, the CONTAINER schema corresponds very naturally to Euler diagrams, therefore making them apt to visualise such semantics [17, pp. 45, 122].[6]

In contrast, when reasoning with the Hasse diagram, we think about paths, links, the vertical orientation, and levels of scales. Some indication that image schemas are implicitly used to cognitively structure diagrams is provided by the informal language researchers use when describing how Hasse diagrams should be used for reasoning [4, 8, 9, 21, 22]. Researchers talk about Hasse diagrams, and the posets they represent, as having *top/bottom* elements and *arrows pointing upward* (VERTICALITY). They mention implications or entailments *going upwards*, line segments *running upwards*, and of diagrams having *upward paths* (PATH, VERTICALITY). Reasoning is done by *following upward/downward edges* and *upward/downward sequences of lines* (PATH, VERTICALITY, LINK). Each line is said to *connect an ordered pair of objects*, and edges are said to *connect adjacent* nodes/elements and to *form sequences* (PATH, LINK). Moreover, nodes and edges can be *traversed*, lines can be *followed* or *traced*, and *arrows* can form *sequences* with consecutive points (PATH). Finally, posets have *levels* and a *largest and smallest* element (SCALE).

Additional support comes from behavioral experiments showing that being upright, as opposed to slanted, explicitly showing levels (i.e., having points placed on horizontal parallels), and having non-crossed lines, makes Hasse diagrams faster to interpret [14, 23]. These findings are consistent with our claims that observation in Hasse diagrams can be modelled as blends of VERTICALITY, SCALE, LINK and PATH. Arguably, being upright, showing levels, and having non-crossed lines, makes it easier to put the structures of VERTICALITY, SCALE, and LINK with PATH respectively, in correspondence with the geometry of a Hasse diagram. Regarding the non-crossed lines, perhaps crossings result in some ambiguity because there are two possible ways to link pairwise the four points involved in the crossing, making sense of them as being adjacent in a path. Theoretical work on diagrammatic reasoning also asserts that Hasse diagrams prioritise visualising the structure of the order they represent, through a vertical organisation, and explicit visualisation of levels [8]. Levels corresponding to elements with the same rank are geometrically orthogonal to the vertical axis. In fact, this axis is the one intended to be interpreted, and elements of the same rank are indeed not comparable semantically with respect to the ordering. This description seems consistent with our description of how VERTICALITY and SCALE may structure the geometrical configuration of a Hasse diagram.

Arguably, there is no definitive way to prove that a user reasons with Hasse and Euler diagrams with the image schemas we have claimed. Therefore, our approach is to show that these integration networks model all the possible observations that Hasse and Euler diagrams allow. In previous work we have followed the same approach to model the inferences we can draw from various diagrams [3]. In the present paper, we specifically discuss facts that emerge as observations, not simply inferences. Moreover, we use our framework to study a case where the observational advantage is equivalent

---

[6] Lakoff and Nuñez mention Venn diagrams in their work, but actually utilise Euler diagrams in their figures [17].

between two diagrammatic representations, but arguably one is much more effective than the other for showing certain information. The reason for this discrepancy could be the mathematical abstraction of the theory of observational advantage. In contrast, our framework accounts for the user as an embodied actor by modeling observation as a conceptual integration network of various image schemas with the diagram geometry. We propose that one diagram may be more cognitively effective than another because the observations it affords can be modeled with a simpler conceptual integration network. Complexity manifests in several ways; we note that the different image schemas, and the different image schema instances, are much more in the integration network for the Hasse diagram. The geometric elements of the diagram itself are also much more, and the integration network overall has much more mental spaces, and more correspondences, than in the case of the Euler diagram. Since mental spaces and their correspondences are proposed to be realised and manipulated in the mind in some way, we conjecture that higher complexity of the integration network modeling the sense-making of a diagram, would correlate with a higher utilisation of the cognitive resources of the user reasoning with that diagram, and thus lower effectiveness of the diagram [10].

An additional contribution of our work is defining in more detail what Stapleton et al. call 'meaning-carrying relationships' [27]. The definition of observation that Stapleton et al. use includes this term, forcing them to address concrete geometric and cognitive properties of the diagram; a meaning-carrying relationship is defined as a visuo-spatial relationship between syntactic elements of a visual representation, that expresses a certain meaning. The term *visuo-* implies an agent with a certain body and perceptual faculties. Cheng et al. [6] also take as a given which relations between symbols of a given representation are meaningful, and should be used for inference. One of our contributions here is that what counts as a meaning-carrying relationship, or valid inference, can be explained in terms of blends with image schemas. At the level of discrete shapes like closed curves, lines etc., a wide range of spatial relationships hold; shapes can be related by having the same or different size, color and shape, by showing symmetry with respect to certain axes, and by their relative position. Someone who has been trained on how to read Euler diagrams knows that only topological relations are meaning-carrying. In contrast, in Hasse diagrams, relative position and topological intersection of lines with points is meaning-carrying, but topological intersection between lines is not. Focusing on the right meaning-carrying relationships and utilising them correctly for reasoning can be challenging for novices. Thus, we believe our approach can have future applications relating to guiding novices on how to use diagrams. Moreover, our theoretical contributions include showing how meaning-carrying relationships can become salient through blending apt image schemas with the geometry of a diagram, making explicit their experiential origins, and finally, providing new avenues for evaluating the cognitive effectiveness of diagrams.

6   Conclusions and Future Work

In this paper we explore the notions of observational advantage and meaning-carrying relation of Stapleton et al. [27] in a more cognitively-inspired way. In this, and most diagrammatic reasoning work, the specific meaning-carrying relations involved are taken as a given, and treated abstractly. In contrast, we believe our framework explores how they can emerge through the interplay of image schemas—which crystallize our early embodied experiences—with the diagram geometry. Our model simply accounts for the differences of the image schemas at play, keeping all else equal. We do not model all processes and factors that could affect the cognitive cost, e.g., the user's experience with the diagrammatic formalism, domain knowledge and cognitive strategies. We study two examples of diagrammatic notations, Hasse and Euler diagrams, with equivalent observational advantage over sentential set-theoretical notation, whereby an Euler diagram is arguably more cognitively effective for many set-theoretic claims than a Hasse diagram. We show that their difference, according to our framework, is the complexity of the integration network modeling how observations on these diagrams become possible. In this paper we discuss the integration networks reflecting only one example of observation. However, we describe how various types of observation about sets can be made with both Euler and Hasse diagrams, and it seems likely that the integration networks modeling most of them would be much simpler in the case of the Euler diagram. Nonetheless, depending on how the observational advantage and the meaning-carrying relations are defined, it might be the case that certain sentences regarding the empty set are not observable from the Euler diagram but only from the Hasse diagram [22, p. 10].

In previous work, we have used first-order logic to formalise and implement the integration networks reflecting reasoning with several diagrammatic formalisms [1–3]. Image schemas provide pointers to the meaning-carrying spatial relations of diagrams, and a cognitive explanation of how an embodied agent uses those relations to reason about the semantics the diagrams represent. Our framework could be used to guide students on which spatial relations of a diagram they must draw meaning from, by making explicit a blend with some image schema. Moreover, by analysing the integration network modeling observations with a particular diagram, we could compare their cognitive effectiveness. The above could be developed into computational systems, as we have already shown that such conceptual blends can be implemented [1–3].

Acknowledgements. The present research was supported by CORPORIS (PID2019-109677RB-I00) funded by Spain's *Agencia Estatal de Investigación*; by DIAGRAFIS (202050E243) funded by CSIC; and by WENET (H2020, grant agreement No. 823783) funded by the European Commission.

References

1. Bourou, D., Schorlemmer, M., Plaza, E.: A cognitively-inspired model for making sense of Hasse diagrams. In: CCIA Proceedings of IOS Press (2021)
2. Bourou, D., Schorlemmer, M., Plaza, E.: Image schemas and conceptual blending in diagrammatic reasoning: the case of Hasse diagrams. In: Basu, A., Stapleton, G., Linker, S., Legg, C., Manalo, E., Viana, P. (eds.) Diagrams 2021. LNCS (LNAI), vol. 12909, pp. 297–314. Springer, Cham (2021). https://doi.org/10.1007/978-3-030-86062-2_31
3. Bourou, D., Schorlemmer, M., Plaza, E.: Modelling the sense-making of diagrams using image schemas. In: CogSci 2021 Proceedings of the UC Merced (2021)
4. Brüggemann, R., Schwaiger, J., Negele, R.: Applying Hasse diagram technique for the evaluation of toxicological fish tests. Chemosphere **30**(9), 1767–1780 (1995)

5. Chapman, P., Stapleton, G., Rodgers, P., Micallef, L., Blake, A.: Visualizing sets: an empirical comparison of diagram types. In: Dwyer, T., Purchase, H., Delaney, A. (eds.) Diagrams 2014. LNCS (LNAI), vol. 8578, pp. 146–160. Springer, Heidelberg (2014). https://doi.org/10.1007/978-3-662-44043-8_18

6. Cheng, P.C.-H., Garcia Garcia, G., Raggi, D., Stockdill, A., Jamnik, M.: Cognitive properties of representations: a framework. In: Basu, A., Stapleton, G., Linker, S., Legg, C., Manalo, E., Viana, P. (eds.) Diagrams 2021. LNCS (LNAI), vol. 12909, pp. 415–430. Springer, Cham (2021). https://doi.org/10.1007/978-3-030-86062-2_43

7. Cheng, P.C.H., Lowe, R.K., Scaife, M.: Cognitive science approaches to understanding diagrammatic representations. In: Blackwell, A.F. (ed.) Thinking with Diagrams, pp. 79–94. Springer, Dordrecht (2001). https://doi.org/10.1007/978-94-017-3524-7_5

8. Demey, L., Smessaert, H.: The relationship between Aristotelian and Hasse diagrams. In: Dwyer, T., Purchase, H., Delaney, A. (eds.) Diagrams 2014. LNCS (LNAI), vol. 8578, pp. 213–227. Springer, Heidelberg (2014). https://doi.org/10.1007/978-3-662-44043-8_23

9. Epp, S.S.: Discrete mathematics with applications. Cengage Learning (2010)

10. Fauconnier, G.: Mental spaces. In: Ten Lectures on Cognitive Construction of Meaning, pp. 1–23. Brill (2018)

11. Fauconnier, G., Turner, M.: The Way We Think. Basic Books, New York (2002)

12. Gärdenfors, P.: Conceptual Spaces: The Geometry of Thought. MIT Press, Cambridge (2004)

13. Johnson, M.: The Body in the Mind. Univ of Chicago Press, Chicago (1987)

14. Körner, C., Albert, D.: Comprehension efficiency of graphically presented ordered sets. In: Current psychological research in Austria. In: Proceedings of the 4th Scientific Conference on Austrian Psychology Social, pp. 179–182. Akademische Druck - u. Verla, Graz (2001)

15. Lakoff, G.: Women, Fire, and Dangerous Things. Univ of Chicago Press, Chicago (1987)

16. Lakoff, G., Johnson, M.: Philosophy in the Flesh, vol. 4. Basic Books, New York (1999)

17. Lakoff, G., Núñez, R.E.: Where Mathematics Comes from: How the Embodied Mind Brings Mathematics into Being. AMC **10**(12), 720–733 (2000)

18. Mandler, J.M.: How to build a baby: II. Conceptual primitives. Psych. Rev. **99**(4), 587 (1992)

19. May, M.: Diagrammatic reasoning and levels of schematization. In: Iconicity. A Fundamental Problem in Semiotics, pp. 175–194. NSU Press (1999)

20. Merleau-Ponty, M.: The structure of behavior. Duquesne Univ Press. (Original published in 1942) (1983)

21. Priss, U.: A semiotic-conceptual analysis of Euler and Hasse diagrams. In: Pietarinen, A.-V., Chapman, P., Bosveld-de Smet, L., Giardino, V., Corter, J., Linker, S. (eds.) Diagrams 2020. LNCS (LNAI), vol. 12169, pp. 515–519. Springer, Cham (2020). https://doi.org/10.1007/978-3-030-54249-8_47

22. Priss, U.: Set visualisations with Euler and Hasse diagrams. In: Cochez, M., Croitoru, M., Marquis, P., Rudolph, S. (eds.) GKR 2020. LNCS (LNAI), vol. 12640, pp. 72–83. Springer, Cham (2021). https://doi.org/10.1007/978-3-030-72308-8_5

23. Purchase, H.: Which aesthetic has the greatest effect on human understanding? In: DiBattista, G. (ed.) GD 1997. LNCS, vol. 1353, pp. 248–261. Springer, Heidelberg (1997). https://doi.org/10.1007/3-540-63938-1_67

24. Sato, Y., Mineshima, K.: The efficacy of diagrams in syllogistic reasoning: a case of linear diagrams. In: Cox, P., Plimmer, B., Rodgers, P. (eds.) Diagrams 2012. LNCS (LNAI), vol. 7352, pp. 352–355. Springer, Heidelberg (2012). https://doi.org/10.1007/978-3-642-31223-6_49

25. Serra Borneto, C.: Liegen and stehen in German: A study in horizontality and verticality. In: Cognitive Linguistics in the Redwoods, pp. 459–506. De Gruyter Mouton (1996)

26. Shimojima, A.: On the Efficacy of Representation. Ph.D. thesis, Indiana Univ (1996)

27. Stapleton, G., Jamnik, M., Shimojima, A.: What makes an effective representation of information: a formal account of observational advantages. J. Logic Lang. Inf. **26**(2), 143–177 (2017)
28. Varela, F.J.: Organism: A meshwork of selfless selves. In: Tauber, A.I. (ed.) Organism and the Origins of Self, vol. 129, pp. 79–107. Springer, Dordrecht (1991). https://doi.org/10.1007/978-94-011-3406-4_5

Evaluating Colour in Concept Diagrams

Sean McGrath[1]([⊠]) [iD], Andrew Blake[2] [iD], Gem Stapleton[3] [iD],
Anestis Touloumis[2] [iD], Peter Chapman[4] [iD], Mateja Jamnik[3] [iD],
and Zohreh Shams[3] [iD]

[1] Goldsmiths, University of London, London, UK
`S.McGrath@gold.ac.uk`
[2] University of Brighton, Brighton, UK
`{a.l.blake,a.touloumis}@brighton.ac.uk`
[3] University of Cambridge, Cambridge, UK
`{ges55,m.jamnik,zs315}@cam.ac.uk`
[4] Edinburgh Napier University, Edinburgh, UK
`p.chapman@napier.ac.uk`

Abstract. This paper is the first to establish the impact of colour on users' ability to interpret the informational content of concept diagrams, a logic designed for ontology engineering. Motivation comes from results for Euler diagrams, which form a fragment of concept diagrams: manipulating curve colours affects user performance. In particular, using distinct curve colours yields significant performance benefits in Euler diagrams. Naturally, one would expect to obtain similar empirical results for concept diagrams, since colour is a graphical feature to which we are perceptually sensitive. Thus, this paper sets out to test this expectation by conducting a crowdsourced empirical study involving 261 participants. Our study suggests that manipulating curve colours no longer yields significant performance differences in this syntactically richer logic. Consequently, when using colour to visually group syntactic elements with common semantic properties, we ask how different do the elements' shapes need to be in order for there to be significant performance benefits arising from using colours?

Keywords: Concept diagrams · Euler diagrams · Perception · Colour

1   Introduction

There is a growing body of evidence that diagrams can help people with logical reasoning, with research primarily focusing on logics with low expressiveness [19,22,23,25]. As particular examples, diagrams have been found to aid some students with deductive reasoning tasks as compared to standard symbolic logic [25], and Euler diagrams have been shown to increase accuracy when performing syllogistic reasoning tasks [23]. In addition, fMRI studies have found, in the context of reasoning, that diagrams provide cognitive offloading and therefore aid cognition, as compared to stylized natural language [22]. Most directly

V. Giardino et al. (Eds.): Diagrams 2022, LNAI 13462, pp. 168–184, 2022.
https://doi.org/10.1007/978-3-031-15146-0_14

related to this paper is work by Alharbi et al. which suggests that concept diagrams[1] support more effective interpretation of information than both OWL (strictly, the Manchester OWL syntax) and description logic [3]. In summary, the prior work covered here compares diagrammatic representations of information with competing notations. The takeaway message is that diagrammatic logics have been shown to effectively support users with tasks, thus giving them an accessibility advantage over their symbolic and textual counterparts. By contrast, this paper sets out to understand the impact of manipulating colour in concept diagrams, in order to increase their efficacy in logical reasoning tasks.

Euler diagrams are the underlying notation of concept diagrams, as well as many other diagrammatic logics [19,22,23,25]. It is known that reducing clutter in Euler diagrams improves cognition [4,27], as does ensuring that they possess so-called *well-formedness properties* [21]. There is no reason to suppose that low clutter and possessing well-formedness properties are not beneficial for concept diagrams. Measures of clutter in concept diagrams were explored in [13]. Empirical research has also focused on the *graphical features* of Euler diagrams. Prior work, such as [6], provides a series of empirically-informed guidelines that point towards effective graphical choices, such as how to use colour, choose curve shapes, and orient diagrams. The guide most relevant to this paper is that for colour: *draw Euler diagrams with curves that have no fill and different colours for each represented set.* An immediate question arises, which we address in this paper: does this guide also apply to concept diagrams?

The study on which this colour-guide, for Euler diagrams, is based was limited to around eight curves. It is estimated that between eight and ten colours can be rapidly distinguished at a time by the human eye [11,20,28]. Whilst the reasons for this are not known [11], it is hypothesized that because humans are only able to store this number of items in their short-term memory [18]. Therefore, since concept diagrams can often include more than ten syntactic elements, varying the hues assigned to them may no longer bring performance advantages. It is important to ascertain whether manipulating colour in concept diagrams can be done in such a way that performance is significantly improved. Appealing to [5], for our study we defined three colour treatments for concept diagrams: (1) monochrome, all diagrammatic elements were black, (2) dichrome, selected diagrammatic elements were blue and the remaining were green (as in [12,14,24]), and (3) polychrome, different colours were assigned to the syntactic elements; none of the curves used a colour fill. Thus, treatment (3) follows the prior guidance and could be expected to outperform (1) and (2), but with the caveat that using more than eight to ten colours may have the potential to be detrimental.

Section 2 summarises concept diagrams. Section 3 describes our study design, with its execution and results covered in Sect. 4. We discuss our results in Sect. 6. The data and materials can be downloaded from [1].

---

[1] Concept diagrams were developed specifically for ontology engineering. Other visual 'ontology' notations include SOVA [15], which is based on node-link diagrams and, thus, is syntactically very different from concept diagrams.

2   A Brief Introduction to Concept Diagrams

Concept diagrams include a variety of syntactic elements in order to convey information [24]. We evaluate a fragment of the notation (we do not need the full expressive power: concept diagrams are a second-order logic). We introduce, by example, the syntax needed for our study. Figure 1 shows two concept diagrams. On the left, the diagram contains one curve inside another to express that (the set of) Korrigans is a subset of Spirits: *all Korrigans are Spirits*. The righthand diagram contains two non-overlapping curves to express that the sets Demon and Elf are disjoint. The boxes are used to indicate the boundaries of each diagram. So, in Fig. 2 there are two juxtaposed diagrams; each individual diagram carries no meaning in this case, and the fact that there are two non-overlapping curves, Mermaid and Giant, does not convey any information since the respective curves are inside distinct rectangles. That is, spatial relationships only convey meaning inside a common bounding box.

In Fig. 3, there are also *two* diagrams. The lefthand *diagram comprises two boxes*, each enclosing some syntax, with an arrow between them. This *solid* arrow, labelled *scares*, is sourced on Boggart and targets an unlabelled curve which is a subset of Midget, asserting that Boggarts scare only Midgets. The righthand diagram is structurally similar but uses a *dashed* arrow labelled by *annoys* annotated with '≥ 1', which is a symbolic device used to convey cardinality information in the following way: Goblins annoy *at least one* thing in the arrow's target set. The arrow's target set is inside Fairy, so we can provide the arrow's meaning in a more succinct way: Goblins annoy at least one Fairy. The use of a dashed arrow does not provide 'only' information as we saw in the case of the solid arrow.

As well as being sourced on curves, arrows can be sourced on the enclosing box. This box is taken to represent the universal set, so we can talk about *everything* or, more simply, *things*. Two examples are given in Fig. 4. On the left, the solid arrow targets a subset of Puck: things chase only Pucks. Essentially, a diagram with this syntactic construction is expressing a *range axiom*: the range of chase is Puck. In the diagram on the right, the arrow's label, *likes*, has an annotation: ⁻. The use of ⁻ is to indicate that we mean the *inverse* of the binary relation *likes*. Thus, the diagram is expressing that things 'like inverse' only Nisses. This is equivalent to *Only Nisses like things* which is a *domain axiom*. Using these basic constructions, more complex diagrams can be formed, like that

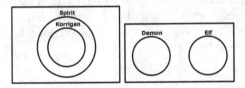

Fig. 1. Subset and disjointness.   **Fig. 2.** Non-disjointness.

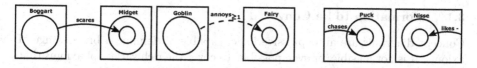

Fig. 3. Diagrams involving arrows.   **Fig. 4.** Range and domain.

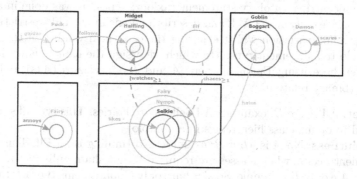

Fig. 5. A more complex diagram which expresses many different statements. (Color figure online)

in Fig. 5 which uses multiple colours for its syntactic elements. It expresses many facts, such as:

- All Halflings are Midgets.   – Elfs chase at least one Fairy.
- No Goblin is a Demon.   – Things guide only Pucks.
- Pucks follow only Halflings.   – Only Demons scare things.

Diagrams with this level of complexity were used to collect performance data.

3   Study Design

We will now describe our between-group study design including: the information conveyed by the diagrams, the colour treatments, participant training, strategies to manage learning effects, performance phase questions, our approach to data collection, and the statistical methods employed. Our study comprised the following phases:

1. Training phase: participants were shown a series of simple diagrams along with their meanings.
2. Learning effect phase: participants were asked two questions, similar to those in the next phase.
3. Performance phase: participants were asked six questions, from which we recorded accuracy and time data.

Each question in the learning effect phase and the performance phase was multiple choice. Before we can describe the three phases, we need to consider the information that was to be conveyed by the performance phase diagrams.

3.1 Information to be Conveyed

Concept diagrams are an expressive logic, capable of defining a broad range of axioms. It is not feasible, or even possible, to cover the rich variety of axioms that one can define using concept diagrams in an empirical study. Given the motivation for developing concept diagrams was to model ontologies, we selected six commonly occurring ontology statement (axiom) types, as was done in a study into the relative efficacy of OWL and description logic in [2]. This restriction provided controlled variation whilst ensuring the ecological validity of the results. The six selected statement types (to which we assign the names shown in bold) are written here using English, where A and B are classes (sets) and p is a property (binary relation)[2]:

1. **Subset:** All A are B; example: All Selkies are Fairies. This type of statement is used to define class hierarchies in an ontology.
2. **Disjointness:** No A is a/an B; example: No Halfling is an Elf. This type of statement occurs when classes are required to not share individuals.
3. **Only:** A p only B; example: Selkies hate only Goblins. This type of statement is used to place a restriction on a property, p: viewing p as a binary relation, if the domain of p is restricted to A, its image must be a subset of B.
4. **Some:** A p at least one B; example: Elves chase at least one Fairy. This type of statement is used to define features of individuals that lie in A.
5. **Domain:** Only A p things; example: Only Demons scare things. This type of statement identifies the domain of a property (binary relation).
6. **Range:** Things p only A; example: Things annoy only Fairies. This type of statement identifies the range of a property.

In what follows, we always write the six types of statements following the conventions illustrated in the examples just given. To generate the eight diagrams needed for the learning effect and performance phases, we needed a systematic approach to selecting the information that they would convey, reflecting the six statement types. Alharbi et al. designed a study to compare sentences expressing these six statement types, focusing on description logic and the Manchester OWL syntax [2]. With permission, we adapted their study materials[3] for our purposes. Their study used eight sets of 14 statements; we used each set of statements to produce a single diagram, one for each question. Each set of statements had ten named sets, eight binary relations, four Subset statements and two of each of the other types of statements; more Subset statements were needed since they were necessary for what we call *indirect* statements to be derived; for an indirect statement, see Sect. 3.3, Fig. 10, where we need to use the information that Ogre

---

[2] We acknowledge the blurring between syntax and semantics here; strictly speaking, A and B are monadic predicates and p is a dyadic predicate.

[3] Whilst [2] reports on OWL and DL, their study also included a third treatment: concept diagrams. None of the diagrams used in our studies were syntactically identical to Alharbi et al.'s diagrams; we adjusted the layouts and represented *Some* statements differently. Our training material was not the same as that provided by Alharbi et al., in part since we followed a crowdsourced approach.

is a subset of Enchanter to deduce that Ogres guide only Nisses. An example of a diagram representing 14 statements can be seen in Fig. 5.

3.2 Colour Treatments

To test whether multiple colour use in concept diagrams brings significant performance benefits over other colour treatments, we identified three different ways of assigning colour. We used colourbrewer [10] to define our colours, ensuring suitability for visualizing qualitative or categorical information rather than sequential or diverging information:

Monochrome: all syntactic elements are coloured the same. We chose to use black, which is often employed when drawing Euler diagrams, see Figs. 1, 2, 3 and 4.

Dichrome: two colours are used for the syntactic elements. We chose to use blue with green arrows, the *de facto* standard for concept diagrams [12,14,24], see Figs. 6,7, 8, 9, 10, 11, 12 and 13.

Polychrome: each set and binary relation takes a unique colour hue, see Fig. 5. Our tasks involved ten sets and eight binary relations, so we needed 18 colours in total. Colourbrewer can only generate sets of up to 12 colours. We generated a set of 10 colours for the named sets and a disjoint set of eight colours for the arrows. Unlabelled curves that were arrow targets took the same colour as their targeting arrow.

3.3 Training Diagrams and Explanations

It was necessary to provide participants with training in the semantics of concept diagrams. We chose to use a sequence of syntactically simple diagrams to explain how the diagrams expressed the six statement types. It should be noted that the training across participant groups differed only due to the nature of the treatment to which they were exposed. For each statement type, we included two training diagrams, which we call a *direct* version and an *indirect* version. The direct version corresponds to information that would naturally be expressed by a single axiom. For example, *All Selkies are Nymphs* and *All Nymphs are Fairies* are expressed by the diagram in Fig. 5 (see the bottom right box). Indirect statements correspond to information that would normally need to be *inferred* from axioms but which is readily visible in a diagram. Using the two statements *All Selkies are Nymphs* and *All Nymphs are Fairies* as a textual example, one can *infer* the *indirect* statement *All Selkies are Fairies*. Referring again to Fig. 5, *All Selkies are Fairies* is naturally expressed by the diagram via circle containment, by virtue of expressing the two statements from which it can be inferred. We now explain the training provided.

Subset Statements. Participants were exposed to two subset training diagrams, with the direct version being shown in Fig. 6. The meaning of the diagram was stated using the convention illustrated in Sect. 3.1, as can be seen in Fig. 6. The indirect subset training diagram can be seen in Fig. 7. In the remaining parts of this subsection, we omit the (simpler) training given for the *direct* statements which adopted a style similar to that illustrated here.

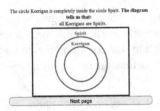

Fig. 6. Training for *direct* Subsets.

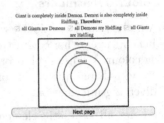

Fig. 7. Training for *indirect* Subsets.

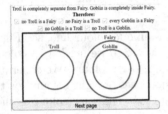

Fig. 8. Training for *indirect* Disjointness.

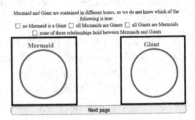

Fig. 9. Training for multiple box use.

Disjointness Statements. Figure 8 shows the indirect disjointness training diagram, which conveys information by the presence of the curves within a *single* box. An important feature of concept diagrams is the use of *multiple* enclosing boxes. This allows a less cluttered representation of classes when they are not known to be disjoint [16]; high levels of clutter leads to less effective diagrams [4, 12]. It was important to train the participants that diagrams exploit distinct boxes in order to avoid expressing a relationship between the represented classes. Figure 9 shows how this was done.

Only Statements. Indirect statements in the case of Only axioms can arise in two ways, depending on the source and the target of the arrow. Referring to Fig. 10, focusing on the arrow source, we see that Ogre is a subset of Enchanter and, since Enchanters guide only Nisses, we can infer that Ogres guide only Nisses. Regarding the target, since Nisses are Demons, we can infer that Enchanters guide only Demons. These indirect statements are perhaps less obvious than those we saw for subset and disjointness statements. In the source case this is, in part, because there is no arrow emanating from Ogre.

Some Statements. Indirect statements in the case of Some axioms can also arise in two ways, depending on the source and the target of the arrow. Focusing on the arrow source in Fig. 11, we see that Ogre is a subset of Giant and, since Giants like at least one Halfling, we can infer that Ogres like at least one Halfling. Regarding the target, since all Halflings are Mermaids, we can infer that Giants like at least one Mermaid. These indirect statements are, as in the case of Only statements, perhaps less obvious than those we saw in the case of subset and disjointness.

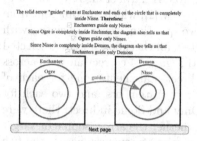 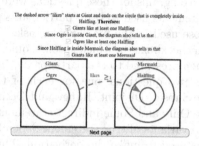

Fig. 10. Training for *indirect* Only.   **Fig. 11.** Training for *indirect* Some.

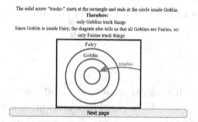 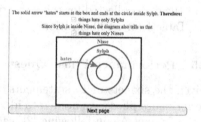

Fig. 12. Training for *indirect* Domain.   **Fig. 13.** Training for *indirect* Range.

Domain Statements. Indirect statements in the case of Domain axioms can only arise in one way, from the target of the arrow. We do not get any indirect Domain statements arising from the source, since Domain axioms are always defined over the universal set which is represented by the enclosing box. In Fig. 12, Goblin is a subset of Fairy and, since only Goblins track things, we can infer that only Fairies track things; that is, if the domain of tracks is Goblin and all Goblins are Fairies then the domain can also be viewed as Fairy.

Range Statements. Indirect statements in the case of Range axioms can also only arise in one way, depending on the target of the arrow. We do not get any indirect Range statements arising from the source, since Range axioms are always defined over the universal set via arrows sourced on the enclosing box. In Fig. 13, Sylph is a subset of Nisse and, since things hate only Sylphs, we can infer that things hate only Nisses. That is, if the range of tracks is Sylph and all Sylphs are Nisses then the range can also be viewed as Nisse.

3.4   Learning Effect Questions

Recall, from Sect. 3.1, each of the six main phase tasks was derived from a set of 14 statements. This meant that the diagrams used in the performance phase were syntactically more complex and more expressive than the relatively simple training diagrams (for example, contrast Figs. 1 and 5). Therefore, two questions were included to reduce the impact of any learning effect that may be present. The diagrams for these questions were derived from Alharbi et al.'s two sets of 14 statements used to train participants in their study [2], which are different from those used in the main phase tasks. These two questions were associated with ten checkboxes of which *seven* should be selected; all checkboxes were deselected when presented to the participants. In total, this gave 14 correct answers across the two questions, one for each of the six direct statements, one for each of the Subset, Disjoint, Range and Domain indirect statements, and two each for the Only and Some indirect statements; for Only and Some indirect, there were two variants of true statement depending on whether the arrow source or target was used to make the derivation. This left six false statements, across the two questions, one for each of the six statement types. This ensured that participants had been exposed to each type of checkbox (direct, indirect and false) for each statement type before performance data was gathered and the two ways in which Only and Some indirect statements could arise. The participants were unaware that the data collected for these two questions would not be used in the analysis. See Table 1 for an illustration.

3.5   Performance Phase Questions

Given the six sets of 14 statements, from which diagrams were derived for the performance phase, we needed to identify suitable sets of checkbox responses for each of them. Again following [2], each type of textual statement occurred as a correct answer six times. This meant we needed 36 statements which appeared as correct answers. For each type of textual statement, we included three *direct*

Table 1. Nine options, six of which are correct.

Option	Checkbox type	Checkmark
Elves chase at least one Fairy	Some – direct	✓
All Selkies are Fairies	Subset – indirect	✓
Things guide only Elves	Range - false	
Selkies hate only Goblins	Only – indirect	✓
All Boggarts are Midgets	Subset – false	
No Halfling is an Elf	Disjoint – indirect	✓
Only Demons scare things	Domain – direct	✓
Pucks follow only Goblins	Only – false	
Things annoy only Fairies	Range – direct	✓

versions of the task and three *indirect* versions. As we are also interested in ensuring that people do not read incorrect information from diagrams, we also included each type of statement as an incorrect answer three times. This gave a total of 54 checkboxes, which were distributed across the six tasks. Thus, each task was associated with nine checkboxes; six of the statements were correct and three were incorrect. Table 1 presents an example of nine statements, their type and the required checkmark (or not). Thus, Table 1 illustrates a correct response to a task. The nine statements were each predicated with an unchecked checkbox when initially presented to a parfticipant.

3.6   Data Collection Method

We adopted a between-groups design. Participants were randomly assigned to a group and were paid £3.25 for their participation. Prolific Academic was used to crowdsource participants from the general population. It is recognised that in crowdsourced studies, participants do not always give questions their full attention, or have difficulties with the language used, and this is hard to control [8]. Varying techniques can be employed for avoiding the recruitment of participants who may have issues with the language or do not give questions their full attention. We chose to limit the participant pool to those who are fluent in English, as well as including other pre-screening criteria covered in Sect. 4. We also included two questions, designed to catch *inattentive* participants, that were trivial to answer if the associated text was read. Answering either of these two questions incorrectly meant that the participant was classified as inattentive. The first of these questions was included in the training phase and the second one was in the performance phase. The inattentive participants were unable to proceed with the study as soon as they answered one of these two questions incorrectly and any data collected up to that point was not retained.

In each phase of the study, each diagram and its associated question was displayed on a unique page. Participants could not return to pages and subsequent pages were not revealed until the 'Next page' button was clicked. The training pages were presented in a fixed order for each participant and, as just indicated, included one of the inattentive questions. The order was: Subset, Subset-indirect, Disjoint, Disjoint-indirect, Disjoint-multiple boxes, Only, Only-indirect, *inattentive question*, Some, Some-indirect, Domain, Domain-indirect, Range, Range-indirect. It was felt that this order began training people using simpler concepts since there were no arrows in the first five diagrams. Once the participant clicked the next button, they were asked to answer the two questions included to reduce learning effect. After that, the next two questions were randomly selected from the six performance phase questions, followed by the second inattentive question, and then the remaining four performance phase questions in a random order.

3.7   Statistical Analysis Method

We view accuracy as more important than time: one representation of information is judged to be more effective than another if users can perform tasks significantly more accurately with it. If no significant accuracy difference exists and performance is significantly quicker then the quicker notation is judged to be more effective. For the analysis, we employed two local odds ratios generalized equation models [26] to analyse the *accuracy* data. For the *time* data, we used a generalized estimation model [17] that allowed us to estimate whether the time taken to provide answers was significantly different. Alternative models such as ANOVA were not deemed appropriate as our data violated their assumptions.

Table 2. Summary of the pilot data.

Group	No. of partici-pants	Accuracy rate	Mean time
Overall	30	81.17%	2 m 52.98 s
M	10	85.37%	3 m 11.10 s
D	10	80.37%	2 m 46.66 s
P	10	77.78%	2 m 38.18 s

Table 3. Main study performance data.

Group	No. of partici-pants	Accuracy rate	Mean time
Overall	261	80.11%	2 m 48.17 s
M	81	77.98%	2 m 52.81 s
D	89	80.96%	2 m 54.74 s
P	91	81.16%	2 m 37.60 s

4 Study Execution and Statistical Analysis

Here we describe our pilot study before presenting the statistical analysis yielding an overall comparison between treatment types and a comparison by task type.

4.1 Pilot Study

When running a pilot study, we pre-screened participants. Pre-screening criteria included having a Prolific approval rate of 95% or higher, the requirement to have completed at least 5 studies on Prolific previously, being fluent in English, and being aged between 18 and 100 (this was imposed by Prolific). This left a pool of 27561 potential participants, out of 63577, so over half were disqualified. Further, we indicated that the study would be supported on desktop and tablet devices, but not mobile devices; Prolific does not guarantee that this means participants will refrain from using a mobile device. A total of 39 participants began the pilot study. Of these, two were classified as inattentive, three timed-out after 50 min, a further three withdrew before completion, and one did not have their data saved due to a read/write error. This left us with data from 30 participants.

The overall accuracy rate and the average time to answer each performance phase question during the pilot study are given in Table 2, accompanied by a breakdown for each group. The pilot data do not indicate a ceiling or floor effect, which would have suggested that the tasks were either too easy or too hard to reveal significant differences. That is, the pilot data suggest that the tasks require some cognitive effort to perform but are not so difficult that the participants are essentially guessing the answers.

We noted a very high error rate for *Disjoint-false* checkboxes: overall, the *Disjoint-false* accuracy rate was 27.78%, with the Monochrome and Polychrome groups both scoring 23.33% and the Dichrome group getting 36.67% correct. Ticking a *Disjoint-false* checkbox would suggest that the participant believed two sets are disjoint when in fact they are not. This could be due to misunderstanding the information provided by multiple rectangle use, so we added further text to the associated training page: "In particular, because Mermaid and Giant are in different rectangles, the diagram **does not tell** us that no Mermaid is a Giant and **does not tell us** that no Giant is a Mermaid." We also observed that the accuracy rates were low overall for *Domain* (50.00%) and *Domain-indirect* questions (37.78%) but we suspected that this was due to the difficulty of understanding the use of inverse. As such no change was made to the study based on this observation.

4.2   Main Study

For the main study, we included an additional pre-screening criterion: no participant who took part in the pilot could take part in the main study. Three participants self-reported as colourblind, one in each group[4]. The statistical analysis is performed on the entire data set; we did not perform a subsequent analysis with the colourblind participants removed. The accuracy rates and mean times are summarised in Table 3. The overall accuracy rate, 80.11%, can be considered high as participants were unlikely to be familiar with concept diagrams prior to taking part. Whilst the accuracy rates and mean times can be seen as an *indicator* of relative performance across groups, it is important to note that the statistical methods employed do not compare these data: the statistical methods that compare means (e.g. ANOVA), do not account for correlated responses from participants and make other assumptions that our data violate.

Learning Effect Questions. We evaluated whether the learning effect questions yielded significantly lower accuracy performance than the six performance phase questions. Based on a Wald test, the learning effect questions had statistically significant lower overall accuracy rate than the performance phase questions (0.8011 vs. 0.7571 with p-value < 0.001). This suggests that participants did improve their accuracy performance during these first two questions. This does not, however, mean that the learning effect was eliminated but suggests that it was reduced by the inclusion of these two questions. It is not appropriate to compare the times taken for the learning effect questions with the performance phase questions due to their differing number of checkboxes (ten versus nine).

---

[4] The impact of the three colourblind participants on the data collected was not significant.

Statistical Analysis: Overall Comparison. Here we report on the overall comparison between the three colour treatment groups. Using a Generalised Estimating Equations (GEE) based [26] statistical model for the accuracy data, we estimated a 95% confidence interval (CI) for the odds of providing a correct answer with one treatment compared to another. Recall that a correct answer means either correctly ticking a checkbox (where the associated statement is true) or correctly not ticking a checkbox (where the associated statement is false). We computed p-values to determine whether the treatments gave rise to significantly different accuracy performance. The estimated odds of correctly answering questions with Dichrome was 1.20 (to 2d.p.) times that of Monochrome with a 95% CI of (0.94,1.53) and p-value of 0.1363 (to 4d.p.). Therefore, there was no significant difference in accuracy performance between Dichrome and Monochrome. Results for the other pairwise comparisons are given in Table 4: there were no significant differences overall in accuracy across treatments.

Using a GEE based statistical model for the time data, we estimated a 95% CI for the ratio of the time (measured in seconds) needed to complete a task with one treatment compared to another. The derived CI and its corresponding p-value allowed us to determine whether two treatments were significantly different. The model estimated that the time needed to complete a task with Dichrome was 1.11 times (2d.p.) that with Monochrome with a 95% CI of $(0.89, 1.37)$ and p-value of 0.3553. Therefore, there is no significant difference in time performance between Dichrome and Monochrome. Results for the other pairwise comparisons are given in Table 5. The analysis revealed no significant differences overall in time taken across the three treatments. Therefore, our accuracy and time

Table 4. Overall comparison: accuracy.

Treatments	Odds	CI	p-value
D versus M	1.20	(0.94, 1.53)	0.1363
D versus P	0.99	(0.78, 1.24)	0.9145
M versus P	0.82	(0.64, 1.05)	0.1174

Table 5. Overall comparison: time.

Treatments	Ratio	CI	p-value
D versus M	1.11	(0.89, 1.37)	0.3553
D versus P	1.12	(0.92, 1.36)	0.2606
M versus P	1.01	(0.82, 1.24)	0.9179

Table 6. Comparison of treatments by accuracy by statement type.

Treatments	Odds	CI	p-value	Most accurate
Only – direct				
Dichrome versus Polychrome	0.58	(0.33, 0.99)	0.0474	Polychrome
Only – indirect				
Dichrome versus Polychrome	0.57	(0.33, 0.98)	0.0436	Polychrome
Some – false				
Monochrome versus Dichrome	2.15	(1.05, 4.41)	0.0364	Monochrome
Monochrome versus Polychrome	2.09	(1.04, 4.22)	0.0391	Monochrome

analysis consistently indicate that there is no *overall difference* in the three colour treatments: *the overall ranking is Monochrome = Dichrome = Polychrome.*

Statistical Analysis: Comparison by Checkbox Type. When seeking to establish whether significant performance differences exist for each of the three variants (direct, indirect, false) of each of the six statement types, we can only consider the accuracy data as it was not meaningful to collect time date for individual checkboxes. As with the overall analysis, we produced a GEE based statistical model. Results for the pairwise comparisons where significant differences were observed are given in Table 6. We can see from the significant results that in two cases Dichrome is significantly less accurate than Polychrome. In the two other cases, Monochrome is significantly more accurate than both Dichrome and Polychrome.

5   Discussion

We observed that for *Only* and *Only-indirect* statements, Polychrome outperformed Dichrome. In these cases, the correct response would have been to select the associated checkbox. These results indicate that Dichrome did not facilitate the extraction of the respective information as well as Polychrome. Surprisingly, however, we also observed that using black curves and arrows was significantly more effective in the case of *Some-false* tasks; these are tasks where the response is incorrect if the associated checkbox is ticked. These results indicate that the Dichrome and Polychrome treatments, which were statistically indistinguishable from each other, did not facilitate the extraction of the respective information as well as Monochrome. Of course, it would be remiss not to remark on the fact that we only had four significant results out of the 60 statistical tests conducted. One would expect to obtain three type-I errors when conducting this number of tests, at the 5% level. Thus, we cannot say with any confidence that any of the treatments significantly differ.

It is particularly surprisingly that we obtained notable evidence that the choice of colour treatment made no difference for those tasks with checkboxes whose associated statements only involved sets (i.e. Subset or Disjoint statements). Here, we expected the polychrome treatment to yield superior task performance because only the information conveyed by the underlying Euler diagrams was necessary for the task. However our observations suggest that, for diagrams with a high level of complexity, the effectiveness of multiple colours for the curves in the underlying Euler diagram is indeed diminished; the Polychrome treatment required 18 colours. Perceptual theory suggests that up to eight to ten colours can be rapidly distinguished by the human eye, after which the perceptual distinction between these colours diminishes [11]. Therefore, we posit that a reduction in the ability to easily distinguish between 10 or more colours has compromised the efficacy that we otherwise anticipated using the Polychrome treatment. Moreover, efficacy is compromised to such an extent that there was no benefit of using multiple colours, compared to Monochrome, and sometimes performance was actually inferior (noting the caveat concerning type-I errors).

In the case of Monochrome, graphical shape is the only differentiator between syntactic elements that represents sets (circles) and those which represents binary relations (arrows). Similarity theory [9] indicates that using different syntactic devices for semantically different entities is sensible: using syntactically similar entities leads to increased search times when seeking to find a particular piece of 'target' syntax. Thus, in the Monochrome case, shape is the only graphical property that may aid a visual search through the diagram when seeking to establish the truth of a given statement. Now, colour can also be used to group syntactic devices that have some semantic commonality, as seen in Dichrome treatment: colours are assigned to syntactic items that represent semantically different types of things: blue curves represent sets and green arrows represent binary relations. In this sense, colour is being used to reinforce the semantic differentiation of syntactic devices via shapes when performing visual search. Thus, we see that using two colours or two shapes has the potential to aid information extraction, with the Dichrome treatment exploiting both and the monochrome treatment exploiting only shape. It is known that colour is a more salient graphical property than form [7], indicating that the use of two colours may be more beneficial than just the use of different shapes. However, our study suggests that using two shapes and two colours (Dichrome) is *not more effective* than using two shapes and just black (Monochrome). We posit that circles and arrows have *sufficiently different visual characteristics* meaning that the additional graphical element of colour does not bring about performance benefits.

6   Conclusion

Based on prior research into Euler diagrams [5], there was evidence to suggest that manipulating colour in concept diagrams had the potential to impact user task performance. However, the case was not clear-cut: concept diagrams express more complex statements than Euler diagrams, exploiting a more diverse set of graphical symbols with which to make statements. Indeed, being designed for use in ontology engineering, the kinds of statements that concept diagrams express can require *each diagram* to include many syntactic elements, as in Fig. 5. These facts suggested that further empirical insight was required in order to understand the role that colour plays in the effective interpretation of concept diagrams. Our study suggests that colour is no longer a useful visual variable to manipulate when seeking to improve user task performance, at least for the kinds of tasks we have evaluated. The take-away message from our study is that, whilst colour is a useful graphical property to manipulate for Euler diagrams, the benefits may be lost in the case of concept diagrams.

The discussion in Sect. 5 alludes to the fact that one reason using two colours may not yield performance benefits – when used consistently with graphical shape to segregate syntactic elements that have differing semantic properties – is that circles and arrows have distinctly different shapes. Thus, our research raises an important question: *when using colour to visually group syntactic elements that have a common semantic property, how different do the elements' shapes need to be in order for there to be performance benefits arising from using colours?* This question is not relevant for just concept diagrams, but all diagrammatic notations that employ a range of graphical shapes to convey information. Finally, we note a further avenue for research is to explore the role of interaction in facilitating information extraction from concept diagrams.

Acknowledgements. This research was partially funded by a Leverhulme Trust Research Project Grant (RPG- 2016–082) for the project entitled Accessible Reasoning with Diagrams. Thanks to Eisa Alharbi for supplying experimental materials, associated with [2], on which some of our materials were based.

References

1. Data: https://research.gold.ac.uk/id/eprint/31899/1/dataSetTidy_forWeb.xlsx, Materials: https://research.gold.ac.uk/id/eprint/31899/
2. Alharbi, E., Howse, J., Stapleton, G., Hamie, A., Touloumis, A.: The efficacy of OWL and DL on user understanding of axioms and their entailments. In: d'Amato, C., et al. (eds.) ISWC 2017. LNCS, vol. 10587, pp. 20–36. Springer, Cham (2017). https://doi.org/10.1007/978-3-319-68288-4_2
3. Alharbi, E., Howse, J., Stapleton, G., Hamie, A., Touloumis, A.: Visual logics help people: an evaluation of diagrammatic, textual and symbolic notations. In: Visual Languages and Human-Centric Computing, pp. 255–259. IEEE (2017)
4. Alqadah, M., Stapleton, G., Howse, J., Chapman, P.: Evaluating the impact of clutter in Euler diagrams. In: Dwyer, T., Purchase, H., Delaney, A. (eds.) Diagrams 2014. LNCS (LNAI), vol. 8578, pp. 108–122. Springer, Heidelberg (2014). https://doi.org/10.1007/978-3-662-44043-8_15
5. Blake, A., Stapleton, G., Rodgers, P., Howse, J.: How should we use colour in Euler diagrams. In: Visual Information Communication and Interaction. ACM (2014)
6. Blake, A., Stapleton, G., Rodgers, P., Howse, J.: The impact of topological and graphical choices on the perception of Euler diagrams. Inf. Sci. **330**, 455–482 (2016)
7. Callaghan, C.: Interference and dominance in texture segregation: hue, geometric form, and line orientation. Percept. Psychophys. **46**, 299–311 (1989). https://doi.org/10.3758/BF03204984
8. Chen, J., Menezes, N., Bradley, A., North, T.: Opportunities for crowdsourcing research on Amazon Mechanical Turk. Hum. Fact. **5**(3), 1 (2011)
9. Duncan, J., Humphreys, G.: Visual search and stimulus similarity. Psychol. Rev. **96**(3), 433 (1989)
10. Harrower, M., Brewer, C.: ColorBrewer.org: an online tool for selecting colour schemes for maps. Cartographic J. **40**(1), 27–37 (2003)
11. Healey, C.: Choosing effective colours for data visualization. In: 7th Conference on Visualization, pp. 263-ff. IEEE (1996)
12. Hou, T., Chapman, P., Blake, A.: Antipattern comprehension: an empirical evaluation. In: Formal Ontology in Information Systems, pp. 211–224 (2016)
13. Hou, T., Chapman, P., Oliver, I.: Measuring perceived clutter in concept diagrams. In: IEEE Visual Languages and Human-Centric Computing, pp. 31–39 (2016)

14. Howse, J., Stapleton, G., Taylor, K., Chapman, P.: Visualizing ontologies: a case study. In: Aroyo, L., et al. (eds.) ISWC 2011. LNCS, vol. 7031, pp. 257–272. Springer, Heidelberg (2011). https://doi.org/10.1007/978-3-642-25073-6_17

15. Itzik, N., Reinhartz-Berger, I.: Sova - a tool for semantic and ontological variability analysis. In: CAiSE 2014 Forum, Advanced Information Systems Engineering, pp. 177–184. CEUR (2014)

16. John, C., Fish, A., Howse, J., Taylor, J.: Exploring the notion of 'Clutter' in Euler diagrams. In: Barker-Plummer, D., Cox, R., Swoboda, N. (eds.) Diagrams 2006. LNCS (LNAI), vol. 4045, pp. 267–282. Springer, Heidelberg (2006). https://doi.org/10.1007/11783183_36

17. Liang, K.Y., Zeger, S.L.: Longitudinal data analysis using generalized linear models. Biometrika **73**, 13–22 (1986)

18. Matsin, L.: Short-term (working) memory. http://www.human-memory.net/types_short.html (2010)

19. Mineshima, K., Sato, Y., Takemura, R., Okada, M.: How diagrams can support syllogistic reasoning: an empirical study. J. Visual Lang. Comput. **25**, 159–169 (2014)

20. Moody, D.: The "physics" of notations: toward a scientific basis for constructing visual notations in software engineering. IEEE Trans. Software Eng. **35**(6), 756–779 (2009)

21. Rodgers, P., Zhang, L., Purchase, H.: Wellformedness properties in Euler diagrams: which should be used? IEEE Trans. Vis. Comput. Graphics **18**(7), 1089–1100 (2012)

22. Sato, Y., Masuda, S., Someya, Y., Tsujii, T., Watanabe, S.: An fMRI analysis of the efficacy of Euler diagrams in logical reasoning. In: Visual Languages and Human-Centric Computing, pp. 143–151. IEEE (2015)

23. Sato, Y., Mineshima, K.: How diagrams can support syllogistic reasoning: an empirical study. J Logic, Lang. Inf. **24**, 409–456 (2015)

24. Stapleton, G., Howse, J., Chapman, P., Delaney, A., Burton, J., Oliver, I.: Formalizing concept diagrams. In: International Conference on Distributed Multimedia Systems, pp. 182–187. KSI (2013)

25. Stenning, K., Cox, R., Oberlander, J.: Contrasting the cognitive effects of graphical and sentential logic teaching: Reasoning, representation and individual differences. Lang. Cognit. Process. **10**, 333–354 (1995)

26. Touloumis, A., Agresti, A., Kateri, M.: Generalized estimating equations for multinomial responses using a local odds ratios parameterization. Biometrics **69**(3), 633–640 (2013)

27. Treinish, L., Rogowitz, B.E.: Why should engineers and scientists be worried about color? IBM, 46, 2009 **69**(3), 633–640 (2013)

28. Ware, C.: Information Visualization: Perception for Design, chap. 6.1: Gestalt Laws, pp. 189–205, 2nd edn.. Morgan Kaufmann Pub. Inc. (2004)

Tables as Powerful Representational Tools

Dirk Schlimm[(✉)] [iD]

McGill University, Montreal, QC H3A 2T7, Canada
`dirk.schlimm@mcgill.ca`

Abstract. Tables are widely used for storing, retrieving, communicating, and processing information, but in the literature on the study of representations they are still somewhat neglected. The strong structural constraints on tables allow for a clear identification of their characteristic features and the roles these play in the use of tables as representational and cognitive tools. After introducing syntactic, spatial, and semantic features of tables, we give an account of how these affect our perception and cognition on the basis of fundamental principles of Gestalt psychology. Next are discussed the ways in which these features of tables support their uses in providing a global access to information, retrieving information, and visualizing relational structure and patterns. The latter is particularly important, because it shows how tables can contribute to the generation of new knowledge. In addition, tables also provide efficient means for manipulating information in general and in structured notations. In sum, tables are powerful and efficient representational tools.

Keywords: Tables · Diagrams · Cognition · Gestalt psychology

1 Introduction

In the wake of the groundbreaking analysis of the use of diagrams by Larkin and Simon [15], the computational efficacy of a representational system for solving particular tasks has become an important criterion for the assessment of such systems. According to Giardino, this raises the question of how this efficacy 'happens to emerge from the interaction between more spontaneous abilities and the production of cultural artifacts' [6, p. 81]. While by far the most work in this area has been done on diagrams, understood more generally, in the present paper a somewhat neglected kind of representation is discussed, namely *tables*. As we shall see below, tables are fairly constrained representations, which explains perhaps why they have not received much attention to so far. If they are mentioned at all, tables are mainly discussed together with other kinds of representations, — e. g., in [7] they are considered together with graphs and illustrations, in [11] and [21] as instances of a much broader category of diagrams, — so that their specific features have often been glossed over. A noteworthy exception are the analyses of relational tables by Shimojima and his colleagues [19,20,26].

The main questions addressed in this paper are: what are the specific features of tables and how do these contribute to the particular uses of tables?

V. Giardino et al. (Eds.): Diagrams 2022, LNAI 13462, pp. 185–201, 2022.
https://doi.org/10.1007/978-3-031-15146-0_15

The structural constraints of tables allow for an explicit identification of their syntactic, spatial, and semantic features and, in turn, of the roles these play in the use of tables as representational and cognitive tools.

In the discussion we attempt to navigate between the Scylla of studying very specific kinds of systems and tasks, which can lead to concrete insights, but raises the question of their generalizability, and the Charybdis of trying to cover a wide range of different systems and thereby running the risk of leading to a high-level analysis that has only little to say about specific cases. In the following, we begin by giving an overview of what we consider tables to be, of their main syntactic, spatial, and semantic features and of the effects of these features on perception and cognition (Sect. 2). We then turn to studying the relation of these features to the, so to speak, *passive* uses of tables: for the general presentation of information, information retrieval, and the visualization of relational structure and patterns (Sects. 3–5). The latter is particularly important, because it shows how tables can contribute to the detection of new patterns and generation of new knowledge. In Sects. 6–8, *active* interactions with tables are discussed, namely operations on tables, tabular manipulations of structured notations, and operations on infinite tables. Together, these discussions aim to shed some light on the power of tables as representational tools and on how this comes about.

2   Tables and Their Features

Definition. Tables are defined here in terms of syntactic, spatial, and semantic features. First, a *table* is a two-dimensional arrangement of $n \times k$ items, so that the position of each cell of the table can be uniquely indexed by a pair $\langle x, y \rangle$ of positive integers, with $x \leq n$ and $y \leq k$. Second, tables are presented spatially as horizontal *rows* and vertical *columns*. Third, it is a characteristic feature of a table that its rows and columns exhibit some *semantic unity*, i.e., that each row and column can be understood as forming a meaningful entity.[1] An arrangement of cells into rows and columns that lacks this kind of semantic unity is an *array* or a *grid* [8]. Examples of particular representations that make use of columns (or rows), but lack the semantic unity of their rows (or columns, respectively), or that are simply grids are abaci, bar charts, and cellular automata.

Syntactic and Spatial Features of Tables. According to the definition given above, a table is an array of cells, such that some of them are adjacent (*neighbors*); the individual indices of neighboring cells differ only by 1. Figure 1 contains an example of a table showing the indices of each cell (on the left) and the relative indices of the neighbors of the cell $\langle x, y \rangle$.[2] Due to the spatial structure of a table, the cells are typically presented in a rectangle and we can easily determine the rows and columns, as well as various diagonals: cells, whose indices that have the same x-coordinate form a row, those with the same y-coordinate a column.

---

[1] Such collections of multiple components of a diagram that 'form a unit with semantic significance' are called 'global objects' in [26, p. 261].

[2] The corner of the table in which cell $\langle 1, 1 \rangle$ is positioned is arbitrary.

$$\begin{array}{cccc}
\langle 1,1\rangle & \langle 1,2\rangle & \ldots & \langle 1,k\rangle \\
\langle 2,1\rangle & \langle 2,2\rangle & \ldots & \langle 2,k\rangle \\
\vdots & \vdots & \ddots & \vdots \\
\langle n,1\rangle & \langle n,2\rangle & \ldots & \langle n,k\rangle
\end{array}$$

$$\begin{array}{ccc}
\langle x-1,y-1\rangle & \langle x-1,y\rangle & \langle x-1,y+1\rangle \\
\nwarrow & \uparrow & \nearrow \\
\langle x,y-1\rangle \leftarrow & \langle x,y\rangle \rightarrow & \langle x,y+1\rangle \\
\swarrow & \downarrow & \searrow \\
\langle x+1,y-1\rangle & \langle x+1,y\rangle & \langle x+1,y+1\rangle
\end{array}$$

Fig. 1. Indices of an $n \times k$ table (on the left) and indices of neighboring cells.

Two cells that differ by 1 in both of their coordinates are diagonal. It is a crucial aspect of tables that their syntactic features are directly related to their spatial features, which will be relevant in our discussion in Sect. 2.

In many cases, the presentation of a table is augmented by *labels* for the rows and columns, which can be used either to denote the rows and columns, or to convey information about the type of their content. Particular presentations of tables frequently also make use of horizontal or vertical lines, coloring or shading of alternate rows or columns, and different spacing between rows and columns to emphasize the semantic unity of the entries and to guide the reading of the table [28, p. 81–95].

Semantic Features of Tables. We can also distinguish certain types of tables on the basis of the content of their cells: in a *homogeneous* table all cells are of the same type (e.g., numbers); in a *relational* table all cells can take only two values, such as empty/nonempty, 0/1, or true/false. Such tables are also called 'feature tables' and are discussed in [19]. More important for their practical use, however, is the *ordering* of the data in some of the rows or columns. Accordingly, Wainer's first rule for the preparation of useful tables is: 'Order the rows and columns in a way that makes sense' [31]. Indeed, hardly any tables we come across do not exhibit some kind of ordering of their rows or columns: ledgers are ordered by date, timetables by time, directories by last name, duty rosters by time and name, inventory lists by item codes, etc. This is a semantic feature, because it does not depend on the spatial arrangement of the cells, but on their content. The ordering (or *sorting*) of a table implies a certain direction of reading ('directedness' is one of the basic aspects of the 'grammar' of diagrams in [11, p. 71–73]), which in turn has the effect that a particular cell is identified as the *origin*, which is typically where one would start reading the entries. As the example of a Japanese train schedule reproduced in [28, p. 47] shows, the origin does not have to be in one of the corners of the table. The rows and columns, together with the origin and directions of reading constitute what Tufte calls the 'viewing architecture' of a table [29, p. 159].

Effects on Perception and Cognition. Since tables are often perceived as a whole, Gestalt psychology provides us with a useful framework for their study. In particular, we will appeal to the Gestalt principles of similarity, proximity, good continuation, and symmetry [5,17]. The spatial arrangement of a table immediately makes us perceive the rows and columns as individual entities. For example, if the columns have entries of different types, e. g., text, dates, numbers, then we tend to perceive these entries as belonging together (i. e., as forming a column), due to the Gestalt principle of *similarity*. By the same principle, coloring can be used so that we perceive the items as belonging together and thereby forming a unit. In addition, we can also employ judicious spacing: if the rows are closer together than the columns, then, according to the Gestalt principle of *proximity*, we perceive the items above each other as being connected, i. e., the columns stand out, and vice versa. This phenomenon is illustrated by the following arrangements:

$$
\begin{array}{ccccc}
\circ & \circ & \circ & \circ & \circ \\
\circ & \circ & \circ & \circ & \circ \\
\circ & \circ & \circ & \circ & \circ
\end{array}
\qquad
\begin{array}{c}
\circ\circ\circ\circ\circ \\
\circ\circ\circ\circ\circ \\
\circ\circ\circ\circ\circ
\end{array}
$$

Not only does the presentation of cell items guide our perception towards the rows and columns, but it also suggests certain axes for reading and moving through the table. That the ordering of entries suggests a particular starting cell (origin) and a direction for reading was already mentioned above. The proximity of neighboring cells similarly suggests a movement in horizontal, vertical, and diagonal directions (indicated by the arrows in Fig. 1, right), and the Gestalt principle of *good continuation* or *continuity of direction*, then, continues to guide our perception along that line.

Materiality. Timetables, which are often adduced as prototypical examples of tables are static, printed on paper or displayed on a computer screen. This limits our possible interactions with them to a mainly passive use of retrieving information. Nevertheless, the particular form and kind of material makes a difference even in this case, e. g., when the table extends over many pages. Moreover, we can also produce tables ourselves, e. g., ledgers, which allows us to further extend and manipulate them. Spreadsheet software allows even further possibilities, such as including formulas that refer to the values of other cells and sorting the entire table according to the entries of a specific row or column.

3   Access to Global Information

After the introduction of the main features of tables, we shall now address how these features contribute to the use of tables as cognitive tools. We begin with the access to global information, before turning to different algorithms for accessing particular cells (Sect. 4) and the visualization of relational patterns (Sect. 5).

Early examples of the arrangement of data into tables are *ledgers*, e. g., to record the sales in a store [8, p. 125–146].[3] Historically, such ledgers often consisted of sheets that could be spread on a table (their modern cousins, called 'spreadsheets', are discussed below, in Sect. 6). In a typical ledger, each row represents an individual sale, recording the date, item, buyer, and price. In addition to simply recording the information, the tabular arrangement offers some very specific ways of assessing it:

---

[3] See [1] for many examples of the use of tables in the history of mathematics.

(1) It affords a quick *overview* of the data,

e. g., regarding the total number of sales, the distribution of customers and prices. Such an overview also allows for

(2) the identification of *singularities*,

such as particularly large numbers in a place-value system, or empty cells in an otherwise filled table; they stand out, because they violate the Gestalt principle of *similarity* and are therefore immediately perceived. Thus, in practical terms,

(3) such an arrangement makes it easier to *detect missing data*

(as the corresponding cells are empty) than a linear presentation. Moreover,

(4) it provides for means to check for the *correctness* of the data,

e. g., dates must have a fixed form; cells in a number-column cannot contain letters; numerical values within a column are typically allowed only within a certain range; if a column is sorted, violations of the order can be detected. Note, that these checks can be performed purely syntactically, i. e., without knowledge of the specific meanings of the entries.

4   Information Retrieval

In discussions about the advantages of tabular representations, it is frequently claimed, on the basis of an appeal to the reader's intuition, that they make it easier to locate information (see, e. g., [6, p. 80]). Consider the example of a timetable, such as the following departure times at a bus station:

8:00	8:20	8:40
9:00	9:30	
10:00	10:20	10:40

Clearly, this information could be represented linearly, but with a tabular representation it is easy to find the next departure time by first finding the appropriate row on the basis of the entries in the left-most column and then going through the columns. Thus, in addition to the quick overview of the data that is provided by a table, we have identified another important advantage of tables, namely the

(5) quick *access* to specific cells.

This property underlies the long-lasting use of tables to represent astronomical data in science and logarithmic tables, as well as addition and multiplication tables in mathematics.

Before moving on, we should pause for a moment and reflect once more on the previous claim. After all, *binary search* is in general the best algorithm for searching for an entry in an ordered list, so let us briefly look at how the representation of the data interacts with the complexity of search algorithms and whether tables really offer an advantage over linear representations.

To find an element in a sorted list consisting of $n \cdot k$ elements using binary search takes $\log_2(n \cdot k)$ steps in the worst case. Now, if these elements are arranged in a $n \times k$ table, applying a binary search to the rows takes $\log_2 n$ steps and applying it again to the columns in that row takes another $\log_2 k$ steps, resulting in a total of $\log_2 n + \log_2 k$ steps. This, however, is equivalent to $\log_2(n \cdot k)$. Thus, when using binary search, it makes no difference whether the data is presented as a table or linearly, so we cannot explain the intuition behind the efficacy of tables for information retrieval on the basis of this search algorithm. (We analyzed only the worst case scenario, but considerations about average cases are analogous.)

While considerations of computational complexity provide a useful means of comparison between different representations, if we want to use them to tell us something about the efficacy of representations for *human* use, we must also take into account the plausibility of the assumptions on which they rely, in this case that each computational step has the same cost. In practice, however, this assumption is frequently unjustified. Consider, for example, the task of searching for a particular name in an old-fashioned telephone book. Given that the entries are sorted by name, we could do a binary search: Open the book in the middle and determine whether the name we are looking for occurs in the first half or in the second; then, go to the relevant half and repeat the procedure, by looking again at the page in the middle of that half of the book, and so on. Instead of applying this procedure, however, what many people will do is to flip through the book until one reaches pages whose entries begin with the same letter as the name we are looking for. Then, one flips back or forth page by page, depending on where one expects the name to be. In terms of complexity theory, this procedure corresponds more or less to a *linear search* through the phone book, which in general involves vastly more steps than a binary search. However, the physical operation of 'flipping through the pages' might well be easier and quicker than 'open the book in the middle of a given block of pages', which would be a good reason for many people's preference for using a linear search algorithm.

So, if we use a linear search algorithm, how does the presentation of the data affect the complexity of the search? A linear search in a sorted list of $n \cdot k$ elements takes $n \cdot k$ steps in the worst case. However, a linear search of the rows takes at most n steps and a linear search of the columns another k, resulting in a total of $n + k$ steps. Here, the difference is considerable, as $n + k$ is usually much smaller than $n \cdot k$. (In a $n \times n$ table, the difference is between $2n$ and n^2 steps, i.e., between linear and quadratic complexity classes.) In other words, when performing a linear search (which presumably comes more naturally to most of us), using a table to represent the data yields much faster search results, just as our intuitions predicted.

In addition to the material conditions that can affect the ease with which certain operations can be carried out, a linear search algorithm might also be preferred because it exploits features of our perceptual apparatus, which allows the scanning of individual elements of a list at a glance (in particular if the list is small), whereas determining the middle element of a list would require additional reasoning. In fact, for lists of relatively short length the actual differences in necessary steps are fairly small and complexity considerations become relevant only with large numbers of elements. Moreover, to rows or columns that are not sorted, as is the case for ledgers and many other tables, binary search cannot be applied at all. Thus, with regard to locating elements, there is a considerable interaction between physical, perceptual, and cognitive constraints, with the content and structural features of the representation.

5 Visualization of Relational Structure and Patterns

As I have argued above, the spatial arrangement of a table allows us to easily perceive some of the items as belonging together (in particular, those arranged in rows, columns, and diagonals). Furthermore, *symmetries* stand out frequently, too, as the recognition of symmetries is also a Gestalt principle. In short, tables

(6) facilitate the perception of particular *patterns* in the data.

If these patterns also correspond to meaningful properties of the represented subject matter, this amounts to an immediate visualization of structural information contained in the data.

Even in the absence of deep structural relations, merely displaying data in a table can focus a researcher's attention to a connection between the ordering of the table and particular features of the data. For example, such connections were found in the tables used for the classification of chemical substances by Doumas and Boullay (1828), which is discussed by Klein in order to illustrate the role of 'paper tools' in the creation of scientific knowledge [9]. Polya quotes Jacob Bernoulli (1713) as noting that 'This table of numbers has eminent and admirable properties'; in his book on problem solving, Polya himself frequently suggests to arrange mathematical formulas 'in suitable tables' [16, vol. 2, p. 193] and encourages the student to ask: 'Do you notice something worth noticing— some law or pattern or regularity?' [16, vol. 2, p. 152].[4]

In order to account for the fact that images and graphs can represent information at various levels of abstraction in a way that makes it immediately available to the users, Kulvicki introduced a notion of 'extractability' of information that is based on a correlation between what is 'syntactically' and what is 'semantically salient' [12]. As we shall see in the following example of tabular representations of binary operations, the specific (syntactic) patterns are straightforwardly recognizable and their correlation to (semantic) properties of the operations that are represented can be easily established. Thus, Kulvicki's analysis of images (as opposed to linguistic representations) seems to apply to tables just as well; indeed, in most examples that he gives himself, the information is actually represented in a table.

To illustrate the previous claim, let us look at some simple examples in which tables that represent the results of binary operations contain easily identifiable

---

[4] Of course, patterns can also emerge from arrangements that are not tables, as Ulam's famous patterns of the distribution of prime numbers show [22].

$$
\begin{array}{c|ccc}
+_3 & 0 & 1 & 2 \\
\hline
0 & 0 & 1 & 2 \\
1 & 1 & 2 & 0 \\
2 & 2 & 0 & 1 \\
\end{array}
\qquad
\begin{array}{c|ccc}
\times_3 & 0 & 1 & 2 \\
\hline
0 & 0 & 0 & 0 \\
1 & 0 & 1 & 2 \\
2 & 0 & 2 & 1 \\
\end{array}
\qquad
\begin{array}{c|cc}
\rightarrow & \mathsf{T} & \mathsf{F} \\
\hline
\mathsf{T} & \mathsf{T} & \mathsf{F} \\
\mathsf{F} & \mathsf{T} & \mathsf{T} \\
\end{array}
$$

Fig. 2. Tables for addition and multiplication modulo 3, truth table for implication.

syntactic patterns that correspond to properties of the operations: the results of addition and multiplication modulo 3 are shown in the first two labeled homogeneous tables in Fig. 2. Here some observations about the distribution of the values in the tables: (i) Each entry consists of one of the values 0, 1, 2, which are also the input values for the operations according to the labels; this corresponds to the fact that the operations are *closed*, i. e., they do not return any value that is not among the inputs. (ii) The fact that the top line of the $+_3$-table corresponds exactly to the labels indicates that the element 0 is the *left-identity* of the operation, just as 1 is the *left-identity* of $\times_3$. These elements are also right-identities, as the elements in their columns match exactly the column labels. These observations together establish 0 as the identity element for $+_3$, and 1 as the identity element for $\times_3$. (iii) Because the identity element for $+_3$ occurs in each row and each column, the operation has an *inverse*, which is not the case for $\times_3$. These observations identify $+_3$ as a *group* operation. (iv) The fact that the entries are symmetrical with respect to the main diagonal from top left to bottom right indicates that both operations $+_3$ and $\times_3$ are *commutative*. Applying the same analysis to the truth-table for classical implication (shown in Fig. 2, right) yields that the operation is also closed, has a left-identity (T), but no right-identity, has no inverse operation, and is not commutative.

Tables that exhibit particular patterns are also easier to memorize, as the historian of mathematics Swetz remarks: 'Multiplication facts were organized into tables, traditionally called *Pythagorean tables*, in which the numerical patterns might be better observed and remembered' [25, p. 84].

6 Operations on Tables

We turn now to the ways in which one can actively engage with tables by performing operations on cells or groups of cells.

Functions on Cells. The notion of 'derivative meaning' was introduced by Shimojima as 'the additional informational relation derivable from, but not included in, the system's basic semantic conventions' of a representation [20, p. 114]. For the case of tables, the basic semantic conventions are those that give the meanings of the values in individual cells. Typical derived information that can be obtained in a table involves those values that are contained in entire rows and columns, for example: how many elements are contained in a row or column, the sum of the elements, the average, or other statistical or arithmetical functions.

Name	T1	T2	T3
A	50	75	85
B	30	50	55
C	40	85	65

Name	T1	T2	T3	Sum
A	50	75	85	210
B	30	50	55	144
C	40	85	65	180
Avg.	40	70	68	

Fig. 3. Simple tabular arrangement of test results with derived meanings.

As a simple illustration, consider the results of three tests (T1, T2, and T3) of three students (A, B, C), as shown in the left table in Fig. 3. This table is used to derive additional information, namely the sums of the results for each student and the averages of each test, recorded in the table on the right. We can readily see that the average of the first test is considerably lower than the other two, and that student A had the highest overall score. I take it that this use of tables is familiar and hardly surprising, but the question arises: *why* do tables lend themselves to this usage? The answer brings us back to the features of tables introduced in Sect. 2. Due to the semantic unity of the rows and columns, to determine the average result of a test or sum of the results of an individual student, only the values in a single column (or row, respectively) have to be consulted; the spatial arrangement makes this task easier, because all cells that have to be taken into consideration are direct vertical (or horizontal, respectively) neighboring cells. This simplifies the symbolic expression that is used to refer to the range of these cells (when formulas on the cells are entered in a spreadsheet) and facilitates shifting the focus of one's attention (in case the derived meanings are obtained 'by hand'). Thus, it is the combination of the syntactic, spatial, and semantic characteristics of tables, together with the effect these have on our perception, that underlies the ease in which derived information can be obtained from a tabular representation.[5]

Spreadsheets. Operations on tables that can be expressed as functions on cells are an essential feature of spreadsheets. However, in addition to simply automating operations that could otherwise also be done by hand, spreadsheets also offer the ability of sorting a table according to the values in a row or column. To achieve this with traditional tables, one would have to create a new, separate table. The fact that spreadsheets allow for in-place sorting, or, to use Stenning's term, an 'agglomerative' mode of reasoning [23, p. 41], puts some pressure on considering the difference between tables and spreadsheets as merely one pertaining to their materiality. Rather, it seems that tables and spreadsheets are

---

[5] Turing's general analysis of computation also begins with a two-dimensional writing surface: 'Computing is normally done by writing certain symbols on paper. We may suppose this paper is divided into squares like a child's arithmetic book. In elementary arithmetic the two-dimensional character of the paper is sometimes used' [30, p. 239]. Although, Turing does not consider this to be an essential feature of computations and thus restricts his model to a one-dimensional tape. Nevertheless, a Turing Machine can also move its head only to adjacent cells on the tape.

really two different kinds of representations. However, we must leave this issue as a topic for future discussion.

Matrices. The study of equations in terms of tabular arrangements of their coefficients was practiced already in ancient China [2], but matrices, as genuine mathematical objects became popular only in the nineteenth century. While they can be understood generally as arrays of numbers, in many applications their rows and columns represent clearly discernible semantic units. Moreover, although many operations on matrices, such as transposition and matrix multiplication, are formally defined in terms of the indices of the elements, they are often conceived, taught, and memorized in terms of operations on rows and columns, thereby appealing directly to the spatial structure of matrices.

7   Tabular Manipulations of Structured Notations

In the previous sections I have argued that the overlapping of the syntactic and spatial features of tables with the semantic unity of the rows and columns allows for, among other things, an immediate perception of patterns and a straightforward formulation of operations on the data. So far, however, we have considered cells as containing only basic elements, e. g., linguistic and numeric items. We come now to a new aspect of the power of tables as representational tools, namely in the case that the cells contain only parts of more complex expressions.

Due to their recursive grammar and compositional semantics, expressions in most mathematical notations are themselves structured. Because of this, we can not only use tables to represent the relations between different expressions, but also to represent the relations of the symbols that constitute an expression. Take numerals, for example. We have already seen examples where numerals were elements in a table, but we can also use a tabular arrangement for the numerals themselves. For the sake of illustration, let us first consider a more exotic example, namely Roman numerals, and then turn to more familiar algorithms for the decimal place-value system and algebraic equations.

Roman Numerals. In the left table of Fig. 4 we see the standard, linear representation of two Roman numerals in the purely additive format. We can perceive at a glance that the first one takes up more space, thus presumably has more symbols, but because of the different width of the symbols ('M' vs. 'I'), we cannot be completely sure about that. On the right side of the figure the same numerals are represented in a tabular format, in which each row contains a numeral expression and there is a column for each group of letters. Here we immediately

Linear representation	Tabular representation					
MDCCCLXXII	M	D	CCC	L	XX	II
MMCXXXVI	MM		C		XXX V	I

Fig. 4. Linear and tabular representations of Roman numerals.

recognize that the second numeral has two M's and thus represents a greater value than the first. The readability of the numerals is greatly enhanced by the tabular representation. Since additions of such numerals are done letter-by-letter (with subsequent simplifications), adding numerals in this format can be done column-wise, thus simplifying the procedure considerably. Indeed, in their discussion of addition and multiplication algorithms for Roman numerals, Schlimm and Neth use such a tabular representation [18].

Addition and Multiplication Algorithms. Most likely we are so familiar with our paper-and-pencil algorithms using the Indo-Arabic decimal place-value system that we tend to overlook the basic assumptions that make them possible in the first place. In particular, most addition algorithms presuppose that the numerals are written underneath each other in a right-aligned way (compare the additions shown in Fig. 5). In fact, if the numerals were left-aligned or not written underneath each other at all, the formulation of an addition algorithm would be much more complex, since it cannot rely on the column-wise processing of the digits. Thus, the (correct) tabular arrangement of the numerals is crucial for our familiar, simple, and efficient addition algorithm.

The tabular arrangement of the addends also plays a crucial role in common multiplication algorithms. Notice the placement of the intermediate results of the addends shown in the first two multiplications in Fig. 6. Here, '115' and '92' are not right-aligned, because they are obtained by multiplication of single digits that have different power-10 factors. In this way, however, the usual column-wise addition algorithm can still be applied. (Historically, this algorithm was known as 'chessboard multiplication', clearly in reference to the tabular arrangement [24, p. 205].) In the third multiplication shown in Fig. 6, the intermediate results are right-aligned, which has the consequence that we have to add the digits *diagonally*, instead of column-wise (which is indicated by the shading of the diagonal). An even more refined algorithm, sometimes called 'lattice multiplication', can be found in the *Treviso Arithmetic* of 1478 [24] (shown in the fourth example in Fig. 6). Here, no intermediate handling of carries is necessary, as the intermediate results of the single-digit multiplications are simply written out, which requires more diagonals to be considered when adding these intermediate results. What is important for our discussion is that all of these algorithms make *essential use* of the fact that a tabular arrangement of the intermediate results allows for a straightforward computation of the final result by processing single digit addition either column-wise or diagonally.

$$
\begin{array}{r} 9\ 2\ 1 \\ +1\ 1\ 5\ 3 \\ \hline 2\ 0\ 7\ 4 \end{array}
\qquad
\begin{array}{r} 9\ 2\ 1 \\ +1\ 1\ 5\ 3 \\ \hline 2\ 0\ 7\ 4 \end{array}
\qquad
921 + 1153 = 2074
$$

Fig. 5. Simple additions with Indo-Arabic numerals.

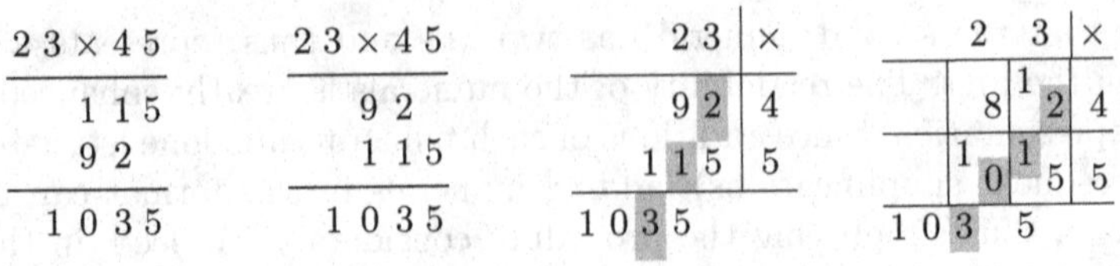

$$
\begin{array}{r}
2\,3 \times 4\,5 \\
\hline
1\,1\,5 \\
9\,2 \\
\hline
1\,0\,3\,5
\end{array}
\qquad
\begin{array}{r}
2\,3 \times 4\,5 \\
\hline
9\,2 \\
1\,1\,5 \\
\hline
1\,0\,3\,5
\end{array}
$$

Fig. 6. Simple multiplications with Indo-Arabic numerals.

Algebraic Equations. To counter the impression that the advantages of the use of tables for structured notations applies only to numerals, let us briefly look at another example, namely algebraic equations. Consider the equations $x^2 + 3x = 2$ and $y^2 = -3y + 2$. A reader with some mathematical experience might be able to parse them quickly, but, in general, the relations between the two equations are easier to detect if they are presented as follows:

$$
\begin{array}{rll}
x^2 & +3x = & 2 \\
y^2 & = & -3y +2
\end{array}
$$

The tabular form of this presentation is determined by the following features: Each of the two rows represents an equation and even without any labels we can readily discern the columns, organized in terms of the powers of the variables, the signs for arithmetical operations, and the equality symbol. By scanning the columns we quickly realize the following differences: In the first column, the elements differ only in the names of the variables ('x' and 'y'), but not in their power; a term corresponding to '$3x$' is missing in the second equation, while a term corresponding to '$-3y$' is missing in the first equation; these two terms occur on different sides of the column with the equation sign and they differ in their leading sign ('+' vs. '−'). With the additional knowledge that a term can be 'pushed' to the other side of the equality symbol while reversing the leading sign, we can *see* that the two equations express the same condition for the free variable and that they only differ in the particular name of this variable ('x' and 'y'). These considerations about the manipulation of algebraic equations are in accord with the 'perceptual account of symbolic reasoning' [13], which is mainly based on empirical work by Landy and Goldstone. In fact, examples given to illustrate this account use a the tabular representation of equations (see, e. g., Fig. 1 in [14, p. 1073]).

8   Operations on Infinite Tables

So far we have considered only finite, two-dimensional tables, but some of their characteristic features remain in place if we generalize the concept to infinitely many rows and/or columns, as will be illustrated in the following two proofs.[6]

---

[6] Extending tables to three or more dimensions is beyond the scope of this paper.

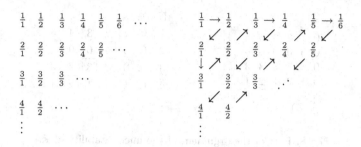

Fig. 7. Tables illustrating the argument for the denumerability of the rationals.

Dovetailing. It is a surprising fact that follows from Cantor's definition of infinite cardinalities, which asserts that two sets have the same cardinality if and only if they can be put into a 1-1 correspondence, that the set of rational numbers has the same cardinality as the set of natural numbers. To establish this, one has to produce a 1-1 correspondence between them, such as

$$\begin{array}{cccccc} 1 & 2 & 3 & 4 & 5 & 6 \ \dots \\ \hline \frac{1}{1} & \frac{1}{2} & \frac{2}{1} & \frac{3}{1} & \frac{2}{2} & \frac{1}{3} \ \dots \end{array}$$

An untrained reader might wonder what exactly the rule is that establishes the correspondence (i.e., which rational numbers follow in the sequence and are correlated to 7, 8, and 9?) and whether this table actually contains *all* fractions. A different arrangement of the fractions gives an answer to these questions in an intuitive way. The table on the left side of Fig. 7 shows an arrangement of the rational numbers, represented as fractions, and the table on the right illustrates how one can count the fractions, i.e., establish a 1-1 correspondence between the natural numbers and the rational numbers. (In fact, the table also shows that some rational numbers are counted more than once, since the fractions $\frac{1}{1}$ and $\frac{2}{2}$, for example, represent the same rational number, so additional restrictions must be imposed to make this work).

Diagonalization. The well-known presentation of the argument that the real numbers between 0 and 1 are *uncountable*, i.e., that it is impossible to establish a 1-1 correlation between them, begins by assuming that it is possible to have a 1-1 mapping f between the natural numbers and the real numbers in question. This is illustrated by a table in which we have the natural numbers as labels for the rows and each element of the decimal expansion of the corresponding real numbers in one column each (as shown in Fig. 8, left; this is another example of a tabular representation of a structured notation, discussed in the previous section). The construction of a real number that cannot be in this table is obtained by changing the first element in the decimal expansion of the first real number in the table, the second element of the expansion of the second number, and so on; these elements are marked in the table on the right of Fig. 8 by boxes. The name of this proof technique, 'diagonalization', clearly refers to the tabular arrangement shown and the fact that this presentation has

```
N  ℝ                          N  ℝ
1  0. 1 2 3 4 5 ...           1  0. [1] 2  3  4  5 ...
2  0. 5 0 0 0 0 ...           2  0. 5 [0] 0  0  0 ...
3  0. 3 3 3 3 3 ...           3  0. 3  3 [3] 3  3 ...
4  0. 1 2 1 2 1 ...           4  0. 1  2  1 [2] 1 ...
   ⋮ ⋮            ⋱             ⋮ ⋮            ⋱
```

Fig. 8. Part of the argument of the uncountability of ℝ.

become the default in textbooks on set theory can be taken as evidence for its pedagogical value (e. g., [4, p. 132]; for the historical development of Cantor's proofs, see [27]).

9 Discussion

Tables as Effective Representations. Because of the semantic unity of the rows and columns of a table, any element is (semantically) related to other elements in two different ways, which also correspond to the syntactic (rows and columns) and spatial arrangement of the elements. Thus, when we see two elements next to each other, we also 'see' their semantic connection: syntactic movement (e. g., in a row) corresponds to spatial movement (e. g., to the right) and the realization that part of the meaning of the element stays the same and part of it changes. This alignment of syntax, semantics, and visual appearance is what makes tables so versatile and powerful representations. For example, we have identified the following aspects of tables in our discussion: (1) They afford a quick overview of the data, (2) allow for the identification of singularities, (3) make it easier to detect missing data, (4) provide for means to check for the correctness of the data, (5) provide quick access to specific cells, and (6) facilitate the perception of particular patterns in the data. Moreover, tables facilitate the expression of functions on their elements and can be used to simplify the manipulations of structured notations.

What is involved in retrieving the information represented in a table is deeply embedded in our reading habits along vertical and horizontal axes (from left to right, from top to bottom) and our background knowledge of ordered sequences (alphabet, numerals, cultural conventions such as the order of first name/last name). The Gestalt principles of proximity, similarity, good continuation, and symmetry, underlie our spontaneous perceptual and cognitive reactions to tabular representations. Due to the two-dimensional organization, binary relations that hold between the elements appear as visual patterns that can be immediately recognized. In this way, tables can be said to translate abstract relations into a perceivable form. If structural relations hold between the components of expressions in some notation, then a tabular arrangement can support the understanding of these expressions as well as their manipulations. Just as formulas can be productive tools in science [9] and numerals can be tools for operating with numbers [10], tables are a powerful tool for our processing of information.

Tables and Diagrams. One motivation to take a closer look at tables, to determine their characteristic features, and to study how these contribute to the efficiency of this kind of representation, has been their relative simplicity and the fact that they are rather constrained. This lack of generality was offset by a clear identification of their structural (syntactic and spatial) and semantic features, and how these affect our perception and our ability to reason with them. If *diagrams* are understood from a semiotic point of view as structured signs, then tables are simply a particular, well-defined category of diagrams. However, diagrams that are frequently discussed in the literature (e. g., [3, 6, 15, 20]) are often *more general* than tables (pace Stenning, who considers directly interpreted diagrams to be subject to more constraints than tables [23, p. 45]), since they do not require any vertical or horizontal arrangement of their elements, and as *more expressive*, since they typically use lines or arrows to represent relations between elements. Nevertheless, it also seems that, whenever possible, such diagrams are presented in such a way that they look very much like tables! The most striking examples are commutative diagrams, in which the elements are arranged in rows and columns in such a way that these also exhibit a semantic unity (see, e. g., [20, p. 122], [3, p. 3,18]). This suggests that it might be fruitful to use the characteristic features of tables identified above and their effects on perception and cognition also as ingredients of a more general discussion of diagrams.

Acknowledgments. Many thanks to Alberto Lopez Garcia, Tyler Marghetis, Valérie Therrien, Theresa Wege, and three anonymous reviewers for comments on an earlier draft. This research was supported by the Social Sciences and Humanities Research Council of Canada.

References

1. Campbell-Kelly, M., Croarken, M., Flood, R., Robson, E. (eds.): The History of Mathematical Tables. From Sumer to Spreadsheets. Oxford University Press, Oxford (2003)
2. Chemla, K.: Different concepts of equations in The Nine Chapters on Mathematical Procedures and in the commentary on it by Liu Hui (3rd century). Hist. Sci. **4**(2), 113–137 (1994)
3. De Toffoli, S.: What are mathematical diagrams? Synthese **200**(2), 1–29 (2022)
4. Enderton, H.B.: Elements of Set Theory. Academic Press, New York (1977)
5. Enns, J.T.: Perception, Gestalt principles of. In: Nadel, L. (ed.) Encyclopedia of Cognitive Science. Nature Publishing, London (2003)
6. Giardino, V.: Behind the diagrams: cognitive issues and open problems. In: Krämer, S., Ljungberg, C. (eds.) Thinking with Diagrams. The Semiotic Basis of Human Condition, pp. 77–101. De Gruyter Mouton, Boston (2016)
7. Guthrie, J.T., Weber, S., Kimmerly, N.: Searching documents: cognitive processes and deficits in understanding graphs, tables, and illustrations. Contemp. Educ. Psychol. **18**, 186–221 (1993)
8. Higgins, H.B.: The Grid Book. The MIT Press, Cambridge (2009)

9. Klein, U.: Paper tools in experimental cultures. Stud. Hist. Philos. Sci. **32**(2), 265–302 (2001)
10. Krämer, S.: Writing, notational iconicity, calculus: On writing as a cultural technique. Modern Language Notes - German Issue **118**(3), 518–537 (2003)
11. Krämer, S.: Figuration, Anschauung, Erkenntnis. Grundlinien einer Diagrammatologie. Suhrkamp, Berlin (2016)
12. Kulvicki, J.: Knowing with images: medium and message. Philos. Sci. **77**(2), 295–313 (2010)
13. Landy, D., Allen, C., Zednik, C.: A perceptual account of symbolic reasoning. Front. Psychol. **5**(275), 1–10 (2014)
14. Landy, D., Goldstone, R.L.: How much of symbolic manipulation is just symbol pushing? In: Proceedings of the 30st Annual Conference of the Cognitive Science Society, Austin, TX, pp. 1072–1077. Cognitive Science Society (2009)
15. Larkin, J.H., Simon, H.A.: Why a diagram is (sometimes) worth ten thousand words. Cogn. Sci. **11**, 65–99 (1987)
16. Polya, G.: Mathematical Discovery. On Understanding, Learning, and Teaching Problem Solving, Combined edn.. Wiley (1981). first ed. 1962–65
17. Rock, I., Palmer, S.: The legacy of gestalt psychology. Sci. Am. **263**(6), 84–90 (1990)
18. Schlimm, D., Neth, H.: Modeling ancient and modern arithmetic practices: Addition and multiplication with Arabic and Roman numerals. In: Sloutsky, V., Love, B., McRae, K. (eds.) Proceedings of the 30th Annual Meeting of the Cognitive Science Society, Austin, TX, pp. 2097–2102. Cognitive Science Society (2008)
19. Shimojima, A.: The inferential-expressive trade-off: a case study of tabular representations. In: Hegarty, M., Meyer, B., Narayanan, N.H. (eds.) Diagrams 2002. LNCS (LNAI), vol. 2317, pp. 116–130. Springer, Heidelberg (2002). https://doi.org/10.1007/3-540-46037-3_16
20. Shimojima, A.: Semantic Properties of Diagrams and Their Cognitive Potentials. CSLI Publications, Stanford (2015)
21. Shin, S.J.: The Logical Status of Diagrams. Cambridge University Press, Cambridge (1995)
22. Stein, M.L., Ulam, S.M., Wells, M.B.: A visual display of some properties of the distribution of primes. Am. Math. Mon. **71**(5), 516–520 (1964)
23. Stenning, K.: Seeing Reason: Image and Language in Learning to Think. Oxford University Press, Oxford (2002)
24. Swetz, F.: Capitalism and Arithmetic: The new math of the 15th century, including the full text of the Treviso arithmetic of 1478. Open Court, La Salle, Ill (1987)
25. Swetz, F.: To know and to teach: mathematical pedagogy from a historical context. Educ. Stud. Math. **29**(1), 73–88 (1995)
26. Takemura, R., Shimojima, A., Katagiri, Y.: Logical investigation of reasoning with tables. In: Dwyer, T., Purchase, H., Delaney, A. (eds.) Diagrams 2014. LNCS (LNAI), vol. 8578, pp. 261–276. Springer, Heidelberg (2014). https://doi.org/10.1007/978-3-662-44043-8_27
27. Therrien, V.: The evolution of Cantor's proofs of the non-denumerability of $\mathbb{R}$. Manuscript (2022)
28. Tufte, E.R.: Envisioning Information. Graphics Press, Cheshire (1990)
29. Tufte, E.R.: The Visual Display of Quantitative Information, 2nd edn. Graphics Press, Cheshire (2001)
30. Turing, A.M.: On computable numbers, with an application to the Entscheidungsproblem. Proc. Lond. Math. Soc. **42**, 230–265 (1936)
31. Wainer, H.: Understanding graphs and tables. Educ. Res. **21**(1), 14–21 (1992)

Why Scholars Are Diagramming Neural Network Models

Guy Clarke Marshall[1]([⊠]), Caroline Jay[1], and André Freitas[1,2]

[1] Department of Computer Science, University of Manchester, Manchester, UK
guy.marshall@postgrad.manchester.ac.uk,
{caroline.jay,andre.freitas}@manchester.ac.uk
[2] Idiap Research Institute, Rue Marconi 19, 1920 Martigny, Switzerland

Abstract. Complex models, such as neural networks (NNs), are comprised of many interrelated components. In order to represent these models, eliciting and characterising the relations between components is essential. Perhaps because of this, diagrams, as "icons of relation", are a prevalent medium for signifying complex models. Diagrams used to communicate NN architectures are currently extremely varied. The diversity in diagrammatic choices provides an opportunity to gain insight into the aspects which are being prioritised for communication and into the conceptualisations of the diagram creators.

Keywords: Neural networks · Systems · Diagrams · Conceptual models

1 Introduction

Diagrams are a signifier, cognitive aid, and mediator of communication. In describing software systems, diagrams often provide a level of abstraction that facilitates an understanding of the overall structure, and the relation between the computational artefacts of the system. Software system diagrams have a dual role bridging between cognition and communication of humans, and representation of mechanisms entailed by machines. In the field of AI, which feature many NN models, the pace of development is high, and as such conferences are the most prestigious academic venues. In their scholarly proceedings, we find that the majority of papers include a system architecture diagram by way of structural explanation. This is common across Computer Science and other model-centric domains. What is less common is the variety of these representations, even when compared with other research and engineering domains. Despite being based on similar and mathematically-well-formalised computational artefacts, such as neural networks, their supporting diagrams have very low consistency. In this paper, we utilise the opportunity provided by the lack of convention to gain insight into the way the creators of NN models are choosing to communicate their models. This follows Even-Ezra's examination of the insight medieval scholastic diagrams may provide into the thinking of their creators [3].

© Springer Nature Switzerland AG 2022
V. Giardino et al. (Eds.): Diagrams 2022, LNAI 13462, pp. 202–209, 2022.
https://doi.org/10.1007/978-3-031-15146-0_16

This study is motivated by a number of questions. Why are diagrams being used to describe NNs? Why are the diagrams so heterogeneous? Progress is made to this end through drawing together recent empirical results [8–11], supported by the following synthesis and reasoning: (i) There is a relation between content included in NN diagrams and their role in the scholarly community as conceptual models, and (ii) There are visual encoding prioritisations which align with subcategories within mental models theories.

2   Background

2.1   Neural Models

AI is materialised as software, written in a programming language, and often based on neural networks. A neural network takes an input (usually text, numbers, images or video), and then processes this through a series of *layers*, to create an output (usually classification or prediction). Each layer contains a set of *nodes* which hold information and transmit signals to nodes in other layers according to their weights and connectivity. Specific mathematical functions or operations are also used in these models, such as sigmoid, concatenate, softmax, max pooling, and loss. Different architectures are used for addressing different types of tasks: Convolutional Neural Networks (CNN), inspired by the human visual system, are commonly used for processing images, and Long Short Term Memory networks (LSTM), a type of Recurrent Neural Network (RNN) which are designed for processing sequences, are often used for text. These neural networks "learn" a function, but have to be trained to do so. Training consists of providing inputs and expected outputs, so the model can learn how a function should be inductively approximated. The model is then tested with unseen inputs, to see if it is able to process these correctly. The explicit data perspective (focused on vectors and matrices) and the functional perspective are fairly distinct and complementary ways of conceptualising the parts of the models, which is part of the problem of communicating in this area. The architectural perspective on the model can be to a greater or lesser extent encompassing the data manipulations, which leads to a broad spectrum of possible representations. Neural networks can also be considered as a set of transitions between latent states (a different way of conceptualising the data). The computation of these latent vectors are at the center of the data representation induced by a NN and are optimised by algorithms such as gradient descent via back-propagation which are sufficiently conventional to be omitted from non-pedagogical diagrams. The functions are not highly heterogeneous, but the architectures are heterogeneous due to the diversity in which its fundamental parts can be composed and configured. An example diagram can be found in Fig. 1.

The diagrams relate the constituting parts of a model at a certain level of abstraction, defining an architecture for the model. The models themselves are comprised of different types of layers and different sizes or parameters for the layers, which are usually encoded in diagrams. The configuration, dependencies between latent dimensions, and attributes of layers are included as the diagrams

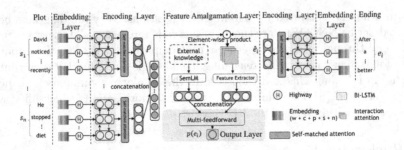

Fig. 1. An example diagram, used by Li et al. [6], using labels for Form, graphical objects variously for Form and State, input and output for Purpose

are utilised by authors attempting to produce a description of these latent states using graphical components. There are fundamental and complex aspects of NNs which are not commonly included in diagrams. Authors put substantial thought into the nature of the loss function, and how to decompose the set of components of the loss, but this is done outside the diagram and articulated through mathematical notation. The mathematics of NN's are well established and have an established representational language. At the system level, diagrams are used but conventions are not well established.

2.2   Mental Models and Mental Operations for NN Diagrams

All three primary mental operations of Apprehension, Judgement, and Inference [5] are at play in using NN diagrams for research. Apprehension, being the forming of a picture in one's mind, is important for depicting and understanding the model. An example of Judgement could be "this is relevant", and Inference "this is a contribution". We focus on the creation of mental representation, i.e. Apprehension. Clark and Chalmers [1] proposed the "Extended Mind Theory" which encompasses diagrams, proposing that diagramming shapes (and is shaped by) cognitive processes. With specific reference to the Computer Science domain, Guarino et al. state that "we may say that a computer program is a conceptual model of the computer's internal behavior, but only as long as its programming language's primitives denote concepts concerning computer behavior. If they rather denote data, we conclude that such a computer program is not a conceptual model." Diagrams make cognitively accessible the models and the computational artefacts of which they are comprised, and therefore have a role to play in the ethics of NNs and AI more broadly. In this way, diagrams are a mechanism for establishing transparency and managing risks around how the model operates.

3 Diagram Content Relates to Conceptual Models

3.1 Heterogeneity in Representation

In principle, the primary purpose of diagrams in scholarly publications is communicative. The authors are attempting to communicate through a diagrammatic
medium some kind of relational structure. Diagrams are ideally suited to this
task, and are used for this purpose in many domains [7]. However, there are other
social aspects. Without passing too critical an eye over the scientific endeavour,
having a efficient diagram in communicative terms (both aesthetically and tech-
nically) may improve perception of a paper, thereby making it more likely to pass
through peer review. While the visual encoding methods are quite unconstrained
and heterogeneous, it is conventional to include an architecture diagram if the
paper presents a novel model. The subsequent discussion attempts to make steps
towards understanding the reasons for, and consequences of, this heterogeneity.

Perhaps due to the complexity of NNs, there are a number of diagrammatic
representational choices that are made by different authors attempting to express
different things. This has been shown by Marshall et al. [11], using VisDNA, a
grammar of graphics [2], to demonstrate the heterogeneity of visual encoding
principles employed in this domain. In an interview study, Marshall et al. [8]
identify heterogeneous use cases and preferences associated with NN diagrams.
The modal use case mentioned by all participants was "how the system works".
Confusions reported were around the "flow" of reading the diagram, the purpose of the system, and gaps or lacks of specificity within the diagram. The
interview study also found a huge range of diagramming tools are used to create
these diagrams, and identified themes in usage. Three major themes were identified, covering visual ease of use, appropriate content and expectation matching.
"Visual ease of use" related to clear navigation, aesthetics, consistency within
the diagram and having distinct process stages. "Appropriate content" referred
to either wanting more or less information in a diagram, or preferring multiple different diagrams to display different information. These contradictions
within these themes reflects the different priorities users had for specificity or
an instantiated example. "Expectation matching" found that users want consistency across the diagram and within the domain, and to have symbols or
abbreviations explained.

Given the social nature of research, it would be practically easier for authors
to directly copy existing styles than devise their own. We argue that there
must be a compelling reason for authors to be creating such different diagrammatic representations. A partial explanation for heterogeneity could be a lack of
appropriate diagramming tools. In a recent interview study involving technical
domain experts, Ma'ayan et al. [7] found that "To illustrate concepts effectively,
experts find appropriate visual representations and translate concepts into concrete shapes. This translation step is not supported explicitly by current diagramming tools". This does not explain why NN diagrams are so heterogeneous
compared to diagrams in other scholarly domains, nor does it explain the lack
of informal conventions.

We hypothesis that a particular representational aspect is prioritised by the author either because it shows what they think is important, or because it is what they would want to see in a diagram authored by their peers. In either case the priority is effective communication. Differences in prioritisation may be causing the creation of bespoke diagrammatic encodings. When representing NNs, the diagram author can prioritise different aspects:

- Abstraction levels in computer systems:
  - Function: Operations which occur, representation transformations, and the purpose of parts of the model
  - Data: The data model, type, dimensionality and how it is manipulated
  - Mathematics: Including specific mathematical functions
  - Code: Important class names and the order in which they are called
- Contextual uses related to scholarly rhetoric:
  - Example: Showing the steps of an example input through that model
  - Contribution: Focusing on the scientific novelty of the approach, giving much more detail in that area
  - Index to text: Using a label structure to allow for easier referencing

These representational priorities result in different content being displayed through different visual encoding mechanisms. It is usual to have aspects of several of these priorities, as it is not the case that the prioritisation of one aspect necessarily inhibits another. In terms of how the diagrams are presented within a paper, some papers include multiple diagrams, either by multiple figures or sub-figures. Often, sub-figures or detailing boxes are used to give both schematic and detailed views within the same diagram. Dependencies are often indicated by arrows. Diagrams almost always represent important content in natural language, such as labels or descriptions.

3.2   NN Models, Mental Models, Conceptual Models and Diagrams

Guarino et al. [4] states that "we may say that a computer program is a conceptual model of the computer's internal behavior, but only as long as its programming language's primitives denote concepts concerning computer behavior. If they rather denote data, we conclude that such a computer program is not a conceptual model." Applying to NN diagrams, it is variable whether the diagram is a conceptual model. In this work we use mental models as a metaphor for mental conceptualisation, as is common practice in human-computer interaction. The conceptual model (the diagram artefact) has a communicative purpose to articulate concepts and the relationships between concepts. Diagrams are often used for representing the creator's conceptual model, and aid learning and reasoning [7].

The focus of this work is the diagrammatic metaphor being used for *what is represented*, rather than the visual encoding. Bringing types of NN diagrams closer to mental models, we can draw parallels with mental model categories [12] and types of diagram observed, as in Fig. 2. Diagrams may have aspects of multiple categories.

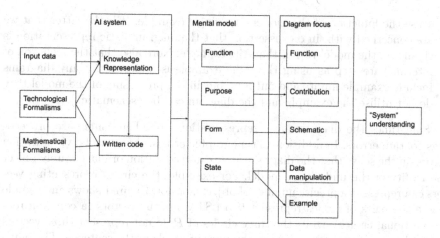

Fig. 2. Representational choices in diagrams of NNs

- Function: Explaining how the model operates by emphasising functional aspects, such as mapping, input and output. Operations used as a verb. For example, "word or sentence embedding" (a general term) rather than "BERT" (a specific architecture for embedding). This type often includes example input and output. Title, caption, other language or images may be used to describe the task.
- Contribution (Purpose): Omits the majority of information other than that required to understand the sub-section of the model that contains the novelty of the model or approach.
- Schematic (Form): Describes the model at a high level, uses probably a block-style without iconic graphical objects. It is succinct, expressive and general, comprised of the representational and functional choices, how they are structured and composed, with emphasis on the dependencies between components. The physical structure analogy is perhaps closest to the classes and modules of code, and the shape of the data. Does not include mathematical or data details. Differing from Function, it commonly uses specific terms such as "BERT" rather than "word or sentence embedding". Also often aggregates graphical objects into modules. (In order to be "state" (i.e. what it is doing) the block diagram should be a verb).
- Data manipulation (State): Includes data dimensions, and usually a visual representation of the data itself. It describes what the model does to the data, so this also includes where operations are primarily labelled arrows (rather than inside blocks).
- Example: How example data transforms. Includes example input, output and intermediate steps. Usually better relates to Function (how it operates) rather than Form (what it looks like), but this depends on the graphical objects used. It is useful to disambiguate this, particularly for Image Processing, where often the diagram is a visual representation of the data manipulation. In one sense this is the Form of the example data manipulation, and in another

sense the Function of the model on a single example. It is the latter that we are concerned with, in our assertion that the diagrammatic representation is signifying the model rather than the example. Note also that the inclusion of intermediate step as using the same example is important. Many diagrams include example inputs and outputs, but in the processing of the model they do not utilise the example and the diagram can be "schematic").

Sometimes the diagrammatic representations found in conference proceedings contain errors. In addition to typographic errors, these can be visualisation errors, in the sense that the diagrams may cause confusion or inaccurately reflect the reality of the underlying model. For example, the circles representing vectors can represent a precise number of objects, or not. Figure 1 shows an example where the pairs of circles represent two LSTM output vectors (a common representational choice), while the three circles of $\hat{P}$ do not represent three vectors but rather j vectors, where j is the number of words in the sentence. The omission of the ellipsis following the embedding layer appears to have led to this visual encoding choice. This unmeaningful 3-vector is repeated perhaps more dangerously in the final concatenation before "multi-feedforward". This can be understood by careful reading of the words and formulae in the text, but could be misleading, as found in an interview study by Marshall et al. [8].

The types of representment employed are of particular interest. Our hypothesis is that the diagrams, and the variety we see exhibiting the above principalities, are a result of the range of cognitive functions being employed by different users. At present, scholars are not using a consistent visual language to communicate. No suitable representation providing as cognitive support such as symbolic equations gave to the mathematicians of ancient Babylon, or the letter x gave to Descartes, has been sought nor found. Another important aspect is reproducibility. Circuit diagrams and other standard diagrammatic representations, often implemented or overseen by professional bodies, have also enabled this standard form of communication and reproducibility across many domains, including Computer Science.

4   Conclusion

We argue that the heterogeneity in diagrammatic representations of NNs is due to the inherent complexity of what is being represented and a lack of obvious visual representational choice for the model themselves. In the case of many other scientific and engineering disciplines, a standard has quickly emerged. It may be that we are too early in the life of "NN science and engineering" to see this, and instead are able to gain insight from the heterogeneity. The heterogeneity seen today is a manifestation of a lack of conventional model elements and visual encoding principles.

NNs are a new medium, which at its most granular representational level are not easily interpretable. Currently there is heterogeneity in diagrammatic representation. Diagrams are a useful, and efficient, way of understanding NNs.

Diagrams are a fundamental signification layer, encoding the design and meta-description of these emerging models. We have hypothesised the diagrams used at present to have relationship to mental models. Interventions designed to improve NN diagrams could aid scholars by providing cognitive support for communicating and reasoning about NN models.

References

1. Clark, A., Chalmers, D.: The extended mind. Analysis **58**(1), 7–19 (1998). ISSN 0003-2638, https://doi.org/10.1093/analys/58.1.7
2. Engelhardt, Y., Richards, C.: The DNA framework of visualization. In: Pietarinen, A.-V., Chapman, P., Bosveld-de Smet, L., Giardino, V., Corter, J., Linker, S. (eds.) Diagrams 2020. LNCS (LNAI), vol. 12169, pp. 534–538. Springer, Cham (2020). https://doi.org/10.1007/978-3-030-54249-8_51
3. Even-Ezra, A.: Lines of Thought: Branching Diagrams and the Medieval Mind. University of Chicago Press (2021)
4. Guarino, N., Guizzardi, G., Mylopoulos, J.: On the philosophical foundations of conceptual models. Inf. Model. Knowl. Bases XXXI **321**, 1 (2020)
5. The Theory of Knowledge. MIP, Macmillan Education UK, London (1970). https://doi.org/10.1007/978-1-349-15442-5_10
6. Li, Q., Li, Z., Wei, J.M., Gu, Y., Jatowt, A., Yang, Z.: A multi-attention based neural network with external knowledge for story ending predicting task. In: Proceedings of the 27th International Conference on Computational Linguistics, pp. 1754–1762 (2018)
7. Ma'ayan, D., Ni, W., Ye, K., Kulkarni, C., Sunshine, J.: How domain experts create conceptual diagrams and implications for tool design. In: Proceedings of the 2020 CHI Conference on Human Factors in Computing Systems, pp. 1–14 (2020)
8. Marshall, G.C., Freitas, A., Jay, C.: How researchers use diagrams in communicating neural network systems. arXiv preprint arXiv:2008.12566 (2020)
9. Marshall, G.C., Jay, C., Freitas, A.: Number and quality of diagrams in scholarly publications is associated with number of citations. In: International Conference on Theory and Application of Diagrams (2021)
10. Marshall, G.C., Jay, C., Freitas, A.: Structuralist analysis for neural network system diagrams. In: Basu, A., Stapleton, G., Linker, S., Legg, C., Manalo, E., Viana, P. (eds.) Diagrams 2021. LNCS (LNAI), vol. 12909, pp. 480–487. Springer, Cham (2021). https://doi.org/10.1007/978-3-030-86062-2_49
11. Basu, A., Stapleton, G., Linker, S., Legg, C., Manalo, E., Viana, P. (eds.): Diagrammatic Representation and Inference. Diagrams 2021. LNCS, vol. 12909. Springer, Cham (2021). https://doi.org/10.1007/978-3-030-86062-2_39
12. Rouse, W.B., Morris, N.M.: On looking into the black box: prospects and limits in the search for mental models. Psychol. Bull. **100**(3), 349 (1986)

A Formal Model of Aspect Shifting: The Case of Dot Diagrams

Atsushi Shimojima[1]([⊠]) and Dave Barker-Plummer[2]

[1] Faculty of Culture and Information Science, Doshisha University,
1-3 Tatara-Miyakodani, Kyotanabe 610-0394, Japan
ashimoji@mail.doshisha.ac.jp
[2] CSLI/Stanford University, 210 Panama Street, Stanford, CA 94305, USA
dbp@stanford.edu

Abstract. Many diagrams can be read in different ways, allowing readers to extract different kinds of information about the represented situation from the same representation. Such diagrams are often used to solve problems that require the combination of information from different views. This has been widely remarked upon in the literature and is sometimes referred to as *aspect shifting*. However, we know of no formal account of the phenomenon, or what an "aspect" of a diagram might be.

In this paper, we give such an account. In an application of our previous work, we describe a theory of representation systems in which the same representation token can be interpreted within multiple distinct representation systems. Each gives a different view of the underlying domain, accounting for multiple readability. We also describe how these different representation systems can be combined into a single overarching system which allows inference across the different aspects given by the component systems. This accounts for why just apprehending a diagram can be a substantial inferential step.

1 Introduction

Many diagrams can be read in different ways, allowing readers to extract different kinds of information about the represented situation from one and the same representation. We say that these diagrams admit *multiple readings* [3,9]. Further, many problems can be solved by combining information of the different kinds drawn from the same diagram. This phenomenon is widely remarked upon [2,5,7], and Giaquinto [4] analyzed it using the term *aspect shifting*. However, we know of no formal account of either multiple readings or aspect shifting, except the one implicit in Jamnik's computational model [5].

In an extension of our model of abstract reading of diagrams [8], we propose such an account. There are two basic ideas in our proposal. The first accounts for multiple readings by viewing a representation token as participating simultaneously in different representation systems. Each provides its own semantics to the diagram token. The second is that these systems can be combined into a single representation system, unifying all of the information, and it is in this combined

© Springer Nature Switzerland AG 2022
V. Giardino et al. (Eds.): Diagrams 2022, LNAI 13462, pp. 210–217, 2022.
https://doi.org/10.1007/978-3-031-15146-0_17

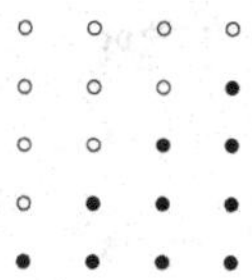

```
o   o   o   o
o   o   o   •
o   o   •   •
o   •   •   •
•   •   •   •
```

Fig. 1. The dot diagram typically used in the proof that $T(4) = \frac{4 \times (4+1)}{2}$.

representation system that problems involving multiple views can be solved. We call the formal operation that combines representation systems *superposition*.

In this paper, we consider the case of "dot diagrams". These diagrams represent particular integers by the number of dots they contain. Many proofs from algebra can be given in this representation, [6]. Figure 1 is an example of the dot diagram used in one such proof. We have used open and closed dots to facilitate perception, but there is no semantic significance to these styles.

The proof appeals to two different ways of viewing this diagram. First, we can view the diagram as a sequence of 4 vertical columns of dots. Each column contains $4 + 1$ dots, for a total of $4 \times (4+1)$ dots. This indicates that the integer that the diagram represents is $4 \times (4 + 1)$. For the second view, notice that the diagram can be divided into two equal triangles, each consisting of $4 + 3 + 2 + 1$ dots. This number is the fourth triangular number, written $T(4)$. This indicates that the integer that the diagram represents is $2 \times T(4)$. Since these views allow us to see the same number both as $4 \times (4 + 1)$ and as $2 \times T(4)$, we can see that $4 \times (4 + 1) = 2 \times T(4)$. This step requires a switch of the two views on the diagram described above, instantiating *aspect shifting*. It is immediate from this equation that $T(4) = \frac{4 \times (4+1)}{2}$.

2   Representation Systems

Our model of representation is based on Barwise and Seligman's general theory of information flow, *channel theory*, [1].

In our terminology, a diagram is a *representation* that carries information about a particular *target*. The target for a dot diagram is a single positive integer $(1, 2, 3, \ldots)$. A representation is constructed to convey information about a represented target. Readers can obtain information about the target by the correct interpretation of a representation. Since readers obtain information from the representation, we often call it the *source* of the system. Information is reliably conveyed by the adoption and maintenance of *semantic constraints*.

The general semantic constraint concerning the diagram in Fig. 1 is that if it is composed of sub-groups of dots $d_1, \ldots, d_n$, the target number is characterizable as the sum of the numbers of dots in $d_1, \ldots, d_n$. When the semantic constraint is successfully followed, readers of this representation can safely read off this information about the target situation.

In our model, a *representation system*, say $\mathfrak{R}$, consists of two *classifications* related by two semantic relations $\Rightarrow_\mathfrak{R}$ and $\rightarrow_\mathfrak{R}$. It is depicted in Fig. 2.

$$\mathrm{typ}(\mathbf{S}) \qquad \Longrightarrow_{\mathfrak{R}} \qquad \mathrm{typ}(\mathbf{T})$$

$$\models_{\mathbf{S}} \qquad\qquad \models_{\mathbf{T}}$$

$$\mathrm{tok}(\mathbf{S}) \qquad \longrightarrow_{\mathfrak{R}} \qquad \mathrm{tok}(\mathbf{T})$$

Fig. 2. The structure of a representation system, $\mathfrak{R}$, where two classifications $\mathbf{S}$ and $\mathbf{T}$ are related by two semantic relations $\Rightarrow_{\mathfrak{R}}$ and $\rightarrow_{\mathfrak{R}}$.

A *classification* consists of a set of *tokens* to be classified, a set of *types* by which they are classified, and a binary relation specifying which tokens have which types. If $\mathbf{S}$ is a classification, then $\mathrm{typ}(\mathbf{S})$ and $\mathrm{tok}(\mathbf{S})$ are respectively the set of types and the set of tokens of classification $\mathbf{S}$. When a token d is of type σ in classification $\mathbf{S}$, we write $d \models_{\mathbf{S}} \sigma$, using the binary relation $\models_{\mathbf{S}}$ associated with classification $\mathbf{S}$.

A representation system requires two classifications: a *source* classification, in which representations are classified by types (on the left in Fig. 2), and a *target* classification, in which the objects that the representations are about are classified by types (on the right in Fig. 2).

Take a representation system used in our sample proof, where we view dot diagrams as a sequence of columns of dots with equal height and interpret them accordingly. In this system, which we call $\mathfrak{R}_{col}$, the set of source tokens to be classified consists of the dot diagrams of the kind illustrated in Fig. 1.

In $\mathfrak{R}_{col}$, the diagrams are classified by the number and height of the columns that they display. Specifically, the source types of this system take the form $\sigma_{col}^{n,n+1}$, meaning "composed of n columns each of $n + 1$ dots." Not every dot diagram is characterizable in this way, and those that are not are left unclassified. The diagram in Fig. 1 is of type $\sigma_{col}^{4,4+1}$, we express this fact as $d \models_{\mathbf{S}_{col}} \sigma_{col}^{4,4+1}$.

The system's target classification, $\mathbf{T}_{col}$, classifies positive integers in a corresponding manner. The classification models a particular way of grasping these numbers, i.e., grasping them as the sum of n terms of the form $n + 1$, i.e., $\sum_{i=1}^{n}(n+1)$. If a target token can be characterized in this way, then we say that it is of type $\tau_{col}^{n,n+1}$. Integers that cannot be characterized as such a sum are left unclassified.

One of the semantic relations involved in a representation system $\mathfrak{R}$ is $\Rightarrow_{\mathfrak{R}}$, which captures the *semantic constraints* that are maintained by people using the system. The semantic constraints of $\mathfrak{R}_{col}$ are that if a diagram is of type $\sigma_{col}^{n,n+1}$, then the number it represents is of type $\tau_{col}^{n,n+1}$. We can write this set of semantic constraints as $\sigma_{col}^{n,n+1} \Rightarrow_{col} \tau_{col}^{n,n+1}$. They hold as constraints because people try not to produce a diagram of type $\sigma_{col}^{n,n+1}$ when the number they represent is *not* of type $\tau_{col}^{n,n+1}$. In general, we call a relation $\Rightarrow_{\mathfrak{R}}$ the *indication relation* of the representation system $\mathfrak{R}$ and say that σ *indicates* τ in $\mathfrak{R}$ whenever $\sigma \Rightarrow_{\mathfrak{R}} \tau$. Thus, $\Rightarrow_{\mathfrak{R}}$ is a binary relation between the sets of types, as shown in Fig. 2.

The other semantic relation involved in the representation system $\mathfrak{R}$ is $\rightarrow_{\mathfrak{R}}$. If there is a representational act that obtains information about a target token w and produces a representation r to convey that information about w, then the relation $r \rightarrow_{\mathfrak{R}} w$ holds. So, $\rightarrow_{\mathfrak{R}}$ is a relation between sets of tokens, as depicted in Fig. 2. We say that r is a *representation* of w in system $\mathfrak{R}$.

A representation system $\mathfrak{R}$, then, is written formally as $\langle \mathbf{S}, \mathbf{T}, \Rightarrow_{\mathfrak{R}}, \rightarrow_{\mathfrak{R}} \rangle$, where $\mathbf{S}$ and $\mathbf{T}$ are the source and target classifications, respectively; $\Rightarrow_{\mathfrak{R}}$ is the indication relation, and $\rightarrow_{\mathfrak{R}}$ is the representation relation.

3   Modeling Aspect Shifting

Our example proof requires that we take different views of the same representation token. These views correspond to two different representation systems, namely, system $\mathfrak{R}_{col}$ introduced above, and system $\mathfrak{R}_{tri}$ introduced below.

Representation system $\mathfrak{R}_{tri}$ has the same sets of source and target tokens as $\mathfrak{R}_{col}$. It lets us view dot diagrams as consisting of two triangles comprising the same number of dots and interpret them accordingly. The source classification $\mathbf{S}_{tri}$ of this system classifies the dot diagrams with the set of types of the form $\sigma_{tri}^{2,T(k)}$, meaning "composed of two triangles each of $T(k)$ dots". Not every dot diagram admits such a partition and those that do not are unclassified in $\mathbf{S}_{tri}$.

On the target side, classification $\mathbf{T}_{tri}$ features types of the form $\tau_{tri}^{2,T(k)}$. They characterize a number as the sum of two identical triangular numbers, i.e., $T(k) + T(k)$ for some k. Not all positive integers are characterizable in this way, and those that are not are left unclassified in $\mathbf{T}_{tri}$.

The semantic constraint of system $\mathfrak{R}_{tri}$ is $\sigma_{tri}^{2,T(k)} \Rightarrow_{tri} \tau_{tri}^{2,T(k)}$, meaning that if a diagram consists of two triangles each of $T(k)$ dots, the represented number is characterizable as $T(k) + T(k)$.

It is significant to note that a diagram can be represented as a pair of triangles of size $T(k)$ without requiring any extra effort on the part of the author of the diagram as long as they adhere to the syntactic convention to shape their diagrams into rectangular arrays of the appropriate dimension. If a diagram has a $k \times (k + 1)$ columnar structure, then it necessarily also consists of a pair of triangles each containing $T(k)$ dots. This geometric constraint underlies the demonstration that the diagram provides.

We propose that a switch between these different representation systems in interpretation is the *shift* referred to in the notion of aspect shifting.

Figure 3 gives the overview, where each system is depicted as a thick horizontal line with its source classification on the left and its target classification on the right. System $\mathfrak{R}_{col}$ occupies the upper row, while $\mathfrak{R}_{tri}$, is depicted in the lower part of the figure. The arrows drawn between some pairs of classifications denote "infomorphisms" between classifications [1].

The key idea is classifications that classify the same set of tokens with different sets of types, where certain instances of classification under the view of one classification are equivalent to certain instances under the view of another. For example, the fact $d \models_{\mathbf{S}_{col}} \sigma_{col}^{4,4+1}$ under classification $\mathbf{S}_{col}$ is equivalent to the

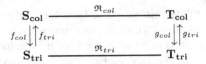

Fig. 3. Systems of representation, $\mathfrak{R}_{col}$, and $\mathfrak{R}_{tri}$, involved in our sample proof. Each thick line represents two semantic relations in a suppressed manner.

fact $d \models_{\mathbf{S_{tri}}} \sigma_{col}^{2,T(4)}$ under classification $\mathbf{S_{tri}}$. Similar relations hold of the target side, between certain facts under classifications $\mathbf{T_{col}}$ and $\mathbf{T_{tri}}$. Thus, to complete our model, we need to explicitly mark which facts under one classification are equivalent to which facts under another. That is what *infomorphisms* do.

The notion of infomorphism was originally developed to mathematically capture different "perspectives" that can be taken on same facts, [1]. Formally, an *infomorphism* is a pair of contra-variant functions between classifications. An infomorphism f from classification $\mathbf{A}$ to classification $\mathbf{B}$ is written $f : \mathbf{A} \rightleftarrows \mathbf{B}$, and the component functions are written $f^{\vee}$ and $f^{\wedge}$, where $f^{\vee}$ is a function from the tokens of $\mathbf{B}$ to the tokens of $\mathbf{A}$, while $f^{\wedge}$ is a function from the types of $\mathbf{A}$ to the types of $\mathbf{B}$. The pair of functions $f^{\vee}$ and $f^{\wedge}$ make an infomorphism if for all tokens $t \in \mathrm{tok}(\mathbf{B})$ and types $\sigma \in \mathrm{typ}(\mathbf{A})$, $t \models_{\mathbf{B}} f^{\wedge}(\sigma)$ if and only if $f^{\vee}(t) \models_{\mathbf{A}} \sigma$. This property is fundamental to infomorphism f, as it lets f do its job to mark the equivalence between facts under different classifications $\mathbf{A}$ and $\mathbf{B}$.

Figure 3 depicts four infomorphisms, f_{col}, f_{tri}, g_{col}, and g_{tri}, responsible for the aspect shift in our sample proof. We exemplify these infomorphisms by considering $f_{col} : \mathbf{S_{col}} \rightleftarrows \mathbf{S_{tri}}$.

As we mentioned above, the fact $d \models_{\mathbf{S_{col}}} \sigma_{col}^{4,4+1}$ under classification $\mathbf{S_{col}}$ is equivalent to the fact $d \models_{\mathbf{S_{tri}}} \sigma_{tri}^{2,T(4)}$ under $\mathbf{S_{tri}}$. The equivalence is actually more general, holding on all dot diagrams and between the types of the form $\sigma_{col}^{n,n+1}$ and $\sigma_{tri}^{2,T(n)}$. Infomorphism f_{col} marks this general equivalence. It consists of the identity function $f_{col}^{\vee}$ from $\mathrm{tok}(\mathbf{S_{tri}})$ to $\mathrm{tok}(\mathbf{S_{col}})$ and the function $f_{col}^{\wedge}$ from $\mathrm{typ}(\mathbf{S_{col}})$ into $\mathrm{typ}(\mathbf{S_{tri}})$ that maps $\sigma_{col}^{n,n+1}$ to $\sigma_{tri}^{2,T(n)}$ for all positive integers n. It is routine to verify that f_{col} is an infomorphism. The fundamental property of f_{col} then says that for all dot diagrams $d_i \in \mathrm{tok}(\mathbf{S_{tri}})$ and all types $\sigma_{col}^{n,n+1} \in \mathrm{typ}(\mathbf{S_{col}})$, the facts $d_i \models_{\mathbf{S_{tri}}} f_{col}^{\wedge}(\sigma_{col}^{n,n+1})$ and $f_{col}^{\vee}(d_i) \models_{\mathbf{S_{col}}} \sigma_{col}^{n,n+1}$ are equivalent, that is, $d_i \models_{\mathbf{S_{tri}}} \sigma_{tri}^{2,T(n)}$ and $d_i \models_{\mathbf{S_{col}}} \sigma_{col}^{n,n+1}$ are equivalent.

This way, infomorphism f_{col} marks the situation where the fact of the form $d_i \models_{\mathbf{S_{col}}} \sigma_{col}^{n,n+1}$ under classification $\mathbf{S_{col}}$ is just a different way of viewing the fact of the form $d_i \models_{\mathbf{S_{tri}}} \sigma_{dim}^{2,T(n)}$ under classification $\mathbf{S_{tri}}$. In other words, it prescribes which facts under $\mathbf{S_{tri}}$ are accessible from which facts under $\mathbf{S_{col}}$ if one switches one's way of viewing diagrams.

Infomorphism $g_{col} : \mathbf{T_{col}} \rightleftarrows \mathbf{T_{tri}}$ does the same job on the target side, and prescribes that facts of the form $i \models_{\mathbf{T_{tri}}} \tau_{tri}^{2,4(n)}$ are accessible from the facts of the form $i \models_{\mathbf{T_{col}}} \tau_{col}^{n,n+1}$ if one switches one's way of viewing numbers. The remaining two infomorphisms, f_{tri} and g_{tri}, depicted in Fig. 3 work similarly.

With this setup, an aspect shift can be seen as a shift of representation systems that are connected via infomorphisms. Take the case of a shift from $\mathbf{S_{col}}$ to $\mathbf{S_{tri}}$. One sees the fact $d \models_{\mathbf{S_{col}}} \sigma_{col}^{4,4+1}$ under the view of classification $\mathbf{S_{col}}$ and interpret it with semantic constraint $\Rightarrow_{col}$ to obtain information $20 \models_{\mathbf{T_{col}}} \tau_{col}^{4,4+1}$. This much is done under representation system $\mathfrak{R}_{col}$. As infomorphism f_{col} marks, the fact $d \models_{\mathbf{S_{tri}}} \sigma_{tri}^{2,T(4)}$ is accessible from the fact $d \models_{\mathbf{S_{col}}} \sigma_{col}^{4,4+1}$ by a switch of view, and if one actually performs the switch, seeing the fact $d \models_{\mathbf{S_{tri}}} \sigma_{tri}^{2,T(4)}$ under classification $\mathbf{S_{tri}}$ and interpreting it with semantic constraint $\Rightarrow_{tri}$ to obtain information $20 \models_{\mathbf{T_{tri}}} \tau_{tri}^{2,T(4)}$, then one is using system $\mathfrak{R}_{tri}$. An aspect shift in our sample proof can be thus modeled as shifts between representation systems $\mathfrak{R}_{col}$ and $\mathfrak{R}_{tri}$ via infomorphisms.

Shifts between source classifications $\mathbf{S_{col}}$ and $\mathbf{S_{tri}}$ are shifts of how we perceptually decompose the given diagram, and so often significantly easier than shifts between target classifications $\mathbf{T_{col}}$ and $\mathbf{T_{tri}}$, which involve shifts of how we conceptually "decompose" a number in the abstract. Yet, they can bring about a shift of entire representation systems between $\mathfrak{R}_{col}$ and $\mathfrak{R}_{tri}$ and provide an alternative conceptualization of the number in question. The presence of diagram d facilitates the aspect shifts necessary and thus our understanding of the proof.

4   Modeling Aspect Integration

In the story that we have told above, the same tokens in the source and the target can be classified in different ways. The tokens are shared by the different representation systems but the types used to classify them differ. However, this story has a problem, namely how tasks that involve multiple views can be solved.

The construction and comprehension of our sample proof are such tasks. With system $\mathfrak{R}_{col}$, we interpret type $\sigma_{col}^{4,4+1}$ holding of our diagram d and obtain information $\tau_{col}^{4,4+1}$ about our target number 20. After shifting our representation system to $\mathfrak{R}_{tri}$, we interpret type $\sigma_{tri}^{2,T(4)}$ of the same diagram and obtain information $\tau_{tri}^{2,T(4)}$ about the same number. Note that the types $\tau_{col}^{4,4+1}$ and $\tau_{tri}^{2,T(4)}$ we have obtained at different stages belong to separate classifications $\mathbf{T_{col}}$ and $\mathbf{T_{tri}}$ of our target number, and crucially, neither classification has both of these types. According to our theory, this means that there is no view in which we can simultaneously attribute these types to our target number. But there must be such a view, for in the final part of the proof, we integrate information $\tau_{col}^{4,4+1}$ and $\tau_{tri}^{2,T(4)}$ about the number and, as they respectively mean that "characterizable as $\sum_{i=1}^{4}(4+1)$" and "characterizable as $T(4) + T(4)$", reach the equation $\sum_{i=1}^{4}(4+1) = T(4) + T(4)$, and then $T(4) = \frac{4 \times (4+1)}{2}$ by algebra.

The notions of classification and infomorphism let us extend our model naturally to capture this integrating view. As Fig. 4 shows, the main component of the extension is an overarching representation system, depicted in the uppermost part. It "superposes" component systems $\mathfrak{R}_{col}$ and $\mathfrak{R}_{tri}$, and in particular gives access to the complete set of types from each representation system.

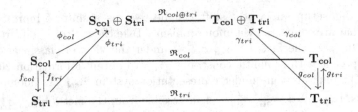

Fig. 4. Superposition of $\Re_{col}$ and $\Re_{tri}$ into a representation system, $\Re_{col\oplus tri}$, which integrates the two views provided by $\Re_{col}$ and $\Re_{tri}$.

Generally, two classifications $\mathbf{A}$ and $\mathbf{B}$ can be superposed if they classify the same set of tokens with disjoint sets of types $\mathrm{typ}(\mathbf{A})$ and $\mathrm{typ}(\mathbf{B})$. The superposed classification $\mathbf{A} \oplus \mathbf{B}$ will classify those same set of tokens with the union $\mathrm{typ}(\mathbf{A}) \cup \mathrm{typ}(\mathbf{B})$ of these sets of types. Its types classify tokens just in the same way they do in the original classifications. Thus, given a token $t \in \mathrm{tok}(\mathbf{A} \oplus \mathbf{B})$ and a type $\alpha \in \mathrm{typ}(\mathbf{A} \oplus \mathbf{B})$, $t \models_{\mathbf{A}\oplus\mathbf{B}} \alpha$ if and only if either $\alpha \in \mathrm{typ}(\mathbf{A})$ and $t \models_{\mathbf{A}} \alpha$, or else $\alpha \in \mathrm{typ}(\mathbf{B})$ and $t \models_{\mathbf{B}} \alpha$.

Thus, $\mathbf{A} \oplus \mathbf{B}$ puts types from different classifications under one umbrella and captures a more diversified way of viewing diagram tokens than the restricted ways of viewing under $\mathbf{A}$ and $\mathbf{B}$. Since classifications $\mathbf{S_{col}}$ and $\mathbf{S_{tri}}$ have the same set of tokens while classifying them with disjoint sets of types, there is a superposed classification $\mathbf{S_{col}} \oplus \mathbf{S_{tri}}$. Similarly for the target side, and there is a superposed classification $\mathbf{T_{col}} \oplus \mathbf{T_{tri}}$ of classifications $\mathbf{T_{col}}$ and $\mathbf{T_{tri}}$.

As a representation system, the superposed system $\Re_{col\oplus tri}$ comes with two semantic relations. The indication relation $\Rightarrow_{col\oplus tri}$ is just the union of the indication relations of the component systems. The representation relation $\rightarrow_{col\oplus tri}$ is identical to $\rightarrow_{col}$, which is identical to $\rightarrow_{tri}$.

Now, it is immediate from the definition of classification $\mathbf{S_{col}} \oplus \mathbf{S_{tri}}$ that any fact of the form $d_i \models_{\mathbf{S_{col}}\oplus\mathbf{S_{tri}}} \sigma_{col}^{n,n+1}$ in this classification is equivalent to the fact $d_i \models_{\mathbf{S_{col}}} \sigma_{col}^{n,n+1}$ in classification $\mathbf{S_{col}}$. We can mark this general equivalence with an infomorphism, say ϕ_{col}, shown in Fig. 4 as the arrow from $\mathbf{S_{col}}$ to $\mathbf{S_{col}} \oplus \mathbf{S_{tri}}$. At the token level, $\phi_{col}\check{}$ is just the identity function from $\mathrm{tok}(\mathbf{S_{col}}) \oplus \mathrm{tok}(\mathbf{S_{tri}})$ to $\mathrm{tok}(\mathbf{S_{col}})$. At the type level, $\phi_{col}\hat{}$ maps every type $\sigma_{col}^{n,n+1}$ in $\mathrm{typ}(\mathbf{S_{col}})$ to its copy $\sigma_{col}^{n,n+1}$ in $\mathrm{typ}(\mathbf{S_{col}} \oplus \mathbf{S_{tri}})$. By the fundamental property of ϕ_{col}, we have:

$$d_i \models_{\mathbf{S_{col}}\oplus\mathbf{S_{tri}}} \phi_{col}\hat{}(\sigma_{col}^{n,n+1}) \quad \text{if and only if} \quad \phi_{col}\check{}(d_i) \models_{\mathbf{S_{col}}} \sigma_{col}^{n,n+1}$$

But the left side is equivalent to $d_i \models_{\mathbf{S_{col}}\oplus\mathbf{S_{tri}}} \sigma_{col}^{n,n+1}$ by the definition of $\phi_{col}\hat{}$ and the right side is equivalent to $d_i \models_{\mathbf{S_{col}}} \sigma_{col}^{n,n+1}$ by the definition of $\phi_{col}\check{}$. Thus, we have the equivalence of $d_i \models_{\mathbf{S_{col}}\oplus\mathbf{S_{tri}}} \sigma_{col}^{n,n+1}$ and $d_i \models_{\mathbf{S_{col}}} \sigma_{col}^{n,n+1}$, successfully marked by infomorphism ϕ_{col}.

The other informorphisms, ϕ_{tri}, γ_{col}, and γ_{tri}, drawn in Fig. 4 work similarly, each marking a general equivalence relation between facts in a superposed classification and facts in one of its component classifications. This tells that aspect shifting is possible to and fro between the superposed system $\mathfrak{R}_{col\oplus tri}$ and the component systems $\mathfrak{R}_{col}$ and $\mathfrak{R}_{tri}$.

5   Conclusion

In this paper we have described a formal model of the semantic base that underpins multiple readings and aspect shifting. To review our main points, a diagram token admits multiple readings when the token participates in multiple representation systems, each making it convey a different type of information about the same target object. Switches of views underlying aspect shifting can occur when facts under different classification schema are equivalent, and the notion of infomorphism from [1] is useful in marking such equivalence across classifications.

Aspect shifting based on a diagram consists of switches of views of equivalent facts across the source and target classifications of disparate representation systems. In particular, the aspect shifting in the example involves (1) a shift between the specialized systems, and (2) a shift toward an overarching system.

Because of our perceptual abilities, multiple views of a diagram are more apparent to us than the corresponding multiple views of the target, resulting in diagrams triggering shifts of representation systems and revealing new truths that are otherwise hard to see about the target. The perceptual grasp of equivalence of facts about a diagram can be transferred to the represented number, and can explain the characteristic persuasiveness of the proof in question.

Our model does not cover all kinds of shifts of views involved in our sample proof. An important question remains how to model the semantic base for shifts of global views of the entire diagram to local views of its sub-parts. Although shifts of this kind are not aspect shifts in the usual sense, they do play an important role in the proof, and their analysis is deferred to future research.

References

1. Barwise, J., Seligman, J.: Information Flow: The Logic of Distributed Systems. Cambridge University Press, Cambridge (1997)
2. Coliva, A.: Human diagrammatic reasoning and seeing-AS. Synthese **186**(1), 121–148 (2012)
3. De Toffoli, S.: Epistemic roles of mathematical diagrams. Ph.D. thesis, Department of Philosophy, Stanford University, Stanford, CA, December 2018
4. Giaquinto, M.: Visual Thinking in Mathematics. Oxford University Press, Oxford (2007)
5. Jamnik, M.: Mathematical Reasoning with Diagrams. CSLI Publications, Stanford (2001)
6. Nelson, R.B.: Proofs Without Words. Number 1 in Classroom Resource Materials. The Mathematical Association of America, NW, Washington DC (1993)
7. Oliveri, G.: Mathematics. A science of patterns? Synthese **112**(3), 379–402 (1997)
8. Shimojima, A., Barker-Plummer, D.: Channel-theoretic account of reification in representation systems. Logique et Anal. (N.S.) **251**, 341–363 (2020)
9. Shin, S.-J.: The mystery of deduction and diagrammatic aspects of representation. Rev. Philos. Psychol. **6**(1), 49–67 (2015)

How to Visually Represent Structure

Axel Arturo Barceló Aspeitia[✉] (iD)

Instituto de Investigaciones Filosóficas, UNAM, 04500 Mexico City, Mexico
abarcelo@filosoficas.unam.mx

Abstract. How does the compositional arrangement of elements in a complex image, like a diagram, a picture or a map, represent the structural features of its content? In this paper I argue that they do so iconically, through the exploitation of relations of visual similarity and dissimilarity. I develop the general claim that our interpretation of this sort of images is guided by the implicit defeasible assumption that things that are patently related represent things that are relevantly related in a similar way. I also identify the usual intrinsic and extrinsic mechanisms we use to represent structural features and illustrate them with an example from real life: a recent infographic from a popular science magazine.

Keywords: Structure · Iconicity · Semantics · Infographics · Interpretation

1 Introduction

Most times, when we use an image to represent something we do not want our audience to just identify the image's reference. Instead we want to convey complex ideas and information. This means that most times, what we want to represent visually will have a structure. In maps, for example, we do not just want to represent towns, rivers, roads, etc. but we want these elements of the landscape to be properly connected between them, i.e., we want to show not only that there is a road, a beach and a town, but that the road goes from the beach to the town and back. The question that drives this work is: how do we communicate this aspect of our content through visual representation?

In recent work, Greenberg [1] has identified a striking feature of many complex visual representations, i.e., that they usually convey structural features iconically, not symbolically. Greenberg found that, in general, the semantic rules linking the relevant features of our representations with the structural features of their referents involve a very small set of general conditions. Consequently, the number of syntactic and semantic categories in these semantic rules is very low [2]. This means that, in order to determine the structural content of our visual representations we usually do not use anything like a dictionary, that is, a set of meaning conventions linking features of the image with features of what it stands for. The aim of this paper is to shed some light on why this is so.

My answer fits and must be understood within a broader Gricean picture of visual representations according to which conventions play a very small role in their interpretation. In other words, we seldom decode visual representations according to some

© Springer Nature Switzerland AG 2022
V. Giardino et al. (Eds.): Diagrams 2022, LNAI 13462, pp. 218–225, 2022.
https://doi.org/10.1007/978-3-031-15146-0_18

previously fixed symbolic conventions, but instead make sense of them by detecting the representational intentions behind them. This means that the inferential process through which we extract structural information from an image usually follows a relevantist process similar to the one guiding pragmatic inferences in linguistic communication [3].

This hermeneutic process might involve conventions, but many of them will be inferred, not learned, and circumscribed to the particular images being interpreted in a way that might not extend to other, novel representations. This means that even when our experience with previous visual representations is helpful in the interpretation of novel representations, the reason might have less to do with representational codes and more with the fact that similar communicative problems require similar solutions, so that so-called representational codes might be better understood not as dictionaries of arbitrarily assigned conventional meanings, but more as general strategies to solve communicative tasks.

2 The Golden Rule of Iconic Representation

The main hermeneutic hypothesis I want to argue for here is that in extracting structural information from a complex image, we postulate defeasible interpretative hypotheses that aim to make sense of particular structural features of the image. For example, if we see the same character repeated in a single image, we assume that it represents the same element in all its occurrences. This assumption can be defeated by other considerations, but it nevertheless guides our search for meaning. In particular, I will develop the hypothesis that when interpreting complex images, we are centrally guided by the general principle that things that are patently related represent things that are also relevantly related, a principle I will call *the golden rule*.

The key notion here, of course is that of a patent relation or difference, which is a generalization of the relevantist concept of ostension [3]. Broadly stated, a fact is patent in my sense if it is complex enough to denote an intentional act of ostension – commonly, one that left the patent fact as its trace. For example, most of what we call "order" or "structure" does not just happen naturally, but is the result of intentional human effort. Thus, when we find objects displayed in patent order, it is rational to assume that someone placed them that way, knowing that we would notice and wonder why she made the effort of displaying them that way. In a well designed visual image, one not only notices the elements that compose the image, but also notices that (at least some of) the way in which they are composed is not random but follows some planned order that calls for an explanation. In other words, we notice how the elements are composed and ask why, i.e., what communicative or aesthetic purpose did the designer pursue in her effort to visually organize the elements of her composition that way and not another.

For a structural feature to be patent in this sense, it must be easily detectable and naturally assumed as intentional. This requires differences and similarities of the right magnitude [8]. Making them too small might confuse the interpreter who might either just miss them or think that they are not intentional. Making them too large, on the other hand, introduces noise, making one's audience wonder why the difference is that big instead of just noticeable enough. In this regards, it is unfortunately easy to make the mistake of assuming that there is something like a normal audience whose cognitive and contextual circumstances determine what is salient or easily detectable, but in actuality audiences are very diverse, and ignoring their diversity commonly results not only in communicative failure, but also in further marginalization of minority bodies. For example, many color differences are not easily detectable by colorblind people, and nearsightedness can make small differences in size difficult to detect. That is why accessibility is essential to good design. It is not a luxury item or an add-on to good design, but a non-negotiable necessary condition [9].

Given our tendency to follow this general rule while generating interpretational hypotheses, it is not surprising that image makers have developed a plethora of mechanisms to exploit it for communicative purposes. In other words, assuming the general explanatory hypothesis that the patent structural features of our visual images usually manifest our communicative intentions to represent analogous structural features allows us to account for many design principles used in all sorts of visual representations, from diagrams and maps to formulas and infographics, as I hope to show in the remainder of the text.

3   Mechanisms of Structural Representation

Derived from the aforementioned general principle – that things that are patently related/similar/different represent things that are relevantly related/similar/different–, we can identify the following general rules: First, in order to represent a structured system, it is necessary to represent its component elements. Structure cannot be represented unless we represent also what is structured. This is usually achieved by using itemized elements like points, geometric figures, letters, etc. One can even use textual labels. As customary, I will call these "characters". They correspond to what Greenberg calls the first order elements of the system, and thus can be as iconic or symbolic as desired [1]. Much can and has been written about how to choose basic characters in order to make their identification and their reference clear, but none of that is relevant to our purposes here, i.e., not how these elements get their referents, but how the relations between these referents are represented. Two sorts of mechanisms are usually used to represent these: intrinsic and extrinsic, depending on whether they rely on internal features of how the elements themselves are represented or involve the introduction of new graphic elements to the image.

3.1   Intrinsic and Extrinsic Mechanisms

Intrinsic mechanisms of structural representation exploit similarities, relations and differences among the characters themselves to represent similarities, relations and differences among the elements they represent: for example, using letters of same or similar color, size, direction, etc. to indicate that the elements represented by those letters are related or of the same kind, while using letters of contrasting color, size, direction, etc. to indicate that they are unrelated or of different kinds [8]. Besides these perceptual similarities and differences, designers, artists and visual communicators usually also use other, more top down intrinsic mechanisms. For example, one might use lower case letters to represent different elements of a single kind and then use the distinction between vowels and consonants, or the early and later letters in the customary alphabetic order to introduce a sub-distinction between them. As a matter of fact, this is very common in algebra, where lower case letters are commonly used to represent numerical values, but the early letters, a, b, c,... are used to represent constant values and the later letters x, y, z,... are used to represent variables. Both sorts of mechanisms, perceptual and top-down, are intrinsic because they pertain to how the characters themselves are represented independently of how they are spatially and temporally distributed or what other elements accompany them.

Extrinsic mechanisms, in turn, can be of two kinds: The first one consists in exploiting the spatio-temporal location of the characters to establish external relations between them. Thus, for example, we can represent two objects as being more similar to a third one by locating the (characters that represent the) first two closer to each other than to the third one [10]. We can also use the center of the image to highlight a character and/or move another to the periphery to represent its lower status.

The second sort consists in introducing new elements to mark the relations or differences between the characters. For example, we can encircle characters that are of a kind, draw a line separating characters that are different, an arrow joining characters that are related, etc. Parentheses, underlining, asterisks, shading, crossing, etc. are also commonly used to represent structural features this way. These mechanisms are extrinsic because they do not rely on intrinsic features of how the characters themselves are represented and instead require the addition of new graphic elements to the image.

3.2 Recursion for Higher Order Representation

We can use the intrinsic features of the mechanisms we use to represent basic structural features to represent structural features of a higher order [11]. Notice that most of the aforementioned mechanisms, both internal and external, have an intrinsic structure. Spatio-temporal location is the obvious example [12], but differences in size, color, etc. are also structured. Thus, for example, if one uses connecting lines of different widths, one would be signaling not only that the relations represented by each sort of line are of three different kinds, but also that these three kinds are themselves ordered in a way that reflects the width order of the lines. Thus, for example, we can use thicker lines to represent stronger relations and thinner lines to represent weaker ones, etc. Regarding lines, one of the most well-known mechanism used to exploit their internal structures is arrows. Arrows are nothing but lines with a marked edge and this asymmetry is what makes them so useful to represent asymmetric relations. A line connecting two elements A and B signals that A and B are related, but an arrow from A to B also signals that the relation is asymmetric, i.e., that the role that A plays in the relation is different that the role B plays. Finally, we can also introduce new extrinsic elements, for example, lines to link lines that link lines, etc. to represent relations between relations between relations, etc.

Yet one of the most powerful tools we have devised to allow for the representation of higher order structural features is indexing (famously studied by Netz on his work on Euclidean diagrams [13]) i.e., using more than one mechanism (usually two different sort of marks) to represent the same relation or kind in order to multiply the possible similarities that can be exploited. For example, we can use a circle to group some elements and then attach a letter or some other symbol to the circle, so that then we can use the features of the letter and of the circle to denote higher order structural features of the represented group. Thus, for example, adding a numerical index to different connecting lines can help us represent a hierarchical order among the relations represented by the lines.

4   A Simple Example

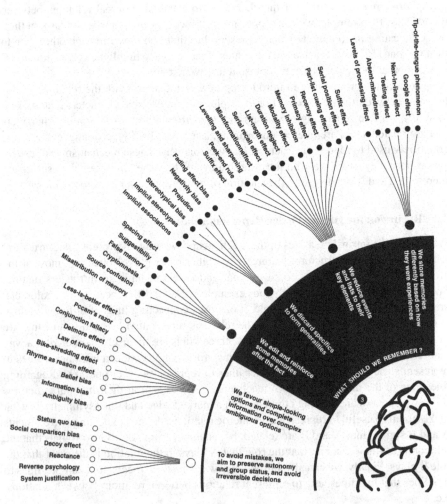

Fig. 1. Detail from Phil Ellis, "The Lazy Brain" 2018.

To illustrate these mechanisms, let me use some simple examples. Since my claim is that these mechanisms are already grounding the visual representation of structure in many of our images, we must find them in effect on regular everyday visual represen-tations. For example, consider the following infographic, designed by Phil Ellis, from Dean Burnett's article "The Lazy Brain" on the BBC Science Focus magazine 2018 issue on the evolutionary value of efficiency (Fig. 1) [14]. Without being a specially innovative or otherwise extraordinary visual representation, it is still a quite successful one, and thus serves perfectly as illustration of how structure is usually depicted.

The first thing to notice is that even though the structured elements are represented by textual labels (the error of confabulation, for example, is represented by the label "Confabulation"), if we do not read the labels, the image still manages to successfully communicate a lot of structural information. Even if we do not know what those labels represent, we can see in the image how they are related. Apart from the abundant text, and except for the picture of the brain at the center, the rest of the elements play structural roles. As predicted by my account, some of them are intrinsic and other extrinsic, some of them are first order and others are higher order. The main intrinsic mechanisms the image uses to represent structural relations are orientation and location. Most noticeably, the orientation of the labels closer to the external edge of the image form a ring. This, in part, tells us that they all have something in common: "Fading affect bias", "Negativity bias", "Prejudice", etc. are stuff of the same kind or play a similar role in the system represented by the image. The same happens for the next ring, closer to the center of the image: "We reduce events and lists to…", "We discard specifics to form generalities…", etc. all represent stuff of the same kind, different from that of "Negativity bias", "Prejudice", etc.

There is more structural information we can also obtain just from the orientation of the text. For example, "We favor simple-looking options…" has the same orientation as "Law of triviality" and this orientation is closer to the orientation of "Delmore effect" and "Bike-shredding effect" that to the orientation of "Suggestibility". This suggests that "We favor simple-looking options…" must be somehow related to "Law of triviality" and perhaps also to "Delmore effect" and "Bike-shredding effect" in a way that it is not treated to "Suggestibility", etc. And this is just orientation. The infographic also uses location as well as similarities and differences in case – upper and lower – to suggest all sorts of relations among the elements represented by the textual labels.

Notice that I have changed the language I am using to describe the content of the image, from talking about what the image "tells" us to what it "suggests". This is because some visual elements are more salient that others and some visual elements more strongly denote intentionality than others. In our example, the fact that the elements in the outer ring form a unity is strongly communicated because it is communicated by many mech-anisms reinforcing one another: location, orientation, size and case. Small differences in orientation, on their own, in contrast, can only suggest differences among their referents.

Let us focus now on the extrinsic mechanisms that are also at play in the image. In this regards, the most obvious are the lines connecting elements in the external ring with elements in the inner ring and the color shading at the center of the image. Once again, their communicative role is very straightforward: the lines tell you that the elements represented at their edges are somehow related, while the color blocks tell us that the elements represented on top of them are also somehow of a same kind.

So far we have been focusing only on first order structural elements, but second order elements also play an important role in this image. The color blocks at the center of the image, for example, are shaped to form a thick ring around the center. Thus, besides representing that the elements enclosed in each shaded surface belong to some sort of unity, this communicates a similarity among the different groups corresponding to each colored surface. Thus, we know that "We discard specifics to form generalities" and "We reduce events and lists to their key elements", "We edit and reinforce some memories after the fact", etc. are somehow related to "WHAT SHOULD WE REMEMBER?" because they are all inside the same colored patch (black in Fig. 1, but blue in Ellis' original image). So far, all that information is first order structural information. But if we factor second-order similarities, we can infer further structure. We can infer that the way "Negative bias" is related to "We discard specifics to form generalities" is the same way that "Cryptomemories" is related to "We edit and reinforce some memories…", even if we do not know what this relation is!

As I had stated above, representing a relation between elements this way suggest no further structure among the elements besides the one already conveyed by other intrinsic or extrinsic mechanisms. In this case, this means that even though "We discard specifics …", "We reduce events and lists …", "We edit and reinforce some memories…", and "WHAT SHOULD WE REMEMBER?" are all located within the same dark patch, and thus their referents must be somehow related, this last element, WHAT SHOULD WE REMEMBER?", must play a different, special role among them, because unlike the others, it is written in upper case and has a radically different orientation. This intrinsic difference in the way the elements in the blue patch are represented defeats the default assumption that everything inside a singular color patch must be somehow the same.

Finally, the infographic also includes indexes. Next to the blue patch, closer to the brain icon, we can see a numeral "3" in a blue circle. Both the color and the location of this visual element point towards it being linked to whatever is represented in the blue patch. The numeral "3" is then used in the accompanying text to make reference to this information outside the image. This is a textbook example of indexing as characterized by Netz [13]. Similar color circles with numerals accompany the other color patches, reinforcing the message that these different patches correspond to information of the same second-order kind. Thus we can see in a common infographic the use of mechanisms of all the kinds we had identified above and thus a clear illustration of how the general principle of using patent visual relations to represent analogous structural relations can be used to visually represent the structural features of our target systems. It remains an open question how general this phenomenon is and, in particular, whether it extends to other non-diagrammatic systems of representation. I will leave its answer for a future time.

References

1. Greenberg, G.: The Iconic-Symbolic Spectrum. Manuscript
2. Giardino, V., Greenberg, G.: Introduction: Varieties of Iconicity. Rev. Philos. Psychol. 6(1), 1–25 (2014). https://doi.org/10.1007/s13164-014-0210-7
3. Sperber, D., Wilson, D.: Relevance : Communication and Cognition. Blackwell, Cambridge, Mass (1995)

4. Ezcurdia, M., Stainton, R.: The Semantics-Pragmatics Boundary in Philosophy, Broadview Press, Peterborough, Canada (2013)
5. Peirce, C.S.: Studies in Logic, by Members of The Johns Hopkins University. Ed. Charles S. Peirce. Little Brown, Boston (1883)
6. Barceló, A.: Las imágenes como herramientas epistémicas. Scientia Studia **14**(1), 45–63 (2016)
7. Barceló, A.: Estructura. Enciclopedia de la Sociedad Española de Filosofía Analítica. http://www.sefaweb.es/estructura/ ISSN 2605-5449 (2018)
8. Dair, C.: Design with Type, University of Toronto Press (1967)
9. Coklyat, B., Finnegan, S.: Alt-Text as Poetry Workbook, Eyebeam/Disability Visibility Project (2020)
10. Dmytryk, E.: On Film Editing: An Introduction to the Art of Film Construction, Routledge (1984)
11. Ginns, P.: Integrating information: a meta-analysis of the spatial contiguity and temporal contiguity effects. Learn. Instr. **16**(6), 511–525 (2006). https://doi.org/10.1016/j.learninstruc.2006.10.001
12. Moktefi, A., Bellucci, F. Pietarinen, A-V.: Continuity, Connectivity and Regularity in Spatial Diagrams for N Terms. In: CEUR Workshop Proceedings 2013, pp. 31–5 (2013)
13. Netz, R.: Greek Mathematical Diagrams: Their Use and Their Meaning. For the Learning of Mathematics **18**(3), 33–39 (1998)
14. Burnett, D., Ellis, P.: The lazy brain. BBC Focus: Sci. Technol. **324**, 48–50 (2018)

Aspect Shifting in Aristotelian Diagrams

Hans Smessaert[1]([⊠])(iD) and Lorenz Demey[2](iD)

[1] Department of Linguistics, KU Leuven,
Blijde-Inkomststraat 21, 3000 Leuven, Belgium
hans.smessaert@kuleuven.be
[2] Center for Logic and Philosophy of Science, KU Leuven,
Kardinaal Mercierplein 2, 3000 Leuven, Belgium
lorenz.demey@kuleuven.be
https://www.logicalgeometry.org

Abstract. Aristotelian diagrams represent logical relations of opposition and implication between formulas or concepts. In this paper we investigate the cognitive mechanism of Aspect Shifting in order to describe various families of Aristotelian diagrams. Aspect shifting occurs when an 'ambiguous' visual representation triggers a perceptual change from one perspective or interpretation to another. In a first part, we consider aspect shifting which takes place on the level of Aristotelian subdiagrams and which switches focus precisely between the oppositional and the implicational perspective. In a second part, aspect shifting is involved in focussing on the ways in which smaller (but complete) Aristotelian diagrams—in particular, Aristotelian squares—are embedded inside bigger diagrams—in particular Aristotelian hexagons. In both parts, special attention is paid to the iterative nature of the aspect shifting.

Keywords: Aspect shifting · Gestalt switch · Opposition/implication relations · Aristotelian diagram · Subdiagram

1 Introduction

Aspect Shifting. The overall aim of this paper is to investigate the cognitive mechanism of Aspect Shifting in order to describe various families of Aristotelian diagrams. The drawing in Fig. 1(a)—which is 'ambiguous' between a leftward facing duck and a rightward facing hare—was first studied by the American psychologist Joseph Jastrow [7]. The drawing in Fig. 1(b)—standardly referred to as Schröder's stairs after the German natural scientist Heinrich G. F. Schröder [10]—is 'reversible' between the view from above descending from left to right, and the view from below rising from right to left.

In contemporary psychology of perception, such drawings illustrate the mechanism of PERCEPTUAL MULTISTABILITY: "under stimulation conditions that

The second author holds a Research Professorship (BOFZAP) from KU Leuven. This research was funded through the research project 'BITSHARE: Bitstring Semantics for Human and Artificial Reasoning' (IDN-19-009, Internal Funds KU Leuven).

© Springer Nature Switzerland AG 2022
V. Giardino et al. (Eds.): Diagrams 2022, LNAI 13462, pp. 226–234, 2022.
https://doi.org/10.1007/978-3-031-15146-0_19

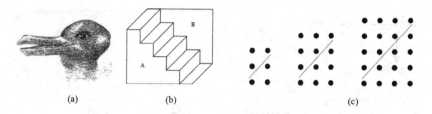

Fig. 1. (a) Duck-hare (b) Schröder's stairs (c) triangular number proof.

elicit perceptual multistability, visual perception continuously vacillates between alternative interpretations of the same, unchanged, sensory stimulus, therefore allowing a complete dissociation of sensory representation from subjective perception [...]. When viewing this stimulus, we realize that two possible interpretations [...] are randomly switching back and forth in our perception" [9, p. 123]. For example, with the Schröder's stairs in Fig. 1(b), "the [A] surface [...] that appears in front suddenly moves to the back and disappears from perception only to be replaced by the perception of the [B] surface that was previously [...] at the back [...]. Within a given temporal window, only one surface is consciously perceived, a phenomenon reflecting the struggle of our visual system to settle on a unique conscious interpretation of the visual stimulus" [9, p. 123].

Inspired by Jamnik [6] and Giaquinto [4], Shimojima [12, pp. 149–154] argues for the importance of this phenomenon of perceptual multistability (sometimes also referred to as *Gestalt switch*) in the realm of diagrammatic proofs for mathematical theorems, by analysing the example of the so-called *triangular numbers*. Given a positive integer k, the triangular number $T(k)$ is the sum of the first k positive integers.[1] It is a theorem of natural number arithmetic that $T(k) = \frac{k \times (k+1)}{2}$. The diagrammatic proof of this theorem is illustrated in Fig. 1(c) for $T(2)$, $T(3)$ and $T(4)$ respectively. It starts by drawing two dot triangles of magnitude k—i.e. with k dots on each of its sides—vertically stacked with their hypothenuses aligned. The resulting dot rectangle contains $2 \times T(k)$ dots, and can also be decomposed into k columns, each containing $k + 1$ dots—i.e. as $k \times (k + 1)$ dots. This makes $k \times (k + 1)$ equal to $2 \times T(k)$, and thus $T(k) = \frac{k \times (k+1)}{2}$. Giaquinto [4] stresses the importance for mathematical discovery of this general process of viewing a figure in two ways—both as a rectangle of equal columns and as composed of two equal triangles—and calls it ASPECT SHIFTING, the term which we also adopt in the present paper.[2]

Aristotelian Relations and Diagrams. In the framework of Logical Geometry [3,14] a central object of investigation is the so-called 'Aristotelian square' or 'square of opposition', visualising ARISTOTELIAN RELATIONS, i.e. logical relations of opposition and implication. Two propositions α and β are said to be:

---

[1] Thus $T(2) = 1 + 2 = 3$, $T(3) = 1 + 2 + 3 = 6$, $T(4) = 1 + 2 + 3 + 4 = 10$, and so on.
[2] In the theory of Shimojima [12, p. 154], aspect shifting involves a layered consequence tracking relation with constraints between two decomposition types of one figure.

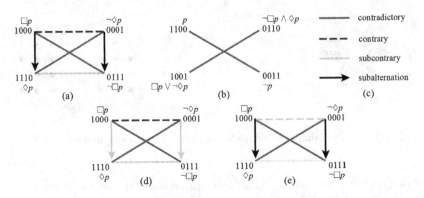

Fig. 2. (a) Classical square (b) degenerate square (c) coding conventions (d) hour-glass = OG perspective (e) bow-tie = IG perspective. (Color figure online)

a. contradictory $CD(\alpha,\beta)$ iff α and β cannot be true together and α and β cannot be false together

b. contrary $CR(\alpha,\beta)$ iff α and β cannot be true together but α and β can be false together

c. subcontrary $SCR(\alpha,\beta)$ iff α and β can be true together but α and β cannot be false together

d. in subalternation $SA(\alpha,\beta)$ iff α entails β but β doesn't entail α

In order to draw an ARISTOTELIAN DIAGRAM (AD for short), we first of all need a fragment F of a language $\mathcal{L}$, i.e. a subset of formulas of that language. The formulas in F are typically assumed to be contingent and pairwise non-equivalent, and the fragment is standardly closed under negation: if formula φ belongs to F, then its negation $\neg\varphi$ also belongs to F. For the language of the modal logic S5 (with operators $\Box$ for necessity and $\Diamond$ for possibility), for instance, a first fragment F_1 could be $\{\Box p, \neg\Box p, \Diamond p, \neg\Diamond p\}$. An Aristotelian diagram AD for F_1 is then defined as a diagram that visualises an edge-labeled graph G. Figure 2(a) presents the AD for F_1. The vertices of G are the elements of F_1, whereas the edges of G are labeled by *all* the Aristotelian relations holding between those elements, using the coding conventions in Fig. 2(c).

Furthermore, we have added the BITSTRING encoding of the formulas involved, in order to facilitate the analysis further on. For this particular fragment, these bitstrings consist of four bitpositions β_n, which have the value 1 or 0, and which correspond to four anchor formulas α_n—together constituting a partition Π of logical space [3].[3] Formulas are classified as level one (L1), level two (L2) or level three (L3) according to the number of values 1 in their bitstring.

The basic building block of any AD is the so-called PAIR OF CONTRADICTORY FORMULAS (or PCD). With the CLASSICAL SQUARE in Fig. 2(a), the two PCDs

---

[3] In this case $\Pi = \{\alpha_1, \alpha_2, \alpha_3, \alpha_4\} = \{\Box p, \neg\Box p \wedge p, \Diamond p \wedge \neg p, \neg\Diamond p\}$ and for every formula $\varphi \in F_1$, its bitstring $\beta(\varphi) = \beta_1\beta_2\beta_3\beta_4$ is such that $\beta_n = 1$ iff S5 $\models \alpha_n \rightarrow \varphi$.

constituting the diagonals of the square connect a L1 and a L3 formula. In Fig. 2(b), by contrast,—which is the AD for the fragment $F_2 = \{p, \neg p, \Box p \lor \neg \Diamond p, \neg \Box p \land \Diamond p\}$ and which is called a DEGENERATE SQUARE—the two diagonal PCDs connect two L2 formulas. More importantly, however, the four pairs of formulas/vertices along the edges of such a degenerate square do not stand in any Aristotelian relation whatsoever (they are said to be *unconnected* [14]).

The ARISTOTELIAN GEOMETRY AG $= \{CD, CR, SCR, SA\}$ is not uniform in the sense that the first three relations are defined in terms of propositions 'being true/false together', whereas the fourth is defined in terms of entailment. In [14] we have argued that AG is 'hybrid' between two other geometries, namely an OPPOSITION GEOMETRY (OG) and an IMPLICATION GEOMETRY (IG).

In Sect. 2 we explore the phenomenon of aspect shifting in the realm of Aristotelian diagrams. We first consider Aristotelian subdiagrams for opposition and implication, which allow us to distinguish between two families of Aristotelian hexagons. Secondly, we go into the ways in which classical Aristotelian squares are systematically embedded inside these two families of hexagons. In Sect. 3 we draw conclusions and mention some questions for future research.

2 Aspect Shifting with Aristotelian (sub)diagrams

Aspect Shifting in the Square. The most basic type of aspect shifting in ADs occurs within the classical square in Fig. 2(a), and holds between the 'hourglass' perspective in Fig. 2(d) and the 'bow-tie' perspective in Fig. 2(e). As with the earlier examples of perceptual multistability, these two perspectives on the square cannot be maintained simultaneously. The two PCD diagonals—which were already shown to be the only common elements in the classical and the degenerate squares in Fig. 2(a–b)—also turn out to be the only common elements in the hour-glass versus the bow-tie perspective in Fig. 2(d–e). Since the hourglass combines the two diagonal CD relations with the two horizontal opposition relations of CR and SCR, it will be called the OG-perspective. Conversely, since the bow-tie combines the two diagonal CD relations with the two vertical implication arrows of SA, it will be called the IG-perspective. It is important to stress that the hour-glass and bow-tie are not themselves Aristotelian diagrams, since *not all* available Aristotelian relations are explicitly represented: the hour-glass ignores the two SA arrows, whereas the bow-tie ignores CR and SCR. These two more elementary shapes are thus called ARISTOTELIAN SUBDIAGRAMS (AsD).[4]

Aspect Shifting in the Sherwood-Czeżowski Hexagon. If we compare the original Aristotelian square for the modal fragment $F_1 = \{\Box p, \neg \Box p, \Diamond p, \neg \Diamond p\}$ in Fig. 2(a) with the hexagonal diagram in Fig. 3(a), we observe that an extra PCD—namely the third diagonal connecting the two L2 formulas $\{p, \neg p\}$—crosses the original square horizontally. We refer to this diagram as a SHERWOOD-CZEŻOWSKI HEXAGON (SC for short) [2,8,13]. The most prominent feature of

---

[4] The hour-glass and bow-tie AsDs have been studied in great detail in our Diagrams 2020 paper [15] in terms of Shimojima's cognitive potential of Free Rides [12].

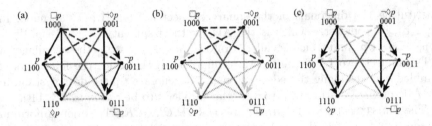

Fig. 3. (a) SC hexagon (b) vase = OG perspective (c) butterfly = IG perspective. (Color figure online)

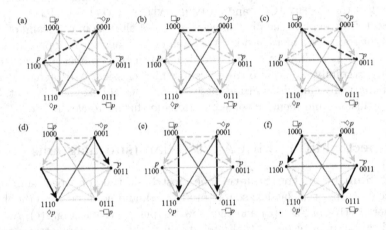

Fig. 4. SC hexagon: OG perspective = hour-glass (a) left (b) center (c) right; versus IG perspective = bow-tie (d) left (e) center (f) right. (Color figure online)

the SC hexagon—serving as a diagnostic for establishing the particular Aristotelian family of hexagons—are the two obtuse triangular shapes defined by three subalternation relations.[5] With all their arrows pointing downwards, these two triangles represent the 'transitive closure' of the SA relation. They also play a crucial role in the aspect shifting which occurs with the SC hexagon between the 'inner' blue/green (rhombic) 'vase' perspective in Fig. 3(b) and the 'outer' black 'butterfly' perspective in Fig. 3(c), which again cannot be maintained simultaneously. Again, the PCD diagonals are shared between the two perspectives. The vase in Fig. 3(b) extends the OG hour-glass perspective in Fig. 2(d), whereas the butterfly in Fig. 3(c) extends the IG bow-tie perspective in Fig. 2(e).

Next to the high-level two-way aspect shifting between vase and butterfly in Fig. 3(b–c), we observe a process of ITERATION, triggering a low-level three-way aspect shifting between the three hour-glass shapes in Fig. 4(a–c) and the three bow-tie shapes in Fig. 4(d–f). Once the overall OG versus IG perspective is fixed, it becomes harder to focus on more than one of the three smaller shapes at once.

---

[5] In our Diagrams 2021 paper [16] identifying such triangular shapes is analysed in terms of Shimojima's cognitive potential of Derivative Meaning [12].

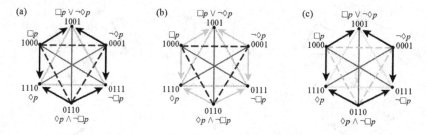

Fig. 5. (a) JSB hexagon (b) star = OG perspective (c) shield = IG perspective. (Color figure online)

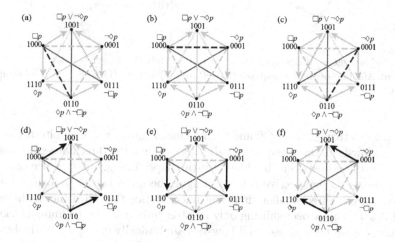

Fig. 6. JSB hexagon: OG perspective = hour-glass (a) left up (b) center (c) right up; versus IG perspective = bow-tie (d) left up (e) center (f) right up. (Color figure online)

Aspect Shifting in the Jacoby-Sesmat-Blanché Hexagon. Comparing the square for the fragment F_1 in Fig. 2(a) with the hexagonal diagram in Fig. 5(a), we observe that the third PCD diagonal connecting the two L2 formulas $\{\Box p \vee \neg \Diamond p, \Diamond p \wedge \neg \Box p\}$ crosses the original square vertically. We refer to this diagram as a JACOBY-SESMAT-BLANCHÉ HEXAGON (JSB for short) [1,5,11,13]. With this JSB the high-level two-way aspect shifting takes place between the inner, blue/green 'star' perspective in Fig. 5(b) and the outer, black 'shield' perspective in Fig. 5(c), which again cannot be maintained simultaneously, but have the three PCD diagonals in common. Like the hour-glass and vase, the star AsD—with its *CR* and *SCR* triangles[6]—has an OG perspective ignoring the *SA* arrows, whereas the shield AsD resembles the bow-tie and butterfly in that it has

---

[6] See [16] for an analysis of these triangular shapes in terms of Derivative Meaning [12]. The 'undirected' triangles for the symmetric relations *CR/SCR* in Fig. 5(b) crucially differ from 'directed' triangles for the asymmetric *SA* relations in Fig. 3(c).

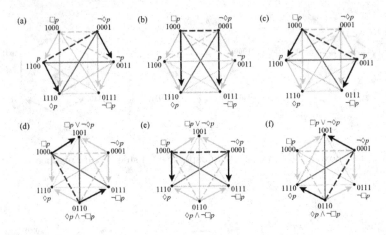

Fig. 7. SC hexagon: AG perspective = square (a) left (b) center (c) right; versus JSB hexagon: AG perspective = square (d) left up (e) center (f) right up. (Color figure online)

an IG perspective ignoring *CR* and *SCR*.[7] Once again, a process of iteration now triggers a low-level three-way aspect shifting between the three hour-glass shapes in Fig. 6(a–c) and between the three bow-tie shapes in Fig. 6(d–f). Once the overall OG versus IG perspective is fixed, it again becomes harder to focus on more than one of the three smaller shapes at once. Notice that with the SC hexagon in Fig. 4(a–f), this aspect shifting only involves 'minimal' 30° (counter)clockwise rotations, i.e. all hour-glasses and bow-ties are basically 'upright'. With the JSB hexagon in Fig. 6(a–f), by contrast, much more 'radical' 120° (counter)clockwise rotations are involved, with two out of the three hour-glasses and bow-ties almost being 'upside down', and hence less easily perceivable.[8]

Aspect Shifting with Embedded Aristotelian Diagrams. So far, high-level aspect shifting with Aristotelian hexagons concerned a two-way split between an OG and an IG perspective, inside of which—by iteration and rotation—a low-level three-way aspect shifting takes place. This overall constellation is 'reversed' with the SC hexagon in Fig. 7(a–c) and the JSB hexagon in Fig. 7(d–e). The high-level three-way aspect shifting adopts an AG perspective by focussing—again basically one at a time—on the three different ways in which a complete classical Aristotelian square is embedded inside these hexagons.[9] For each of these embedded squares, the iteration process then triggers a low-level two-way aspect shifting between the respective OG hour-glass perspectives in Fig. 4(a–c) and Fig. 6(a–c) and the IG bow-tie perspectives in Fig. 4(d–f) and Fig. 6(d–f).

---

[7] Notice that it is perfectly possible in theory to highlight other subparts for aspect shifting, as long as the crucial property of closure under negation is observed.

[8] They are problematic for the Apprehension Principle by which the structure/content of the visualisation should be readily/accurately perceived or comprehended [17].

[9] Differences between 'minimal' SC and 'radical' JSB rotations directly carry over.

3 Conclusion

The present study of the mechanism of aspect shifting in Aristotelian diagrams constitutes a next step in a recent research line inspired by the theory of cognitive potentials of Shimojima [12], elaborating on the notions of Free rides [15] and Derivative meaning [16]. By studying the Aristotelian diagrams from the perspective of perception and cognition, we also try to take a next step in establishing an exhaustive typology of diagram families, as well as a place for Aristotelian diagrams (and logical geometry) within the broader realm of logical diagrams research. Two topics for further research immediately suggest themselves at this point, namely (i) more (experimental) research concerning the differences in perceivability related to the degree of rotation involved in various types of hexagons, and (ii) extending aspect shifting to embedded squares versus hexagons in Aristotelian octagons.

References

1. Blanché, R.: Structures Intellectuelles. J. Vrin, Paris (1969)
2. Czeżowski, T.: On certain peculiarities of singular propositions. Mind **64**(255), 392–395 (1955)
3. Demey, L., Smessaert, H.: Combinatorial bitstring semantics for arbitrary logical fragments. J. Philos. Logic **47**, 325–363 (2018)
4. Giaquinto, M.: Visual Thinking in Mathematics: An Epistemological Study. Oxford University Press, Oxford (2007)
5. Jacoby, P.: A triangle of opposites for types of propositions in Aristotelian logic. New Scholasticism **24**, 32–56 (1950)
6. Jamnik, M.: Mathematical Reasoning with Diagrams: From Intuition to Automation. CSLI Publications, Stanford (2001)
7. Jastrow, J.: The mind's eye. Popular Sci. Monthly **54**, 299–312 (1899)
8. Khomskii, Y.: William of Sherwood, singular propositions and the hexagon of opposition. In: Béziau, J.Y., Payette, G. (eds.) New Perspectives on the Square of Opposition, pp. 43–59. Peter Lang, Bern (2011)
9. Panagiotaropoulos, T.I., Logothetis, N.K.: Multistable visual perception as a gateway to the neuronal correlates of phenomenal consciousness. In: Albertazzi, L. (ed.) Handbook of Experimental Phenomenology, pp. 119–143. John Wiley (2013)
10. Schröder, H.G.F.: Ueber eine optische Inversion bei Betrachtung verkehrter, durch optische Vorrichtung entworfener, physischer Bilder. Annalen der Physik und Chemie **181**, 298 (1858)
11. Sesmat, A.: Logique II. Hermann, Paris (1951)
12. Shimojima, A.: Semantic Properties of Diagrams and Their Cognitive Potentials. CSLI Publications, Stanford (2015)
13. Smessaert, H.: Boolean differences between two hexagonal extensions of the logical square of oppositions. In: Cox, P., Plimmer, B., Rodgers, P. (eds.) Diagrammatic Representation and Inference, pp. 193–199. Springer, Berlin/Heidelberg (2012). https://doi.org/10.1007/978-3-642-31223-6_21
14. Smessaert, H., Demey, L.: Logical geometries and information in the square of opposition. J. Logic Lang. Inf. **23**, 527–565 (2014)

15. Smessaert, H., Shimojima, A., Demey, L.: Free rides in logical space diagrams versus Aristotelian diagrams. In: Pietarinen, A.V., et al. (eds.) Diagrammatic Representation and Inference, pp. 419–435. Springer, Cham (2020). https://doi.org/10.1007/978-3-030-54249-8_33
16. Smessaert, H., Shimojima, A., Demey, L.: On the cognitive potential of derivative meaning in Aristotelian diagrams. In: Basu, A., et al. (eds.) Diagrammatic Representation and Inference, pp. 495–511. Springer, Cham (2021). https://doi.org/10.1007/978-3-030-86062-2_51
17. Tversky, B.: Visualizing thought. Topics in cognitive. Science **3**, 499–535 (2011)

Epistemic Roles of Diagrams in Short Proofs

Henrik Kragh Sørensen[(✉)] and Mikkel Willum Johansen

Section for History and Philosophy of Science, Department of Science Education,
University of Copenhagen, Copenhagen, Denmark
{henrik.kragh,mwj}@ind.ku.dk

Abstract. Recent case studies in the philosophy of mathematical practice have pointed out that certain types of diagrams play epistemic roles in mathematical proofs. To complement such case studies and provide a quantitative basis for further analysis and discussions, we undertake an empirical study based on a large and contemporary corpus of mathematical texts. Following an *a priori* assumption that diagrams in *short* proofs carry more epistemic warrant, we focus on 1- or 2-sentence proofs that refer to diagrams, and we build a corpus of such proofs from the arXiv. Based on this corpus we analyze and develop a typology of such proofs in order to conduct selected qualitative close-readings of diagrams in their argumentative contexts. This leads us to discuss tensions between visual and syntactical aspects of diagrams that suggest that *hybrid* diagrams play distinct roles in mathematical practice.

1 Introduction

The philosophical study of diagrams in mathematical practice has recently gained new impetus through detailed studies of their prevalence and support for mathematical cognition. Recent quantitative investigations have shown that diagrams were relatively frequent in mathematical publications throughout the past century despite the fact that such prominent mathematicians as David Hilbert considered them to be insufficient as epistemic support for mathematical claims. Diagrams were relatively frequent around 1900, but between 1910 and 1950 the prevalence of diagrams in mathematics publications decreased noticeably. After 1950, their use increased again especially due to the use of commutative diagrams in emerging fields such as category theory and K-theory, before the use of diagrams found in publications diversified towards the end of the past and into the 21st century [9].

Today, a wide variety of different diagrams are commonly used in mathematical publications, but despite their prevalence the epistemic roles of diagrams in contemporary mathematical practice are still in need of investigation.

The connection between diagrams and logical inference was investigated in the 1990s [e.g. 13]. These studies clearly demonstrated the epistemic potential in diagrammatic reasoning, but they were somewhat removed from mathematical

© Springer Nature Switzerland AG 2022
V. Giardino et al. (Eds.): Diagrams 2022, LNAI 13462, pp. 235–242, 2022.
https://doi.org/10.1007/978-3-031-15146-0_20

practice. More recent studies have addressed this issue through case studies analyzing the roles that knot, commutative, and similar diagrams play in concrete mathematical practice [5]. The overall conclusion is that such diagrams can play integral roles in both proving and understanding mathematical theorems. With a key term coined by De Toffoli, certain diagrams have a *hybrid* nature in the sense that they share features with both algebraic and geometric representations [4]. Such diagrams are designed for the typographical layout to support intuitive, visual reasoning, while simultaneously being part of a formalism that supports syntactic considerations and manipulations. Diagrams of this type thus offer a compromise between demands for (formal) rigour and the cognitive economy afforded by visual intuition. For that reason hybrid diagrams have the potential to play special epistemic roles in mathematical argumentation.

In the following we investigate various epistemic roles played by diagrams in mathematical proofs. We do so by first assessing the frequency of hybrid diagrams among the diagrams used for epistemic purposes in short mathematical proofs before we turn to close readings of two cases chosen to be rich in information and perspectives.

2   Methods and Materials

2.1   Preparing the Corpus

Mathematical manuscripts uploaded to the arXiv provide a comprehensive corpus of texts for digital studies of mathematical practice. Each manuscript is provided with metadata about its date of uploading and self-ascribed research field chosen from 32 mathematical categories. Additionally, LATEX source files are openly available for almost all of the manuscripts. In our project we have built a pipeline for processing these LATEX source files, which contain substantial structural information, into *contexts* corresponding to structural elements of mathematical research publications. Among these contexts, the *proof context* contains structural components that pertain to proving statements (which are captured in *theorem contexts* etc.). Thus we have direct access to structural elements of mathematical texts which are intended as demonstrations. Moreover, we can identify and process other LATEX instructions which correspond to diagrams constructed using special advanced figure-drawing packages for LATEX. Combining these two elements of our pipeline—the *proof context* and the source for mathematical diagrams—we are able to automatically extract those diagrams that feature (directly, i.e. not by reference only) in short proofs, defined as only consisting of one or two sentences. We detect the length of proofs in terms of sentences using a standard NLP sentence tokenizer.

For the current project, we built a corpus of all the manuscripts uploaded to arXiv in 2021 within the mathematics section; this comes to 34 426 papers of which our pipeline gives us access to the structural information of 32 276 papers (93.8%). This total corpus contains no less than 335 113 proofs, but we chose to focus on only short proofs which contain or refer to diagrams. Thus, our inclusion criteria are:

1. Either the *proof text* contains (at least) one of the *indicator words* `diagram`, `figure`, `sketch` or `drawing` (or derived forms), or
2. the proof contains (at least) one of the follow LaTeX constructs:
   (a) Either the command `\xymatrix`, or
   (b) any one of the environments `tikzpicture`, `tikzcd`, `psmatrix`, `pspicture`, `knot` or `ytableau`, which are frequently used to typeset diagrams of various sorts, or
   (c) a graphics file included by the command `\includegraphics`.

When we extracted the proofs meeting these criteria, we ended with 900 proofs, containing 366 identified diagrams and referring to more diagrams outside the proof context. These short proofs with their diagrams were then extracted and compiled using LaTeX into a document which provided the basis for our subsequent, qualitative and human-centred analyses.

2.2 Coding and Categorization

Of the 268 single-sentence proofs in the corpus 215 were coded and categorized in NVivo using a mixed theoretical and grounded approach: Instances that include diagrams were first categorized according to *types* known from the literature (see Sect. 1) while instances not including diagrams were categorized using grounded categories that emerged during the first round of coding [2]. A second round of coding was performed to ensure consistency with the final code book. Subsequently, instances that include diagrams were further categorized according to their *type*, if the type could be discerned. Instances where the type could not be discerned were categorized as either *other hybrid* or *other non-hybrid* depending on a judgement of the epistemic role of the diagram (see Table 1).

Instances that did not include diagrams but referred to them were categorized with the following emergent *categories*:

- *1D diagram*: One dimensional diagram such as exact sequence. These are not included in the analysis as diagrams in this paper [see [8], for discussion].
- *Hypothetical diagrams*: Reference to a diagram that could be made or imagined, often with instructions or reference to similar diagrams in the literature.
- *Chart*. The indicator word "figure" picked up the use of charts. These are not considered diagrams in this analysis.
- *Not diagram, other*: Indicator words refer to the literature or are used in a non-visual sense.

Three instances were further removed from the data set as they could not be identified in the current online versions on `arXiv`, presumably because the paper had been revised. Three more instances were further removed as the diagram referred to did not play a clear epistemic role in the proof.

This categorization was complete and unique in the sense that all instances were coded as belonging to precisely one of the categories described above.

3   Types and Uses of Diagrams in Short Proofs

Based on our quantitative study of the 2021 corpus, a few initial observations can be made. First, and unsurprisingly, we found that the prevalence of short proofs that refer to diagrams varies considerably across mathematical fields. On average, in category theory, almost every second paper contains such as proof; and in K-theory and homology, algebraic topology, quantum algebra, and geometric topology more than 10% of papers include short proofs referring to diagrams. On the other hand, such proofs were much rarer in (most) other fields.

We also tested whether larger prevalence of short proofs referring to diagrams led to other features that we could hypothesize, such as perhaps fewer equations, shorter proofs in general, etc. but it seemed to have no significant impact.

We did not directly analyze the function of the concrete diagrams categorized as commutative, graphs and knots, but diagrams of these types are generally associated with hybrid functions. Given this assumption, it is clear from the overall distribution of diagram types (Table 1) that hybrid diagrams were the dominating type in our sample, with commutative diagrams as the most common sub-type. This being said, instances including non-hybrid diagrams formed a substantive minority.

Table 1. Instances including diagrams: Distribution of diagram *types*.

Diagram type	#
Commutative	102
Graph	7
Knot	1
Other hybrid	18
Other non-hybrid	20
Total	147

Table 2. Instances not including diagrams: Distribution of *categories*.

Category	#
1D-diagram	8
Chart	2
Hypothetical diagram	29
Not diagram (other)	23
Total	62

In the categories of non-diagrams (Table 2) it is especially worth noting the prevalence of hypothetical diagrams. This was an emergent category we did not expect, and its presence in the data set illustrates the diverse roles diagrams play in mathematical epistemic practice. To explore the category further, we only give two examples from the data set, leaving many more for separate discussion:

Proof [of four identities]. They can be checked by diagram computation [10, p. 22].

Proof. The statement (4.2) is immediate from a picture, for example Figure 16 in [external reference], using that between any such pair of points, there is almost surely a unique maximizing path [12, p. 15].

The two examples are extreme cases illustrating the breadth of the category as we used it. In the first case diagrams are merely stipulated, while in the second particular features of a diagram type known in the literature is hinted at. These hypothetical diagrams are invoked but not present in the argumentation, and as such they are placeholders for gaps in the proofs that are left to the reader [see also 1], just as tedious calculations or computer experiments are sometimes used.

4 Epistemic Roles of Diagrams

To further explore the data set, we chose two cases for close analysis. Following the method of information-oriented selection we sought two abnormal cases [6, p. 230], one belonging to the category "Other non-hybrid diagrams" and the other to the category "Other hybrid diagrams".

4.1 Case Study 1

The paper "Lamps in Slim Rectangular Planar Semimodula Lattices" was uploaded by G. Czédli onto `arXiv` in January 2021 and classified as dealing with rings and algebras [3]. It contains 11 figures of diagrams, all but two of which include the central object of the paper, the so-called *lamps*.

The paper was included in our corpus because its single-sentence proof of Lemma 3.1 contains the indicator word 'figure' [3, p. 18]:

Proof. The proof is trivial by Fig. 1 and (2.10). ☐

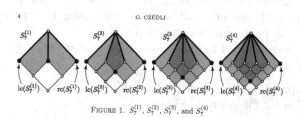

4

G. CZÉDLI

FIGURE 1. $S_7^{(1)}$, $S_7^{(2)}$, $S_7^{(3)}$, and $S_7^{(4)}$

Fig. 1. Figure 1 in [3, p. 4].

The figure, to which the proof refers, occurs many pages earlier in the paper and is reproduced here in Fig. 1. It came with a brief introduction, pointing to an earlier paper:

For example, the lattices $S_7^{(n)}$ for $n \in \mathbb{N}^+ := \{1, 2, 3, \dots\}$, defined in Czédli [2] and presented here in Fig. 1 for $n \leq 4$, are slim rectangular lattices. [3, p. 3]

The reference '(2.10)' in the proof refers to a statement about lamps:

> [E]very internal lamp comes to existence from a multifork extension. Furthermore, if a lamp K comes by a multifork extension at a 4-cell H_i, then CircR(I) is a geometric region determined by H_i; [3, p. 12]

This explanation provides another way of describing the formation of lamps and their properties, cast in a different language and invoking carefully named objects and processes.

Based on this short case, we first notice that Czédli's figure plays an epistemic role in his proof as it is part of making the proof "trivial". Yet, although the figure suggests a pattern of expansion, there is nothing to suggest that the figure is dynamic or supports any form of syntactical reasoning, so it does not seem to classify as a hybrid diagram. When Czédli introduced his Fig. 1, he spoke of it as an example, suggesting that the epistemic role of the figure lies mainly in suggesting instances of these objects along with the processes of generalizing such instances. This would help the reader to construct mental representations. Thus, this case suggests a situation in which a diagram plays an epistemic role by exposing co-exact features and abstracting away from complications [11]. It serves as an integral part of the reasoning by fostering familiarity with the object and expressing key insights in the form of generation of (a family) of lamps.

4.2   Case Study 2

In February 2021, K. Wada uploaded his paper "CF-moves for virtual links" to the arXiv [15]. The paper was classified as general topology, and in it Wada studied transformations of virtual links, which are generalizations of knots. As is the case with knots, virtual links have a specific syntax which Wada illustrated along with the lists of Reidemeister moves R1–R3 and V1–V4 and the so-called CF-move [15, p. 1]. These introductions were given using the first four of a total of 16 figures in the paper which spans 14 pages.

This paper was included in our collection because of the 1-sentence proof of its Lemma 2.1 [15, p. 4]:

> *Proof.* The proof in the case $\epsilon\epsilon' = 1$ follows from Figure 2.4, and that in the case $\epsilon\epsilon' = -1$ follows from Figure 2.5.   □

The figures immediately follow the proof, and Wada's Fig. 2.4 is shown here as Fig. 2. This figure shows a dynamic and linear structure with a clear syntax: It is to be read from top-left to bottom-left as a process in which one virtual link is transformed into another through a sequence of operations (R2, R3, CF, CF, R2). This epistemic use of diagrams is well-known also in other branches of knot theory [5], but in this example, the syntax of links is adapted, and the operations go beyond standard Reidemeister moves.

Therefore, this case illustrates that Wada's Fig. 2.4 plays an epistemic role as a hybrid diagram. But it also highlights how new syntax and manipulations are to be introduced visually before they can be brought to use, even in simple proofs such as this [see also 7].

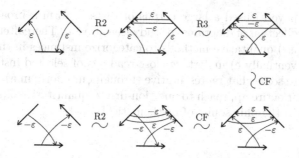

FIGURE 2.4. Proof of Lemma 2.1 in the case $\varepsilon\varepsilon' = 1$

Fig. 2. Figure 2.4 in [15, p. 5].

5   The Epistemic Role of Diagrams in Short Proofs

The purpose of this study was to shed light on the epistemic roles that diagrams play in mathematical practice. In our approach, we combined quantitative and qualitative corpus studies to gain additional content for discussions about diagrams in mathematical practice and begin methodological triangulation.

We operationalized the notion of diagrams having high epistemic warrant by focusing on diagrams that appear or are referred to in short (one- or two-sentence proofs). This proxy proved to be effective in that the vast majority of those proofs we identified indeed rely essentially on a diagram for their argument.

Unsurprisingly, the prevalence of diagrams in short proofs varies across disciplines, and we have found empirical support for the intuition that fields like category theory and K-theory rely more on diagram-based proofs than other fields.

Furthermore, our qualitative coding of the identified instances led to some expected and a few quite surprising results. The vast majority of diagrams identified were *commuting diagrams* which are known to have a hybrid function in mathematical proofs [4]. More surprisingly, we also found other forms of hybrid diagrams, in the form of knot diagrams (case study 2), combinatorial manipulations and several other types of diagram. Thus our project has added detail and discussion to the notion of *hybrid diagrams*.

As noted in the introduction, hybrid diagrams are in line with an epistemology emphasizing formal rigour. Seen in this light the use of such diagrams as epistemic warrant in proof contexts is less surprising. On the other hand we were quite surprised to see a substantial amount of non-hybrid diagrams playing somewhat similar epistemic roles (case study 1). This suggests that the use of diagrams in mathematical proofs in some cases challenges a traditional epistemology emphasizing formal rigour, for instance by using co-exact features of a diagrams as steps in a proof (see case study 1). Finally, from a methodological viewpoint, our process has shown a successful implementation of what we refer to as our research agenda—*the Copenhagen Program for using ML in studying diagrams*: We have a) used a large corpus of texts to form a broad and (relatively) varied collection of diagrams to study [see also 14]. Thereafter, we have b) used (in this case) qualitative methods to categorize instances in the collection, leading us to eventually c) undertake close-readings of selected instances which we can claim are somewhat representative through our efforts in a) and b). This encapsulates our entire approach to question-driven quantitative *and* qualitative corpus studies in the philosophy of mathematical practice.

References

1. Andersen, L.E.: Acceptable gaps in mathematical proofs. Synthese **197**(1), 233–247 (2018). https://doi.org/10.1007/s11229-018-1778-8
2. Charmaz, K.: Constructing Grounded Theory. Sage Publications, London (2006)
3. Czédli, G.: Lamps in slim rectangular planar semimodular lattices (2021). https://doi.org/10.48550/ARXIV.2101.02929
4. De Toffoli, S.: 'Chasing' the diagram: the use of visualizations in algebraic reasoning. Rev. Symbol. Logic **10**(1), 158–186 (2017). https://doi.org/10.1017/S1755020316000277
5. De Toffoli, S., Giardino, V.: Forms and roles of diagrams in knot theory. Erkenntnis **79**(4), 829–842 (2013). https://doi.org/10.1007/s10670-013-9568-7
6. Flyvbjerg, B.: Five misunderstandings about case-study research. Qual. Inquiry **12**(2), 219–245 (2006)
7. Giardino, V.: Manipulative imagination: how to move things around in mathematics. THEORIA. Int. J. Theory History Found. Sci. **33**(2), 345 (2018). https://doi.org/10.1387/theoria.17871
8. Johansen, M.W., Misfeldt, M., Pallavicini, J.L.: A typology of mathematical diagrams. In: Diagrammatic Representation and Inference, pp. 105–119. Lecture Notes in Computer Science, Springer International Publishing, Cham (2018). https://doi.org/10.1007/978-3-319-91376-6_13
9. Johansen, M.W., Pallavicini, J.L.: Entering the valley of formalism: trends and changes in mathematicians' publication practices 1885–2015. Synthese **200**(3) (2022). https://doi.org/10.1007/s11229-022-03741-8
10. Katada, M.: Actions of automorphism groups of free groups on spaces of Jacobi diagrams. II (2021). https://doi.org/10.48550/ARXIV.2105.09072
11. Manders, K.: The Euclidean diagram. In: Mancosu, P. (ed.) The Philosophy of Mathematical Practice, chap. 4, pp. 80–133. Oxford University Press, Oxford (2008)
12. Schmid, D.: Mixing times for the TASEP in the maximal current phase (2021). https://doi.org/10.48550/ARXIV.2104.12745
13. Shin, S.J.: The Logical Status of Diagrams. Cambridge University Press, Cambridge (1994)
14. Sørensen, H.K., Johansen, M.W.: Counting mathematical diagrams with machine learning. In: Pietarinen, A.V., Chapman, P., Smet, L.B.D., Giardino, V., Corter, J., Linker, S. (eds.) Diagrammatic Representation and Inference, pp. 26–33. No. 12169 in Lecture Notes in Computer Science (LNAI), Springer (2020). https://doi.org/10.1007/978-3-030-54249-8_3
15. Wada, K.: CF-moves for virtual links (2021). https://doi.org/10.48550/ARXIV.2102.12930

Diagrams and Applications

Ancillary Diagrams: A Substitute for Text in Multimedia Resources?

Richard Lowe[1,2]([⊠]) and Jean-Michel Boucheix[1]

[1] University of Burgundy Franche-Comte (LEAD-CNRS), Dijon, France
[2] Curtin University, Perth, Australia
`r.k.lowe@curtin.edu.au`

Abstract. Multimedia resources conventionally convey their subject matter through a combination of descriptive and depictive representations. However, responsibility for explaining that content is typically skewed heavily towards multimedia's descriptive components. This theoretical paper considers likely perceptual and cognitive processing requirements for internalizing these two sources of information during mental model construction. It uses the example of a multimedia resource consisting of written text and an accompanying overview picture to propose that much of the role usually allocated to text in such a resource could conceivably be reallocated to a set of ancillary diagrams. This proposal is based on an analysis suggesting that these diagrams are a better foundation for mental model building than is text. Consequently, replacing the text in a multimedia resource with appropriately designed ancillary diagrams should result in superior understanding. Likely benefits and costs of this approach as well as possibilities for its further development are discussed.

Keywords: Multimedia explanation · Internal and external representations · Ancillary diagrams · Mental model construction

1 Introduction

Our current information-rich society is one in which visual forms of information are increasingly pervasive. Along with this rise in our reliance on such visualizations, the way that society uses verbal information has also been changing significantly. These changes are particularly evident in the growth of short form text-based communications (mobile phone text messaging, social media platforms, news websites, etc.). There has also been a complementary rapid uptake of various types of static and dynamic visuals across these avenues of communication. However, one area that has lagged somewhat behind this trend is that of explanatory multimedia (as commonly found with technology-based educational and training resources, electronic product manuals etc.). In multimedia resources, words (written or spoken) still typically carry the primary responsibility for presenting information to the target audience. Although it is certainly true that such resources are usually generously illustrated these days, the included pictorial material is rarely relied on for conveying the bulk of the content – that remains largely the job of the text.

© Springer Nature Switzerland AG 2022
V. Giardino et al. (Eds.): Diagrams 2022, LNAI 13462, pp. 245–259, 2022.
https://doi.org/10.1007/978-3-031-15146-0_21

In this chapter, we propose that the 'over-reliance' on text-based explanation evident in much current multimedia design may limit a resource's effectiveness for developing understanding. Historically, researchers and practitioners have advocated replacing text with pictures for audiences who are not native speakers of a local language or whose language skills are otherwise deficient [1]. However, this is not the theme of the present chapter. We do not propose doing away with text because the target audience lacks a basic level of comprehension of text *per se*. Instead, we argue for visualizations to be given greater explanatory responsibility than they have had hitherto, and for the role of text used together with explanatory visuals to be re-conceptualized. Our proposal is that static or animated diagrams (provided that they are properly designed) could fulfil much the same role as has traditionally been done by explanatory text, and that the purpose of text could be changed to one of supporting visual interpretation of these ancillary diagrams. The rationale for suggesting such changes is based on differences in the extent to which the fundamental characteristics of descriptive (textual) and depictive (pictorial) representations align with those posited for mental models [2, 3]. We raise the possibility that our proposed changes to the design of multimedia resources could substantially improve their effectiveness for fostering understanding.

1.1 An Example

The example of a manual caulking gun (Fig. 1) will be used to illustrate the proposal being put forward in this chapter.

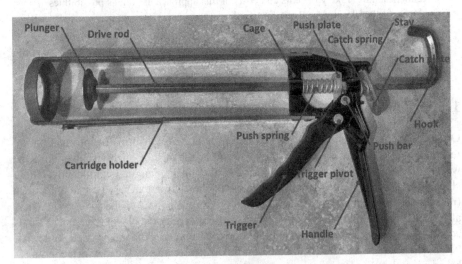

Fig. 1. Caulking gun overview picture

Let us suppose for the purposes of our discussion that we wish to develop a multimedia resource to explain how the mechanism of a caulking gun allows this device to perform its overall function. Caulking guns are typically used in housing construction and maintenance to extrude a continuous bead of viscous caulking compound (such as silicone sealant) that fills gaps between adjacent non-mating surfaces. After a cartridge of caulking compound is fitted into the gun, its contents are progressively extruded by means of successive squeezes of the trigger. Successful functioning of the caulking gun system relies on the interaction of the mechanism's two main sub systems:

1. The 'push' sub system that moves the drive rod through the cartridge so that its plunger pushes out the caulking compound. With each squeeze of the trigger, this sub system ejects a dose of the cartridge contents.
2. The 'catch' sub system that ensures the drive rod progressively moves through the cartridge so that all the contents are ultimately ejected. It does this because the grip that the catch plate exerts on the drive rod prevents the rod from slipping backwards after each trigger press.

The 'push' and 'catch' sub systems perform their individual roles that together contribute to the mechanism's proper overall functioning via two complementary causal chains. Each of these chains consists of a series of components that propagate activity between primary cause and ultimate effect by means of inter-component contact interactions. For example, consider the chain of events that occurs when the initial *cause* (a squeeze of the trigger) leads to the final overall *effect* (extrusion of some caulking compound). When the trigger is given its first squeeze, the 'push' causal chain begins with depression of the trigger towards the fixed handle of the gun. As the pivoted trigger rotates, the movement of its push bar in contact with the push plate causes that plate to change from a vertical to an angled orientation. This angling of the push plate in turn causes it to grip the drive rod then push it a limited distance along inside the cylinder so that the first dose of the caulking compound is ejected by the plunger. In concert with the operation of this 'push' causal chain, a second parallel 'catch' causal chain operates by which the tendency of the drive rod to retreat to the original position it occupied before the trigger squeeze (*cause*) is counteracted by grip from the catch plate that arrests its movement (*effect*). Successful functioning of the caulking gun mechanism depends on a coordinated and finely calibrated interplay between these two causal chains. Fundamental to this interplay is the relationship of a long, strong push spring (impinging on the push plate) to a short, weaker catch spring (impinging on the catch plate).

It is clear from the above account that despite the caulking gun being a common, easily operated device, the mechanism responsible for the gun's functionality is rather sophisticated. From the point of view of comprehending precisely how this mechanism works, this actually makes it quite complex. Consequently, designing an effective explanation to help people fully understand the way its numerous individual components (about a dozen of them) contribute individually and collectively to its overall functioning presents a considerable challenge. Currently, a popular response to such a challenge would be to develop a multimedia resource that uses a combination of descriptive and depictive information to explain this content.

This 'text plus picture' approach to multimedia has several common present day variants that can involve modifications such as using spoken rather than written text or using animated rather than static pictures [4]. Nevertheless, the way that multimedia resources of this type are currently designed still typically reflects their heritage from traditional printed textbooks where text was the primary carrier of information and pictures were generally treated as subservient adjuncts to the text-based explanation. In the next section, we consider various types of representation on the basis of a relatively straightforward multimedia implementation consisting of a written text that explains the functioning of a caulking gun accompanied by an overview picture (as per Fig. 1) that shows its main parts.

2 Representations

Representations have a 'stand-for' relationship with their referents (i.e., the subject matter to which they refer). They can be either external to a person (such as printed and spoken text, or static and dynamic pictures) or internal (such as mental images, propositional knowledge, or mental models) [5–7]. Comprehension of the subject matter referred to by external representations requires the operation of 'bottom-up' perceptual and cognitive processes to extract then internalize relevant aspects of the available information. This internalized information is complemented 'top-down' by stored knowledge gained from prior experience to construct a mental representation of the referent subject matter. Ideally, this mental representation is a coherent knowledge structure that captures the subject matter sufficiently well to act as a basis for successful task performance.

Table 1 summarizes some key attributes of the types of representation that are the focus of this paper: mental models, depictive representations (pictures), and descriptive representations (text). It should be referred to when reading the following sections.

Table 1. Comparison of mental models, depictive and descriptive representations.

	Mental Model (internal tokens/relations)	Depictive (external picture)	Descriptive (external text)
Structure	Non-linear	Non-linear	Linear
Interrogation	Not prescribed	Not prescribed	Conventional reading direction (L to R; T to B)
Information Type	'Quasi-visuospatial'	Visuospatial	Non visuospatial
Representation	Analog but tokenized	Analog	Propositional
Processing Route	Mental construction	Direct processing as visuospatial	Multi-step: Interpretation then conversion into analog

2.1 External Versus Internal Representations

A mental model is a particular type of internal knowledge structure that individuals can acquire via bottom-up and top-down processing. A good understanding of a topic is assumed to be the result of constructing a high quality mental model. These internal representations have been posited to consist of mental tokens and relationships that are organized in an analog, quasi-visuospatial manner that reflects the information structure of the subject matter they represent [6, 7]. A high quality mental model is one having a close correspondence with its referent subject matter and that therefore makes it very useful in tasks such as prediction and inference. One crucial factor that can determine the quality of a mental model formed from an external representation is the level of processing challenge involved in internalizing that information source [8–10]. More specifically, mental model construction is likely to be facilitated if differences between characteristics of the type of external representation upon which it will be based, and the characteristics posited for mental models, are kept to a minimum. The greater the differences between these two classes of representation, the more demanding will be the processing required and the higher the possibility of errors. In particular, if an external representation requires a substantial amount of preliminary processing in order to make the information it is carrying readily compatible with the requirements for mental model building, the likely outcome will be a lower quality internal representation.

2.2 Descriptive Versus Depictive Representations

The words comprising a piece of text are constituted from agreed sub sets of alphabetic symbols organized in a particular sequence. Groupings of these words are in turn are arranged according to rules of syntax and semantic constraints. Their physical layout in space is linear and ordered left to right, top to bottom. In terms of the visual nature of the individual elements and their spatial arrangement, none of these levels of descriptive representation directly maps onto the visuospatial structure of the subject matter it represents. Descriptive representations can therefore be thought of as *arbitrary* in the sense that there is essentially no discernible one-to-one correspondence between the representation and its referents [2]. However, mental models supposedly represent their referents in a far more analog fashion. The external subject matter that is modelled internally via these knowledge structures is represented by tokens (mental entities that stand for the external referent entities) arranged in a relational organization paralleling the key referent relationships. In other words, a mental model is partly isomorphic in that it has a high degree of correspondence at a fundamental level with the referent subject matter it represents. It follows that a person engaged in reading a piece of text about content that is markedly visuospatial in nature must carry out extensive conversion of that representation in order to process it into a form that is well suited for mental model construction. This transformational 'side-task' can be a very resource intensive process in its own right and hence tie up capacity that could otherwise be devoted to the main task of mental model construction. Table 2 summarizes some types of conversion activities that a reader of text may need to carry out during this transformational processing.

Table 2. A list of possible activities required for text-to-visuospatial conversion.

Identify all task-relevant entities referred to (directly or indirectly) by the text	Mentally organise tokens into an arrangement analogous to the structure of the referent situation
Determine the material properties of all relevant entities	Assign task-relevant dynamic information to mental tokens
Determine the geometric properties of all relevant entities	Introduce appropriate constraints on tokens' dynamics
Convert non-analog (linearized) account of visual and spatial information into analog visuospatial account	Form sequences of functionally-related tokens to represent causal chains
Abstract information about entities to generate appropriate mental tokens	Incorporate higher-order relations governing the coordination of different causal chains

In contrast, the visuospatial properties of a well-designed *depictive* representation of the same content already closely match those of its referent subject matter. It typically has a high degree of one-to-one correspondence to its referent in terms of both the entities it portrays and how those entities are related to one another. Unlike text, there are few arbitrary conventions (such as linearity and sequencing rules) that intrude to distort the layout of the represented information. Instead, in all but the most extreme cases of abstraction and manipulation in diagrammatic depictions, mapping between representation and referent is relatively straight forward. This means that the task of going from a depictive representation to a mental model is likely to involve far less side-task transformational processing than would be the case for a corresponding descriptive representation. In the next sections, we expand on how differences in descriptive and depictive representations fundamentally affect the way they are processed in a multimedia context.

2.3 Reconciling Representations: Processing Implications

Consider a conventional multimedia resource that presents complex, unfamiliar subject matter via a text and an accompanying overview picture. The text shown in Fig. 2 addresses the 'push' subsystem of the caulking gun mechanism using such an approach.

A person encountering this combination must make many back-and-forth comparison transitions between the text component and the picture component while trying to build a coherent unified mental representation of the referent system. This involves repeated shifts of attention and attentional adjustments in order to process corresponding or complementary target aspects of these two very different types of representation. In addition to navigating these transitions, the individual must also perform various mental conversions in order that the information carried by these two very different media can be reconciled and then combined on a common representational basis (see Table 2). Both the continual to-and-fro activity and the ever-present requirement for such conversions are resource-intensive processing activities. For subject matter of any complexity, they result in this being a very demanding form of processing, both perceptually and cognitively.

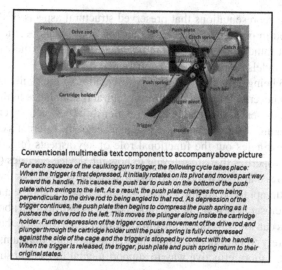

Fig. 2. Multimedia presentation of caulking gun subsystem

Now consider how the situation (and concomitant processing demands) would likely change if the text was replaced by ancillary diagrams depicting the same content as would normally be presented by that text. We hypothesize that although some back-and-forth comparison transitions would still be needed, fewer of them should likely be required and they would impose a much smaller processing overhead. This is because of the far greater similarity between the diagrams and the picture than between text and picture. As a result, search within the diagrammatic depictions would be substantially lower than within the body of text and would be less demanding. Then, once corresponding representations of the same information items were located, much less processing would be required to reconcile them.

Keeping in mind the limits on human information processing, the second scenario should be considerably less demanding and therefore likely to leave more processing resources free for mental model building than would the text-based scenario. Further, because any inter-representational conversions that are required would be far more modest, there should be less danger of errors creeping in with the diagram-based scenario.

3 Constructing a Mental Model: Diagrams Instead of Text?

In this section, we consider in more detail the task of constructing a mental model from an overview picture accompanied by ancillary diagrams (rather than text). To assist our consideration of this task, we devised Fig. 3 as a notional way to show some key features of a mental model in concrete form. Note that we do not claim Fig. 3 to be anything more than a hypothetical expression of these features. It is intended solely to facilitate comparison between a mental model and the type of ancillary diagrams discussed above. This is an important point to make because there is currently no definitive account of how mental models are actually manifested in the mind. Johnson-Laird [6, 7, 10] considered them to be analog representations that preserved structural aspects of the referent and although grounded in perception, were abstract and not modal-specific. Their abstract nature means that rather than representing *particular* situations (the case with mental images), mental models represent *sets* of situations.

Despite Fig. 3 being a much simplified representation of the caulking gun that lacks veridical detail, it nevertheless bears a close structural resemblance to the gun's mechanism. Although it preserves the fundamental relationships between the entities that exist in a real caulking gun, abstract tokens are used in place of the referent's entities. Further, the representation singles out the functional role of key aspects (e.g., the pivots) and captures certain properties that are relevant to how the device operates (e.g., the tokens representing entities that are fixed versus those that are moveable). For the sake of clarity, Fig. 3 does not attempt to be comprehensive - other aspects could be added that would probably bring it closer to a 'real' mental model (such as information about the direction and extent entities can move, sequencing information, etc.). However, the purpose of this realization is merely to help demonstrate that using ancillary diagrams in multimedia resources may be a more effective way to support mental model construction than the conventional use of text.

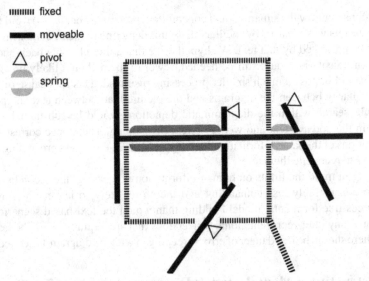

Fig. 3. Possible information in a mental model of the caulking gun mechanism (hypothetical)

Let us assume that Fig. 3 is a not unreasonable concrete expression of what an individual is trying to construct when processing a multimedia resource on the caulking gun mechanism. We can then use Fig. 3 as a basis for hypothesizing about the processing routes and activities that might be involved if an individual was to be given ancillary diagrams (instead of text) as a basis for mental model construction. The type of situation envisaged here is that the block of text provided in Fig. 2 would be replaced by several diagrams intended to serve the same content presentation purpose. Figure 4 shows a possible implementation of such a combination.

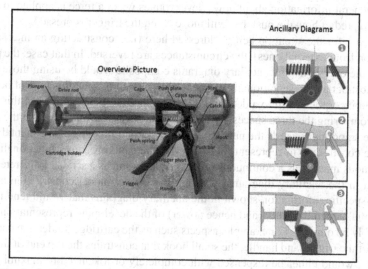

Fig. 4. Ancillary diagrams used in place to text to accompany overview picture

Note that the ancillary diagrams incorporate various features that are designed to boost their explanatory power (e.g., colour coding, transparency, additional symbols, alignment to aid inter-diagram comparisons, etc.). For comparison purposes, Fig. 5 places the first ancillary diagram beside the information set constituting the hypothetical mental model.

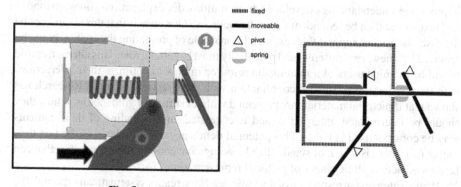

Fig. 5. Ancillary diagram/mental model comparison

Although they are various superficial differences between the two representations, at a deeper structural level they have a great deal in common. This makes it relatively easy to map between their corresponding aspects. It is also quite possible to do similar mapping with the other two ancillary diagrams shown in Fig. 4 if the mental model is progressively 'run' forwards in time. For example, the relation between the solid line token representing the trigger and its adjacent pivot token in the mental model allows domain general information about how a lever rotates when a force is applied to one of its arms to predict how the push bar will move when the trigger is pressed.

However, for the situation being addressed here (i.e., constructing an internal representation from external ones), the circumstances are reversed. In that case, the person studying the overview-plus-ancillary diagrams composite would be using those depictions to abstract a representationally efficient generalization about this type of behavior in order to incorporate it into a developing mental model. We can envisage this would involve comparing the three successive ancillary diagrams and inferring that the trigger can move smoothly towards the handle by rotating around its pivot. The mental model would be constructed to represent this aspect of the caulking gun's functionality in a parsimonious manner as a continuous process (rather than as a series of discrete stages as shown in the ancillary diagrams). During this mental model construction activity, instance-specific information shown in the ancillary diagrams that would tend to limit the potential generalizability (and hence power) of the developing representation would presumably be omitted. For example, aspects such as the cartridge holder, the particular shaping of the trigger and handle, the small hook that constrains the top end of the catch plate, etc., would either be dispensed with completely or tokenized to maximize their generalizability. This would mean that the mental model could be applied not only to the particular instance of a caulking gun shown in Fig. 1, but also to a host of other superficially different but functionally similar design variants of this device that are available in the market place.

4 Repurposing Multimedia's Text Components

If empirical studies were to show that replacing text with ancillary diagrams did indeed improve the understandings developed from multimedia explanations, does this mean that text would then be redundant for such resources? Our view is that this should not be the case. Rather, we suggest that text's traditional role of presenting the content could be replaced by a new, very different and potentially most beneficial role. This alternative role would be to guide users of a multimedia resource in how to optimize their interactions with the ancillary diagrams (in coordination with the overview picture). Research has shown that if pictorial materials are presented without sufficient guidance as to how they should be interrogated, interpreted, and inter-related, understanding of their contents may be compromised [11, 12]. This potential deficiency can be related to the fact that, unlike text, there is a lack of standardized reading conventions and approaches that can be applied across all instances of pictorial representation.

Well written text, irrespective of the topic, leads the reader systematically through the presentation of its subject matter by taking advantage of its standardized linear structure and syntactical rules. However, there are no corresponding constraints on how pictures are to be 'read' because the presented information is structured according to the structure of the depicted subject matter (and not according to a universally applicable set of conventions and rules). Consequently, individuals who lack background knowledge about the subject matter portrayed in a depictive representation may prioritize which aspects they attend to and how they sequence their interrogation of those aspects according to the depiction's superficial perceptual characteristics [c.f. 13]. This may result in key information going un-noticed and errors of interpretation.

Because depictive representations such as the ancillary diagrams being addressed here lack the inbuilt features for supporting appropriate navigation etc. that are present for text, it would make sense to accompany them with some form of add-on guidance. In contrast to text's limitations for representing visuospatial information, it can be a highly effective way to convey sequenced procedural instructions. Our suggestion therefore is that rather than removing text from multimedia resources altogether, it instead be repurposed as a way of guiding the viewer through appropriate and fruitful processing of the ancillary diagrams that we suggest might take over text's traditional role. An illustration of how such an approach might be implemented is given in Fig. 6.

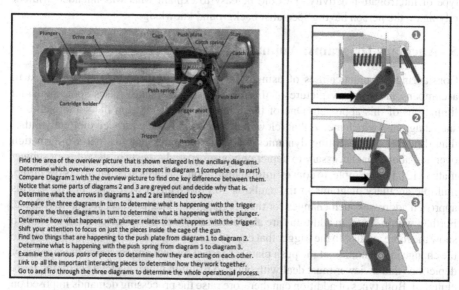

Find the area of the overview picture that is shown enlarged in the ancillary diagrams.
Determine which overview components are present in diagram 1 (complete or in part)
Compare Diagram 1 with the overview picture to find one key difference between them.
Notice that some parts of diagrams 2 and 3 are greyed out and decide why that is.
Determine what the arrows in diagrams 1 and 2 are intended to show
Compare the three diagrams in turn to determine what is happening with the trigger
Compare the three diagrams in turn to determine what is happening with the plunger.
Determine how what happens with plunger relates to what happens with the trigger.
Shift your attention to focus on just the pieces inside the cage of the gun
Find two things that are happening to the push plate from diagram 1 to diagram 2.
Determine what is happening with the push spring from diagram 1 to diagram 3.
Examine the various *pairs* of pieces to determine how they are acting on each other.
Link up all the important interacting pieces to determine how they work together.
Go to and fro through the three diagrams to determine the whole operational process.

Fig. 6. Guiding text could support interrogation of depictive representations

Another justification for changing the role of text to guiding interrogation of ancillary diagrams (instead of presenting content) is that this could largely avoid the issue of requiring possession of domain-*specific* background knowledge (almost unavoidable when text is used to present content). Most text-based explanations of content that is in some ways complex or unfamiliar implicitly assumes a certain existing level of relevant background knowledge (often wrongly, which hinders the reader's interpretation). It is really very challenging for a text author to provide for a range of readers who have widely differing prior knowledge of relevance to the particular content involved.

Converting from a text explanation of some content to an analog representation typically requires the person to elaborate the entities mentioned. So, if the text mentions a spring, the reader will need to 'flesh out' that item in order to convert it… such as what shape springs usually are, what they are made of, how they behave when subjected to force, their ability to return to their original shape/size once the force is removed, etc. A person who lacks such 'spring-specific' background knowledge could be at a real disadvantage with a text-based explanation of our caulking gun mechanism. However, this issue could be tackled with additional ancillary diagrams. A broader issue warranting empirical investigation is the generalizability of this approach to other types of subject matter, such as non-mechanical (biological) content.

If text was instead used for guidance, not content presentation, it would rely only on domain *general* background knowledge, such as what is meant when someone is asked to focus attention on a specific area of a diagram, notice a particular aspect of that diagram, or compare two of its aspects, etc. These guiding instructions are extremely generic and are universally applicable, irrespective of the content involved. It would be almost unheard of that someone would not understand what they were required to do having received such an instruction. Even if guiding text introduced some unfamiliar type of interrogation activity, it would be easy to explain what was intended without relying on the person having specialist background knowledge.

5   Ancillary Diagrams: Animated Alternatives

Considering the practicalities of using a set of ancillary diagrams instead of text to accompany an overview picture of the referent subject matter raises some potential limitations of this approach. One of these limitations arises from the static nature of such diagrams (which means that relevant dynamics must be portrayed indirectly rather than directly). Representing dynamics via static diagrams requires extra information over and above that necessary to depict only visuospatial aspects of the referent subject matter [12]. For example, to convey information about changes in components over time, multiple ancillary diagrams of the caulking gun mechanism were used in Fig. 4. This approach addresses such changes for the trigger, push plate, push spring, drive rod, etc. Further, within-diagram additions are also necessary, such as the inclusion of arrows (to show the force applied to the trigger that causes it to move) and the dotted line (to indicate the change in orientation of the push plate). These extras not only increase the number of depictions that a viewer must deal with but also result in those displays becoming more cluttered. Both types of addition can therefore raise the processing demands imposed on viewers. Another potential downside of these static ancillary diagrams is that the viewer is required to correctly interpret their extra dynamics-related information (e.g., via mental animation). This interpretation relies on the viewer possessing and successfully applying appropriate background knowledge about the conventions used to indicate dynamics via a static depiction. For viewers who are young or who lack such knowledge, this requirement can result in difficulties and interpretation errors.

Using animations instead of static diagrams may offer a way to avoid these potential problems. It could reduce or eliminate the need not only for multiple diagrams, but also for within-diagram additions. Further, it provides an opportunity to make explicit the relationship between the information in an overview depiction and in its accompanying ancillary diagrams. For example, animation could be used to single out a target sub system from the overview depiction and convert it into an ancillary diagram. It could also be used in a related way to show the origin of ancillary diagrams that provide views of the subject matter that are different from those given in the overview depiction.

However, research indicates that animations are by no means a universal panacea. Ironically, the very strength they have in terms of being able to represent dynamics directly can be problematic when it comes to viewers extracting task relevant information from animated displays [14]. Avoiding such problems seems to rely on fundamentally changing how animations are designed so that the way they present information is more closely attuned with human information processing capacities. The Composition Approach to animation design has been developed to address the mismatch between these two aspects that too often compromises the effectiveness of conventionally designed ('Comprehensive') animations. This novel approach is founded on the Animation Processing Model (APM) that characterizes the construction of a mental model from an animation in terms of five interdependent processing phases [15].

If animated rather than static depictions were to be used as ancillary diagrams in the approach canvassed above, it is important that their design be optimized in terms of providing support for mental model construction. One important consideration in designing more effective animations is the fine-grained, content-specific characterization of likely perceptual and cognitive challenges that could arise from presenting information about the referent subject matter in a temporally veridical manner. Complex, unfamiliar dynamic subject matter tends to have features that makes it difficult for viewers to process successfully if an animated representation faithfully reproduces its actual dynamics. This typically occurs if the dynamics involve substantial simultaneity, as is the case with the caulking gun example. Here, the 'push' causal chain and the 'catch' causal chain have an intimate functional relationship (the gun will not work as it should unless both operate properly and in concert). However, if an animation was actually to depict these two central aspects of the gun simultaneously (i.e., as they would occur in real life), a likely result would be inadequate viewer processing of the presented information. Consequently, the quality of a mental model built from exposure to this animation would probably be severely compromised.

Empirical research indicates the benefits of a Composition Approach to animation design in which counterproductive simultaneity is removed by sequential rather than parallel presentation of such information [16, 17]. A necessary pre-cursor to this design approach is a thorough analysis of the referent subject matter that can reveal which of its aspects have the potential to impose excessive information processing demands on the viewer if presented in a veridical manner. The results of such an Event Unit Analysis [18] can then be taken into account in the design of an animation to tailor its presentation characteristics to those of the particular subject matter being addressed. Event Unit Analysis is therefore a content-specific technique whose results will differ according to the nature of the subject matter involved.

6   Discussion and Conclusion

A dominant concern of orthodox approaches to multimedia design is to find ways of staging presentation of their constituent descriptive and depictive representations so that their combination works as effectively as possible. Typically however, these approaches do not fundamentally question the roles that are assigned to these two broad types of representation within such combinations. In this paper, we considered the potential effectiveness of multimedia resources from the perspective of the extent to which their design was likely to provide support for an individual's construction of high quality mental models. From an analysis of their likely processing demands, we concluded that descriptive representations (e.g., text) should be far less suited to conveying content information than depictive representations. Using the example of a caulking gun mechanism, we explored an alternative approach to multimedia design that replaced explanatory text with ancillary diagrams and repurposed text as a guiding resource for supporting more effective processing of the depictive content presentation. Results from a recent pilot study indicate that the use of ancillary diagrams (as exemplified in Fig. 4) can be an effective alternative to a conventional multimedia design. Potential limitations of this approach were flagged, and a suggestion made that they could be circumvented by using animated instead of static ancillary diagrams [19]. Cautions about the possibility of negative effects from conventionally designed animations were raised and the use of Composition Approaches and Event Unit Analysis introduced to ameliorate these effects. The theoretical proposals put forward in this paper are intended to stimulate empirical research into more principled ways to design explanatory multimedia. Suitable experiments could range from straightforward comparisons of the relative effectiveness of text versus ancillary diagram accompaniments in multimedia, to the potential of more tokenized animated ancillary diagrams for fostering higher quality mental models [18]. However, we recommend that this research gives more consideration to the benefits of 'working backwards' from posited attributes of high quality mental models rather than merely 'working forwards' from the characteristics of the external representations that supply the raw material from which those internal representations are built.

References

1. Wright, P.: Presenting technical information: a survey of research findings. Instr. Sci. **6**, 93–134 (1977)
2. Schnotz, W.: Integrated model of text and picture comprehension. In: Mayer, R.E., Fiorella, L. (eds.) The Cambridge Handbook of Multimedia Leaning, pp. 82–99. Cambridge University Press, Cambridge (2020)
3. Butcher, K.R.: The Multimedia Principle. In: Mayer, R.E. (ed.) The Cambridge Handbook of Multimedia Learning, 2nd edn., pp. 174–205, Cambridge University Press, Cambridge (2014)
4. Low, R., Sweller, J.: The modality principle in multimedia learning. In: Mayer, R.E. (ed.) The Cambridge Handbook of Multimedia Learning, 2nd edn., pp. 227–262. Cambridge University Press, Cambridge (2014)
5. Kintsch, W.: Comprehension: A Paradigm for Cognition. Cambridge University Press, Cambridge (2003)
6. Johnson-Laird, P.N.: Mental Models. Harvard University Press, Cambridge (1983)
7. Johnson-Laird, P.N.: How We Reason. Oxford University Press, Oxford (2006)
8. Bétrancourt, M.: The animation and interactivity principles in multimedia learning. In: Mayer, R.E. (ed.) The Cambridge Handbook of Multimedia Learning (1st Edition) pp. 487–512. Cambridge University Press, Cambridge (2005). https://doi.org/10.1017/CBO9780511816819.019
9. Lowe, R., Boucheix, J.-M., Menant, M.: Perceptual processing and the comprehension of relational information in dynamic diagrams. In: Chapman, P., Stapleton, G., Moktefi, A., Perez-,

S., Bellucci, F. (eds.) Diagrams 2018. LNCS (LNAI), vol. 10871, pp. 470–483. Springer, Cham (2018). https://doi.org/10.1007/978-3-319-91376-6_42

10. Johnson-Laird, P.N.: Mental models and human reasoning. PNAS, **26**, 107 (43) 18243–18250 (2010). https://doi.org/10.1073/pnas.1012933107

11. Hegarty, M., Just, M.A.: Constructing mental models of machines from text and diagrams. J. Mem. Lang. **6**(32), 717–742 (1993)

12. Mayer, R.E., Hegarty, M., Mayer, S., Campbell, J.: When static media promote active learning: annotated illustrations versus narrated animations in multimedia instruction. J. Exp. Psychol. Appl. **11**(4), 256–265 (2005)

13. Lowe, R., Boucheix, J.-M.: Learning from animated diagrams: how are mental models built? In: Stapleton, G., Howse, J., Lee, J. (eds.) Diagrams 2008. LNCS (LNAI), vol. 5223, pp. 266–281. Springer, Heidelberg (2008). https://doi.org/10.1007/978-3-540-87730-1_25

14. Lowe, R.K.: Animation and learning: Selective processing of information in dynamic graphics. Learn. Instr. **13**, 157–176 (2003)

15. Lowe, R.K., Boucheix, J.M.: Dynamic diagrams: a composition alternative. In: Cox, P., Plimmer, B., Rogers, P. (eds.) Diagrammatic Representation and Inference, LNAI, pp. 233–240. Springer, Berlin (2012)

16. Lowe, R.K., Boucheix, J.M.: Principled animation design improves comprehension of complex dynamics. Learn. Instr. **45**, 72–84 (2016). https://doi.org/10.1016/j.learninstruc.2016.06.005

17. Lowe, R.K., Schnotz, W., Boucheix, J.M.: The Animation composition principle in multimedia learning. In: Mayer, R.E., Fiorella, L. (eds.) The Cambridge Handbook of Multimedia Learning, 3rd edn., pp. 313–323. Cambridge University Press, New-York (2021)

18. Lowe, R., Boucheix, J.-M.: Event unit analysis: a methodology for anticipating processing demands of complex animated diagrams. In: Pietarinen, A.-V., Chapman, P., Bosveld-de Smet, L., Giardino, V., Corter, J., Linker, S. (eds.) Diagrams 2020. LNCS (LNAI), vol. 12169, pp. 307–322. Springer, Cham (2020). https://doi.org/10.1007/978-3-030-54249-8_24

19. Ploetzner, R., Berney, S., Bétrancourt, M.: A review of learning demands in instructional animations: The educational effectiveness of animations unfolds if the features of change need to be learned. J. Comput.-Assisted Learn. **36**, 838–860 (2020). https://doi.org/10.1111/jcal.12476

Diagrams for Learning to Lead in Salsa Dancing

Erica de Vries[✉] [ID]

Univ. Grenoble Alpes, LaRAC, 38000 Grenoble, France
Erica.deVries@univ-grenoble-alpes.fr

Abstract. Diagrammatic and symbolic notations play a role in the performing arts, such as music, dance, and drama. Some notations for documenting movement of the human body in time have been developed for research and practice. However, contrary to music and drama, learning to dance does not require the mastery of dance notations. The goal of the paper is to examine the potential of diagrammatic notational schemes for learning to lead in salsa dancing. First, goals and functions of dance notation are considered and an existing diagrammatical system is examined as a representational system. Subsequently, a systematic analysis of moves between salsa position diagrams is undertaken and learning tasks are suggested for empirical study.

Keywords: Dance notation · Performing arts · Modelling moves and positions

1 Introduction

Diagrammatic and symbolic notations play a role in the performing arts, such as music, dance, and drama. However, whereas actors learn to read a script and musicians learn to read sheet music, notational schemes are much less used for learning to dance. This paper focuses on linear salsa, a partnered dance with simple moves and positions at beginner salsa performance and extremely sophisticated patterns at advanced levels. An existing diagrammatic scheme for salsa positions [9] is presented and analyzed on its representational properties. Moreover, using the scheme for learning to lead requires enlarging the set of positions and developing a systematic way of describing genuine salsa moves. Finally, directions for empirical testing of the usefulness of salsa position diagrams for learning to lead in salsa dancing will be outlined.

2 About Functions of Diagrams in Dance

The documentation of performance arts in notations, diagrams, scores, and sketches, has been theorized by Goodman [5]. Dance notation is the documenting of human dance movement using symbols similar to what musical notation is to music and what the written word is to drama. As highly complex organisms, humans can adopt an infinite number of positions by moving individual body parts and exploit subtle bodily expressions. Moreover, humans move in three-dimensional space individually or two or more dancers can coordinate amongst them to move in patterns. As a consequence of this complexity, any notational system can only take into account a very small subset of all positions, moves and expressions. Thus, as a modelling device, a dance notation is a discretization of continuous movement for a particular purpose.

According to Goodman [5], the primary function of a score in the arts is to specify the essential properties that a particular performance must have in order to belong to the work. Thus, dance notation is used to document a choreography or a dance composition. Other functions emerged for research purposes, such as the construction of a formal model of positions and transitions for studying human movement, programming robots, or for teaching robots how to dance [2, 6, 7]. Indeed, partnered dances involve moving as a couple, which is an interesting case of non-verbal communication [2].

Learning a specific style of dancing entails learning to adopt its bodily positions and to execute its moves. Positions and moves are the elementary components of a dance designated by generic or specific names, e.g., first position, handshake position, pas de bourrée, grapevine, box step, and enchufa. Nowadays, dance moves and positions are accessible on the Internet with keywords "how to" or "moves and positions" associated to the name of a dance, such as hip-hop, ballet, salsa, country, tango, etc. Search results primarily display text, pictures, how-to-videos, and on-line classes. Diagrammatic or notational systems are not habitually used in teaching and learning to dance.

3   Learning to Lead in Advanced Salsa Dancing

Salsa, as a patterned dance, involves a lead and a follow (most frequently, but not necessarily, a man and a woman). The lead takes the follow through a series of moves and turns to salsa music. The basic step occurs on beats 1, 2, 3 and 5, 6, and 7 in an eight count rhythm (two bars of four beats each). Linear salsa, as opposed to circular Cuban salsa, involves moving on an imaginary line, also called slot. Figure 1 shows an elementary move using von Renesse and Eck's diagrammatic notation [9]. From basic position, the lead makes way by stepping backwards out of the slot, guides the follow across the body, and steps back into the slot to basic position rotated 180°. Although highly schematic, the diagram contains all crucial information from a salsa dance perspective: identification of lead and follow, their orientation, handholds (connecting arcs), and changes in position during the eight counts.

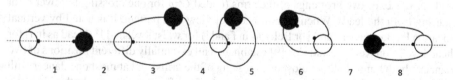

Fig. 1. Top view of a Cross Body Lead (CBL) for switching places in the slot (dotted line).

Beginner salsa performance has very few moves and requires only basic communication skills. Beginners learn elementary moves by imitation and practice in salsa classes. Although partner changes during the lesson ensure that any lead dances with any follow, leading actually plays only a minor role during classes because all dancers practice the same move at the same time. At the end of a lesson, student dancers film the learned moves for future reference (examples available online, e.g., video[1] with basic steps and several CBLs from 0:00 to 0:17, followed by a sophisticated pattern).

Salsa dancers share a repertoire of positions and moves that constitutes the language of salsa. The goal of learning is not just to execute salsa moves as a couple, but to be able to participate in "social dancing". Social dancing is spontaneous much like improvising when playing an instrument (numerous videos available online through keyword search "salsa social dancing"). In order to participate in social dancing, one has to learn to lead or to follow any salsa move with any partner in any setting. Learning intermediate and advanced salsa therefore entails extending one's "alphabet of moves" [2], and learning to dance with familiar and unfamiliar partners without a planned sequence of moves. Indeed, the lead extemporaneously decides on each move in the flow of the activity. An important skill for leads is thus to recall and initiate moves, and to communicate them to the follow through body language. However, beginner leads tend to instigate the same moves over and over again out of habit[2]. How could salsa diagrams help to overcome this difficulty in learning to lead?

4   An Existing Notational Scheme for Salsa Positions

Von Renesse and Eck [9] developed a notational scheme from a mathematical point of view. Their aim was to systematically explore the repertoire of different positions available to the salsa dancer. The discretization proceeds by considering the beginning and end positions of the eight beats in salsa music (see Fig. 1). Moreover, positions that require very small adjustments to transition from one to the other are not relevant either from a dance or from a mathematical perspective. For example, hand and feet positions and slight angular differences in the bodies of the dancers are not modelled. Thus, each of the positions is discrete for a large set of slightly different positions, comparable to knots in knot theory [2, 6, 7]. To obtain a mathematical knot, one starts with a string, ties a knot, and then joins the ends [1]. Similarly, two dancers start with one handhold, take intricate positions, and close the human string by the second handhold.

Figure 2 shows some salsa diagrams and their formal notation. The lead (filled circle) and follow (blank circle) face their partner or turn their back (coded 1 and 0 respectively). There can be zero, one or two handholds (coded RL for lead's right to follow's left hand) and zero, one, or two crossings of the arms (coded C^L_R for one crossing left over right starting from the lead). When an arm is out of view of a partner, it is noted by vertical location B (Back as in c and j or Belly as in f and i) for waist level and H (Head as in f) for head level. Von Renesse and Eck [9] established all essentially different positions of two dancers, both hands held, at most one crossing of the arms, and at most one dancer with an arm behind the body. They found a total of 156 different positions both physically possible and danceable (see Fig. 2d, f, h, i, j, k, and l).

---

[1] Crazy Lion Productions: Super Mario, Salsa on1 Partnerwork@HotSalsaWeekend, https://www.youtube.com/watch?v=oJpF7z5yWA4.

[2] Dance Dojo: How to Remember Salsa Moves (the mistake that's holding you back), https://www.youtube.com/watch?v=6W58JLb04AA.

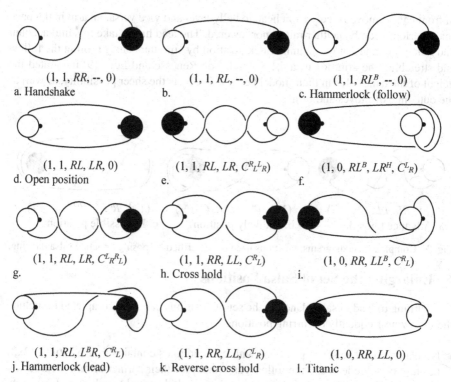

a. Handshake $(1, 1, RR, --, 0)$

b. $(1, 1, RL, --, 0)$

c. Hammerlock (follow) $(1, 1, RL^B, --, 0)$

d. Open position $(1, 1, RL, LR, 0)$

e. $(1, 1, RL, LR, C^R_L{}^L_R)$

f. $(1, 0, RL^B, LR^H, C^L_R)$

g. $(1, 1, RL, LR, C^L_R{}^R_L)$

h. Cross hold $(1, 1, RR, LL, C^R_L)$

i. $(1, 0, RR, LL^B, C^R_L)$

j. Hammerlock (lead) $(1, 1, RL, L^B R, C^R_L)$

k. Reverse cross hold $(1, 1, RR, LL, C^L_R)$

l. Titanic $(1, 0, RR, LL, 0)$

Fig. 2. Salsa positions in diagrammatic and formal notation (adapted from [9]).

5   Analyzing the Diagrammatical Scheme

Salsa position diagrams belong to the category of extrinsic representational systems [8]. In contrast to intrinsic representations, structures in extrinsic representations exist solely by virtue of a truth-preserving correspondence with a state of affairs in the represented world [8]. In other words, all position diagrams need to be verified because the diagrammatic formalism in and of itself allows states of affairs which cannot exist in the real world. Let us examine the diagrams in Fig. 3. A diagram with three crossings of the arms (Fig. 3a) seems rather awkward, but both physically possible and danceable in advanced salsa dancing. In contrast, a position with two crossings of the arms as in Fig. 3b can be adopted by two dancers by touching finger tips, but the lead has no danceable move for leading the dancers into or out of the position. It is therefore highly unlikely to naturally occur in dancing. Finally, Fig. 3c. is a diagram of an impossible position since it cannot be taken due to morphological constraints (arms are not long enough for two handholds in hammerlock position).

Interpretation of the salsa position diagrams requires internal rules, i.e. some information is not encoded in the diagram and needs to be memorized by the dancers [11]. In particular, the view from above does not allow appreciating the vertical position of the handholds. Although not important in distinguishing between static positions, the height of the handholds is crucial for selecting moves for two reasons. First, whereas an arm in front can be moved freely from head to belly level and vice versa, an arm in the back (hammerlock) can be neither raised nor lowered. The lead has to take this into account and guide into and out of a hammerlock position by simultaneously turning the follow and stretching the arm downwards. Second, Von Renesse and Ecke [9] integrated the height of the handholds in their model because it affects the sheer possibility, as well as the outcome, of moves and turns.

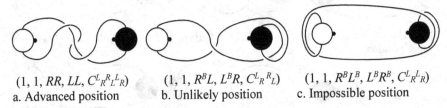

$(1, 1, RR, LL, C^L{}_R{}^R{}_L{}_R)$ $(1, 1, R^B L, L^B R, C^L{}_R{}^R{}_L)$ $(1, 1, R^B L^B, L^B R^B, C^L{}_R{}^L{}_R)$
a. Advanced position   b. Unlikely position   c. Impossible position

Fig. 3. Complex salsa diagrams: positions need to be verified by posing or actual salsa dancing.

6   Enlarging the Set of Salsa Positions

For learning to lead in salsa dancing, the set of positions has to be completed to include the following frequently occurring positions.

- No handholds. The set of positions with no handholds contains four positions (2x2) because both the lead and the follow can either face their partner or turn their back.
- Single handhold. The set of positions with a single handhold such as in Fig. 2a, b, and c. This set can be obtained by multiplying the number of relative orientations of the two dancers (4), the number of single handholds (4) and the number of handhold positions (no dancer has an arm hidden from the partner, either lead or follow has a hidden arm either at waist or at head level (5). A total of 4x4x5 = 80 positions were drawn and verified.
- Two handholds with two arm crossings. Two frequent positions have two crossings of the arms. Starting from basic position (Fig. 2d), these are obtained by a full turn of either the lead or the follow with both handholds passing above the head to the right (produces Fig. 2g) or to the left (produces Fig. 2e).

The enlarged set for intermediate salsa dancing englobes $156 + 4 + 80 + 2 = 242$ positions.

7   Characterizing Genuine Salsa Moves

Von Renesse and Ecke [9] modelled a space of transition spaces starting from basic position (Fig. 2d) generating all positions obtained by one or more half turns of the follower to the left or to the right. However, these are only minimal dance moves which are not representative of the repertoire of actual moves. The current purpose of learning to lead in salsa dancing does require such a systematic characterization of genuine salsa moves. Indeed, several variables can be identified that define salsa moves as transitions between salsa positions (see Table 1 for example moves to be applied to Fig. 2).

- Slot change (no change, pass on lead's left or lead's right). At the end of the move, both dancers may end up in the same slot position, i.e. they stay in place. Alternatively, the lead may instigate a slot change which involves travelling in the slot by leading the follow to pass either on the lead's left (as in Fig. 1) or on the lead's right.
- Individual dancer turns. Lead and/or follow may turn in multiples of 180° with a maximum of two turns for most nonprofessional dancers. Thus, lead and follow each have nine options for turning: no turn, or a half turn, a whole turn, a one and a half turn, or a double turn either to the left or to the right.

Table 1. List of twenty elementary moves and their names. The letters for initial (In.) and final (Fi) positions refer to Fig. 2 (* rotated 180°, ** turn executed by couple in closed position).

Nr	In.	Handholds		Slot	Turns		Fi.	Name
		Right	Left	Change	Lead	Follow		
1	a	up	-	none	0°	1 R	a	right turn
2	b	up	-	none	1 R	0°	b	lead right turn
3	b	up down	-	none	0°	2 R	c	double right turn
4	d	up	up	none	0°	1 R	g	right turn
5	d	up	down	none	1 R	0°	j	lead right turn
6	d	up	up	none	0°	1 L	e	left turn
7	h	up	up	none	0°	1 R	k	right turn
8	h	up	up	none	1 R	0°	k	lead right turn
9	k	up	up	none	0°	1 L	h	left turn
10	b	-	-	none	1 R**	1 R**	b	natural turn
11	d	-	-	on left	½ L	½ L	d*	cross body lead
12	d	-	-	on left	½ R	½ L	d*	CBL variation
13	a	up	-	on left	½ L	½ R	a*	walk
14	d	up	up	on left	½ L	1½ L	e	inside turn
15	e	up	up	on left	½ L	1½ R	d	outside turn
16	d	down	up	on left	½ L	1½ L	f	inside turn
17	h	up	down	on left	½ L	1 L	i	inside turn & check
18	k	up	up	on left	½ L	1 L	l	butterfly or titanic
19	a	up	-	on right	½ R	1½ R	a	reverse outside turn
20	d	-	-	on right	½ R	½ R	d*	reverse CBL

- Height of the handholds. The effect of a turn depends on the height of the handholds (down or up). When a handhold is up, the arms go over the head of the dancers, when it is down, the arms of the dancers loop around their bodies resulting in a different final position. There are at least four configurations for this variable: both hands up, left up & right down, left down & right up, both hands down. For the current purpose, we do not consider changes in the height of a handhold during a move (this occurs in intermediate salsa, see Table 1 move number 3).

- Handhold changes. There are at least seven handhold configurations, i.e. no handhold (1), one handhold (4), two handholds (3). During a move, the lead can let go of a handhold, change hands, or ask for a handhold. This is necessary for switching between positions, for example between the parallel handhold position and one of the crossed handholds (e.g., change from Fig. 2d to h or to k). For the current purpose, we consider at most one change in handhold configuration during a move.

Table 1 shows twenty of the most common moves. The initial position and the particular combination of values on all variables determines the final position. For example, moves 14 and 16 only differ in the height of the right handhold, but they produce strikingly different final positions. The question arises whether an exhaustive list of moves can be established. At beginner level, learned patterns, even very sophisticated ones, start from a very small set of elementary positions such as Fig. 2a, b, or d. but any position in the set of 242 can in principle be designated as the initial position of a move. Furthermore, three of the four variables can be independently and systematically varied to create an exhaustive set of combinations (3 slot changes x 9 lead turns x 9 follow turns = 243 different moves). However, their actual practicability depends on the initial position (242 different positions), the height of the handholds, and whether or not handhold changes are taken into account. The systematic variation of all values of all variables would produce over 1.5M different moves that all need to be checked in actual dancing. In comparison, the Tower of Hanoi studied by Zhang and Norman [11] has only 27 legal out of 60 positions of three disks on three pegs, and at most three legal out of six moves from any position. In salsa, the list of potential moves is extremely large and there is no straightforward way of enumerating and verifying all of them.

8   Directions for Future Research

The analysis and elaboration of a diagrammatical scheme showed the complexity of salsa as a performance art and the immense magnitude of the space of positions and moves. Three approaches could build on the systematic charting of the salsa space.

First, empirical study may focus on memory for salsa positions and moves. Such an approach may proceed by comparing diagrammatic and formal notations, as well as pictures and text. Moreover, adopting the classical paradigm for studying chess [4], diagrams could serve in the study of memory for salsa positions. The tasks include presenting dancers of varying skill with an unfamiliar position and ask them to think aloud as they analyze the position and chose what move to make. Moreover, more skillful dancers should show superior recall when presented with the more complex positions. Comparing leads and follows of similar level of skill would inform about the specificity of leading in partnered dances.

Second, video is the more appropriate learning technology for sensory-motor procedures, such as tying a knot and first aid procedures. Studies into learning with videos often comprise a learning phase for understanding and encoding, and a recall phase including a demonstration of the procedure [3]. Thus, future research could compare leads and follows learning with video and with diagrams for salsa patterns of different length and complexity.

Finally, the specificity of leading resides in the necessity of selecting moves in the flow of sensory-motor activity. Although under time constraints, salsa dancing can be seen as crisscrossing a landscape and compared to chess as complex decision making or search in a position space [4]. Future research could study spatial knowledge of salsa positions and moves by "learning through navigation", i.e. by dancing, compared to learning from a map [10] of position diagrams and moves. Indeed, mental simulation tasks could be an effective strategy for learning to lead. From a given initial position, dancers could be asked to apply as many moves as possible and predict the final position. Dancers may also be asked to generate all the moves that allow going back and forth between two positions. As a concluding remark, the study of diagrams in learning to lead in salsa dancing will require appropriate performance measures to complement those for conceptual understanding and execution of short sensory-motor procedures.

References

1. Adams, C., et al.: Encyclopedia of Knot Theory. CRC Press (2021)
2. Baillieul, J., Ozcimder, K.: The control theory of motion-based communication: Problems in teaching robots to dance. In: 2012 American Control Conference (ACC), pp. 4319–4326. IEEE, Montreal, QC (2012). https://doi.org/10.1109/ACC.2012.6315286
3. Boucheix, J.-M., Forestier, C.: Reducing the transience effect of animations does not (always) lead to better performance in children learning a complex hand procedure. Comput. Hum. Behav. **69**, 358–370 (2017). https://doi.org/10.1016/j.chb.2016.12.029
4. Connors, M.H., et al.: Expertise in complex decision making: the role of search in chess 70 years after de Groot. Cogn. Sci. **35**(8), 1567–1579 (2011). https://doi.org/10.1111/j.1551-6709.2011.01196.x
5. Goodman, N.: Languages of art. An approach to a theory of symbols. Hackett, Indianapolis (1976)
6. Ozcimder, K.: Communication through motion in dance with topological constraints. In: 2014 American Control Conference, pp. 178–183 IEEE, Portland, OR, USA (2014). https://doi.org/10.1109/ACC.2014.6859167
7. Ozcimder, K., et al.: Perceiving artistic expression: a formal exploration of performance art salsa. IEEE Access. **6**, 61867–61875 (2018). https://doi.org/10.1109/ACCESS.2018.2871003
8. Palmer, S.: Fundamental Aspects of Cognitive Representation. In: Rosch, E., Lloyd, B. (eds.) Cognition and Categorization. pp. 259–303. Lawrence Elbaum Associates, Hillsdale, NJ (1978)
9. von Renesse, C., Ecke, V.: Mathematics and Salsa dancing. J. Math. Arts **5**(1), 17–28 (2011). https://doi.org/10.1080/17513472.2010.491781
10. Thorndyke, P.W., Hayes-Roth, B.: Differences in spatial knowledge acquired from maps and navigation. Cogn. Psychol. **14**(4), 560–589 (1982). https://doi.org/10.1016/0010-0285(82)90019-6
11. Zhang, J., Norman, D.A.: Representations in distributed cognitive tasks. Cogn. Sci. **18**(1), 87–122 (1994)

The Use of Diagrams in Planning for Report Writing

Emmanuel Manalo[1](✉) and Laura Ohmes[2]

[1] Graduate School of Education, Kyoto University, Kyoto, Japan
manalo.emmanuel.3z@kyoto-u.ac.jp
[2] Institute of Pedagogy, Carl von Ossietzky University of Oldenburg, Oldenburg, Germany
laura.ohmes@uni-oldenburg.de

Abstract. In this study, we investigated 32 undergraduate university students' use of diagrams in planning to write two coursework reports. For both reports, the students were asked to submit a diagrammatic plan for what they were going to write. Prior to their first plan, no instruction was provided about how to use diagrams for planning. However, prior to the second plan, the students were provided instruction on the use of sketchnoting, which is one method for creating visual notes and organizing ideas. For the first plan, only 31% actually submitted a diagram plan, with the majority submitting a text-based plan. However, for the second plan, the proportion who submitted a diagram plan increased to 66%, but they also reported experiencing more difficulty in creating their plans compared to those who submitted text-based plans. The students' plans and reports were scored for various quality features, analysis of which revealed that, for the second report, diagram plans had a better logical structure than text plans. More importantly, second reports created with diagram plans were also found to have a better logical structure than those created with text plans. The findings indicate that many students require instruction to be able to create diagrammatic plans, but that creating such plans can be helpful in structuring their written work.

Keywords: Diagrammatic plans · Report writing · Diagram use instruction · Sketchnoting

1 Introduction

To write effectively, it is generally considered beneficial to plan before and during actual text production. In that planning, the writer needs to critically consider the purpose of the writing and the needs of the intended audience, and to generate ideas and organize those in a cohesive manner (i.e., decide what to say, in what order, and how to say it) [1]. Poor planning can negatively impact the logical flow and comprehensibility of the written work, and its capacity to meet the intended purpose [2].

There are different ways to plan what to write. For example, Flower and colleagues distinguished between three approaches to planning based on how the writing is structured: schema-driven (following an externally-sourced schema for structuring the output), knowledge-driven (focused on conveying what the writer knows), and constructive

© The Author(s) 2022
V. Giardino et al. (Eds.): Diagrams 2022, LNAI 13462, pp. 268–276, 2022.
https://doi.org/10.1007/978-3-031-15146-0_23

(aimed at addressing the writing task requirements) [3]. On the other hand, Isnard and Piolat examined three approaches based on the form of organization used: free organization of ideas (i.e., no guidance or constraints), organization of ideas into an outline (i.e., text format), and graphic organization of ideas (i.e., requiring the production of diagrams to connect ideas) [4]. When considering the cognitive processes that diagrams can facilitate, constructing a diagrammatic plan would appear to present some useful advantages over a text-based plan. For instance, diagrams have the capacity of grouping together all information that needs to be used together [5], which is important in planning as relationships between ideas can become more explicit and apparent, which in turn can enable necessary inferences to be drawn and a holistic overview to be apprehended. Empirical findings from a couple of studies have also indicated that diagrams can facilitate critical reasoning [6, 7]. As critical thought is important at least in academic writing, diagram use may prove beneficial when planning what to write.

However, evidence from the few studies that have examined the value of diagrammatic planning have not supported the notion of such advantages. For example, in the Isnard and Piolat study which was conducted with university students, those in the graphic organization group did not generate any more ideas compared to those in the other groups [4]. In other areas of research concerning the use of self-constructed diagrams for various learning purposes (e.g., problem solving, communication), numerous problems have been identified, including students' inability to appropriately use diagrams to meet task requirements [8, 9]. Such problems are considered hindrances to realizing the benefits that diagram use can bring to a wide variety of learning tasks. There are a number of studies that have shown however that with appropriate and adequate instruction, those problems can be overcome [10].

The extent to which problems in diagram use might exist where planning in writing is concerned has not been adequately examined. The present study therefore aimed at filling in gaps in current understanding. It addressed the following questions:

(i)   Are students able to create diagrammatic plans for reports they have to write? Does the provision of instruction make a difference?
(ii) How do students view the construction of a plan for their reports? Do those views vary according to the kind of plan they create?
(iii) Are there qualitative differences between diagram and text plans?
(iv) Are there detectable quality differences between reports constructed with diagram plans compared to text plans?
(v)   What factors influence students' decisions in planning methods to use?

In this study, instruction provided was based on the sketchnoting method for note taking and organizing information. Sketchnotes are visual notes which contain "a mix of handwriting, drawings, hand-drawn typography, shapes, and visual elements like arrows, boxes & lines" [11: p. 2]. They can be used to summarize information, collect ideas, and to prepare plans for learning activities [12]. The potential of sketchnoting is seen, for example, in synthesizing information, drawing connections, and identifying patterns [13], which makes the method potentially useful for planning in writing.

The difference compared to other diagrammatic plans is that the sketchnote plan consists not only of diagrammatic structures (e.g., arrows, lines, boxes), but also drawings/illustrations (e.g., people, objects, situations), which clarify, supplement, or enhance the written notes aesthetically [11]. The use of drawings/diagrams in notes is not new (e.g., Darwin and da Vinci used them in their legendary notes). What is new and innovative about sketchnoting is the application of the idea that everyone can draw and that even stick figures can represent ideas and knowledge. This helps enable learners who want to use drawings but have previously not felt confident.

2 Method

Ethics approval for this study was obtained in the first author's institution. The participants were 32 Japanese undergraduate university students (females = 20) who were taking a course in education taught by the first author, all of whom consented to the use of their coursework for this research. The course was conducted in English, which was a foreign language for the students, but they all had at least an adequate command of it. In the course, the students had to write two reports (each requiring a summary of a research article and an appraisal of that article) and, for each report, they were asked to construct a diagrammatic plan for their report and submit that ahead of the report deadline. The reports were the same in value: each counted 15% toward the students' final grade (3% of which was allotted to the quality of their plan).

Apart from being asked to create a diagrammatic plan prior to the first report, no other instruction or guidance was provided. However, during the grading of the first report (including the plan for it), the students were provided comments to let them know in cases where their plan was not a diagram. Plans were considered as diagrammatic if they included visual elements such as boxes or other shapes, illustrations, arrows and other lines to indicate various relationships. Plans that included only words, phrases, sentences, and/or bulleted points on their own were considered as text plans.

Between the two reports, the second author provided two 90-min instruction sessions on the use of sketchnoting [11]. The students were shown examples of sketchnotes, and informed about their usefulness in reflection, and in creating plans and writing reports [12, 14]. They were taught how to draw and use visual forms (e.g., shapes, boxes, arrows, illustrations) to represent and organize information, and they were given exercise sheets to practice drawing and create their own sketchnotes.

For this research, we analyzed the plans and reports the students produced. Together with their plans, the students were also asked to respond to three questions about how easy/difficult they found creating their plans, how much they liked/dislikes them, and how useful they considered them. We examined their responses to these. In addition, at the end of the course, we invited the students to participate in a brief interview and two students volunteered. We also analyzed their responses to questions we asked about planning.

We categorized the students' plans as either text or diagram plans and, if the latter, whether they were sketchnote-type or not. We then scored the plans for content, including the number of key points and views/opinions included, and the presence of various features (e.g., word connectors, lines, arrows, boxes, etc.). We scored the two reports for essentially the same content and features. These categories for scoring were based on those used in previous similar research [4]. In addition, we gave each plan and report overall scores for clarity of logical flow (Logic) and message conveyed (Message). The scoring of logical flow focused on the summary of the research article, while that for clarity of message focused on the students' appraisal/opinion of that article.

To ensure reliability in scoring, we first drew up and discussed the scoring definitions and rubrics to use. Then we independently scored an initial batch of students' plans and reports, compared and discussed our scoring, and made adjustments to the definitions and rubrics. We then scored half each of the remaining plans and reports. We duplicated scoring on 25% of all the data to determine inter-scorer reliability, which we found to be satisfactory. All categorical scoring had perfect congruence (Cohen's $\kappa = 1.00$). The scale-based scoring all returned Cronbach's α values above .70, except for the scoring of Logic in Plan 1 ($\alpha = .67$), which we re-scored, after which we reached perfect agreement. A research assistant with no vested interest in the outcomes of this research also independently scored the same 25% of data, and all reliability indicators (Cohen's κ and Cronbach's α values) reached acceptable agreement levels.

3 Results and Discussion

3.1 Students' Ability to Create Diagrammatic Plans

For the first report plan (Plan 1), 10 of the 32 students (31.25%) created a diagram plan, while 19 students (59.38%) submitted a text plan. Three (9.38%) did not submit a plan. For the second report plan (Plan 2), which was after the sketchnoting instruction, the number who submitted a diagram plan increased to 21 (65.63%), while those who submitted a text plan decreased to 6 (18.75%). Five students (15.63%) did not submit a plan. Of the 21 diagram plans submitted, 7 (21.88% of the total) were sketchnote-type plans. Examples of those different types of plans are shown in Fig. 1.

McNemar's test showed that the pattern of change in students' construction of a diagrammatic plan was significant, χ^2 (1, N = 32) = 8.07, $p = .005$. This means that, following instruction, the proportion of students who constructed a diagram plan significantly increased. These findings, first of the initially low proportion of students able or willing to construct diagrams, and second of increases in those able to construct diagrams following instruction, are congruent with previous empirical findings about diagram use in mathematical word problem solving and in writing explanations [10, 15]. They confirm that student limitations in diagram use – in this case, in planning – can largely be overcome with the provision of appropriate and adequate instruction [10].

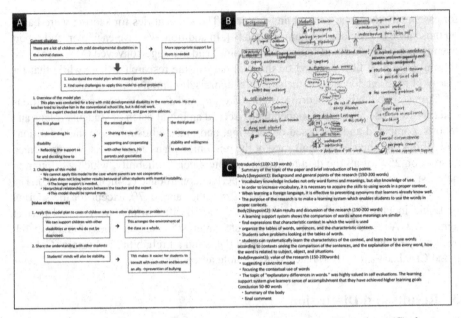

Fig. 1. Examples of the students' diagram (A), sketchnote-type (B), and text (C) plans

3.2 Views About Plan Construction

As noted earlier, the students were asked about their experiences of ease/difficulty and liking of construction, and usefulness of their plans. They were asked to answer on 1 to 5 scales (e.g., very difficult to very easy), and to briefly explain their answers. In Plan 1, no statistically significant differences were found. However, in Plan 2, students who created a diagram plan indicated that they found it more difficult ($M = 2.79, SD = 1.25$) compared to those who created a text plan ($M = 4.33, SD = .58$), and the difference was marginally significant with a large effect size, $F(1, 16) = 4.22, p = .058, \eta^2 = .220$. Content analysis of explanations revealed a number of sources of those difficulties, including understanding the content of the research paper they had to write about, and integrating visual elements, such as illustrations, into the diagram plans. Those who created sketchnote plans reported that it was time consuming and challenging to ensure the plan was easy to understand. In contrast, while those who created text plans also noted some difficulties in summarizing key points, they also indicated familiarity with creating such plans, which made the planning easy for them.

Students who created a diagram plan (including sketchnotes) viewed creating the plan as "helpful" because it assisted them in correctly understanding the content and structure of the paper they were writing about. Moreover, they felt that the diagram helped them to write a well-structured report and to write "smoothly". Similarly, a number of students who constructed a text plan perceived the plan they made as helpful even if they modified the plan while they were writing.

Reasons for liking or disliking the creation of the plans were related to students' experiences of difficulty and helpfulness. For example, students indicated they liked diagramming (including sketchnoting) because it helped to organize their thoughts, and to clarify connections between their own opinion and the content of the research paper.

3.3 Qualitative Differences Between Diagram and Text Plans

Regarding Plan 1, when comparing diagram plans and text plans, understandably, there were significantly higher inclusions of lines, arrows, and other visual connectors (Lines) in diagram plans ($M = 7.00$, $SD = 5.92$) compared to text plans ($M = 1.21$, $SD = 1.75$), $F(1, 28) = 19.30$, $p < .001$, $\eta^2 = .417$; and of Boxes in diagram plans ($M = 7.50$, $SD = 4.86$) compared to text plans ($M = .68$, $SD = 2.36$), $F(1, 28) = 26.29$, $p < .001$), $\eta^2 = .493$. In the number of Key points included, there was also a marginally significant advantage of text plans ($M = 4.74$, $SD = 2.35$) compared to diagram plans ($M = 3.20$, $SD = 2.20$), $F(1, 28) = 2.92$, $p = .099$, $\eta^2 = .097$ (medium effect size).

After instruction, in Plan 2, the diagram plan advantage remained for Lines (diagram plan $M = 8.05$, $SD = 6.80$; text plan $M = .83$, $SD = 2.04$), $F(1, 26) = 6.42$, $p = .018$), $\eta^2 = .204$; and for Boxes (diagram plan $M = 8.00$, $SD = 4.51$; text plan $M = 1.50$, $SD = 3.67$), $F(1, 26 = 10.41$, $p = .003$), $\eta^2 = .294$. There was also a significantly higher count of Sequencing and grouping for diagram plans ($M = 3.48$, $SD = 1.94$) compared to text plans ($M = 1.50$, $SD = .84$), $F(1, 26) = 5.79$, $p = .024$, $\eta^2 = .188$. Furthermore, the marginally significant difference in number of Key points included was no longer present: in fact, the mean number of Key points in diagram plans ($M = 6.19$, $SD = 3.36$) was higher than in text plans ($M = 4.50$, $SD = 4.34$), but not significantly so.

These qualitative differences between diagram and text plans suggest two important points. The first is that diagrams by their very nature may facilitate the manifestation of certain useful plan features such as connection and grouping of information [cf. 5]. The second is that, if students are not familiar with diagram use, they may construct diagram plans that are inferior to text plans (e.g., as in Plan 1, they may include fewer key points). With instruction, however, such disadvantages appear possible to overcome: as the results here indicate, in Plan 2, the diagram plans were no longer inferior to text plans where inclusion of Key points was concerned.

3.4 Differences Between Reports Constructed with Diagram and Text Plans

When comparing the overall scores for Logic (i.e., clarity of logical flow) and Message (i.e., clarity of message conveyed) of diagram plans and text plans for Report 1, no significant differences were found. Likewise, when comparing Report 1s created with diagram plans, text plans, and no plan, no significant differences were found.

However, diagram plans for Report 2 had a significantly higher Logic score ($M = 4.19$, $SD = .75$) compared to the text plans ($M = 3.17$, $SD = .98$), $F(1, 26) = 7.61$, $p = .011$, $\eta^2 = .233$ (i.e., large size effect). Perhaps more importantly, a significant effect was found when comparing Report 2 Logic scores according to whether they were created with diagram plans, text plans, or no plan, $F(2, 31 = 4.48$, $p = .020$), $\eta^2 = .236$ (i.e., large size effect). Simple main effects using Fisher's LSD revealed that the Logic scores of reports written with a diagram plan ($M = 4.62$, $SD = .50$) were significantly higher compared to the scores of reports with a text plan ($M = 4.00$, $SD = .63$), $p = .023$, and the scores of reports with no plan ($M = 4.00$, $SD = .71$), $p = .033$.

This finding is important because it suggests that, following the provision of instruction, many students were able to construct diagram plans that were deemed as having a clearer logical flow and structure. More importantly, there is evidence to suggest that those plans led to reports that were also superior in logical flow and structure.

3.5 Factors that Influenced Students' Decisions on Planning Methods to Use

The responses of the two students who volunteered to be interviewed revealed that the *instruction* influenced their decision to use diagrams in two ways. Firstly, the instruction enabled both students to draw crucial visual elements: "I had no confidence in my drawing skills. So before, I wrote only sentences or words, but by learning about sketchnoting I understood that I only have to draw simple illustrations like arrows or squares or circles" (Student 2). Secondly, the instruction to create a visual plan itself was decisive for the use of sketchnoting for Student 1: "I also wrote notes in literal [meaning text] first as I always do and then I drew the drawings because you told me that I should use drawings, sketchnoting when submitting the visual plan". Their *ability level* also affected the students' decisions. For example, Student 2 who created a diagram but not a sketchnote explained: "I can draw simple illustration if someone teaches me, 'Please draw this illustration', but it is difficult for me to create original illustrations". *Time* consideration was closely related to *ability level*, as shown in a statement by the same student: "I am not good at drawing complex illustrations or drawings, so it takes me a lot of time".

Furthermore, certain *goals* can go hand in hand with the use of certain graphical elements. For example, Student 1 reported that she used different boxes in order to organize the content. Finally, *habits* also determined the decision for using a certain method. For example, Student 1 mentioned that she used a text plan before creating the sketchnote because that is what she always does before writing.

3.6 Conclusion

The findings of this study suggest that when appropriate instruction is provided, the majority of students can effectively use diagrams for planning reports they are going to write. Perhaps more importantly, evidence was found indicating that diagrammatic planning benefitted not only the functionality of the plans that were constructed, but also the quality of the reports that were written. The benefits were congruent with what previous research has indicated as the computational efficiencies that diagram use brings to information processing [5]: in the present study's case, better *logical structuring* appears to have been facilitated in both the plans and the reports.

However, even after instruction, constructing diagram plans was still generally experienced by the students as more difficult compared to constructing text plans. This may be attributable to inadequate experience and practice in such construction. Similar findings have previously been reported in cases where sketchnoting had been taught for use in note taking and memorization. Students perceived sketchnoting as interesting and useful, but they also found it more difficult and time consuming compared to methods they were more familiar with and had previously employed [16]. This problem may be possible to resolve through the provision of more detailed instruction and practice [15] – which ought to be examined in future research. Likewise, it would be beneficial to investigate which thinking and writing processes diagrammatic planning may be able to facilitate particularly in relation to the requirements of the writing tasks administered. Flower and colleagues, for example, noted variations in approaches to planning according to how the writing is structured [2, 3]. It would therefore be useful to examine the extent to which diagrams may facilitate the objectives corresponding to those structural forms. In this study, we only found effects on logical flow, but depending on the writing task and diagram use instruction provided, other effects may be possible.

Acknowledgment. This research was supported by a grant-in-aid (20K20516) received from the Japan Society for the Promotion of Science.

References

1. Harris, K.R., Santangelo, T., Graham, S.: Metacognition and strategies instruction in writing. In: Waters, H.S., Schneider, W. (eds.) Metacognition, Strategy Use, and Instruction, pp. 226–256. Guilford, New York (2010)
2. Flower, L., Hayes, J.R.: A cognitive process theory of writing. Coll. Compos. Commun. **32**, 365–387 (1981)
3. Flower, L., Schriver, K.A., Carey, L., Haas, C., Hayes, J.R.: Planning in writing (ED313701). ERIC (1989). https://eric.ed.gov/?id=ED313701
4. Isnard, N., Piolat, A.: The effects of different types of planning on the writing of argumentative text. In: Eigler, G., Jechle, T. (eds.) Writing. Current Trends in European Research, pp. 121–132. Hochschul Verlag, Freiburg (1993)
5. Larkin, J.H., Simon, H.A.: Why a diagram is (sometimes) worth ten thousand words. Cognitive Sci. **11**, 65–99 (1987)
6. Nussbaum, E.M.: Using argumentation vee diagrams (AVDs) for promoting argument-counterargument integration in reflective writing. J. Educ. Psychol. **100**, 549–565 (2008)
7. Uesaka, Y., Igarashi, M., Suetsugu, R.: Promoting multi-perspective integration as a 21st Century skill: The effects of instructional methods encouraging students' spontaneous use of tables for organizing information. In: Jamnik, M., Uesaka, Y., Schwartz, S.E. (eds.) Diagrams 2016, LNAI **9781**, pp. 172–186. Springer, Berlin (2016)
8. Van Garderen, D., Montague, M.: Visual-spatial representation, mathematical problem solving, and students of varying abilities. Learn. Disabil. Res. Pr. **18**, 246–254 (2003)
9. Manalo, E., Uesaka, Y.: Students' spontaneous use of diagrams in written communication: Understanding variations according to purpose and cognitive cost entailed. In: Dwyer, T., Purchase, H., Delaney, A. (eds.), Diagrams 2014. LNAI, LNCS, vol. 8578, pp. 78–92. Springer, Berlin (2014)
10. Manalo, E., Uesaka, Y., Chen, O., Ayabe, H.: Showing what it looks like: teaching students to use diagrams in problem solving, communication, and thinking. In: Manalo, E. (ed.) Deeper Learning, Dialogic Learning, and Critical Thinking: Research-based Strategies for the Classroom, pp. 231–246. Routledge, New York (2020)
11. Rohde, M.: The Sketchnote Handbook. Peachpit Press, Berkeley (2013)
12. Tatar, N., Seker, M.: The effects of learning styles of pre-service teachers on their skills to prepare sketchnotes. In: Proceedings of the International Conference on Education and New Developments, pp. 165–168. http://end-educationconference.org/2019/wp-content/uploads/2020/05/2019v1end035.pdf (2019)

13. Paepcke-Hjeltness, V., Mina, M. Cyamani, A.: Sketchnoting: a new approach to developing visual communication ability, improving critical thinking and creative confidence for engineering and design students. In: Proceedings of the 2017 IEEE Frontiers in Education Conference, pp. 1–5 (2017). https://ieeexplore.ieee.org/document/8190659
14. Perry, K., Weimar, H., Bell, M.A.: Sketchnoting in School. Discover the Benefits (and Fun) of Visual Note Taking. Rowman Littlefield, London (2018)
15. Manalo, E., Uesaka, Y.: Hint, instruction, and practice: the necessary components in promoting spontaneous diagram use in students' written work? In: Jamnik, M., Uesaka, Y., Schwartz, S.E. (eds.) Diagrams 2016, LNAI **9781**, pp. 157–171. Springer, Berlin (2016)
16. Bratash, V.S., Riekhakaynen, E.I., Petrova, T.E.: Creating and processing sketchnotes: a psycholinguistic study. Procedia Comput. Sci. **176**, 2930–2939 (2020)

Logical Diagrams

From Euler Diagrams
to Aristotelian Diagrams

Lorenz Demey[1]([⊠])[iD] and Hans Smessaert[2][iD]

[1] Center for Logic and Philosophy of Science, KU Leuven,
Kardinaal Mercierplein 2, 3000 Leuven, Belgium
lorenz.demey@kuleuven.be
[2] Department of Linguistics, KU Leuven,
Blijde-Inkomststraat 21, 3000 Leuven, Belgium
hans.smessaert@kuleuven.be

Abstract. Euler and Aristotelian diagrams are both among the most well-studied kinds of logical diagrams today. Despite their central status, very little research has been done on relating these two types of diagrams. This is probably due to the fact that Euler diagrams typically visualize relations between sets, whereas Aristotelian diagrams typically visualize relations between propositions. However, recent work has shown that Aristotelian diagrams can also perfectly be understood as visualizing relations between sets, and hence it becomes natural to ask whether there is any kind of systematic relation between Euler and Aristotelian diagrams. In this paper we provide an affirmative answer: we show that every Euler diagram for two non-trivial sets gives rise to a well-defined Aristotelian diagram. Furthermore, depending on the specific relation between the two sets visualized by the Euler diagram, the resulting Aristotelian diagram will also be fundamentally different. We will also link this with well-known notions from logical geometry, such as the information ordering on the seven logical relations between non-trivial sets, and the notion of Boolean complexity of Aristotelian diagrams.

Keywords: Euler diagram · Aristotelian diagram · Square of opposition · Logical geometry · Information ordering · Boolean complexity

1 Introduction

Euler diagrams are among the most well-studied kinds logical diagrams today [1, 20, 24, 26, 27]. They have a rich history, which obviously includes the work of Leonhard Euler in the eighteenth century, but also goes back much further,

The first author holds a Research Professorship (BOFZAP) from KU Leuven. This research was funded through the KU Leuven research project 'BITSHARE: Bitstring Semantics for Human and Artificial Reasoning' (3H190254, 2019–2023).

© Springer Nature Switzerland AG 2022
V. Giardino et al. (Eds.): Diagrams 2022, LNAI 13462, pp. 279–295, 2022.
https://doi.org/10.1007/978-3-031-15146-0_24

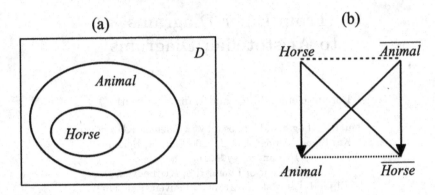

Fig. 1. (a) Euler diagram for *Horse* ⊂ *Animal*; (b) the corresponding square of opposition. (Solid, dashed and dotted lines respectively stand for contradiction, contrariety and subcontrariety; arrows stand for subalternation.)

at least to medieval manuscripts from the eleventh century [11,16–18]. Similarly, Aristotelian diagrams (such as the square of opposition) are also studied intensively today, especially in the burgeoning research program of logical geometry [3,9,10,25], and they, too, can boast a long and well-documented history [13,21,23]. The history of both types of diagrams is further described in [22].

Despite their central status, very little research has been done thus far on relating Euler and Aristotelian diagrams.[1] One explanation for this lacuna might be that Euler diagrams typically visualize a relation between *sets/terms*, whereas Aristotelian diagrams typically visualize relations between *propositions/sentences*. However, recent work has shown that the mathematical background structure required for obtaining a well-defined Aristotelian diagram is that of a Boolean algebra, and it does not matter whether this is an algebra consisting of propositions or of terms (or yet some other notion) [4]. Consequently, it becomes a mathematically well-defined and conceptually natural question to ask whether there is any kind of systematic connection between Euler and Aristotelian diagrams. Our goal in this paper is to provide an affirmative answer to this question. In particular, we will show how each Euler diagram for two (non-trivial) sets gives rise to a well-defined Aristotelian diagram. Furthermore, depending on the specific relation between the two sets visualized by the Euler diagram, the resulting Aristotelian diagram will also be fundamentally different.

The paper is organized as follows. Section 2 presents a motivating example and describes some of the necessary theoretical background. Section 3 contains the main results of this paper, and shows how each two-set Euler diagram gives rise to an Aristotelian diagram. Section 4 presents some further discussion of these results, and mentions some questions for future research.

---

[1] A notable exception, albeit in a very different direction than the one we will take in this paper, is the work of Bernhard [2].

2   Motivating Example and Theoretical Background

Consider the Euler diagram shown in Fig. 1(a). What does this diagram represent or visualize? The standard answer is that the diagram visualizes two sets, *Horse* and *Animal* (which exist inside some domain of discourse D), and the relation *Horse* $\subset$ *Animal*, i.e., *Horse* is a strict subset of *Animal*. Relative to a Boolean algebra of sets, this means that there exists a subalternation from *Horse* to *Animal*.[2] However, according to a less standard answer, the diagram in Fig. 1(a) shows *more* than what has just been mentioned. First of all, by showing the set *Horse* inside the domain of discourse D, it also shows, if only implicitly, the complement set $\overline{Horse} = D \backslash Horse$. The same goes for the set *Animal* and its complement $\overline{Animal} = D \backslash Animal$. Secondly, the Euler diagram also shows, again only implicitly, five more relationships that these two new complement sets enter into:

- *Horse* $\cap$ $\overline{Horse}$ $= \emptyset$ and *Horse* $\cup$ $\overline{Horse}$ $= D$,
  i.e., *Horse* and $\overline{Horse}$ are contradictory to each other,
- *Animal* $\cap$ $\overline{Animal}$ $= \emptyset$ and *Animal* $\cup$ $\overline{Animal}$ $= D$,
  i.e., *Animal* and $\overline{Animal}$ are contradictory to each other,
- *Horse* $\cap$ $\overline{Animal}$ $= \emptyset$ and *Horse* $\cup$ $\overline{Animal}$ $\neq D$,
  i.e., *Horse* and $\overline{Animal}$ are contrary to each other,
- *Animal* $\cap$ $\overline{Horse}$ $\neq \emptyset$ and *Animal* $\cup$ $\overline{Horse}$ $= D$,
  i.e., *Animal* and $\overline{Horse}$ are subcontrary to each other,
- $\overline{Animal} \subset \overline{Horse}$, i.e., there is a subalternation from $\overline{Animal}$ to $\overline{Horse}$.

Taken together, these four sets and the six relations holding among them can be visualized by means of a square of opposition, as shown in Fig. 1(b).[3] This Aristotelian diagram thus contains exactly the same information (i.e., the same sets and the same relations among them) as the Euler diagram in Fig. 1(a). The only difference between both diagrams is that the Euler diagram strongly emphasizes two sets, viz. *Horse* and *Animal*, and one relation, viz. the subalternation from *Horse* to *Animal*, while strongly 'downplaying' the two other sets and the five other relations. By contrast, the Aristotelian diagram attributes equal status

---

[2] Given an arbitrary Boolean algebra $\mathbb{B}$, we say that x and y are contradictory iff $x \wedge_\mathbb{B} y = \perp_\mathbb{B}$ and $x \vee_\mathbb{B} y = \top_\mathbb{B}$, that they are contrary iff $x \wedge_\mathbb{B} y = \perp_\mathbb{B}$ and $x \vee_\mathbb{B} y \neq \top_\mathbb{B}$, that they are subcontrary iff $x \wedge_\mathbb{B} y \neq \perp_\mathbb{B}$ and $x \vee_\mathbb{B} y = \top_\mathbb{B}$, and that they are in subalternation iff $x <_\mathbb{B} y$. If $\mathbb{B}$ happens to consist of subsets of some given set D, this means that X and Y are contradictory iff $X \cap Y = \emptyset$ and $X \cup Y = D$, that they are contrary iff $X \cap Y = \emptyset$ and $X \cup Y \neq D$, that they are subcontrary iff $X \cap Y \neq \emptyset$ and $X \cup Y = D$, and that they are in subalternation iff $X \subset Y$. See [4, Section 2] for further explanation and motivation.

[3] This square might look a bit strange, since it contains sets rather than propositions. However, we emphasize once again that Aristotelian relations (and thus also diagrams) can be defined relative to arbitrary Boolean algebras, regardless of whether these algebras consist of propositions, sets, or something else. The square of opposition in Fig. 1(b) is thus perfectly well-defined, just like any other, more ordinary-looking square of opposition that contains propositions rather than sets.

to all four sets and all six relations alike.[4] Some of these ideas were already mentioned in passing in a recent, more historically oriented paper:[5]

> one can view the original Euler diagram in Fig. [1(a)] as a visual represen-
> tation of both proper inclusion relations—albeit, perhaps, with different
> degrees of visual perspicuity. More generally, from this alternative perspec-
> tive, the single Euler diagram in Fig. [1(a)] at once visualizes six relations
> among *Horse, Animal, D\Horse* and *D\Animal*, all six of which are also
> visualized by the classical square of opposition in Fig. [1(b)].
>
> [5, p. 192, references to figures updated to the present paper]

In this paper, we will investigate these ideas more systematically. More specifically, we will show that this kind of transformation not only works for Euler
diagrams representing a subalternation relation, but also for Euler diagrams
depicting any other kind of relation between two sets. In [25] it is shown that
every pair of non-trivial[6] sets X and Y (within a domain of discourse D) stands
in exactly one of the following seven relations:[7]

1	contradiction (CD):	$X \cap Y = \emptyset$	and	$X \cup Y = D$,
2	contrariety (C):	$X \cap Y = \emptyset$	and	$X \cup Y \neq D$,
3	subcontrariety (SC):	$X \cap Y \neq \emptyset$	and	$X \cup Y = D$,
4	bi-implication (BI):	$X \subseteq Y$	and	$X \supseteq Y$, i.e. $X = Y$,
5	left-implication (LI):	$X \subseteq Y$	and	$X \not\supseteq Y$, i.e. $X \subset Y$,
6	right-implication (RI):	$X \not\subseteq Y$	and	$X \supseteq Y$, i.e. $X \supset Y$,
7	unconnectedness (UN):	$X \cap Y \neq \emptyset$	and	$X \cup Y \neq D$ and
		$X \not\subseteq Y$	and	$X \not\supseteq Y$

The first three relations are sometimes called *opposition relations*, while the next
three are the *implication relations*. Note that left-implication corresponds to the
ordinary Aristotelian relation of subalternation. Unconnectedness can be viewed

---

[4] In earlier work [7,8], we have argued that the idea that a square of opposition
attributes *exactly* the same status to all six relations should be somewhat nuanced.
For example, based on principles like center/periphery or on considerations regarding
distance, one could argue that contradiction (on the two diagonals, in the center of
the square) is visualized more prominently than the other relations (on the edges,
at the periphery of the square). However, these subtle differences in an Aristotelian
diagram completely vanish in comparison to the more drastic differences in emphasis
that occur in Euler diagrams—e.g. the explicit subalternation from *Horse* to *Animal*
versus the more implicit subcontrariety between *Animal* and $\overline{Horse}$ in Fig. 1(a).

[5] The theoretical core of [5] consists of its Sections 3, 4 and 5. The present paper can
be viewed as building upon Section 3, while [19] elaborates on Sections 4 and 5.

[6] Given a domain of discourse D, a set X is said to be *non-trivial* iff $\emptyset \neq X \neq D$.

[7] These seven relations could also be defined for arbitrary Boolean algebras instead of
just for sets. However, for the purposes of this paper this will not be necessary.

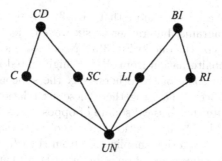

Fig. 2. Information ordering on the seven relations between two non-trivial sets [25].

as the absence of any other relation: X and Y are unconnected iff they do not stand in any of the other relations. These seven relations constitute a refinement of the five so-called 'Gergonne relations', which are perhaps more widely known [12,14]. The Gergonne relations $X = Y$, $X \subset Y$ and $X \supset Y$ straightforwardly correspond to *BI*, *LI* and *RI*, respectively; furthermore, the Gergonne relation $X \cap Y = \emptyset$ corresponds to $CD \cup C$, and $X \cap Y \neq \emptyset$ corresponds to $SC \cup UN$. Finally, these seven relations are ordered according to their information levels [25]: it can be shown that contradiction and bi-implication are the most informative relations, unconnectedness is the least informative, and the four other relations' information levels are in between. This information ordering is shown in Fig. 2.

3   The Seven Euler Diagrams for Two Sets and Their Corresponding Aristotelian Diagrams

We will now consider Euler diagrams for each of the seven possible relations between two (non-trivial) sets, and investigate what kind of Aristotelian diagram they give rise to. We start with the implication relation of *left-implication*, which boils down to re-examining the motivating example from the previous section. The Euler diagram in Fig. 3(a) shows a left-implication (i.e., subalternation) from A to B. In order to highlight the six relations that are shown by this diagram, we will use thick black and grey ellipses for resp. A and B, and thick black and grey dashed lines, together with a thickened rectangle for the domain of discourse, for their complements, resp. $\overline{A}$ and $\overline{B}$.[8] Using this high-lighting convention, Fig. 3(c) and (d) show the very same Euler diagram as in (a), but now highlighting the subalternations from A to B and from $\overline{B}$ to $\overline{A}$, respectively. Similarly, Fig. 3(e) highlights the contrariety between A and $\overline{B}$, while Fig. 3(f) highlights the subcontrariety between $\overline{A}$ and B. Finally, Fig. 3(g) and (h) highlight the contradictions between A and $\overline{A}$ and between B and $\overline{B}$,

---

[8] The overall idea is thus that a set corresponds to the region delimited by a thick solid line (either an ellipse or the outer rectangle), subtracting (if necessary/applicable) the region inside the thick dashed line.

respectively. We emphasize once more that Figs. 3(c–h) should not be viewed as six separate Euler diagrams, but rather as six ways of looking at one and the same Euler diagram, viz. the one in Fig. 3(a). Needless to say, some of these six relations—e.g. the subalternation from A to B highlighted in Fig. 3(c)—are far easier to process than some of the others—e.g. the subcontrariety between $\overline{A}$ and B shown in Fig. 3(f). Taken together, these six relations (all of which are Aristotelian) constitute the classical square of opposition shown in Fig. 3(b).

Secondly, we consider the implication relation of *right-implication*. The Euler diagram in Fig. 4(a) shows a right-implication from A to B, i.e. a subalternation from B to A. Using the same convention as before, Fig. 4(c) and (d) show the very same Euler diagram as in (a), but now highlighting the subalternations from B to A and from $\overline{A}$ to $\overline{B}$, respectively. Similarly, Fig. 4(e) highlights the subcontrariety between A and $\overline{B}$, while Fig. 4(f) highlights the contrariety between $\overline{A}$ and B. Finally, Fig. 4(g) and (h) highlight the contradictions between A and $\overline{A}$ and between B and $\overline{B}$, respectively. Taken together, these six relations (all of which are Aristotelian) constitute the classical square of opposition shown in Fig. 4(b).

Thirdly, we switch over to the opposition relations, and consider the relation of *contrariety*. The Euler diagram in Fig. 5(a) shows a contrariety between A and B. Figure 5(c) highlights the contrariety between A and B, while Fig. 5(d) highlights the subcontrariety between $\overline{A}$ and $\overline{B}$. Similarly, Fig. 5(e) and (f) highlight the subalternations from A to $\overline{B}$ and from B to $\overline{A}$, respectively. Finally, Fig. 5(g) and (h) highlight the contradictions between A and $\overline{A}$ and between B and $\overline{B}$, respectively. Taken together, these six relations (all of which are Aristotelian) constitute the classical square of opposition shown in Fig. 5(b).

Fourthly, we consider the opposition relation of *subcontrariety*. The Euler diagram in Fig. 6(a) shows a subcontrariety between A and B. Figure 6(c) highlights the subcontrariety between A and B, while Fig. 6(d) highlights the contrariety between $\overline{A}$ and $\overline{B}$. Similarly, Fig. 6(e) and (f) highlight the subalternations from $\overline{B}$ to A and from $\overline{A}$ to B, respectively. Finally, Fig. 6(g) and (h) highlight the contradictions between A and $\overline{A}$ and between B and $\overline{B}$, respectively. Taken together, these six relations (all of which are Aristotelian) constitute the classical square of opposition shown in Fig. 6(b).

Fifthly, we switch back to the implication relations, and consider the relation of *bi-implication*. The Euler diagram in Fig. 7(a) shows a bi-implication between A and B. Figure 7(c) and (d) highlight the bi-implications between A and B and between $\overline{A}$ and $\overline{B}$, respectively. Similarly, Fig. 7(e) and (f) highlight the contradictions between A and $\overline{B}$ and between $\overline{A}$ and B, respectively. Finally, Fig. 7(g) and (h) highlight the contradictions between A and $\overline{A}$ and between B and $\overline{B}$, respectively. Taken together, these six relations constitute the pair of contradictories (PCD) shown in Fig. 7(b). This PCD contains two identical sets at both of its vertices, which correspond to the bi-implications A/B and $\overline{A}/\overline{B}$ (which are themselves not Aristotelian). The single solid line corresponds to *four* contradiction relations $A/\overline{A}$, $A/\overline{B}$, $B/\overline{A}$ and $B/\overline{B}$ (which are Aristotelian).

Sixthly, we switch back one more time to the opposition relations, and consider the relation of *contradiction*. The Euler diagram in Fig. 8(a) shows a contradiction between A and B. Figure 8(c) and (d) highlight the contradictions

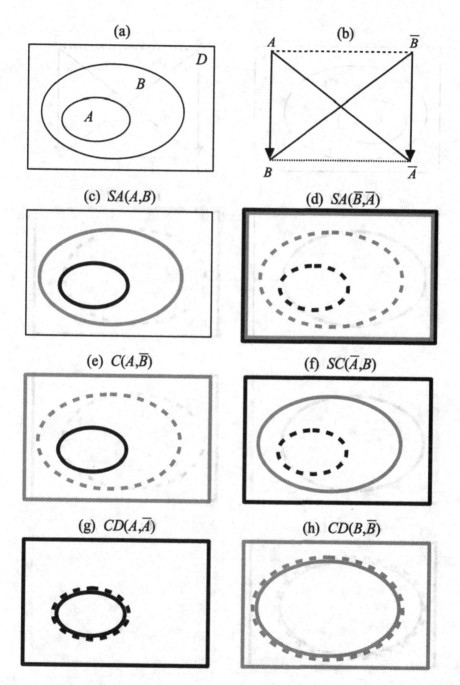

Fig. 3. (a) Euler diagram for the left-implication from A to B. (b) The corresponding classical square of opposition. (c–h) Highlighting the six relations among A, B, $\overline{A}$ and $\overline{B}$ in the Euler diagram (note: all six of them are Aristotelian relations).

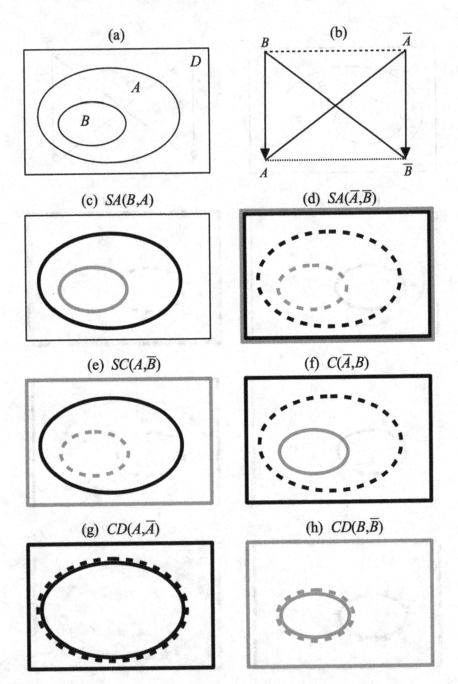

Fig. 4. (a) Euler diagram for the right-implication from A to B. (b) The corresponding classical square of opposition. (c–h) Highlighting the six relations among A, B, $\overline{A}$ and $\overline{B}$ in the Euler diagram (note: all six of them are Aristotelian relations).

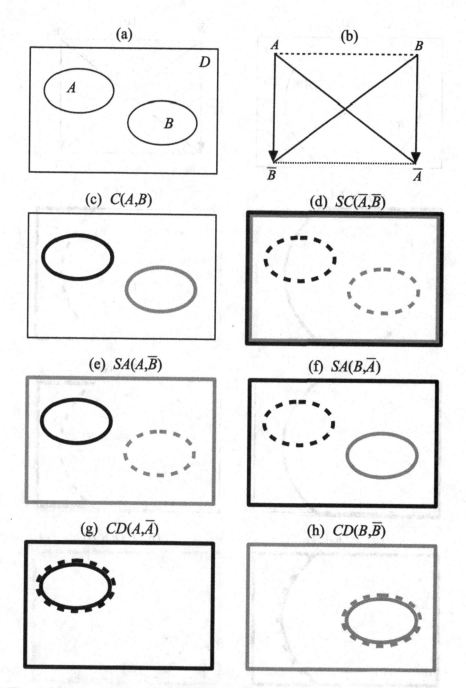

Fig. 5. (a) Euler diagram for the contrariety between A and B. (b) The corresponding classical square of opposition. (c–h) Highlighting the six relations among A, B, $\overline{A}$ and $\overline{B}$ in the Euler diagram (note: all six of them are Aristotelian relations).

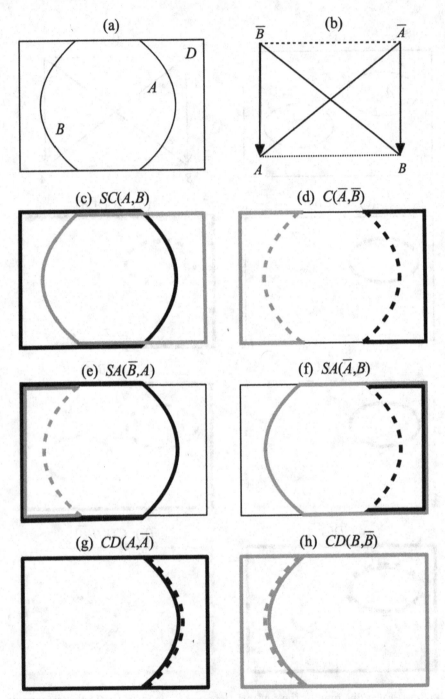

Fig. 6. (a) Euler diagram for the subcontrariety between A and B. (b) The corresponding classical square of opposition. (c–h) Highlighting the six relations among A, B, $\overline{A}$ and $\overline{B}$ in the Euler diagram (note: all six of them are Aristotelian relations).

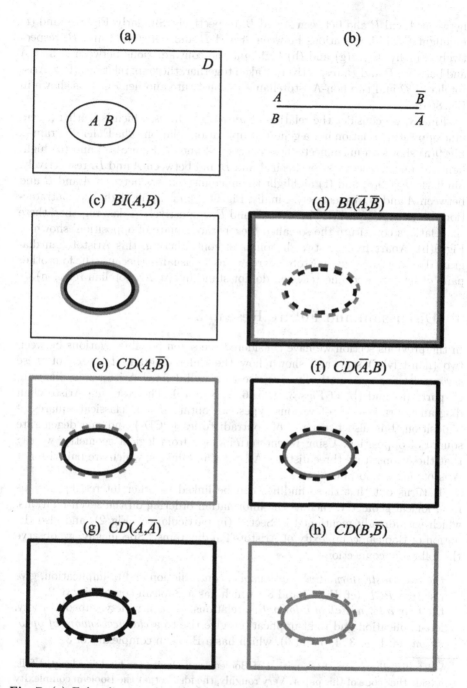

Fig. 7. (a) Euler diagram for the bi-implication between A and B. (b) The corresponding PCD. (c–h) Highlighting the six relations among A, B, $\overline{A}$ and $\overline{B}$ in the Euler diagram (note: the four CD are Aristotelian relations, but the two BI are not).

between A and B and between $\overline{A}$ and $\overline{B}$, respectively. Similarly, Fig. 8(e) and (f) highlight the bi-implications between A and $\overline{B}$ and between $\overline{A}$ and B, respectively. Finally, Fig. 8(g) and (h) highlight the contradictions between A and $\overline{A}$ and between B and $\overline{B}$, respectively. Taken together, these six relations (four Aristotelian CD and two non-Aristotelian BI) constitute another PCD, as shown in Fig. 8(b).

Finally, we consider the relation of *unconnectedness*, which is neither a genuine opposition relation nor a genuine implication relation. The Euler diagram in Fig. 9(a) shows an unconnectedness between A and B. Figure 9(c) and (d) highlight the unconnectedness between A and B and between $\overline{A}$ and $\overline{B}$, respectively. Similarly, Fig. 9(e) and (f) highlight the unconnectedness between A and $\overline{B}$ and between $\overline{A}$ and B, respectively. Finally, Fig. 9(g) and (h) highlight the contradictions between A and $\overline{A}$ and between B and $\overline{B}$, respectively. Taken together, these six relations constitute the so-called 'degenerate square of opposition' shown in Fig. 9(b). Apart from its two diagonals of contradiction, this Aristotelian diagram does not have any Aristotelian relations to visualize (because the four other pairs of sets are unconnected, i.e., do not stand in any Aristotelian relation).

4 Discussion and Future Research

In the previous section we have considered the seven possible relations between two (non-trivial) sets, and shown how the Euler diagrams for each of these seven relations systematically give rise to a well-defined Aristotelian diagram; cf. parts (a) and (b) of Figs. 3, 4, 5, 6, 7, 8 and 9. The resulting Aristotelian diagrams turn out be of various types: we obtained four classical squares of opposition, but also two pairs of contradictories (PCDs) and one degenerate square of opposition. Using recent terminology from logical geometry, we say that these constitute three distinct Aristotelian families, which are pairwise not Aristotelian isomorphic [3,9].

It turns out that these findings can be linked to other interesting notions from logical geometry, such as the information ordering on the seven relations, which was already mentioned in Sect. 2 (in particular, cf. Fig. 2), and also the notion of Boolean complexity of Aristotelian diagrams.[9] Specifically, we observe the following connections:

– the two *most informative* relations, i.e. contradiction and bi-implication, give rise to a *PCD* (cf. Figs. 7 and 8), which has a Boolean complexity of 2,
– the four *intermediately informative* relations, i.e. contrariety, subcontrariety, left-implication and right-implication, give rise to a *classical square of opposition* (cf. Figs. 3, 4, 5 and 6), which has a Boolean complexity of 3,

---

[9] A detailed discussion of the notion of Boolean complexity (or bitstring length) falls outside the scope of this paper. Very roughly, the idea is that the Boolean complexity of a diagram D is the smallest number n of bits that are required to faithfully encode D. Formally, given a Boolean algebra $\mathbb{B}$ and diagram $D = \{x_1, \ldots, x_n\}$, we have $n = |\{\pm x_1 \wedge_{\mathbb{B}} \cdots \wedge_{\mathbb{B}} \pm x_n \mid \pm x_1 \wedge_{\mathbb{B}} \cdots \wedge_{\mathbb{B}} \pm x_n \neq \perp_{\mathbb{B}}\}|$ (where $+x = x$ and $-x = \neg_{\mathbb{B}}x$); see [9] for much more mathematical details, motivation and examples.

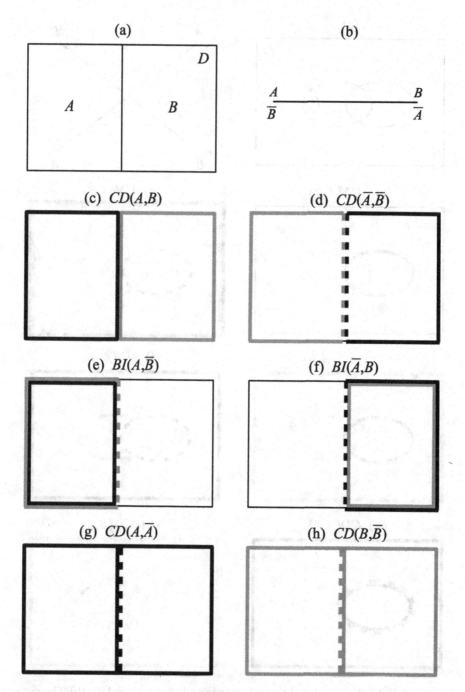

Fig. 8. (a) Euler diagram for the contradiction between A and B. (b) The corresponding PCD. (c–h) Highlighting the six relations among A, B, $\overline{A}$ and $\overline{B}$ in the Euler diagram (note: the four CD are Aristotelian relations, but the two BI are not).

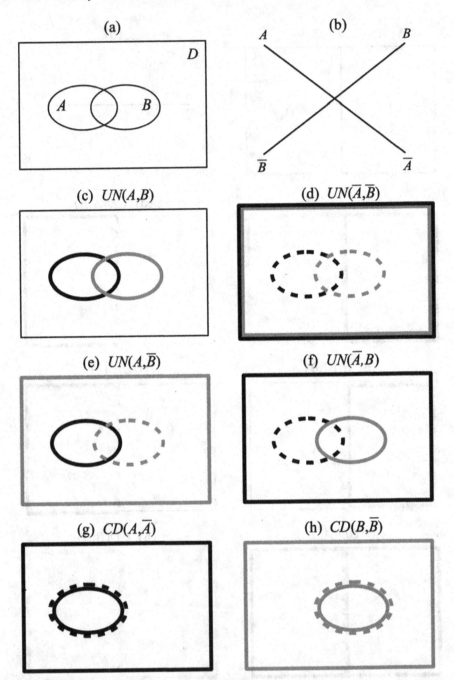

Fig. 9. (a) Euler diagram for the unconnectedness between A and B. (b) The corresponding degenerate square of opposition. (c–h) Highlighting the six relations among A, B, $\overline{A}$ and $\overline{B}$ in the Euler diagram (note: the two CD are Aristotelian relations, but the four UN are not).

– the *least informative* relation, i.e. unconnectedness, gives rise to a *degenerate square of opposition* (cf. Fig. 9), which has a Boolean complexity of 4.

We thus find an inverse correlation between (i) the information level of the relation visualized by the Euler diagram and (ii) the Boolean complexity of the corresponding Aristotelian diagram.

The true significance of these results is not yet fully understood at this point, but they clearly illustrate the theoretical fruitfulness of this approach within logical geometry. Furthermore, and even more importantly, by systematically linking Aristotelian diagrams with Euler diagrams, we have taken an important next step in charting the place of Aristotelian diagrams (and thus of logical geometry) within the broader landscape of logical diagrams research.[10] Since there exists a vast amount of work on diagrammatic reasoning with Euler diagrams, establishing a bridge to Aristotelian diagrams will hopefully inspire new, analogous work on diagrammatic reasoning with Aristotelian diagrams as well.

Thus far we have focused exclusively on (Aristotelian diagrams corresponding to) Euler diagrams for two non-trivial sets A and B. This suggests several avenues for further research; we finish this paper by mentioning three of them:

– What happens if we remove the restriction that the sets should be *non-trivial*, in other words, if we allow that $A = D$ or $A = \emptyset$ or $B = D$ or $B = \emptyset$? The Euler diagrams for these cases should be fairly straightforward, but the corresponding Aristotelian diagrams will violate the condition (which is usually considered to be fundamental in logical geometry) that Aristotelian diagrams should only contain non-trivial elements.
– What about Aristotelian diagrams corresponding to Euler diagrams for *more than two* sets? A special case is when these multiple sets constitute a partition of the domain of discourse; it is known that in this special case, the corresponding Aristotelian diagram will be a (strong) α-structure [5,19]; however, there are currently no results yet about the general case.
– What about other types of diagrams, e.g. *spider diagrams* [15]? Can these also be transformed into well-defined Aristotelian diagrams?

References

1. Bernhard, P.: Euler-Diagramme: Zur Morphologie einer Repräsentationsform in der Logik. Mentis, Paderborn (2001)
2. Bernhard, P.: Visualizations of the square of opposition. Log. Univers. **2**, 31–41 (2008)
3. Demey, L.: Computing the maximal Boolean complexity of families of Aristotelian diagrams. J. Log. Comput. **28**, 1323–1339 (2018)
4. Demey, L.: Metalogic, metalanguage and logical geometry. Logique et Anal. (N.S.) **248**, 453–478 (2019)

---

[10] An earlier step in this direction was our paper [6], which explores the interaction between Aristotelian diagrams and Hasse diagrams.

5. Demey, L.: From Euler diagrams in Schopenhauer to Aristotelian diagrams in Logical Geometry. In: Lemanski, J. (ed.) Language, Logic, and Mathematics in Schopenhauer, pp. 181–205. Springer, Cham (2020)
6. Demey, L., Smessaert, H.: The relationship between Aristotelian and Hasse diagrams. In: Dwyer, T., Purchase, H., Delaney, A. (eds.) Diagrams 2014. LNCS (LNAI), vol. 8578, pp. 213–227. Springer, Heidelberg (2014). https://doi.org/10.1007/978-3-662-44043-8_23
7. Demey, L., Smessaert, H.: The interaction between logic and geometry in Aristotelian diagrams. In: Jamnik, M., Uesaka, Y., Elzer Schwartz, S. (eds.) Diagrams 2016. LNCS (LNAI), vol. 9781, pp. 67–82. Springer, Cham (2016). https://doi.org/10.1007/978-3-319-42333-3_6
8. Demey, L., Smessaert, H.: Logical and geometrical distance in polyhedral Aristotelian diagrams in knowledge representation. Symmetry 9(10)(204) (2017)
9. Demey, L., Smessaert, H.: Combinatorial bitstring semantics for arbitrary logical fragments. J. Philos. Log. 47, 325–363 (2018)
10. Demey, L., Smessaert, H.: Geometric and cognitive differences between Aristotelian diagrams for the Boolean algebra $\mathbb{B}_4$. Ann. Math. Artif. Intell. 83, 185–208 (2018)
11. Edwards, A.W.F.: An eleventh-century Venn diagram. BSHM Bull. 21, 119–121 (2006)
12. Faris, J.: The Gergonne relations. J. Symb. Log. 20, 207–231 (1955)
13. Geudens, C., Demey, L.: On the Aristotelian roots of the modal square of opposition. Logique et Anal. (N.S.) 255, 313–348 (2021)
14. Grattan-Guinness, I.: The Gergonne relations and the intuitive use of Euler and Venn diagrams. Int. J. Math. Ed. Sci. Tech. 8, 23–30 (1977)
15. Howse, J., Molina, F., Taylor, J., Kent, S., Gil, J.Y.: Spider diagrams: a diagrammatic reasoning system. J. Vis. Lang. Comput. 12, 299–324 (2001)
16. Lemanski, J.: Periods in the use of Euler-type diagrams. Acta Baltica Historiae et Philosophiae Scientiarum 5, 50–69 (2017)
17. Lemanski, J.: Logic diagrams in the Weigel and Weise circles. Hist. Philos. Logic 39, 3–28 (2018)
18. Lemanski, J.: Euler-type diagrams and the quantification of the predicate. J. Philos. Log. 49, 401–416 (2020)
19. Lemanski, J., Demey, L.: Schopenhauer's partition diagrams and logical geometry. In: Basu, A., Stapleton, G., Linker, S., Legg, C., Manalo, E., Viana, P. (eds.) Diagrams 2021. LNCS (LNAI), vol. 12909, pp. 149–165. Springer, Cham (2021). https://doi.org/10.1007/978-3-030-86062-2_13
20. Linker, S.: Sequent calculus for euler diagrams. In: Chapman, P., Stapleton, G., Moktefi, A., Perez-Kriz, S., Bellucci, F. (eds.) Diagrams 2018. LNCS (LNAI), vol. 10871, pp. 399–407. Springer, Cham (2018). https://doi.org/10.1007/978-3-319-91376-6_37
21. Londey, D., Johanson, C.: Apuleius and the square of opposition. Phronesis 29, 165–173 (1984)
22. Moktefi, A., Shin, S.J.: A history of logic diagrams. In: Gabbay, D.M., Pelletier, F.J., Woods, J. (eds.) Handbook of the History of Logic, vol. 11. Logic: A History of its Central Concepts, pp. 611–682. North-Holland, Amsterdam (2012)
23. Read, S.: John Buridan's theory of consequence and his octagons of opposition. In: Béziau, J.Y., Jacquette, D. (eds.) Around and Beyond the Square of Opposition, pp. 93–110. Springer, Basel (2012)
24. Rodgers, P.: A survey of Euler diagrams. J. Vis. Lang. Comput. 25(3), 134–155 (2014)

25. Smessaert, H., Demey, L.: Logical geometries and information in the square of opposition. J. Logic Lang. Inform. **23**, 527–565 (2014)
26. Stapleton, G., Moktefi, A., Howse, J., Burton, J.: Euler diagrams through the looking glass: from extent to intent. In: Chapman, P., Stapleton, G., Moktefi, A., Perez-Kriz, S., Bellucci, F. (eds.) Diagrams 2018. LNCS (LNAI), vol. 10871, pp. 365–381. Springer, Cham (2018). https://doi.org/10.1007/978-3-319-91376-6_34
27. Stapleton, G., Shimojima, A., Jamnik, M.: The observational advantages of euler diagrams with existential import. In: Chapman, P., Stapleton, G., Moktefi, A., Perez-Kriz, S., Bellucci, F. (eds.) Diagrams 2018. LNCS (LNAI), vol. 10871, pp. 313–329. Springer, Cham (2018). https://doi.org/10.1007/978-3-319-91376-6_29

Visualizing Polymorphisms and Counter-Polymorphisms in S5 Modal Logic

Pedro Falcão[(✉)]

São Paulo, Brazil

pedroalonsofalcao@gmail.com

Abstract. We present a graphical representation that allows us to easily determine if a certain modal function is or is not a polymorphism of a given relation. While doing so, we provide a comparison between two ways (a calculative and a diagrammatic one) to analyze a claim about the Sheferness criterion in the theory of clones of (S5) modal functions.

Keywords: Modal logic · Clone theory · Sheffer functions

1 Introduction

We exhibit a rather complex logical/mathematical problem involving calculations that are pretty laborious when done by ordinary means, but which can be readily seen using diagrams.

In his excellent paper 'On functional completeness in the modal logic S5' [8] the Moldavian logician M. F. Ratsa commits a slight imprecision: he claims that a certain formula (f_{21}) is an example of an exclusive polymorphism (in a sense to be defined precisely) of a certain relation (R_{21}). We use an extension of the technique presented in an earlier paper [5] in order to show that his claim is incorrect (the technique is not necessary but, as we expect to show, useful), and we provide an alternative formula.

We start by giving an interpretation of S5 formulas as operations on n-dimensional cubes (we will focus on $n \leq 4$); then we define the *relation expressed* by a formula. Next, we define the notion of *polymorphism* of a relation, after giving a list of relations whose polymorphisms are maximal clones of modal operations. All these notions and results can be found in [8].

We then proceed to the elaboration and refutation of the claim about f_{21}, and we finish our paper presenting the above-mentioned alternative formula. We try to keep this material self-contained, but acquaintance with [5] can be helpful while interpreting the diagrams presented here.

2 Modal Formulas as Operations on Cubes

Following Ratsa, we will associate formulas of propositional S5 to operations on the structures A_1, A_2, and A_3 (cf. Fig. 1). We can think of each A_n as an

© Springer Nature Switzerland AG 2022
V. Giardino et al. (Eds.): Diagrams 2022, LNAI 13462, pp. 296–311, 2022.
https://doi.org/10.1007/978-3-031-15146-0_25

n-dimensional cube or (using the familiar notion of a *proposition* as a set of possible worlds) as the set of all propositions in a model with n possible worlds.

An interesting way to interpret the structures A_n is thinking of them as the set of all bitstrings (i.e. sequences of 0's and 1's) of length n (cf. [2]). In fact, the bitstrings of length n can be seen as a sort of *characteristic function* of the propositions in the models with n possible worlds; e.g. in the model with two possible worlds the necessary proposition will be characterized as **11**, the contingent propositions as **10** and **01**, and the impossible proposition as **00**.

One advantage of thinking of propositions as bitstrings is that it is simple to define how boolean (and modal) operations behave on bitstrings, and if we wish we can translate these definitions back into the more philosophical realm of propositional operations.

The boolean operations on bitstrings can be defined in terms of bitwise (usual) boolean operations. Let $B = b_1, ..., b_n$ and $S = s_1, ..., s_n$ be bitstrings of length n. We define the *bitstring negation* $\neg B$ as the bitstring whose terms are, respectively, $\neg b_1, ..., \neg b_n$; and we define the *bitstring conjunction* $B \wedge S$ as the bitstring whose terms are, respectively, $b_1 \wedge s_1, ... , b_n \wedge s_n$. The modal operator $\square$ has the rule: $\square B = B$ if B has 1 in every bit, otherwise $\square B =$ the bitstring of same length as B which has 0 in every bit.

Since we are here dealing with Ratsa's results, we also present the names he uses to refer to the elements of the structures A_1, A_2, and A_3. The elements of A_1 he calls simply 1 and 0. As for the elements of A_2: 1 stands for **11**, ρ stands for **10**, σ stands for **01**, and 0 stands for **00**. For A_3: 1 stands for **111**, ω stands for **110**, ν stands for **101**, σ stands for **011**, ρ stands for **100**, μ stands for **010**, ε stands for **001**, and 0 stands for **000**. Ratsa also has names for the elements of A_4 but, since we will not enter into details about A_4 here, we will omit them.

On top of all that, we decided (cf. Fig. 1) to give *colors* to the elements of each structure! The choice of colors is quite arbitrary, but we tried to organize them. The colorful colors in $A3$ are arranged almost like a rainbow, going from infrared to ultraviolet. The choice of black for 0 was suggested by the fact that the RGB code for black is (0, 0, 0). This use of colors allows us to represent operations over these structures (cf. Figs. 2 and 3).

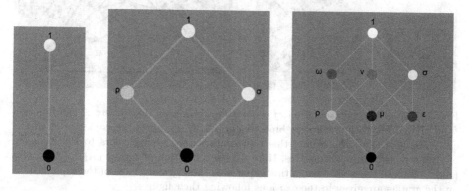

Fig. 1. Structures A1, A2, and A3

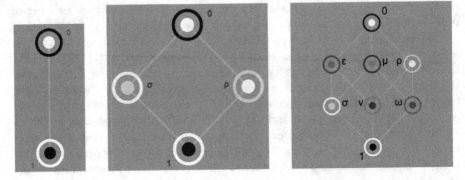

Fig. 2. A1, A2, and A3 under the effect of ¬. It is helpful to notice that the complementary elements of each structure (other than 0 and 1) have names that are either graphically similar (ω, ε / σ, ρ) or phonetically similar (ν, μ).

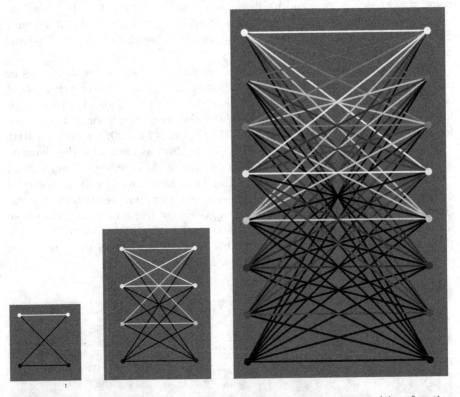

Fig. 3. The *graph representation of a binary operation on a structure A* is a function *from* the edges of the complete bipartite graph whose parts are copies of A *to* the elements of A. We 'abbreviate' this representation by giving colors to the elements of A and to the edges themselves. Here we see the action of $\wedge$ over $(A_1)^2, (A_2)^2$, and $(A_3)^2$. Much of the work done in this paper uses these graphs; most of the explanations on the graphs are given in the captions following their figures.

3   Modal Formulas as Relations on Cubes

For any formula $\phi(p_1, ..., p_n)$ of propositional S5, and any m-dimensional cube A_m, we can think of the A_m-*relation expressed by* ϕ as the set of n-tuples $\langle t_1, ..., t_n \rangle \in (A_m)^n$ such that $\phi(t_1, ..., t_n) = 1$. For instance, the formula $p \veebar q$ expresses the A_1-relation of *difference* $\{\langle 0, 1 \rangle, \langle 1, 0 \rangle\}$ (it also represents the relation of complementarity for every A - cf. Fig. 8). Also, the formula $p \rightarrow q$ expresses the A_1-relation *less than or equal to* $\{\langle 0, 0 \rangle, \langle 0, 1 \rangle, \langle 1, 1 \rangle\}$. To give an example involving modality and a bigger cube, we note that the formula $p \leftrightarrow \Box q$ expresses the A_2-relation $\{\langle 0, 0 \rangle, \langle 0, \rho \rangle, \langle 0, \sigma \rangle \langle 1, 1 \rangle\}$. We give plenty of other examples in the next section.

4   Ratsa's Relations

The relations presented in this section (together with a pair of relations on A_4, omitted here for the sake of simplicity) constitute a *functional completeness criterion for sets of operations of propositional S5*. The proof of this fact is beyond the scope of this paper (details can be checked in [8] or in [4]), but some elaboration on it will be found in the next sections.

We start by considering some A_1-relations. Here $E^4(p, q, r, s)$ means: *there is an even number of truths among p, q, r, s* (a definition of E^4 in terms of the usual connectives is: $E^4(p, q, r, s) =_{df} (p \leftrightarrow q) \leftrightarrow (r \leftrightarrow s)$). When defining a relation, we simply state a formula that expresses it. There is a correspondence between relations and matrices, to be clarified in the next section.

$$R_0 =_{df} \neg p, R_1 =_{df} p, R_2 =_{df} p \veebar q, R_3 =_{df} p \rightarrow q R_4 =_{df} E^4(p, q, r, s).$$

The corresponding A_1-matrices are:

$$M_0 = \begin{bmatrix} 0 \end{bmatrix}$$

$$M_1 = \begin{bmatrix} 1 \end{bmatrix}$$

$$M_2 = \begin{bmatrix} 0 & 1 \\ 1 & 0 \end{bmatrix}$$

$$M_3 = \begin{bmatrix} 0 & 0 & 1 \\ 0 & 1 & 1 \end{bmatrix}$$

$$M_4 = \begin{bmatrix} 0 & 0 & 0 & 0 & 1 & 1 & 1 & 1 \\ 0 & 0 & 1 & 1 & 0 & 0 & 1 & 1 \\ 0 & 1 & 0 & 1 & 0 & 1 & 0 & 1 \\ 0 & 1 & 1 & 0 & 1 & 0 & 0 & 1 \end{bmatrix}$$

We proceed to consider some A_2-relations. Here $\triangledown p$ reads 'it is contingent that p' and is defined as $\Diamond p \wedge \Diamond \neg p$; $\triangle p$ reads 'it is rigid that p' and is defined as $\neg \triangledown p$; $\triangledown^+ p$ reads 'it is contingently true that p' and is defined as $\triangledown p \wedge p$; $\triangledown^- p$

reads 'it is contingently false that p' and is defined as $\bigtriangledown p \wedge \neg p$; $\neg \bigtriangledown^- p$ reads 'it is not contingently false that p'; $\neg \bigtriangledown^+ p$ reads 'it is not contingently true that p'. (Roderick Batchelor devised this notation for the more exotic unary modal functions. See [1].)

$R_5 =_{df} \bigtriangledown^- p$, $R_6 =_{df} \neg \bigtriangledown^- p$, $R_7 =_{df} \bigtriangledown p$, $R_8 =_{df} \Box(p \leftrightarrow \Box q)$, $R_9 =_{df}$ $\Box(p \leftrightarrow \Diamond q)$, $R_{10} =_{df} (\Box p \wedge q) \vee (\neg \Diamond p \wedge \neg q)$, $R_{11} =_{df} \Box(p \leftrightarrow \Box q) \vee \Box(p \leftrightarrow \Diamond q)$, $R_{12} =_{df} \Box(p \leftrightarrow \Box q) \vee \Box(\neg p \leftrightarrow \Diamond q)$, $R_{13} =_{df} \Box(\neg p \leftrightarrow \Box q) \vee \Box(p \leftrightarrow \Diamond q)$, $R_{14} =_{df} \Box(\bigtriangledown^+ p \leftrightarrow \bigtriangledown^+ q)$, $R_{15} =_{df} \triangle p \leftrightarrow \triangle q$, $R_{16} =_{df} (p \leftrightarrow q) \vee (\bigtriangledown p \leftrightarrow \bigtriangledown q)$, $R_{17} =_{df} \triangle p \vee \triangle q$, $R_{18} =_{df} \triangle p \wedge \triangle r \wedge ((p \leftrightarrow r) \vee \triangle q)$, $R_{19} =_{df} \triangle p \wedge \triangle r \wedge ((p \leftrightarrow r) \vee \bigtriangledown q)$.

The corresponding A_2-matrices are:

$$M_5 = \begin{bmatrix} \rho \end{bmatrix}$$

$$M_6 = \begin{bmatrix} 0 & \sigma & 1 \end{bmatrix}$$

$$M_7 = \begin{bmatrix} \rho & \sigma \end{bmatrix}$$

$$M_8 = \begin{bmatrix} 0 & 0 & 0 & 1 \\ 0 & \rho & \sigma & 1 \end{bmatrix}$$

$$M_9 = \begin{bmatrix} 0 & 1 & 1 & 1 \\ 0 & \rho & \sigma & 1 \end{bmatrix}$$

$$M_{10} = \begin{bmatrix} 0 & 0 & 1 & 1 \\ 0 & \rho & \sigma & 1 \end{bmatrix}$$

$$M_{11} = \begin{bmatrix} 0 & 0 & 0 & 1 & 1 & 1 \\ 0 & \rho & \sigma & \rho & \sigma & 1 \end{bmatrix}$$

$$M_{12} = \begin{bmatrix} 0 & 0 & 0 & 0 & 1 & 1 \\ 0 & \rho & \sigma & 1 & 0 & 1 \end{bmatrix}$$

$$M_{13} = \begin{bmatrix} 0 & 0 & 1 & 1 & 1 & 1 \\ 0 & 1 & 0 & \rho & \sigma & 1 \end{bmatrix}$$

$$M_{14} = \begin{bmatrix} 0 & 0 & \rho & \sigma & 1 & 1 \\ 0 & 1 & \rho & \sigma & 0 & 1 \end{bmatrix}$$

$$M_{15} = \begin{bmatrix} 0 & 0 & \rho & \rho & \sigma & \sigma & 1 & 1 \\ 0 & 1 & \rho & \sigma & \rho & \rho & \sigma & 0 & 1 \end{bmatrix}$$

$$M_{16} = \begin{bmatrix} 0 & \rho & \rho & \sigma & \sigma & 1 \\ 0 & \rho & \sigma & \rho & \sigma & 1 \end{bmatrix}$$

$$M_{17} = \begin{bmatrix} 0 & 0 & 0 & 0 & \rho & \rho & \sigma & \sigma & 1 & 1 & 1 & 1 \\ 0 & \rho & \sigma & 1 & 0 & 1 & 0 & 1 & 0 & \rho & \sigma & 1 \end{bmatrix}$$

$$M_{18} = \begin{bmatrix} 0 & 0 & 0 & 0 & 0 & 0 & 1 & 1 & 1 & 1 & 1 & 1 \\ 0 & 0 & \rho & \sigma & 1 & 1 & 0 & 0 & \rho & \sigma & 1 & 1 \\ 0 & 1 & 0 & 0 & 0 & 1 & 0 & 1 & 1 & 1 & 0 & 1 \end{bmatrix}$$

$$M_{19} = \begin{bmatrix} 0\,0\,0\,0\,0\,0\,1\,1\,1\,1\,1\,1 \\ 0\,\rho\,\rho\,\sigma\,\sigma\,1\,0\,\rho\,\rho\,\sigma\,\sigma\,1 \\ 0\,0\,1\,0\,1\,0\,1\,0\,1\,0\,1\,1 \end{bmatrix}$$

Finally, we consider the A_3-relations corresponding to the following matrices. We do not have S5 formulas expressing these relations.

$$M_{20} = \begin{bmatrix} 0\ \rho\ \mu\ \nu\ \sigma\ 1 \end{bmatrix}$$

$$M_{21} = \begin{bmatrix} 0\ \rho\ \mu\ \varepsilon\ \omega\ \nu\ \sigma\ 1 \\ 0\ \sigma\ \sigma\ \sigma\ \rho\ \rho\ \rho\ 1 \end{bmatrix}$$

$$M_{22} = \begin{bmatrix} 0\ \rho\ \mu\ \varepsilon\ \omega\ \nu\ \sigma\ 1 \\ 0\ \rho\ \nu\ \omega\ \varepsilon\ \mu\ \sigma\ 1 \end{bmatrix}$$

$$M_{23} = \begin{bmatrix} 0\ \rho\ \mu\ \varepsilon\ \omega\ \nu\ \sigma\ 1 \\ 0\ \sigma\ \omega\ \nu\ \mu\ \varepsilon\ \rho\ 1 \end{bmatrix}$$

5 Polymorphisms and Counter-Polymorphisms

We say that an n-ary operation $f(p_1, ..., p_n)$ is a *polymorphism* of an m-ary *A-relation* R if for every $\alpha_{ij}(i = 1, ..., m; j = 1, ..., n) \in A$:
if

$$R(\alpha_{11}, \alpha_{21}, ..., \alpha_{m1}) \wedge R(\alpha_{12}, \alpha_{22}, ..., \alpha_{m2}) \wedge ... \wedge R(\alpha_{1n}, \alpha_{2n}, ..., \alpha_{mn})$$

then

$$R(f(\alpha_{11}, \alpha_{12}, ..., \alpha_{1n}), f(\alpha_{21}, \alpha_{22}, ..., \alpha_{2n}), ... , f(\alpha_{m1}, \alpha_{m2}, ..., \alpha_{mn})).$$

In this definition, the relation R can be replaced by a matrix M whose columns are the m-sequences of elements of A satisfying R (say, arranged in the 'alphabetical' order induced by the order: $0, \rho, \mu, \varepsilon, \omega, \nu, \sigma, 1$). We say that *a matrix M' is a submatrix of a matrix M* if all columns of M' are columns of M. If M' is a submatrix of M we may write $M' \subseteq M$. Given an n-ary formula f and a matrix M with n columns, by $f(M)$ we mean the column generated applying f in each row of M. If c is a column of matrix M we may write $c \in M$ (or, if that is not the case, $c \notin M$). Using these notions, the above definition can be restated (equivalently, but perhaps more clearly) as follows:

A *formula f is a counter-polymorphism of matrix M* if there is an $M' \subseteq M$ such that $f(M') \notin M$.

A *formula f is a polymorphism of matrix M* if f is not a counter-polymorphism of M. If f is a polymorphism of M, we may write $f \in Pol(M)$.

Given a formula f and a family of relations $R^* = \langle R_1, ..., R_k \rangle$, the *polymorphic profile of f w.r.t. R^** is the k-tuple whose i-th term is 1 if $f \in Pol(R_i)$, and 0 otherwise. We say that *f is an exclusive polymorphism of R_i* (w.r.t. R^*) if the polymorphic profile of f has a single occurrence of 1, in its i-th place.

302   P. Falcão

Let R^* be the family of the relations in Sect. 4 supplemented by the omitted A_4-relations R_{24} and R_{25}. Ratsa established that a set of modal operations F is *functionally complete* (i.e. sufficient to define every modal operation) if, for every relation $r \in R^*$ there is an operation $f \in F$ such that $f \notin Pol(r)$.

In the reminder of this paper we only consider the family of relations presented in Sect. 4, so when we say *the polymorphic profile of f* we mean the polymorphic profile of f w.r.t. the family of relations in Sect. 4.

6   Diagrams for Polymorphisms and Counter-Polymorphisms on A_1

In this section we consider a simpler version of the diagrams that will be presented in the end of this paper. In Figs. 4 and 5 we consider the polymorphic profile of the functions $\wedge$ and $\downarrow$ w.r.t. the relations $R_0 - R_4$. These are the relations whose sets of polymorphisms are precisely the pre-complete systems of two-valued functions, determined by Emil Post in [7].

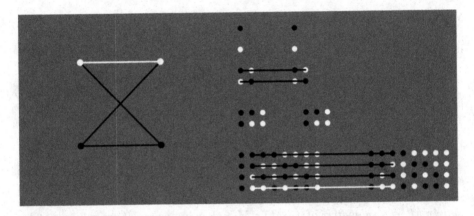

Fig. 4. The action of $\wedge$ on $(A_1)^2$ (on the left) and its polymorphic profile (on the right). We can see that $\wedge$ is a polymorphism of R_0 since the line connecting the black nodes in the left part is black; it is also a polymorphism of R_1 since the line connecting the white nodes in the left part is white; it is a counter-polymorphism of R_2 since, as the figure indicates $0 \wedge 1 = 0$ and $1 \wedge 0 = 0$, i.e. we can use arguments which are different to get values that are equal; it is a polymorphism of R_3, as the absence of lines connecting the copies of M_3 indicates, and is a counter-polymorphism of R_4, since (as indicated) with $\wedge$ we can construct, using arguments in M_4, a column of values that is not in M_4.

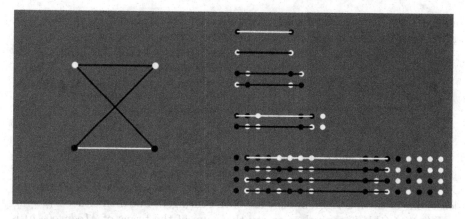

Fig. 5. $\downarrow$ and its polymorphic profile. It is well known that Peirce's arrow is a function in terms of which every other truth-function can be defined. This follows immediately from the fact that it is a counter-polymorphism of all relations $R_0 - R_4$, which characterize the maximal pre-complete systems of truth-functions.

7 Ratsa's Alleged Exclusive Polymorphism

Ratsa claims that a certain formula (which we call f_{21}) is an exclusive polymorphism of the relation R_{21} (or, what is the same, of the matrix M_{21}). He is interested in such a formula because it helps him to prove that his criterion for determining if a single function is functionally complete (i.e. if it is a Sheffer function for S5) is as good as it can be (cf. [8], p. 278).

To properly present Ratsa's formula, we introduce some preliminary notions (which are interesting in themselves). We start by defining the straightforward propositional relations of *independence, connection, compatibility*, and *incompatibility*:

$$Ind(p,q) =_{df} \Diamond(p \wedge q) \wedge \Diamond(p \wedge \neg q) \wedge \Diamond(\neg p \wedge q) \wedge \Diamond(\neg p \wedge \neg q).$$
$$Con(p,q) =_{df} \neg Ind(p,q).$$
$$Comp(p,q) =_{df} \Diamond(p \wedge q).$$
$$Incomp(p,q) =_{df} \neg \Diamond(p \wedge q).$$

It is interesting to notice that for $A_i (i \in \{1, 2, 3\})$ the A_i-relation expressed by $Ind(p, q) = \varnothing$. In order to find a pair of independent propositions, we need to resort to A_4 (this fact is noted w.r.t. bitstrings in [2], except that what we call independence is there called *unconnectedness*. In their terminology: 'unconnectedness requires bitstrings of length at least 4').

Since the compatibility relation will be significant in our next definition, we give an explicit characterization of its A_3-instances, from which the other instances may be derived. We start the characterization by listing some compatible elements of $(A_3)^2$: $\langle \mu, \omega \rangle, \langle \mu, \sigma \rangle, \langle \varepsilon, \nu \rangle, \langle \varepsilon, \sigma \rangle, \langle \nu, \omega \rangle, \langle \nu, \rho \rangle, \langle \nu, \sigma \rangle, \langle \omega, \rho \rangle, \langle \omega, \sigma \rangle$

and we finish it by noticing that everything different from 0 is compatible with 1 and with itself, and that compatibility is a symmetric relation.

The *modal profile* of a pair of propositions p, q is the 4-tuple $Modpro(p, q) =_{df}$ $\langle Comp(p, q), Comp(p, \neg q), Comp(\neg p, q), Comp(\neg p, \neg q) \rangle$.

To present f_{21} we need to introduce some formulas used in its definition.

$$S(p, q) =_{df} \Box(p \lor q) \lor \Box(p \to q) \lor \Box(q \to p).$$
$$V(p, q) =_{df} S(p, q) \land S(p, \neg q) \land S(\neg p, q) \land S(\neg p, \neg q).$$

S 'says' that p and q are connected even if we disregard its (possible) incompatibility (or equivalently: there is at least one 0 in the last three entries of $Modpro(p, q)$), while V 'says' that p and q are *strongly connected*, i.e., either (at least) one of them is rigid, or they are both contingent but then either $\Box(p \leftrightarrow q)$ or $\Box(p \veebar q)$ (this is equivalent to say that sum of the terms of $Modpro(p, q)$ is less than 3).

Ratsa's formula is:

$$f_{21} = (V(p, q) \to ((p \to q) \land \neg\Box q)) \land (((p \leftrightarrow S(p, q)) \land (q \to S(p, q))) \lor V(p, q)).$$

To see that this is not an exclusive polymorphism of R_{21} it is enough to notice that it is not a polymorphism of R_{21}. This is obvious given that $\{\langle \rho, \sigma \rangle, \langle \mu, \sigma \rangle\} \subseteq R_{21}$ and $f_{21}(\rho, \mu) = \varepsilon$, $f_{21}(\sigma, \sigma) = 1$ and that $\langle \varepsilon, 1 \rangle \notin R_{21}$. This last claim can perhaps be more easily checked by considering Fig. 10, where we present the action of f_{21} over A_1, A_2, and A_3, and its polymorphic profile.

8   Moody Truth-Functions

The definition in this section is essentially the same found in [3], p. 35. Recall the definition of *Modpro*, given in the last section.

The *moody truth-functional representation of a binary modal operation f* is a sequence of eight binary truth-functions $\langle f_1, f_2, f_3, f_4, f_5, f_6, f_7, f_8 \rangle$, together with the proviso:

if $Modpro(p, q) = \langle 1, 1, 1, 1 \rangle$, apply f_1;
if $Modpro(p, q) = \langle 1, 1, 1, 0 \rangle$ or $\langle 0, 0, 0, 1 \rangle$, apply f_2;
if $Modpro(p, q) = \langle 1, 1, 0, 1 \rangle$ or $\langle 0, 0, 1, 0 \rangle$, apply f_3;
if $Modpro(p, q) = \langle 1, 0, 1, 1 \rangle$ or $\langle 0, 1, 0, 0 \rangle$, apply f_4;
if $Modpro(p, q) = \langle 0, 1, 1, 1 \rangle$ or $\langle 1, 0, 0, 0 \rangle$, apply f_5;
if $Modpro(p, q) = \langle 1, 1, 0, 0 \rangle$ or $\langle 0, 0, 1, 1 \rangle$, apply f_6;
if $Modpro(p, q) = \langle 1, 0, 1, 0 \rangle$ or $\langle 0, 1, 0, 1 \rangle$, apply f_7;
if $Modpro(p, q) = \langle 1, 0, 0, 1 \rangle$ or $\langle 0, 1, 1, 0 \rangle$, apply f_8.

Since we are here ignoring A_4, when using moody truth-functions, we will restrict ourselves to the 7-tuples corresponding to $f_2 - f_8$.

We claim that the operation expressed by $\langle \top, \land, \leftrightarrow, \uparrow, \land, \downarrow, \to \rangle$ is an exclusive polymorphism of R_{21}. We support our claim with Fig. 11 and with the captions of the figures preceding it.

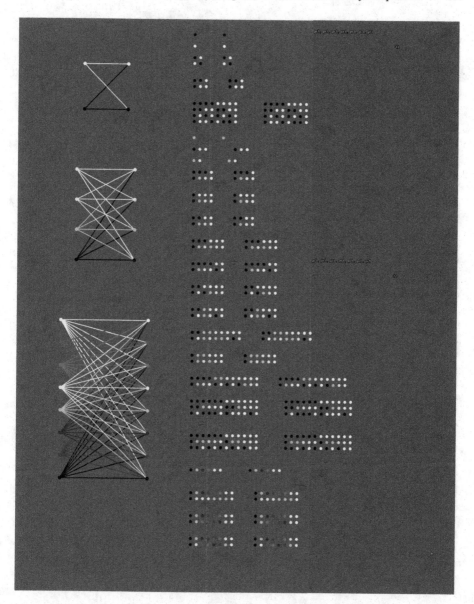

Fig. 6. The projection of the first argument (π_1^2) is a universal polymorphism. We take advantage of the space left by the absence of counter-polymorphisms of this operation to present the framework we are working with. On the right side of this figure you can see (pairs of) the translation into colors (following Fig. 1) of the relations presented in Sect. 6.

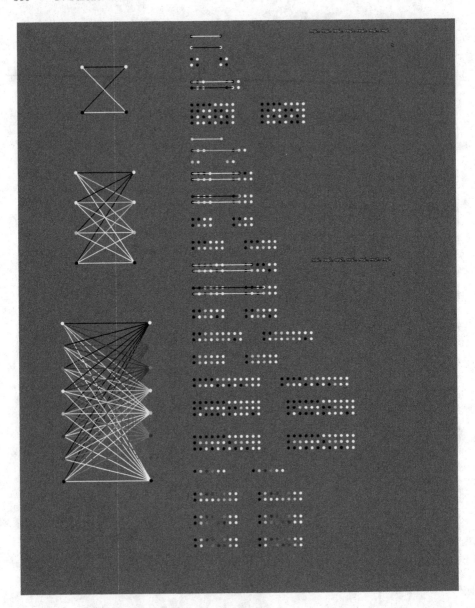

Fig. 7. The negation of the second argument $\neg\pi_2^2$ over A_1, A_2 and A_3 and its polymorphic profile. Notice that the counter-polymorphisms are indicated by horizontal lines connecting relevant columns of the matrices. Notice also that the polymorphic profile of $\neg\pi_2^2$ w.r.t. $R_0 - R_4$ $(0, 0, 1, 0, 1)$ is complementary of that of $\wedge$ $(1, 1, 0, 1, 0)$ (cf. Fig. 4).

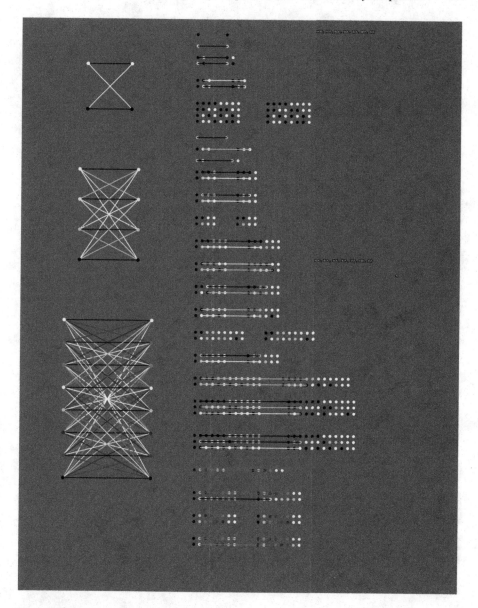

Fig. 8. This graph represents the action of $\underline{\vee}$. It is interesting that the white lines on the left side represent precisely the relation of complementarity in the structures A_1, A_2 and A_3.

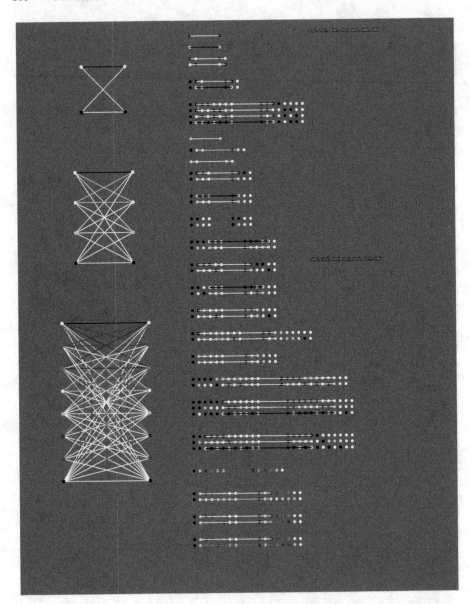

Fig. 9. This is the representation of the very well known (boolean) operation ↑ (the Sheffer stroke). Notice that it is an exclusive polymorphism of R_{10}.

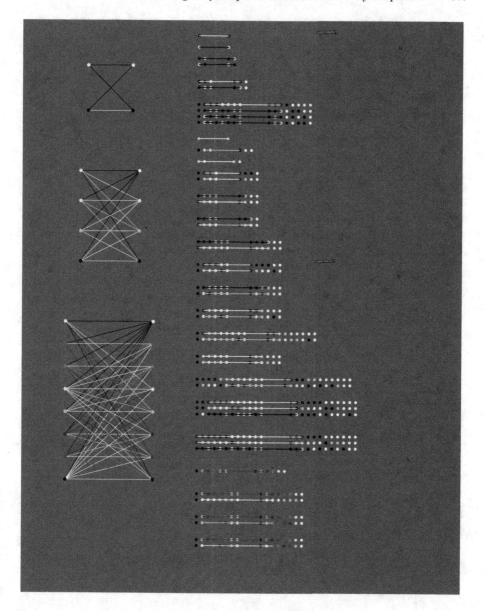

Fig. 10. f_{21} over A_1, A_2 and A_3 and its polymorphic profile.

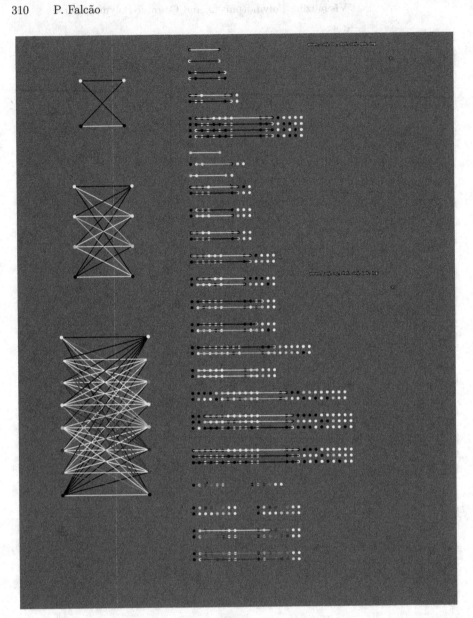

Fig. 11. $\langle \top, \wedge, \leftrightarrow, \uparrow, \wedge, \downarrow, \rightarrow \rangle$ is an exclusive polymorphism of M_{21}.

9 Conclusion

We are glad to give an exoteric presentation of a somewhat esoteric result, and we hope that this paper is not too enigmatic. We believe that the techniques presented here are also useful in the investigations on clones of k-valued functions (cf. [6]) and we expect to give some new results on this matter soon.

References

1. Batchelor, R.: Clone theory: Modal functions (2020). Unpublished manuscript
2. Demey, L., Smessaert, H.: Combinatorial bitstring semantics for arbitrary logical fragments. J. Phil. Logic **47**(2), 325–363 (2017). https://doi.org/10.1007/s10992-017-9430-5
3. Falcão, P.: Aspectos da teoria de funções modais. Master's thesis, University of São Paulo (2012). https://doi.org/10.11606/D.8.2012.tde-11042013-104549
4. Falcão, P.: On pre-complete systems of modal functions. PhD thesis, University of São Paulo (2017). https://doi.org/10.11606/T.8.2019.tde-19122019-182332
5. Falcão, P.: New representations of modal functions. In: Basu, A., Stapleton, G., Linker, S., Legg, C., Manalo, E., Viana, P. (eds.) Diagrams 2021. LNCS (LNAI), vol. 12909, pp. 271–278. Springer, Cham (2021). https://doi.org/10.1007/978-3-030-86062-2_28
6. Lau, D.: Function Algebras on Finite Sets: A Basic Course on Many-Valued Logic and Clone Theory. Springer, Heidelberg (2006). https://doi.org/10.1007/3-540-36023-9
7. Post, E.L.: The Two-Valued Iterative Systems of Mathematical Logic. Annals of Mathematics Studies, No. 5. Princeton University Press, Princeton (1941)
8. Ratsa, M.F.: On functional completeness in the modal logic S5. Investigations in Non-Classical Logics and Formal Systems, Moscow, Nauka, pp. 222–280 (1983). (in Russian)

Representing Formulas of Propositional Logic by Cographs, Permutations and Tables

Michał Sochański[✉] [ID]

Adam Mickiewicz University, ul. Wieniawskiego 1, 61-712 Poznań, Poland
michal.sochanski@amu.edu.pl

Abstract. The paper presents how formation trees, a type of syntax trees for a formula, can be used to represent semantic information about formulas of classical propositional logic in form of graphs, permutations and tables. The three representation types are discussed in terms of the construction process as well as their cognitive potentials and observational advantages.

Keywords: Diagrams · Logic · Combinatorics

1 Introduction

In this paper I present three diagrammatic methods of representing the structure of semantic dependencies between occurrences of literals in formulas of classical propositional logic. The discussed representations – cographs, bar-charts based on permutations, and tables – are constructed using formation trees, a type of syntax trees for formulas. Each representation type carries information about satisfying assignments in a way analogous to disjunctive normal forms. Their crucial characteristic is that they can be seen as representing the information simultaneously for a formula and its negation, thereby carrying information about validity.

The idea of representing logical formulas and Boolean functions as cographs is not new, and can be traced at least to [7]. In recent years, a group of logicians in particular D. Hughes and L. Strassburger, have used the interpretation of logical formulas as cographs to construct a new type of proof system for classical propositional logic, called "combinatorial proof". The method has been introduced in [6] and developed (among others) in [5].[1] The approach taken in this paper is different in several ways. Firstly, formation trees are used, which allow construction of the cograph representation for formulas with broad class

---

[1] Proof of a formula, in this context, consists in finding a particular homomorphism between graphs, and so has been characterised by Hughes as "graphical" [6].

My work was supported financially by National Science Centre in Poland, grant no 2017/26/E/HS1/00127.

© Springer Nature Switzerland AG 2022
V. Giardino et al. (Eds.): Diagrams 2022, LNAI 13462, pp. 312–320, 2022.
https://doi.org/10.1007/978-3-031-15146-0_26

of connectives. Secondly, new representation of logical formulas are introduced: permutations, permutation-based bar charts and T-tables. Thirdly, the representations are not used to provide a proof method, but to extract information about the structure of semantic dependencies between occurrences of literals.

The next two sections introduce the representation types in some formal detail, omitting proofs of their properties. The reader can refer to [1] in which cographs and permutations are discussed in a more formal and comprehensive form, with applications to computational logic and the theory of synthetic tableaux. The final section compares all the discussed representation types in terms of (among others) their cognitive potentials and observational advantages.

2   Formation Trees

All the representations analysed in the paper are constructed using formation trees, a type of syntax trees with inner nodes labelled with formulas of α and β type according to Smullayn's notation. The idea of labelling syntax trees in this way comes from Dorota Leszczyńska-Jasion and is described in more detail in [1] and [2], with application to computational logic.

To start with, classical propositional logic is defined in a standard way, with logical connectives $\neg, \rightarrow, \wedge, \vee$ and propositional variables denoted by the symbols $p, q, r, \ldots$. A *literal* is a propositional variable or its negation. Furthermore, formulas expressed in this language may be divided into four types according to Smullyans uniform notation: literals, formulas of the form '$\neg\neg A$', α-formulas and β-formulas, see Table 1 (please note, that contrary to Smullyan, formulas of type '$\neg\neg A$' are not treated as an α- or a β-formula).

Table 1. Uniform notation after [4].

α	α_1	α_2	β	β_1	β_2
$A \wedge B$	A	B	$\neg(A \wedge B)$	$\neg A$	$\neg B$
$\neg(A \vee B)$	$\neg A$	$\neg B$	$A \vee B$	A	B
$\neg(A \rightarrow B)$	A	$\neg B$	$A \rightarrow B$	$\neg A$	B

Formation trees are finite trees labelled with formulas such that:

1. if a node of the tree is labelled with a formula of the form '$\neg\neg B$', then the node has exactly one child labelled with B,
2. if a node of the tree is labelled with an α-formula (β-formula), then the node has exactly two children labelled with α_1, α_2 (β_1, β_2, respectively).

Figure 1 depicts a formation tree T for the formula

$$\neg[(\neg p \rightarrow (\neg r \wedge q)) \rightarrow \neg(q \vee \neg p)]$$

314   M. Sochański

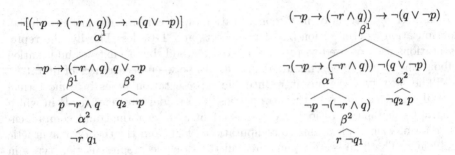

Fig. 1. Formation tree for the formula $\neg[(\neg p \to (\neg r \wedge q)) \to \neg(q \vee \neg p)]$ and its negation.

further denoted as F_1, as well as a formation tree T_N for $\neg F_1$. Please note that, in general, formation tree for a formula $\neg F$ may be obtained by negating all the formulas in inner nodes and leaves in the formation tree for F.

If T is a formation tree, the set of occurrences of literals in the leaves of T will be denoted by $L(T)$. In case of the formula F_1, $L(T) = \{p, \neg r, q_1, q_2, \neg p\}$. This set is of particular interest to us, as all the introduced representation types contain elements that directly refer to it.

Further, if x, y are leaves of T, their **lowest common ancestor** is the lowest inner node in T that has both x and y as descendants. If the lowest common ancestor of x and y in T is an inner node of type α, we will call x and y **semantically dependent** in T; if their lowest common ancestor is an inner node of type β, we will call x and y **semantically independent**. If we consider the formation tree for F_1 depicted on Fig. 1, the lowest common ancestor of $\neg r$ and q_2 is α_1 and the lowest common ancestor of p and q_1 is β_1; thus $\neg r$ and q_2 are semantically dependent whereas p and q_1 are not. Finally, we will call $C \subseteq L(T)$ a **maximal α-clique in T** if it fulfills the following two conditions:

1. $\forall x, y \in C$: x and y are semantically dependent
2. $\forall x \in L(T) \setminus C \; \exists y \in C$: x and y are semantically independent

The set of all maximal α-cliques of a formula F will be denoted by M_F; for example, $M_{F_1} = \{\{p, q_2\}, \{p, \neg p\}, \{\neg r, q_1, q_2\}, \{\neg r, q_1, \neg p\}\}$.

We will further call a maximal α-clique **consistent** if it does not contain contradictory literals; for example, $\{p, q_2\}$ is consistent, while $\{p, \neg p\}$ is not. The crucial property of any consistent maximal α-clique C is that every valuation that satisfies C also satisfies the formula F for which T was constructed. Intuitively, it is enough to know the values of literals in C to know that F is satisfied, regardless of all the values assigned to other variables.

The set M_F may be used to construct a disjunctive normal form (DNF) of F, with every maximal α-clique corresponding to one of the terms of the DNF. For example, such DNF for F_1, after omitting inconsistent maximal α-cliques and repetitions of literals in particular terms and the subscripts, is the following:

$$(p \wedge q) \vee (\neg r \wedge q) \vee (\neg r \wedge q \wedge \neg p)$$

The DNF of $\neg F_1$ constructed in a similar way has the form:

$$(\neg p \wedge r) \vee (\neg p \wedge \neg q) \vee (\neg q \wedge p)$$

It can be shown that the DNF based on M_F is equivalent to F. One important consequence of this fact is that a formula is a tautology if and only if all the elements of $M_{\neg F}$ are inconsistent (see [1] for further details; this fact is also used in construction of the "combinatorial proof" system in [6]).

In the next section, three types of diagrammatic representations will be introduced, constructed using information about semantic (in)dependency contained in formation trees. The representations enable, among others, locating maximal α-cliques and thereby visually checking the validity of formulas of classical logic.

3 Graphs, Permutations and T-tables

The first representation type, graphs, are familiar combinatorial objects: a graph G is a pair (V, E), where V is the set of vertices and E is the set of edges, $E \subseteq \{\{v_i, v_j\} : v_i, v_j \in V\}$. If T is a formation tree, a **semantic graph** $G_T = (V, E)$ is a simple, undirected, labeled graph such that $V = L(T)$ and for $v_1, v_2 \in V$, $\{v_1, v_2\} \in E$ if v_1, v_2 are semantically dependent in T. Labels of the semantic graph G_T correspond to the occurrences of literals in $L(T)$. If G is a semantic graph for F, then its complement, labelled by $\overline{G}$, is a semantic graph for $\neg F$, with all the occurrences of literals in labels switched to their complements. Note that many formulas may correspond to the same semantic graph. Thus, semantic graphs can be seen as representing semantic information common to a class of formulas. Figure 2 depicts semantic graphs for the formulas F_1 and $\neg F_1$.

The crucial property of semantic graphs is that they are cographs [5,6], that is graphs that can be generated recursively from single-vertex graphs by join and disjoint union operations. If $G_1 = (V_1, E_1)$ and $G_2 = (V_2, E_2)$ then the disjoint union of G_1 and G_2 is the graph $G = (V_1 \cup V_2, E_1 \cup E_2)$. Join of G_1 and G_2 is a graph G created by adding edges between all vertices from G_1 and G_2.[2] Please note, that if T_F is a formation tree for a formula F, maximal α-cliques of T_F correspond to maximal cliques in G_F. Additionally, maximal α-cliques of $T_{\neg F}$ correspond to maximal independent sets of G_F, after switching all the literals to their complements. In what follows, I will refer to maximal cliques, skipping the α.[3]

---

[2] In discrete mathematics, cographs are often represented by cotrees and parse trees, the latter corresponding to formation trees. Parse trees are binary trees, with inner nodes of types 1 and 0, corresponding to $\alpha-$ and $\beta-$nodes of the formation tree. Their structure mirrors the recursive procedure of construction of cographs, with 1-nodes corresponding to join operation and 0-nodes to disjoint union. See [3,7] for other properties of cographs.

[3] A clique in a graph G is a complete induced subgraph H of G. A maximal clique is a clique that cannot be extended to a greater clique by adding new vertices. An independent set in a graph G is a subgraph H of G such that no $v_1, v_2 \in H$ are adjacent. Similarly, a maximal independent set in G is one that cannot be extended by adding new vertices to it.

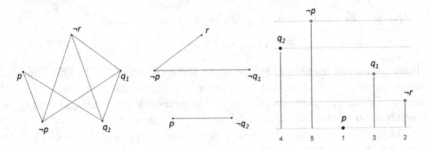

Fig. 2. Semantic graphs corresponding to F_1 and $\neg F_1$ and a permutation chart for F_1. (Color figure online)

Information about semantic (in)dependency of occurrences of literals contained in the formation trees can also be represented by permutations and permutation-based bar charts. It is known that every cograph is a permutation graph [3], hence any cograph G with n vertices corresponds to a permutation $\pi = [\pi_1, \pi_2, ..., \pi_n]$. In case of semantic (co)graphs, the resulting permutations will additionally be labelled with occurrences of literals. For a given semantic graph $G = G(T)$ we can construct π_G recursively from the formation tree T using the function Perm. To do that, let us introduce a function $C : L(T) \mapsto \{1, 2, ..., n\}$, where $n = |L(T)|$, such that every leaf of T is labelled according to its position from left to right in T (for leftmost leaf x, $C(x) = 1$, etc.). Then π_G is defined as follows, where $X^\frown Y$ denotes the concatenation of two sequences forming a permutation:

$$\text{Perm}(x) = [C(x)]$$
$$\text{Perm}(\alpha) = \text{Perm}(\alpha_2)^\frown \text{Perm}(\alpha_1)$$
$$\text{Perm}(\beta) = \text{Perm}(\beta_1)^\frown \text{Perm}(\beta_2)$$

Permutation representation π of a semantic graph $G(T) = G[\pi]$ has several important properties. First of all, if leaves x and y of T are semantically dependant, their order in π is reversed. Maximal cliques of $G[\pi]$ correspond to decreasing subsequences of π; the latter are such subsequences $S = [\pi_{i_1}, \pi_{i_2}, ..., \pi_{i_k}]$, that $\pi_{i_r} > \pi_{i_s}$ for $r < s$ and such that S cannot be enlarged by adding new elements from π in a way that this property still holds. For example, F_1 is represented by the permutation $[4, 5, 1, 3, 2]$ and its decreasing subsequences are $[4, 1]$, $[5, 1]$, $[4, 3, 2]$ and $[5, 3, 2]$ (they correspond, respectively to maximal α-cliques: $\{p, q_2\}$, $\{p, \neg p\}$, $\{\neg r, q_1, q_2\}$ and $\{\neg r, q_1, \neg p\}$). Further, maximal independent sets of G correspond to increasing subsequences of π (defined in an analogous way).

Permutations are linear and in this sense it is debatable whether they can be considered as diagrams. However, one can represent them in a 2-dimensional form by drawing simple bar charts. In Fig. 2 permutation for F_1 is depicted, together with the labelling and the associated chart. Maximal cliques and maximal independent sets can be read off the chart by visually tracing decreasing and increasing subsequences (an example is indicated with color).

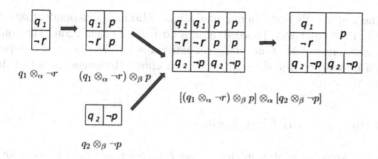

Fig. 3. Construction process of the T-table for F_1.

The third method of representing semantic (in)dependency makes use of tables, defined recursively using formation trees. The definition draws from [8], which presents a method of representing any cograph as a Ferrers diagram, a type of dot diagram used to represent and reason about partitions. In the remaining part of this section, an extension of this idea is proposed that allows expressing similar semantic information as semantic graphs and permutations, with use of a different 2-dimensional language.

We say that a table X is of size $n \times m$ if X has n rows and m columns. Let $X \otimes_\alpha Y$ denote the following operation on tables X and Y, where X is of size $n \times m$ and Y of size $k \times l$: first duplicate each column of X l times, obtaining m subtables of size $n \times l$, placed next to each other horizontally; next we attach a copy of Y below each such subtable, obtaining the resultant table of size $(n + k) \times (ml)$, denoted by $X \otimes_\alpha Y$. Secondly, let $X \otimes_\beta Y$ denote the following operation on similar tables X and Y: first duplicate each row of X k times, obtaining n subtables of size $m \times k$, placed next to each vertically; next we attach a copy of Y to the right of each such subtable, obtaining the table of size $(nk) \times (m + l)$, denoted by $X \otimes_\beta Y$. The defined operations can be used to formulate a *quasi*-formal recursive method of constructing a table based on a formation tree T, further denoted as T-**tables**:

Table$(x) = \overline{x}$
Table$(\alpha) = \alpha_1 \otimes_\alpha \alpha_2$
Table$(\beta) = \beta_1 \otimes_\beta \beta_2$

Note that x denotes the leaf of T and $\overline{x}$ denotes a table consisting of one cell containing the label of x (occurrence of literal). Figure 3 depicts an example of the construction process, with an additional step added, in which cells containing the same occurrence of a literal are merged in order to improve readability.

In consequence of the construction process of the T-tables, cliques are arranged vertically and independent sets horizontally. To read off a maximal clique from the diagram, one has to start with any rectangle in the top row, and proceed downwards, by subsequently taking rectangles such that share a side (not just a point) in the vertical orientation. This way we obtain a sequence of rectangles that corresponds (after omitting possible repetitions) to a set of occurrences of literals that is a maximal clique. Maximal independent sets can be obtained in a similar way, proceeding in a horizontal orientation. The construction process ensures that *all* the maximal cliques (and maximal independent sets) can be read off the diagram, and each clique (independent set) is in fact maximal.[4]

4 Summary and Conclusion

Semantic graphs, permutation charts and T-tables make use of formation trees to represent information about semantic (in)dependency of literals occurring in its leaves in a diagrammatic form. The building blocks of all three diagrams are representations of occurrences of literals: vertices in semantic graphs, numbers and bars in permutations charts and cells (or sets of cells) in T-tables. In graphs, semantic dependency is represented by the presence of an edge between the vertices, in permutation charts by the relative height of the bars and in T-tables by vertical alignment of relevant cells. It seems that maximal cliques and maximal independent sets are easier to read off from permutation charts than graphs, and easiest to read off from T-tables (although such comparison is subjective). This is due to the fact that checking vertical alignment of cells seems to involve smaller cognitive cost than looking for sets of edges in a graph or decreasing sequences of bars. Additionally, relevant visual properties of graphs are becoming difficult to read off very quickly with rising graph size, whereas the two other representation types retain readability also for relatively big formulas.

Semantic information contained in all the representation types is important and useful in at least two ways, which may be seen as their cognitive potentials. Firstly, maximal cliques point at minimal sets of literals, such that their satisfiability implies the satisfiability of the formula. Such information is crucial in many applications, for example in Binary Decision Diagrams or SAT. Secondly, visual inspection of the independent sets may be used to check validity of the formula. Further, all representations have potential to generate "derivative meaning" [9], in that they represent some global, or high-level, aspects of formulas; for example, connected components of a graph inform which sets of occurrences of literals are semantically dependent and the shape of a T-table may indicate whether there are more maximal cliques or independent sets. In a final example, Fig. 4 depicts all three diagrams for the following formula:

$$((p \land q) \to r) \to ((p \to r) \lor (q \to r))$$

Validity of the formula may be checked by inspecting all independent sets, all increasing sequences or all horizontally aligned sequences of rectangles.

---

[4] Note that each horizontal path crosses each vertical path in exactly one point (occurrence of a literal). This is consistent with an interesting property of cographs: any maximal clique of a cograph intersects any maximal independent set in a single vertex.

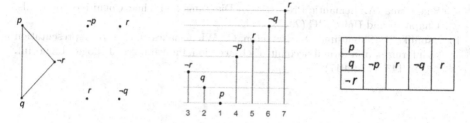

Fig. 4. Three diagrammatic representations of $((p \wedge q) \to r) \to ((p \to r) \vee (q \to r))$.

Semantic graphs, permutation charts and T-tables can also be compared to other representations of logical formulas in terms of their observational advantages, as discussed in [10]. Firstly, they allow direct observability of statements about semantic dependency and in consequence about satisfiability and validity that cannot be observed from the standard representation of formulas of classical propositional logic. On the other hand, all the diagrams represent in a compact form similar information as that contained in disjunctive normal form, maximal cliques corresponding to terms. Their crucial advantage over DNF is that they allow simultaneous representation of the terms of a DNF for a formula and a DNF for its negation, as every maximal independent set in T_F corresponds to a maximal clique in $T_{\neg F}$, after switching all the literals to their complements. This parallel reading may be seen as a kind of *aspect shift*.

References

1. Leszczyńska-Jasion, D., Sochański, M.: Methods of construction of synthetic tableaux based on cographs and permutations (manuscript available on https://ddsuam.wordpress.com/publications/)
2. Chlebowski, S., Jukiewicz, M., Leszczyńska-Jasion, D., Sochański, M., Tomczyk, A.: Synthetic tableaux: minimal tableau search heuristics. In: Proceedings of the 11th International Joint Conference on Automated Reasoning. Springer LNCS (2022). ISBN:978-3-031-10768-9
3. Golumbic, M.C.: Algorithmic graph theory and perfect graphs. Ann. Disc. Math. **57** (2004)
4. Smullyan, R. M.: First-Order Logic. Springer-Verlag (1968). https://doi.org/10.1007/978-3-642-86718-7_4
5. Ralph, B., Strassburger, L.: Towards a combinatorial proof theory. In: Proceedings of the International Conference on Automated Reasoning with Analytic Tableaux and Related Methods, pp. 259–276. Springer LNCS (2019). https://doi.org/10.1007/978-3-030-29026-9_15
6. Hughes, D.: Proofs without syntax. Ann. Math. **164**, 1065–1076 (2006)
7. Corncil, D.G., Lerchs, H., Burlingham, L.S.: Complement reducible graphs. Discret. Appl. Math. **3**(3), 163–174 (1981)
8. Epple, D.A., Huang, J.: (k, l)-colourings and Ferrers diagram representations of cographs. Eur. J. Combinat. 91, 103208 (2021)

9. Shimojima, A.: Semantic Properties of Diagrams and Their Cognitive Potentials. Chapman and Hall/CRC (2015)
10. Jamnik, M., Shimojima, A., Stapleton, G.: What makes an effective representation of information: a formal account of observational advantages. J. Logic. Lang. Inf. **26**(2), 143–177 (2017)

The Notion of Diagrammatic Isomorphism in Venn-Peirce Diagrams

Sumanta Sarathi Sharma(✉)🄳

School of Philosophy and Culture, Shri Mata Vaishno Devi University Katra,
Union Territory of Jammu and Kashmir 182 320, India
ss.sharma@smvdu.ac.in

Abstract. In assertoric syllogism, Aristotle was concerned with pairs of premises that may or may not produce a valid conclusion. Medievals and contemporaries are interested in the number of valid syllogisms and figures. This paper proposes the notion of diagrammatic isomorphism using Venn-Peirce diagrams to offer remarkable insight into the theory of syllogisms. The exercise aims to realign the debates on the assertoric syllogistic to its primogenitor's path.

Keywords: Syllogistic · Concludent pairs · Diagrammatic congruence · Diagrammatic isomorphism · Venn-Peirce diagrams

1 Historical Preliminaries

Aristotle meticulously worked out cases wherever *a pair of premises produced a valid conclusion*(concludent pair) and dispensed such *pairs that cannot produce a syllogism*(inconcludent pair) [20]. In later antiquity, Aristotle's 'assertoric' syllogisms were called 'categorical' syllogisms' [4], which has a well-documented history from a 'discourse' to a 'consequence' and from a 'demonstration' to an 'argument form' [8,23,31]. Aristotle discussed the formation of 14 syllogisms valid in three figures [17,20], after considering 48 pairs of premises [16]. Ariston of Alexandria introduced 'subaltern' syllogisms into the Aristotelian syllogistic [4]. Later, Galen added the fourth figure [24] though it is marred with some controversies [26]. The medieval analysis added 'subaltern' moods and the fourth figure, which resulted in 24 valid syllogisms in four figures.

Syllogistic witnessed many debates, regarding the number and relevance of figures [11,13,22,25,27], where either these studies highlight the 'symmetry' of the fourth figure or relegate it to a 'transformed first figure.' A recent study suggested that eight syllogisms are valid using the notion of distinct and indistinct moods [27], whereas only six are claimed as basic syllogisms using indirect proof and inversion [7]. A fascinating study reveals that there can be as many as 262,144 syllogisms, out of which only 48 are valid [34]. Nevertheless, logicians mostly agree that there are 256 syllogisms in four figures out of which 15 are valid as found in logic manuals [6,10,15,30]. Admittedly, this math is intriguing, and its numbers – enticing. In this study, we explore syllogisms through Venn-Peirce diagrams to put an end to this above enticement.

© Springer Nature Switzerland AG 2022
V. Giardino et al. (Eds.): Diagrams 2022, LNAI 13462, pp. 321–328, 2022.
https://doi.org/10.1007/978-3-031-15146-0_27

2   Venn-Peirce Diagrams for Syllogisms

There was some confusion in the past regarding Euler and Venn diagrams as they both used closed curves. Interestingly, Peirce himself discussed 'Venn diagrams' under the heading of Euler diagrams [29]. However, Venn criticized Euler's diagrams at great length before suggesting his diagrams [32]. Moreover, Euler and Venn's systems appeal to different methods of representation [19]. What we refer to as Venn diagrams for syllogistic incorrectly – are actually 'Venn-Peirce' diagrams [18, 19, 21, 32, 33]. In short, Venn gave us 'shading' to depict *emptiness* for universal propositions and Peirce gave us 'X' mark to show *existence* for particular propositions (Fig. 1).

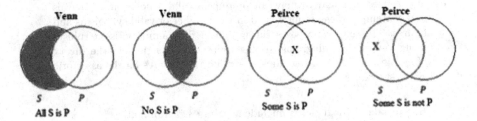

Fig. 1. Venn-Peirce diagrams for propositions

Both Euler and Venn-Peirce diagrams display many diagrammatic properties like free rides [28], well-matchedness [9], etc. Another property, called 'counterpart equivalence' ($\mathcal{CE}$) was initially proposed for Euler diagrams, where "[we] call two diagrams D and D' counterpart equivalent if and only if every minimal region of D has a counterpart in D' and every minimal region of D' has a counterpart in D" [12]. For example, the following two diagrams, as shown in Fig. 2, are counterpart equivalent:

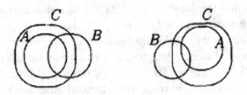

Fig. 2. $\mathcal{CE}$ in Euler diagram

Both the diagrams in Fig. 2 represent the same information i.e., B intersect with both A and C, while A along with the intersection part of A and B are fully contained in C. $\mathcal{CE}$ is also a fundamental property of Venn-Peirce diagrams. For instance, Fig. 3. represents 'all M is P' and 'all S is M':

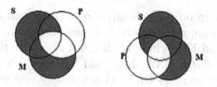

Fig. 3. $\mathcal{CE}$ in Venn-Peirce diagram

$\mathcal{CE}$ depicts the equivalence of two or more sets of information although the diagrams do not seem congruent. In the next section, we reintroduce and expand the notion of diagrammatic congruence for Venn-Peirce diagrams using $\mathcal{CE}$.

2.1   On Diagrammatic Congruence

"Two or more moods are diagrammatically congruent if they have identical Venn-Peirce diagram" [27]. The notion of diagrammatic congruence ($\mathcal{DC}$) was proposed keeping in mind the idea of the Venn-Peirce framework for syllogisms. Hence, the definition mentions moods and Venn-Peirce diagrams. Broadly, any two diagrams D and D' are diagrammatically congruent, if they are identical. Identical here must be understood as isomorphic or homomorphic, as discussed in [2,14]. For example, EIO-1, EIO-2, EIO-3, and EIO-4 (i.e., Ferio, Festino, Ferison, and Fresison) are diagrammatically congruent, as shown in Fig. 4:

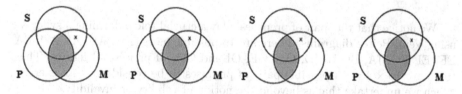

Fig. 4. $\mathcal{DC}$ of EIO-1,2,3,4

It may be noted that EIO-1,2,3,4 are considered as separate syllogisms. Similarly, EAE-1 and EAE-2 (i.e. Celarent and Cesare) are also diagrammatically congruent as shown in Fig. 5:

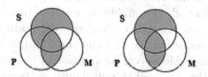

Fig. 5. $\mathcal{DC}$ of EAE-1,2

EIO-1,2,3, and 4 can be symbolically shown equivalent by using simple *conversion* and *commutation* respectively. The same is true for EAE-1 and 2. Interestingly, EIA, EIE, and EII (which are invalid) also have the same Venn-Peirce diagram as EIO. Similarly, EAA, EAI, and EAO (which are also invalid) are diagrammatically congruent to EAE. This anomaly and seemingly discomforting observation can well be understood by appealing to the fact that Venn-Peirce (or any diagrammatic technique) draws the premises (and never the conclusion) of a syllogism. With this observation in mind, let us enlarge and extend the scope of $\mathcal{DC}$ and introduce a new notion called 'diagrammatic isomorphism.'

2.2 Diagrammatic Isomorphism ($\mathcal{DI}$)

Two or more illustrations are diagrammatically isomorphic, if and only if they have identical Venn-Peirce diagrammatic depiction, irrespective of them being valid or invalid. $\mathcal{DI}$ supersedes its predecessor $\mathcal{DC}$. It is plain from the above that EIA, EIE, EII, and EIO from any figure have the following diagram (Fig. 6):

Fig. 6. $\mathcal{DI}$ of EIA, EIE, EII and EIO

We notice that the 'pair of premises' play a crucial role in forming a syllogism using Venn-Peirce diagrams. There are 16 possible pairs (AA, AE, AI, AO, EA, EE, EI, EO, IA, IE, II, IO, OA, OE, OI and OO) of premises 4 figures. Thus, there are $16 \times 4 = 64$ possible pairs of premises to be considered—an exercise, which we undertake that is beyond the notion of validity or invalidity.

3   Beyond Validity and Invalidity

We find that there is more to just the notions of validity and invalidity while re-examining A, E, I, and O propositions using Venn-Peirce diagrams. First, E and I propositions remain diagrammatically identical even if we replace their subject and predicate terms. However, A and O types of propositions have non-identical depictions. Second, the middle term's position in the major premise and the minor premise changes twice. Precisely, the position of the middle term in the case of major premises in the first and third figures is the same and in the second and fourth figures. Moreover, the position of the middle term in the case of minor premises in the first and second figures is the same, and in the third and fourth figures, it remains the same. Computing the above, we obtain:

a. AA, AO, OA, and OO have four iterations since A and O are diagrammatically incongruent as shown in Fig. 7.

AA-1   AA-2   AA-3   AA-4

AO-1   AO-2   AO-3   AO-4

OA-1   OA-2   OA-3   OA-4

OO-1   OO-2   OO-3   OO-4

Fig. 7. $\mathcal{DI}$ for AA, AO, OA and OO using Venn-Peirce diagrams

b. AE, AI, EA, EO, IA, IO, OE, and OI have two iterations as one premise is diagrammatically congruent, and the other is diagrammatically incongruent as shown in Fig. 8.

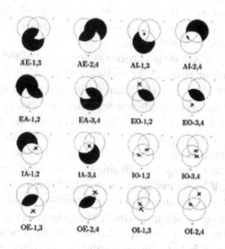

AE-1,3   AE-2,4   AI-1,3   AI-2,4

EA-1,2   EA-3,4   EO-1,2   EO-3,4

IA-1,2   IA-3,4   IO-1,2   IO-3,4

OE-1,3   OE-2,4   OI-1,3   OI-2,4

Fig. 8. $\mathcal{DI}$ for AE, AI, EA, EO, IA, IO, OE and OI using Venn-Peirce diagrams

c. EE, EI, IE, and II have just one iteration each since both E, and I have diagrammatically congruent illustrations as shown in Fig. 9.

Thus, the actual number of premise pairs in four figures (iterations) to be considered will be $(\mathbf{a} + \mathbf{b} + \mathbf{c})$ i.e., $[(4 \times 4) + (8 \times 2) + 4] = 36$. This treatment is neither unique nor novel if we recall an important fact in traditional syllogistic, which has skipped our attention for a while. In his theory of the syllogism,

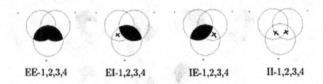

EE-1,2,3,4   EI-1,2,3,4   IE-1,2,3,4   II-1,2,3,4

Fig. 9. $\mathcal{DI}$ for EE, EI, IE and II using Venn-Peirce diagrams

Aristotle was deeply interested in pairs of propositions, which entail a valid conclusion [3]. In numerous passages (say, from 26a10 up to 68b10) of *Analytica Priora*, we find expressions such as 'there will be a syllogism', 'there is a syllogism', 'a syllogism is formed', 'a syllogism is possible', vis-à-vis expressions like 'there will be no syllogism', 'a syllogism is not possible', etc. [17]. This line of argument and analysis suggested by Aristotle is the same as a concludent and an inconcludent pair of premises. For e.g., EI is a concludent pair of premises (as O can be validly inferred from EI), whereas EE is an inconcludent pair. With time, this information evanesced along with its perusal, and what came to the fore was the number of syllogisms, number of figures, number of valid moods, etc. These possible depictions of syllogisms (or pairs of premises) using the Venn-Peirce framework bring us back to an impinging question which is, "Does Venn-Peirce diagrams depict a syllogism (in Aristotle's sense) or just a pair of propositions"? To this, Buridan observes, "*It seems to me that Aristotle takes a syllogism not to be composed of premises and conclusion, but composed only of premises from which a conclusion can be inferred* [5]."

Buridan's reading of Aristotle clarifies syllogism's valued exploration of concludent and inconcludent pairs. A Venn-Peirce diagram certainly depicts a pair of propositions, but so does any (diagrammatic) system of syllogistic reasoning. The ratiocinator is also asked to decide whether the conclusion follows from it. If the conclusion can be made explicit by drawing the premises, the syllogism has formed (or is valid), else it is not. This shows the need to delve beyond the notions of validity and invalidity to do justice to the theory of syllogisms. Questions like, whether *Darapti* or *Bramantip* are valid? or why Aristotle did not mention *Barbari*, if he knows *Barbara* is valid? can all be answered, provided that we pick the call of concludent pair of premises. If the notions of validity or invalidity of a syllogism are important, then the concepts of concludent and inconcludent pair of premises are pivotal. Once we understand how a syllogism becomes valid or why it fails to become valid, we address the root cause of the issue rather than dealing with its effect.

4   Concluding Remarks

An analytical and diagrammatic exercise on the pairs of premises (of a syllogism) is required to understand the trajectory of syllogistic reasoning. Successes (valid syllogisms) often hide certain critical information, which failures (invalid syllogisms) reveal. Several passages of *Analytica Priora*, suggest that Aristotle was interested in how syllogism forms and may not form. He was interested in the notion of validity (formation of a syllogism) and wanted to demonstrate the reason for invalidity (i.e., the error occurring while reasoning). Bacon correctly pointed out that *"truth emerges more quickly from error than from confusion* [1]". The overemphasis on 'how many' (or the number of syllogisms, figures) is a later outcry. It has taken off the essence of syllogism. Our inquiry should focus on how syllogisms form. Once we address this, the rest all fall in place. The findings of this paper are reiterated below:

First, there are very few syllogisms (valid or invalid) contrary to our prevailing belief. Second, the notion of $\mathcal{DI}$ allows us to infer identical Venn-Peirce diagrammatic depictions, valid in one case and invalid in many others. Third, there is no visual representation or iteration (of a syllogism), which is exclusively valid; however, some illustrations are solely invalid. Fourth, the notion of concludent and inconcludent pairs (of premises) is much more significant than the validity or invalidity of syllogisms. Lastly, there are eight concludent pairs, AA, AE, AI, AO, EA, EI, IA, and OA; the other eight possible pairs are EE, EO, IE, II, IO, OE, OI, and OO are inconcludent.

Acknowledgment. The author sincerely expresses gratitude to the anonymous reviewers for their comments and suggestions on an earlier draft.

References

1. Bacon, F.: The New Organon. CUP, Cambridge (2000)
2. Barwise, J., Etchemendy, J.: Visual information and visual reasoning. In: Allwein, G., Barwise, J. (Eds.), Logical Reasoning with Diagrams, pp. 3–26. OUP, New York (1996)
3. Boger, G.: Completion, reduction and analysis: three-proof theoretic processes in Aristotle's prior analytics. Hist. Philos. Log. **19**, 187–226 (2007)
4. Bobzien S.: The Stanford Encyclopedia of Philosophy. https://plato.stanford.edu/archives/sum2020/entries/logic-ancient/. Accessed 15 Apr 2020
5. Buridan, J.: Treatises on Consequences. (S. Read, Trans.) Fordham University Press, New York (2015)
6. Copi, I.M.: Introduction to Logic, 4th edn. Macmillan Publishing, New York (1972)
7. Dyckhoff, R.: Indirect proof and inversions of syllogisms. Bull. Symb. Log. **25**, 196–207 (2019)
8. Dutilh Novaes, C.: The syllogism as defined by Aristotle, Ockham, and Buridan. In: Pelletier, J., Roques, M. (Eds.) The Language of Thought in Late Medieval (2017)
9. Gurr, C.: Effective diagrammatic communication: syntactic, semantic and pragmatic issues. J. Visual Lang. Comput. **10**, 317–342 (1999)
10. Guttenplan, S.D., Tamny, M.: Logic: A Comprehensive Introduction, 2nd edn. Basic Books Inc., New York (1978)
11. Hadgopoulos, D.J.: The principle of the division into four figures in traditional logic. Notre Dame J. Formal Log. **20**, 92–94 (1979)
12. Hammer, E., Shin, S.-J.: Euler's visual logic. Hist. Philos. Log. **19**, 1–29 (2007)
13. Henle, P.: On the fourth figure of the syllogism. Philos. Sci. **16**, 94–104 (1949)

14. Howse, J., Molina, F., Shin, S.-J., Taylor, J.: On diagram tokens and types. In: Hegarty, M., Meyer, B., Narayanan, N.H. (eds.) Diagrams 2002. LNCS (LNAI), vol. 2317, pp. 146–160. Springer, Heidelberg (2002). https://doi.org/10.1007/3-540-46037-3_18

15. Hurley, P.J.: A Concise Introduction to Logic, 7th edn. Wadsworth Publishing, California (1999)

16. Lear, J.: Aristotle Logical Theory. CUP, New York (1980)

17. McKeon, R.: The Basic Works of Aristotle. Random House, New York (1941)

18. Moktefi, A., Pietarinen, A.-V.: On the diagrammatic representation of existential statements with Venn diagrams. J. Log. Lang. Inf. **24**(4), 361–374 (2015). https://doi.org/10.1007/s10849-015-9228-1

19. Moktefi, A., Shin, S.-J.: A history of logic diagrams. In: Gabbay, D.M., Pelletier, F.J. (Eds.), Handbook of the History of Logic, pp. 611–680. Elsevier, Amsterdam (2012)

20. Patzig, G.: Aristotle's Theory of Syllogism: A Logico-Philological Study of Book A of the Prior Analytics. D. Reidel Publishing Company, Dodrecht-Holland (1968)

21. Peirce, C.S.: Collected Papers. HUP, Cambridge (1933)

22. Plochmann, G.K.: Professor Henle on the four figures of syllogism. Philos. Sci. **19**, 333–341 (1952)

23. Read, S.: Aristotle's Theory of Assertoric Syllogism. https://www.st-andrews.ac.uk/~slr/The_Syllogism.pdf. Accessed 21 June 2020

24. Rescher, N.: New light from the Arabic sources on Galen and the fourth figure of the syllogism. J. Hist. Philos. **3**, 27–41 (1965)

25. Rose, L.E.: Aristotle's syllogistic and the fourth figure. Mind **74**, 382–389 (1965)

26. Sabra, A.: A twelfth-century defence of the fourth figure of the syllogism. J. Warburg Courtauld Inst. **28**, 14–28 (1965)

27. Sarathi Sharma, S.: Depicting the redundancy of fourth figure using Venn-Peirce framework. In: Chapman, P., Stapleton, G., Moktefi, A., Perez-Kriz, S., Bellucci, F. (eds.) Diagrams 2018. LNCS (LNAI), vol. 10871, pp. 689–696. Springer, Cham (2018). https://doi.org/10.1007/978-3-319-91376-6_61

28. Shimojima, A.: Operational constraints in diagrammatic reasoning. In: Allwein, G., Barwise, J. (Eds.), Logical Reasoning with Diagrams, pp. 27–48. OUP, New York (1996)

29. Shin, S.-J.: Peirce and the logical status of diagrams. Hist. Philos. Log. **15**, 45–68 (2007)

30. Strawson, P.: Introduction to Logical Theory. Metheun, London (1952)

31. Thom, P.: The syllogism and its transformations. In: Dutilh-Novaes, C., Read, S. (Eds.) The Cambridge Companion to Medieval Logic, pp. 290–315. CUP, Cambridge (2016)

32. Venn, J.: On the diagrammatic and mechanical representation of propositions and reasonings. Philos. Mag. **10**, 1–18 (1880)

33. Venn, J.: Symbolic Logic. Macmillan and Company, London (1881)

34. Williamson, C.: How many syllogisms are there? Hist. Philos. Log. **9**, 77–85 (1988)

Generalizing Aristotelian Relations and Diagrams

Stef Frijters[✉][iD]

Institute of Philosophy, Centre for Logic and Philosophy of Science,
KU Leuven, 3000 Leuven, Belgium
stef.frijters@kuleuven.be

Abstract. The square of opposition is a type of diagram that graphically represents the Aristotelian relations between sentences or formulas. It has been noted in the literature that certain extensions of the square have several Boolean subtypes. However, the traditional Aristotelian relations themselves cannot be used to distinguish these different subtypes. Furthermore, the traditional Aristotelian relations are relations between two individual formulas. In this paper I propose a very natural generalization, resting on elementary set-theoretical notions, of these relations to sets of formulas of arbitrary size. I show that this generalization can be used to construct new diagrams, viz. generalized squares of opposition, that can express information that could not be expressed by the traditional squares. Furthermore, I show that the generalized Aristotelian relations can be used to classify Boolean subtypes of extensions of the square that could not be distinguished by the traditional relations.

Keywords: Square of opposition · Aristotelian relations · Logical geometry

1 Introduction

The *square of opposition* and its extensions, together called the Aristotelian diagrams, have been used to teach logic, to investigate logical and philosophical questions, and have found applications in research domains as varied as computer science, psychology and linguistics. For these reasons, the square and its extensions have themselves become the object of research in the domain of *logical geometry* [1].

Logical geometry studies both the Aristotelian diagrams and the logical relations they depict, known as the four Aristotelian relations. Each of the Aristotelian relations expresses a logical relation between two individual formulas. In this paper, I propose a generalization of each of the four Aristotelian relations to sets of formulas. I show that this generalization can be used to construct new diagrams and to distinguish different subtypes of existing Aristotelian diagrams.

The paper is structured as follows. In Sect. 2 the traditional Aristotelian relations and the square of opposition are presented. In the next section (Sect. 3)

© Springer Nature Switzerland AG 2022
V. Giardino et al. (Eds.): Diagrams 2022, LNAI 13462, pp. 329–337, 2022.
https://doi.org/10.1007/978-3-031-15146-0_28

Fig. 1. (a) a traditional square of opposition for classical propositional logic, and (b) one for the modal logic **S5**.

I propose a generalization of the Aristotelian relations and show how they can be used to construct a new generalized square of opposition. Section 4 expands on this and proves that the new generalizations are not reducible to the traditional relations. I then show (Sect. 5) how the generalizations can be used to distinguish different Boolean subtypes of Aristotelian diagrams that have been studied in the literature, but cannot be distinguished with the traditional Aristotelian relations. Finally, Sect. 6 gives a short summary and mentions some possible directions for further research.

2   The Traditional Aristotelian Relations

The four traditional Aristotelian relations are formally defined in Definition 1. When this does not lead to confusion, I will drop the reference to the logic **S**. I will also use the abbreviations $CD(\varphi, \psi)$, $C(\varphi, \psi)$, $SC(\varphi, \psi)$ and $SA(\varphi, \psi)$.

Definition 1. *Let* **S** *be a logical system, which is assumed to have Boolean operators and a model-theoretic semantics* $\models$. *The formulas* $\varphi, \psi \in \mathcal{L}_{\mathbf{S}}$ *are*

$$
\begin{aligned}
&\textbf{S}\text{-}contradictory &&iff \models \neg(\varphi \wedge \psi) \ and \models \varphi \vee \psi\\
&\textbf{S}\text{-}contrary &&iff \models \neg(\varphi \wedge \psi) \ and \not\models \varphi \vee \psi\\
&\textbf{S}\text{-}subcontrary &&iff \not\models \neg(\varphi \wedge \psi) \ and \models \varphi \vee \psi\\
&in\ \textbf{S}\text{-}subalternation &&iff \models \varphi \to \psi \quad and \not\models \psi \to \varphi
\end{aligned}
$$

We can represent these Aristotelian relations graphically in a square of opposition. Two such squares are depicted in Fig. 1. The contradiction relation is represented with a solid line, the contrariety relation with a dashed line, the subcontrariety relation with a dotted line and subalternation with an arrow.

3   Generalizing the Aristotelian Relations and Squares

3.1   Generalized Aristotelian Relations

In this section we give a generalization of the classical Aristotelian relations of Definition 1. One way of looking at the first three relations in Definition 1 is to treat them not as relations between two individual formulas, but as properties of a two-element set of formulas. For example, we can say that $\Gamma = \{\varphi, \psi\}$ is contradictory iff any model of **S** validates exactly one formula in Γ iff the class of all models of **S** is partitioned by Γ. Of course, this idea of the class of models being partitioned does not need to be limited to two-element sets. We can define it for sets of formulas of arbitrary size. This is a very natural generalization of the contradiction relation to sets of formulas. As it turns out, the relations of contrariety and subcontrariety can be generalized in a similar way, by using elementary set-theoretical notions (Definition 4). However, before doing so we first give two preliminary Definitions (Definitions 2 and 3).[1]

Definition 2. *Let $\mathcal{M}_{\mathbf{S}}$ be the class consisting of all models of* **S**.
$$[\![\varphi]\!]_{\mathbf{S}} =_{df} \{M \in \mathcal{M}_{\mathbf{S}} \mid M \models \varphi\}$$
$$[\![\Gamma]\!]_{\mathbf{S}} =_{df} \{[\![\varphi]\!]_{\mathbf{S}} \mid \varphi \in \Gamma\}$$

Definition 3. *A set Γ consisting of sets is*
disjoint *iff for all $\Delta, \Theta \in \Gamma$ such that $\Delta \neq \Theta$, $\Delta \cap \Theta = \emptyset$*
a covering *of a set Δ iff $\Delta \subseteq \bigcup \Gamma$*

Definition 4. *Let $\Gamma \subseteq \mathcal{L}$, such that $|\Gamma| > 1$. Then Γ is:*

contradictory *iff $[\![\Gamma]\!]$ is a partition of $\mathcal{M}$, i.e. is disjoint and a covering of $\mathcal{M}$*
contrary   *iff $[\![\Gamma]\!]$ is disjoint, but is not a covering of $\mathcal{M}$*
subcontrary *iff $[\![\Gamma]\!]$ is not disjoint, but is a covering of $\mathcal{M}$*

The case for subalternation is slightly different. The relations CD, C and SC are, in the terminology of [4], *opposition relations*, whereas SA is an *implication relation*. The opposition relations are symmetric, e.g. $C(\varphi, \psi)$ iff $C(\psi, \varphi)$. In contrast, the relation SA is asymmetric: if $SA(\varphi, \psi)$, then not $SA(\psi, \varphi)$. Thus it makes sense that the generalizations of the opposition relations should be unary relations, but the generalization of SA should remain a binary relation. Keeping this in mind I propose Definition 5 as the generalization of SA.

Definition 5. *Let $\Gamma, \Delta \subseteq \mathcal{L}$, such that $\Gamma \neq \emptyset \neq \Delta$. Then:*
Γ and Δ are in subalternation *iff $\bigcup [\![\Gamma]\!] \subset \bigcup [\![\Delta]\!]$.*

Informally, $SA(\Gamma, \Delta)$ can be read as 'if a formula in Γ is true, then a formula in Δ is true, but not vice versa'. Similarly, $CD(\Gamma)$ can be read as 'there is always exactly one formula in Γ that is true', $C(\Gamma)$ as 'no two formulas in Γ can be true together, but all formulas in Γ can be false together', and $SC(\Gamma)$ as 'there is always at least one formula in Γ that is true, and it is possible that multiple formulas in Γ are true together'. Of course, Definitions 4 and 5 are only an actual *generalization* of the classical Aristotelian relations if: $CD(\varphi, \psi)$ iff $CD(\{\varphi, \psi\})$, $C(\varphi, \psi)$ iff $C(\{\varphi, \psi\})$, $SC(\varphi, \psi)$ iff $SC(\{\varphi, \psi\})$ and $SA(\varphi, \psi)$ iff $SA(\{\varphi\}, \{\psi\})$. This is easily checked by comparing Definition 1 with Definitions 4 and 5.

3.2   Generalized Squares of Opposition

Given the generalized Aristotelian relations, we can draw new *generalized squares of opposition* with sets of formulas at the vertices (instead of individual formulas). The general format of a generalized square of opposition is depicted in

---

[1] Again, we omit the subscript **S** when no ambiguity is possible.

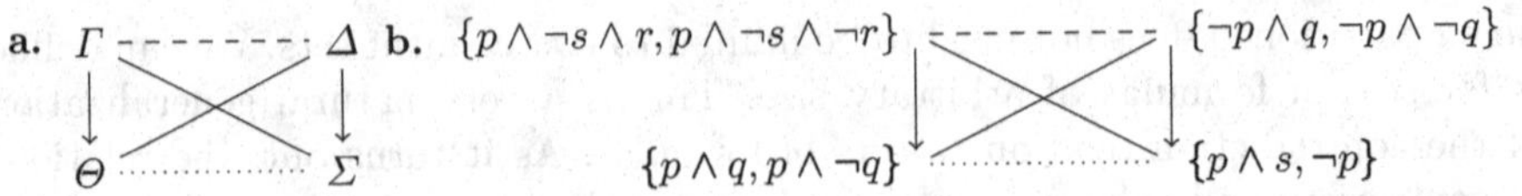

a. Γ - - - - - - - - Δ **b.** $\{p \wedge \neg s \wedge r, p \wedge \neg s \wedge \neg r\}$ - - - - - - - - $\{\neg p \wedge q, \neg p \wedge \neg q\}$

Θ .... Σ $\{p \wedge q, p \wedge \neg q\}$ .... $\{p \wedge s, \neg p\}$

Fig. 2. (a) general format of a generalized square of opposition and (b) one example

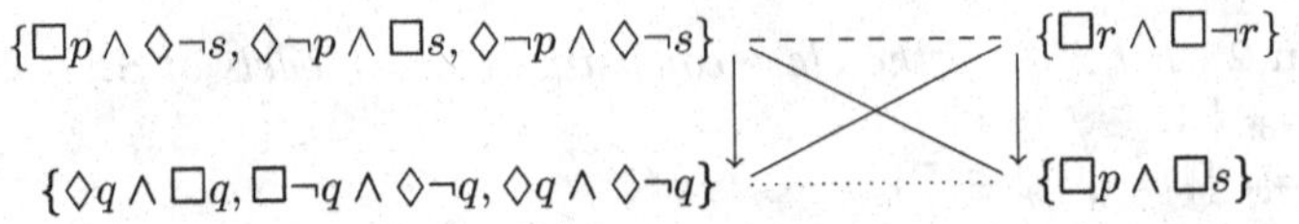

$\{\Box p \wedge \Diamond \neg s, \Diamond \neg p \wedge \Box s, \Diamond \neg p \wedge \Diamond \neg s\}$ - - - - - - - - $\{\Box r \wedge \Box \neg r\}$

$\{\Diamond q \wedge \Box q, \Box \neg q \wedge \Diamond \neg q, \Diamond q \wedge \Diamond \neg q\}$ .... $\{\Box p \wedge \Box s\}$

Fig. 3. A generalized square of opposition for the modal logic **K**

Fig. 2a. The solid lines signify that the union of the two sets at the vertices is contradictory. A dashed line signifies that the union of the two sets is contrary, the dotted line that the union is subcontrary and the arrow from a set Γ to a set Θ signifies that SA(Γ, Θ). Figures 2b and 3 show two concrete examples of generalized Aristotelian squares.

4 The Generalization is a Proper Generalization

In Sect. 3.1 we have seen that Definitions 4 and 5 are a generalization, meaning that the generalized relations say at least as much as the traditional relations. In this section I show that the generalized Aristotelian relations are a *proper* generalization: they say strictly *more* than the original relations, i.e. the generalized relations cannot be reduced to the original relations. I discuss two ways one might expect such a reduction to work, and I prove that neither of these two reductions holds. Section 4.1 proves that the generalized relations are not reducible to Aristotelian relations between disjunctions, and Sect. 4.2 proves that the generalized relation holding of a set Γ cannot be reduced to statements about the traditional Aristotelian relations between all of the formulas in Γ.

4.1 Generalized Relations and Relations Between Disjunctions

It follows from Definition 5 that SA(Γ, Δ) iff SA$(\bigvee \Gamma, \bigvee \Delta)$. Thus, the generalization of SA is reducible to the traditional SA relation. Suppose that for every R $\in \{CD, C, SC\}$ and non-empty $\Gamma, \Delta \subseteq \mathcal{L}$, R$(\Gamma \cup \Delta)$ iff R$(\bigvee \Gamma, \bigvee \Delta)$. In that case all generalized relations would be reducible to the traditional relations, and would not say anything really new. As the left side of Theorem 1 shows, one might initially be inclined to think that this reduction would go through. However, the "not the other way round"-results of Theorem 1 show that the generalized relations are not reducible to the traditional relations in this way.

Theorem 1. *Let $\Gamma, \Delta \subseteq \mathcal{L}$ be finite and let $\Gamma \neq \emptyset \neq \Delta$. In addition, assume there are no $\varphi \in \Gamma$ and $\psi \in \Delta$ such that $\models \varphi \leftrightarrow \psi$, then:*

$$
\begin{array}{lll}
CD(\Gamma \cup \Delta) & implies & CD(\bigvee \Gamma, \bigvee \Delta) \;\; but \; not \; the \; other \; way \; round \\
C(\Gamma \cup \Delta) & implies & C(\bigvee \Gamma, \bigvee \Delta) \;\;\; but \; not \; the \; other \; way \; round \\
SC(\bigvee \Gamma, \bigvee \Delta) & implies & SC(\Gamma \cup \Delta) \;\;\;\; but \; not \; the \; other \; way \; round \\
SA(\Gamma, \Delta) & iff & SA(\bigvee \Gamma, \bigvee \Delta)
\end{array}
$$

Proof. We only prove the cases for $CD(\Gamma \cup \Delta)$ and $SC(\bigvee \Gamma, \bigvee \Delta)$. The other cases are then left safely to the reader. For the first implication, suppose that Γ and Δ are as in Theorem 1, and that $CD(\Gamma \cup \Delta)$. By Definition 4, $[\![\Gamma \cup \Delta]\!]$ is a partition of $\mathcal{M}$. Hence, every model of the logic makes at most one $\varphi \in \Gamma \cup \Delta$ true; since there are no $\varphi \in \Gamma$ and $\psi \in \Delta$ such that $\models \varphi \leftrightarrow \psi$, Γ and Δ are disjoint; thus $\varphi \notin \Gamma$ or $\varphi \notin \Delta$. Hence, $\models \neg(\bigvee \Gamma \wedge \bigvee \Delta)$. Since $[\![\Gamma \cup \Delta]\!]$ is a partition of $\mathcal{M}$, every model makes at least one $\varphi \in \Gamma \cup \Delta$ true. Thus, $\models \bigvee \Gamma \vee \bigvee \Delta$. By Definition 1, $CD(\bigvee \Gamma, \bigvee \Delta)$. For the other direction, consider $\Gamma = \{p, q\}$ and $\Delta = \{\neg p \wedge \neg q\}$. Then $CD(p \vee q, \neg p \wedge \neg q)$, but not $CD(\{p, q, \neg p \wedge \neg q\})$.

For the other case, suppose that $SC(\bigvee \Gamma, \bigvee \Delta)$. By Definition 1, $\not\models \neg(\bigvee \Gamma \wedge \bigvee \Delta)$ (1) and $\models \bigvee \Gamma \vee \bigvee \Delta$ (2). By (1), $[\![\Gamma \cup \Delta]\!]$ is not disjoint. By (2), $[\![\Gamma \cup \Delta]\!]$ is a covering of $\mathcal{M}$. By Definition 4, $SC(\Gamma \cup \Delta)$. For the other direction, consider $\Gamma = \{\neg p, \neg p \wedge q\}$ and $\Delta = \{p\}$. Then $SC(\{\neg p, \neg p \wedge q, p\})$, but not $SC(\neg p, p)$.

4.2 Generalized Relations and Sets of Traditional Relations

In the previous section, one strategy for reducing the generalized relations to the traditional relations was proven not to work. However, there is another possible strategy. Perhaps the generalized Aristotelian relations, as holding of a set Γ, determine the original Aristotelian relations as holding between all of the pairs of formulas in Γ, and vice versa. Theorems 2 and 3 show this to be untrue.

Theorem 2. *There exist sets Γ, Δ such that the formulas of Γ stand in precisely the same traditional Aristotelian relations as those of Δ, and yet Γ and Δ do not stand in the same generalized Aristotelian relation.*

Proof. Consider $\Gamma = \{p \wedge q, p \wedge \neg q, \neg p\}$ and $\Delta = \{p \wedge q, p \wedge \neg q, \neg p \wedge \neg q\}$. For all distinct $\varphi, \psi \in \Gamma$, $C(\varphi, \psi)$ and for all distinct $\varphi, \psi \in \Delta$, $C(\varphi, \psi)$. However, it is also easy to check that $CD(\Gamma)$, while $C(\Delta)$.

Theorem 3. *There exist sets Γ, Δ such that Γ and Δ stand in the same generalized Aristotelian relation, and yet the formulas in Γ do not stand in the same traditional Aristotelian relations as those of Δ.*

Proof. Consider $\Gamma = \{p \vee q, \neg p \vee q, p \vee \neg q, \neg p \vee \neg q\}$ and $\Delta = \{p, q, \neg p, \neg q\}$. By Definition 4, $SC(\Gamma)$ and $SC(\Delta)$. However, for all distinct $\varphi, \psi \in \Gamma$ it holds that $SC(\varphi, \psi)$, while for no distinct $\varphi, \psi \in \Delta$ does it hold that $SC(\varphi, \psi)$.

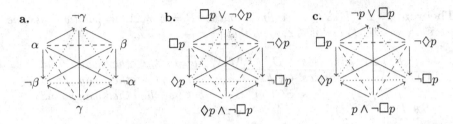

Fig. 4. (a) general format of a JSB hexagon, (b) a strong and (c) a weak JSB hexagon

Theorem 2 clearly illustrates that the Aristotelian relations holding between the formulas in a set do not uniquely determine the generalized Aristotelian relation holding of that set itself. Conversely, Theorem 3 proves that the generalized Aristotelian relation holding of a set does not uniquely determine the Aristotelian relations holding between the formulas in that set. Thus, the generalized Aristotelian relations are not reducible in this way.

From the fact that the Definitions 4 and 5 are a generalization of Definition 1, it follows that the generalized relations can be used to express all the information that can be expressed with the traditional Aristotelian relations. In addition, this section has shown that the traditional Aristotelian relations cannot express everything that the generalized relations can express. Thus we can conclude that the generalized relations are a proper generalization of, and thus say strictly more than, the traditional relations.

5   Using the Generalized Relations to Classify Traditional Diagrams

In this section I show that we can use the generalized Aristotelian relations to classify existing logical diagrams. Section 5.1 describes how the generalized Aristotelian relations can be used to differentiate weak and strong Jacoby-Sesmat-Blanché hexagons, and Sect. 5.2 explains how the generalized relations can be used to differentiate different kinds of Buridan octagons.

5.1   Jacoby-Sesmat-Blanché hexagons

The diagram in Fig. 4a shows the general form of a JSB hexagon. As in Fig. 1, the connecting lines in Fig. 4 represent the traditional Aristotelian relations. I use the symbols α, β, γ and their negations to refer to the formulas in those positions in the hexagon.

The other two diagrams in Fig. 4 are examples of JSB hexagons. These diagrams belong to two different Boolean subtypes of JSB hexagons. Diagram 4b is a *strong* JSB hexagon, and Diagram 4c is a *weak* JSB hexagon. A JSB hexagon is *strong* iff the disjunction of the formulas on its contrariety triangle is a tautology, i.e. iff $\models \alpha \lor \beta \lor \gamma$. Otherwise, the JSB hexagon is weak [1,2].

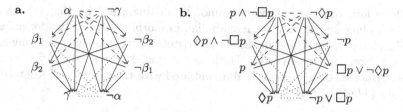

Fig. 5. (a) general format of a Buridan octagon and (b) one example

The traditional Aristotelian relations cannot be used to distinguish the weak and strong JSB hexagons. After all, they are *Aristotelian isomorphic* [1]: any two formulas in a strong hexagon stand in the same Aristotelian relation as any two formulas that are on the same positions in a weak hexagon. In contrast, Theorems 4 and 5 prove that the generalized Aristotelian relations can be used to distinguish strong and weak JSB hexagons.

Theorem 4. *For any JSB hexagon D: D is strong iff CD($\{\alpha,\beta,\gamma\}$).*

Proof. For the left to right direction, suppose that diagram D is a strong JSB hexagon. By the definition of a *strong* JSB hexagon, $\models \alpha \vee \beta \vee \gamma$. Hence, $[\![\{\alpha,\beta,\gamma\}]\!]$ is a covering. Since D is a JSB hexagon, C($\{\alpha,\beta\}$), C($\{\beta,\gamma\}$) and C($\{\gamma,\alpha\}$). By Definition 1, $\models \neg(\alpha \wedge \beta)$, $\models \neg(\beta \wedge \gamma)$ and $\models \neg(\gamma \wedge \beta)$. Hence, $[\![\{\alpha,\beta,\gamma\}]\!]$ is disjoint. By Definition 4, CD($\{\alpha,\beta,\gamma\}$). For the right to left direction, suppose CD($\{\alpha,\beta,\gamma\}$). By Definition 4, $\models \alpha \vee \beta \vee \gamma$.

Theorem 5. *For any JSB hexagon D: D is weak iff C($\{\alpha,\beta,\gamma\}$).*

Proof. For the left to right direction, suppose D is a weak JSB hexagon. Hence, $\not\models \alpha \vee \beta \vee \gamma$. Thus, $[\![\{\alpha,\beta,\gamma\}]\!]$ is not a covering of $\mathcal{M}$. Since C(α,β), C(β,γ), and C(γ,α), $[\![\{\alpha,\beta,\gamma\}]\!]$ is disjoint. By Definition 4, C($\{\alpha,\beta,\gamma\}$). For the right to left direction, suppose C($\{\alpha,\beta,\gamma\}$). By Definition 4, $\not\models \alpha \vee \beta \vee \gamma$.

5.2   Buridan Octagons

We now turn our attention to Buridan octagons. The diagram in Fig. 5a shows the general format of a Buridan octagon, and the diagram in Fig. 5b shows one example of such an octagon. As is the case for JSB hexagons, different Boolean subtypes of Buridan octagons have been distinguished. In [1] the four subtypes of Buridan octagons of Definition 6 are identified.[2]

Definition 6. *A Buridan octagon is of subtype*
1 iff $\models \alpha \leftrightarrow (\beta_1 \wedge \beta_2)$ and $\models \gamma \leftrightarrow (\beta_1 \vee \beta_2)$
2 iff $\models \alpha \leftrightarrow (\beta_1 \wedge \beta_2)$ and $\not\models \gamma \leftrightarrow (\beta_1 \vee \beta_2)$
3 iff $\not\models \alpha \leftrightarrow (\beta_1 \wedge \beta_2)$ and $\models \gamma \leftrightarrow (\beta_1 \vee \beta_2)$
4 iff $\not\models \alpha \leftrightarrow (\beta_1 \wedge \beta_2)$ and $\not\models \gamma \leftrightarrow (\beta_1 \vee \beta_2)$

---

[2] The subtypes 2. and 3. are each other's mirror image and could be folded into one category. They are Boolean isomorphic [1].

These four different subtypes cannot be distinguished by the Aristotelian relations. Once again, they are Aristotelian isomorphic [1]: any two formulas in one Buridan octagon stand in the same Aristotelian relation as two formulas in the same positions in any other Buridan octagon. However, the different subtypes of Buridan octagons can be differentiated with the generalized Aristotelian relations (Theorem 6).

Theorem 6. *A Buridan octagon is of subtype*
  1. *iff* $SC(\{\alpha, \neg\beta_1, \neg\beta_2\})$ *and* $SC(\{\neg\gamma, \beta_1, \beta_2\})$
  2. *iff* $SC(\{\alpha, \neg\beta_1, \neg\beta_2\})$ *and* $not\ SC(\{\neg\gamma, \beta_1, \beta_2\})$
  3. *iff not* $SC(\{\alpha, \neg\beta_1, \neg\beta_2\})$ *and* $SC(\{\neg\gamma, \beta_1, \beta_2\})$
  4. *iff not* $SC(\{\alpha, \neg\beta_1, \neg\beta_2\})$ *and* $not\ SC(\{\neg\gamma, \beta_1, \beta_2\})$

Proof. I prove that $\models \alpha \leftrightarrow (\beta_1 \wedge \beta_2)$ iff $SC(\{\alpha, \neg\beta_1, \neg\beta_2\})$. The other cases are safely left to the reader. For the left to right direction, suppose that $\models \alpha \leftrightarrow (\beta_1 \wedge \beta_2)$. It follows that $\{\alpha, \neg\beta_1, \neg\beta_2\}$ is a covering of $\mathcal{M}$. By the properties of a Buridan octagon, neither $CD(\neg\beta_1, \neg\beta_2)$ nor $C(\neg\beta_1, \neg\beta_2)$. By Definition 1, the set $\{\alpha, \neg\beta_1, \neg\beta_2\}$ is not disjoint. By Definition 4, $SC(\{\alpha, \neg\beta_1, \neg\beta_2\})$.

For the right to left direction, suppose $SC(\{\alpha, \neg\beta_1, \neg\beta_2\})$. By Definition 4, $\{\alpha, \neg\beta_1, \neg\beta_2\}$ is a covering of $\mathcal{M}$. Hence $\models \alpha \vee \neg\beta_1 \vee \neg\beta_2$. Thus, $\models (\beta_1 \wedge \beta_2) \rightarrow \alpha$. By $SA(\alpha, \beta_1)$, $SA(\alpha, \beta_2)$, and Definition 1, $\models \alpha \rightarrow (\beta_1 \wedge \beta_2)$.

6   Conclusion

In this paper I have presented a generalization of the Aristotelian relations that are depicted by squares of opposition. I have shown that this generalization can be used to construct new generalized squares of opposition. In addition, I have illustrated that the generalized relations can be used to distinguish different Boolean subtypes of well-known extensions of the square of opposition.

This opens up several avenues for further research. Firstly, it would be worthwhile to investigate whether Boolean subtypes of other extensions of the square of opposition (e.g. the Moretti octagon [2,3]) can also be distinguished by the generalized Aristotelian relations. Secondly, we might want to explore the properties of extensions of the generalized square of opposition, e.g. generalized JSB hexagons. Lastly, in this paper I have only presented one generalization of the Aristotelian relations. It is possible to construct other generalizations. It could be fruitful to construct and compare these other possible generalizations.

Acknowledgements. I would like to thank Lorenz Demey, Hans Smessaert, Jan Heylen and Joost Vennekens for valuable comments on earlier versions of this paper. This research was financially supported by the BITSHARE-project (IDN-19-009, Internal Funds KU Leuven).

References

1. Demey, L., Smessaert, H.: Combinatorial bitstring semantics for arbitrary logical fragments. J. Philos. Log. **47**(2), 325–363 (2018)
2. Lemanski, J., Demey, L.: Schopenhauer's partition diagrams and logical geometry. In: Basu, A., Stapleton, G., Linker, S., Legg, C., Manalo, E., Viana, P. (eds.) Diagrams 2021. LNCS (LNAI), vol. 12909, pp. 149–165. Springer, Cham (2021). https://doi.org/10.1007/978-3-030-86062-2_13
3. Moretti, A.: The geometry of logical opposition. Ph.D. thesis, Université de Neuchâtel (2009)
4. Smessaert, H., Demey, L.: Logical geometries and information in the square of oppositions. J. Logic Lang. Inform. **23**(4), 527–565 (2014)

John Cook Wilson's Hanging Plants:
A Contribution to the History of Early
Logic Trees

Dave Beisecker[1] and Amirouche Moktefi[2([⊠])]

[1] Department of Philosophy, University of Nevada, Las Vegas, USA
beiseckd@unlv.nevada.edu
[2] Ragnar Nurkse Department of Innovation and Governance, Tallinn University of Technology,
Tallinn, Estonia
amirouche.moktefi@taltech.ee

Abstract. It is known that Lewis Carroll's method of Trees anticipated modern decision procedures using Tree and Tableau devices. We present another method independently designed by John Cook Wilson in the mid-1890s. This forgotten episode offers an interesting case of simultaneous invention and directs attention to the specific kind of problems tackled by early mathematical logicians and the need for such methods of solution. For the purpose, we briefly sketch Carroll's method of Trees. Then, we present Cook Wilson's logic and motivations. We subsequently introduce the main graphical conventions of his method. Finally, we apply it to a complex problem and compare it with Carroll's Trees.

Keywords: Trees · Lewis Carroll · John Cook Wilson · Logic diagram · Sorites

1   Introduction

The use of Trees in logic is old [9]. However, modern tree-like decision procedures were developed from the mid-1950s onwards by Evert Willem Beth, Jaakko Hintikka, Richard Jeffrey, Raymond Smullyan and others [3]. Lewis Carroll's method of Trees, developed in the mid-1890s, is often regarded as a precursor of these modern methods [2, 4, 5, 16, 19, 21]. The idea of Carroll's method of Trees is simple: one postulates an entity and draws its necessary inferences in search for a contradiction. It has been suggested that Carroll might have been influenced by his reading of Christine Ladd-Franklin's work [1, 10, 14]. Yet, it was Carroll's merit to offer a visual implementation of this method for the solution of complex problems. In this paper, we show that Carroll was not alone in this line of research. Indeed, we present a hitherto unknown tree-like method independently developed by John Cook Wilson in the mid-1890s. It has the same procedure as Carroll's but makes use of different visual conventions.

© Springer Nature Switzerland AG 2022
V. Giardino et al. (Eds.): Diagrams 2022, LNAI 13462, pp. 338–346, 2022.
https://doi.org/10.1007/978-3-031-15146-0_29

2 Carroll's Method of Trees

Carroll invented his method of Trees in 1894 [20, p. 155]. However, he did not expose it
in the first part of his logic treatise, issued two years later. Indeed, he planned its inclusion
in subsequent parts, which he never completed. The method eventually appeared in an
edition of Carroll's *Nachlass* in 1977 [5]. There, it is described as follows:

> Its essential feature is that it involves a *Reductio ad Absurdum*. That is, we begin by
> assuming, *argumenti gratia*, that the aggregate of the Retinends (which we wish to
> prove to be a *Nullity*) is an *Entity*: from this assumption we deduce a certain result:
> this result we show to be *absurd*: and hence we infer that our original assumption
> was *false*, i.e. that the aggregate of the Retinends is a *Nullity*. [5, p. 280]

This procedure was used to solve Sorites problems involving a high number of
premises. Such complex problems played an essential role in the shaping of early mathematical logic. Indeed, logicians engaged in a friendly contest to compare the merits
of their systems for the solution of such problems [15]. Venn precisely invented his
diagrams due to his dissatisfaction with earlier Eulerian schemes [18]. It is for the same
purpose that Carroll designed his method of Trees. Let us illustrate Carroll's method by
solving a problem involving seven premises, as shown in (Fig. 1). Here, x' stands for
non-x. To ease illustration, we dropped the existential import, as it does not bear on our
discussion. The purpose is to find what conclusion follows form this set of premises.

(1) There is no $h\,m\,k$.
(2) There is no $d'\,e'\,c'$.
(3) There is no $h\,k'\,a'$.
(4) There is no $b\,l\,h'$.
(5) There is no $c\,k\,m'$.
(6) There is no $h\,c'\,e$.
(7) There is no $b\,a\,k'$.

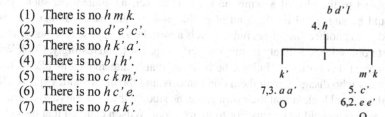

Fig. 1. Carroll's method of Trees [5, p. 292–295]

In the premises, b, d' and l are the terms that do not appear with opposite signs, their
aggregation forms the root of the tree. We postulate the existence of a 'Thing' that has
the attributes $b\,d'\,l$. Premise (4) states that whatever is $b\,l$ is necessarily h. Hence, our
'Thing' must also be h. We write h under the root. Premise (1) states that whatever is h
is necessarily $(m\,k)'$. Hence, it is either k' or $m'\,k$. Consequently, we place alternative
branches under h: one branch for k' and the other for $m'\,k$. Let us first consider the
branch k'. Premise (7) states that whatever is $b\,k'$ is necessarily a'. Hence, our 'Thing'
that has (so far) the attributes $b\,d'\,l\,h\,k'$ has also the attribute a'. However, Premise (3)
states that whatever is $h\,k'$ is necessarily a. Hence, our 'Thing', which already has the
attribute a', has also the attribute a. We place both a and a' under k' in the tree. Since
their coexistence is inconsistent, we place 'O' under $a\,a'$ to indicate the end of this first
branch. Let us, now, consider the other branch $m'\,k$. Premise (5) states that whatever is

$m'\,k$ is necessarily c'. We write c' under $m'\,k$ in the tree. Premise (6) states that whatever is $h\,c'$ is necessarily e'. Hence, our 'Thing' that has (so far) the attributes $b\,d'\,l\,h\,m'\,k\,c'$ has also the attribute e'. However, Premise (2) states that whatever is $d'\,c'$ is necessarily e. Hence, our 'Thing', which already has the attribute e', has also the attribute e. We place both e and e' under c' in the tree. Since their coexistence is inconsistent, we place 'O' under $e\,e'$ to indicate the end of this second branch. Since all branches of the tree have been shown to be lead to inconsistency, it follows that the root is forbidden. Hence, the conclusion of the argument is: "There is no $b\,d'\,l$".

3   Cook Wilson's Hanging Plants

Although hardly remembered today, Cook Wilson played in his time a key role in the British philosophical scene and had an important influence on subsequent Oxford philosophers [11]. He was the *Wykeham Professor of Logic* at the University of Oxford from 1889 to his death in 1915. His logical studies appeared posthumously in 1926 [7]. Cook Wilson's modern reputation as a logician is rather poor. Peter Geach even described him as an "execrably bad logician" [8, p. 123]. This disesteem seems to rest primarily on Cook Wilson's opposition to modern mathematical logic.

Indeed, Cook Wilson objected to the new logic and criticised its mathematical inspiration and dress. Given that it is the business of logic to study the (inference) methods of other sciences, "it is incredible that any particular scientific method, for example the mathematical, should be the method of logic itself" [7, p. 636]. Cook Wilson did not utterly object to the idea of a symbolic logic. However, he argued that such symbolism should be suggested by the kind of problems logicians tackle, rather than being imported from another discipline. Indeed, "it is a mistake to suppose that the symbolism adapted to one science is likely to suit another" [7, p. 640]. Interestingly, Cook Wilson did not stop at this criticism. Indeed, he believed that "mathematicians like to say the philosophers who disagree with them don't understand the mathematics" [7, p. xl]. To beat mathematical logicians at their own game, he studied their systems and constructed his own, which he held to be superior to theirs. Cook Wilson claimed that his calculus "solves with ease and simplicity all the problems attacked by the symbolic logicians whose calculus is in comparison very cumbrous" [7, p. xcv].

Carroll famously constructed devilish problems, which he circulated for opinion among his colleagues, including Cook Wilson. The two men exchanged on various topics in mathematics from the mid-1880s onwards [17]. In 1892, they engaged in a fierce dispute on hypotheticals, which expanded to a large controversy among British logicians [13]. In subsequent years, they challenged each other to solve complex problems of their invention [12]. Cook Wilson admitted that Carroll "was clever in the construction of difficult problems" [7, p. 638], but claimed that Carroll "was astonished [...] as he freely said, at the way in which [Cook Wilson] solved all such problems" [7, p. xcv].

Cook Wilson revealed one of his methods in a letter to Carroll on 3 November 1896:

"Your mention of a method of '*Trees*' makes me wonder whether you have really been using a quasi-graphic method, identical with one which I have used for years. I suppose 'Trees' have branches and this makes me curious.

I should rather have called my method a method of 'Hanging Plants' but my 'Hanging Plant' inverted becomes a "Tree"'. [6].

Cook Wilson apparently invented his method before being acquainted with Carroll's. In his (unpublished) letter, he sketched the construction of his 'hanging plants' and applied it to a problem (no 32), involving twelve premises, which Carroll had sent him [5, p. 403]. Three versions of his solution were included: a graph constructed upwards like a tree, another graph developed downwards like a hanging plant, and finally an alternative version of the hanging plant where the "connexion of premises [is] shown more fully" [6].

Cook Wilson's account reveals the key conventions of his method. Its principle is similar to Carroll's method of Trees. One sets an aggregate of attributes as the root of a graph and draws necessary inferences from the premises. When a necessary contradiction is reached, the root is denied. In this respect, Carroll and Cook Wilson's methods might be said to be the very same. However, their visualizations of this procedure differ. In the following, we present and comment on Cook Wilson's main conventions.

4   Conventions

The nodes of the graph are called 'Fruits'. Positive terms are encircled while negatives are squared, as shown in (Fig. 2). These devices, introduced to "aid the eye" [6], are superfluous since signs are already indicated on terms. Hence, these shapes do not play a non-redundant role in the graph. Contradictions are detected when a term is found once affirmed and once negated, i.e. once circled and once squared. As such, these shapes may be said to play some role in conveying the contradiction to the eye.

Fig. 2. Representation of the terms x (left) and x' (right).

It is unclear how the root ought to be represented. Alternative conventions are found in Cook Wilson's illustrations, as shown in (Fig. 3). One option consists in depicting terms (and their shapes) separately. Here, nothing formally distinguishes the root from the fruits. In a second option, the root's terms (and their shapes) are jointly enclosed. The third option consists in concatenating the terms and encircling them within a single shape. Here, the specificity of the root is stressed since it (alone) contains an aggregate of terms, whereas each 'Fruit' contains a single term.

Fig. 3. Alternative representations of the root $x\,y'$

Cook Wilson used arrows to depict inferences, as shown in (Fig. 4). One kind of arrows has an arrowhead directed to the fruit that is produced. We are told that the "arrowhead shows something necessary follows from what is above it (in conjunction with the root or some other necessary fruit)" [6]. For instance, a headed arrow from x to y simply expresses "x is y". Multiple (independent) headed arrows may leave or arrive at the same node. This form of branching is interpreted as a conjunction of inferences. Finally, when several terms jointly entail another, the separate arrows that leave the antecedent terms merge before reaching (with a single arrowhead) the consequent term.

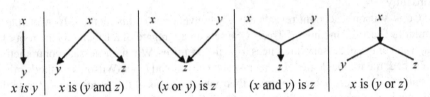

x	x	x y	x y	x
y	y z	z	z	y z
x *is* y	x is (y and z)	(x or y) is z	(x and y) is z	x is (y or z)

Fig. 4. Representation of inferences

A second kind of arrows, with no arrowheads, expresses alternatives. Suppose x necessarily entails either y or z. Here, one draws a headed arrow which points at a branch that terminates (with no arrowheads) at y one side and z on the other, as shown in (Fig. 4).

At this stage, some essential differences with Carroll's conventions appear. Indeed, Cook Wilson's system seems (more) visual and makes a use of arrows similar to that of contemporary argument graphs. Carroll rather adopted somewhat symbolic notations that dispense with most of the arrows. Inference itself is indicated by placing the consequent term under its antecedent. The only branching found in Carroll's is divergent, stands for alternatives, and resembles Cook Wilson's. Other kinds of branching are circumvented. On the one hand, (divergent) conjunctive branching is avoided by aggregating terms. For instance, if x is known to entail y and z, one places the aggregate y z under x. On the other hand, convergent branching is absent in Carroll's system. For instance, if it is known that, on different branches, terms x and y independently entail z, one would expand each branch separately and simply place one occurrence of z under x and another under y. If premises allow so, Cook Wilson would rather point his arrows at a single occurrence of z. Although each set of conventions has its merits and shortcomings, their dissimilarities produce important visual differences. In particular, Cook Wilson's graphs prove far 'bushier' than Carroll's are.

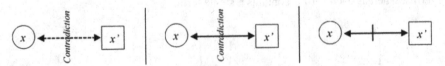

Fig. 5. Alternative representations of contradiction

When a contradiction is reached, namely a term and its opposite are affirmed, Cook Wilson connects those opposites with a double-headed arrow to express their contradiction. Three versions are found in Cook Wilson's illustrations, as shown in (Fig. 5). Although these variations are not essential, they attest to Cook Wilson's concern for the visualization of each step in his procedure.

5 Application

Let us illustrate John Cook Wilson's method by addressing the same problem we solved earlier with Carroll's trees. We obtain the hanging plant, shown in (Fig. 6). The procedure is quasi-similar to Carroll's, as one readily observes from the order in which terms appear and the contradictions that are reached. To aid conviction, we develop here the construction of the hanging plant.

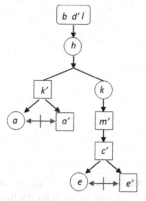

(1) There is no $h\,m\,k$.
(2) There is no $d'\,e'\,c'$.
(3) There is no $h\,k'\,a'$.
(4) There is no $b\,l\,h'$.
(5) There is no $c\,k\,m'$.
(6) There is no $h\,c'\,e$.
(7) There is no $b\,a\,k'$.

Fig. 6. Cook Wilson's Hanging Plant (our solution).

Again, we place $b\,d'\,l$ at the root. Premise (4) states that whatever is $b\,l$ is necessarily h. Hence, our root $b\,d'\,l$ is h. We draw a headed arrow from the root to a circled fruit h. To accommodate further premises, we divide by dichotomy h into alternative branches k and k'. Let us first consider the branch k'. Premise (7) states that whatever is $b\,k'$ is necessarily a'. Since b and k' are necessary fruits (in this branch), they entail a'. We draw an arrow from k' to a squared a'. Premise (3) states that whatever is $h\,k'$ is necessarily a. Since h and k' are necessary fruits (in this branch), they entail a. We draw an arrow from k' to a circled a. Here, we have a and a' as necessary fruits. We draw a double-headed arrow between them to mark their contradiction and end this branch. Now, we consider the other branch k. Premise (1) states that whatever is $h\,k$ is necessarily m'. We draw an arrow from k to a squared fruit m'. Premise (5) states that whatever is $k\,m'$ is necessarily c'. Since k and m' are necessary fruits (in this branch), they entail c'. We draw an arrow from m' to a squared c'. Premise (6) states that whatever is $h\,c'$ is necessarily e'. Since h and c' are necessary fruits (in this branch), they entail e'. We draw an arrow from c' to a squared e'. Premise (2) states that whatever is $d'\,c'$ is necessarily e. Since d' and c' are necessary fruits (in this branch), they entail e. We draw an arrow from

c' to a circled e. Here, we have e and e' as necessary fruits. We draw a double-headed arrow between them to mark their contradiction and end this second branch. Since all alternative branches of the plant have been shown to be lead to inconsistency, it follows that the root is forbidden. Hence, the conclusion of the argument is: "There is no $b\,d'\,l$".

The main difference between Carroll and Cook Wilson concerns the treatment of disjunctive branching, as shown in the portions of graphs in (Fig. 7). Here, Premise (1) asserts that h is $(m\,k)'$. Thus, h is either $m\,k'$ or $m'\,k'$ or $m'\,k$. Carroll commonly used a binary branching. Here, $m\,k'$ and $m'\,k'$ are merged to form k' on one side while the compound term $m\,k'$ occupies the other side. Cook Wilson's conventions do not *a priori* forbid expressing the disjunction of three terms. However, the fruits in his graphs do not seem to contain compound terms. Hence, Cook Wilson first divides h by dichotomy into k or k', then explores each branch separately. Here, Premise (1) asserts that No $h\,k$ is necessarily m', hence, it is possible to derive m' as a necessary fruit in this branch. From this point, Carroll and Cook Wilson's methods proceed similarly again.

Carroll's *Tree*   Cook Wilson's *Hanging Plant*

Fig. 7. Disjunctive branching

A look at the graphs suggests another key difference. Indeed, Carroll kept a trace of the premises used at each step whereas Cook Wilson did not. This absence is aggravated by the partial depiction of inferences. Consider the derivation of m' in the plant. Premise (1) states that h and k jointly entail m'. Thus, we ought to draw convergent arrows that leave h and k, merge and reach m' with an arrowhead, as shown in (Fig. 8-a). However, Cook Wilson does not require this complete scheme. It suffices, indeed, to connect m' to one of its antecedents, here k, in such a way as to express its necessity. In this example, m' could not be connected to h alone since the necessity of m' holds only within the k branch of the alternative. Let us now consider the derivation of c'. Premise (5) states that k and m' jointly entail c', as shown in (Fig. 8-b). However, Cook Wilson merely demands

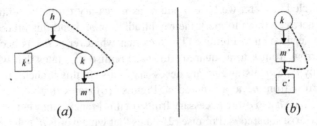

(a)   (b)

Fig. 8. (Complete) representation of inferences

an arrow that connects c' to either k or m'. Indeed, the aim of the procedure is to derive the fruits until contradiction is found. Keeping trace of the construction is not required by the search itself, although it is helpful to revise or communicate the graph. It should also be reminded that, unlike Carroll's Trees, Cook Wilson's plants do not demand that every branch is ended. It suffices to establish the necessity of a contradiction, e.g. a necessary contradiction in each side of an alternative, if any.

Carroll did not depict full inferences either, since terms are placed under their predecessors without reference to those that entailed them. Yet, it is easy to reconstruct each step of the procedure. It is also possible to draw Hanging Plants displaying full inferences but that would needlessly increase their bushiness, and thus, their inconveniency.

Let us conclude with a trivial difference between Trees and Hanging Plants. Both graphs grow head-downwards but only Cook Wilson's appellation is suggestive of this direction. Carroll justified the use of 'Trees' by the practice of genealogy writers: "A *Genealogical* "Tree" *always* grows *downwards*: then why may not a *Logical* "Tree" do likewise?" [5, p. 281]. Yet, there is more to this difference of naming. Indeed, Carroll's graphs have a 'trunk' because he places new terms under their antecedents and abstains from introducing branches whenever possible. Contrariwise, Cook Wilson's plants frequently require branching, possibly even at the root. This feature, regardless of their direction, also makes Cook Wilson's graphs closer to hanging plants than to trees[1].

References

1. Abeles, F.F.: Lewis Carroll's method of trees: its origins in *Studies in Logic*. Mod. Logic **1**(1), 25–35 (1990)
2. Abeles, F.F.: Toward a visual proof system: Lewis Carroll's method of trees. Log. Univers. **6**(3–4), 521–534 (2012)
3. Anellis, I.: From semantic tableaux to Smullyan trees: a history of the development of the falsifiability tree method. Mod. Logic **1**(1), 36–69 (1990)
4. Beisecker, D.: Regions of force: Peirce, Frege, Carroll, and bilateral proof trees. Logique et Anal. (N.S.) **251**, 317–340 (2020)
5. Bartley, W.W., III.: Lewis Carroll's Symbolic Logic. Clarkson N Potter, New York (1986)
6. Cook Wilson, J.: Letter to Charles L. Dodgson. Cook Wilson Papers, Bodleian Library, University of Oxford, The Wilson – Dodgson Box, 3 November 1896, pp. 57–58 (1896)
7. Cook Wilson, J.: Statement and Inference, vol. 2. Clarendon Press, Oxford (1926)
8. Geach, P.T.: Review of Lewis Carroll's symbolic logic. Philosophy **53**, 123–125 (1978)
9. Hacking, I.: Trees of logic, trees of Porphyry. In: Heilbron, J.L. (ed.) Advancements of Learning, pp. 221–263. L. S. Olschki, Florence (2007)
10. Ladd-Franklin, C.: On the algebra of logic. In: Peirce, C.S. (ed.) Studies in Logic, pp. 17–71. Little, Brown, and Company, Boston (1883)
11. Marion, M.: John Cook Wilson. In: Zalta, E.N. (ed.) The Stanford Encyclopedia of Philosophy (2010). <http://plato.stanford.edu/archives/spr2010/entries/wilson/>
12. Marion, M., Moktefi, M.: La logique symbolique en débat à Oxford à la fin du XIXe siècle : les disputes logiques de Lewis Carroll et John Cook Wilson. Revue d'Histoire des Sciences **67**(2), 185–205 (2014)
13. Moktefi, A.: Lewis Carroll and the British nineteenth-century logicians on the barber shop problem. Proc. Canadian Soc. Hist. Philos. Math. **20**, 189–199 (2007)

---

[1] The second author benefited from the support of the TalTech internal grant SSGF21021.

14. Moktefi, A.: Are other people's books difficult to read? The logic books in Lewis Carroll's private library. Acta Baltica Historiae et Philosophiae Scientiarum **5**(1), 28–49 (2017)
15. Moktefi, A.: The social shaping of modern logic. In: Gabbay, D., et al. (eds.) Natural Arguments: A Tribute to John Woods, pp. 503–520. College Publications, London (2019)
16. Moktefi, A.: Why make things simple when you can make them complicated? An appreciation of Lewis Carroll's symbolic logic. Log. Univers. **15**(3), 359–379 (2021)
17. Moktefi, A., Abeles, F.F.: The making of 'What the Tortoise said to Achilles': Lewis Carroll's logical investigations toward a workable theory of hypotheticals. The Carrollian **28**, 14–47 (2016)
18. Moktefi, A., Edwards, A.W.F.: One more class: Martin Gardner and logic diagrams. In: Burstein, M. (ed.) A Bouquet for the Gardener, pp. 160–174. LCSNA, New York (2011)
19. Simons, P.: Tree proofs for syllogistic. Stud. Logica. **48**(4), 539–554 (1989)
20. Wakeling, E.: Lewis Carroll's Diaries, vol. 9. The Lewis Carroll Society, Clifford (2005)
21. Wilson, R., Moktefi, A. (eds.): The Mathematical World of Charles L. Dodgson (Lewis Carroll). Oxford University Press, Oxford (2019)

Peirce's Complex Diagrams

Reetu Bhattacharjee[1]([✉]) and Amirouche Moktefi[2]

[1] Classe di Lettere e Filosofia (Faculty of Humanities), Scuola Normale Superiore, Pisa, Italy
reetu.bhattacharjee@sns.it
[2] Ragnar Nurkse Department of Innovation and Governance, Tallinn University of Technology, Tallinn, Estonia
amirouche.moktefi@taltech.ee

Abstract. It is known that early modern logic tackled complex problems involving a high number of terms. For the purpose, John Venn, and several of his followers, designed algorithms for the construction of complex logic diagrams. This task proved difficult because diagrams tend to lose their visual advantage beyond five or six terms. In this paper, we discuss Charles S. Peirce's work to overcome this difficulty. In particular, we reconstruct his algorithm for the purpose and compare it with those of his contemporaries Venn and Lewis Carroll.

Keywords: Peirce · Venn diagram · Carroll diagram · Complex diagrams

1 Introduction

Charles S. Peirce (1839–1914) made significant contributions to the tradition of Euler and Venn diagrams. Recently, Ahti-Veikko Pietarinen's [22] opened the way to several studies that explored Peirce's work in this area [3, 4, 23]. This paper is a contribution in this direction. It addresses Peirce's procedures for the construction of complex diagrams, a topic that is overlooked in both diagram and Peirce studies.

The old syllogistic hardly needed such complex diagrams since the Syllogism has only three terms and complex arguments, known as Sorites, were commonly treated as a series of syllogisms. One of the merits of Boolean logic which developed in Peirce's time was precisely to expand the old doctrine. It aimed at notations and methods that would produce the conclusion that follows for an argument involving any number of terms [7]. This task occupied post-Boolean logicians who invented symbolic, diagrammatic and even mechanical methods for the purpose together with sets of complex problems to test these methods. On the one hand, the supporters of the new logic engaged in a friendly contest to compare the merits and shortcomings of their solutions. On the other hand, they challenged the opponents of the new logic to solve such problems with the old

The first author benefited from the support of the research grant "Quod erat videndum: heuristic, logical and cognitive aspects of diagrams in mathematical reasoning" as part of the research project MIUR – "Departments of Excellence", call 2017 - Faculty of Humanities at Scuola Normale Superiore. The second author benefited from the support of the TalTech internal grant SSGF21021.

V. Giardino et al. (Eds.): Diagrams 2022, LNAI 13462, pp. 347–355, 2022.
https://doi.org/10.1007/978-3-031-15146-0_30

methods [13]. The solution of such complex problems was regarded as both the business of the new logic and the justification of its mathematical dress [17].

It was precisely for tackling such complex elimination problems that John Venn designed his diagrams. In the following, we first sketch Venn's procedure to adapt his diagrams when the number of terms increases. Then, we address Peirce's own algorithms to construct complex diagrams. Finally, we compare Peirce's method with those of Venn and Lewis Carroll to assess its merits and shortcomings.

2 Venn's Diagrams for n Terms

Unlike earlier Eulerian diagrams, Venn's method consists in two steps: first, one draws a 'primary diagram' that represents the possible subclasses of a term. Then, cells are marked to express actual knowledge about those subclasses. For a number of terms n, Venn's primary diagram consists of 2^n compartments exhibiting all the combinations between those terms. For $n = 1$, Venn uses a circle whose interior stands for the affirmation of the term. For additional terms, it suffices to add closed figures, "subject to the one condition that each is to intersect once and once only all the existing subdivisions produced by those which had gone before" [24, p. 8]. For $n > 3$, Venn suggested an inductive algorithm to draw continuous diagrams, with "comb-like" shapes [25, p. 118, 6]. This method produces the diagrams shown in (Fig. 1).

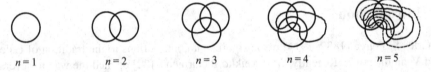

$n = 1$ $n = 2$ $n = 3$ $n = 4$ $n = 5$

Fig. 1. Venn diagrams constructed with the inductive method

However, when $n > 3$, Venn was unhappy with these schemes. Indeed, he preferred the use of "only symmetrical figures, such as should not merely be an aid to the sense of sight, but should also be to some extent elegant in themselves" [24, p. 8]. Consequently, he designed alternative diagrams, shown in (Fig. 2).

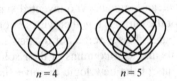

$n = 4$ $n = 5$

Fig. 2. Venn diagrams for four and five terms

For four terms, Venn simply made four ellipses intersect in such a way as to obtain "the simplest and neatest figure" that would exhibit desired subdivisions [24, p. 7]. Finally, for five terms, he introduced an annulus that stood for the fifth term, and hence broke its negative into two disjoint areas: the outer region and the inside ellipse. Venn admitted this shortcoming but argued that this diagram remains superior to alternative methods "to grapple effectively with five terms and the thirty-two possibilities which they yield" [24, p. 7][1].

For six terms, which is the highest number he addressed, Venn reluctantly suggested using two 5-term diagrams, one for the affirmation of the sixth term and the other for its negation. Venn reverted here the method that guided the construction of his previous figures. Indeed, hitherto, Venn added a curve for each term to divide into two all existing cells. This technique amounts to inserting a 1-term diagram for the nth term inside each cell of an $(n - 1)$-term diagram. However, for his sixth term, Venn did the opposite since he rather inserted the existing 5-term diagram in each cell of a 1-term diagram standing for the sixth term. Venn admitted that this scheme "to some extent loses the advantage of the *coup d'oeil* afforded by a single figure" [24, p. 8].

3 Peirce's Algorithm

Peirce was familiar with Venn's diagrams, which he regarded as an amended version of Eulerian diagrams. In his manuscript "On logical graphs" (1903)[2], he identified several limitations of Euler's diagrams and suggested amendments to overcome them [20]. Despite their shortcomings, Peirce praised Euler's diagrams in the form that includes both Venn's and Peirce's own amendments. He notably acknowledged their utility for the solution of complex problems:

> "Complicated questions of non-relative deductive reasoning are rare, it is true; still, they do occur, and if they are garbed in strange disguises, will now and then make the quickest minds hesitate or blunder. Euler's diagrams are the best aid in such cases, being natural, little subject to mistake, and everyway satisfactory. It is true that there is a certain difficulty in applying them to problems involving many terms; but it is an easy art to learn to break such problems up into manageable fragments." [20, p. 59]

In the design of his complex diagrams, Peirce applied this strategy of breaking up complex problems into 'manageable fragments'. Indeed, although he unhesitatingly adopted Venn's diagrams up to four terms, he rejected Venn's proposals for higher numbers. Instead, he suggested the following procedure of construction:

> "With more than four terms the system becomes cumbrous; yet, by having on hand lithographed blank forms showing the four-term figure on a large scale [...] all the compartments containing repetitions of one figure, whether that for one term, for two terms, for three or for four, and considering corresponding regions

---

[1] Hugh MacColl immediately contended that his algebraic methods were superior to Venn diagrams for such complex problems [10]. Venn strongly opposed MacColl's work. This hostility led MacColl to abandon his logical studies for over thirteen years [2].

[2] This manuscript (MS 479) is accessible on the Peirce Archive repository (https://rs.cms.hu-berlin.de/peircearchive/pages/search.php). In this paper, page numbers refer to the file titles.

of all sixteen of the large compartments to represent together the extension of one term, it is possible without much inconvenience to increase the number of terms to eight" [20, pp. 36–37].

Peirce did not produce diagrams to exemplify this procedure, except for one 8-term diagram. However, it is easy to provide illustrations of the missing diagrams. In each case, a large 4-term diagram stands for the first four terms. Then, a small diagram is inserted in each cell to represent the remaining terms. For five terms, the small diagram represents one term; for six, two; for seven, three. For eight terms, the small diagram is itself a 4-term diagram. Hence, we obtain the diagrams shown in (Fig. 3).

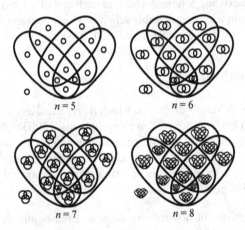

Fig. 3. Peirce's complex diagrams

Peirce's algorithm has several advantages. It is simple, ensures continuity between the figures and, importantly, requires little since it merely reproduces, within each cell, the already known expansion from 1- to 4-term diagrams. The trick consists in having a diagram in which each cell contains another diagram. This technique amounts to having a Venn diagram of Venn diagrams.

Evidently, these (discontinuous) schemes have limitations that are inevitable when the number of terms increases[3]. Peirce did not consider diagrams for more than eight terms. For the purpose, he rather suggested making "a list of the regions numbered in the dichotomous system of arithmetical notation, one numerical place being appropriated to each term" [20, pp. 36–37]. This technique is reminiscent of pre-Venn procedures, such as William S. Jevons' *Logical alphabet* [8].

4   Peirce's Alternative Diagram

To solve complex problems, Peirce acknowledged the merits of algebraic methods for those who have acquired sufficient expertise and practice. Yet, he did not discourage

---

[3] Interestingly, Peirce also knew Venn's inductive method to construct continuous complex diagrams [6, p. 31]. Yet, he preferred to proceed with discontinuous figures.

the usage of diagrams. We are rather reminded that "the diagrams are always ready." [20, p. 60]. To illustrate their applicability, Peirce provided a diagrammatic solution to a problem which he held to be "more complicated than anybody is likely to meet with in a long life, elsewhere than in a logic-book" [20, p. 60]. This problem was first published by his former student Christine Ladd-Franklin:

> "Six children, a, b, c, d, e, f, are required to obey the following rules: (1) on Monday and Tuesday no four can go out together; (2) on Thursday, Friday, and Saturday, no three can stay in together; (3) on Tuesday, Wednesday and Saturday, if b and c are together, then a, b, e, and f must remain together; (4) on Monday and Saturday b cannot go out unless either d, or c, e, and f stay at home. b and f are first to decide what they will do, and c makes his decision before a, d or e. Find (α) when c must go out, (β) when he must stay in, and (γ) when he can do as he pleases" [9, p. 58].

Peirce treats each day separately by considering what the rules tell us on those children's constraints on that day. Hence, each day involves six terms which are the courses of events in which those children a, b, c, d, e, f stay at home, respectively. For instance, the term a indicates that the child a is inside the house while not-a rather designates the circumstances in which the child a is outside. Since six terms are involved in the argument, Peirce makes use of a 6-term diagram for each day. Surprisingly, however, Peirce did not employ the 6-term scheme which he designed with his algorithm, namely a 4-term diagram with a 2-term diagram in each cell. Peirce rather preferred the use of an alternative diagram made of a 3-term diagram containing another 3-term diagram in each cell, as shown in (Fig. 4).

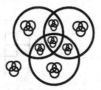

Fig. 4. Peirce's alternative 6-term diagram

The construction of this alternative diagram resembles that of the previous diagrams. Indeed, it also consists in inserting a small m-term diagram in a $(6-m)$-term large diagram. The difference merely pertains to the distribution of the terms, indicated by the value of m. Previously, Peirce held $m = 2$, while, in this alternative scheme, $m = 3$.

Peirce did not justify this change. He simply proceeds with the new diagram and solves the problem at hand. In brief, he selects for each day the rules that apply on it. Then, he marks the cells that are forbidden by those rules. For instance, we are told that on Monday "no four can go out together". Accordingly, Peirce marked all the cells that are outside at least four terms in the diagram of that day. After reporting all the data, Peirce reads what each diagram tells on each child's presence in the house. Peirce's final answer is not important for our purpose since we are merely concerned with the construction of his diagrams. Yet, we observe that his answer coincides with those of Ladd-Franklin's algebraic method [9, p. 61].

Although Peirce did not state what motivated the usage of this alternative 6-term diagram, it is interesting to note the resemblance between it and Peirce's 8-term diagram. Indeed, these are the only complex diagrams, for more than four terms, found in Peirce's manuscript. Both are constructed with similar-looking Venn diagrams. For a number of terms n, a small $(n/2)$-term diagram is inserted in each cell of a large $(n/2)$-term diagram. This common feature gives an elegant appearance to each diagram. Peirce did not indicate whether this feature reflects a general method of construction. If it is so, one needs to keep in mind that such a procedure has a limited scope of application since it does not apply to diagrams involving an odd number of terms.

5   Comparison with Venn and Carroll

Peirce was not alone in his attempt to construct adequate complex diagrams. Indeed, the publication of Venn diagrams in 1880 opened the way to several rival schemes that aimed at overcoming Venn's difficulties when the number of terms increased [19]. Early candidates included Allan Marquand's tables [14] and Alexander Macfarlane's stripes [11]. Both readily abandoned continuous figures to ensure the regularity of their diagrams [18]. Later, Carroll offered a new method of construction for up to ten terms [5]. Carroll's complex diagrams are commonly regarded to be superior to Venn's [12, 27, p. 197].

Carroll used simple figures for up to four terms. His diagrams resemble Venn's but include an outside square that encloses the logical universe. This square is dichotomously divided to tackle successive terms, up to $n = 4$, as shown in (Fig. 5).

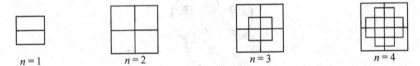

$n = 1$ $n = 2$ $n = 3$ $n = 4$

Fig. 5. Carroll diagrams for one, two, three and four terms

To construct 5-, 6-, 7- and 8-term diagrams, Carroll simply inserts a small 1-, 2-, 3- and 4-term diagram, respectively, in each cell of a large 4-term diagram, as shown in (Fig. 6)[4]. Carroll did not illustrate diagrams for more than eight terms but he suggested a method for their construction[5].

---

[4] Like Venn, Carroll constructed continuous 5-term diagrams [26, p. 434]. Yet, he also eventually preferred a discontinuous figure. It is unclear why his published version has a diagonal line in each cell of a 4-term diagram. This orientation does not match with subsequent figures. In a private leaflet, Carroll rather used a horizontal line [1, p. 58].

[5] For 9 terms, Carroll places two 8-term diagrams next to each other, one for the ninth term and the other for its negative. This amounts to inserting an 8-term diagram in each cell of a 1-term diagram. For ten terms, he suggested inserting an 8-term diagram in each cell of a 2-term diagram. Carroll stops at ten but this plan evidently can be pursued [12].

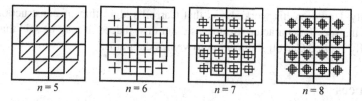

Fig. 6. Carroll diagrams for five, six, seven and eight terms

It is interesting to compare the methods of Venn, Carroll and Peirce for the construction of complex diagrams. In (Table 1), their procedures (for $n > 4$) are summarized for convenience. Up to four terms, Carroll and Peirce followed Venn's technique of adding a curve to represent the last term. All three abandoned continuous figures at five terms but Carroll and Peirce's approach differ from Venn's. Indeed, the latter represented the fifth term with a single figure while the formers 'dispersed' it within the sixteen cells of a 4-term diagram. For six terms, all three logicians adopted 'fragmented' diagrams, with varying repartitions of terms. Peirce notably offered two possible configurations. Venn does not go beyond six terms. Carroll and Peirce continue up to eight terms with similar algorithms but Carroll alone continues up to ten terms.

Table 1. Summary of the methods ($a \times b$ indicates an a-term diagram of b-term diagrams)

n	Venn (1880)	Carroll (1897)	Peirce (1903)	Peirce's alternative (1903)
5	4×1	4×1	4×1	
6	1×5	4×2	4×2	3×3
7		4×3	4×3	
8		4×4	4×4	4×4
9		1×8		
10		2×8		

This appraisal shows that Peirce shared his predecessors' preference for regular (albeit discontinuous) diagrams to ease manipulation. In this respect, his alternative diagrams, which make use of similar-looking figures, can be regarded as a shift in this direction. Although he adopted Venn's schemes for up to four terms, Peirce departed from Venn in his treatment of higher numbers of terms. He rather independently developed an original algorithm that proves similar to Carroll's[6]. As such, Peirce cannot make claims

---

[6] It is unclear the extent to which these logicians knew each other's work. Carroll referred to Venn in his late writings but there is no evidence that the latter influenced the early development of Carroll's diagrams [16]. Peirce certainly knew Venn's (early) writings but there is no evidence that he knew Carroll's. His only mention of it is a handwritten note on Carroll's barbershop paradox [21, p. 650] (see [15]).

for priority. However, his work shows that Carroll's algorithm of construction is not rooted in the specific characteristics of his diagrams. Indeed, it may be said that Peirce has equally applied Carroll's algorithm to Venn's diagrams.

References

1. Abeles, F.F. (ed.): The Logic Pamphlets of Charles Lutwidge Dodgson and Related Pieces. LCSNA, New York (2010)
2. Abeles, F.F., Moktefi, A.: Hugh MacColl and Lewis Carroll: crosscurrents in geometry and logic. Philosophia Scientiae **15**(1), 55–76 (2011)
3. Bhattacharjee, R., Moktefi, A.: Peirce's inclusion diagrams, with application to syllogisms. In: Pietarinen, A.-V., Chapman, P., Bosveld-de Smet, L., Giardino, V., Corter, J., Linker, S. (eds.) Diagrams 2020. Lecture Notes in Computer Science (Lecture Notes in Artificial Intelligence), vol. 12169, pp. 530–533. Springer, Cham (2020). https://doi.org/10.1007/978-3-030-54249-8_50
4. Bhattacharjee, R., Moktefi, A.: Revisiting Peirce's rules of transformation for Euler-Venn diagrams. In: Basu, A., Stapleton, G., Linker, S., Legg, C., Manalo, E., Viana, P. (eds.) Diagrams 2021. LNCS (LNAI), vol. 12909, pp. 166–182. Springer, Cham (2021). https://doi.org/10.1007/978-3-030-86062-2_14
5. Carroll, L.: Symbolic Logic. Macmillan, London (1897)
6. Edwards, A.W.F.: Cogwheels of the Mind: The Story of Venn Diagrams. Johns Hopkins University Press, Baltimore (2004)
7. Green, J.: The problem of elimination in the algebra of logic. In: Drucker, T. (ed.) Perspectives in the History of Mathematical Logic, pp. 1–9. Birkhäuser, Basel (1991)
8. Jevons, W.S.: The Principles of Science, 3rd edn. Macmillan, London (1879)
9. Ladd-Franklin, C.: On the algebra of logic. In: Peirce, C.S. (eds.) Studies in Logic, pp. 17–71. Little, Brown, and Company, Boston (1883)
10. MacColl, H.: On the diagrammatic and mechanical representation of propositions and reasonings. Phil. Mag. **10**, 168–171 (1880)
11. Macfarlane, A.: The logical spectrum. Phil. Mag. **19**, 286–290 (1885)
12. Macula, A.J.: Lewis Carroll and the enumeration of minimal covers. Math. Mag. **68**(4), 269–274 (1995)
13. Marion, M., Moktefi, M.: La logique symbolique en débat à Oxford à la fin du XIXe siècle : les disputes logiques de Lewis Carroll et John Cook Wilson. Revue d'Histoire des Sciences **67**(2), 185–205 (2014)
14. Marquand, A.: Logical diagrams for n terms. Phil. Mag. **12**, 266–270 (1881)
15. Moktefi, A.: Lewis Carroll and the British nineteenth-century logicians on the barber shop problem. Proc. Canadian Soc. Hist. Philos. Math. **20**, 189–199 (2007)
16. Moktefi, A.: Are other people's books difficult to read? The logic books in Lewis Carroll's private library. Acta Baltica Historiae et Philosophiae Scientiarum **5**(1), 28–49 (2017)
17. Moktefi, A.: The social shaping of modern logic. In: Gabbay, D., et al. (eds.) Natural Arguments: A Tribute to John Woods, pp. 503–520. College Publications, London (2019)
18. Moktefi, A., Bellucci, F., Pietarinen, A.-V.: Continuity, connectivity and regularity in spatial diagrams for N terms. In: Burton, J., Choudhury, L. (eds.) DLAC 2013: Diagrams, Logic and Cognition, vol. 1132, pp. 31–35. CEUR Workshop Proceedings (2014)
19. Moktefi, A., Edwards, A.W.F.: One more class: Martin Gardner and logic diagrams. In: Burstein, M. (ed.) A Bouquet for the Gardener, pp. 160–174. LCSNA, New York (2011)
20. Peirce, C.S.: On logical graphs. Houghton Library, Harvard University, MS 479 (1903). Peirce Archive: https://rs.cms.hu-berlin.de/peircearchive/

21. Peirce, C.S.: Logic of the Future, vol. 1. De Gruyter, Berlin (2020)
22. Pietarinen, A.-V.: Extensions of Euler diagrams in Peirce's four manuscripts on logical graphs. In: Jamnik, M., Uesaka, Y., Elzer Schwartz, S. (eds.) Diagrams 2016. Lecture Notes in Computer Science (Lecture Notes in Artificial Intelligence), vol. 9781, pp. 139–154. Springer, Cham (2016). https://doi.org/10.1007/978-3-319-42333-3_11
23. Sautter, F.T., Mendonça, B.R.: Validity as choiceless unification. In: Basu, A., Stapleton, G., Linker, S., Legg, C., Manalo, E., Viana, P. (eds.) Diagrams 2021. LNCS (LNAI), vol. 12909, pp. 204–211. Springer, Cham (2021). https://doi.org/10.1007/978-3-030-86062-2_18
24. Venn, J.: On the diagrammatic and mechanical representation of propositions and reasonings. Phil. Mag. **10**, 1–18 (1880)
25. Venn, J.: Symbolic Logic, 2nd edn. Macmillan, London (1894)
26. Wakeling, E.: Lewis Carroll's Diaries, vol. 8. The Lewis Carroll Society, Clifford (2004)
27. Wilson, R., Moktefi, A. (eds.): The Mathematical World of Charles L. Dodgson (Lewis Carroll). Oxford University Press, Oxford (2019)

Posters

How to Build and Convert Complex Propositions in the Marlo Diagram

Marcos Bautista López Aznar(✉) (iD)

Logic, Language and Information Research Group (HUM 609), Huelva University, Huelva,
Spain
marlodiagram@gmail.com

Abstract. Marlo diagrams are a novel method of representing logical propositions
that the author has used successfully with hundreds of high school students for
instructional purposes. The examples of construction and conversion of complex
diagrams that we offer in this work have a double objective: on the one hand,
we hope that the reader becomes familiar with our notation, which, due to its
novelty, is complex for those not initiated in our diagrams. On the other hand, we
want to illustrate how our graphic conversions are articulated with those of natural
language, always preserving the conclusions that follow from the premises.

Keywords: Logic diagrams · Quantification of predicate · First order logic

1 How to Build and Convert Complex Propositions in the Marlo Diagram

Marlo diagrams [1, 2] are a renewed and improved version of the Doctrine of the Quantification of the Predicate which, although abandoned due to its limitations at the time, also allowed Charles Stanhope and William Stanley Jevons to build the first logic machines in history [6]. Following this doctrine, we can represent both the classical propositions of the syllogism and any other proposition of first-order logic in the following way: the total-partial association of the possible combinations of one variable with another. For example, A → B, means that: *toto A = at least part of B*. You should keep in mind that when we say that *All Londoners are English,* we mean that at least "part" of the English are equal to "all" Londoners. So, we just need to remember now that in our notation we add a subscript x to express that all possible combinations of a variable (a) are of a single type (b). However, the associated variables without subscript x must be considered in a particular way. Then, $a_x b$ means *toto A = part B*, that is, A → B. If we want to represent the proposition *No A is B* or A → ¬B, then we will write $b_x ¬a$: *toto A = part ¬B*. For example, if we say that *No vegetarians eat meat*, we say that *Part of the people who do not eat meat is equal to all vegetarians.* And at the same time, we affirm that *All people who eat meat are part of the people who are not vegetarian* (remember that *part* means at least part). The disjunction A ∨ B means *toto ¬B = part A*. At this point, we recommend the reader visit the web version of Marlo's diagram [7],

V. Giardino et al. (Eds.): Diagrams 2022, LNAI 13462, pp. 359–363, 2022.
https://doi.org/10.1007/978-3-031-15146-0_31

read the instructions, run classic inference examples, and solve the proposed exercises starting from number one. This will make it easier to understand how these diagrams work. Figure 1 shows how to convert and transform the model of *No vegetarians eat meat*. Recall that when converting we only change the order of the variables while when transforming we permute the subscript x between the variables and, at the same time, we change the quality of the variables.

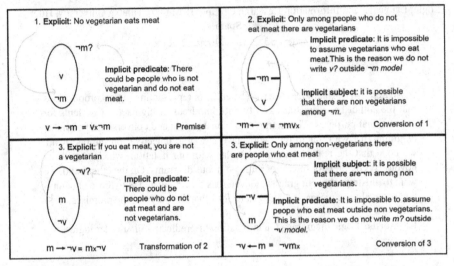

Fig. 1. Four equivalent models for the conditional proposition $V \rightarrow \neg M$.

We always place the letter that represents the subject of the propositions in the center of the models. If this subject is universal, we do not divide the model. But if the subject is particular, then we divide the model. Therefore, in model 1 of Fig. 1 we observe that *All v are ¬m*. However, in model 2 of Fig. 1 we observe that part of the people who do not eat meat are vegetarians, but the possibility of not eating meat without being a vegetarian is also represented in the upper region of $\neg m$, which is not determined nor as v or $\neg v$. On the other hand, when the letter that represents the predicate is taken universally, it is only located within the model of the subject. But if only part of the predicate is associated with the subject, then this predicate must also be placed outside the subject model with a question mark. For example, in model 1 in Fig. 1, $\neg m$ is also placed outside v because the proposition *No vegetarian eats meat* still allows us to assume that it is possible not to eat meat and not to be a vegetarian ($\neg m?$). Remember that, just like in Venn diagrams, the exterior of any φ region in Marlo diagrams always represents $\neg \varphi$. Of course, we also apply the rule that any region of a model φ contains φ. For example, all subclasses of dogs are dogs. If we now look at model 2 in Fig. 1, we can see that the predicate v is not placed outside $\neg m$ *model* because it is impossible to think that there are vegetarians who eat meat. In this way, the only v that appears inside the $\neg m$ *model* now means that *toto v is ¬m*. No other kind of v is possible. And if we have understood how to build simple propositions, we can try to move on to the construction and conversion of more complex diagrams by considering the toto-partial relations that the premises establish between its variables (see Fig. 2).

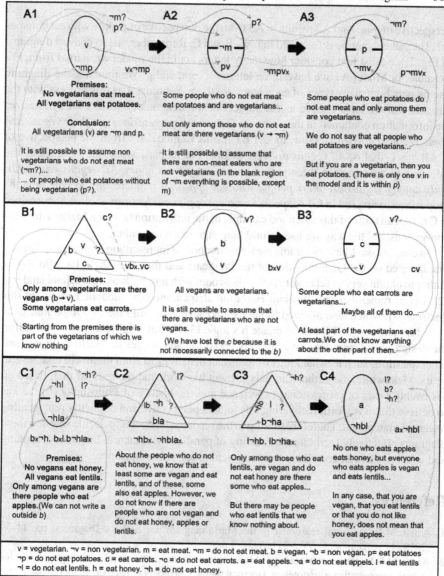

Fig. 2. Examples of conversion of complex models in Marlo diagram.

Now, you must remember that letters that occupy the same region of a model or that are written together and at the same level outside the model are necessarily associated. On the contrary, letters that are placed in different regions within a model or at different levels outside the model are not necessarily associated, although they are potentially combinable. In the first row of diagrams of Fig. 2, starting from the premises *No vegetarians eat meat* and *All vegetarians eat potatoes*, we reach the same conclusions from different perspectives (we will not explain again here the inference processes that allow us to synthesize all the information in A1[1]). Model A1 results in model A2 from the perspective of ¬*m*. And A2 results in A3 from the perspective of people who eat potatoes (*p*). The same dynamic is followed in rows B and C. Remember that to convert diagrams in Fig. 2, we must first consider how many letters are in the model we started from. For example, in Model A1 we have three letters: *v*, ¬*m*, and *p*. We then ask the diagram, one by one, how many types of each letter are there. We must start this process with the variable that we have chosen as the subject of the new model. Model B1 synthesizes the information contained in the premises *Only among vegetarians are there vegans* and *Some vegans eat carrots*. Now, model B1 results in model B2 from the perspective of *b*. All *b* is *v*, that is, *all vegans are vegetarians*. For its part, Model C1 synthesizes the information contained in three premises: *No vegans eat honey. All vegans eat lentils. Only among vegans are there people who eat apples*. It is interesting to note how the proposition expressed in C4 *All people who eat apples eat lentils* was already contained in C1. We can think of this as a good example of the integration between Marlo's diagram conversions and the way we use natural language when reasoning.

In conclusion: Marlo diagrams are a new method of representing logical propositions that is based on the Quantification of the Predicate and that since 2014 has allowed its author to obtain very good results in the classroom with hundreds of high school students [2]. Let us remember that William Hamilton also claimed the didactic benefits of this doctrine [4], which also allowed Stanhope and Jevons to build the first logic machines in history and inspired Boole to create his logic [3–5]. But empirical studies are still in the design phase, and definitive answers about the advantages of Marlo diagrams and other questions such as what kinds of users can benefit most from them will take several years. Meanwhile, the author can only present his work and the reasons that, based on his twenty years of professional experience and the history of Philosophy [6], he has to believe that it is worth recovering this logical perspective and explicitly representing uncertain statements. Therefore, it is up to the reader at this point to decide whether these diagrams effectively facilitate the drawing of parallels with natural language reasoning and whether this can contribute to strengthening logical competence.

References

1. Aznar, M.B.L.: Visual reasoning in the Marlo diagram. In: SetVR@Diagrams, pp. 44–59 (2018). http://ceur-ws.org/Vol-2116/paper3.pdf
2. Aznar, M.B.L.: Diagramaslógicos de Marlo para el razonamiento visual y heterogéneo: válidos en lógica matemática y aristotélica. Doctoral thesis, University of Huelva, Spain (2020). http://hdl.handle.net/10272/19769
3. Boole, G.: An Investigation of the Laws of Thought. Dover, New York (1854)
4. Hamilton, W.: Lectures on Metaphysics and Logic, vol. 4. William Blackwood and Sons, Edinburg (1860)
5. Jevons, W.: Pure Logic or the Logic of Quality. Stanford, London (1864)
6. Mays, W., Henry, D.P.: Jevons and logic. Mind, n.s. 62, pp. 484–505 (1953)
7. Soler-Toscano, F., Aznar, M.B.L.: fersoler/MarloDiagrams (2022). https://fersoler.github.io/MarloDiagrams/. Accessed 16 June 2022

Perception of Node-Link Diagrams: The Effect of Layout on the Perception of Graph Properties

Elektra Kypridemou[1,2]([✉]) [iD], Michele Zito[1], and Marco Bertamini[2] [iD]

[1] Department of Computer Science, University of Liverpool, Liverpool, UK
{e.kypridemou,michele}@liverpool.ac.uk
[2] Visual Perception Lab, Department of Psychological Sciences,
University of Liverpool, Liverpool, UK
marcob@liverpool.ac.uk

Abstract. The way we choose to draw the networks on the plane (layout) is found to be important for the readability of networks by humans. In this study, we examine how different layouts affect our perception of specific properties of small networks of 16 nodes each. We compare a simple grid layout to the planar and force-directed layouts, which are some of the most well-established layout algorithms. We also introduce an alternative 'improved' grid layout, which optimizes the outcome layout in terms of specific aesthetics. When people had to decide whether a network is a tree given a node-link diagram, the layout significantly affected their performance. The same pattern appeared for the detection of the connectedness property. However, when people had to detect two properties at a time, the layout didn't affect their performance. The results show that the layout we choose for representing a network is crucial for our perception of some of the network's basic properties. However, when people had to detect more than one property at a time, the chosen layout didn't seem to significantly affect their performance.

Keywords: Graph drawing · Perception · Graph layout · Network visualization

1 Introduction

Node-link diagrams are commonly used to visually represent entities (nodes) and their relationships (links), also known as networks. They are widely used to visualize and communicate linked data. There is a great amount of graph drawing algorithms that generate such visual representations of graphs (also called layouts). These algorithms usually aim to optimize some visual characteristics (or 'aesthetics') of the drawing, that are found to affect the readability of the graph [1,2]. Previous empirical studies explored the perception of node-link diagrams in terms of their aesthetics, usability and readability [3]. The first study to investigate the effect of different layouts on the human perception of specific

© Springer Nature Switzerland AG 2022
V. Giardino et al. (Eds.): Diagrams 2022, LNAI 13462, pp. 364–367, 2022.
https://doi.org/10.1007/978-3-031-15146-0_32

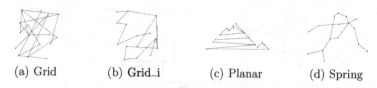

(a) Grid   (b) Grid_i   (c) Planar   (d) Spring

Fig. 1. The four layouts.

graph properties was published by Soni et al. [4]. They used graphs of order 100 for all the experiments, which resulted in stimuli that looked like clouds of lines and dots. Hence, their approach can not necessarily be generalised for the perception of other graph properties. Kypridemou et al. [5,6] explored the perception of graph properties in much smaller graphs of 16 nodes.

In this study, we further extend the previous work of Kypridemou et al. on graphs of the same size (16 nodes), using some common properties (connectedness, tree), as well as a new property that is expressed as a combination of two other properties. We compare a simple grid layout with well known planar and spring layouts. We also introduce an alternative 'improved' grid layout, which reduces the number of crossings while keeping most of the simplicity of the original grid layout. We use signal detection theory (SDT) [7] to analyse the d prime (d') and bias (c) dependent variables that will give us a better understanding of the sensitivity and the bias of participants' performance.

2   Method

The experiment consisted of three different tasks, which we call Treeness, Connectedness and Multi. For the Treeness task, participants had to detect whether the given graph was a tree or not. For the Connectedness task, participants had to decide whether the represented graph was connected or not. Finally, for the Multi task, participants had to decide whether the graph 'has at least one of the following features: a) a loop/cycle of length 3 *or* b) at least a node with degree higher than 4'.

All stimuli were drawings of planar simple graphs of 16 nodes each, which were visually represented as node-link diagrams using the following layouts: a random grid layout (Grid), an improved version of a grid layout (Grid_i), a planar layout (Planar), and a spring layout (Spring). Exemplar stimuli for each of the four layouts are provided in Fig. 1. A more extensive description of the specific algorithms and procedures used for drawing each of the layouts can be found in [8]. The resulting 200 drawings of each task were depicted as node-link diagrams of red dots of fixed size and black lines of fixed thickness (Fig. 1). Figure 2 shows the sequence events of a trial. In the study participated 16 participants (7 male, 9 female, 18 to 41 years old), with no prior knowledge on graphs.

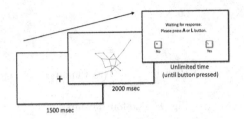

Fig. 2. Event sequence of one of the experiment's trials.

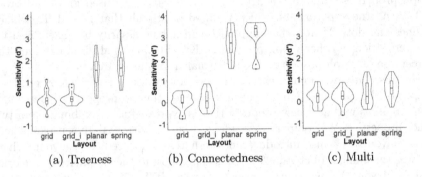

(a) Treeness   (b) Connectedness   (c) Multi

Fig. 3. Violin plots of sensitivity (d') per layout for each property.

3   Results and Discussion

The qualitative results about the specific strategies used in each task are described in [8]. The results of the SDT analysis are shown in Figs. 3 and 4. For the treeness property, there was a significant main effect of layout on the sensitivity ($F(3, 45) = 32.81; p < 0.001$) and the bias ($F(3, 45) = 7.18; p < 0.001$) metrics. Similarly, for the connectedness task, the layout was found to have a significant main effect on the sensitivity ($F(3, 45) = 191.64; p < 0.001$) and the bias ($F(3, 45) = 55.62; p < 0.001$) metrics. For the multi task, the layout was not found to have any significant main effect on the performance for the sensitivity metric ($F(3, 45) = 2.32; p > 0.05$), but there was a significant main effect of the layout on the bias metric ($F(3, 45) = 14.42; p < 0.001$). Additional statistical analyses are described in [8].

The results on the treeness and the connectedness properties are consistent with the previous findings of Kypridemou et al. [5] on the same tasks on graphs of the same size. This indicates that the findings are generalised from comparison tasks to detection tasks. Furthermore, the SDT framework of this study provided more in-depth understanding of the ability of the participants to detect the signals on the stimuli. The two versions of the grid layouts biased the participants towards identifying non-connected graphs as connected. This bias is probably because these two layouts tend to draw the two connected components of the non-target graphs as overlapping shapes, which makes the graphs look as connected.

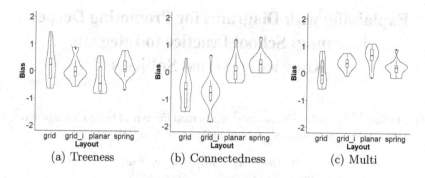

Fig. 4. Violin plots of bias per layout for each property.

The Multi task revealed some new findings, extending the previous study. The results show that the layout we choose for representing a network is crucial for our perception of some of the network's basic properties. However, when the task becomes harder and people have to detect more than one property at a time, the chosen layout doesn't seem to significantly affect performance.

There is a large variety of other graph properties to be explored in future work. The results of such studies could lead to better understanding as per which layouts are most appropriate for visualizing graphs, when the aim is for humans to be able to detect specific graph properties. Looking towards this direction, graph visualization will not be discussed as a one-solution-fits-all approach, but will rather be a more customized solution per case, given the task at hand.

References

1. Bennett, C., Ryall, J., Spalteholz, L., Gooch, A.: The aesthetics of graph visualization. Comput. Aesthet. **2007**, 57–64 (2007)
2. Purchase, H.: Which aesthetic has the greatest effect on human understanding? In: DiBattista, G. (ed.) GD 1997. Which aesthetic has the greatest effect on human understanding?, vol. 1353, pp. 248–261. Springer, Heidelberg (1997). https://doi.org/10.1007/3-540-63938-1_67
3. Yoghourdjian, V., et al.: Exploring the limits of complexity: a survey of empirical studies on graph visualisation. Vis. Inform. **2**(4), 264–282 (2018)
4. Soni, U., Lu, Y., Hansen, B., Purchase, H.C., Kobourov, S., Maciejewski, R.: The perception of graph properties in graph layouts. In: Computer Graphics Forum, vol. 37, pp. 169–181. Wiley Online Library (2018)
5. Kypridemou, E., Zito, M., Bertamini, M.: The effect of graph layout on the perception of graph properties. In: EuroVis (Short Papers), pp. 1–5 (2020)
6. Kypridemou, E., Zito, M., Bertamini, M.: The effect of graph layout on the perception of graph density: an empirical study. In: EuroVis (Short Papers) (2022)
7. Stanislaw, H., Todorov, N.: Calculation of signal detection theory measures. Behav. Res. Methods Instrum. Comput. **31**(1), 137–149 (1999)
8. Kypridemou, E., Bertamini, M., Zito, M.: Perception of node-link diagrams: the effect of layout on the perception of graph properties (2022). https://osf.io/4b5k7

Explaining with Diagrams for Promoting Deeper Learning: School Practice to Integrate Knowledge Across Subjects

Yuri Uesaka[1]([X]), Tsubasa Kurosawa[2], Kazumasa Furuya[2], Shigeru Yanagimoto[2], Mengshi Liu[1], Satomi Shiba[1], and Nao Uchida[1]

[1] The University of Tokyo, Tokyo, Japan
yuri.uesaka@ct.u-tokyo.ac.jp
[2] Saitama Prefectural Ina Junior High School, Saitama, Japan

Abstract. Diagrams are considered a powerful strategy for understanding and problem-solving. Self-explanation is believed to be behind the effectiveness of diagrams. However, it is not clear to what extent students engage in self-explanation. The possibility that students do not always engage in self-explanation is suggested by empirical studies showing that diagrams do not always produce efficacious outcomes. Ichikawa [1] also argued that it is unclear how students interpret diagrams and discussed the need to have students explain themselves using diagrams. In science learning, diagrams effectively help students learn the principles behind phenomena. Having students use diagrams to explain phenomena may help them understand the principles of the phenomena correctly and integrate their knowledge effectively across subject areas. Therefore, in this study, we developed lesson instructions in which students were required to explain the phenomenon using diagrams after the teacher had explained it. Students were also given the opportunity to solve the problem collaboratively after the explanation had been provided. The study involved 71 8th-grade students in one school. Fifty-eight same grade students from a traditional public school also participated in the study and served as the control group. A "basic knowledge test", which tested students' knowledge in a fill-in-the-blank format, and a "principle understanding test" and "transfer test," which tested students' knowledge in an explanation format, were administered. The results demonstrated no significant difference in the basic knowledge test, but the score in the principle understanding test and the transfer knowledge test was higher for the students who received the experimental instruction. This study indicates that deeper understanding is facilitated by combining the experience of using diagrams with peer explanation.

1 Introduction

While the traditional goal of education has focused on solving problems efficiently, recent changes in global educational goals have made it more essential to promote deeper learning among students. This "deeper learning" involves conceptual understanding and the transfer of learned knowledge in different contexts.

V. Giardino et al. (Eds.): Diagrams 2022, LNAI 13462, pp. 368–372, 2022.
https://doi.org/10.1007/978-3-031-15146-0_33

Diagrams may play an important function in achieving this goal. Diagrams have been considered a valuable strategy for problem-solving and suitable tools for communication. However, they may also be important as a tool to promote deeper understanding. In particular, diagrams may help in learning the principles behind phenomena in science learning (e.g., [2]). They may help students understand phenomena correctly and integrate knowledge effectively across subject areas.

As for the reason why diagrams contribute to promoting deeper learning, Ainsworth and Th Loizou [3] argued that diagrams facilitate self-explanation. However, some studies have shown that diagrams are not always effective (e.g., [4]), so not everyone spontaneously self-explains when using the diagrams taught. Ichikawa [1] also argued that it is unclear how students interpret diagrams and discusses the need for students to explain what they have learned using diagrams.

When considering how diagrams are used in the classroom, many teachers actively use them in instruction. However, the activity in which students themselves explain the principle with the use of diagrams is not always done sufficiently. For example, although teachers teach problem solving well with the use of diagrams in Japan, not much time is given to students for them to explain what they have learned using diagrams as teachers do, or to solve applied problems using diagrams. However, under these circumstances, students may not correctly understand the principles underpinning the phenomena. If teachers want to share the principles behind the phenomena with more students, they need to allow students to explain themselves with diagrams.

Based on the awareness of these issues, in this study, educational psychologists and teachers in school collaboratively designed and conducted a science class in which students got opportunities to explain the principle behind the phenomena they were learning with diagrams. The important point is that the teacher explains to students by using diagrams and ensures that the students themselves have the opportunity to explain using diagrams. We also examined the effect of the instruction compared to the traditional style of instruction in schools (i.e., this study is a practice-based research).

2 Outline of Practice Proposed in this Study

This practice was conducted at a public junior high school in the Kanto region of Japan. The class concerned a one-hour science class for 8th-grade students. The first instructional plan was written by the second and third authors, who are public school teachers, and it was later modified in discussions with other authors including psychologists.

There were two major topics to be covered in the class. One was "sea winds and land winds", and the other was "monsoons". A common principle can explain both. More specifically, due to the difference in specific heat between the ground and water, during relatively hot weather (daytime or summer), an updraft rises from the ground (land or content) and a downdraft is generated in the water (ocean), and that causes the wind to blow from the ocean to the land. On the other hand, during relatively cold periods (night time and winter), updrafts are generated in the water (ocean) and downdrafts are generated on the ground (land and continents), and that causes winds to blow from the land to the sea. Visual representation for understanding this was given.

Students with only a shallow understanding might memorize this content as a one-to-one correspondence, so that they just remember the facts of "sea breezes during the day" and "land breezes at night". They might also memorize that "the Japanese monsoon blows from the southwest in summer and from the northeast in winter". On the other hand, students with deeper understanding comprehend the principle behind the winds through strategies such as diagram use so that they can remember and reconstruct those wind movements from the principle and remember the contents for a longer time.

The explanations of the phenomena and the principle are usually included in the textbook, which is often accompanied by diagrams, and many teachers explain to students with the use of diagrams in class. However, as mentioned in the introduction, it is not sufficient for many students to simply listen to the explanations by a teacher. It might be necessary to give students opportunities to explain the principle and the phenomena by themselves with diagrams. Therefore, in this practice, activities were incorporated during which students explained the content to their peers with the use of diagrams. The content relating to seasonal winds is not only covered in the 8th-grade science class but also in social studies. For example, the monsoon in India is included in the 7th-grade social studies curriculum. However, it is thought that such deep understanding across subjects is not sufficiently covered in class. Therefore, activities that required consideration of the monsoon in other areas of the world, with diagram use, were also included in the class session as applied problem-solving.

The "thinking-after-instruction" approach proposed by Ichikawa [1] was used in these teaching methods. This teaching method consists of four stages: teacher's explanation, checking comprehension, deepening understanding, and reflection (Fig. 1). This framework was used to design the lesson. More specifically, the following flow of lessons was conducted. (1) The teacher explained the phenomena of sea wind and land wind, and the principle that explained the wind movement direction. (2) The students checked their understanding of "sea wind and land winds" with each other. Specifically, using diagrams, the students checked whether they could explain the phenomena and the principle behind them in their own words (see Fig. 1). (3) The teacher explained the phenomena and the principle of the Japanese monsoon. (4) The students checked their understanding of the Japanese monsoon with each other. Using diagrams, they checked whether they could explain the phenomena and the principle behind them in their own words. (5) Students worked in groups to think about the monsoons in Southeast Asia, India, and Africa. (6) Representative students were asked to explain the phenomena and the principle by taking on the role of TV newscasters. (7) As a reflection activity, the teacher asked the students to write on paper what they understood, what they still did not understand well, and what they wanted to know more about.

This study also took data from classes from a normal public school in Tokyo to obtain comparable control group data. Seventy-one students participated in the survey in the practicing school and 58 students in the base-line group. The teacher explained the phenomena and a principle in the classes, and the students were asked to solve the problems in class or at home. For the students in this "base-line group", the teacher explained the principle (as would be typical in most classrooms). There was no activity in which the students themselves explained the principle using diagrams. In addition, the importance of diagrams was not specifically mentioned, and the applied problem-solving was not included. To examine the effectiveness of this practice, a post-test was conducted 1 to 2 weeks after implementing the lesson.

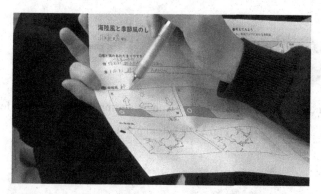

Fig. 1. A student explaining to other students using diagrams

3 Evaluation and Discussion

The post-test comprised three parts: the first part was a "basic knowledge test" which is fill-in-the-blank question; the second was a "principle understanding test" and the third was a "transfer test" that required descriptive answers. The first part was a question, in which students were asked to answer "sea wind" or "land wind" for daytime wind and night time wind. The second part had a question that asked students to explain the principle of why such differences in the wind occur according to the day/night time. The third part had a question requiring integrating the knowledge they learned in science and social study, in which students were asked to explain why the direction of the monsoon is different between Japan and India. The results are shown in Fig. 2. No difference was found in the "basic knowledge test". On the other hand, "principle understanding test" and "transfer test" scores were higher in the classes where the practice was implemented than in the control group. Detailed results are shown in Fig. 2.

This study conducted a practice incorporating a learning activity in which students themselves explained using diagrams. The results showed that the students' deeper understanding, such as explaining a principle, was promoted compared to the regular classes. The principle behind the phenomena was taught in both schools. In the control group, the teacher only used diagrams to explain. As a result, only some students who reached a deeper understanding on their own could explain the principle. On the other hand, in classes with practice developed in this study, many more students were able to explain the principle even though they were given only a few minutes to explain it using diagrams. In addition, the transfer test indicated that students got a comprehensive understanding across subjects. The present study was practice-based, and many areas have not been rigorously tested between the experimental and control groups. It is desirable to conduct a more detailed investigation of the effects of students' own explanations using diagrams in the future.

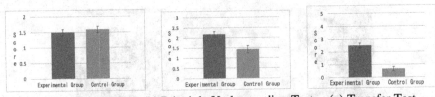

(a) Basic Knowledge Test (b) Principle Understanding Test   (c) Transfer Test

Fig. 2. Results of post-tests

References

1. Ichikawa, S.: Cognitive counseling to support Learning: A new intersection of psychology and education (1993)
2. Ainsworth, S., Prain, V., Tytler, R.: Drawing to learn in science. Science **26**, 1096–1097 (2011)
3. Ainsworth, S., Loizou, A.T.: The effects of self-explaining when learning with text or diagrams. Cogn. Sci. **27**(4), 669–681 (2003)
4. Van Essen, G., Hamaker, C.: Using self-generated drawings to solve arithmetic word problems. J. Educ. Res. **83**(6), 301–312 (1990)

Visually Analyzing Universal Quantifiers in Photograph Captions

Yuri Sato[1]([⊠]) [ID] and Koji Mineshima[2]

[1] The University of Tokyo, Tokyo, Japan
satoyuri0@g.ecc.u-tokyo.ac.jp
[2] Keio University, Tokyo, Japan
minesima@abelard.flet.keio.ac.jp

Abstract. Universal quantifiers have been the subject of much work in symbolic and diagrammatic logic. However, little attention is paid to the question of how they can be visually grounded, that is, depicted in real images such as photographs. To investigate this question, we focus on universal quantifiers such as "all" and "every" used in an image captioning dataset and present a qualitative analysis of these expressions. The analysis revealed that although the use of universal quantifiers in image captions is rare, there are interesting patterns in their usage in terms of the semantics of visual representations. We distinguish two ways in which universal quantifiers are used in image captions. One is *object-based quantification*, which involves quantification over multiple discrete objects in a definite domain. The other is *region-based quantification*, where some property is ascribed to a salient continuous region in an image. We compare these two ways of visually representing universal quantification with two major representation systems studied in diagrammatic logic.

Keywords: Visual representation · Universal quantifier · Photograph · Image caption · Grounding · Object · Region

1 Introduction

Universal quantifiers have been used as important tools and the subject of logical formalization. This is true not only for symbolic logic but also for diagrammatic logic [12] and spatial logic [1]. For example, Euler diagrams have been intensively studied as visual representations of logical statements [8,13]. However, while there are various ways to represent universal quantifiers in symbolic and diagrammatic systems, it is not fully clear how they can be depicted by real images such as photographs; less attention is paid to the question of how universal quantifiers can be *visually grounded*. The aim of this study is to address this question. Recently, photographs have been studied intensively in relation to machine learning techniques to automatically generate captions describing images, and large amounts of human-generated caption data have been collected in the Vision and Language research [3,4]. It was often claimed that logical

© Springer Nature Switzerland AG 2022
V. Giardino et al. (Eds.): Diagrams 2022, LNAI 13462, pp. 373–377, 2022.
https://doi.org/10.1007/978-3-031-15146-0_34

expressions such as universal quantifiers are rarely found among textual captions for images [14]. To our knowledge, however, little is known about what relationship holds between logical expressions and images.

We collect caption data of universal quantifiers and analyze what pattern exists in the type of photographs that ordinary people give sentences containing universal quantifiers (cf. [7]). This study is a sequel to [9–11], whose overall goal is to understand the visual grounding of logical concepts and the spectrum of symbolic and visual representations, thereby seeking to provide an explanatory theory of representations and broaden the realm of the study of diagrams.

2   Analyzing Textual Descriptions of Image Contents

We used the Microsoft COCO dataset [6] (164,000 images for training) and their caption annotation data for our analysis. In this dataset, five captions were independently given to a single image by different annotators via crowdsourcing. Thus, the higher the match among the caption contents, the more reliable the linkage between the image and the caption. We extracted images according to whether or not there were at least three out of five captions containing expressions for universal quantifiers; we call it 3/5 criteria.

Among the various ways in which universal quantifiers are realized in natural language [15], we use *all* and *every* as representative expressions in English. We searched captions containing these two expressions. We removed captions that come from road/traffic signs (such as *stop! all way*). There were only seven items satisfying the 3/5 criteria. Figure 1 shows all the images and the captions.

Although the use of universal quantifiers in image captions is rare as is expected, there are interesting patterns in their usage; we can distinguish two types of the uses of *all/every*. One type is *object-based* universal quantification, which involves quantification over objects in a domain and thus can be represented in the form *all objects in a domain have a property F*. Typically, quantifiers of this type are associated with count nouns in the plural form such as *all four paws*. In Fig. 1, this type of quantifier is shown in red. All the captions in (a) are of this type. The quantifier expression *everything* in (f-2) and (f-4) can also be classified as object-based.

Another type is *region-based* quantification, which can be paraphrased as *the entire region has a property F*. A characteristic of region-based quantification is that the quantifier is associated with a noun in the singular form that specifies an area to which some property is ascribed. In Fig. 1, this type of quantifier is shown in blue. All the captions in (b), (c), and (d) are of this type. The quantifier expression *everywhere* is classified as region-based. The same situation can sometimes be described in terms of object-based and region-based quantification; thus, images (e-g) were a mixed case annotated with both types of quantifiers.

Compared to existing representation systems in diagrammatic logic, object-based quantification used in image captions have much in common with that used in Tarski's World [2], the type of quantification that visually refers to multiple discrete objects. On the other hand, region-based quantification in image

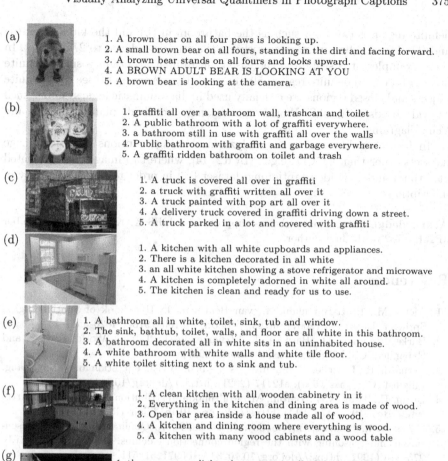

(a)
1. A brown bear on all four paws is looking up.
2. A small brown bear on all fours, standing in the dirt and facing forward.
3. A brown bear stands on all fours and looks upward.
4. A BROWN ADULT BEAR IS LOOKING AT YOU
5. A brown bear is looking at the camera.

(b)
1. graffiti all over a bathroom wall, trashcan and toilet
2. A public bathroom with a lot of graffiti everywhere.
3. a bathroom still in use with graffiti all over the walls
4. Public bathroom with graffiti and garbage everywhere.
5. A graffiti ridden bathroom on toilet and trash

(c)
1. A truck is covered all over in graffiti
2. a truck with graffiti written all over it
3. A truck painted with pop art all over it
4. A delivery truck covered in graffiti driving down a street.
5. A truck parked in a lot and covered with graffiti

(d)
1. A kitchen with all white cupboards and appliances.
2. There is a kitchen decorated in all white
3. an all white kitchen showing a stove refrigerator and microwave
4. A kitchen is completely adorned in white all around.
5. The kitchen is clean and ready for us to use.

(e)
1. A bathroom all in white, toilet, sink, tub and window.
2. The sink, bathtub, toilet, walls, and floor are all white in this bathroom.
3. A bathroom decorated all in white sits in an uninhabited house.
4. A white bathroom with white walls and white tile floor.
5. A white toilet sitting next to a sink and tub.

(f)
1. A clean kitchen with all wooden cabinetry in it
2. Everything in the kitchen and dining area is made of wood.
3. Open bar area inside a house made all of wood.
4. A kitchen and dining room where everything is wood.
5. A kitchen with many wood cabinets and a wood table

(g)
1. there are many lights that are on in all of the buildings
2. The buildings on the street are all covered in bright lights.
3. A nighttime shot of the Las Vegas strip and all the neon signs.
4. a street at night cars and signs and lights
5. Night time street view of hotels and lighted signs on the Vegas Strip.

Fig. 1. Photograph images expressing *all* and/or *every* with full five captions (#COCO-ID, #flickr-ID, Author): (a) #238960, #2363513312, Steven Martin, (b) #306560, #8311906187, Ezmo Dreams, (c) #487353, #4667382943, ercwttmn, (d) #424337, #4780553791, M W, (e) #289654, #7536472060, BJBEvanston, (f) #66327, #8180557127, Mitch Barrie, (g) #61732, #6462876055, john flanigan. Words in red and blue indicate object-based and region-based universal quantification, respectively. (Color figure online)

captions is comparable to topological representations used in Euler diagrams [8] and Region Connection Calculus [5]; it ascribes a property or a relation to the salient area (region) in an image or a diagram.

Furthermore, a closer look reveals that in these images, a single definite object can be seen in its entirety such as the bear in (a) and the truck in (c) or a closed definite region is captured such as the bathroom in (b) and the kitchens in (d) and (f). The number of images satisfying the criteria reduced to 2/5 was 71. In these examples, it is still often the case that an image contains a single definite object or a closed definite region: 59 items (83.1%). We can also see that definite objects and closed regions are crucially used in diagrammatic logic systems, such as grid boards in Tarski's World and rectangles to divide planes in Euler and Venn diagrams.

In future work, we plan to analyze more image captions by using image datasets other than COCO (e.g., NLVR2 [14], where two images are presented at a time) and use video captioning dataset [16] in order to obtain a variety of descriptions.

Acknowledgments. This work was supported by JSPS KAKENHI Grant Number JP20K12782 to the first author.

References

1. Aiello, M., Pratt-Hartmann, I., van Benthem, J.: Handbook of Spatial Logics. Springer, Dordrecht (2007). https://doi.org/10.1007/978-1-4020-5587-4
2. Barker-Plummer, D., Barwise, J., Etchemendy, J.: Tarski's World: Revised and Expanded. CSLI Publications, Stanford (2007)
3. Bernardi, R., Pezzelle, S.: Linguistic issues behind visual question answering. Lang. Linguist. Compass **15**(6), e12417 (2021). https://doi.org/10.1111/lnc3.12417
4. Bruni, E., Tran, N.K., Baroni, M.: Multimodal distributional semantics. J. Artif. Intell. Res. **49**, 1–47 (2014). https://doi.org/10.1613/jair.4135
5. Cohn, A.G., Bennett, B., Gooday, J., Gotts, N.M.: Qualitative spatial representation and reasoning with the region connection calculus. GeoInformatica **1**(3), 275–316 (1997). https://doi.org/10.1023/A:1009712514511
6. Lin, T.-Y., et al.: Microsoft COCO: common objects in context. In: Fleet, D., Pajdla, T., Schiele, B., Tuytelaars, T. (eds.) ECCV 2014. LNCS, vol. 8693, pp. 740–755. Springer, Cham (2014). https://doi.org/10.1007/978-3-319-10602-1_48
7. van Miltenburg, E., Morante, R., Elliott, D.: Pragmatic factors in image description: the case of negations. In: VL 2016, pp. 54–59. ACL (2016)
8. Mineshima, K., Okada, M., Takemura, R.: A diagrammatic inference system with Euler circles. J. Log. Lang. Inf. **21**(3), 365–391 (2012). https://doi.org/10.1007/s10849-012-9160-6
9. Sato, Y., Mineshima, K.: Depicting negative information in photographs, videos, and comics: a preliminary analysis. In: Pietarinen, A.-V., Chapman, P., Bosveld-de Smet, L., Giardino, V., Corter, J., Linker, S. (eds.) Diagrams 2020. LNCS (LNAI), vol. 12169, pp. 485–489. Springer, Cham (2020). https://doi.org/10.1007/978-3-030-54249-8_40
10. Sato, Y., Mineshima, K.: Can humans and machines classify photographs as depicting negation? In: Basu, A., Stapleton, G., Linker, S., Legg, C., Manalo, E., Viana, P. (eds.) Diagrams 2021. LNCS (LNAI), vol. 12909, pp. 348–352. Springer, Cham (2021). https://doi.org/10.1007/978-3-030-86062-2_35
11. Sato, Y., Mineshima, K., Ueda, K.: Visual representation of negation: real world data analysis on comic image design. In: CogSci 2021, pp. 1166–1172 (2021)

12. Shin, S., Moktefi, A. (eds.): Visual Reasoning with Diagrams. Birkhaüser, Basel (2013)
13. Stapleton, G.: A survey of reasoning systems based on Euler diagrams. Electron. Notes Theoret. Comput. Sci. **134**, 127–151 (2005). https://doi.org/10.1016/j.entcs.2005.02.022
14. Suhr, A., Zhou, S., Zhang, A., Zhang, I., Bai, H., Artzi, Y.: A corpus for reasoning about natural language grounded in photographs. In: ACL 2019, pp. 6418–6428 (2019). https://doi.org/10.18653/v1/P19-1644
15. Vendler, Z.: Each and every, any and all. Mind **71**(282), 145–160 (1962)
16. Xu, J., Mei, T., Yao, T., Rui, Y.: MSR-VTT: a large video description dataset for bridging video and language. In: CVPR 2016, pp. 5288–5296. IEEE (2016). https://doi.org/10.1109/CVPR.2016.571

Comparison of Diagram Use for Visualizing Probability Problems in U.S. and Chinese Textbooks

Chenmu Xing$^{(\boxtimes)}$ ⓘ, Megan R. Bender, and Leticia Cossi de Souza

Minot State University, Minot, ND 58707, USA
{chenmu.xing,leticia.cossidesouza}@minotstateu.edu,
megan.bender@ndus.edu

Abstract. The present work compared the use of visual representations in textbooks for teaching basic probability. Textbook chapters on basic probability were compared across three educational systems for high school students (U.S. regular-level, U.S. advanced-level (AP), and Chinese regular-level). Results revealed great disagreements in the use of visual representations by textbook types: Although more visualizations are present in both types of U.S. textbooks, the regular-level textbook shows a higher tendency for using pictorial images, which are visual representations irrelevant to problem solving. The advanced-level U.S. textbook and the regular-level Chinese textbook both use schematic visual representations (e.g., diagrams) more often when visualizing problems. Use of visual representations also seems to be linked with specific problem-solving stages. The current study findings offer insights for instructional design and warrant further evaluation of the efficacy of mathematics textbook design for visual aids.

Keywords: Diagram design for math problem solving · Probability education · Textbook analysis

1 Introduction

Visual representations have been widely used as tools for math problem solving including probability [1–4]. However, their effects on math problem solving vary by visual representation types. Pictorial images, which focus on the concrete entities described in a problem, have been found to impair problem solving because they contain distracting information irrelevant to the essential information for problem solving [2, 3]. On the other hand, structurally congruent schematic visual representations (e.g., diagrams), which represent the essential problem structure and elements while removing irrelevant details, are linked with higher problem-solving success [1–3].

Current knowledge about how standard instructional resources such as textbooks use visual representations to teach probability remains scarce. Meanwhile, textbook analyses conducted in some other critical school math domains have revealed inconsistency between the ways target content is presented in widely used textbooks and evidence-based recommendations for instructional design [e.g., 5]. Therefore, this work aimed

© Springer Nature Switzerland AG 2022
V. Giardino et al. (Eds.): Diagrams 2022, LNAI 13462, pp. 378–381, 2022.
https://doi.org/10.1007/978-3-031-15146-0_35

to explore whether textbooks for teaching probability have followed evidence-based principles when designing visual representations for the learning content.

This exploratory investigation focused on comparing textbooks used for teaching high school probability in three educational systems: (1) the U.S. regular-level, intended for the regular high school math curriculum in the U.S.; (2) the U.S. advanced-level, for U.S. high school students who take Advanced Placement (AP) statistics; and (3) the Shanghai (China) regular-level, used for the regular high school math curriculum in the region. Of particular interest are the comparisons of the U.S. regular-level textbook with the other two types, one targeting a more advanced level of probability education in the U.S. educational system and the other also targeting the regular high school level but from a top performing educational system on international math assessment measures like PISA [6]. The comparison results may provide useful insights for instructional design of visual aids for formal school math education in domains such as high school probability.

We asked two main research questions: First, when these textbooks accompany probability problems with visual representations, what types of visual representations (effective vs. ineffective for problem solving) do they primarily rely on? Second, is the use of schematic visual representations (e.g., diagrams) for probability problems similar and consistent across the textbook types?

2 Method

For each textbook type, a representative textbook (student edition) was chosen based on popular market share of their textbook publishers (for the U.S. textbooks) or dominant use of its textbook series in the region (for the Shanghai textbook): *enVision Algebra 2* for the U.S. regular level [7], *Introduction to Statistics and Data Analysis (AP Edition)* for the U.S. AP level [8], and *Mathematics for Grade 12* for the Shanghai textbook [9]. A qualified problem instance must be from the probability chapters in these textbooks and presents an opportunity to seek a mathematically based solution or answer to the given problem instance. Such problems include worked example problems that demonstrate step-by-step solution procedures as well as exercise and review problems for practice. Each problem was coded by whether it is accompanied by any visual representation and if visualized, the type (see Fig. 1 for examples).

Fig. 1. An example problem with pictorial and schematic visual representations comparable to instances found in the textbooks

A problem was coded as pictorially represented if it is accompanied by any visual representation that depicts the real-world appearance of the concrete entities described in the problem [2]. A problem was coded as schematically visualized if a schematic visual representation is used to encode or organize the mathematical structure or elements of the problem [2]. Schematic visual representations found in the textbooks include trees, tables, Venn diagrams, networks, other graph types (e.g., distribution graphs), and schematic outcome/sample space listings. A problem may be accompanied by multiple types of visual representations. Therefore, each visual type was coded independently with dichotomous codes (yes or no).

3 Results and Discussion

A total of 827 problem instances affording problem-solving opportunities were found across the three textbooks (U.S. regular: $n = 292$; U.S. AP: $n = 373$; and Shanghai regular: $n = 162$). Most of these problems ($n = 766$) present opportunities that may prompt students to develop a solution first. But 61 problems only involve the execution of a given solution, which is typically the last problem-solving stage after a solution has become available [4] (e.g., Calculate $_{10}C_3$, a problem instance for students to just learn or practice how to calculate the formula for combination step by step). Almost all the execution-only problems were found in the Shanghai textbook ($n = 60$) and none in the U.S. AP textbook.

The main analysis was conducted including all problem instances ($n = 827$), regardless of the problem-solving stages they may involve. The two U.S. textbooks showed more similar frequencies of visualizing problems (U.S. regular: 43.5%; U.S. AP: 46.4%), whereas it is much less often for the Shanghai textbook (20.4%) to do so, $\chi^2(2) = 33.723, p < .001$, *Cramer's V* $= .202$ (medium effect). However, a closer examination focusing on the types of visual representations used for those visualized problems suggested dramatically different visual design preferences by textbooks. Where problems are accompanied by visual representations ($n = 333$), the U.S. regular textbook has most heavily relied on the use of pictorial images ($n = 76$ out of 127 visualized problems, or 59.8%), compared to 45.5% ($n = 15$ out of 33 visualized problems) by the Shanghai textbook, and a much more limited use of such representations by the U.S. AP textbook ($n = 30$ out of 173 visualized problems, or 17.3%), $\chi^2(2) = 58.504, p < .001$, *Cramer's V* $= .419$ (large effect). We also compared the use of schematic visual representations for visualized problems by textbooks: $n = 65$ (51.2%) by the U.S. regular textbook, $n = 150$ (86.7%) by the U.S. AP textbook, and 26 (78.8%) by the Shanghai textbook, $\chi^2(2) = 46.977, p < .001$, *Cramer's V* $= .376$ (large effect).

To check whether the observed difference by textbooks were a result from including execution-only problems, we conducted an additional analysis just on problems that present solution development opportunities ($n = 766$). Textbook differences in the overall visualization tendency remained a similar pattern: 43.6% of the problems are visualized by the U.S. regular textbook, 46.4% by the U.S. AP textbook, and now up to 32.4% by the Shanghai textbook, $\chi^2(2) = 6.419, p = .040$, *Cramer's V* $= .092$ (small effect). Textbook differences in pictorial and schematic visual representation for their visualized problems remained the same as found in the main analysis, because none of the execution-only problems have visual representations.

Thus, the current work found great disagreements across textbook types in how they visualize probability problems. The U.S. regular textbook shows a higher tendency for visualizing problems with pictorial representations that relevant research has found ineffective and sometimes even harmful for problem solving [2]. And although it has provided schematic visual representations like diagrams for about half of its visualized problem instances, this rate was not as high as those of the U.S. AP or the Shanghai textbooks. An interesting finding from this exploratory work is that no visual representation was given to problems that only require solution execution. This may suggest that the utility of visual representations for probability problem solving is stage dependent. It seems that visual (including diagram) representations are much more likely to be provided at the stage of solution development than at the stage of solution execution. This finding, showing the textbook designers' perspective, is consistent with a similar tendency of visualization strategies for probability problem solving observed in solvers [4]. However, the current results should be carefully interpreted because almost all those execution-only problems were linked with a single textbook. Future research is needed to systematically investigate this matter to evaluate whether the stage-visualization interaction pattern in probability problem solving is generalizable.

Acknowledgements. This work was supported by the Small Grants for Faculty Research program at Minot State University.

References

1. Xing, C., Corter, J.E., Zahner, D.: Diagrams affect choice of strategy in probability problem solving. In: Jamnik, M., Uesaka, Y., Elzer Schwartz, S. (eds.) Diagrams 2016. LNCS (LNAI), vol. 9781, pp. 3–16. Springer, Cham (2016). https://doi.org/10.1007/978-3-319-42333-3_1
2. Hegarty, M., Kozhevnikov, M.: Types of visual–spatial representations and mathematical problem solving. J. Educ. Psychol. **91**, 684–689 (1999)
3. Presmeg, N.C.: Visualization in high school mathematics. For Learning of Mathematics **63**, 42–46 (1986)
4. Zahner, D., Corter, J.E.: The process of probability problem solving: use of external visual representations. Math. Think. Learn. **12**, 177–204 (2010)
5. McNeil, N.M., et al.: Middle-school students' understanding of the equal sign: the books they read can't help. Cogn. Instr. **24**, 367–385 (2006)
6. Organization for Economic Co-operation and Development (OECD): PISA 2018 Technical Report. https://www.oecd.org/pisa/data/pisa2018technicalreport/ (2019)
7. Kennedy, D., Milous, E., Thomas, C. D., Zbiek, R. M., & Cuoco, A.: enVision Algebra 2. Savvas Learning Company (2018)
8. Peck, R., Short, T., Olsen, C.: Introduction to Statistics & Data Analysis, 6th Edition (AP Edition). Cengage (2020)
9. Yuan, Z., Zhao, X. (eds.): Mathematics for Grade 12. Shanghai Education Publishing House (2008)

Author Index

Printed in the United States
by Baker & Taylor Publisher Services

Printed in the United States
by Baker & Taylor Publisher Services